THE MIDDLEMOST AND THE MILLTOWNS

BOURGEOIS CULTURE AND POLITICS IN EARLY INDUSTRIAL ENGLAND

Brian Lewis

D1745161

Stanford University Press
Stanford, California
2001

Stanford University Press
Stanford, California
©2001 by the Board of Trustees of the
Leland Stanford Junior University

Printed in the United States of America on acid-free,
archival-quality paper.

Library of Congress Cataloging-in-Publication Data
Lewis, Brian, 1965-
    The middlemost and the milltowns : bourgeois culture and
politics in early industrial England / Brian Lewis.
      p. cm.
   Includes bibliographical references and index.
   ISBN 0-8047-4174-3 (alk. paper)
      1. Middle class – England – History – 18th century. 2. Middle
class – England – History – 19th century. I. Title.

   HT690.G7 L39   2002
   305.5'5'0942 – dc21   2001049442

Original printing 2001

Last figure below indicates year of this printing:
00 09 08 07 06 05 04 03 02 01

Typeset by Janet Gardiner in 9.5/12.5 Sabon

Exmouth

University of Plymouth Library

Subject to status this item may be renewed
via your Voyager account

http://voyager.plymouth.ac.uk

Exeter tel: (01392) 475049
Exmouth tel: (01395) 255331
Plymouth tel: (01752) 232323

THE MIDDLEMOST AND THE MILLTOWNS

BOURGEOIS CULTURE AND POLITICS
IN EARLY INDUSTRIAL ENGLAND

For My Parents

ACKNOWLEDGMENTS

I have incurred many debts during the research and writing of this book. In one sense the research began when I was a teenager at Queen Elizabeth's Grammar School, Blackburn, where the late Lynne Martindale and the late David Ramm guided my first, faltering steps in the study of history, and Alan Petford piqued my interest in the methods and promise of local history. At Balliol College, Oxford, where I was an undergraduate, Colin Lucas stimulated a fascination with the French Revolution and its ramifications across Europe. John Prest, my tutor in modern British history, then and ever since has been an unfailing source of wisdom and support, a model Oxford tutor. His very helpful critique of the book manuscript is only the most recent example of his generosity.

This book is based on my Ph.D. dissertation at Harvard University, where my graduate work was generously funded by a Frank Knox Memorial Fellowship, the Harvard Krupp Foundation, and research grants from the History Department. I received much encouragement and advice at Harvard from the late John Clive (my first adviser), Simon Schama (who became my adviser), Caroline Ford, Charles Maier, and Susan Pedersen. David Blackbourn gave me valuable feedback on the dissertation and has been very supportive ever since. Boyd Hilton, my supervisor during a productive year as a graduate visiting student at Trinity College, Cambridge, suggested a number of new avenues to explore, and I benefited from a research grant from the college's Eddington Fund. I received early guidance and suggestions from John Brewer, Graeme Davison, John Garrard, Patrick Joyce, R. J. Morris, Linda Colley, V. A. C. Gatrell, Gareth Stedman Jones, Leonore Davidoff, Michael Rose, and Roger Schofield.

I have spent months at a time in a number of libraries and record offices: I am deeply indebted to the staff at Bolton Archives and Local Studies, the Lancashire Record Office in Preston, Blackburn Reference Library, Preston Reference Library, the Public Record Office at Kew, Cambridge University Library, the Widener Library at Harvard, and the McLennan Library at McGill for their efficient and friendly service, and to those at the other libraries and record offices in London, Lancashire, and Cambridge (listed in the footnotes) where I spent briefer periods. Letters of the Rev. John William Whittaker in the library of St. John's College, Cambridge, are quoted with the permission of the Master and Fellows. For accommodation during research trips to London I must thank above all Carolyn and Jeremy Bradburne for allowing me the use of their flat in Kew, and Steve and Debi Maughan for putting me up in Camden Town. For much-needed help with computing and printing, my thanks to David Wu and Jesse Wen. Friends, colleagues, and students at the Center for European Studies at Harvard, in the Department of Modern History at the University of Manchester (where I spent a semester as a sabbatical-leave replacement), and for the last five years in the Department of History at McGill have provided inspiration and congenial environments for the writing and rewriting of this study.

Two of my McGill colleagues, Nancy Partner and Kate Desbarats, read the manuscript in its entirety and have been particularly generous in proffering advice. Catherine LeGrand, the then Chair, allowed me some welcome relief from teaching during a critical phase of the writing, and Suzanne Morton, the current Chair, has been very supportive. My coworkers in British history, Colin Duncan, Elizabeth Elbourne, and Michael Maxwell, have made the pursuit of the British past at McGill a pleasure. Georgii Mikula and her staff in the departmental office perform miracles on a daily basis, and their assistance has been enormous. A McGill internal grant from the Social Science and Humanities Research Council of Canada facilitated a further summer in Lancashire archives, and McGill conference-travel grants enabled me to present some of my thoughts at conferences in Manchester and Washington, DC. Comments on these occasions, and at seminars in a number of different venues in and around McGill, have been most helpful. Katie Sams's editorial work on the manuscript and Sebastian Normandin's help with proofreading and indexing have been painstaking and meticulous. At Stanford University Press Norris Pope has been a most courteous editor—I am particularly grateful to him for accommodating such a stout manuscript—and the sharp eyes of Janet Gardiner and Louise Herndon have prevented many remaining errors. I am indebted to Carman Miller, Dean of the Faculty of Arts at McGill, for a grant toward the cost of publication.

My greatest debt is to my parents for all of their support and for providing the home in Blackburn where much of this book was researched and written. It would not have been possible without them, and it is dedicated to them, with love and gratitude.

Brian Lewis

CONTENTS

LIST OF TABLES

The Middlemost and the Milltowns

Bourgeois Culture and Politics in Early Industrial England

INTRODUCTION

'Tis observed . . . that oysters, when placed in their barrel,
Will never presume with their stations to quarrel.
They still make the best of their present condition,
Tho' preference is due to the middle position.
When the top is turn'd downward, the highest must fall
And the lowest will rise to the top of them all.
Not so with the middlemost—*their* situation
No change can experience, or feel degradation.
The middlemost, too, their bland juices bestow,
On their poor piping brethren embedded below.
From this let us learn what an oyster can tell us,
And we all shall be better and happier fellows.
Acquiesce in your stations whenever you've got 'em,
Be not proud at the top, nor repine at the bottom,
But happiest they in the middle who live,
And have something to lend, and to spend, and to give.

*The Rev. Thomas Wilson, in his capacity as Deputy Rhymesmith of
the Preston Oyster and Parched Pea Club, 1808.*[1]

   This book investigates the lives, ideologies, and actions of women and men
like the Rev. Wilson, in the Lancashire cotton towns of Blackburn, Bolton,
and Preston between the late-eighteenth and mid-nineteenth centuries. He
called them the middlemost; I shall generally call them the bourgeoisie, maybe
envisaging a narrower segment of society; others prefer upper-middle class(es),
local elite, urban gentry, urban patriciate, leading or respectable inhabitants.[2] I
am referring to the merchants, manufacturers, professionals, substantial retailers, and their families—people who exercised the most power locally,
whose voice was loudest in the public square, and who played the most critical role in the formation of urban Britain. The nation, in the long run,
emerged closer to their multifarious norms and values than to those of any alternative groups or discourses.[3]
   The book follows these people from boardroom to bedroom, assembly to
art gallery, garden to ghetto, through their volunteer corps, vacation cottages,

churches, and chapels. It is a social and cultural history in which politics is central, a local history in which the development of church and state are to the fore. Beginning in 1789 with the onset of revolution abroad, and ending with the Great Exhibition of 1851, a symbol of mid-Victorian stability, it is organized around the quest for order: how members of the bourgeoisie sought to bring order to their own lives and to create an orderly society within the context of rapid urbanization and the ever-increasing reach of the state. Each of the chapters speaks to an aspect of this search. The chapter sequence disrupts the narrative and thematic flow to convey a sense of this simultaneous creating and being created—to suggest that the whole cannot be understood without a perpetual oscillation between public and private or the interleaving of culture and politics. More broadly, the study revisits an old favorite in the historical repertoire: Why was there no French-style revolution in Britain? How was stability maintained in a volatile society of brutal inequalities of wealth and power?[4] How did the nation weather the aftermath of defeat in America, the crisis of the French Revolutionary and Napoleonic Wars, the postwar depression and radical agitation, the Reform Act turmoil, Chartism, the traumas of early industrialization and rapid urbanization—with, at the end of it all, the monarchy still intact, Victoria's head and shoulders still attached, the House of Lords unchanged, the House of Commons somewhat broadened but still highly restricted, and the great parties, Whigs/Liberals and Tories/Conservatives, still under the control of a small group of aristocratic families?

A brief sketch of some of the competing explanations is in order. The first set of explanations latches onto the findings of economic historians over the last quarter century that have flattened out the growth curve of the "Industrial Revolution."[5] The "Tory" version tends to deny that there is a problem needing explanation. Gradual growth meant that no great fault lines of class or extreme ideological cleavages developed.[6] The loyal, deferential, patriotic lower orders remained substantially more important than radical and disruptive elements; clergymen preaching a gospel of social quiescence and acceptance of one's station in life always had a greater impact than Thomas Paine and his successors. In sum, as *socioeconomic* change was not cataclysmic, it is hardly surprising that *political* change was not cataclysmic. A more "liberal" version contends that because British industrialization was so protracted and uneven, labor was able to adapt.[7] Political agitation, sometimes violent, was *part* of the worker response, but the development of trade societies, friendly societies and benefit clubs proved more durable, easily expanding into the tradition of reformism and laborism that characterized Britain's labor movements later in the century.

The second set of explanations does not dissent from the premise that a violent revolution was possible and even likely given the intensity of economic upheaval, exploitation, and state repression. But the lower-class attempts at emancipation failed, and Britain continued (continues?) to labor under an antique political system with real power in the hands of a privileged few, and the nation suffered (suffers?) from not experiencing a democratic, let alone a socialist, revolution.[8] One way to explain this failure is to point to key figures—Methodists, the labor aristocrats—who were bought off, co-opted, seduced into conformity to the established order.[9] Another way, more plausibly, emphasizes the effectiveness of repression. The state remained strong—it lost no wars after 1782, did not run out of money like the French monarchy in 1789 and could attract the united support of the propertied classes in defense of law and order—so was able to defeat popular radicalism by brute force. Though the state bureaucracy was tiny by Continental standards, it could speedily mobilize adequate coercive power to subdue and control any likely scale of unrest in Britain or Ireland.[10]

A somewhat more subtle variant places most weight on the notion that at key, potentially revolutionary moments in British history, the propertied classes remained united—quite unlike the disastrous situation in France in 1789, 1830, and 1848 when division in the middle and upper classes heralded revolution. As Lenin was to argue, what is needed beyond the acute suffering and consequent agitation of the oppressed classes is "a crisis . . . among the 'upper classes', a crisis in the policy of the ruling class, leading to a fissure through which the discontent and indignation of the oppressed classes burst forth."[11] In Britain there was no such fissure. Michael Mann, in the most strongly stated recent version of this thesis, underlines the scope, intensity, and organization of Chartism—more impressive than anything prior to the revolutions in France—and suggests that the movement failed because there was no weakness on the other side. The working class encountered an equally resolute, class-conscious, and self-righteous ruling regime and capitalist class. They clashed head-on, there was no dialectical resolution, and the working class lost, plain and simple.[12]

A third constellation of explanations revolves around the notion of a "quiet revolution." One take on this is the Whig narrative. The British constitution and state were sufficiently adaptable to accommodate the strains and stresses in society, hence there was no need for a violent revolution. The ruling elite made concessions to the newly volatile classes in society, ultimately ensuring a graceful, peaceful transition from aristocracy to democracy. This is the language of incorporation, accommodation, and compromise as enlightened rulers shepherded bigger and bigger flocks into the fold. A nonconservative variant acknowledges the success of radicalism. The Chartists failed in their immediate political objectives, still less provoked a revolution, but the strength and the size of the movement forced the state to make concessions—factory legislation, Repeal of the Corn Laws, the dismantling of Old Corruption, steady reductions in taxation, a shift in emphasis from indirect to direct taxation.[13] This was not a process of calm adaptation, but the panicky reaction of the old order to seething discontent. The emphasis is on conflict and instability, not consensus.[14] But the end results were similar: further steps in a quiet transformation, reducing the prospects or need for a noisy revolution.

A final star in this particular galaxy is the "bourgeois hegemony" argument—an answer to those puzzled as to why the middle classes failed to enact a revolution in spite of the continuing predominance of the aristocracy in church and state. It contends that the bourgeoisie controlled all the economic levers—all the important aspects of a capitalist society—and that aristocratic political control at the center was largely irrelevant. As long as governments followed policies broadly favorable to the economic interests of manufacturers and industrialists, the latter were quite content for the old elite to remain in nominal power at the top. This quiet revolution of the bourgeoisie, which succeeded in establishing middle-class norms as the common sense of nineteenth-century Britain, meant a political revolution was unnecessary. Like the other quiet revolutionary models, it implies a transformation that was deeper and more enduring than the surface froth of the French model.[15]

These, in very broad, monochromatic brush-strokes, have been the principal interpretations. In practice most scholars have dabbed at colors from a variety of such palettes to create vibrantly subtle compositions and to paint over some of the many imperfections. The considerable growth in the number of studies of the middle classes in the past few years—an attempt to correct the depiction of the faceless bourgeoisie or propertied ranks seen in the great foundational social histories fixated on working-class formation and lower-class radicalism—is, implicitly or explicitly, a recognition (and in turn a demonstration) that none of these interpretations make sense without a detailed examination of the middle-class role.

But what is meant by "the middle classes"? After the assaults in recent years is there much left of the idea of class, or at least of broad classes establishing through conflict a form of consciousness as the motor of history? Empirical research, contemporary politics, the challenge of academic feminism, the linguistic turn: all have left the class narrative bloodied and bowed.[16] Vigorous mental gymnastics are now required to claim a particular date or period when the middle class was "made," consciousness achieved, the finish line crossed. The confident assumption that in the generation after the French Revolution the middle class passed along the highway to consciousness, refueling at familiar stations—Pitt's income tax, the Orders in Council, the trade embargo against the United States, the Corn Laws, Peterloo, the Queen Caroline Affair, Reform, Repeal, 1848—has withered.[17]

Partly this doubt stems from backward glances at the rich scholarship on the late-seventeenth- and eighteenth-century middling sort, which has depicted a pulsating, rapidly urbanizing commercial society nurturing ever greater numbers of merchants, professionals, and retailers.[18] Add to this historians' haymaking with the Habermasian notion of the development of an independent bourgeois public sphere in later-Stuart and Hanoverian England,[19] stretch out the time frame of British industrialization, and all kinds of questions of the timing of class consciousness are raised. More fundamentally, the politics of identity and the assault of postmodernism have caused irreparable damage to the grand narratives of history, rupturing all necessary links between economic forces and social formations, emphasizing the linguistic construction of multiple forms of personal and collective identity, and demolishing the notion that class has any primacy over other forms of identity. Central to much post-Marxian and/or left-libertarian thinking is an uneasy sense of liberation from constrictive paradigms—a shattering of the anachronistic shackles that once tamed the teeming past, and an emergence, blinking in the sunlight, from the labeled, controlled, and constructed "reality" of nineteenth-century theorists. The stress now is on the fragmented nature of human experience and on differences—of ethnicity, gender, age, sexual orientation, region—as opposed to lumping into broad classes. Class has no particular explanatory priority in social and historical analysis, but is simply one of a plurality of oppressions, each rooted in a different form of domination—sexual, racial, national, or economic.[20]

Yet the concept of class remains crucial because the Hanoverians used class terminology interminably. Asa Briggs, in a pioneering study of language, assumed that the frequency of the use of the term "middle class" in the 1790s reflected social reality.[21] But if we are going to draw out the massing of the middle of society over a much longer period, recognize the strength in numbers of the middling sort much earlier in the century, and deny the revolutionary nature of the late-eighteenth and early-nineteenth-century economic transformation, then this supposition is clearly inadequate. Class was a linguistic construct that had to be thought, talked, and propagated. It was thus vulnerable both to alternative discourses that might present themselves as superior ways of explaining the numbingly complicated reality that makes up an individual's existence, and to discursive reconstructions and remodelings of its own internal coherence. This helps move us away from the depiction of a mature class society riding the crest of an industrial revolution and somehow establishing itself as a permanent fixture on the beach, and makes us confront the fluidity of the contested language of self-description. David Cannadine's valuable recent synthesis convincingly describes three basic models of society in open competition during this period: society as an ordered, onion-skin-layered hierarchy of ranks, orders, sorts, or classes—the most frequently encountered usage; society as a triad of upper, middle, and lower groups; and society as an adversarial dichotomy between "us" and "them," "patricians" and "plebeians," "tax-eaters" and "taxpayers."[22] Dror Wahrman's detailed examinations of the use of the term "middle class" illuminate how oppositional groups from the Friends of Peace in the 1790s to liberal-radicals in the mid-nineteenth century made strategic use of the term—an attempt to accrue political advantage by an appeal to the alleged merits of a social middle, an intervention within an evolving world rather than a straightforward reflection of it.[23]

In the midst of the great debate on class, scholars of the middlemost have written complex, nuanced interpretations, discovering both forces for division and for cohesion. Those intent on atomization can unfurl a scroll of divisive factors: party and sectarian rivalries; tensions within denominations; gender, generational, and regional divisions; vast income disparities; status and organizational schisms within the professions; clashes between an ethos of duty and service and the desire to make pots of money; fissures between export- or domestic-market-oriented, tariff or free trade, labor- or capital-intensive businessmen—to name but a few. But, as those intent on depicting cohesion point out, a number of these factors could also prove class formative. Religion might array portions of the bourgeoisie into hostile camps, but the denominational community could stretch across the fine layers of status division, structuring kinship networks, aiding the transfer of capital, providing the necessary collective infrastructure for later cross-denominational commingling. Professional and business rivalries tended to rest on a substantial unity of attitudes conducive to capital accumulation: self-help, hard work, strict discipline, a strict accountability to God, the need for a quiescent workforce. Gender divisions could similarly provide a common level of understanding by finding expression in idealized separate spheres and the cult of domesticity.[24]

When middlemost historians have joined the dots between their work and the lack of a revolution, they have, by and large, searched most eagerly for the forces of cohesion, arguing that middle-class formation and a greater degree of class consciousness were essential in the creation of effective collective leadership for Britain to weather the crises of early industrialization with the political structure substantially intact. If these historians have failed to find this class consciousness at the political or the economic level, they have sought it at the cultural level—such as the shared values of domesticity or the proliferation of voluntary associations, both of which papered over the divisions of sect or party.[25]

Although there are evident difficulties in implying that these values were the exclusive property of the middle classes, much of this is beguiling and—in putting the position of the middle classes at the heart of the debate—very welcome. Yet, in raising the flag of dissent, I would like to suggest that community studies of the middle classes (focusing on the creation of local stability without looking much beyond their boundaries)[26] and stability studies (centering on the evolution of the state and on national politics, without paying close attention to local particularities) have not communicated with each other particularly effectively, nor with the radical challenge to the class narrative. Much can be learnt from a range of high-political and social histories that, in attempting to explain relative stability, place considerable emphasis on divisions in the ruling elite. For example, historians of high politics have contended that the dissenting Whig rump kept open the channels to popular radicalism from the 1790s, ultimately providing the necessary flexibility in the constitution in 1832; this top-level schism in the propertied ranks presented reformers with the possibility of effecting change *within* the constitution and political system.[27] Roger Wells's explanation for the failure of the famished to revolt during the direst years at the turn of the century rests heavily on the perception and reality of divided responses from a disunited ruling class.[28] Robert Gray's dissection of the short-time movement in the 1830s and 1840s subtly teases apart national and local elites' disparate approaches to the question of order, pointing to the—faltering, spasmodic, but real—potential for cross-class negotiation.[29]

Similarly, in arguing for a kaleidoscopic view of class and power relations, my contention is that a major part of the explanation of stability lies in the diversity and cross-cutting agendas of the disunited bourgeoisie. Paradoxically, a lack of solidarity or rigidity helped maintain bourgeois preeminence at the local level during the most unstable period of modern British history—an inversion of commonsensical logic. Throughout the following pages, stress is placed on the wide and fluctuating range of measures of coercion, concession, indoctrination, and incorporation as various members of the bourgeoisie and fractions of capital in conjunction with the state devised their own halting, conflicting, and incomplete solutions.

The role of the state is germane to the argument in two main respects. Firstly, Chapters 1 and 12 detail the elaboration of religious-based narratives both of accommodation and of opposition to the structure and institutions of the state—critical local-elite divisions mirroring the schisms in national politics. Secondly, two chapters examine the apparatus and impact of state-sanctioned authority. In its most blatant form, state power meant armed force, the maintenance of authority through violence. No history of the bourgeoisie and of order can ignore the barracks, the cavalry, the infantry, the yeomanry, the spies, the special constables, the selective use of the law to make examples, the web of information feeding back to the home secretary, and the facility of troop movements enhanced by better roads and by railways. These are the subjects of Chapter 3. Chapter 5 investigates the sea change in policing and punishment. The era of warfare, the population explosion, and the increased ease of communication created both a greater need by the state to keep a check on its citizens and the greater ability to do so. Enlightenment rationality had bequeathed a dual legacy: the rhetoric and something of the reality of liberty and juridical equality, and the creation of a potentially vastly more coercive state.[30] As theorists from Weber to Foucault to Giddens have argued (in very different ways), the modern nation-state operates by rendering its citizenry more "legible," by increasing the means of surveillance and by heightening the distance between conformist and "deviant" elements. Policing and reformed prisons—as well as the New Poor Law (Chapter 7)—were attempts to modify behavior and to swell the ranks of the conformist and the respectable by inculcating self-discipline, the "internalized gaze," meeting the agendas of the forces of order and the Christian moralist.[31]

The effectiveness of these coercive aspects of the attempt to create an ordered society and the role of members of the bourgeoisie in supporting them will be dissected. Alone they were insufficient. From a sense of fear, or Christian duty, or enlightened thinking, or the desire to recruit as many as possible to one's party or denomination to undercut the opposition, different individuals and bourgeois fractions pursued a plethora of alternative and—at times—mutually incoherent solutions. One of these was short time and a second was paternalism, both discussed in Chapter 9. A third possibility was the incorporation of the lower orders into hierarchical parties, either popular fronts behind reform and free trade, or Operative Conservative Associations (Chapter 12). A fourth was to engineer the environment: clean bodies, clean minds (Chapter 10). A fifth was simply indoctrination, from the pulpit or in the schoolroom, and a sixth was religious paternalism, the creation of a jigsaw of denominational hierarchies (Chapter 6).

All of these were responses to the inseparable forces of fear (of popular unrest, disorder and disease in an unfamiliar, industrializing, urbanizing, and well-peopled landscape) and of optimism (in the creation of wealth, in progress, in the providential choice of the British nation to show the world, by example, a new civilization). And members of the bourgeoisie carried them out while weaving together a patchwork of ideologies and identities to create order in and make sense of their own lives—the foci especially of Chapters 2, 4, 8, and 11. The attempts were confused, partial, often contradictory, often unsuccessful. But the divisions, the cross-cuttings, and the polarities, by dividing and ruling the local rulers as well as the divided and ruled, prevented the cracks of class from yawning into chasms.[32]

The Gramscian notion of hegemony remains useful in this context. In the words of E. P. Thompson, hegemony is a "dominant discourse, which imposes a structure of ideas and beliefs—deep assumptions as to social proprieties and economic process and as to the legitimacy of relations of property and power, a general 'common sense' as to what is possible and what is not."[33] Hegemony does not depend upon a dominant class but on dominant belief-systems; the concept of *bourgeois* hegemony is much too restrictive. Nor does it depend on brief periods of revolutionary upheaval but—in the case of the hegemony of liberal-capitalism—on longer-term processes of economic change and state-building (what Thompson, again, described as the "Great Arch").[34]

Bourgeois political or denominational participation and voluntary associationism—however internally contradictory—constantly reaffirmed a market and a civic culture, and kept open that public space in which bourgeois freedoms operated. The thrust and parry of debate, the rivalries and animosities, reworked and reordered the relationships of power and authority upon each different layer, perpetually constructing and reconstructing the hegemony of the liberal-capitalist system. But hegemonies depend on the consent of the governed, a consent won through negotiation (peaceful or violent). They are constructed on a daily basis by human agents and can be deconstructed or demolished by them too. The divided bourgeoisie's array of different beliefs and values multiplied the access-points for a challenge from below to each aspect of the dominant belief-systems. But ultimately this apparent vulnerability, by provoking alteration and accommodation, aided in the acquisition of the "consent" of the lower as well as the higher orders, a consent resting on ideological conviction *or* a recognition of the strength of the existing order *or* the debilitating power of "dull economic compulsion" *or*—most likely—a combination of all three.[35]

The model I am suggesting diverts our gaze from class consciousness and onto the longer-term civic and institutional framework wrought by the interplay of capitalist and state-building forces. Radical rather than Tory, it denies that slower-than-once-thought economic change or the fragmented nature of classes eroded all potential for revolution at a time of political-ideological tumult exacerbated by war and early industrialization.[36] It argues for the (always imperfect) consolidation—through consensus *and* conflict—of a diversity of political and socioeconomic fractions and discourses behind the "common sense" of liberal capitalism, rather than the victory of one class and the failure of another, or the simple imposition of the ideas of one class on another. And it allows a wide latitude for radical change—and appropriation of the dominant language—within common sense's overarching framework.[37] Above all, while not denying that elite divisions can be disastrous for those anxious to avoid revolution, it maintains that—to stave off the buildup of revolutionary pressures or to avoid the alternative of holding the country down by armed force—elite cohesion, the united face of the properted ranks over a sustained period, can be equally catastrophic.

The study is largely confined to the four parishes (typically northern in their vastness) of Blackburn, Preston, Bolton, and Deane (which covered much of the area to the immediate south and west of Bolton, and was often spelled "Dean")—an area of over 110,000 acres.[38] This choice was made not because

TABLE 1
Population Growth

	1801	1811	1821	1831	1841	1851
Blackburn						
Township	11,980	15,083	21,940	27,091	36,629	46,536
Parish	33,631	39,899	53,350	59,791	71,711	84,919
Preston						
Township	11,887	17,065	24,575	33,112	50,131	68,537
Parish	14,300	19,528	27,300	36,336	53,482	72,136
Borough						69,542
Bolton						
Great Bolton	12,549	17,070	22,037	28,299	33,449	39,923
Little Bolton	4,867	7,079	9,258	12,896	15,707	19,888
Borough						61,171
Parish	29,826	39,701	50,197	63,034	73,905	87,280
Deane						
Parish	12,843	16,129	18,916	22,994	26,217	29,819

SOURCE: *Census of Great Britain, 1851: Population Tables*, Division VIII (London, 1852). The municipal and parliamentary borough of Blackburn was the same as the township; that of Preston included the township of Fishwick; and that of Bolton included the townships of Great and Little Bolton and part of the township of Tonge with Haulgh. As an indication of growth prior to the first census, Dr. John Aikin noted in 1795 that the population of Bolton (both townships) had grown from 5,339 in 1773 to 11,739 in 1789: J. Aikin, *A Description of the Country from Thirty to Forty Miles Round Manchester* (London, 1795), 261-62.

the parishes were any longer of great administrative or emotional significance in themselves (except to their vicars, who will be prominent players in what follows), but because they provide a mid-sized boundary between the county or hundred and the township, they were in existence throughout the period (unlike, say, the Poor Law Unions), and they cover a substantial swath of Lancashire countryside. They incorporate not only the three towns but also a number of smaller industrializing settlements and most of the bourgeois families who lived in the countryside surrounding the urban nuclei. Most but not all, and when these families breach the boundaries (for example, in the developing desirable suburb of Penwortham, just across the river Ribble from Preston but in Penwortham Parish), I follow in their footsteps.

I am a product of the Blackburn middle classes. Familiarity with the region, its people, and its history is the first reason for my choice of the town and its neighbors for this case study. The second is more substantial. These towns spearheaded the cotton-manufacturing revolution and experienced explosive growth (Tables 1 and 2). Here the problems of early industrialization

TABLE 2

Other Populous Townships
(greater than 3,000 in 1851)

	1801	1811	1821	1831	1841	1851
Blackburn Parish						
Over Darwen	3,587	4,411	6,711	6,972	9,348	11,702
Lower Darwen	1,646	1,805	2,238	2,667	3,077	3,521
Walton le Dale	3,832	4,776	5,740	5,767	6,659	6,855
Bolton Parish						
Farnworth	1,439	1,798	2,044	2,928	4,829	6,389
Halliwell	1,385	1,828	2,288	2,963	3,242	3,959
Horwich	1,565	2,374	2,873	3,562	3,773	3,952
Kearsley	1,082	1,388	1,833	2,705	3,436	4,236
Little Hulton	1,498	1,886	2,465	2,981	3,052	3,184
Little Lever	1,276	1,586	1,854	2,231	2,580	3,511
Sharples	873	1,374	2,065	2,589	2,880	3,904
Turton	1,369	1,782	2,090	2,563	3,577	4,158

SOURCE: *Census of Great Britain, 1851: Population Tables*, Division VIII (London, 1852).

were at their most acute, and the attempts to recreate stability at their most intense.[39] Since large landowning interests did not predominate, the bourgeoisie was at the forefront of this endeavor. Two titled families did have important influence. The Stanleys, earls of Derby, were considerable property owners in Preston,[40] but as we shall see, socially, politically, and in terms of proportionate wealth and property-holding, their importance steadily diminished during the town's industrial expansion. The Bridgemans, earls of Bradford, possessed much property (including coal mines) to the immediate south and west of Bolton, and some within the town itself;[41] but although their agent, George Piggot, figured prominently in local affairs, they largely remained aloof, politically and socially, from the town's elite.

Members of the bourgeoisie therefore navigated their presence through a landscape of squires,[42] some of them buying wholesale or piecemeal small-to-middling estates within the rural penumbra of their respective towns and melding with the lesser gentry in lifestyle and marriage. Within the squirearchical patchwork, before the advent of steam power, the three towns served as the warehousing and marketing centers for the pacesetters of rural industry: the calico printers in the townships east of Blackburn and on the river Darwen near Preston;[43] the spinners, bleachers, and papermakers on the streams north

TABLE 3
Bourgeois Heads of Household in 1851

	Preston	Blackburn	Bolton
Occupation			
Industrial			
Textile manufacturing	60	70	99
Textile finishing	1	3	31
Other industrial	13	17	44
Banking	4	1	2
Managerial	0	4	4
Professional			
Armed forces	7	1	3
Law	49	23	23
Medicine	31	22	29
Church	21	20	32
Nonconformist ministers	8	12	18
Roman Catholic priests	6	6	2
Other "professionals"	17	14	17
Retail and wholesale	59	39	48
Craft	15	23	22
Independent means	49	34	46
Landowners	18	13	11
Totals	358	302	431

SOURCE: 1851 Census Enumerators' Returns, on microfilm at BRL, BALS, PRL, Leyland Public Library, and the PRO. Analyzed with the aid of a FileMaker Pro database on a Macintosh computer. For an explanation of methods, categories, and problems, see Appendix 1.

of Bolton, in Horwich, and in the townships to the south on the river Irwell and its tributaries;[44] and the merchants, putters-out or chapmen who employed armies of rural handloom weavers across the district.[45] Preston, as a surrogate county town boasting an urban gentry, was different from its neighbors; but after the introduction of manufacturing by the Watsons and the Horrockses toward the end of the eighteenth century, the town increasingly came to resemble its sisters. Nevertheless, by the end of our period what outsiders saw as unsightly clones, still to their inhabitants and historians contained significant differences. A comprehensive analysis of the 1851 census in an attempt to quantify the local bourgeoisie (Tables 3 and 4) clearly highlights

TABLE 4

Leading Occupations, Not Heads of Household, 1851

	Preston	Blackburn	Bolton
Textile manufacturing	26	19	17
Textile finishing	0	1	14
Other industrial	7	7	9
Banking	2	1	1
Managerial	9	16	10
Armed forces	1	2	2
Law	10	4	8
Medicine	4	1	4
Church	8	2	9
Ministers	2	1	0
Priests	6	0	0
Other "professionals"	14	10	9
Retail and wholesale	11	18	18
Craft	1	9	15
Totals	101	91	116

SOURCE: As Table 3. This table does not include those still in training and listed as "apprentice," "student," or "assistant," nor those of independent or landed means or in "non-bourgeois" occupations. Nearly all of those listed are relatives of the head of the household, with the exception of, for example, the Catholic priests, and ten living as lodgers in Preston (five curates, an attorney, a barrister, a physician, a Unitarian minister, and a Primitive Methodist minister), three in Blackburn (a clergyman, a Wesleyan minister, and a surgeon), and nine in Bolton (seven clergymen, a solicitor, and a surgeon).

the predominance of the textile industry, particularly of cotton, in all three towns and their hinterlands, and a substantial if subsidiary retailing, wholesale, and craft sector. But it also reveals the markedly higher textile-finishing presence (thirty-eight bleachers and seven calico printers) and a greater industrial diversification (including sixteen ironfounders/engineers, eight coalmasters, and six papermakers) in the Bolton area, which were partly associated with the South Lancashire coalfield. And, still clinging to its status as one of Lancashire's legal and administrative centers, Preston had more than twice the number of lawyers.

This, in briefest outline, introduces the arguments, the places, and the people that fill this book. At every stage in the odyssey, I shall try to depict members of the bourgeoisie as individuals—the magistrate, parish curate, prison chaplain, governess, society lady, medical officer, coalowner, manufacturer, barrister, and so on—with their own trials, troubles, and triumphs, as well as fractions of the bourgeoisie as collective ideological and organizational actors. I shall continue to pillage a number of items from the warehouse of theoretical ideas to approach a clearer understanding of the bourgeoisie's many different forms of class, gendered, national and regional identity, its role at the thrusting center of modern British society, and its multiple varieties of public and private expression. Not all aspects of these people's lives are here: I say little, for example, about wealth creation and economic sinews, partly because they are well covered elsewhere, partly because I am focusing on what people did with their wealth and power rather than on how they derived it, partly (some might add) because the text is long enough already. There are also notable omissions where the local record is surprisingly sparse or silent—nothing on the antislavery movement, for instance. But the critical elements pertaining to the question of stability and in the building of bourgeois order are here, and each of the threads I shall discuss is as closely interwoven in the fabric of bourgeois life as the warp and weft of a cotton piece. The period begins under the shadow of revolution and war, and our first step is into that particularly charged atmosphere.

CHAPTER 1: WARTIME

Major General Daniel Hoghton, riddled with perhaps twenty bullets, lingered for an hour before he died on May 16, 1811, near Albuerta. "His noble exit was at the head of his troops," the death notice in the *London Gazette* had it; "he was advancing to the enemy, his sword in his hand, the cheer of a charge in his mouth, and victory in his imagination!" This was an enviable death, confirmed by his divisional commander in a letter to his brother, Sir Henry Philip Hoghton: "[N]o officer ever parted from this Life under circumstances more honorable to Himself, or more glorious to the cause for which He contended." A more prosaic and less flattering account insisted that he was struck down while mounting a horse; but for public consumption the official idiom was resolutely heroic.[1]

Another casualty of Wellington's war in the Peninsular was Lieutenant Robert Knowles, son of Robert Knowles of Eagley Bank, a Bolton coalowner, who volunteered from the First Royal Lancashire Militia into the Seventh Regiment of Fusiliers in May 1811. He began in dashing, swashbuckling mode, reporting back from Aldea de Bisboa in October that "It was a beautiful sight to see our Cavalry skirmishing with [the enemy]." Proud "that I have fought for my country abroad," he made light of the dangers: "One ball grazed my cap, another cut my canteen-strap in two, but I am happy to say there was not one billeted upon my body." He was killed in action at the Pass of Roncesvalles in the Pyrenees in July 1813. This brought him a memorial in Bolton Parish Church, erected by his fellow townsmen in 1816 as a tribute to his heroism and worth.[2]

Death and glory in the nation's noble cause; scions of the Lancashire gentry and bourgeoisie uniting for God, king, country, and the defense of the social order; the realization that "Success abroad insures quiet at home," as Sir Henry put it to his brother, "and we are resting under your labors":[3] a substantial number of the local bourgeoisie read from this loyalist script.[4] But some did not, or at least they made their loyalty very heavily conditional. The French Revolutionary era and the war years witnessed the elaboration of two contrasting bourgeois narratives: a dominating narrative of accommodation under the broad mantle of church, state, and the prevailing power structure, and a narrative played in minor key defining itself in opposition to and seeking to supersede that power structure.[5] Both were to be of enduring importance in the long-term stabilization of the milltowns.

Polarization and Patriotism

A liberal-radical bourgeois minority largely drew its inspiration, collective identity, and sense of grievance with the existing structure of state and society from the fact that most of them were religious Dissenters.[6] Beyond helping define the extent of marriage, business, social, and political ties, this form of identity colored an individual's whole sense of history and experience of second-class citizenship.[7] As with all baggy generalizations, this requires qualification: Not all bourgeois radicals were Dissenters, by no means all bourgeois Dissenters were radical; "middling sort," Wilkite radicalism against stockjobbers, speculators, and high taxation did not necessarily have any religious content;[8] and, in spite of the statutory discrimination against Dissenters, most in practice scarcely felt its sting.[9] Nevertheless, to the relatively small but disproportionately affluent and self-confident rational Christians in particular, the legislated privileges for one church and the stigmatization of the rest remained deeply, woundingly offensive. "It is said, we are in possession of a *free* and *compleat* TOLERATION," wrote the Rev. John Holland, the Bolton Unitarian minister, soon after the outbreak of the French Revolution; but "We are threatened with *pains* and *penalties*, if we speak against the doctrine of the TRINITY in UNITY. Is this TOLERATION?"[10]

Holland was confident that Truth would ultimately prevail through the application of reason and argument. But his pamphlet intervention, in attacking the doctrines of the Trinity and consubstantiation, did not speak for the majority of Dissenters. It came after the failure to secure the repeal of the Test and Corporation Acts, which exacerbated local divisions in Dissenting ranks and helped rally conservative support in defense of the Church on a scale unprecedented since the sectarian rage of the early-eighteenth century. The first two attempts to secure repeal, in March 1787 and May 1789, were partly coordinated and the motions seconded by Sir Henry Hoghton, the Presbyterian MP for Preston and the leading Dissenting voice in the Commons. John Burgoyne, his fellow Preston MP, and Thomas Stanley, the Whig county member, joined him in voting in favor of repeal, but the motions were defeated largely because of the unexpected opposition of William Pitt. Before a third vote, repealers took the campaign outside Parliament and London in an attempt to whip up Dissenting support across the country.[11] One of the most significant such meetings was held in Warrington in early February 1790. This was chaired by Thomas Cooper of Lever Hall, Bolton, an Enlightenment polymath, lawyer, scientist, freethinker, and nominal Unitarian, a prominent figure in the Manchester Lit. and Phil., who had moved north from London in 1785 to become a member of the firm of Baker, Teasdale, Bridges, and Cooper, calico printers, at Raikes, near Bolton.[12] It was clear at Warrington that Cooper and other advanced, rational Christians—Unitarian and Presbyterian—wished to push a more radical agenda of religious reform, precipitating a split when the Bolton Independents, led by Samuel Fletcher, stormed out and subsequently succeeded in separating the area's Independents and Baptists from the original campaign. In published letters to Thomas Plumbe, a Bolton Anglican, who had chaired a meeting of repealers in Bolton, Fletcher explained his opposition on the grounds that the radicals wanted to target such matters as tithes and the Anglican liturgy, that they had denied Independents and Baptists fair representation on the local repeal committee, and that they had demanded repeal "as a right," not "by supplication."[13] He strikingly revealed the extent of Dissenting divisions in his comment to Cooper that Unitarianism "has no more foundation in Divine Revelation, than *Mahomet's;* and that persons of your sentiments have no more right to the name of *Christian*, than his disciples."[14]

Edmund Burke read out a copy of Fletcher's description of the Warrington meeting in the Commons, and MPs' recognition of the splits within Dissent and the radicalism of a part of it resulted in a crushing defeat for the third repeal motion in March 1790. In the aftermath, local Anglicans, their tails up and concerns aroused, organized Church and King Clubs wherever the repealers had been most active; Manchester's Church and King Club, formed in March 1790, was in turn answered by the Manchester Constitutional Society, with Thomas Cooper a leading player.[15]

The polarization of bourgeois society was given a fillip and a particular cast at the start of the revolutionary era through this fundamental disagreement about the state's role in religious affairs. But there is no doubt which side claimed the overwhelming majority of adherents as the French Revolution veered from its controlled and benign constitutional pattern into a violent and expansionist threat. In August 1793, fleeing the loyalist backlash, Cooper set sail for the United States, there to become an important figure in a somewhat more congenial political environment.[16] In Lancashire, the contours of the type of loyalism that drove him out are plainly visible. In Bolton, for example, in December 1792 the Rev. Robert Dean chaired a meeting to form a branch of John Reeves's Association for the Preservation of Liberty and Property Against Republicans and Levellers, the attendees pledging themselves "as good and faithful subjects" to defend the constitution from attack and to counteract seditious writings. The committee of seventy-four gentlemen included thirty improvement commissioners, a clear indication that the wealth of the town was stating its position and closing ranks. In January 1793 a large crowd in the marketplace witnessed the burning of an effigy of Thomas Paine and copies of his writings and other "seditious" works as part of the cleansing of the local public library of the pernicious influence of radicals.[17] On other occasions the Rev. John Holland, the Unitarian minister, was also burnt in effigy and represented as chief mourner, riding on an ass, at a mock funeral for Paine.[18] All this followed closely patterns of loyalism, partially orchestrated by the government, across the country.[19]

As the pit-props of the established order buckled and collapsed in France, the intensity of the trumpeting from press and pulpit of the virtues of the status quo in Britain increased correspondingly. The appropriation of a robust patriotism involved the championing of a domesticated monarch, the rule of law, and religious observance in opposition to barbarism, anarchy, and infidelity.[20] "[T]he contest in which we are engaged," proclaimed the Rev. Thomas Dunham Whitaker of the Holme early in 1794, "has no parallel in the history of mankind: every thing dear to us as men, or as Christians, is at issue: it is a war of Property against Pillage—of Humanity against Barbarism—of Order against Confusion—of Religion against Atheism—of Allegiance against Rebellion."[21] Order demanded unquestioned obedience: "Submit yourselves to every Ordinance of man for the Lord's sake," the vicar of Blackburn, the Rev. Thomas Starkie, preached to a congregation of friendly societies on New Year's Day 1793, "whether it be to the King, as supreme; Or unto Governors, as unto them that are sent by him for the punishment of evil doers, and for the praise of them that do well" (1 Peter 2:13-14).[22] Avoid dangerous "new-fangled opinions . . . fabricated in the pretended schools of Reason and Philosophy," the Rev. Thomas Bancroft, vicar of Bolton, exhorted a friendly society of weavers at the time of the 1797 invasion threat; "Your load of suffering, whatever it be, will be much relieved by patience and piety; and a rest in a better world is the sure reward of the heavy-laden, who have borne their burdens with faithfulness in this."[23] More emphatically still, he urged a congregation of local volunteer corps men in 1802 to reason thus:

"As a social being, Providence has placed me in a community and country where there is an established Order and Government—Governors must command and Subjects must obey—I am a Subject—I am not to search back into the records of a thousand years to find a ground for this duty. I am not to perplex myself with Declarations of Right and Speculations of Reform. I must consider that Protection and Obedience are mutual. I must acknowledge that God the Fountain of all wisdom and right has demanded this subjection, and it will be inconsistent in me to resist a divine ordinance, who have dedicated myself to the obedience of God. By God's especial favor I live under a Government nearer perfection than any which the changeful discontents of modern times have been able to hit upon."[24]

The Church did not have a monopoly on appeals to obedience demanded and justified by the national ideal. In June 1793 the Catholic clergy of Preston organized a performance of *The Messiah* and the Coronation Anthem in their new chapel, St. Wilfrid's, a conspicuous display of loyalty as a calculated claim to inclusion within the national community, both in the spirit of rendering unto Caesar and in an attempt to remove accusations of according precedence to an extraterritorial master.[25] The Rev. Joseph Barrett, preaching to Darwen Dissenters in 1795, called for an end to party spirit and for fidelity to the overruling providence of God. All lovers of their country should be aware that a house divided against itself could not stand.[26]

The developing forces of property, order, and quiescence reinforced pulpit pronouncements in a number of ways. The *Blackburn Mail*, for example, which started shortly after the war began, was replete with patriotic enthusiasms, ranging from advertisements playing the patriotic card (for Barnard's *History of England*, with an engraving of Boadicea, "who bravely Opposed the Roman Invaders"; for Blackstone's *Commentaries*, extolling the virtues of the British constitution), to detailed accounts and maps of the progress of the army and navy, to appropriate songs and poetry, and to the iconography of the medallion on the paper's heading (featuring Britannia, the British Lion, and the Wooden Walls of Old England in a typical mixing of British and English emblems).[27] Recruiting parties, such as that conducted by Capt. Daniel Hoghton in Blackburn in July 1793, drew on local-elite participation: the principal inhabitants paraded the streets with cockades in their hats, the church bells rang most of the day, and ale was distributed among the people.[28] The regaling of the lower orders with beef, plum pudding, and beer by landowners, merchants, and manufacturers took on a new intensity, displays of patriotic, quasi-squirearchical paternalism reinforcing one central message: "While the opulent are thus bountiful to the poor, the latter can have no reason to complain of the unequal distribution of property, or to think they would be happier in any other country."[29] The celebration of the anniversary of Charles II's Restoration took on new significance. The number of oak boughs on show in May 1794 in Blackburn was conspicuously high, "and the sight at this time was truly pleasing, as it evinced the detestation entertained of French tyranny, &c. by the loyal inhabitants of this town."[30] Celebrations of victories were also, naturally, occasions for symbolic and patriotic display. News of Admiral Howe's victory in the Channel on June 1 was greeted by the customary bells during the day and by picturesque transparencies during the night, one of them showing the *"Disturber of Nations,"* Thomas Paine, pinioned on the ground under the paws of the British Lion. Admiral Duncan's victory over the Dutch fleet in October 1797 occasioned bells, bonfires, a general illumination, and the roasting of a sheep for the populace.[31] An attack on the king's carriage in October 1795 was helpful, since it allowed the loyalists of Preston and Blackburn to express outrage; the Blackburn address talked of "the numerous and unexampled blessings we have hitherto enjoyed under your Majesty's civil administration—blessings, at this time, so powerfully contrasted with the miseries and horrors of anarchy experienced in a neighboring

Nation."[32] In addition, repeated Fast Days and "National Humiliations" brought many people to their knees in churches and chapels, in displays of national unity "for the Pardon of our Sins, for imploring God's Assistance on his Majesty's Arms by sea and land, and to avert so great a Scourge as an invasion upon this Island."[33]

The various wartime subscriptions combined both charitable and patriotic statements, giving a further indication of who was supporting the war effort. The Blackburn elite subscribed to supply British troops in Flanders with winter clothing in November 1793, to relieve distress and discontent at home in January 1794 (the promotion of domestic tranquillity, explained the *Mail*, being a most unequivocal test of genuine patriotism), and to help the wounded and widows and orphans after Duncan's victory in 1797. The committee organizing this subscription, begun at a nonsectarian victory dinner in St. John's Tavern, included the vicar, the Rev. Thomas Starkie, the Catholic priest, Dr. William Dunn, and the Rev. J. M'Quhae, the Independent minister.[34] The most impressive subscriptions came in response to the government's appeal for voluntary contributions for the defense of the country in February 1798. In Preston the urban gentry contributed in force.[35] In Blackburn, the putters-out and merchants led the field: Henry Sudell gave £700, Messrs. Cardwell, Birley, and Hornby £500, Henry Feilden £300 and his brother William £200.[36] At Peel, Yates and Company's counting house in the village of Church, Jonathan Peel of Accrington House headed the subscription list with £1,000, and it tailed down to a long list of their workpeople subscribing £83 17s. between them.[37] Whether cajoled or spontaneous, workforce donations bought a stake in the patriotic effort, a means of heightening loyalty; similar lists of donations were published for Messrs. Feildens' warehousemen and warpers, Henry Feilden's laborers at Witton House, the servants of Mrs. Feilden and John Fowden Hindle, and the house servants and colliers of R. G. Lomax of Clayton.[38]

It would be easy, but mistaken, to conflate all this under the banner of loyalism. Men and women who rallied in defense of the nation against possible French invasion did not necessarily support fighting abroad; those who celebrated British victories were not necessarily loyal to the existing structure of the state, Church, and society. Between the pontificating parson preaching obedience for a Manichean struggle of purity against pestilence, and the rational Christian committed to patriotic self-defense, lay a considerable acreage of nuance.[39] The same is true of the volunteer corps, ostensibly set up to give the rudiments of training for a reserve of armed force in case of invasion or domestic upheaval, but legible on a number of levels by different participants: as a key component in the creation of a party of order, defending the chattels and values of men of property; as the manly defense of women tending the hearth and home; as a means of disciplining the lower orders by their institutionalization into an armed hierarchy; as a vehicle for claims on the nation and sectional self-assertion by segments of the local bourgeoisie; or, more radically, as the notion of "a people in arms," a *levée en masse* with its hint of the democratic subversion of the established military order.[40]

All of these motivations, singly or combined, were visible among the gentlemen volunteers of Blackburn, Bolton, and Preston, organized first in 1794 and more comprehensively in the spring of 1798 under the threat of invasion and internal unrest. Much depended on local whim and enthusiasm: there was no standardization, little sense of duties, and no quality control of officers;[41] each volunteer had to kit himself out and serve without pay; the corps were not to be marched more than six miles (later extended to eight miles) from the town except by voluntary consent. Local elites sorted themselves out along predetermined notions of status, wealth, and worth. John Clayton of Little Harwood Hall became major-commandant of the Loyal Blackburn Volunteer Association, Henry Sudell and Henry Feilden his captains; William Feilden became captain-commandant of the Blackburn Volunteer Troop of Cavalry, with Richard Cardwell, merchant, his first lieutenant; in both, the cream of the town's gentlemanly capitalist, cotton-mercantile, largely Anglican elite made up the remainder of the officer ranks.[42] The Loyal Bolton Volunteer Infantry, first enrolled in July 1794, was officered by Lt. Col. Peter Rasbotham of Birch Hall, Farnworth, Major Ralph Fletcher, coalowner, and an array of bleachers, manufacturers, spinners, and retailers. Given its participation at a Church-and-King gathering in March 1797 to celebrate the anniversary of the 1790 vote retaining the Test and Corporation Acts (it fired three volleys to mark the occasion), its sectarian composition can be inferred.[43] The Bolton Light Horse Volunteers, on the other hand, were headed by John Pilkington, a prominent Unitarian merchant and manufacturer.[44] There were two sets of volunteers in Preston, the Royal Preston Volunteers under Nicholas Grimshaw of Barton Hall, which apparently incorporated the Tory-Anglican, corporation, predominantly professional elite, and the Loyal Preston Volunteers under John Watson, millowner, a principal supporter of Lord Derby's Whig interest in Preston.[45] To an extent this was the perpetuation of party politics by other means; but the Loyal Preston was also different from its neighbor in that its rank and file mainly consisted of men from, or close to, Watson's factories in Preston, Penwortham, and Walton-le-Dale. Jonathan Peel similarly gathered the workmen of Peel, Yates and Company's printworks at Church into a regiment of five hundred under his command, a state-sanctioned means of extending mill-time discipline to millhand "volunteers." The *Blackburn Mail* saw this patriotic arming of workpeople as a way of convincing the enemy that Britain, too, could become a nation in arms, and therefore it urged other large concerns to follow suit.[46] There was some calculated risk to this, in that disaffected men in uniform with rifles and bayonets were more dangerous

than unarmed rioters. The Rev. Thomas Bancroft, JP, vicar of Bolton, recruited his first spies in 1798 to watch and infiltrate radical organizations,
prompted by the fear of "Jacobins" seizing the Bolton Volunteer Corps'
weapons;[47] and a letter from Bolton to Lord Portland in 1800, purporting to
be from the "Vicker," inhabitants, and rank-and-file Volunteers, claimed that
they would not fire on the half-starved wretched rioters should disturbances
occur. They were laboring under "a sett of the most Damnable Infernal Vil-
lains that ever Existed on the face of the Earth and if any Disturbances does
arise we will fire upon our Commanders for we Shall not be so desparate as to
murder our fellow Creatures, that is starving to death"; "before we will see
our own Neighbours deing [dying] for want we will blow the Town to Ashes
wich we can verry soon." But, while Bancroft believed that "There is a spirit
of dissatisfaction more generally diffused than at any known period, & the
coalition between Jacobinism & Distress is really alarming," he and his spy
were unable to find any certain traces of an intended insurrection, and he did
not believe that the volunteer ranks were disloyal; the officers and subalterns
spoke with unqualified confidence of their men.[48] Locally, this confidence
proved well founded. When the Loyal Bolton Volunteers were disbanded in
1802, Bancroft could praise them both for expressing the "disinterested virtue" of ancient Rome—"when the ruling passion of each man's breast was a
love of his country, when ease, profit, domestic comfort, conjugal and filial
love were all sacrificed on the altar of his country"—and for enforcing self-
discipline. "You have learned from your military profession the duties of subordination, discipline and obedience," he told them. "Transfer these habits to
your moral conduct. The order of society depends upon your contentedness
and industry in the station allotted to you."[49]

There seems little doubt that the volunteers were popular with the propertied. Singleton Cooper, son of the innkeeper of the Man of Scythe, Churchgate, Bolton, joined a group of lads in forming a mock volunteer regiment.
"We used to march to Church in Military order. We grew in repute and in favour too; for we frequently were invited by the neighbouring Gentry to their
Mansions, where on the Lawn in front of the house we used to go through our
exercise and evolutions to the seeming great amusement of our inviters, and
they never failed to regale us with bread and cheese, and ale."[50] Officership of
the different corps conferred status. Nicholas Grimshaw of the Royal Preston
Volunteers chose to have himself portrayed resplendent in full uniform in
front of his home, Barton Hall.[51] With their fancy uniforms, and titles to
match the officers of the line and of the militia, volunteer officers were just
that little bit more worthy of notice, easing their acceptance into the cross-
mercantile-professional-gentry world of notables. They would almost certainly
be singled out for a toast at any constitutional dinner; when, for example, the
earl of Derby gave his annual dinner at Preston for about seventy gentlemen in

July 1800, the borough MPs, the mayor and aldermen, the clergy, and the officers of the two volunteer corps were particularly mentioned among the list of guests.[52] According to his funeral oration, Nathaniel Aspden, Blackburn surgeon, devout Methodist and member of the Gentlemen Cavalry, believed

that in the bible, which he made the rule of his faith and practice, religion and loyalty were joined together; and being sensible of the many privileges, both civil and sacred, we enjoy, under the reign of his most gracious Majesty; and hearing and seeing gentlemen come forward, and voluntarily enrolling and embodying themselves, to stand by, and defend, our rights and privileges, as men and Britons, he thought it his duty to join them, which he did, and never deviated from his sentiment to the last.[53]

If status were of any concern to him, the cavalry and most of the infantry attended the funeral in full uniform and he was despatched with due pomp.[54]

Whether the local corps actually did much more than bolster egos and mingle messages is doubtful. They did not have the opportunity to repel invaders, nor much occasion to stamp out domestic disorder. It is notoriously difficult to estimate the revolutionary threat during the French Revolutionary wars.[55] The Rev. Bancroft and Ralph Fletcher, Bolton magistrates, gathering dubious information from their spies and passing it along to the Home Office, gave the impression that Bolton and vicinity teetered on the brink.[56] At times the vicar cast doubt on the value of his intelligence, downplaying alarmist statements;[57] at others he—and Fletcher almost invariably—sounded the tocsin about "the Hellish schemes of these perturbed Spirits."[58] In the spring of 1801 in particular, both feared the impact of dear food and high unemployment, and saw a Jacobinical plot behind a petition of cotton weavers to Parliament. Thomas Ainsworth, a Bolton millowner, claimed that at least fifty thousand had been combined by oath in that part of the country, that "every link that bound subjects to government seems broke," the product of pinching hunger, and that "if government does not interfere in respect to the price of provisions every day will grow worse and in the end it will not have it in its power to quel [*sic*] the rising spirit of the people and I think and many others the time is at no great distance—if ever there is an invasion or other comotion [*sic*] to employ the regular force of ye country I make no doubt but that opportunity will be seized." This alarmism of whisper and rumor was compounded by some riotous scenes in Bolton in March on the committal of three radicals to Lancaster Castle.[59] One of them, a youth called William Moor, had sworn in an informer who promised to "persevere in my endeavours to obtain a brotherhood of affection amongst Englishmen of every religious denomination; and to obtain an equal representation of all the people of England." For this, Moor was found guilty after a second trial and sentenced to transportation for seven years, the first ten months of which he spent in Lancaster Castle, the rest on a hulk in Langston harbor.[60] In May, radicals held meetings on Horwich Moor and on Rivington Pike, where twenty-one were arrested, and other arrests followed, including the unfortunate William Gallant, the only radical organizer to be hanged in the period.[61]

"They say," wrote Fletcher in June, with suggestive vagueness, "that the French are determined to invade the United Kingdom in every quarter and that immediately on their arrival within sight of our coasts, signals will be made and the knowledge of their approach will be conveyed from London to Edinburgh in four hours and then the rising unwarrantly [*sic*] to take place."[62] But there is little to suggest that anything like this sophisticated degree of organization existed. The authorities found it relatively easy to disrupt radical plans through a process of surveillance, containment, and use of the law. There was no invasion, no weakening of governmental resolve, no disastrous split within the ranks of the propertied, and no mutinies by either regular or volunteer troops, all well-nigh essential for a revolution to break out. The volunteers had played *some* role in all this. Thomas Ainsworth had raised again the fear that they could not be trusted; but they are recorded as acting as an armed escort of the three radicals to Lancaster Castle in March, and, the previous October, helping disperse a large crowd in Darwen Street, Blackburn. "The great utility of the Volunteer Corps has always been readily admitted," commented the *Blackburn Mail* on this occasion, "but their importance to the safety of the country, is now most clearly proved. The zeal and energy they every where display, are, at this moment, the chief means of preventing, perhaps, the introduction into this country of Revolutionary horrors."[63] The juxtaposition of "preventing," "perhaps," and "introduction" indicates that this assessment rested on hypothetical speculation.

The volunteers, in reality, tended to be rather less polished than their buttons or boots, their zeal neither uniform nor free from tensions. The Bolton Volunteer Corps, for example, expecting voluntary contributions for its expenses, soon ran out of money in 1796 and applied to the government to be bailed out.[64] Many of the volunteers had businesses to run, and their enthusiasm for soldiering could diminish after an invasion scare. William Feilden, in charge of the Blackburn cavalry corps, wrote to Lord Derby in July 1802 that his troop of no more than twenty to twenty-five privates was now too small, and in any case they no longer wished to continue, as a further neglect of their pursuits would be inconvenient.[65] When the Napoleonic Wars began in 1803, impressive numbers rallied to reconstitute the various corps. More than seven hundred volunteered on the first day of recruitment for the Preston Royal Volunteers, for example, and over £3,000 in funding was soon raised.[66] In Blackburn, John Cardwell, at the behest of several principal inhabitants, offered a new corps of at least forty rank and file for service in any part of the North West Military District; but he added "that the Members of this proposed Association are to a Man engaged in Business at Home, and that it would be very inconvenient to them to be removed from the Town—but in Case of actual Necessity they will come forward with the greatest Chearfulness [*sic*]."[67] In May 1805, after the whole of the Chorley Division of the Preston and Chorley Cavalry resigned, Captain William ffarington and his fellow officers also resigned their commissions because of the difficulty in mustering the remaining half and in finding more recruits prepared to put up the necessary money to equip themselves. They did, however, reassure the government that in the event of an emergency they intended to join Major Pilkington's Bolton troop, "and to take with us those few that still remain true to the cause in which we embarked."[68]

Two sets of volunteer infantry in one town could generate rivalries, especially if they reflected partisan divisions. In Preston, John Watson wrote to Derby on July 23, 1803, to offer his services again in a revival of his Loyal Preston Volunteers, a corps of between three hundred and five hundred men. On the twenty-fifth a meeting of inhabitants resolved to re-embody the Royal Preston Volunteers under Nicholas Grimshaw, to consist of more than eight hundred men.[69] The Loyal Preston was sanctioned slightly ahead of the Royal Preston, according precedence and seniority to Watson, a reversal of their former standing. Watson claimed that this was just, because he was first on the field, Grimshaw and his officers that it had only been obtained through private solicitation (perhaps the influence of Derby). The dispute dragged on, publicly, with the Royal Preston failing to gain redress; they conceded defeat at the end of 1804 with as much gentlemanly aplomb as they could muster, promising to serve in any situation or rank to which His Majesty chose to appoint them. But they could not resist a parting shot across Watson's bows, with the

hope that Lieutenant Colonel Watson will, at length, with equal sincerity, join in regretting, that, at the first raising of the Volunteer Force, he refused to concur in the only effectual means of prevention, (and which were most anxiously and unremittingly pressed upon him, both in public and in private,) viz. a thorough union of the whole town in the formation of *one respectable and united Corps of eight or nine hundred Men, all collected round one common standard, in the glorious cause of their common King and Country.* This desirable measure was however rejected, and it was readily foreseen and pointed out that disunion and jealousy would be the natural consequences.[70]

If jealousy and waning enthusiasm bedeviled volunteering, it could also be the victim of business failure. In 1807 Watson's cotton-manufacturing concern, the second biggest in Preston after the Horrocks's, collapsed. In October, Bertie Markland, deputy lieutenant, reported that the partners, Lt. Col. Watson and his sons, Lt. Col. John Watson Jr. and Capt. Joseph Watson, were in insolvent circumstances beyond redemption. As the Loyal Preston consisted chiefly of their own workmen and mechanics, on the point of being laid off, there was a danger that neither form of discipline, mill nor military, would hold; "and as the Winter is fast approaching & the Trade here in a most depressed state some Danger may be apprehended from the discontent of these Men among whom there are many Irish of the lowest Class." Further investigation revealed the insolvency of Captains Paul Catterall and David Ainsworth, both heavily connected with the Watsons, and Capt. Joseph Myers, expected to be a bankrupt, had left the county. The remaining officers made considerable but fruitless efforts to find an adequate complement of new officers and resigned their commissions in the summer of 1808. Another corps in the town, the Preston Rifle Corps, was more fortunate. Its commandant, Capt. Thomas Ogle, merchant, found himself in Lancaster Castle with debts of more than £44,000, "and not likely to be liberated." Although initially no "proper gentleman" had wanted to take command of it because of the expense, William Brade, liquor merchant, took on the charge in June and the corps survived.[71]

But its independence was short-lived. The government had readily disbanded the volunteers and reverted to the militia during the intermission between wars in 1802, and in 1808 Lord Castlereagh at the War Office did so again by integrating the volunteer corps into a new Local Militia. This reflected continued doubts about the reliability, efficiency, and commitment of the volunteers. The Local Militia was based on the principle of universal service, not volunteering, and on more rigorous training and discipline (officers' authority being underscored by the Mutiny Act); this would enable a better flow of trained recruits from militia to army, and free up more regular soldiers to serve in the European campaigns.[72] The Preston Volunteer Infantry and the Preston Rifle Corps became part of the Amounderness Regiment of Local Militia, with Nicholas Grimshaw as Lt. Col. Commandant, the Bolton Regiment of Local Militia came under Lt. Col. Ralph Fletcher, the Blackburn Hundred Local Militia, Lower Division, was led by Lt. Col. Henry Hulton of Preston, a former army officer, and the Higher Division by Lt. Col. Hargreaves.[73] The erstwhile volunteer officers maintained their ranks (though still a notch behind those of their grade in the regular militia), and they and their men had become part of the county hierarchy headed by the lord lieutenant.[74]

The volunteers, recruited either in towns or from the workforces of mill colonies, are often seen as enhancing urban or urban-elite self-assertiveness, opening up a greater public space for bourgeois participation. This is undeniable, but it oversimplifies. For one thing, in these small towns, where the town-and-country borders were so permeable, the boundaries between minor gentility, leading professions, and wealthy merchants so fluid, it is difficult to classify the leadership of the volunteer corps as wholly urban bourgeois. For another, the older militia, augmented with supplementary battalions and regiments throughout the wars, was staffed by officers who had to meet precise property qualifications,[75] and so it—like the county magistracy and the deputy lieutenancy—became increasingly open to professional men and gentlemanly capitalists who invested their wealth in land, whether or not they relinquished the firm or the factory. Here the trend was toward a blurring of the lines of gentry and bourgeoisie within a broader class of notables, distinguished by wealth and standing rather than by birth.[76] So, particularly after the integration of the volunteers into the Local Militia and the county structure, did volunteering challenge the structure of the aristocratic state or buttress its walls? Perhaps that is a false dichotomy. Whether individuals, while uniting in defense of the nation, were anxious to assert their dignity and claims independently of the landed hierarchy or to gain access to those very social strata, they subverted the rigidities of the old order, testing its elasticity.

Politics in Preston

The tension between aspirations for independence and for amalgamation was visible at the same time in the politics of Preston, and initially at least this had little to do with the war. It was the culmination of a long-standing battle for supremacy between Tory-Anglicans who had control of the common council and the Whig-Dissenter interests of the Stanleys and the Hoghtons, leading landowners in and around the borough. In a violent showdown election in 1768—when, on appeal, Parliament determined that "the inhabitants at large" and not merely the freemen could vote, creating one of the broadest franchise boroughs in the country and tipping the advantage against the corporation[77] —John ("Gentleman Johnny") Burgoyne (husband to Lady Charlotte Stanley, daughter of the eleventh earl of Derby, and subsequently to gain notoriety for his generalship during the American War of Independence) along with Sir Henry Hoghton, sixth baronet, defeated two other local landowners in the Tory-Anglican corporation interest, Sir Peter Leicester of Tabley and Sir Frank Standish of Duxbury. They retained their seats until Burgoyne's death in 1792 and Hoghton's in 1795, and were succeeded in turn and without competition by W. Cunliffe Shawe of Preston and of Singleton Lodge (who retired after one term in favor of Lord Stanley, who had come of age) and Sir Henry's son, Sir Henry Philip Hoghton. This apparently smooth succession belied intense party rivalry. William Dobson, local historian and chronicler of parliamentary elections in Preston, points to the extent of factional division within the town: separate horse races between 1786 and 1791, held under the auspices of each party; two party packs of hounds; leisured ladies transported to separate soirées in sedan chairs sporting different colors; corporation addresses to the throne delivered by John Blackburne, Tory county MP, rather than by the two MPs. Even so, the Tories did not seem to represent much of an electoral challenge. For example, at the end of 1788, John Watson Jr., a strong partisan of the Stanleys (a Watson mill lay on Stanley property), wrote privately and cynically that they could afford to be parsimonious in distributing the traditional Christmas beef to the poor: "In my opinion I see no prospect of opposition, I'm persuaded we are upon too firm a rock for any one to risk an attack, this alone has Induc'd me to be very sparing in supplying the wants of the needy."[78]

All this changed in 1796 when a new economic interest became powerful enough to bid for a share of political influence. John Horrocks, founder of the cotton dynasty and in the midst of a spectacular rise, stood on the corporation ticket; the "new and important Rank which this Town has of late Years assumed in the *Great National Scale of Trade*," he claimed, demanded "that the Representation of the Town, should be entrusted to those who are *conversant* and *interested* in its *Trade* and *Prosperity*." Lord Derby ignored the warning of a supporter over a year earlier that it might be time to come to some arrangement with Horrocks, and that of another in May 1796:

The account he [Horrocks] gave me of his success on the canvass, amounts to this; either he has been deceived by false promises, or Lord Derby has not that force in the Borough which will enable his Lordship to return two Members; *and between ourselves*, I am afraid his Lordship does not know his *real* strength in Preston; This you will please to observe is only an opinion offered *to you*, but I think his Lordships *real* friends ought to examine this point very carefully, and not suffer him to expend a large sum of money without there is a fair probability of gratifying his wishes.[79]

"A Freeman of Preston," charging Derby and his committee with dirty tricks (putting up a £3,000-£4,000 building "for the sole purpose of blocking up the lights in another building belonging to Mr. Horrocks"), argued that it was to no avail:

[Y]ou must be sensible that the trading interest, if it does not now, must in a short time preponderate over your own. The inhabitants are no longer the same class of men they were when your influence was at its height—differing from your Lordship in sentiments and politics, they will no longer be dictated to; but, independent alike in their principles and in their means of subsistence, they are determined to convince the world that their borough is not the property of any man. . . . Leave us, my Lord, to ourselves—Let us exert the dearest privilege of Britons, that of electing our own representatives.[80]

Horrocks apparently secured the backing of the earl of Liverpool, who was in Pitt's cabinet as chancellor of the Duchy of Lancaster and president of the Board of Trade, and of the Manchester Church and King Club,[81] and so to some extent at least the language of interests and independence, draped in patriotic rhetoric, served as a proxy for aristocratic and sectarian rivalries. In the event the Derby coalition won, albeit narrowly; the polls stood at Stanley 772, Hoghton 756, and Horrocks 739 at the end of the tenth day, after which Horrocks declined to continue. The local elite was fairly evenly divided: one 1796 poll book reveals that of the voters from the leading occupations, fifty plumped for Horrocks, forty-one voted for Stanley and Hoghton, three for Horrocks and Stanley, and one for Horrocks and Hoghton. But it had been an expensive and chastening experience for the Whigs. Drink, palm-greasing, and associated expenditure cost them an exorbitant £11,550; at least thirty-three pubs across Preston benefited from their largesse, ranging from £95 2s.10d. spent at the Castle Inn to more than £550 at the Legs of Man.[82]

With Horrocks's mills continuing to expand, there was every indication that at the next election an even greater Whig expenditure would be insufficient. So the Stanleys and the corporation struck a deal to avoid the turmoil and expense of a contest. Under their new coalition, Stanley and Horrocks were returned unopposed in 1802; and the coalition, represented by a succession of Derbyite and corporation MPs—entailing joint campaigns, joint manifestoes, and at times contradictory voting records in Parliament[83]—remained firm until 1826, incorporating the vast majority of voters and considerably decreasing party tension and the potential for popular election-time carnival. As one election address put it in 1807, with somewhat tortured logic, the peace and prosperity of a large and trading town greatly benefited when the leaders of the two great parties, including all the respectable inhabitants, whose contests had distracted the borough for the previous forty years, agreed to forget their disputes and each offer a respectable candidate to the free choice of the electors.

Having secured local parliamentary representation for Tory-Anglicanism and the manufacturing interest, leading inhabitants were quite happy with a distinctly non-radical propertied compromise. This might be seen as one more instance of bourgeois self-promotion within the elastic boundaries of the old order, the rallying of property in return for the negotiation of a greater space. The dissenting middle-class voice was all but crowded out by this conditional, questioning loyalism. But the electoral process in Preston provides a prime example of the survival of a frail strand of bourgeois radicalism. In a by-election in 1804, when Samuel Horrocks was elected after his brother's early death, broadsides protested against the "Junto" of five or six individuals who had stitched up the town by forming the coalition, but no alternative candi-date materialized. In the 1807 election, one election squib railed against the eight or ten men—the numbers varied—who "did actually, without conven-ing a meeting to take the sense of the town, sign an Agreement, forsooth, and for what purpose? [W]hy, not to buy, or sell, or convey an estate or property of their own, but, *monstrous deed!* agree to sell and compromise your liberties."

This time an independent candidate, Joseph Hanson of Strangeways Hall, Manchester, was put forward. Hanson, born in 1774, the prosperous son of a Manchester merchant and manufacturer, was a radical, Unitarian, Friend of Peace who favored manhood suffrage. In 1803 he became Lt. Col. Commandant of his own corps, the Manchester and Salford Rifle Regiment of Volunteers—a good indication of how politically broad volunteering could be. In the Preston election he campaigned on a platform of independence from the coalition, an end to the war, and for a minimum wage for handloom weavers. He claimed that under the coalition system "the person who has the most extensive manufactory will be sent to Parliament, whatever good grounds of objection there may be to his politics, his integrity, or his ability." Certainly the bulk of the respectable classes voted for the coalition ticket, in spite of Samuel Horrocks's alleged dullness: accounts of his oratorical contribution in Parliament ranged from a charge of complete silence to an assertion that he once uttered an expressive "oh!" Most of Hanson's vote came from disgruntled weavers, and that was not sufficient to ruffle the coalition unduly. But he was not without an element of bourgeois support, and Dobson states that his committee included Thomas Wilson, banker, Thomas Sudell, attorney, and Thomas Emmett, timber merchant.[84]

Hanson subsequently became involved in a petitioning campaign for peace, and in May 1808 addressed a crowd of weavers in Manchester protesting about the rejection of a minimum wage bill. The authorities considered him a dangerous man, accused him of sedition and inciting the disturbances that followed the meeting, and gaoled him for six months. This only enhanced his popular appeal but with his health wrecked, his political activities after his release were limited to supporting a weavers' petitioning movement and giving evidence in 1811 to a parliamentary committee. Here he called for peace, a revocation of the Orders in Council, an act for the arbitration of wages, and parliamentary grants for the distressed manufacturing districts. Shortly afterwards, in September 1811, he died.[85] His younger brother, Edward, stood for the independent interest in Preston in the 1812 election, but once again the coalition survived, represented by Horrocks and Edmund Hornby of Dalton Hall, who was keeping the seat warm for the son of Lord Stanley (who had transferred to a county seat).[86]

Evolving Bourgeois Narratives

Joseph Hanson was an inspirational figure for the "small but determined" band of liberal reformers, largely Unitarian, who were later active in Manchester politics and who laid the groundwork for Manchester School liberalism.[87] He was exceptional for his status as popular hero and martyr, but he was not alone. The economic distress of 1807 that had brought the collapse of the Watson enterprise and the Loyal Preston Volunteers, and fueled weaver agitation for a minimum wage and their support for Hanson in the Preston election, was exacerbated at the end of the year by Napoleon's Continental Blockade denying access to European markets for British goods. This was the background to a large-scale weavers' strike in Lancashire and Cheshire from May to June 1808, attended by sizable crowd gatherings in and around all three towns and the smashing of many windows. The military and volunteers contained disorder, and the strike ultimately ended with a 20 percent increase in piece rates.[88] The economic malaise coincided with the military campaigning in Europe going badly; fifteen years after the start of the struggle, the end of the beginning still seemed far distant. A peace agitation had begun in Lancashire cotton towns in late November 1807. A peace petition in Bolton from the end of January 1808 gathered over seventeen thousand signatures. This was largely the work of lower-class radicals, but Ralph Fletcher and his informers singled out the influence of three or four wealthier Unitarians, particularly an "opulent manufacturer" called John Brandreth. Indeed, "the Ostensible Leader of these Clamourers for Peace is Brother to Doctor Brandreth (MD) of Liverpool—who is much connected with *Roscoe*"—that is, William Roscoe, MP for Liverpool 1806-1807, one of the chief opponents of the Napoleonic War. These Unitarians allowed people to sign the petition in the Bolton Unitarian meeting house, and Brandreth organized the petitioners in such numbers as to block the adoption of a loyalist counter-petition at a public meeting in the Sessions Rooms.[89]

The following year, the Duke of York's mistress, a married woman, was caught trafficking in promotions in the army and the Church. He was cleared after a Commons inquiry, but resigned anyway as Commander-in-Chief of the army. Sensing the opportunity to censure a man at the heart of the state and the running of the war, nearly a hundred "landowners, housekeepers, and manufacturers" in Bolton signed a requisition to the borough reeves and constables to call a public meeting. A counter-requisition, led by the vicar, declared such a meeting to be both inexpedient "and must necessarily wound the parental feeling of our beloved and revered Sovereign," and the authorities agreed. A precise matching of names and faces is not possible, but there is little doubt from the contrasting requisition lists that bourgeois individuals and families that were later to be prominent in liberalism and conservatism were already in substantial numbers staking out their positions on the conduct of the state.[90] George III's Golden Jubilee in the same year provided plenty of ammunition for a loyalist counter-attack,[91] but it should be borne in mind that the somewhat frenetic expressions of joy were not overly spontaneous, were heavily marshalled and were sandwiched between unmistakable signs of grave dissatisfaction.

Further demonstration of divisions in Bolton and Blackburn came during the disturbances of 1812, when Luddite outbreaks in the Midlands spread to

Lancashire and the West Riding. In Bolton in mid-April, incendiaries set fire to a hayrick of Joseph Ridgway and to Rothwell's ropewalk. Ralph Fletcher and his fellow magistrates coordinated the forces of order in response: two hundred infantry (some regular army from recruiting parties in town, mostly his own Local Militia), sixty regular cavalry (Capt. Bullen's Greys), forty of Major Pilkington's Light Horse Volunteers, and around eighteen hundred special constables. None of this prevented the most serious incident, the razing of Rowe and Duncough's factory at Westhoughton on April 24. The authorities, informed by Fletcher's spies, were well aware that this was being planned but they did not coordinate adequately to ensure a military presence at the crucial moment. Subsequently, the Local Militia rounded up twenty-two suspects, four of whom (including a boy) were hanged at Lancaster.[92] In light of this and other riotous incidents, the County Lieutenancy met in Preston on May 1 and ordered Local Militia commanders to muster their men across the county for use in an emergency as stopgaps before a regular military force could arrive.[93]

These arrangements helped keep the crisis under control, and the military commander of the district, Lt. Gen. Thomas Maitland, did not believe that martial law or the suspension of habeas corpus was necessary.[94] In the aftermath, a body of leading inhabitants headed by Thomas Ainsworth presented a silver vase to Ralph Fletcher for his zeal in the cause of order. But, although the response of the local authorities to the disturbances may have elicited the praise of one sector of the bourgeoisie, it antagonized another, which resolved to present Dr. Robert Taylor, a Bolton Unitarian physician, with a piece of plate worth a hundred guineas in appreciation of his contribution to exposing the so-called blackfacing spy system. Taylor responded in an address "To the Friends of Freedom in the Town and Neighbourhood of Bolton," leveling a series of accusations at the local authorities: that they had made house-raids and arrested people at night contrary to law, as they had during "the worst periods of the French Revolution, or the Irish Rebellion"; that they had tormented those imprisoned with offers of pardon and protection if they fingered their social superiors—in some instances, individuals pointed out to them; and that they had labored mightily to prove that the origins of the disturbances lay not in hunger, the doubling of the price of potatoes, and a hatred of machinery, but in political or religious disaffection. The government had stiffened law-and-order measures during the crisis, including making machine-breaking a capital offense; but Taylor and his friends had insisted that the common law was perfectly adequate to deal with the scale of violence: "We ventured to doubt the existence of the *numerous armies* said to be *arrayed* in the disturbed districts, of their *trainings and drillings by night and by day,* and of their *extensive depôts of concealed arms.*" He believed that the destruction of Westhoughton Factory had been pushed forward by spies with disguised, blackened faces—more active in raising recruits than any others, the only ones in the habit of attending nocturnal meetings armed ("it . . . becomes a matter of serious inquiry how, or where, or by whom, they were furnished with fire-arms")—and that the activities of the military on the night in question looked suspiciously like a concocted scheme to keep the field free for arson. The sum total of the allegations was that the party of order had deliberately played up and incited the radical threat in order to justify increasingly repressive measures and also to precipitate the flight of the middle classes into conservative ranks.[95]

This was essentially a bitter dispute over responses and tactics. Taylor and his friends were *not* expressing approval of the rioters' methods or goals[96] but simply measuring the activities of the authorities against their alternative reading of constitutional rights. They were not even suggesting that there had been no need for the use of force, merely that, if it had suited their plans, the magistrates could have dispersed a meeting, arrested three or four ringleaders, and broken the conspiracy's back. Whether true or not, the blackfaced-spy scandal of 1812 (and its subsequent incarnations in the years up to the Peterloo Massacre in 1819) figured in an ongoing, polarizing political rhetoric, a fixed point of reference in the evolving histories of conservatism and political dissent. For example, during the 1820s the Bolton Church and King Club allegedly drank a standing toast to "The Memory of Samuel Fletcher Esq.," a distant relative of Ralph Fletcher and, according to Robert Heywood, Unitarian manufacturer, who wrote furious letters to the *Morning Chronicle* and to Henry Hunt's *Examiner* in 1828, a principal coordinator of the spy system.[97] In 1835, on the formation of Operative Conservative Associations, a correspondent in the liberal *Bolton Free Press* warned the Bolton operatives not to be deceived: "[M]any of you will be able to tell who were the oppressors of the poor in those days of bitter humiliation to Bolton;—the times of the 'Flash fight,' the burning of Westhoughton Mill, the Peterloo, the orangery and black-facing which never had an equal except in the annals of France." At a gathering in 1838, Tories drank a toast to the conservative magistracy of the county and eulogized the part played by Col. Fletcher and William Hulton between 1812 and 1819, and in reply the *Free Press* editor attacked the black-facing system as an un-English and unparalleled attempt to crush the progress of freedom.[98] A year later, Timothy Grimshaw wrote that 1812 was a remarkable year "for the troubles then existing in the country under the Castlereagh and Sidmouth administration, and how peculiarly Bolton was doomed to feel the tyranny, carried into effect by our own townsmen; who, I blush to say it, were so far lost to every feeling of justice and humanity, as to lend themselves the willing agents in sacrificing the innocent blood of their neighbours to their own individual interest and aggrandizement. O it was foul play!"[99]

If 1812 gave verbal ammunition for both sides, it also provided a tangible victory for the Friends of Peace: the repeal of the Orders in Council. In Blackburn, a deferential petition of March 1811 to the Prince Regent had drawn attention to local distress and the impact of government policies on the country's commercial interests.[100] A year later, a more hard-hitting petition to the Commons lay for signature in various booksellers' in the town center. High prices, falling wages, frequent interruptions of labor, and an unprecedented number of failures and bankruptcies added up to a picture of misery:

What those causes are, to which evils of such enormity and magnitude may be traced, it is not difficult to ascertain. Your Petitioners submit, that they may be discovered in the impolicy which suggested, adopted, and still continues unrevoked—the Orders in Council; in the absence of conciliatory measures towards the United States; and in the want of clear, prompt and satisfactory explanations in diplomatic negociations [*sic*] with that Country. But they are imperiously compelled to specify, what, in their apprehensions, is the primary cause of their sufferings:—As natives of a Country professing the Christian Religion, they deplore the moral effects of war; as men, they lament the miseries of their fellow-creatures; as Britons, they feel convinced that war is inimical to their interests—that its continuance is more injurious to a commercial Country like their own, than to one which possesses within itself, greater physical resources—that the subjugation of the enemy is more impracticable than ever, and that his power is more firmly compacted by the opposition he has encountered.[101]

This attack, couched in terms of masculine patriotism (as *men* and as *Britons*), elevating commercial interest and Christian morality to the pinnacle of national good, formed part of an orchestrated campaign. Antiwar liberals and some northern manufacturers, seeing exports wither for the second time in under five years and fearing war with the United States, spearheaded an agitation that was partly ridden and partly spurred by Henry Brougham and the Whigs in Parliament.[102] It encountered considerable loyalist opposition. Counterpetitions followed swiftly in Blackburn. The first claimed that the initial petition had been privately prepared, that signatures had been industriously sought, and that many had signed in the hope of an end to the war "without any consideration whether Peace was attainable, except on terms which would, probably, produce our own subjugation." But it is a curiously phrased, far-from-unambiguous document. It too was "deeply interested in the revival of Commerce," but presumed "not to express a wish that the Orders should be rescinded," trusting "that the united Wisdom of your Honourable House will adopt such Measures as may ultimately tend to the national Prosperity." As for the East India Company's monopoly, which the peace petition had attacked, "we think it indecorous to *dictate* what ought to be done, in full confidence that your Honourable House will comply with the general wish."

Likewise, "we have the firmest reliance that no opportunity will be lost to cultivate a friendly intercourse with the United States of America, and to procure a general Peace, upon terms of honour to the Crown." A second petition, to Spencer Perceval, was much less equivocal, patronizingly contending that the antiwar petition had been signed mostly by "poor industrious Men and *Boys*" who were unable "to appreciate the merits of many of the complicated questions of Policy," that the depiction of distress had been exaggerated, and that "the language of despondence" propagated "*discontent at home.*" As for the Orders in Council, the petitioners "firmly rely on the Wisdom of Parliament, and his Majesty's Government, to *rescind, continue, extend or modify them,* as may be most conducive to the lasting welfare of the country."[103]

As the peace petitions and agitations continued across the region, the magistrates, clergy, and other inhabitants of the Bolton area signed a syrupy address to the Prince Regent, professing the highest confidence in the talents of himself and of his government. It went on,

We clamour not for peace, believing that a safe and honourable peace, is altogether unattainable in present circumstances. We complain not of the Orders in Council, being fully persuaded that they are not the cause of our sufferings, and that an adherence to them is a necessary and politic measure. We trust that under the auspices of your Royal Highness, our trade will ere long again flourish, and we believe that every measure that true wisdom can suggest, will be adopted in the mean time to assist and promote it.[104]

"True wisdom" suggested, for a variety of economic, political, and diplomatic reasons, the revoking of the Orders in Council; the state proved its responsiveness to influential interests.[105] Although it gave no answer to the prayers for peace, antiwar activity subsided with a revival in trade and the success of allied armies in the remaining years of the conflict. The protests since 1807 had shown a bourgeois house divided, but could not disguise the fact that the wars strengthened the bourgeois commitment to an evolving Tory ideology: the sacred rights of property and an ordered hierarchy in church and state had been rhetorically buttressed through the contrast with a republican or usurping barbarism, and the appropriation of a language of national identity.[106] At the center was the Protestant constitution and a suitably domesticated and unobtrusive monarch, and propping up the edifice ever more securely were the songs, the beef, the ale, the loyalist readings of history, the key texts of Toryism (such as "Fear God and Honour the King," and "Meddle not with them that are given to change"),[107] and whatever else could be called into service in the patriotic cause, particularly the twisting of the memory of Pitt into a useful shape that rendered him historically unrecognizable.[108]

Throughout the wars, the majority of the local bourgeoisie associated bourgeois progress with the progress of the aristocratic state. This was not co-option—an early "selling out" by the bourgeoisie even in the early stages of industrialization—but the calculation of interest and the economic and social advancement of themselves vis-à-vis their superiors and inferiors, a step in the "quiet revolution" of the bourgeoisie. The wars tended to bolster bourgeois self-identity: commercial expansion and periodic trade disruption, the revolutionary stirrings of the lower classes, the chance to dress up in volunteer regiment uniforms to express both loyalty *and* a measure of independence from patrician control, *could* foster a more cohesive and coherent class awareness among the loyalists, *or* this same sectional self-assertion could be used as a vehicle for those who wished to climb into the ranks of the broadening band of mixed-wealth notables, *or* it could bolster the small knot of radicals in their opinions. The price members of the bourgeoisie demanded for their taxes, donations, mobilization, and vocal support was a responsive and responsible state, and it was principally in judging this that the bourgeoisie displayed its divergent voices during the wars, ensuring that just as it had been heavily divided before 1793 it would not emerge after 1815 pounded into a homogeneous Tory mold. The bourgeois radicals were confident enough to challenge the wisdom of the state's actions at home and abroad; the loyalists still broadly trusted the judgment of the executive and legislature.

CHAPTER 2: SERIOUSNESS

Convinced that the Word of God was about to be fulfilled, William Whittaker, failed Manchester merchant and father of the future vicar of Blackburn, predicted in 1795 that

this Country, Scotland[,] Ireland and all Europe will be involved in War—the most Cruel Wars that ever happend on Earth which will be accompanied with Famine & Pestilence Earthquakes & Fire from Heaven what the Jews sufferd is not to compare with what Christendom is doomd to suffer—The French will invade and conquer this Country and will itself be conquerd by the Turks and made tributary; and the Turks & Swedes will overrun all the Continent of Europe.[1]

The rise to hegemony of the Swedes is rather an idiosyncratic touch, but in its essentials this was an oft-repeated apocalyptic message. God intervened directly and cataclysmically in human affairs as a punishment for human transgressions. The Puritan-evangelical tradition of individuals and nations locked in mortal combat with satanic forces confronted the Renaissance legacy of gentility, politeness, and civility and the Enlightenment legacy of Reason; the duties of frugality, abstinence, and otherworldliness challenged the imperative of a capitalist economy for energetic and conspicuous consumption; the ethic and necessity of work contradicted the ideal of leisured refinement. For middling families on the rise, the reconciliation of these legacies—when commercial and industrial wealth was making the latter ever more realizable ever lower down the social scale—was a considerable source of tension and anxiety. A reconciliation of sorts was effected in the ideal of the Christian gentleman or lady—refined, but not overly indulgent; tasteful, but not frivolous—but there were many different nuances along the road of the bourgeoisie's ever unstable, ever fluctuating, always schizophrenic cultural formation.[2] All three legacies suggested a distancing from a "traditional" and an (increasingly exclusive) popular culture.[3]

Clerical Seriousness

The battle was fought out among all groups of the professional, mercantile, and manufacturing bourgeoisie. It is especially vividly expressed by the ministers, the chief propagandists of cultural ideology in the cotton district, who had embarked upon the last great crusade in British history in order to reclaim the nation for God.[4] In 1786, in the aftermath of defeat in America, the Rev. Edward Whitehead, vicar of Bolton, bemoaned the state of the nation:

Look through every Rank and Station, and you cannot but observe the Propensity to Luxury, to Dissipation, to Extravagance which universally prevails;—the Dress, the Diet, the Wages of the common People are such as former Times never knew.—Content seems flown, Industry and Œconomy are in a Manner vanished;—every Thing implies a Disrelish for the Post in which Providence hath fixed Mankind.

He looked to exemplary hangings and to Sunday schools for at least "a Reformation of Manners among the lower Ranks of People."[5]

In the dark days of the 1790s, the specter or reality of war, revolution, and famine were especially propitious for messianic pronouncements, like the one delivered by the Rev. Thomas Jones, minister of St. George's, Little Bolton, in 1797, in an appeal for donations for Sunday schools for the new church. The times were awful. The righteous arm of the Lord was stretched out.

And what is the cause of all these massacres, these torrents of blood, of weeping parents, of weeping children, and of weeping friends? *Sin*; Sin is the cause of all the evils that prey upon and distract nations, families, and individuals. What then has not *this nation* to fear, where infidelity, profaneness, hypocrisy, and sin in every form, even among all ranks, so generally prevail?

Thank God for a virtuous king.[6] Jones wielded the cudgel again the following year, with a call for radical moral reform among the higher classes:

[W]hile the servants see that these times make no difference in their masters [*sic*] usual course of living, that their feasts, their merry meetings, their drunken revels are as common as ever, the servants will not like to be starved and worked to death to support the extravagance of their masters. No reform in these things has yet been observed in any of the masters or mistresses in this town or neighbourhood.

Without reform, ruin was certain, and the judgment of God upon France, Flanders, and Holland would be visited upon England. All places of public amusement and all promoters of French principles and vices must be shut up at least for the duration of the war.[7] The Rev. Thomas Stevenson of St. John's, Blackburn, was more sanguine about Britain's chances of survival in 1807, even as Napoleon, "Selected by divine Providence as a scourge to punish sinful nations," was felling less virtuous peoples. The nation had been spared thus far—above all because of its pure faith, and the genuine piety and holiness of life of many of its members and of many Dissenters. But there was no room for complacency; the occasional observance of fast days would serve no purpose without a sincere abhorrence of past transgressions and a real change in manners and morals. All ranks of society were guilty of a lack of religious principle, an indifference to public worship, the systematic neglect of the Lord's Supper, dissoluteness, luxury, extravagance, and the immoderate love of pleasure.[8]

Dr. Thomas Dunham Whitaker, vicar of Whalley and of Blackburn, squire of the Holme, was the epitome of the Christian gentleman, the evangelical patrician. A student of law at Cambridge, he married into Leeds mercantile wealth (the Thoresby family), turned to the Church, inherited his father's estates and nominated himself to the family curacy of Holme. Most of his life he dedicated to a cultivated, gentlemanly lifestyle of tending to his estates, antiquarian studies, and improving the standing of the Church. He brought together the neighboring clergy—the Rev. Thomas Starkie, vicar of Blackburn, the Rev. William Barton of Samlesbury, the Rev. Robert Smith of Waddington, and the Rev. Thomas Wilson, master of Clitheroe School—in a literary club, dining at each others' houses, to discuss the Church, literature, and politics. Such meetings, we are told, displayed elegant hospitality, pleasurable conversation and quiet enjoyment. Whitaker's daily schedule, at least before he became vicar of Blackburn, was to breakfast before eight and directly enter his study to begin writing. He nearly always read a page or two of Tacitus, except on Saturdays when he read one of the Fathers, preferring Chrysostom. About noon he joined his workmen in the woods for three hours, and he liked to have his two greyhounds with him; he was awarded the Gold Medal of the Society of Arts in 1794 for planting 64,135 larches in one year: planting was the great delight of his life. He dined at three, then did little until tea at six or half past six, before returning to the study for an hour. At half past seven his family joined him, and while the ladies sewed, one of the sons read aloud from Clarendon, Robertson, Southey, or—especially—Scott's novels, which he reviewed for the *Quarterly*.[9]

Such was the relatively leisured life of a clerical squire, when not involved in magisterial duties. But Whitaker's thought, partial though it was to a vanished, settled, gentry hierarchy, and more generous than most Establishment clerics to the achievements of Roman Catholicism, was suffused with evangelical doctrine. Take, for example, his unrealized project: to write a history of the Roman Empire fit for Christians to read. His aim was to recognize the splendor of Gibbon's *Decline and Fall*, but "the work will be given to the public merely as one which the pious may read without a sigh, and the modest without a blush, neither of which can be said to be the case with respect to that great but depraved and mischievous performance."[10] More directly, the "topographical" books that he did complete were concerned with "vindicating the present constitution of England, and of serving the interests of religion by the occasional introduction of such remarks as appeared to arise out of the subject." These included railing against the awful state of the Church, its internal decay in vigor and spirit. There should be less interference by the civil power in spiritual matters, much more attention paid by patrons to clerical merit rather than family interests, the solicitations of friends, and literary claims, and more accommodation provided to meet the competition from Dissenters in manufacturing towns.[11]

In his history of Leeds in 1816 these thoughts came out even more strongly. He praised the purchasing of the advowson of the vicarage of Leeds by the parishioners:

Had it not been for this judicious and well-timed step, the cure of many thousand souls might at every avoidance have been consigned to some younger son, or some worthless favourite of a great family, raw, dissipated, and ignorant; the advowson might have been advertised, and brought under the hammer from time to time, with the usual recommendations—the vicinity of a pack of foxhounds, or the certainty of good society and evening card parties.

On the question of leisure, he was glad that the theater had been shut up for four years because of lack of patronage. Here his ambivalence about polite society and Christian values was at its most acute. He thought theatrical entertainment the most elegant and fascinating of all amusements, and therefore the most dangerous: "Of every thing which tends to corrupt the principles, to debauch the heart, and above all to dishonour the Almighty, I should, in its connexion with the present subject, wish and pray that it might assume a shape the most repulsive and brutal possible." The modern stage was profane. Thus voluntarily to court temptation, merely because the object was attractive, might be used with equal force as an apology for sins from which many of the unreflecting advocates of stage plays would shrink with horror.[12] So here Dr. Whitaker drew the line between cultivated gentility (entirely laudable) and worldliness that fondled the outer fringes of sin (the theater, and fox-hunting, card-playing parsons). Maintaining such a leaky barrier would not be easy.

Another influential minister who tried at the same time was the Rev. Dr. Joseph Fletcher of Chapel Street Independent Chapel, Blackburn. He came from a very different background. Born in 1784 in Chester, the son of a gold-smith, he entered his father's business before proceeding to Hoxton Academy and then on to Glasgow University. He came to Blackburn for the first time in 1806. The Rev. Joseph France recalled in 1846,

Such was the effect of his early ministrations amongst us, both in public and private, that a considerable revival took place of "pure and undefiled religion," which had previously fallen to a low ebb even in the church itself. Cards, dancing, the theatre, which had before been tolerated to a greater or less extent among even the members of the church, soon gave place to the voice of prayer and praise, both at the prayer-meeting and in the social circle.

In practice, this opposition to "the world, the flesh, and the devil" could take the form of a rebuke to Thomas Clayton, high sheriff of Lancashire in 1808, for deciding to hold his progression on a Sunday, thus disturbing the day's tranquillity, order, and religious devotion. At the private level, he wrote to a friend, Mrs. C. [Cunliffe?], in 1813, disapproving of her presence at certain places of amusement:

I should, perhaps, find some difficulty in proving to an irreligious person the evil of cards and of dancing—of assemblies and of theatres; for they are all parts of ONE AND THE SAME SYSTEM—the system of worldly dissipation; but I should hope that every reflecting and serious mind would feel at once their evil and their inconsistency. Little reasoning would be necessary to convince a sincere inquirer after the will of Christ.

Conformity to the dictates of fashionable dissipation would also be setting the wrong example to family, servants, and worldly associates. The latter "see no more harm in cards and dancing at home than in the assembly—they think the theatre no worse than either! Where will they stop?"[13] Where indeed. The slope was devilishly slippery.

Yet assemblies flourished. The experience of theaters in the doldrums in the cotton towns during Regency England might say something about where most committed or lip-serving Christians were prepared to draw the line. But the question of which entertainments were or were not actually or potentially sinful itself drew a jagged line among the clergy of different denominations. J. W. Whittaker, vicar of Blackburn, had no problems in attending French theater when he was in Paris. The Rev. William Thistlethwaite of St. George's, Little Bolton, son of a Yorkshire clergyman and resolutely Evangelical, was also rather tolerant of some entertainments. He was a diligent and dedicated minister, a man who, after a year of family tragedies, could write in October 1817 a memorandum in his diary: to be more watchful against evil thoughts, strenuous in repressing desires of worldly honors for his children, earnest in suppressing all feelings of vanity, less careful about the things of this world, more regular, long, and spiritual in his private devotions, more *serious* in the whole state of his mind and conversation. Yet he noted in his diary in November 1823 that he had consented for "my young people" to go to a concert in Manchester. The matter obviously troubled him. He really did not see anything wrong in it. Did it draw the mind from God and dispose it to love the world? He thought not, unless inordinately pursued. He would go himself without any scruple, if it would not cause offense to the minds of some of his Christian brethren.[14]

Clerical seriousness demanded a life of exemplary piety and constraint and a vigorous didacticism. This seriousness was recorded in a received narrative structure, which is not to say that it was artificial, merely that thoughts were recorded, structured, and molded by an available language of experience. First one had to recognize how monstrous a sinner one was, before one could be refreshed by the cathartic power of the spirit. John M'Kenzie, Particular Baptist minister at Vauxhall Road Chapel, Preston, kept a diary recording the state of his soul and ubiquitous satanic temptations. For example, on May 29, 1841: "This morning dissolved and broken hearted in prayer, wept, from a sense of sin, helplessness, and the Lord's long absence." On March 19, 1842: "O what a blessed morning has this been to me! Ever memorable morning! The dear Lord has answered my request; he has experimentally saved my soul." But the road to salvation had to negotiate many perils; on September 1, 1846:

For many weeks I have been distressed and plagued with vile thoughts in the heart. It has brought me at times into great guilt, and even dreadful terrors have seized me, lest the Lord should strike me dead for the vile thoughts, and indulging in them. I have wept, grieved, and prayed against them, but could not overcome them. They have made my very heart groan, and filled my mind with gall. But the Lord has pleased to hear my cry: he took away the power of the temptation, and delivered my mind from it; and on Saturday blessed me with the sweetness of the truth in Isa. xxvii. 1-6.

When dangerously ill in 1848, the sins of his youth paraded themselves before his eyes. He praised God for his affliction.[15]

The Rev. Peter Houghton, assistant curate at Walton-le-Dale Church, likewise was thankful to God for punishing him for his vices via an injury in sword practice in 1821. According to a posthumous morality tale penned by the Rev. Roger Carus Wilson, Evangelical vicar of Preston, Houghton's later youth was characterized by unlimited license and wholesale sin. Contrition followed ruin, but this was insufficient: "[N]o symptom in any man's case can be less hopeful than a disposition to extenuate his culpability, by ascribing his failings rather to his circumstances than his evil propensity, and to rely with unshaken trust upon his own strength and ability to amend." It took the sword injury to create in him a true spiritual appetite through divine mercy. As he put it in his journal, October 19, 1821, "O how gracious was the Lord thus to afflict me, and then mercifully bring to my mind as a refuge, that pure and holy religion which I could never have received or adopted in the false security of health and worldly prospects!" An exemplary life followed, of devotion, study of the Scriptures, and family worship, before his ordination, and soon after his early, but peaceful and victorious, death from consumption. The moral was contained in Wilson's parting benediction: "Happy soul! thou art now beyond the reach of trial and distress! May many readers be incited, by thy example, to choose 'that good part,' which shall terminate in 'glory, and honour, and immortality!'"[16]

According to Lord Charles Thynne, the vicars of Deane and Bolton "were like the poles, Mr. G[irdlestone] being Evangelical and Mr. Slade a Churchman." But both were worshippers at the altar of seriousness. Slade rose early every morning, exercised his horse before breakfast, then said prayers with his family and servants, before visiting the parish church schools. He diligently saw to parochial business, strove to visit every case of sickness known to him, and was a prolific author of religious works. John Hick, ironfounder and later MP, recounted the story Slade told a dinner party about the time he had drunk nearly a pint of wine at college, "and he dwelt upon the recollection of this with evident and unfeigned regret, and he had never so far committed himself again; we did not think it so very dreadful." Luke Boardman, later the founder of a Ragged School, described the turning point in his search for God when, as a servant to Slade, he wandered into the vicarage drawing room at two in the morning. "All was dark, except from the glimmer of a candle I carried in my hand. In one corner of that room I found [the vicar] on his knees in deep mental agonising prayer. He heeded me not, even knew not of my presence."

For five years from 1825 Slade recorded his thoughts in his diary. Although eschewing any form of enthusiasm or innovation, he could acknowledge in October 1825 that "I am lamentably wanting in the complete formation of the true Christian character." On New Year's Day 1827 one of his children broke out with measles, an apparently ominous start to the year. But "Afflictions are commonly to be remembered amongst our greatest blessings, and so the beginning of the year might rather be deemed auspicious, as opening with a mark of heavenly favour, of salutary instruction and warning, 'for whom the Lord loveth He correcteth, and chasteneth every son whom He receiveth.'" Finally, on his death in 1860, a letter was found commending his spirit to God with the words, "Unworthy, most deeply and abominably and infinitely unworthy, have I been of the divine mercy and grace so abundantly manifested to me; but the price of the atoning sacrifice is infinite and in the blood of the spotless Lamb is all my hope."[17]

The Rev. Edward Girdlestone's attitude toward seriousness can be approached via a pamphlet he wrote on the family in the 1850s. Family prayer—"now happily . . . almost universal, at least once a day, amongst the higher and middle classes"—provided a shield "against the attacks with which Satan assails us all." He entreated parents,

have you endeavoured to convince your children practically of their own sinful nature and sinful conduct? Have you laboured to make them aware of their own personal weakness, their inability to save themselves, their need of the anointing of the Holy Spirit and the Redeemer's love? Have you led, actually led, them to the foot of the cross?

He earnestly warned young people leaving home against yielding to the pomp and vanities of a wicked world, and the sinful lusts of the flesh. They would hear things called by strange names. Pleasure would be—happiness, a cunning man—ingenious, the prodigal—generous. Father's house, with its morning and evening prayer, opened Bible, and mild code of discipline and counsel, would be held up as an object of ridicule. Satan was sure to beset one's path with the great temptation of worldly-minded companions.[18]

Lay Seriousness

We have moved a long way from the cheerful ribaldries of the Rev. Thomas Wilson or the days in the late-eighteenth century when the Rev. James Folds, lecturer of Bolton Parish Church and curate of Walmsley, used to lose money at cards.[19] Clergymen had their own thresholds where respectability left off and sin began, but there can be no doubt that the cult of seriousness was well-nigh universal and that that threshold was high, be it for the clerical squire, the High Churchman, the Evangelical Anglican, or the Dissenting minister. The perils of the outside world were to an extent tamed and domesticated by the ideology of the Christian family—finery, show, elegance, taste were acceptable to many more inside the home than outside—and we will explore this in due course. But what of lay people and the cult of seriousness? Here the examples are legion, from personal testimony, through fast days, to campaigns against the profanation of Sundays.

In terms of conforming to a received narrative, leading Methodists—or at least their biographers—were particularly practiced. The essential plot figured worldliness, an overwhelming sense of personal sin after a long struggle, a flooding of the soul with the spirit of God, a sure knowledge of salvation, and a triumphant death. It was remarkably consistent. Nathaniel Aspden, born in 1766 in Harwood, trained as a surgeon and set up practice in Colne. He married in 1788, and the couple indulged themselves for a while in the fashionable circles of society. Soon they both agreed to hear the Methodists, and then the struggle began between his own sense of unworthiness and the violent assaults of the powers of darkness. He was admitted as a Methodist in 1790 and came to practice in Blackburn the following year. "When called out, particularly on the midwifery business, it was usual with him, either before or after delivery, to acknowledge God, and call upon him for help, or return him thanks for mercies received; and so directed all around him to God, in Christ, as the great Author and Giver of all good." He became ill in 1798 and died of consumption three months later, resigned, confident, and serene.[20]

James Hemmington Wood was born in 1795 the son of a minister and educated as a surgeon in Manchester. Once his parents moved to Stockport, "he did then, considering himself more at liberty, though he knew it wrong, frequently visit the theatre. This conduct, being in direct opposition to his religious education, and the voice of parental instruction and example, had a powerful tendency to blunt in him the edge of moral feeling." In 1813, aged seventeen, he was elected surgeon, apothecary, and man-midwife to the Blackburn Dispensary and workhouse, hoping at the end of the stipulated time to attend the requisite lectures in London and so begin practice for himself. But the symptoms of consumption had taken hold and were gathering pace, and he had to resign. In June 1814 his father wrote to him that he considered him near the eternal Word:

O my James, it is true, you have sinned, and that with a high hand; but, if you despair of mercy on that account, and consequently do not pray for salvation, that is the most effectual way to perish. . . . O come, do not despair, but trust in the Lord. He has pardoned crimes as numerous and aggravated as yours. . . . My heart and my eyes are full. What, a child of mine *go to hell*! God forbid! for the sake of Jesus Christ, who came into the world to save sinners, even the chief.

But the affliction from God was concentrating James's mind and had brought him to prayer. He now sought out the company only of the righteous. On a journey to France for the sake of his health, the habits of foreigners acted—as they did for so many other British travelers—as a foil for his own newly awakened and patriotic self-righteousness. France was a wicked place of bold infidelity and blind superstition, where shops were open, people gambled and danced and went to the theater on the Lord's Day. Back in England, at the end of the year he confessed to his mother his wickedness in the past in attending the theater and other places of fashionable resort. The real danger was, as the writer of the account editorialized, that

Many Novels, Plays, and Romances, are so full of infernal poison, written with so much subtilty [*sic*], painting the worst vices in the most pleasing colours, that they seem to have been inspired by the great deceiver and enemy of mankind. How dangerous then must it be to see these represented, when rendered engaging by soft music, beautiful scenery, pleasant voices, and a just and agreeable action! These things dissolving the mind in pleasure, leave it quite unguarded; and the fatal poison entering at every sense, diffuses itself through the whole soul.

Wood died victoriously on December 30.[21]

Mary Crompton, daughter of Peter Rothwell, prominent Bolton iron-founder and Methodist, delighted in music and dancing when she was young and thus was heading straight for perdition. Only the prayers of her sisters and the affliction of a friend, who came to see herself as the chief of sinners, persuaded her to give her heart fully to God. The first defining moment came at a prayer meeting on September 1, 1810: "I had such a view by faith of the Saviour hanging upon the cross for me, that I never durst doubt afterwards. I came running home to announce the joyful intelligence to my dear sisters, who had longed for my salvation." The second arrived in May 1818 when she received witness of the Holy Ghost that the blood of Christ had cleansed her from all sin. She started a school for women and instructed poor children in sewing. After marrying R. S. Crook, a Liverpool barrister, in 1828, she diligently pursued charitable objectives, including spreading the Word at the penitentiary.[22]

The marriage of Margaret, daughter of Edward Crompton of Bolton, to a French nobleman, Leonard Thomas de Manneville, proved to be an unsuccessful attachment and ended with a long Chancery suit over possession of their child, whom the father allegedly wished to have educated in a Catholic convent abroad (see below, Chapter 4).[23] But partly through the blessings of these trials she found true religion, both within the Church (she remained a member to the end of her life) and as a Wesleyan (she joined in 1829). Alone this was not enough. The Almighty saw fit to take unto Himself her child and mother within the same year: "The Lord saw the only way to bring me to Himself, was to remove all my earthly props; and though I can never cease to mourn the loss of my beloved relatives, I can bless God for their removal to heaven, that my own salvation might be insured." She realized that happiness lay in basking in the sunshine of her Savior's love rather than in worldly pleasures. At times this could be peculiarly intense; on September 7, 1833, she wrote in her diary,

How richly do I deserve the lowest hell for my portion! but instead of that, my soul this morning seemed to be quite overwhelmed with the love of my dying Saviour, and I was, whilst dressing, in such an ecstacy, that I was compelled to cry out, Glory! Glory! Glory! Oh! that this was always the frame of my soul.

She was permitted a further period of personal suffering in the three or four years before she died in 1842.[24]

Thomas Crouch Hincksman, Preston flax spinner and Wesleyan, testified through his life to the enduring power of the darkness-to-light narrative. Born the son of a London draper in 1799, he was placed in the business of Garner and Outram, being sent to their Bolton branch to learn bookkeeping and a practical knowledge of the cotton trade at the age of sixteen. At Bolton, "I was surrounded with vice and immorality, and in nine long months saw more of the dark side of this world than either before or since." He found true religion while staying with the family of Robert Gardner, Wesleyans, in Manchester. His conversion experience occurred in 1818, a light from heaven touching him while he lay in bed: "I was overwhelmed with a sense of peace and joy which I had never before conceived of. It kept me long awake in praise and thanksgiving."

He moved to Chorley and then on to Preston, still in the employ of Gardner, before starting up his own factory, Ribble Bank Mill, with two partners. His life was one of rigorous rectitude within the ranks of Preston Methodism, as circuit steward, class leader, treasurer of Lune Street Chapel, and active promoter of day and Sunday schools. When he moved to Lytham in 1848 for the sake of his wife's health, he played the principal role in the promulgation of Methodism there. He was, as his biographer put it, "essentially a man of order, a most pronounced *method*-ist in all he did." Principled, prosperous, but not covetous, the bearer of a lofty standard of home rule, he rarely attended dinner parties or drawing-room gatherings and never hosted them except in connection with his church and the Bible Society. Duty, order, punctuality: Hincksman had seriousness engraved all over him.[25]

So did his wife, Dorothy. She was the daughter of a small master potter in the Potteries. In her late teens she started attending Methodist services. She described one night, upon hearing a preacher at Hanley:

I was thinking over the words . . . "*Christ Jesus came into the world to save sinners.*" Well, I said; but not for one so vile. It was repeated, "*Christ Jesus came into the world to save sinners,*" all sinners, even the worst. Then, I said, I must be one. In a moment light broke forth. I had "joy unspeakable and full of glory," and my mouth was filled with praise.

Thus began her new life of piety, which resulted in a temporary rupture with her father. In 1824 she married Thomas Jones, a Wesleyan missionary, and set sail with him to the West Indies. Fifteen months later, she was the only survivor when a mail boat between the islands was wrecked off Antigua, claiming the lives of her husband, four other missionaries, their families, servants, and crew. Back in England, she married Hincksman in 1832. They made a formidable couple. She too, her biographer relates, was a determined enemy to indolence and extravagance. She took a warm interest in the circulation of the Scriptures and religious tracts, and her reading toward the end of her life (in 1859; he died in 1883) was concentrated particularly on the prophetic parts of the Scriptures, especially those bearing on the restoration of the Jews.[26]

A slightly different type of narrative concerned the child growing up already within a vigorously religious household, who had to wrestle with the Almighty as much as anyone, but for whom tales of the deepest sinfulness of worldliness were somewhat inappropriate. Anne Eliza was the daughter of Roger Crane, one of Preston's earliest well-to-do champions of Methodism. "From her first years, she was accustomed to bow at the family altar; to reverence the word of God; to listen quietly and attentively to His ministers in His house; and to esteem them, and all who loved the Lord Jesus, very highly, for

His sake." She married George Fishwick of Springfield near Garstang in 1819, who developed the mill colony at Scorton; "On her marriage, Mrs. F. had not, like many harmless, thoughtless young ladies, to give up habits of self gratification and indulgence, and to acquire those of self-denial and control." But she still needed to be tested. For example, after she gave birth to a delicate son, "Many times during his infancy, were her faith and resignation keenly tested; but when she was fully willing to make the sacrifice, God said, as in the ancient days, 'It is enough,' and restored the child to his mother."[27]

The Wesleyan Methodists were the most prolific narrators of the personal transition from worldliness to seriousness, but they were not alone. Some Dissenters described the lives of their most prominent members using a very similar narrative form. Joseph Topp of Kearsley built the first Independent Chapel in Farnworth. His daughter Elizabeth was born in 1803 into a highly religiously charged household. Her biographer records with evident delight that one day when young she was seen rocking in her little chair with her youngest sister on her knee, singing

> There is a dreadful hell,
> And everlasting pains,
> Where sinners must with devils dwell,
> In darkness, fire, and chains.

Inevitably she felt for a time that she was too vile for salvation, but at length she cast herself entirely on the mercy of God, through the atoning blood of Christ, and found the joy and peace of believing. She married George, eldest son of J. R. Barnes of Summerfield, and dedicated much of her life to prayer, the study of the Scriptures, the distribution of tracts, and teaching in the Sunday school, urging on the children, often with tears, to an immediate and entire decision for God.[28] George himself, a worshipper at Halshaw Moor Independent Church, had had frequent doubts and fears in his late teens that he was not a child of God, and withdrew from church, believing that he had no right to be there. But after the deaths of a younger brother, his sister-in-law, and his sister in quick succession in the mid-1830s he gave himself afresh to God and became both a liberal supporter of religious societies and a Sunday school teacher.[29]

Most of the evidence for seriousness comes not from structured narratives from hagiographers or autobiographies but from comments or observations in correspondence, diaries, and accounts that reveal a particular cast of mind and guiding principle. Seriousness was extraordinarily widespread across the ranks of the lesser gentry and the bourgeoisie. It long predated the French Revolution, but William Whittaker and the clerical moralists were not alone in treating that cataclysm as a major portent, an indication of God's wrath, and a call to moral arms. Take the retrospective of Lady Shelley (as she became), daughter of Thomas Winckley of Preston. Her account is over-generalized and sanctimonious, but it can stand as an example of the Revolution's impact on a young child (she was born in 1787) and on polite society. She recalled the grief of those around her at the execution of Louis XVI and Marie Antoinette. She was taken to see, in a convent in Preston, Princesse Louise de Bourbon, who had fled from a convent near Paris during the Terror: "Thus was the instability of rank and prosperity impressed upon my mind, in a manner far more eloquent and convincing than by any amount of books or sermons relating to that painful episode." As for polite society,

The awakening of the labouring classes, after the first shock of the French Revolution, made the upper classes tremble. They began to fear that those who had hitherto been treated as helots might one day, as in France, get the upper hand. Never, in the history of our country, was a better proof afforded of the good sense of the Anglo-Saxon character. Practical measures were adopted to improve the condition of the poor. Land allotments, clothing clubs, and many other philanthropic measures were promoted. Village schools sprang up in many parts of the country. The parson no longer hunted; or shot, five days in the week, cleaning his fowling-piece on the sixth, prior to the preparation of a drowsy sermon, delivered on the seventh day to a sleeping congregation. Every man felt the necessity for setting his house in order.[30]

The Hultons of Hulton Park, with extensive landed and coal-owning interests, influential members of the Bolton elite, occupied that uncertain social layer of the lesser gentry and the haute bourgeoisie. William Hulton, magistrate of Peterloo notoriety, reinforced his political notions by subscribing fully to the cult of Church-evangelical seriousness. According to his obituarist, he conscientiously set himself in his early days against the prevailing laxity of the gentry and Established clergy and allied himself with those bent upon resuscitating the spiritual life of the Church. For fifty years his seat at Deane Church

was never empty at either of its services, nor did he ever fail in his attendance at the Lord's table. Among his tenants he did everything in his power to keep alive the same reverence for holy things which he entertained himself, and always urged and encouraged them to avail themselves of religious ordinances both by precept and by example.[31]

Jonathan Peel of Accrington House, manufacturer, comes across in the description by his granddaughter, Catherine Jacson, as the very epitome of patriarchal authority. He practiced a personal asceticism after, apparently, an early manhood of living freely. Gout induced abstemious habits and the close study of scriptural subjects. But the frugality of the master did not diminish the comforts and abundance of the rest of the household, and domesticity (or bourgeois gentility) cohabited with a streak of puritanism. Jacson's vivid recollection of her grandfather is of his powerful form through the window of his sitting room, seated in an uncushioned wooden armchair, holding a large, quarto, parchment-bound Bible, with one or two other books, probably sermons or meditations, on an oak table beside him. The day at Accrington House was unvaried: family prayers at half past seven, at which no family member, guest, or servant would be missing or late. Peel sat motionless by the dining table, where the Bible and Prayer Book were laid ready, ten minutes before the prayer bell rang. Breakfast followed at eight, with a saucer of oatmeal porridge, a small pot of treacle, and a soft sour oatcake for the master. Dinner was at one, abundant for the family, spare for its head. Tea at six was a repetition of breakfast, and prayers at eight an exact reprise of the morning session. Grandfather rarely appeared at supper at nine. Such was the life of one octogenarian near-millionaire in the 1820s.[32] While the asceticism might have been extreme, the devotion, regularity, and family prayers were not.

John Fowden Hindle, a gentleman-merchant and High-Church Tory, who lived in one of the grand townhouses on King Street, Blackburn, wrote a letter to his son, William, in 1817, after William had chosen to make a career in the army. Like a letter from Lord Chesterfield to his son, it was intended to be kept for perusal ("If you love me do not *destroy this letter* but treasure it up for *my sake*"); but it could scarcely have been more different in tone and content. He wrote,

I my dear Boy have packed up in your Box a Bible, and a Prayer Book, and also a new Weeks preparation for the holy Sacrament which I pray & beseech you regularly to peruse and which will be the means of securing your happiness in this life, but above all will prepare you for that eternal & brighter happiness in the world that is yet to come; be ever my dear Boy regular in your attendance at Church, and you have *promised* me (by permission of Providence) to receive the holy Sacrament with your dear Sister Custance at Edinburgh; this is an *essential* part of your duty which I *beg* & *entreat* you will *never* omit.

He reminded him that the good and pious Christian was an honorable and brave soldier, and he beseeched him to be obedient to his superior officers and gentle and polite to his equals and inferiors. He fixed his allowance at £150 a year, but suggested this might be raised to £200 if he were frugal and conducted himself well. Moreover,

let me also caution my dear Boy against Gaming, a vice onst learnt is never cured and which inevitable woud [*sic*] bring you to ruin, to Poverty, & to Jail, be sober and on your guard against every vice and may you prove your self an ornament to your Profession & merit ye esteem of all your brothers in Arms, and the continued affection of your fond Parents.[33]

Examples of seriousness can be readily multiplied throughout the bourgeoisie. Roger Cunliffe, principal in the Blackburn banking firm, an Independ
ent, wrote to a fellow Sunday school teacher, Thomas Ainsworth, in 1817,

Since my arrival in London I have had many conflicts against the vicious influences which abound, but have hitherto been able to withstand them. The temptations in this place have arrived at a very great pitch,—to a magnitude which you
cannot conceive in the country. . . . I am at a great loss here on the Sabbath day,
for there is very little doing in the Sunday School, and there is no school at all
where I attend. Do value your privileges in this respect, and be concerned about
making a right improvement of them. Let me urge you to be very serious with the
children you teach, for it is a more solemn charge than many are aware of.[34]

Thomas Thomasson, the Bolton cotton lord, a former Quaker whose thoughts
turned to a freethinking Christianity, was a democrat, free trader, lover of the
commercial spirit, and campaigner for the political equality of the sexes. Muscular, freethinking independence to this extent was unusual among the bourgeoisie. But, like many others, he was deeply scarred by the puritanical legacy.
He was extremely wealthy, but according to his obituarists, he lived plainly,
not spending his wealth in selfish gratification. Thrifty forethought was his
practice as well as his recipe for success. He scorned all those who lived an
idle, self-indulgent life on the labors of others, those who rode on the backs of
the world's toilers.[35] James Simpson Sr., who owned the Foxhill Bank Printworks, amassed considerable wealth, retired, bought a country estate, became
a magistrate, and was reputedly fond of show, the liveries of his servants being especially fine. But his son, James Jr., deviated from this standard tale of a
maturing cottonocracy. He abandoned his intention to enter law "from a conscientious scruple as to the duty that may devolve upon an advocate in plead-
ing an unjust cause," and succeeded his father to the estate (since his older
brother became a clergyman). He was an ardent Leaguer, an advocate of
peace and of the prohibition of the liquor traffic. As a Bible Christian he
wrote pamphlets advocating vegetarianism, and in September 1847 the Vege-
tarian Society was formed on his proposition, he becoming its first president.[36]
James Barlow, Blackburn surgeon, was said to be "something of a rake," and
after separating from his wife he had an illegitimate son, James Barlow Stewardson Sturdy, in 1808 who went on to become a solicitor and mayor.[37] Even
so, Barlow inculcated a moralizing seriousness in his published works. In a
lecture to the Blackburn Scientific Institution in 1831 he held up the marvels
of nature as abundant evidence of the goodness of the Almighty, calculated to
produce gratitude and obedience among humans. Therefore the reading of
novels and other trivial matter must be subordinated to the extension of the
bounds of human knowledge.[38] In some of his medical writings he attributed
prostatic enlargement to, among other things, "high living" and "excessive

sexual intercourse," and difficult and painful parturitions to "habits of dissipation and voluptuousness."[39] Joseph Livesey, Preston cheesemonger, publisher, and radical, at the lower fringes of the bourgeoisie, lived the abstemious life one would expect from the leading advocate of teetotalism. In his autobiography he described how his wife, after they hired their first servant, always continued to do household chores; "A lady's life of soft indulgence, rising late in the morning, lolling on a sofa most of the forenoon reading novels, with little exercise, fed with rich food, and pampered with delicacies—these have killed many a thousand with better constitutions than Mother Livesey's." None of his sons were profligate, because he accustomed them all to work, maintaining that "Idleness, whether in young or old, nearly always leads to evil." He sent none of them away from home for education or to learn a profession or business, "and hence they were not exposed to the numerous temptations which are always surrounding young people, unshielded by the watchful care of parents."[40]

William Hulton's nephew, Campbell Basset Arthur Grey Hulton, the son of Capt. Henry Hulton, had imbibed from the same fountain of seriousness as his uncle. He began a diary while at Brasenose College, Oxford, in 1832, in which he recorded on one occasion a Sunday evening resolution never to go to a Sunday breakfast party again: "The party yesterday I find has got too great a hold on my mind . . . In a word, I am unsanctified, just as a person is unsanctified on the Sunday when he has been to the opera on the Saturday night."[41]

The *Preston Pilot* took the queen herself to task in 1839 for being just so unsanctified. She was the head of the Church and supposedly a shining example of rectitude. But the previous week she and her suite had attended the Italian opera on Saturday night.

Now without entering into any examination affecting the morality of the Italian Opera performances, (although there is too much reason to believe that it is a very questionable one) we would respectfully ask if the being present to witness them is a proper or becoming manner of preparing the mind and feelings for the discharge of the Christian's duties and privileges on the succeeding day?

To compound the offense, she was in the habit of going out for a ride or in a carriage on Sunday afternoons. Evidently the young queen was not yet sufficiently bourgeoise for some of the respectable of Lancashire.[42] But at least she had not attended the opera on the day itself, unlike the profane French, fond of desecrating the Sabbath by indulging in "unlawful" pleasures. Look at what had happened to the Duc de Berri, assassinated on his return from the Italian Opera House in Paris on a Sunday. "We do not wish to infer that so serious a misfortune as a violent death might have been anticipated from such a profanation of the day, but in having so engaged himself, he had in an impious manner proclaimed his disregard for the protection of the Lord of the Sabbath," and suffered accordingly. The destruction of the Italian Opera House by fire, on a Sunday, after a performance, was not coincidental.[43]

The sanctity of Sunday was a reiterated theme. As one scholar at William Hoole's Independent Academy on King Street, Blackburn, later lamented, "Oh! those terrible Sundays, when except to walk to and from Chapel-street to listen to two long sermons, the chapel being like an ice house in winter, we were kept solemnly in doors, hardly venturing to smile or talk except in the language of Canaan!"[44] Jane Pedder of the Preston banking family took an equally absolutist view as the Blackburn Independents regarding the Sabbath. When she heard that her brother, Richard, was going to move from Fishergate to a house on the outskirts, she wrote to him voicing her concerns. She was worried that his new house was too close to the town, so that his friends might walk down to spend part of each Sunday with him. She told him, "to those who value their souls there should be no going to each others houses on that sacred day to pass on the time; no going to any but the house of God which is always open to receive all who are anxious to consecrate His *own* day to His service."[45]

Alderman William Walker of Bolton, a Wesleyan, rose from being an apprentice currier to owning an extensive tannery business. He and his family attended chapel or Sunday school at least three times each Sunday. No secular books or periodicals were displayed around the home on the Sabbath, and the children were forbidden to whistle or to show any trace of high spirits.[46] Thomas Hincksman, the Preston Wesleyan millowner, would have approved. He became concerned about how the working classes occupied their leisure time, most specifically on the Marsh between his mill and the Ribble. As his biographer put it,

There, on a Sunday afternoon, men and boys were accustomed to assemble to spend the sacred hours in dog-racing, pigeon-flying, gambling, wrestling, and (it is said) sometimes, prize-fighting. And, as may readily be supposed, the homes in the adjacent streets, and whose male occupants were generally present at these scenes, were utterly ignorant and godless.

Hence Hincksman began a small Sunday school in the area in 1827.[47]

Organized attempts to keep the Sabbath were sporadic and tended to need outside prompting. In April 1836 the vicar of Preston, the Rev. Roger Carus Wilson, called a meeting to form a society in connection with the London Lord's Day Observance Society. He railed against the number of bathing carts to be seen, and newsrooms open, and a general attention to the things of this world rather than a care for souls and a preparation for eternity. The members pledged to abstain from employment on the Lord's Day inconsistent with its sacred character and to avoid all secular engagements (business, convivial meetings, traveling) unless absolutely necessary. But the society immediately ran into protests because it excluded Dissenters and Catholics from the committee (see Chapter 6).[48]

With the advent of the railway and the mass excursion, a problem posed itself: should the lower orders be encouraged to travel into the country on Sundays (the only time they generally *could* travel) by cheapening the rates? The Rev. John Shepherd Birley of Bolton brought up the issue at a meeting of the North Union Railway in August 1845. The *Preston Chronicle* summarized the two main lines of thought. One camp believed that it would foster a desire to escape from the duties, restraints, and obligations of home, would spiral into a passion, bringing in its wake unsettled habits, domestic misery, and improvidence. The other camp, supported by the newspaper, argued that the working classes did not have the financial means to make cheap, short trips habitual. Besides, those likely to travel were unlikely to be the habitués of alehouses but the more prudent and economical, those who were able to retain a Sunday suit for themselves and their families.[49]

Peter Rothwell, the Bolton ironfounder, took his Sabbatarianism so seriously that at the time of his sudden death in 1849, he was in Glasgow, where he had traveled expressly to attend the half-yearly meetings of some railway companies of which he was a shareholder, to vote against Sunday trains.[50] The Rev. John Clay, the Preston prison chaplain, a pre-Tractarian High Churchman, on the other hand was vehemently opposed to Sabbatarianism: "I would have the religion of Sunday made as pleasant as possible to the working man." In giving evidence to the 1853 Parliamentary Committee on Public Houses he said that he could see no religious objection to playing cricket or visiting museums on Sundays, and to the contrary that these activities should be encouraged, as they would compete with pubs.[51] But he too could sound quasi-evangelical when describing the pleasures and temptations of larger towns like Manchester and Liverpool, enticing one to deep iniquity or habitual vice: "To these dangers the educated and the uninstructed are alike exposed: theatres and gaming-houses, with all their vicious appendages, entice the former, while dram-shops and beer-houses seduce the latter."[52]

Vice obviously included sex, and seriousness extended to a heightened concern about sexuality and the body. This was of particular concern to those denizens of the cotton district who might venture to the Lancashire watering places. One disturbed correspondent wrote to the *Preston Chronicle* in 1826,

I was really surprised to observe men bathing on the beach opposite the houses at Lytham; and most shamefully exposing their persons, to the great annoyance of females, who are thereby prevented from the enjoyment of refreshing sea breezes, during such disgusting and disgraceful scenes. At Southport there are some excellent rules for the regulations of bathers;—one is, that no man shall bathe from a caravan within a hundred yards from the caravans of females, and the other, that no man shall bathe within a given distance on the beach marked out by posts.[53]

Such a fear of flesh was similarly expressed in 1831 by Peter Whittle, the Preston historian, when he criticized bathing machines without screens on the Southport beach at high tide, mixed without regard to their occupants' sex:

We would not contend for any hypocritical fastidiousness of delicacy, but there are certain limits of decorum, beyond which modesty, sensitive as it is, ought not to pass; and though there may be no real or moral contamination, 'tis well to observe them even for appearance sake, for it is not enough to avoid actual criminality, but the very semblance also.[54]

Footraces could be a problem for the sensitive. Nelly Weeton, governess in the service of Edward Pedder of the Preston banking family at his house, Dove's Nest, near Ambleside, has left us a delicious description of a "blackguard" footrace at a regatta in the Lakes. Four men took part.

Two of them ran without shirts; one had breeches on, the other only drawers, very thin calico, without gallaces [braces]. Expecting they would burst or come off, the ladies durst not view the race, and turned away from the sight. And well it was they did, for during the race, and with the exertion of running, the drawers did actually burst, and the man cried out as he run [*sic*]—"O Lord! O Lord! I cannot keep my tackle in, G—d d—n it! I cannot keep my tackle in."

The ladies, including many of fashion and rank, disgusted, "all trooped off."[55] This was in 1810. Three decades later "A Lover of Decency" in a letter to the *Blackburn Standard* was no less concerned about skimpily clad athletes as an outrage to public morality. These footracers were apparently clogging up the turnpike roads, particularly the Preston-Blackburn road, on Saturday afternoons. Is it not monstrous, he asked,

that men almost in a state of nudity should be permitted day after day to expose themselves to the public gaze on the most frequented of our ways, close to a town which is not quite in a state of barbarism? This is a season of the year in which many respectable families are travelling to and from watering places and elsewhere, and I know it has excited both their astonishment and disgust to encounter scenes on the turnpike road in question that would not be tolerated in the back settlements of America, and which would be scouted by the New Zealanders. If such practices are to be continued, I would recommend the trustees to put out handbills informing the community on what *particular* days and at what hours the road cannot be travelled along by females, on account of its being wanted for races by demi-savages.[56]

Four Serious Men

We can examine the attitudes toward seriousness of four men—John Taylor, William Cross, John Horrocks Ainsworth, and Robert Heywood—in rather more detail. All were participants in the cult, but each approached it with a different philosophy and interpreted it in very different ways. John Taylor, future coroner, was born in Bolton in 1811. After training to be a surgeon for six months and not finding it to his taste, he was articled to James Knowles, Bolton solicitor, in 1828. His real love was the stage, and he joined an amateur society which met weekly to recite lines and study and rehearse plays. He filled every leisure moment with the repetition of poetry and self-correction in voice, address, and memory.[57] In the winter of 1830 he took the risky step (since "Those who professed religion held the Theatre to be an abomination") of appearing at the Bolton Theatre, playing the part of Gambia in Thomas Morton's *The Slave*. He dared not tell his parents.[58] But in subsequent years as his career progressed he played a number of other roles. In April 1832 he and part of the Bolton theatrical corps were invited to Horwich by the stagestruck John Bridson, brother of the bleacher Thomas Ridgway Bridson and nephew of Joseph Ridgway of Ridgmont. On one evening, when Bridson was going to appear in a role, the village constable arrived just before the curtain went up and told him that he had received instructions from Ridgway—"the magistrate of the village, whose word was law"—to take him into custody if he attempted to act. Bridson was forced to comply.[59]

Taylor married Jane, daughter of John Salt of Bolton, in 1835. The wedding prompted him to consider whether he could with propriety carry on his profession and still continue to act: "At the time of my marriage my habits ill became domestic life—much company keeping—habitual attendance at inns and other public resorts—a habit at that time very general amongst persons in what ought to have been called decent circumstances."[60] These thoughts were apparently reinforced as he moved upwards in his profession, was elected the first borough coroner in 1839, took a pew at St. George's, moved out of town to Ainsworth House on the Bury Road, and his family grew.[61] He rented a family pew at the newly consecrated Christ Church, Harwood, and at the first sacrament of the Lord's Supper he presumed to join the communicants.

My conscience told me I ought; my ignorance of God was such that I did not think it wrong to go; and yet I ventured in my own righteousness and strength and stole like a thief to the Table, supposing amongst others—and all meeting for the first time there—that they would not know but that I had been accustomed to attend at some previous place of worship; and thus I got rid of the novelty of this my first positive engagement to join the Lord's people.

He began to read more of a religious character, confessing to little knowledge of God, of the plan of salvation, of his own sinfulness and need for a Savior, other than the occasional pricks of conscience, caused by reflection on the increase of his family "and of my habits of life, which were expensive, foolish, and unbecoming a professor of Christ."[62]

Seriousness increased its grip on him, and he responded partly out of conviction, partly from calculation. Although he gave a series of lectures in March 1841 on "the Genius and Influence of Shakespeare" to benefit the Mechanics' Institute, by the end of the year he had concluded that acting on stage "was detrimental to my position in society, and that any remembrances of the stage were best put out of the way." He gave his collection of more than five hundred plays to a London theatrical friend.[63] In 1843 he and his wife began reading aloud the Scriptures systematically, ten chapters a night. In the spring of 1844 he gave up spirits and tobacco, and shortly after began keeping a diary, with resolutions to pursue a more diligent course of reading and to avoid resorting to pubs except on urgent professional business.

He never reached the stage of equating theater with sin—in September 1844, for example, he read a paper on *Hamlet* to the Delta Society (see Chapter 8)—but the whole trend of his thought, at least as he relates it, was toward a liberal application of a coating of seriousness and respectability. After his mother's death in February 1845 he abstained entirely from alcohol and took the pledge.[64] While not doubting the earnestness of the following diary entry at the end of September, we should be aware of the extent to which it fitted narrative conventions, saying what a professor of Christ would have been expected to say, in the way he would have been expected to say it (and, given that Taylor himself published it in his autobiography, maybe all along was intended for public consumption). He wrote,

Having faithfully kept my pledge against drinking, and having totally abstained from using tobacco in every shape since the 16th February last, I have had more time for private reading, and have confined that reading chiefly to books of a religious character. I have also perceived my religious feelings advance—the Sabbaths are really a delight—and I feel quite anxious for the advancement of my Saviour's kingdom on earth. Until this year commenced I had no clear conception of the influence of the Holy Spirit. I now am assured that His work upon the heart and affections is a work of divine instrumentality, producing Love to Christ, and giving to everyday life a relish for heavenly and a distaste for earthly things. Believing the day-spring from on high to have visited me, I am anxious to grow in grace—to waste no opportunity of religious communion—to attend upon every means of grace within my power, and to check every rising sin, unholy desire, and worldly inclination that may interfere and increase the distance between me and Jesus Christ. I also clearly perceive the daily advantage of daily communion with God in family prayer, which is firmly established in the house morning and evening, as well as private prayer. So easily are we led astray; so prone are our thoughts to wander after the sinful lusts of the flesh; so tempted am I by worldly men who use unholy means to advance their worldly interests, and fearful of being injured in professional practice unless I employ their weapons, I am sorely beset; yet by the kindness of God I have succeeded beyond my expectations, and hope by perseverance to maintain my standing in my profession, and at the same time "read my title clear to mansions in the skies."[65]

Thereafter Taylor's life was one of continuing devotion to the Lord. In January 1847 he fitted up a building next to Ainsworth Hall where he could expound the Scriptures on Sunday and Tuesday evenings, the clergyman at Ainsworth having been removed from the living by the bishop for improper conduct. This proved so popular that he transformed a brewhouse into a larger chapel the following spring. Meanwhile his religious reading continued, including the works of the Rev. Octavius Winslow on "Atonement," "Holy Spirit," and "Glory of the Redeemer," and he traveled to Leamington on several occasions for earnest conversation with the author. He spent much of his spare time in hearing sermons—he was a regular communicant Anglican but attended and supported a wide variety of Dissenting chapels as well—in reading divinity, in visiting religious friends, and in supporting the temperance cause. He clearly spelled out the didactic message: "I rather wish to indicate how it is possible to do a long daily work for the benefit of a family, and yet by abstinence from many worldly modes of mixing in society to do many services for God in advancing His cause and aiding in raising the tone of the neighbourhood in which we live."[66]

Three further points of interest indicative of the mantle of seriousness that he had assumed can be extracted from a familiar litany of piety. Firstly, on a trip to the Continent in September 1849, he noted while at Frankfurt on a Sunday that the shops were open as usual, there was music in the streets, and an opera was advertised for the evening; "Retired at 9 p.m., and thanked God that he was ever present with His church although the world forgot Him."[67] Secondly, at the close of 1850 he mused in his diary,

Fretting often that I cannot convert all those around me—relations, servants, neighbours, friends—to the truth as it is in Jesus; testifying in cottage lectures and otherwise for Jesus the crucified; struggling to maintain a decent appearance in the flesh; to educate my family; to assist in spreading the glorious Gospel of Christ; to relieve the wants and necessities of the poor. And Thou, O God, alone knowest my sincerity, earnestness, and faithfulness.[68]

Finally, in October 1852 he attended the ordination of the Rev. W. Hope Davison at Duke's Alley Chapel. He had been present back in 1818 when the Rev. Joseph Fox had been ordained and had given a darkness-to-light account of his conversion. Davison on the other hand gave an elaborate statement of theological doctrine. Taylor made his preference for the former clear: it was nearer the Truth than "all the so-called advantages of German reading and philosophy so-called that form the staple of much of our modern pulpit talk."[69]

William Cross, Preston attorney, deputy prothonotary, deputy lieutenant for the county, and Anglican Tory, felt that gentility had to make far fewer concessions to seriousness and that the two were quite compatible. Born in 1771, he came to assume a leading place in the local elite, just like his father and other family members, being on dining terms with the local notable families, taking an active part in electioneering, frequently attending the Oyster and Parched Pea Club (see Chapter 8), assemblies, plays, concerts, vestry meetings, dispensary meetings, agricultural meetings, and so on, and rising to become a major in the Royal Preston Volunteers. At the same time, from early in life he was, according to his son, deeply read in theology and familiar with the writings of many of the great Church divines. He was an intimate friend of the Evangelical vicar, the Rev. Roger Carus Wilson, seems to have taken a great interest in church extension, particularly the building of Trinity, St. Peter's, and St. Paul's, and assiduously attended the meetings of the Church Missionary and Christian Knowledge Societies. He regretted the laxity into which the Church had fallen, and looked for its ordinances to be more fully observed and rites and ceremonies more duly and frequently administered. He was ever watchful of his own conduct as a Churchman, always attended communion when he could, went to church two or three times every Sunday and to whatever weekly services, lectures, confirmations, and visitations there might be, and jotted down his "Heads of Self-Examination—as to Duties towards God." His son wrote, "He was a church man from conviction & I believe the Church had never a more faithful member or warmer advocate or a truer friend than my Father."

How did he reconcile this with his active social life, his reputation for being a real wit and a joy in company? His was a flexible, worldly seriousness, his religion one which, as he himself noted, "excludes no pleasure hinders no business interrupts no occupation but goes forth with us in our walks mingles in Society gilds our Home Sanctifies our closet and tranquillizes our slumbers." His son John's godfather, Mr. Justice James Allan Park, held him up as a shining example that "*true* religion is neither gloomy nor fanatical . . . her ways are ways of pleasantness and all her paths are peace."[70]

A second Bolton Anglican who left a valuable record in his diary was the prominent bleacher John Horrocks Ainsworth of Moss Bank. At a tea party in St. Paul's schoolroom at the start of 1849 he reminded his audience,

You are warned by the Bible, that fearful events, such as are without parallel for their horror, will take place before the consummation of all things; and you know that mighty convulsions have already commenced in the kingdoms of Europe; how does it then behove us to take heed to our ways, and to pray God that He will of His infinite mercy ward off the evil days, as He was pleased to do in the case of

Josiah, till we and our children, and our children's children, shall be sleeping in the grave.[71]

The patron and chief financier of two churches and their attendant schools, a man who once intervened in theological debate with a twenty-four-page publication of New Testament quotations, and whose charitable contributions to all types of religious institution were extensive, Ainsworth was the epitome of the serious Christian.[72]

This impression might be reinforced by perusing his diary, which he started at the age of twenty-three, and spattered with self-admonitions, homilies and reflections. For example, on January 17, 1823, he wrote of the advantages of early rising, clearing the head and fitting the mind for business; "The good example set to your servants is not the least advantage." On October 25, "Never let your amusements interfere too much with business." On January 31, 1824, "Novel-reading tends rather to weaken the mind and check the exertion of reflecting." On October 30, "Do not allow yourself more than 1/2 an hour for dressing; it is quite sufficient, and you will thus gain much time, which has hitherto been wasted." On the following day, "the reason, why Christianity is so much opposed, is that its professors attend so little to their Christian duties." And so on over the years, exhorting himself to perseverance, to the improvement of his manners and conversation, to the conquering of mental indolence, to fill up his leisure hours with reading only good books, to "Severe Mathematical study" and the study of geometry as ways to improve the mind. He fed on a steady diet of improving literature; that for December 1847 was not untypical: the Old and New Testaments with *Notes* by Mant, Bland's *Latin Verses*, Goldsmith's *Geography*, Alexander Jamieson's *Conversations on General History*, the *Grammar of Commerce*, Walker's *Themes*, Nelson's *Fasts and Festivals*, *The Spectator*, *Geography by a Lady*, Jay's *Morning and Evening Discourses*, Budd's *Preface on Baptism and Puseyism*, plus a sermon by same, a *Life of Ignatius Loyola*, *The Novitiate*, and Manning's *Sermons*. During the same month he translated Luke's Gospel from Latin into English and some collects into Latin and French.[73]

Yet we shall later (Chapter 8) catch a glimpse of Ainsworth the religious attender of balls and assemblies, and of his hectic social schedule during the 1822 Preston Guild. During his trips to Paris, London, and elsewhere in the 1820s he reveled in the theatrical and musical offerings, recorded plentiful dinners swilled down with five or six glasses of sherry or port, went to the races, and indulged in hunting and shooting.[74] So far so conventional if the "progression-to-seriousness" narratives we have examined were to act as our guide. This, after all, was during his "reckless youth," from which he might have been expected to repent at his leisure. But Ainsworth did not follow that route. His exhortations to self-improvement ran concurrently with his active and indulgent social life. There was no hint that the two were incompatible, that seriousness could not be leavened with a full, unself-conscious, non-guilty gentility. His theater-going and dancing might have waned, but with age rather than disapproval, and his excessive eating and drinking continued, for which the reward was bouts of gout.[75] At the end of 1831 he attended a meeting of the anti-spirits Bolton Temperance Society and in his diary expressed himself fully satisfied of the need for temperance.[76] Either he intended this as a prescription for others, or he changed his mind, or his opinion of what constituted temperance was inflated rather above the average. From 1835 the annual amount of wine and spirits drunk at his home, Moss Bank, was recorded in his wine book. This steadily built up to a crescendo, so that in the year from July 1, 1847, the household disposed of 1,284 bottles: 209 sherry, 272 port, 57 Madeira, 38 claret, 86 hock, 99 champagne, 70 brandy, 10 gin, 8 rum, and 1 lunell, with 51 sherry, 12 port, 1 Madeira, and 14 brandy used in the kitchen, 21 port donated for use at Holy Communion, and 121 sherry, 199 port, 4 brandy, 9 gin, and 2 rum distributed to the poor.[77]

Robert Heywood, Bolton counterpane manufacturer, bleacher, and liberal Unitarian, is the final layman who can be studied in some depth. As a member of a professedly rational religion that denied emotional religious experience and the notion of the holy spirit, there was no sense in his writings of a transition from darkness to light, or of an awakening, or of daily wrestling matches between good and evil for possession of his soul. He enjoyed dining, the theater, glee clubs, and billiards, but his form of seriousness was ever ready to rail against luxury, aristocratic overindulgence, and mean-spiritedness. As he noted in his diary in November 1830, "May God above send down his love with swords as sharp as sickles / To cut the throats of gentlefolks who grudge poor men their victuals." Perhaps somewhat more seriously he quoted with approval this conception of the *via media* between seriousness and gentility a decade earlier: "An elegant sufficiency—content, Retirement, rural quiet, friendship[,] books, Ease and alternate labour—useful life[,] Progressive virtue and approaching heaven."[78]

In 1828 he penned a letter to the *Bolton Chronicle* clearly indicative of his rationalist and anti-hypocritical stance on the observance of the Lord's Day. James Kearsley, a newly created magistrate, had stopped a poor Irishman outside his house on a Sunday evening for transporting a number of calves in a cart and fined him five shillings for violating the Sabbath, in spite of the Irishman's statement that he had only just hired the cart because the calves were tired. Eventually the Irishman paid up, "at the same time telling his worship that though he was master here he would not be so in hell." Heywood commented,

Without entering into a long dissertation on the propriety of strictly observing the sabbath as being well adapted for both man and beast one cannot but observe the great inequality of law which permits coaches and all sorts of jaunting on this holy day and at the same time visits with such severity the trivial offence just mentioned. It may fairly be asked which is a greater crime in the sight of heaven the poor Irishman alleviating his wearied animals or the common practice of our nobility gentry and *magistrates* devoting the after part of this sacred day to eating and drinking and sometimes *speaking* unworthily.[79]

Heywood's correspondence reveals repeated exhortations to his relatives and acquaintances to sobriety and plain—though not puritanical—living. In March 1824 he chided his cousins for continuing to live off their father at home, thus not displaying a due sense of independence, and for dressing above their station.[80] An advocate of temperance, he urged James Heywood, a cousin, to the strictest sobriety in 1836 by joining the temperance society "as the only safeguard." He held up two examples: Uncle Robert, living a prolonged life through sobriety and securing the respect of numerous relations and friends; and William Smith, a man formerly in his employ who had been discharged because drink had addled his brain.[81] In 1838 he chided Jacob Brettell, a minister, for lack of economy. He asked, "Why should you indulge so much or at all in the habit of smoking it is not needed for health and besides the expense it often leads to other excesses which greatly interfere with bodily if not mental activity." He also complained of "the very needless and unusual expense of curling your hair," which "would be better left to the other sex," and of Brettell's intention of sending his son to a boarding school, "which under any circumstance I should scarcely approve and certainly not where instruction can be so well imparted by one of the parents."[82] In July 1842 he thought that John McKeand, his nephew, working at his Crescent Bleachworks in Salford, should be at the works precisely at eight, and he insisted that he be called at six so that he might spend an hour in reading before breakfast. Two years later young John was evidently not improving in the way his uncle had hoped. Heywood complained that "you are indulging in the nasty disgraceful habit of smoking. Such practices lead very often to drunkeness [sic] and other gross irregularities." He insisted that he abandon it. It also seems that John had been wearing showy dress. This would not do: anything approaching foppishness was despised in business.[83]

Heywood was an advocate of rational recreation. George Egerton, manager of the theater, wrote to him as mayor in 1840, requesting his patronage on one evening in the coming week. For the first time in many years "the Theatre is now not unfit for the reception of the gentry of this Town in comfort and accommodation." Heywood replied in a manner that perhaps suggested certain doubts whether the theater, which he enjoyed, really could be seen as rational recreation:

I do not object to rational amusements for the people and if the Theatre be so improved as you represent shall not withhold my name on the occasion proposed. At the same time I beg to inform you that my patronage in this way must be very limited as but few of my personal friends are in the habit of attending such performances. I should also wish that no allusion of an official nature should take place in the course of the evening.[84]

Although heavily involved in local Unitarianism and a frequent attender of different chapels, Heywood did not often leave religious reflections in his diaries and correspondence. But when he did he made it plain that he regarded this life as a trial for the next. On the death of his father in 1832 he wrote, "I ought not to murmur, rather should I be thankful for past favors and strive so to live that I may hope for an everlasting reunion with that most endeared relative." To a friend, Noah Makinson, in 1840, he wrote,

You say truly that our time on earth will be short and implore that it may be devoted to the will of God to which I respond amen at the same time whilst we live we should be active in the discharge of our duties and thus be better prepared for that awful event whenever it shall arrive when we may hope never to part again.[85]

Seriousness and Gentility

Thus across the elite and the bourgeoisie, clerical and lay, the widely diffused cult of seriousness manifested itself in numerous different forms as each individual drew his or her own line between God and the world. It was a real tension, one that could to an extent be subsumed under the rubric of respectability, which contained elements of both seriousness and gentility but could not be reduced to either. Seriousness was not in itself sufficient to ensure respectability. A devout Primitive Methodist handloom weaver living in a cellar, however clean, was not and could never be respectable. Wealth and status alone could ensure that; then respectability would be assumed and could only possibly be forfeit by extreme vulgarity or wayward behavior. It was easiest to be respectable within the Established Church. As Louisa Potter sniffed, "Who ever heard of a genteel Methodist, or an elegant Baptist, or an extremely polished Ranter? The thing is impossible."[86] Yet among the more devout, the Church ever bordered on the margins of worldliness and non-seriousness. For them, Potter's "Mr. Weston" would have been typical. Only with his failing health were "the account-book and ledger, which were hitherto his principal studies . . . laid aside for 'Blair's Sermons' and 'Porteous's Lectures,' steady, respectable divinity that could be taken in moderate doses, and was doing something towards preparing for the inevitable journey."[87] Or the Rev. Geoffrey Hornby, as described by Lady Shelley, who had "a perfect understanding of the art of rising in his high calling." He pursued and married the "very ugly" daughter of Lord Strange, eldest son of the earl of Derby, entitling him to the rich living of Winwick. "The parson squire troubled himself but little in the parish; but being very clever, he preached sermons which were above par, wore a shovel hat, a clerical-cut coat, and looked every inch a Dean and embryo Bishop."[88]

But this is reverting to something of a caricature of Church-laxity against Nonconformist-rigor, which as we have seen is far from being the whole story. As both seriousness and gentility waxed together, the twain had to be confronted at many different levels and within each denomination. Both tended to reinforce a decline in emotional forms of worship toward the more controlled, quieter, less exuberant, more orderly, more repressed. When Anthony Hewitson did a tour of the Preston churches in the late sixties, he brought out this generational and social-hierarchical sea change well. At Cannon Street Independent Chapel, for example, he found "a good deal of pride, vanity, scent, and silk-rustling," rather than "ill-clad screamers," "roaring enthusiasts," "fanatics," and "ejaculators." At Lune Street Wesleyan Chapel, the most fashionable Methodist establishment in town,

Now and then a few worshippers of the ancient type drop in from some country place, and explode at intervals during the course of some impulsive prayer, or gleeful hymn, or highly enamelled sermon. You may occasionally at such a time, hear two or three in distant pews having a delightful time of it. At first they only stir gently, as if some one were mildly pinching or tickling them. Gradually they become more audible, and as the fire of their zeal warms up, and the eloquence of the minister enflames, they get keener, fiercer, more rapturous; the intervals of repose are shorter, the moments of ecstacy are more rapid and fervent; and this goes on with gathering desperation, until the speaker reaches his climax, and stops to either breathe or use his handkerchief. But hardly a scintilla of this is perceived on ordinary occasions; indeed it has become so unpopular that an exhibition of it seems to quietly amuse—to evoke mild smiles and dubious glances—rather than meet with reciprocity or approval. It must be some great man in the region of Wesleyanism, some grand, tearing, pathetic, eloquent preacher who can stir to a point of moderate audibility the voices of the multitude of worshippers.

Even Saul Street Primitive Methodist Chapel, largely working class and tremendously boisterous twenty or thirty years before, was becoming comparatively quiet. The Quaker Meeting House in Friargate was attended by "decorous, respectable, middle-class people . . . who dislike shoddy and cant as much as they condemn spangles and lackered gentility." Here the old-style dress was in decline among the younger members, and when Mr. Jasper, a principal speaker, prayed, "there was not much of 'the old Foxian orgasm' manifested by him; he was serene, did not shake, was not agonised."[89]

This partial retreat from puritanism in the Society of Friends can be seen as a result of the direct impact of gentility and respectability, leavened by consumerism and boosted by the rise in the social scale of many of its members.

The rules and disciplines of the Friends were clearly set out, including exhortations to plain dealing, the avoidance of "all vain Sports, places of Diversion, Gaming, and all unnecessary frequenting of Alehouses or Taverns, excess in drinking, and Intemperance of every kind," and by example and precept "to train up their children, servants and those under their care in a religious life and conversation consistent with our Christian profession and in plainness of speech behaviour and apparel." The minute book of the Women's Preparative Meeting of Edgworth and Bolton added against this last item in March 1846, "all do not appear to be equally impressed with the importance of the latter part of this Query."[90]

The most influential local Quaker family was the Ashworths, and the extent to which they were willing to comply with the Friends' precepts of puritanism and seriousness is instructive. Henry Ashworth remained true to the Quaker tradition of refusing to bear arms and to use force. As a county magistrate this placed him in a difficult position. During the Plug Plot crisis of August 1842, William Ford Hulton called a meeting of the county magistrates, but Ashworth asked to be excused, "as I am well known to attend religious scruples on those grounds."[91] He wrote to Robert Heywood, "my absence is not from Cowardice,—but rather that my peculiar principles may not in any way interpose to the supposed disadvantage of the ends of justice."[92] Hulton informed the earl of Derby, the lord lieutenant, who had "grave doubts of the fitness of Mr. Ashworth to continue to hold the office of Justice of the Peace." The home secretary, Sir James Graham, concurred, but neither the chancellor of the Duchy of Lancaster, Lord Granville Somerset, nor the lord chancellor, Lord Lyndhurst, would agree to Ashworth's removal, apparently largely because of the length of time that had elapsed since his appointment.[93]

But when it came to his social life Ashworth strayed from Quaker principles. While it could just about be argued that the family parties and dances, the billiards and the extensive wine cellar at his home, The Oaks, remained on the right side of the line, being dedicated to the goddess of domesticity and the family hearth, Ashworth's love of hunting and shooting clearly could not. For the Friends, "Hunting and Shooting for diversion is ranked among vain sports."[94] But Ashworth resisted repeated censure and even began hiring shooting lodges and estates in Scotland from the 1850s, at one point reportedly saying that "It would give him extreme pain should he be compelled to withdraw from the body rather than surrender what he considered to be a manly and legitimate recreation."[95] At least two of his sons smoked cigars and went to the horse races, his sons and daughters went to the theater, his brother, Edmund, rode to hounds, and a number of his offspring married non-Quakers, meaning automatic disownment by the Society. Henry remained a Quaker, though he began using the pagan names of the month in his letters from mid-century, but Edmund joined the Established Church in the late 1870s.[96]

Dealing with Death

There is one further matter that deserves attention: how the serious bourgeois dealt with death.[97] For those who believed that God intervened directly in the affairs of humankind, that life was a struggle between the forces of good and evil for the capture of their souls, and that only faith in the saving grace of God through the atonement of Christ could snatch one from the jaws of everlasting perdition, frequent early deaths could only be explained in terms of trial, special favor, or an impenetrable master plan. It is easy to point out the contradictions from a rational perspective, if faith were susceptible to reason, which it self-confessedly is not. There is something wonderfully malleable about a faith that could proclaim the survival of a sick child as a special sign of favor (the parents having passed the test of faith) and its death as precisely the same (the child being preserved from the horrors of worldly temptation). Logically the child must have been the loser in the first case, and the parents must have failed the test in the second. But logic was not a factor, except maybe among some Unitarians and a small number of skeptics. Logic and reason provided no comfort in dealing with the death of a baby or young child, but faith that it was all to the good just might.

"[S]urely your heavenly Father is dealing graciously and mercifully with you in taking your choicest and most precious jewels before they are contaminated with the temptations which abound on every hand," Mrs. George Barnes of Farnworth wrote in February 1845 on the death of her sister's baby. "Could you see what she has escaped by this painful dispensation, your joy would be greater than your sorrow now is; but the evil which she has escaped, and the glory she is now enjoying, are both veiled in order that you may live and walk by faith."[98] Dr. William St. Clare of Preston wrote in 1802 to Thomas Parker of Newton Hall on the death of a child:

This my Dear Sir, must be considered as one of these afflicting trials, these awful warnings which are inflicted to remind us that the present is not intended to be a state of perfect happiness; and that Husband and Wife, Parents & children, and the dearest Friends must sooner or later, all, all separate, to meet in brighter and more blissful realms.

He could urge nothing in consolation "which your own fortitude, & christian resignation will not more readily suggest."[99] In 1825 Esther Mary Grimshaw became godmother to the sons of Mr. and Mrs. James Palmer. They named them George and Charles after the Grimshaw brothers (sons of Nicholas Grimshaw, Preston attorney and seven-times mayor) who drowned in the Ribble in 1822. Mrs. Grimshaw thanked the Palmers for perpetuating "the remembrance of Those who are no Doubt in Mercy taken from this World of Trial, & who I have piously resigned to the Wise Disposer of all human Events."[100] John Taylor recorded in his diary the loss of his third child, Gertrude. On January 3, 1846, she became ill with croup. She died on the fifth.

I never knew the loss of a child until this day. I never before felt the utter prostration of heart and soul I this day experienced—the suddenness of the attack—the recollection of her little tricks and gambols—the sight of her clothes, playthings, and other recollections recurred to my mind on the sudden, and tears flowed beyond power of repression.

On the sixth: "Felt that our visitations here on earth are sent to humble our pride and lead us into the way of peace." On the eighth, when she was buried: "Happy, happy loved one, thrice blest, made perfect through suffering and kept from the evil that is in the world!" Finally on the eleventh he recorded Mr. Bingham's sermon at Harwood: how it was well for the parents that the child was dead, and how it was well for the child to die, since children dying young escape many trials and temptations (2 Kings 4:26).[101]

Thus the Wise Disposer in His mercy spared the innocent and tested the faithful in "this ocean of troubles."[102] Death taught a lesson. For the Rev. H. W. McGrath of Walton-le-Dale in a letter to his vicar, Dr. Whittaker, this was the horror of popery. One of Whittaker's children had passed to a happier and better world: "our's[sic], whatever our little shades of difference, is not the creed that consigns to perdition Infant little ones!"[103] For the Rev. William Thistlethwaite of St. George's, Little Bolton, in a Sunday school pamphlet, it was the rewards of submission and subordination. He related the story of Betty Ann Hawkins, a docile, sweetly disposed, industrious scholar at the Sunday school, brought up to the handloom. As she wove, she learned the scriptures by heart or sang hymns. She died from consumption at the age of fifteen, in 1809, patient, submissive, resigned, welcoming the approach of death, entirely relying on the Savior's blood and merits. "Now I am ready;—come Lord Jesus;—receive my spirit," she said on her deathbed.[104] For the biographer of James Wood, a young Blackburn surgeon and Methodist who died at the end of 1814, death was a mark of distinguishing favor for the truly pious. God sometimes called them away so as to spare them the calamities he was about to bring upon a nation, a place, or a family. At other times He spirited them away as a rebuke to their parents for excessive indulgence and fond expectations, turning their children into idols or images of jealousy. Wood died in exemplary manner: "[R]aising one hand in joyful triumph, and lifting his longing eyes to heaven, without a sigh or groan, he breathed his last."[105] The deathbed of John Parke of Longton, a fellow Methodist, was equally blessed. He died in April 1847, aged ninety-two: "[T]he summons came; he lifted up his hand, as if to betoken the completeness of his victory over death and the grave, and his happy spirit departed."[106] According to the Rev. William Jones, Bolton Independent minister and fellow-laborer in the Bible Society with Thistlethwaite, his colleague died showing calmness and serenity of mind, a steady, humble, confident reliance on his Lord. Thistlethwaite had had an affliction of a very distressing nature in the latter part of his life. What was the lesson to be drawn? That "the afflictions of the righteous, are not *judicial*, but *corrective*; and the greatest indications of their Father's parental tenderness and regard."[107]

Through wrestling with the demon of doubt, the faithful in Christ were tried and tested, the ultimate goal being absolute and unquestioning obedience before the power of the divine will. In 1840 "it pleased God to commence a series of afflictions" against William Hulton. "The first blow was the loss of a beloved Son, by a fall from his horse; the last—the death of my dear friend and relation Mr. Langford Brooke, by drowning. Other calamities fill'd up the interstices." He "suffered most severely," but made it plain that he was "not murmuring at [God's] will, or witholding [sic] entire acquiescence in his dispensations."[108] Reconciliation with loved ones would occur in Heaven. When Mrs. Barnes's brother-in-law died in 1844, she wrote to her sister, "You know where Jesus is—go with Mary to his *footstool*; whilst your dear partner is at *his throne, there you can meet* YET." The final, fervent belief, an epitaph for those who wrapped themselves in the mantle of seriousness in an age assailed by uncertainty, hope, fear, and flux, was that "'all things work together for GOOD to them that love God.'"[109]

CHAPTER 3: CONTAINMENT

In December 1794, the innkeepers and publicans of Bolton felt aggrieved. They met to protest about the great losses they incurred in the quartering of troops, temporarily resident in town. There was a war on, so they dutifully resolved to acquiesce in their hardship for the greater good rather than to pen a petition.[1] But they had raised a valid point, especially as it seemed increasingly likely that the spirit of radicalism and periodic depression would between them require a more-or-less continuous military presence in the manufacturing districts. For the government and military commanders, inns were more convenient and less controversial than quartering troops in private houses, but barracks would be better still. During the war the government began building barracks in the larger northern towns, a practice extended to the smaller towns in the postwar period. Bricks and mortar came to represent a practical solution and to epitomize the most overt phase of containment in modern British history, abated only around mid-century by the maturation of industrial capitalism, the re-creation of a more stable hegemony and ideological consensus, and the institutionalization of a mesh of new forms and techniques of industrialist and state-led discipline. This was containment at the behest of local elites; before they began to organize sanitary improvements on a large scale or to express local pride through monumental administrative architecture, they demanded barracks to house the troops that were to maintain or impose order.

Although troops flooded the cotton district in 1812, it was only in the postwar context of political radicalism, labor unrest, and election riots in the mushrooming milltowns that the apparatus of repression became more permanent and institutionalized. Was the ugly scaffolding of armed force essential in the construction of a stable edifice? Historians have tended to choose between two paths. One path meanders between consensus and quiescence. It points to the startlingly low level of popular and governmental violence on the British mainland in comparison to Ireland and the Continent, stressing that the higher orders of society remained relatively unconcerned about the threat of revolution, and were quite right to do so: those magistrates who did give credence to the most unlikely of plots were largely deluding themselves and glorifying their own roles in stamping out radical unrest. The revolutionary challenge was more low-key than elsewhere and hopelessly unsynchronized, so the army's role and response was correspondingly limited.[2]

The second path weaves among periods of intense revolutionary potential or at least bouts of serious popular commotion, edging nervously over the moors by night to the seething sounds of men drilling, arming, and preparing, signaling to each other across the hills by torchlight, hoots, or gunshots. According to this depiction, only armed force maintained order, more by the highly visible movement of troops than by the "salutary example" of bullet, saber, or bayonet impacting on flesh, and without infantry, cavalry, a vigilant magistracy, and a network of spies, the House of Hanover would have shared the same fate as the House of Bourbon.[3] The *violence douce* of other forms of control was effective only with the permanent threat of *violence ouverte.*[4]

The difficulty is in assessing how much potential violence might have been unleashed had the structure of authority broken down. It is certainly true that only rarely and briefly in the three milltowns did the authorities lose control: for a few hours in Blackburn in 1826, for two hours in Bolton in 1839, and for a few days less categorically in all three towns in 1842. Given the abundance of the combustible material assembled during this period of harsh measures and recurring, desperate want, the surprise is perhaps that a spark was struck so infrequently and doused so rapidly. In the country as a whole, the relatively small casualty list after decades of crowd dispersal suggests both limited violence and a disciplined military force intent on minimizing injuries.[5] It is not possible to make out a case for the Leninist notion that it was only armed repression that kept government and society intact. But, as we shall see, there *is* a sense in which the encroaching arm of the disciplinary state in its most transparent and unsubtle form upheld all the other attempts at control, co-option, coercion, or consensus.

Confronting Postwar Disorder

The clamor for barracks among sections of the local bourgeoisie began during the tense half-decade following Waterloo. There were no formidable outbreaks in the local area, but many members of the local elite, landed and bourgeois, believed economic unrest (especially the weavers' strike in Lancashire from May to September 1818) and radical ferment across the manufacturing districts (particularly in the summer and autumn of 1819, climaxing at Peterloo) to be sufficiently threatening and frightening to necessitate a permanent military presence.[6] "[T]he Peace & Security" of Blackburn "cannot be preserved without the Aid of Military Force," Dr. Thomas Dunham Whitaker, JP and vicar of Blackburn and of Whalley, wrote to Lord Sidmouth, the home secretary, early in 1820. He chaired a meeting of the magistrates in Whalley in February in response to a government proposal for permanent barracks for Blackburn Hundred, and after a couple of months of fairly heated debate over the location (most of the county JPs arguing the merits of their own end of the Hundred) Robert Townley Parker's offer of land about half a mile from Burnley was accepted.[7] The government paid the bulk of the bill, but these county JPs were eager enough for the barracks to subscribe substantial amounts themselves.

The towns were rather less enthusiastic. Troops had been stationed in Bolton since 1816 at the request of magistrates and dispersed in billets throughout the town; but Lt. Gen. Sir John Byng, like most commanders, found such an arrangement unsatisfactory and threatened to withdraw his men unless a temporary barracks were provided. In December 1819 the boroughreeve and constables contracted for premises to turn into infantry and cavalry barracks at a rent of £200 a year and spent £600 in fitting them up. The town was to provide the building, the Barracks Department the bedding, fuel, and furniture. But the townships within the division refused to contribute in proportion to the property tax assessment, and the local authorities appealed to the Treasury to be bailed out.[8] Already a pattern was being established: military leaders welcomed barracks as a more efficient mode of maintaining discipline in the ranks; they were widely supported among the magistracy and landowners, but encountered a high level of resistance from lower and indeterminate levels of the propertied, opposed either to the cost or the concept.

The first real crisis for the milltowns, a step in the education of the propertied about the merits of armed force, came in the spring of 1826 with unprecedented levels of unemployment and its consequences: families of malnourished weavers, an increase of political agitation, heightened troop movements, the setting up of relief committees and soup kitchens, and letters flying thick and fast between London and the provinces. In mid-April, the Rev. John William Whittaker, vicar of Blackburn, commented that the lower classes were bearing their privations well; "We are, notwithstanding, glad to have the protection of a military force, preferring the *preventive* rather than the *corrective* system."[9]

The trouble began in Blackburn ten days later, with a highly disciplined attack on newly installed powerlooms, identified as the root cause of the distress.[10] The military presence in town was small, consisting of one troop of the King's Dragoon Guards—thirty-two men—under Capt. Bray billeted at the Hotel, and a recruiting party of eight infantrymen. Bray and sixteen of his men were called away to riots in Accrington. They encountered a crowd, several thousand strong, that had gathered on Enfield Moor and was heading in the direction of Blackburn. Bray "drew up the cavalry and commanded them to charge as though they were going to fire right into the mob: the leader of the mob said with spirit and a loud voice, 'Blow away we are ready for you'," David Whitehead, a Rawtenstall millowner, wrote in his diary. "The officer said that was 'real English.' He did nothing more but let the mob pass on and marched according to his orders to Accrington."[11]

The crowd proceeded to Blackburn. John Kay, the constable, reported that they were headed by a group of forty or fifty with clubs and sticks, three with large iron weights on poles, followed by pikemen with more than fifty pikes, one man with a gun, and one with a blunderbuss, and then the rest of the crowd, all the men variously armed with pikes, pike shafts, hammers, and other weapons. Walking as fast as they could in a compact body they made directly for Banister Eccles and Company's factory on Jubilee Street, the largest and earliest steam-powered mill in town. Eccles Shorrock, one of the partners, stated that the pikemen formed themselves into two lines each side of the yard while others entered the mill and demolished the powerlooms. The military arrived too late to save the machinery; but as soon as the alarm was given that soldiers were coming, the people in the yard began to make their escape.[12]

Sixteen men on horseback were clearly inadequate to prevent the crowd fulfilling its very precise, focused mission. Few arrests could be made: there was insufficient force to detain those captured. While the soldiers were diverted for a few minutes in driving the rioters away from the canal banks, the rioters destroyed the looms at John Haughton's mill.[13] Unable to protect property, at 5:30 p.m. the commanding officer sent for reinforcements from Major Eckersley in Manchester. A troop of the Second Dragoon Guards marched for Blackburn at 9:30 p.m., followed the next morning at daybreak by a company of the Sixtieth Regiment. Neither of these, nor a troop sent to Haslingden, could prevent the following day's wrecking of looms by a crowd of two or three thousand at William and George Carr's mill and Grime's mill in Over Darwen, and at William Turner's factory at Helmshore. The next day they smashed the Whiteheads' looms at Rawtenstall.[14]

With powerloom mills also coming under attack along the river Irwell on the twenty-sixth, the Bolton magistrates readied themselves. They mustered sixty or seventy of the yeomanry cavalry under Capt. Kearsley and around thirty of the Bolton Local Militia under Capt. Warr, but feared that the looms could not be saved without additional force. With one or more field pieces from Manchester, guarded by the hundred or so Chelsea Pensioners in town, plus whatever cavalry could be spared, Ralph Fletcher, William Hulton, and Joseph Ridgway, JPs, predicted "that any attack on the Peace of our Town may be prevented, or should it be made, may be successfully resisted."[15]

The government moved swiftly to reinforce the artillery, infantry, and cavalry in Lancashire, "so that in a very few days there will be an irresistable [*sic*] military force in that County."[16] Four hundred of the Seventy-third Regiment arrived from Ireland and marched for Accrington, Wigan, and Bolton, convincing Gen. Byng that—if the millowners played their part—there were now sufficient troops stationed in all of the principal manufacturing towns for peace and property to be preserved. This proved accurate, and both Bolton and Preston avoided the riots.[17] Charles James Darbishire later wrote, "there was certainly a great deal of alarm excited in Bolton but the presence of the yeomanry & the regulars which began to pour into the country from all quarters (for ministers were evidently seriously alarmed) succeeded in preventing any disturbance whatever."[18]

The moment had passed and the mopping up could begin, with the arrest of loom-breakers identified by special constables.[19] Capt. Skinner of the King's Dragoon Guards at Blackburn reported on May 5 that at two o'clock that morning he had been called on to supply twenty men and horses with an officer to aid in the apprehension of marked characters at Belthorn, a weaving village on the moors above the town. Although the alarm spread from hill to hill, ten or twelve people were arrested. He concluded, "the panic spreading thro' the Country by these Midnight apprehensions is calculated to produce the best effects—In Darwen & vicinity there will be about 60 leading Rioters to take up when reported 'at Home'." Arrests continued by night and day throughout the month. Even so, this was only a partially successful measure: the magistrates reported toward the end of May that most of the Darwen suspects had still not returned, and those arrested by the constable had been rescued; and even when prisoners were taken by military escort to stand trial at Lancaster, it was difficult to find witnesses to give evidence.[20]

It was an uneasy summer. As the depression deepened, spies sent in reports of small groups or "classes" of people gathering in the out-townships, of meetings with "delegates" on the moors around Blackburn, of plans to break more looms, to murder named millowners, to seize a cannon and an iron foundry to cast balls. Millowners and commanders believed that fresh trouble was imminent. Early in July, two Blackburn mills—Banister Eccles and Company and Feilden, Throp and Townley—urgently requested and received arms for self-defense;[21] and Byng put forward a plan for temporary barracks at the government's expense in the recent troublespots. These barracks, in Bolton, Blackburn, Oldham, Clitheroe, Haslingden, Bury, Accrington, Halifax, and Bradford, hired in September, were fitted up to his satisfaction by October. He also began negotiating for land for a permanent barracks in Blackburn, a central location to serve as a new focal point of armed force north of the principal military node of the region at Manchester.[22] Although this came to nothing, it marked the recognition by successive military commanders that from now on the military would not be departing, and that a large, permanent structure would reduce the reliance on temporary quarters elsewhere.[23]

By the autumn, propertied nervousness began to abate as trade improved; and in early December, there were more powerlooms at work than there had been before the wrecking.[24] But as the volatile mixture of the year's events cooled, a residue was left behind: barracks in Blackburn and Bolton were

there to stay, a permanent extension of the sabered arm of the state. The rioters had only been able to achieve their limited and well-ordered objectives because of the paucity of troops at the scene; neither the government nor many
of the principal inhabitants wanted to make that mistake again. Even so, for
many local players the level of urgency ebbed and flowed with the particular
crisis. Besides, the military alone was not enough. Long-term stability required
a more constructive response to the demands of popular mobilization. As
Lord Lieutenant Derby put it in May 1826, military force might prevent riot
and destruction, but it would not relieve want and distress, could not effect a
permanent cure.[25] There comes a point when a government cannot maintain
legitimacy if its only means of preserving the peace is through the display of
rifle and bayonet. But in the short term it was effective. As Thomas Rogerson,
secretary of the Blackburn Relief Committee, said with approval, "Indeed I
think the presence of the military assist very much to overawe the half-fed
poor and keep them quiet."[26]

The authorities remained vigilant, but in the next two years the only disturbances in the towns involved Bolton colliers in a turnout over wages, and
brawls between the townspeople and the troops in Blackburn.[27] The situation
deteriorated in the spring of 1829, with ominous signs of an imminent reprise
of 1826. The same ingredients were present: high unemployment, low wages,
high prices for basic necessities, and men gathering in groups on the moors or
in the handloom-weaving villages to talk, complain, define targets, consider
the risks, and plan. The Rev. Whittaker was convinced at the start of May
that a descent on Blackburn was being organized. A rumor on the fourth
spread the word that a large meeting at Enfield had planned an attack on
manufacturing property. A military patrol paraded the streets all night. Sir
Henry Bouverie, Byng's successor, thought that the whole district appeared
"to be in a state ready for any mischief," and that he did not have sufficient
troops to meet magistrates' requests.[28]

While Home Secretary Peel took measures to increase the military force in
the Northern District, magistrates swore in three hundred special constables in
Blackburn. They were not optimistic about being able to preserve the peace,
but this time the civil and military authorities were ready, as were the millowners in Blackburn, placing strong armed guards in their mills at night. No
outbreak occurred that summer, in spite of Bouverie's fears that further wage
reductions could yet provoke trouble, and then "it will be necessary to be prepared at all points to guard against the destruction which will sooner or later
be attempted by the Working Classes when entirely driven to despair."[29]

As part of these preparations, Bouverie, like his predecessor, pressed for
permanent barracks in Blackburn, and in 1830 the Ordnance purchased
twenty acres of land between the canal and the Burnley road at Bottomgate.

He argued that the temporary barracks were old and dilapidated, and they brought the troops into contact with milltown populations, endangering discipline and rendering them less effective in cowing the people. Since trade fluctuations made troop reductions unwise, he stressed on this occasion and when he pushed the same case three years later, military discipline and popular order could best be maintained by having battalions housed in purpose-built structures on the outskirts of a limited number of towns—Stockport, Manchester, Burnley, and Blackburn—providing good coverage of the manufacturing district in an emergency.[30] But while schemes for building or extending had gone ahead or were shortly to do so at the first three, the government held fire on the plan for Blackburn.[31]

Over the next few years the army continued to play a significant role in the governing of the three towns. Two issues in particular required their intervention: labor disputes and election riots.[32] None of these were as significant as the 1826 riots or some of the key events during the Chartist era, but they were part of an ongoing drama of violence and counterviolence in which the military was appealed to as the first line of defense. The deployment of the armed forces on these occasions generally followed a familiar pattern. Either predicting trouble in advance or deciding that the civil forces were inadequate soon after disturbances had begun, the authorities and substantial property owners screamed for troops and then were reluctant to part with them, even though military leaders hankered after leaving as soon as possible for the sake of morale, discipline, and to deal with other problems elsewhere.

In a by-election in Preston at the end of 1830, Henry Hunt defeated the Hon. E. G. Stanley in one of the shock-symbolic results of the time. Stanley demanded a scrutiny of the poll, and this along with the victory unleashed considerable excitement, with lighted tar barrels, torch-lit processions, flags, and all the panoply of lower-class visual and aural challenge. The mayor and the magistrates had sworn in a hundred special constables, but did not have recourse to troops, in spite of the appeals of frightened property owners. The mayor, Nicholas Grimshaw, present at almost every contested election since 1768 and returning officer at five of them, asserted that "less outrage prevailed at the recent Election, than at any former within living Memory, and if I had yielded to the weakly grounded Requisitions with which I was assailed, to call in a Military Force during the Poll, I should have endangered the general Safety of the Town, and have invalidated the Election." Except for the expected tumult at the scrutiny, "I have not hitherto felt one Moments serious Alarm."[33]

Meetings of the magistrates and deputy lieutenants at the end of the month in Preston, Salford Hundred, and Blackburn Hundred reflected the anxieties of the lord lieutenant and the home secretary in the face of the Preston disturbances, and the activities of Political Unions and of the General Trades Union movement across the region, rather than any pressing local worries. But the meetings variously called for the mustering of Pensioners and the swearing-in of special constables as precautionary measures, and for legislation to put down the trades unions. An appeal at one of the Preston meetings for a permanent military presence in the town "for the Protection of the Property of the Spinners, Manufacturers and Trades-People" was deferred as yet unnecessary.[34]

Disturbances broke out again in Preston in November 1831, shortly after Hunt left town following a tour of his constituency. Although he had been greeted with crowds, flags, music, and lighted tar barrels, his stay was peaceful. The trouble came when "Hunt's mob" attempted to enforce a turnout to increase numbers at a political meeting. The postmistress wrote excitedly on the seventh that they had attacked Swainson, Birley and Company's factory that afternoon, cutting the straps to close down the works, demolishing a large part of the counting house, defacing and throwing the books and papers into the lodge, breaking all the windows, and forcing out the workpeople. After that they proceeded to the lockup, released two prisoners, and set fire to the books and papers. But "the military are expected to arrive at every moment, pray God to protect us from a lawless band of ruffians." The county House of Correction was also threatened, but the crowd drew back on the sight of cannon and muskets. The arrival of three companies of the Eightieth Regiment from Blackburn the following morning "has relieved the Inhabitants from great Anxiety," as the town clerk put it.[35]

Preston was becoming educated in the need for a more permanent military presence. In the aftermath, Charles Swainson related how his mill had been at the mercy of the mob because of the lack of soldiers; some cavalry, he wrote, needed to be constantly stationed in the town. A rich swathe of leading inhabitants—clergymen, manufacturers, merchants, bankers, and professional men—requested that Patton House, the unoccupied townhouse of the earl of Derby and the only suitable building in town, be used as a barracks for the Eightieth Regiment, the commander complaining that billeting his men was not conducive to discipline. Derby agreed. Thomas Batty Addison, Samuel Horrocks, William Marshall, and Laurence Rawstorne, JPs, similarly pointed to the need for a continued military force, especially as they believed many of the special constables to be leading Huntites who could not be trusted.[36]

Simultaneous political meetings in Blackburn sparked the swearing in of 450 volunteers—including a healthy representation of the local elite of all parties and all denominations—as special constables for six months.[37] In the light of reports of the activities and possible arming of Political Unions, the authorities in all three towns took similar precautions preceding and during the Reform election toward the end of 1832. Rioters in Bolton partially demolished the polling booths, but the town became comparatively peaceful as soon as the military arrived. When the intention of Col. Burrell to march his men out became known, more than a hundred of the most respectable inhabitants remonstrated with the magistrates. In Preston, the mayor called in a troop of horse and two companies of foot. Peace was preserved, though he urged that the men be kept in town for a few days until the excitement generated by Hunt's losing the election had subsided. But with no further disturbances, the army left both towns soon after the polls closed.[38]

The Reform crisis weathered, the government and military commanders could take stock. In the summer of 1833 Lord Melbourne inquired whether the force in the Northern District could be reduced, but Sir Henry Bouverie advised against. The magistrates, he stated, were almost all so dependent on troops that they desired a larger rather than a smaller force. Trade was good and political agitation limited, but trades unions were widespread, and trouble from the distressed and discontented was only ever a trade-cycle crisis away. He did not have much faith in potential substitutes: an enlarged police force would be expensive, unpopular, and ineffective; the deeply disliked yeomanry could only be used sparingly and when the use of force became inevitable, for the sight of it could be expected to provoke a riot; and although special constables did not attract as much hostility as the ordinary police, and their conduct found more favor with juries, they tended to act vigorously only in the presence of troops. In contrast, "the timely employment of the Military in sufficient Force, to render successfull [*sic*] opposition to it vain, has constantly been successfull & without unfortunate Results." For those reasons, he continued to favor the prevailing arrangements for emergencies: the small regular police, special constables, and Pensioners, headed by magistrates and supported within sight by troops.[39]

In the rather improved economic circumstances of the next few years the forces of order in the vicinity of the three towns could largely stand aside. They were troubled only by the elections of 1835 and 1837—the latter being combined in Preston with unrest and animosities occasioned by large numbers of Irish navvies used as a cheap form of labor in constructing the railways—and by the bitter Preston strike of 1836-37. This was the most serious labor dispute of the decade. A struggle over wages and unionization by the cotton spinners led to the shutting down of the mills with fifteen thousand thrown out of work. In early November, just before the lockout began and after cotton mills in Euxton and Hoghton had been torched, Home Secretary Russell responded to an appeal from the municipal authorities and other gentlemen of Preston and dispatched reinforcements to the town. By the twelfth there was a troop of the King's Dragoon Guards and a company of the Seventh Royal Fusiliers in Preston (billeted at the Bull and the Red Lion, since Patton House had been demolished), and a troop of the King's Dragoon Guards at Chorley if need be. The army remained there until, after suffering a cruel winter, the workforce capitulated. Thomas Miller, mayor and a principal millowner, spelled out starkly the reason for having soldiers at hand. The unemployed, losing £1,000 in wages a day, would be harder hit than the master spinners, "so that, unless violence prevails, the men must ultimately submit."[40] This was the task of the army: to prevent violence prevailing.

Meeting the Chartist Challenge

The most serious challenge from below to the status quo came in the initial phase of Chartist agitation from 1839 to 1842. The biographer of General Sir Charles Napier, the new commander in the Northern District, believed that insurrection in this period was only prevented by the presence of the military, the emphasis being on *presence*, since any large-scale bloody confrontation with the people could well have ignited insurrectionary pressures and radically altered the course of British history.[41] Certainly, if the discipline of the troops and the nerve of the propertied classes held, the forces of order were likely to emerge victorious, at least in the short term, and the main question given the resources at the command of the government was whether the country would trek along a liberal-capitalist or an authoritarian-capitalist trail. Both options were underpinned by men in red and on horseback.

The state's strength was clearly spelt out by Napier and government leaders during the crisis years. Napier, humane, radical, appalled at the prospect of civil war and at the misgovernment he saw both at a local and a national level, and a more reliable, candid witness than most, wrote on August 6, 1839,

The Duke of Portland tells me there is no doubt of an intended general rising. Poor people! They will suffer. They have set all England against them and their physical force:—fools! We have the physical force, not they. They talk of their hundred thousands of men. Who is to move them when I am dancing round them with cavalry, and pelting them with cannon-shot? What would their 100,000 men do with my 100 rockets wriggling their fiery tails among them, roaring, scorching, tearing, smashing all they came near? And when in desperation and despair they broke to fly, how would they bear five regiments of cavalry careering through them? Poor men! Poor men! How little they know of physical force![42]

Beyond a formidable advantage in the means of violence, another weapon in the hands of the government was the law. During the August 1842 crisis, Wellington wrote that the Chartists must be brought to see "that the Government is too strong for them not only by its Executive Means. But by means of the Law." Peel agreed: "The inherent power of the Law is greater than most people suppose," and the friends of order should be instructed in how to wield it to maximum effect. But "law and civil rights must be upheld by Power," Sir

James Graham summed up, "and cannot with safety be left to the unaided protection of moral influences or even religious restraint."[43]

Military force was necessary, but never alone sufficient. Repression can be effective for so long but only for so long before a crisis of legitimacy becomes acute, and the government's failure to deliver the material goods and to ensure order and stability becomes critical. The sight of an army firing into a more-or-less peaceful crowd is often a crucial moment in the cracking of legitimacy, which is why Peterloo had such resonance in radical and liberal circles over so long a period, and even the firing into a riotous crowd is a risky affair. But in the short term the physical force of the state can tide a government over a troubling period and give it a chance to work out a new agenda, re-order its hegemony, renegotiate its legitimacy, in response to the mobilization of "people power."

A test of resolve confronted the liberal administration in Bolton in the summer of 1839. In office partly by virtue of a Tory boycott of the new council while its legal validity was being tested, the liberals found themselves in the position of having to reconcile their principles with the need for law and order. There was little doubt as to which would emerge triumphant, but the fact that the mayor, Charles James Darbishire, had supported the Charter as recently as the autumn of 1838 was an indication that there would be little enthusiasm for the use of force. In July 1839, with reports circulating that pikes were being manufactured in considerable quantities in two or three places in town and large meetings being held spouting inflammatory language, he wrote that he wished to avoid any collision with the people "unless upon the most extreme necessity." In early August the borough magistrates decided to appoint around eleven hundred special constables—all those eligible to vote in parliamentary elections—in the face of repeated Chartist meetings and the threat of a strike. Darbishire made arrangements with the churchwardens and the military commander in case of disturbances during the Chartist procession to the parish church, but "The most perfect decorum prevailed during the service." On August 11 the mayor was confident that the magistrates would succeed in maintaining the peace, but he had already requested that a detachment of dragoons be stationed in Bolton as a precautionary measure. The following day groups began to assemble before 6 a.m., and alternated between processing around the town and hearing speeches in the marketplace. In response the special constables patrolled the streets, a party of around twenty-seven dragoons had arrived from Manchester, and a warrant had been issued for the arrest of one leader, George Lloyd.[44]

On the thirteenth the careful preparations briefly seemed to break down and the party of order to lose control. The day's events began with the arrest of two Chartist leaders, Lloyd and Warden. The crowd stoned the soldiers taking them to Manchester, and it remained in commotion for the rest of the day, breaking the windows of the police office and turning out some of the factories. The authorities read the Riot Act at 6 a.m. and again in the afternoon, and made two ineffective attempts to clear the streets. Darbishire had stipulated to Col. Cairncross that the troops should not fire unless absolutely necessary, and although he was criticized after the event for so restraining the military, he defended himself by claiming that the opportunity to fire had not arisen: the crowd in the streets had mainly consisted of women and children, and had offered no resistance. The real trouble began later on, when word reached the magistrates in the police office that the crowd was assailing about forty special constables trapped in the upper room of Little Bolton Town Hall. The emergency of the day had brought together the—predominantly Tory— county magistrates with the—exclusively liberal—borough magistrates for the first time, and John Fletcher, a county JP, was deputed to call out the military (so the mayor and others understood) or to hold them in readiness (so Fletcher and others believed). Through a series of mishaps which some—including the *Bolton Chronicle* and Lord Lyndhurst in Parliament—attempted to blame on the weakness or radical sympathies of the mayor, and others attributed to the intense party animosities and divided authority in town, the hapless special constables were left for a considerable time to defend themselves as best they could in the town hall. By making effective use of the stones and brickbats hurled at them, they prevented the rioters from ascending the stairs, and the assailants fled—their attempts to set fire to the building thwarted—on the eventual arrival of a company of the Ninety-sixth.[45]

The event was relatively trivial and inflated to score party political points. The attack on the town hall may only have caused damage amounting to £60-70, and the authorities were keen to play down what had occurred. Alderman John Mangnall wrote, "with the exception of window breaking & a determination of forcing work men from their employ there was nothing concerted and much more has been said of it than it deserves as the whole outrage did not exceed more than two hours." Col. Wemyss visited the town and reported that apart from the damage done to the town hall and some windows broken at the public reading room, the place did not bear any of the marks of riot. Only two or three shots had been fired, and James Winder, the town clerk, thought it a matter of congratulation that all had passed off without loss of life.[46]

Still, while the crisis lasted the authorities mobilized all the resources at their command, the millowners placed extra watchmen around their factories and all business came to a standstill. Prisoners were surreptitiously transported by rail at 3 a.m. to Kirkdale Gaol in Manchester because the directors of the railway feared that the track would otherwise be sabotaged. On the fourteenth a grenadier company of the Eighty-sixth arrived from Chorley and took up quarters in the damaged town hall, while two troops of the Eighth

Hussars marched into town from Ireland en route to Bury, one of them being detained overnight. This was in addition to the two troops of the Ninety-sixth already in Bolton. The magistrates also ordered out the Bolton Troop of the Duke of Lancaster's Yeoman Cavalry; its commander reported that the troop and a company of the Ninety-sixth were out much of the day, clearing the streets.[47]

The local liberals in conjunction with the county authorities had survived the crisis and, with the odd tremor, successfully rallied the forces of order at their disposal. Traditionally more fearful of Crown and executive power than of the people, Whigs and then liberals had frequently been hesitant in the face of the crowd. In recent decades they had been compelled to negotiate a path for the security of property between the Scylla of the party of order (Pittite repression, Peterloo, the Six Acts) and the Charybdis of popular radicalism (drilling on the moors, pike-making, Luddism, the burning of Bristol). The Whig government in 1839 was not as exercised about public order as Liverpool and Sidmouth had been, and was anxious to avoid any counterproductive debacle like Peterloo. It gave local liberals the space to see Chartist agitation as more of a threat than state violence.[48] This was not the end of any working-class/bourgeois rapprochement: as we shall see (Chapter 12) there were ongoing attempts to sustain a "popular front" which clearly prefigured the later compromise of Gladstonian Liberalism, and we shall later note the continuing opposition to barracks and military force of a minority of leading members of the bourgeoisie like Thomas Thomasson and John Bowring. But it did signify that in time of crisis the party of order could rely on wider propertied support, and popular radicalism could be left largely to the people.

The law, as Sir James Graham said, had to be upheld by power; but, Napier sardonically remarked, "it is not decent to have the law of the land upheld by soldiers at every turn: if it is necessary what sort of law must it be!"[49] He was under no illusions about the nature of his task if radical reforms were not introduced: "if, when these dense masses starve by the rise of a farthing per pound in cotton we still go on as hitherto, let us prepare for keeping the operatives down by force, building barracks like fortresses, holding military possession of the country, establishing a paid magistracy and increasing the force with more troops, or a rural police."[50] He had nothing but contempt for magistrates and their persistent demands for troops: "Alarm! Trumpets! Magistrates in a fuss," he wrote in July 1839, "Troops! Troops! Troops! North, South, East, West. I *screech* at these applications like a gate swinging on rusty hinges, and swear! Lord, how they make me swear!"[51] In urging the need for more permanent barracks, like his predecessors, he was also well aware how fluctuating the support of the local magistracy could be: "When the Chartists put them in a funk, Oh, barracks! yes as many as you please.

When they get soldiers and the Chartists are quiet, Really we can't afford barracks, they are too costly."[52]

Lancashire had permanent barracks at Burnley, Manchester, and Stockport, and temporary ones at Blackburn, Bury, Liverpool, Ashton, Todmorden, Rochdale, Bolton, Wigan, and Haydock.[53] Napier found the quarters at Rochdale, Todmorden, Blackburn, Bolton, and Wigan insecure and "absolutely disgusting."[54] He resurrected the notion of permanent barracks for Blackburn and settled on building at Mellor, just outside the town, close to the new turnpike road to Preston. This would house a battalion of infantry of eight hundred men, a squadron of cavalry, a demi-battery of artillery (two field pieces and about forty men), and all the conveniences for the headquarters of a regiment. Parliament voted £12,000 for it.

With Parliament prepared to stump up the money, and in an atmosphere of recurrent alarms during the next two years, the local propertied expressed considerable enthusiasm for barracks. John Fowden Hindle was prepared to exchange land at Mellor for the patch of ground that the Ordnance already owned at Furthergate, and in January 1842 some of the leading inhabitants of Blackburn and area, mostly Tories, memorialized Peel to offer to buy jointly a farm at Livesey and donate it to the government. Their objective was to secure the continuation of "that protection for persons and property and that encouragement in the peaceable carrying on of their extensive mercantile concerns, with which they have been so long indulged, and which—if deemed requisite for upwards of twenty years last past, and enjoyed, without interruption, during that long period—is, your Memorialists believe, more necessary now, than at any former time, both from the vast increase of population and the rapid growth of manufactures in this district."

The problem was that, already by the summer of 1840, the strategic reasons for building an establishment near Blackburn seemed less compelling. Attention began to switch toward a barracks at Preston because of the proximity of the new railway for troop movements from the south and from Ireland. Once the new port at Fleetwood opened up an even quicker passage of troops and supplies from Ireland and Scotland, there was really no contest.[55] The county magistrates of Blackburn Lower Division tried one last time after the riots of the summer of 1842, memorializing the Duke of Wellington for a change of heart, and deploying familiar arguments: the immensity of the population in and around Blackburn, the vast size of the mills and of the capital employed, the inevitability of occasional riots in as fluctuating a trade as cotton, and hence the need of "the moral restraint" imposed by the presence of the military. If the riots were "not repressed by the most prompt and energetic measures," there would be "a dreadful destruction of property, as well as of the means of supplying future employment to the poor," as happened in 1826, while the rioters often proceeded so rapidly and furtively that a military stationed at a distance would not arrive in time "to prevent outrage and the destruction of property, if not of life." Hindle followed this up by writing, "although this question is entirely unconnected with politics, yet it would be highly gratifying to the Conservative Inhabitants of this place, after their repeated and successful struggles in a cause which they have much at heart, to find her Majesty's Government disposed both to excuse and to lend a favourable ear to their importunity on the subject of the Barracks." But the government listened to its military advisors rather than to its local partisans and built the Fulwood Barracks, on the outskirts of Preston, over the next few years.[56]

The authorities of unincorporated Blackburn were largely law-and-order Tories, but the liberal council and borough magistracy of Bolton also had to confront the question of barracks. Liberal leaders had no doubt that armed force, on the spot, was essential. As Col. Wemyss reported in October 1841, they concurred that it would not be prudent to withdraw the troops from Bolton because of the size of the population, the extent of the distress of the lower classes, and the total inadequacy of the police forces and of special constables, who "are thought nothing of by riotous assemblages, unless Troops are at hand to protect them." The mayor, Thomas Cullen, and five borough magistrates[57] stressed that when a riot occurred it would be impossible to procure troops from Manchester in time, even by railway, since it would only take half a dozen men with a pickax or a crowbar to do damage to the line that would take hours to repair. But, although the magistrates were apparently well disposed toward providing improved accommodation for the soldiers, they had neither funds nor powers to levy a rate for the purpose.[58]

As the commander threatened to withdraw the force because of the state of the barracks, and as the local authority remained impotent, the question was effectively thrown open to a wider segment of the town. An awkward squad of propertied dissenters took the opportunity to state their views at a meeting of the largest property owners and ratepayers called in response to the threat of withdrawal. But as only nineteen men were present, this can tell us little about the magnitude of an alternative voice. Samuel Taylor (cotton spinner?), Thomas Lever Rushton, attorney, and Peter Rothwell Arrowsmith, cotton spinner, spoke in favor of a military presence, but the weight of the meeting was resolutely opposed. William Naisby, draper, thought that the government was anxious to distribute soldiers all over the country, to make the starving people die quietly; the parsons and the aristocracy, not the people, were the greatest threats to property. For Isaac Barrow, timber merchant and builder, the army was merely an excuse for the aristocracy to live on public money. Thomas Thomasson, cotton spinner, attacked the unconstitutional nature of the standing army, a band of hired assassins; he would rather trust property in the hands of his poorer neighbors than in the hands of the aristocracy. The meeting resolved, with only two voting against, "That this meeting sees in the present movement of the Executive a very alarming indication of their intention to bring the Country under the operation of a System of extended military despotism having for its object the maintenance of the system of abuse in the Government of the Country which has reduced it to its present depressed and alarming condition," and that no assistance be given to the arrangements to make Bolton a military station. Passing on these resolutions to the Home Office, Col. Wemyss concluded bluntly, "I consider the Radical sentiments they express, a strong corroberative [*sic*] proof of the necessity of continuing a military Force at Bolton."[59]

The Bolton station did remain, and in May of the following year Major General Sir William Gomm, the new commander of the Northern District, suggested that until a permanent barracks be built at Bury it was not safe to abandon it. This meant the government had to set about repairing the Bolton barracks at its own expense, while the local authorities raised a subscription to provide accommodation for the troops in the shambles in the interim. Wemyss noted in June that, while the Chartists were placarding the town with posters like "Bread not Barracks," "a very different feeling prevails among those who have property at Stake."[60]

The Plug Plot

The propertied of Preston thought similarly. Apprehensive of Chartist movements in June 1842, Samuel Horrocks, the mayor, itemized the civil forces in the town—seventeen unarmed constables of the borough police, sixty special constables, and two hundred men of the county constabulary who could be assembled within twenty-four hours if there were no disturbances elsewhere—but made it clear (with arrangements for dragoons and their horses to stay at the Bull and the Red Lion, and for sixty foot to be quartered at the Corn Exchange) that the Preston authorities intended to rely above all on military support.[61]

The preparations across the region were barely adequate for the events of August, when the milltowns experienced their most traumatic few days at the juncture between popular and state or propertied violence. The plug plotters—strikers from southeast Lancashire attempting, with some Chartist support, to enforce a general turnout by drawing the plugs from factory boilers—arrived in Bolton on the eleventh and started going from mill to mill to stop them from working. On the twelfth the police successfully dispersed the crowd and arrested several of the ringleaders, while the millowners met to coordinate defenses, each agreeing to supply a number of their workpeople to act as special constables. Further commotion led to a reading of the Riot Act later in the afternoon, and the military and the police patrolled the streets during the evening. On the thirteenth a crowd of several thousand men armed with bludgeons again entered the town and succeeded in stopping a number of mills, collieries, and other works and demanded or helped themselves to bread and money from shops and houses. A further reading of the Riot Act and the calling out of the Bolton Yeomanry failed to deter the plug plotters, by this stage considered too numerous and intimidating to attempt to disperse: "It may fairly be said," wrote the town clerk, "that the whole of the District is at their mercy." No additional troops could immediately be spared from Manchester.[62]

On a summons to the whole of the electoral body, the mayor and magistrates swore in many more special constables on the fifteenth, bringing the total to nearly six hundred, and a party of the Fifty-eighth arrived from Manchester. The turnouts returned in the afternoon, but given the much greater show of resistance, the town clerk reported that only a few hundred remained to hear the Riot Act read. The police began making arrests amid considerable resistance, but on the soldiers being commanded to load, the people fell back. They fled as the police and the military advanced, and "a part of the mob was vigorously pursued by several of the Yeomanry along the canal bank frightening some of them into the canal and others into the fields in all directions." The military and the yeomanry patrolled the streets all evening. Robert Heywood reported of the day's events, "We are well satisfied with our proceedings having put down the tumult without loss of life or even with much injury."

The next day the work of stopping the mills recommenced. Millowners from the surrounding countryside were coming into town to ask for help, "stating that they are almost prostrate and at the mercy of the roving Bands and the people have lost all Energy to resist them." This was the pattern over the next few days, with groups of strikers touring the countryside turning out mills or intimidating farmers and other rural residents for food. Although James Winder, the town clerk, and Thomas Cullen, the mayor, repeatedly called for additional soldiers to patrol the country areas and prevent the men from gathering, Gen. Sir William Warre in Manchester could not spare the troops.[63]

In the surrounding industrial villages, millowners took all possible precautions. At John Horrocks Ainsworth's bleachworks at Halliwell, on the sixteenth "The mob came to the works & let off the boilers"; on the seventeenth he attended a meeting at the Commercial Inn in Bolton, when an association was formed for the protection of property; on the eighteenth Robert Heywood swore in as special constables all the men aged over twenty-one at the works; no bells rang at the usual times, since "the ringing of a bell should be the signal of the approach of the mob." At Farnworth, men were drilled at Thomas Bonsor Crompton's paper mills, and from the sixteenth a committee met daily at the Bowling Green Inn to coordinate arrangements for the protection of persons and property. A lookout party stationed in the church tower could communicate with others at Bull Hill and in the Burnden area, and by the hoisting of a flag, a chain reaction could be initiated to Bolton Parish Church and from there to the military officers quartered in the Swan Hotel.[64]

The fabric of containment in Blackburn was stitched together from an equal patchwork of expedients. Men armed with bludgeons had started to gather in Blackburn on the thirteenth, and information arrived that a large body of turnouts had been stopping the mills three or four miles from the town. The magistrates swore in a number of respectable inhabitants as special constables. On the morning of the fifteenth Col. Arbuthnot drew up his troops as early as 4 a.m., but they were not called out until mid-morning when word came that a considerable number of strikers, advancing down the Accrington road in the direction of Rodgett and Brierley's mills, had reached the vicinity of the Mother Red Cap pub. Magistrates, police, and military met them at the mill. The police skirmished with the rioters and arrested about thirty of them, but the arrival of large groups from the Haslingden area swelled the crowd, and repeated readings of the Riot Act over several hours proved fruitless. Only gradually did the crowd disband after the capture of several men who appeared to be the ringleaders. During the afternoon Arbuthnot and his men dispersed a crowd attacking Feilden and Townley's mill in King Street, and subsequently responded to requests to protect Hopwood's, William Eccles's and Joseph Eccles's mills. After driving the rioters away from the latter mill, the soldiers took a number of prisoners to the barracks. They were pelted with paving stones on the way, and "to prevent a rescue and the destruction of life, it was found necessary to order the Soldiers to fire." Two men and a woman were wounded.[65]

By the end of the week the magistrates were congratulating themselves that their plan to prevent the mobs entering the town and to disperse them whenever they gathered for destructive purposes had worked well. In addition,

The respectable classes of Society in the Town and neighbourhood are disposed to give us every support and, at our request, a number of them have voluntarily organized themselves as a protective force. They divide themselves into small parties and perambulate the Township during the whole of the night. . . .We have directed them to apprehend all suspicious persons who cannot give a good account of themselves.

As gangs roamed the countryside extorting and intimidating, the magistrates determined to extend voluntary protective associations to the out-townships by recommending that six or eight respectable householders be sworn in as constables for each township and that they should patrol the country night and day. Meanwhile on the eighteenth a party of soldiers dispersed a crowd in Over Darwen, and the following day a detachment came to protect the Hargreaves's large mill at Accrington, where one of the partners, anticipating a visit from the turnouts, had sworn in several hundred of the workpeople as special constables.[66]

Unusually, the conduct of the magistracy was applauded by a military commander. Col. Arbuthnot wrote, "The conduct of the magistrates of Blackburn is *beyond all praise*, & no expressions of mine can convey to you how much I feel, & at the same time am obliged to them for their gallant conduct, whenever employed against a mob, and their determination to uphold the laws of their country." A couple of months later, as part of his bid to have barracks in Blackburn, John Fowden Hindle boasted that the town had established a national precedent of going out to meet the mob on the highroad, something that could not have been accomplished without the presence of the military. This and the on-the-spot arrests of many of the ringleaders, "had the effect of striking sudden terror into the minds of the rioters, of paralysing their plans, and inspiring the peaceable inhabitants of the neighbourhood, for many miles round, with courage and a fixed determination to offer the most vigorous resistance to mob violence."[67]

The proceedings had been rather different in Preston. The turnouts had visited the mills in succession on the twelfth, and there was insufficient force in town to offer effective resistance, though a small party of the Seventy-second arrived in the course of the evening. The following morning the magistrates, the police, and the military met the rioters in Lune Street and attempted to disperse them. The crowd stoned the authorities from front and rear, and Chief Constable Woodford was among the wounded. The mayor, Samuel Horrocks, read the Riot Act to no effect, and later reported that the military had to fire in self-defense, killing or severely wounding several men. Sir William Warre regretted the deployment of such a small detachment; immediately on hearing of the riot he sent off by railway 150 men of the Sixtieth Rifles under Major Wilford and requested Lord Francis Egerton to send the Bolton and Wigan troops of the Lancashire Yeomanry with the least possible delay. The calling out of ninety Pensioners during the course of the day completed the lineup of the forces of order.[68]

The mayor and the magistrates were not slow to point out the moral of the tale. They postered the town the same day with a message exhorting the people to maintain the peace, since an overwhelming military force had arrived and additional troops were on the march: "Whilst we deplore the melancholy consequences which many of the misguided Persons engaged in the Riot this morning have brought upon themselves, we shudder to think of what may be the effect of any further resistance to the force now at our disposal, and which it will be our duty to employ, if any resistance be made." Horrocks wrote to the home secretary the next day, "I beg to acquaint you that the measures taken here yesterday appear to have entirely suppressed the insurrection in this town."[69] The *Preston Pilot* predicted that the event would be looked back on with both

regret, in the remembrance that so many of our fellow-creatures could have been so infatuated as to surrender their better judgments, and thereby become the ready tools for carrying out the evil designs of wicked men; and of devout satisfaction in having the cheering fact brought to mind, that there were not wanting in the hour of need a chosen band of men, who hesitated not fearlessly to throw themselves in the gap of threatened danger, and by their magnanimous courage and gallantry became the honoured instruments of staying the plague of anarchy and confusion, and a reign of terror.[70]

Between five and six o'clock the following morning a number of magistrates assembled to make plans. While the mayor and the recorder remained at the headquarters with Major Wilford and a reserve including a troop of the Bolton Yeomanry under Lord Francis Egerton, Lt. Col. Austen took a body of police and a detachment of riflemen to a station at the east end of town, his fellow magistrates Jacson and Lowndes took another group toward the north, and Bairstow and Taylor another toward the west. Their presence "encouraged the well disposed & awed others." The workpeople had largely returned to work, and two of the casualties had died. Horrocks commented, "Deeply as I regret that any of the misguided [party?] engaged in the riot should have suffered so severely the consequences of their own misconduct, I trust a beneficial example has been made" which may "materially contribute to the saving of life and property."[71]

But that was not the end of the trouble. Information arrived on the seventeenth that a large body of navvies and others had assembled at Chorley and intended to advance on Preston. Woodford, a superintendent, and sixteen constables of the county force, supported by Major Wilford, two officers, and ninety-six men of the Sixtieth Rifles took their positions at Walton Bridge where the Chorley road crossed the Ribble. Lesser forces stationed themselves at the other bridges over the river, with magistrates in attendance at each. As the crowd approached armed with clubs, iron bars, and cutting instruments, magistrates and police advanced toward it and, supported by the Rifles, dispersed it, arresting twenty-seven.[72]

In the Preston area the picture was similar to that at Bolton and Blackburn: large bodies of men roamed the surrounding countryside without let or hindrance while the authorities rapidly restored order in the towns where the army was stationed. After a number of the factories voluntarily turned out, the mayor and magistrates resolved to punish in the courts all those who induced the workpeople to quit without giving proper notice. They also applied for additional troops following the withdrawal of a division of the Sixtieth; as George Jacson put it, "if we can get the additional force we have applied for I have little doubt that with care and great exertion we shall be able to keep the Peace of the Town."[73]

Here was a combination of force and the full rigor of the law that the prime minister, the home secretary, and the commander in chief advocated. When on the twenty-third Ainsworths' spinners turned out, the justices immediately issued warrants for the arrest of thirteen of the ringleaders. The next morning the magistrates committed twelve spinners, taken up during the night, to the House of Correction for a month when they refused to return to work. The Walton rioters were tried between August 25 and 27 and mostly sentenced to terms of from one month to two years in Kirkdale or Preston gaols.[74]

During the week or more of commotion Sir James Graham had coordinated the government's response. As all the law-enforcement and surveillance agents—military commanders, local authorities, lord lieutenants, postmasters, postmistresses—reported to him directly or indirectly, he was one of the best-informed men in the kingdom on the spread of the disturbances and how they were being dealt with. He authorized battalions of Guards to be sent from London by railway and a regiment from Portsmouth. He approved of Warre sending for a regiment from Dublin, and of his plan of drawing the regular cavalry from York, to be replaced in the barracks with yeomanry; he suggested that the cavalry be drawn likewise from Leeds and Sheffield to the Lancashire border.[75]

Graham applauded the measures taken at Blackburn, Bolton, and Preston, particularly in contrast to what he saw as the weak conduct of some magistrates elsewhere, whom he suspected of doing little to prevent the riots because of their support for the Anti-Corn Law League. "At Preston," he wrote to the queen, "the good effect of vigorous measures has been demonstrated by the Peace of the Town and by the return of the work-people to their employment. At Blackburn Col. Arbuthnot resisted the entrance of the Mob into the Town with success." When reports from Lancashire were favorable on the seventeenth he commented, "The Mobs are somewhat overawed by the vigor with which the troops have acted at Preston, at Blackburn, and at Bolton, where several Prisoners have been taken, where the troops in self defence have been compelled to fire, and where several Persons have been killed and wounded among the Rioters." The queen approved: "At Preston the lesson (& a severe one it was) has done good,—for it is worse to let these Riots get ahead than to *act* with severity at first."[76]

1848

Acting "with severity at first" was the very essence of containment. Between them, ministers of state, military officers and men, local notables, and the bulk of the propertied nation—the massed ranks of the party of order—

rallied to make sure these riots did not "get ahead." After decades of experience in policing crowds, the army was a well-disciplined instrument of power and, with the advent of the railway, it could be deployed significantly more rapidly than at any time in the past, wherever a well-informed government and army command might consider appropriate.[77] There is little doubt that, while the mosaic of containment was being pieced together, the party of order had accrued further support during the events of 1839-42 and the voice of dissent and doubt had diminished. For the bulk of propertied Lancastrians, the threat and use of violence was, if regrettable, essential.

The apparatus of order was scarcely tested again until 1848, when it proved to be functioning very smoothly. An excellent illustration of this was the meeting in January of about three thousand at Craven Brow, Darwen: it was chaired by Daniel Duckworth, Blackburn beerseller, and addressed by Richard Marsden (formerly the leading light in Preston Chartism but for the past year secretary of the Blackburn Weavers' Union) and William Beesley, Blackburn chairmaker. Beesley called on the people to have firearms ready in their houses and to use them in defense of themselves and their rights, now that the military was engaged with the Irish in Ireland. The meeting voted unanimously in favor of a general strike in the face of a threatened 10 percent wage cut in the Eccles and Shorrock mills. This was well discussed by the authorities. Superintendent Robert Carswell of the county police was present with an inspector and ten constables, and an inspector from the Manchester Division attended in plain clothes. Chief Superintendent Sheppard suggested that "the clipping of [Beesley's] wings would go a long way to ensure the peace of the neighbourhood in which he resides." Lt. Gen. Sir Thomas Arbuthnot drew the attention of Sir George Grey at the Home Office to Beesley's language, along with the opinion of the chairman of the Quarter Sessions at Manchester that, while indeed seditious, it would be impolitic to take notice of it in the prevailing tranquil state of the country. An aide wrote to Major Temple, commander of the detachment of the Sixtieth at Blackburn, "From experience the Lieut. GenL. does not apprehend that a strike of the operatives on account of misunderstandings between them and their masters on the score of wages is likely to be attended with a breach of the public Peace at least in the first instance." The magistrates would not interfere with them if they remained peaceable; but the detachment should be kept ready, just in case.[78] And so finely judged decisions were taken in weaving the web of containment from latent spools of information.

Eighteen hundred and forty-eight was not a year of crisis in the three milltowns; the authorities remained vigilant but apparently not unduly alarmed. In coordination with London they drew up elaborate contingency plans to mobilize special constables and Pensioners alongside regular troops in case of a general insurrection at the time of the Kennington Common meeting on

April 10. However, these proved unnecessary, and the manufacturing district remained calm—attributable, Arbuthnot thought, to the complete failure of the meeting in London.[79] The immediate crisis, such as it was, passed; but the surveillance continued, along with sporadic troop movements and swearings in of specials as and when deemed necessary. Radical activity in Britain and Ireland peaked again in a particularly intense period in July and August,[80] and the reverberations spread to Bolton. An attempt was made in the early hours of July 27 to blow up the bed-quilt-manufacturing premises of Robert Lomax and William Pownall (only minor damage was sustained), and groups of Chartists on two occasions held demonstrations of marching and countermarching, eight to ten abreast, through the principal streets. The magistrates readied the usual means of force at their disposal, placarded the town with warnings about the illegality of drilling, requested millowners and employers to protect their property from arson and to use their influence with their operatives to abstain from illegal assemblies, and called on ministers of all denominations to impress on their congregations the duty of obedience to the law.[81]

The much more frightening events of 1839-42 had rallied many bourgeois reformers to the flag of order; "1848," locally, might have been a relative nonevent, but it is reasonable to assume that the fears generated by the insurrectionary wave across Europe completed the process of education. Town councils and local newspapers, breathing a collective sigh of relief after Kennington Common, tumbled over each other to express their loyalty to state and constitution, and their gratitude to the forces of order. Bolton Council, combining an address of congratulations to the queen on the birth of another princess with a loyal declaration, assured Her Majesty "of our great thankfulness and joy that the foolish attempts which have been recently made to unsettle your Majesty's Government and to disturb the quiet and good order of the Land have signally failed having been so promptly met and so effectually repressed by the almost unanimous energy and exertion of your Majesty's faithful subjects."[82] The loyal memorial initiated by Preston Council attracted 3,423 signatures, 253 from the "upper middle classes," 813 from the "lower middle," and 2,357 from "operatives."[83]

And yet: this was still a loyalism that was conditional on the state showing itself to be responsive and responsible. As even the effusive loyal address from Preston pointedly remarked, "Public order and loyalty have been preserved, not by measures of coercion or intimidation, but by a deeply rooted reverence and affection towards Your Majesty, implanted in the minds of the people by the prompt solicitude uniformly evinced by Your Majesty for the redress of all real grievances and abuses, and for the promotion of the welfare and prosperity of all orders and conditions of men."[84]

The quid pro quo for bourgeois liberal support was continued movement in the direction of reform and liberalization. This voice was expressed by two of the Preston newspapers, the only two fairly liberal papers still surviving in the three towns. The *Preston Guardian* contended that progressive change was necessary: "The bullet and the bludgeon may in some measure silence the demand for political rights, but they cannot suppress the desire for justice."[85] The *Preston Chronicle* took the opportunity both to damn the Chartists and to argue that the bourgeoisie, having gained political emancipation and free trade with the aid of the people, now owed it both to the lower orders and to their own long-term best interests to share their rights; "indeed, they will not be long able to retain what they possess in security, without being content to share the privileges they enjoy with those whose efforts procured them what they possess." If Chartism were not eradicated by the obliteration of the grievances in which it had had its birth, the leaven of disaffection would continue to ferment, "and the fate of the aristocracy and *bourgeoisie* of England may be eventually as humiliating and disastrous as that which has recently overtaken the same branches of the social community throughout France." An extension of the franchise would be a true measure of conservation and not of destruction: "It would draw round all the institutions of the empire an immense accession of volunteer strength; men proud of their privileges, feeling and valuing their rights and liberties, and determined to defend and cherish what they love."[86]

This was the voice of enlightened self-interest, recognizing that on occasions it might be necessary for the privileged, propertied, and powerful to give a little to preserve much. It readily leant itself to a classic concessionist narrative of recent British history, outlined toward the end of the year:

Powerful as is the aristocratic element of our constitution,—upon every occasion when it has been opposed to the declared public feeling of the country, it has succumbed. The history of the last twenty years is a record of the progress of legislative measures, extending civil rights and ameliorating social evils; and herein is the true cause of England's freedom from the tide of revolution. Timely concession, seasonable reforms, the adaptation of institutions to the spirit of the age, and the extension of constitutional privileges, by securing the adhesion of her people, have placed England in her present position in the scale of nations.

The middle and upper classes were in danger of misreading this narrative, misunderstanding recent events on the Continent, and rushing headlong toward reaction, away from social and political reform; they must remember that "Despotic power is the cause of revolutionary frenzy, not its cure."[87]

This was a perceptive summary of recent British history, pointing to the fact that even in the year of revolutions the propertied classes were far from monolithic, the dissenting voice—however well tutored in the need for order—

remaining alive. The stress on the state's repeated tactical withdrawals under-lines the role and success of containment. The troops remained in place after 1848, and it would be an exaggeration to say that a plateau of tranquillity had been reached by mid-century. Industrial disputes—1853-54 in Preston, 1874 in Blackburn—continued to provide flashpoints. But it became much more difficult to envisage the military as playing a crucial role in perpetuating liberal-capitalist society. The permanent barracks were now mostly in place, and the crowded and unhealthy temporary expedients could gradually be abandoned. Thanks to railways, troops could be more concentrated and kept apart from the expensive, cramped, vulnerable, and potentially contaminating sites in towns. The reduction in numbers of troops through much of the mid-forties' prosperity could continue, leaving an institutionalized, disciplined, and by no means insignificant residuum—in 1849 there were 1,174 officers and men in the Fulwood Barracks at Preston, and still 137 and 217 in temporary barracks at Blackburn and Bolton respectively.[88] The army remained in readi-ness, but it had fulfilled its main purpose: to stand by and intervene when nec-essary, while the country's rulers, national and local, constructed on the back of a stabilizing economy a new and consensual hegemony.[89]

CHAPTER 4: DOMESTICITY, SEX, AND MARRIAGE

Against the Grain

After a busy assizes in the spring of 1790, William Cross, his father John, and a Mr. Aspden (presumably Joseph Seaton Aspden, attorney) set out from Preston with their servants for a tour on horseback through north Wales. Their route took them to Llangollen and to a celebrated and curious anomaly in the patterning of domesticity. Like many more-distinguished guests, they visited Miss Butler and Miss Ponsonby, the "romantic owners" of The Cottage or Plas Newydd, a rural idyll of fine rooms and beautiful gardens. Aged about thirty-five, the two ladies were of great family and fortune in Ireland, one Catholic, one of the Established Church, but they had eschewed marriage and settled down together in quasi-conjugal bliss at the age of around nineteen. Cross found them handsome and very sensible women, but he clearly disapproved of their living arrangement, noting, "The motives from which they have thus deviated so widely from the general and I think more useful and natural modes of life, are and must remain dark and mysterious." Such a same-sex relationship might therefore be tolerated or even lauded (on the taken-for-granted assumption that lesbian sexual activity was inconceivable), but only as a curiosity, and only then among women of rank and wealth. Even so, a Preston attorney found it unnatural and deviant, contrasting it unfavorably with the "natural," pair-bonded conjugal unit.[1]

Nelly Weeton and Catherine Jacson—two strong-willed women closer to home—also sought to some degree to transgress the norms of domesticity. Nelly Weeton was born in 1776, her father a ship's captain in the African slave trade, her mother a Preston butcher's daughter, a lady's maid who later, as a widow, kept a school. Nelly's brother, Tom, supported by mother and sister, entered the law, becoming articled to Nicholas Grimshaw in Preston and eventually settling in practice at Leigh.[2] Partly in the hope of furthering Tom's career, Nelly became governess for Edward Pedder at the end of 1809. Pedder, of the Preston banking family, had whisked away his dairymaid from his home, Darwen Bank, to a Gretna Green marriage the previous summer, to the chagrin of his family. She was not yet eighteen, he nearly twice her age. Such an unequal social relationship severely complicated a more typical power relationship between the sexes. First Mrs. Pedder had to be trained so as to be "a little better fitted for the society he wishes hereafter to introduce her to," "fit to appear in the presence of his relations." She had to be taken out of circulation for a few years, so he rented a house, Dove's Nest, near Ambleside, overlooking Lake Windermere and well out of range of Preston's polite society. Nelly Weeton's job was to see to Mrs. Pedder's education and refinement, as well as to oversee the education of Mary Gertrude, Pedder's ten-year-old epileptic daughter by his late first wife.[3] Weeton, as a governess, was in that most difficult of all nineteenth-century women's positions, tiptoeing along the boundaries of class and gender, a lady who was employed and receiving wages, a woman who was supposed to act as an asexual being when admitted to the sanctity of the domestic hearth.[4]

As governess, Weeton was able to penetrate beneath the lacquered surface of the family's public display. In her letters and journal she depicts Pedder as a boorish man inclined to drunken rage,[5] scarcely educated in spite of his progression through public school, university, and army. "Mr. P., like many of the wealthy, possesses a library of little real use. He himself reads little, so that the shelves make a display of knowledge he possesses not; many a volume, I dare say, has never been opened." His notion of a gentleman "is one who has many dependents, whom he may use and abuse as he pleases." At times he was lavish in his expenditure, at others he could fly into a rage with his wife for ordering some boot-blacking or buying a few yards of ribbon or thread. He gave nothing to charity "except where he can put his name to a subscription list." Later on, "before his Preston friends, he appears so doatingly fond, so lavish of his money upon her! He will, there, force cloaths and ornaments upon her, which when he gets home he is continually reproaching her with." Quarrels, beatings, locking her in or out of the house all prompted her on two occasions to flee to her father's farmhouse.[6]

Out of this sorry tale arose Weeton's reflections on the nature of domesticity and how it had become distorted in the Pedder household. Mrs. Pedder was unable to carry out the normal duties of a lady, "no ladies of any rank visiting Mrs. P., and she not choosing on Mr. P.'s account, to visit with those who do not rank as high as his friends in Preston." Marrying above herself, she had to endure "numberless mortifications"—his relatives snubbing her, his verbal abuse of her in front of the male servants, and so on. She was far from being mistress of her house: "Mr. P. is master, mistress, housekeeper." At this extreme, a wife's position, with the law against her, could be in some respects worse than a servant's. Weeton wrote,

I have wondered and wondered again, why he should treat the wife he has endured so much from his friends for, so much more unkindly than the commonest servant in the house—but so it is. . . . She has no help for herself; she cannot escape—the laws of the realm prevent that. "A servant," as he said one day, "must not be spoken harshly to, for they can quit you when they please."—What a sorry motive! what a contemptible reason for using a servant well. . . . A wife, I suppose, may be treated in any way, according to the whim of the moment, because she is tied by the law, and cannot quit you when she pleases.[7]

Weeton could quit; she did so in March 1811 when she could stand it no longer. But there was more to her rebelliousness than simply this. She was beginning to question the whole notion of the position of women in society. On occasions she could sound conventional on the notions of masculinity and femininity ("I say it is a disgrace to the dignity of the female character for any woman to strive to become master in her husband's house, or to make her husband afraid of her. It is an equal disgrace to a man, so to submit"; and on going out in a little boat, "I have not been very often in it, though fond of the amusement, as I consider it rather a masculine one for a female.") At other times she could take the binary-opposite, dualistic view of the sexes, the separate-and-distinct-but-equal philosophy, to its logical conclusion. In a little essay in the autumn of 1810 she wrote,

Woman almost ever since the creation has been a humbled, degraded being indeed, when compared with man. With as just a sense of right and wrong, as strong a feeling of liberty and oppression, the same warmth of gratitude and resentment, she has been treated as if her capacity were little above the level of a brute . . . I would not be understood to argue that woman is superior to man . . . I would only affirm that they are *equal*, and ought to be treated as such in every respect. For though their virtues and their vices, their mental and their corporeal qualifications necessarily differ greatly, yet, placed in opposition to each other, they would form so exact an equipoize, that a truly impartial mind, whatever kind of a form encompassed it, could perceive not the smallest line of difference.

In barbarous societies, bodily strength was looked to as the most admirable qualification, but in enlightened societies, where mental superiority was most desired, women would inevitably rise to the level of men in wisdom, virtue, and dignity.[8] Yet she realized that this was still some way off. As she wrote to her brother,

I often feel as if I were not in my proper sphere, as if I possessed talents that only want awakening . . . Why are not females permitted to study physic, divinity, astronomy, &c., &c., with their attendants, chemistry, botany, logic, mathematics, &c.? To be sure the mere study is not prohibited, but the practise is, in a great measure. Who would employ a female physician, who would listen to a female divine, except to ridicule? I could myself almost laugh at the idea.[9]

Catherine Formby, who married Charles Roger Jacson, a Preston cotton lord, provides a second instructive example. When she was aged fourteen, in

1832, her father, Henry Greenhalgh Formby, laid down the acceptable limits of feminine activity. He

valued scholarship. Henry's [her brother's] success had been so deep a gratification to him, and why not her's [*sic*], if it were in a minor degree. Alas! The question was a natural one, but it was founded on ignorance. Feminine grace, feminine dignity, feminine usefulness, who prized those and the like feminine gifts more than that so loved father? But feminine ambition!—*that* he reckoned destroyed them all. And he thought his young daughter, who was becoming so much to him—so much his companion, so easy to influence, to inspire, to bind to him in heart and mind, he thought her to be growing dangerously ambitious.

While her brothers Henry and Richard were educated at Oxford, her father sent her for a short time to a London school to learn "behavior," to be "finished." In the summer of 1834, a day or two before he contracted the cholera that swiftly killed him, he walked with her in the Regent Street area:

[T]he time was the close of June, and wealth and fashion in pompous equipages almost choked the streets. "This," said my father, "is one picture of life; now we will look on another;" and, turning aside into narrow dingy streets, he took me through Drury Lane, and the surrounding purlieus, pointing out the sad evidences of drunkenness and degradation, and speaking with unusual gravity and seriousness on the solemnity of life in its various phases.

He spoke of the motives that should influence one's course in life and warned against ambition and the desire of distinction in woman as injurious to the grace and delicacy of the feminine character. She had brought home some school prizes, and he detected in her a force of purpose that alarmed him.[10]

Here was a strong-minded woman, writing from the more liberated vantage point of the 1890s, who evidently wished for a more extended role for women. And yet she bathed her childhood and upbringing in a nostalgic aura that had limited room for regrets. She wrote of a "loyal and loving domestic conformity that secured the combined comfort and order of the home life";

Truly I cannot repeat too often my grateful sense of the debt I owe to the "old custom," which made obedience an easy habit, and deference a natural tribute. I cannot too often repeat my grateful sense of the blessing of that pure atmosphere which surrounded me in childhood and youth, making honour and deference to age and authority a natural sense—so fitly was it demanded—so justly was it paid—so much was it rewarded at the time, so fruitful has it been, and is now, in sweet and sacred memories.[11]

Both Weeton and Jacson, expressing differing gradations of early feminist thought, took stock of a powerfully hegemonic "separate spheres" ideology (the man immersed in the sordid details of the business world and public life,

the woman restricted to the home and harmless philanthropy) and retreated
into a self-policed self-doubt. This suggests the pervasiveness of the cult of
domesticity and the ideal of the separation of spheres, but also the contradictions and uncertainties of women's language. Weeton, like Mary Wollstonecraft, tentatively argued a radical feminist case based on difference. But her
concession and even celebration of those gendered differences used to justify
consignment of women to the private sphere illustrates clearly enough the difficulties involved in breaking out from a dominant discourse and in subverting
a dominant language.

This raises a number of important questions about the nature of that discourse, about challenge or affirmation, transgression or compliance. For example, how effective were the normative pronouncements on domesticity of
clergymen, doctors, and assorted public moralists? Or did reality often run
counter to rhetoric, as a number of scholars have claimed, women finding active ways to become involved in the public sphere and to challenge patriarchal
domination? Did the spheres become *increasingly* separate in this period as the
process of industrialization put a greater distance between workplace and
bourgeois home (see Chapter 11), and a public, political sphere was expanded
for males? Or have the separation and the separating out been exaggerated,
umbilically tied to unworkable models of industrial takeoff and class formation? Above all, to what extent were women active participants in the creation
and re-creation of the structure of ideological constraint they variously deplored and welcomed?[12]

The Language of Domesticity

It is clear that the ideology of domesticity was by no means a newly minted
phenomenon during the revolutionary era, but—like the bourgeoisie itself—
was constantly being reformulated and refabricated through the power of language under the twin impact of political upheaval and economic change.[13] It
was reinforced at every possible opportunity by a legion of male and female
commentators. Clergymen of all shades were its most active proponents
through command of the pulpit and ready access to the printing press. In
1797, when fears of French invasion were in the air, the Rev. Thomas Bancroft, vicar of Bolton, preached a sermon to a weavers' friendly society exhorting obedience, the rights and duties pertaining to each station in society,
the rejection of all the newfangled philosophies of Reason, so called, and the
glories of the British constitution. Equally predictable was his contrast between the wise and the improvident humble laborer. The latter spent his time
in the alehouse, while his family languished in the miserable home; maybe he
would end up in gaol or the poorhouse, his children become vagabonds, and
his wife die of a broken heart. The former was all that Hannah More could
desire. "As his character is good, he is sure of meeting with employ; and he

depends upon the favour of God and his own diligence for the rest." His fare was coarse but sufficient, his clothing plain but whole, his dwelling humble but clean, with a comfortable fire, clean and healthy children, a frugal and loving wife. Something would be laid aside for old age and infirmity. On Sundays the family, decent, comely, and cheerful, would prepare themselves early for the duties of the day, before proceeding to the house of God.[14]

This was a standard picture, essentially prescriptive of large doses of one vision of bourgeois norms for the lower orders. It was part offense and part defense: partly didactic, unrolling the bourgeois map into unconquered territory, partly desperately seeking to shore up the levees marking out the boundaries between the different God-given categories of life, currently being radically challenged by revolutionaries abroad and rationalists at home. Earlier in the crisis-ridden 1790s, when Armageddon seemed so close at hand, the Rev. Thomas Starkie, vicar of Blackburn, had made this quite clear. Inequality, he said, was of God's own appointment.

This natural inequality in the condition of men was designed by providence for the most important purposes—for purposes subservient to the chief end of our existence: it constitutes our trial and probation in this life. The inequality of the sexes has its foundation in nature. They were formed for each other's solace and support; and the duties—of protection in the stronger sex, of submission in the weaker, and of mutual affection in both—rest on a divine command.[15]

The message was clear: there must be no tampering with any of the relationships of authority, subordination and power, whether of rank or gender.

Women had special responsibilities as the most virtuous sex. The Rev. Joseph Fletcher, Blackburn Independent minister, knotted himself in a skein of double standards in a sermon he preached to youth in 1811. "Detested above all beings," he lectured, "be that monster who first allures by artifice and deceit, an unsuspecting female from the path of rectitude—and still more detested be he who leaves her a prey to the villainy of others, or the subject of incessant remorse to herself." But once a woman forfeited her virtue, she was rightly excluded from all decent society on the grounds that "'the best things when corrupted become the worst.'" Fletcher lamented that male unchastity did not make a similar outcast of the man.[16] He was ever engaged in the crusade against "the world, the flesh, and the devil," and it is especially interesting to note his views on the woman in marriage and the home. When in July 1819 his sister, Mary, married a minister, he wrote to her reminding her of her duties:

It is particularly the duty of a minister's wife, next to the preservation of her own consistency and circumspection, to be in every thing alive to the usefulness, and comfort, and honour, and influence of her "lord." Next to the glory of God, and the salvation of your own soul, you must live for your husband, not merely in relation to personal and domestic duties, but for him as a Christian minister, so that your prudence, your zeal, and your discretion, may always render you as much the object of his ministerial confidence as of his conjugal attachment. . . . Determine, as a general rule, to be never absent from your own home on the evenings, except some very particular circumstances may seem to justify your deviation from your general rule. Never contradict your husband in the presence of others. Let it always appear that you respect him as well as love him, for there may be love where there is little or no respect.[17]

The Rev. William Jones, minister of the Mawdsley Street Independent Chapel in Bolton, explained his views on the position of women in an essay on marriage in 1842. He wrote,

Because woman was the "first in the transgression," she was put under the authority and dominion of man. But this is not an argument for his tyranny; it is a reason why he should render the yoke easy, and the burden light. She feels sufficiently the effects of the curse—in the weakness of her frame—in the debility of her constitution—and in the sufferings inseparably connected with child-birth. Therefore, the man should do her "honor as unto the weaker vessel."

The wife's obedience was unlimited, except where the salvation of her soul was endangered. In return the husband's duties were to give her his undivided attention and to maintain, comfort, and protect her.[18]

Being a wise mother was one of the most important of all female duties. As the Rev. Edward Girdlestone, vicar of Deane, put it in the 1850s, the corruption of human nature began early in life, and the Christian mother had to correct it:

For yours it is, with a tenderness and skill which a father's rude hand in vain endeavours to rival, to twine the young tendrils of the vine around the cedar of Lebanon. Yours it is to nurse your little ones for Jesus, by guiding to His blessed name the first feeble accounts of their infant tongues, while as yet they are too indistinct for a father's ear to understand them. Yours it is to behold the first bended knee—to dictate the first petition to the throne of grace—to listen to the first outpourings of gratitude to Him who suffers even little children to come to Him.[19]

These then were some of the core elements of the ideology of domesticity and of the role of women across the early-nineteenth century. There might be different nuances among the clerical propagandists, but there was nothing that the Rev. Starkie said on the subject in the 1790s that the Rev. Girdlestone would not have understood six decades later. Domesticity was, in effect, the fluvial deposit of three swelling streams of thought in a rich delta where all of the bourgeoisie and many besides could wallow. One stream, gentility, descending from the high peaks of aristocracy, carried with it the concept of the refined lady in the drawing room who certainly did not work but directed the management of the house by a gaggle of servants and helped create a network of social alliances through entertaining and visiting.[20] A second stream, seriousness, fed by evangelicalism, similarly treated the sexes as fundamentally different but compatible, each fulfilling a preordained role in God's greater design. It treated the home as a sanctuary against worldly pollution, with the wife taming male lust, creating the contented home and bringing up the children in the paths of virtue. In so far as it was bourgeois, it acted as a means of self-definition against unevangelicalized aristocrats and the uncontrolled populace.[21] The third stream, rationality, had most problems with the ideology, witness a goodly number of Enlightenment radicals from Mary Wollstonecraft and William Godwin through Robert Owen and the utopians to Harriet Taylor and John Stuart Mill. But these were nonconformists going against the grain even in the world of economic, political, and religious rationalism. For most rationalists a modicum of gentility and seriousness only confirmed their opinion that the sexes were on earth to perform different roles, and that the protective cocoon of the home was an ideal to be striven for in a world of economic and political uncertainty, flux, and anxiety, a very foundation of civil society and of highly valued independence. From this position there were few dissenters. But beyond this core of values the diverse genealogy of domesticity allowed plentiful scope for competing visions, even within the partially reconciled medley of contradictions that made up each individual's personal beliefs.

If the French Revolution and its repercussions prompted a forceful restatement of the philosophy of hearth and home and segregated roles, just as the American Revolution had done before it,[22] further crises in political affairs throughout the early-nineteenth century precipitated repeated reformulations of domesticity—displacements of wider anxieties about the pace and nature of social and economic change. One of the most celebrated instances is the Queen Caroline Affair. The intriguing aspect of this affair was the way in which both supporters of the king and advocates of the queen could draw on the ideals of domesticity in presenting their case. Some historians have pointed to the success of the queen's backers in propagating a vision of a wronged woman bravely defending her honor against a libertine king and court, a further step in the delineation of a bourgeois domesticity against a degenerate nobility.[23] This was probably true for the more radical and any of the lower orders who welcomed any opportunity that embarrassed the government.[24] But it was not true for the loyalist majority of the local bourgeoisie, who could strengthen an ever-flexible domesticity by drawing on another strand in its composition and describe the queen as little better than a whore, having violated the most sacred vows and duties of her sex.

The loyalists could be under no illusions about the character of George IV. The Rev. Jackson Porter of St. John's, Blackburn, for example, in a funeral address for the king a decade later, could not refrain from adding to his eulogy, "we must, with sorrow, confess, that his early life was lamentably defective in moral correctness and virtuous prudence."[25] This was understood, but in 1820 it was not the king's virtue but Caroline's that was most at issue for the loyalists and the evangelicals, not only from a reflex loyalty but also on the grounds that women, from the queen down, had the furthest to fall. A letter from "A widowed Wife" to the queen in the *New Times*, quoted with approval in the *Blackburn Mail*, spelled out some of the issues. She told her, "the rank of no female whatever can exalt her above the duties which God and man have alike imposed upon her." She asked,

Did you studiously endeavour to conform to his taste, to model your character by his ideas? . . . Did you oppose submission to his will, gentleness to his impetuosity, and tenderness to his coldness? . . . You are a subject, a wife, a woman, and should be a Christian: on which of these characters can you justify the languages you have held?—a language which is calculated to stir up sedition and anarchy, to fill our land with lamentations, and our streets with blood![26]

A letter from "Civis" charged the queen's court with being "the rendezvous of demoralizing principles and Bacchanalian devotees" and asked husbands whether they would really wish their own wives to imitate her conduct.[27] The loyal petition from Blackburn married both the duties of females with those of subjects, speaking of "a decided opinion of reprobation on the conduct of the Queen, both on the Continent, as a woman, and since her return to England, as the first Subject of the Crown."[28] But perhaps most telling of all was the use of role models to enhance the cause of family and hearth, the tale of two Charlottes and one Caroline. The *Mail* drew the explicit contrast between one queen, charged with adultery, and the feminine virtue of another, the consort of George III, speaking of "the countless blessings which for nearly sixty years this nation derived from the scrupulous vigilance of Queen Charlotte, in watching over female morals."[29] The second virtuous Charlotte, still fresh in the memory, was Princess Charlotte Augusta, daughter of the Prince Regent and wife of Prince Leopold of Saxe-Coburg, who died in childbirth in November 1817. The baby, a prince, did not survive, terminating the direct succession. The sorrow, the mourning, and the solemn services formed a greater bourgeois moment than the divisive affair three years later. The worthy of Blackburn took the opportunity to pontificate on loyalism and domesticity. On the day of the funeral, business was suspended, a solemn procession took place to the parish church, people in mourning cloaks carrying lighted flambeaux lined the streets, and clerics gave sermons in all of the chapels. The Rev. Thomas Starkie, the vicar, addressed the young, unmarried women in the congregation. Charlotte "in her single state was a Mirror in which every young female might view herself to advantage." She combined filial affection and prompt obedience. Turning to the wives, he reminded them that she had blossomed in marriage:

I would recall to your minds that constant and increasing affection to her husband, which bore so prominent a part in the subject of our sorrow. It was after she had entered into the holy state of marriage, that her discretion, her affections, & all the amiable qualities of her heart burst forth, and became more manifest to the world. . . . As a pattern then of conjugal duty and affection her example may be followed by females in every rank and condition of life.[30]

This could not be applied to Caroline. The respectable, loyalist bourgeoisie chose their icons from the national family accordingly.

A later famous crisis in gender roles concentrated on the workplace as the locus for displaced fears of industrial transformation. The 1842 parliamentary report on conditions in the mines, with its depiction of female semi-savages stripped to the waist hauling coal trucks, was influential in building or reinforcing a consensus from paternalist peer to trades unionist against women working.[31] But the cotton mill was more important in the textile district, and here there was no consensus. As we shall see (Chapter 9), outsiders' attacks on the mills as hotbeds of vice and exploitation met vigorous rebuttals from members of the local bourgeoisie, manufacturing, clerical, legal, and medical. Most manufacturers needed the labor of women, found it cheaper, and hence remained self-interestedly mute when it came to the extension of separate spheres further down the social scale. Few paternalists followed Henry Ashworth (see Chapter 9) in attempting to exclude all married women from their works.[32] Most were willing to rely on such defenses of the "moral tone" of the factory system as that penned by the Rev. Franklin Baker, the Bolton Unitarian minister. He stressed the disciplining nature of the mill, the order and regularity imposed through close managerial surveillance, to counter the charges that the indiscriminate mixing of the sexes converted mills into schools of vice and immorality.[33]

Few if any members of the local bourgeoisie found fault with unmarried women working, and no one denied the importance of female domestic servants (preferably single and by implication asexual), essential to the efficient functioning of the bourgeois home. But many were willing to spell out the incompatibility of married women working and an ideology of happy homes and hearths as a desirable standard for all classes. The liberal *Blackburn Gazette* in the summer of 1833, for example, in defending the millowners against the charges of "white slavery" and "infanticide" put about by the Ten Hours advocates, alleged that if children were restricted in working, more mothers would be forced to go to the factories instead. Predictably, it found the answer in cheaper bread through Repeal of the Corn Laws, so that fathers might support their families as of yore by the fruits of their own individual labor.[34] The

Rev. Francis Henry Thicknesse, vicar of Deane, an outsider who probably had
no close manufacturing ties, provided a good later example. He railed against
husbands who permitted their wives to work in factories: "Why, what in the
name of common sense does a man marry a wife for? To come home after a
hard day's work to a black fire, no dinner or supper, a dirty house, and perhaps one of his children run over by a cart just for want of somebody to look
after it?"[35] Explicit in this critique was the notion that a married woman could
only fulfill her allotted duties on earth when tending to the home and the children, and that to do otherwise was to offend against Christianity and the cardinal virtues of thrift and good order.

The image of the clean, comfortable cottage fitted very snugly the agenda
of the sanitary reformers of the 1840s, who readily appropriated the language
of domesticity and its gendered ideal (see Chapter 10).[36] Short-timers, too,
countering the *Blackburn Gazette's* logic, argued that only with sufficient free
time for all—men, women, and children—could domesticity flourish. This is
well represented in a medal struck to commemorate the passage of the Ten
Hours Act in 1847. "God Save the Queen" was inscribed on the obverse and
on the reverse "Evenings at Home," with a family grouped at a table by the
kitchen hearth, a clock on one wall as a sign of relative prosperity and conformity to a well-ordered time discipline, mother ironing, father reading, the
son reading or doing sums, the daughter knitting, sewing, or darning.[37]

Women in Public

Contrast a painting of the Addison family around the breakfast table in
their large residence in Winckley Square, Preston. The scene breathes dignified
abundance, the blending of refinement and seriousness. Mrs. Addison is
holding the sugar tongs, John Jr. is reading the *Preston Chronicle*, and Thomas Batty has just paused from a perusal of a parliamentary blue book.[38] The
thickening of the nation's midriff with mercantile, industrial, and professional
wealth in the late-eighteenth and early-nineteenth centuries allowed increasing
numbers to aspire to such representations of well-ordered domestic contentment and to the confinement of the woman in the private sphere as a leisured
lady. But it is somewhat ironic that, at the level of the Addison family, upon
the sunny uplands of relative financial security, separate spheres allowed the
time and scope for privileged women to carve out a greater role for themselves, to be more insistent upon their own importance, and to begin the work
of political and cultural emancipation.[39] It could well be the case that separate
spheres mattered more urgently to *lower*-middle-class families on the rise,
seeking to distinguish themselves from the working wives of the lower orders.

Many lower-middle-class women worked, principally as shopkeepers,
farmers of small to medium holdings, and schoolteachers. The first two involved working at home, often in a supervisory capacity, and none of them

involved much risk of sexual impropriety, the constant fear of the factory fantasists. School-teaching, true, usually meant working away from home, but women teachers only taught girls and, occasionally, small boys; and no one seriously expected that girls could be taught sewing or needlework by male teachers. These women workers tended to fall into three categories: unmarried women who would sometimes be able to relinquish work on marriage; married women who helped their husbands in the draper's shop or provision store; and widows who had to carry on the family business once their husbands had died, and possibly before their sons were of age to take over.[40] Landladies of pubs and hotels tended to fall into this latter category, teetering on the lower edge of respectability because of the nature of their profession, even though the size of their establishments often indicates substantial potential wealth.[41] All this was below the level of the bourgeoisie. Bourgeois ladies simply did not work if they could afford not to; and if they *had* to work, they were scarcely bourgeois.[42] This was a minimum criterion for entry to the club, and the reason why a rigorously defined ideology of public and private was more important to the arriving and newly arrived than the securely settled.

Ladies might not work, but they could bring capital into a business enterprise or a profession by way of marriage.[43] In the textile towns this does not seem to have been a massive contribution[44] and presumably had a greater importance in the lower branches of the middle class at the smaller retail or embryo-manufacturing level than in the higher. Besides, the woman's dowry was more properly a limited transfer of resources from one family to another, organized by men. Some women invested in canal or railway shares, but the contribution was minor, and the chief point of interest was that at shareholders' meetings they were barred from attending, being able to vote only by proxy. For example, the initial subscription list for shares in the Manchester, Bolton and Bury Canal in 1790 included £1,100 from five women; but this compared with £46,600 subscribed by ninety men.[45] At a meeting of the shareholders to the Bolton and Preston Railway in 1842, seven women were present by proxy, representing 119 shares, as against ninety-eight men, in attendance or present by proxy, holding 4,514 shares.[46]

The exclusion of the bourgeois lady from a political voice was well-nigh total. It may be true to say that the Great Reform Act extended and made uniform the parameters of this exclusion, as £10 males in corporate boroughs across the country came within the pale of the political nation. But this would be to overestimate the significance of the measure for relations of gender and to treat it as more of a defining moment than in reality it was. The extended franchise in Preston had since the mid-eighteenth century ensured male political representation all down the social scale, and 1832 merely reduced that voice. Here and in the other towns it would be an exaggeration to say that bourgeois men were excluded from the political nation before 1832, since many of them qualified for a county vote by being forty-shilling freeholders, and within the towns the various organs of local government—the corporation in Preston, select vestries, vestries, court leets, improvement commissions, and so on—were confined to men, and largely men of the middle classes. Eighteen thirty-two was simply an incremental extension of this, not a radical departure.

The exclusion of women from the franchise was largely taken for granted, but the question was raised among lower-class radicals and gives a further indication of the difficulties in subverting a dominant discourse. Take an address from an unnamed female radical reformer in a Huntite publication in Preston early in 1832:

[Man] has been enthralled, enslaved, deprived of his natural rights by the odious inventions of despotic tyranny, and the natural consequence of the degradation of his mind has been that in all the relations of domestic life he has become as great a tyrant as any despot on the face of the earth, recompencing [*sic*] himself for the loss of public freedom by being a private despot. Of course, in domestic as well as political government, it is necessary for the oppressed to be ignorant, and for this reason—Ignorance has been represented as perfectly meritorious in woman.[47]

This is a powerful statement about the logical indivisibility of rights, doing what feminism does best: exploiting the "inconsistencies, contradictions, and possibilities inherent in the politics of the moment."[48] If males outside the political nation could claim the right of freedom from unnatural oppression, so too could females; if these men could demand inalienable political and civil rights, denying them to women would require especial ingenuity.[49] The potential vulnerability of the masculine political sphere was revealed strikingly in a speech at a Reform meeting in Blackburn in 1831 by the radical reedmaker George Dewhurst:

[I]n the marriage vow the woman gave up her rights to her husband; and he from that time became responsible for their exercise (hear). If it [the vote] were extended to females, it might create disturbance in many families, as the husband and wife might be at variance as to the candidate whom they ought to support. (Laughter.) He was aware that women were as capable of judging either in political or religious matters as men; and in most matters they were far superior to them, being more virtuous, more sober, and more persevering than men. He thought, however, that it would be quite sufficient if the franchise were extended to men.[50]

This was hardly a watertight argument. As a number of scholars have convincingly described, with the levees beginning to spring leaks, just as they had in France more spectacularly in the 1790s, male, lower-class radicals sought to shore them up using the masonry of domesticity. Traditionally, plebeian women had assumed a prominent role in communal protest and ritualized riot to secure a just price for bread and to enforce other aspects of the moral economy, all in the name of the family. But in the gradual decline in crowd and street politics and their replacement by the more formalized mechanisms of union and party, female militancy was increasingly sidelined.[51] Borrowing from notions of middle-class domesticity, plebeian male radicals grounded their claims to citizenship in chivalrous notions of respectability and masculinity: the male breadwinner would provide for the family, and skilled labor could then stake its claim alongside other forms of property to equality in political rights.[52]

Yet this was not solely the achievement of men. Plebeian women's "militant domesticity"[53] provides the most flagrant and ironic example of what might be termed "transgressive compliance." A famous instance was the appearance of members of the Blackburn Female Reform Society on the platform at a radical reform meeting in the town in July 1819, presenting an embroidered cap of liberty.[54] Radicals saw this female activism, in the words of Barbara Taylor, "not as a challenge to women's traditional family role, but as a necessary extension of it, at a time when the rights and needs of all family members were under attack."[55] In other words, if a good wife and mother needed to step into the public arena in order to defend her family, this she must be prepared to do, however regrettable such action might be. The ambiguity here is plain enough. The very act of political participation, however hedged and hesitant, was transgressive of gendered norms and, once secured, the reality or the memory of such a space was difficult to close down. And yet, by deploying the language of domesticity the logical inference was that these women could measure their success in terms of whether or not they felt the need to break out of the private sphere again.[56]

Again, the shaping of a rhetoric of protest from an available language of domesticity proved (from a feminist perspective) self-defeating and more potent in the short term than exploitation of the inconsistencies in the rhetoric of the rights of man. As a logical extension by mid-century, during the brutal lockout and strike in Preston in 1853, an operative cotton spinner, Margaret Fletcher, addressed a public meeting to complain that the

natural order of things was reversed, and women had to go out to work whilst men remained at home, made beds, washed clothes etc. Under these circumstances it behoved her sex to bestir themselves. If capital had its right, labour had *its* right. If capital claimed the right to keep its wife at home and have half a dozen servants to wait upon her, surely the working man had a right to keep *his* wife at home too. . . . It was a disgrace to an Englishman to allow his wife to go out to work.[57]

What is interesting here is not whether the "natural order" of gender roles had indeed been turned inside out—whether striking male cotton operatives really were making beds and washing clothes—but that this woman had adopted so completely the dominant language of domesticity. Elite notions that separate spheres constituted an important facet of English national superiority—a construction given added force by the exclusion of women from mines in the 1840s and the further restriction on women's hours in cotton mills[58]—sat uncomfortably beside masters' treatment of their millhands, hence her argument that working-class women demonstrate publicly for their *right* to be confined to the domestic sphere.

Bourgeois women rarely spoke on public occasions, and when they did they adopted an apologetic tone, a reflexive sense of how they were supposed to present themselves. At the presentation of a clock to William Taylor, manager for Horrocks, Miller and Company, by the workpeople in 1835, the wife of Thomas German, Preston cotton lord, stood up to say a few words: "Although I am deeply sensible that I am not altogether in place, as it is not usual for females to speak in public assemblies, though they do sometimes usurp that privilege at home—and I request, while I say a few words to you, that the gentlemen will stop their ears." And a little further on, "I do feel so much out of my proper place."[59] The presence of women at public agitations, where numbers were important, carried little weight. An editorial charge that women and boys were in a majority in a gathering could be damning. The Rev. Hugh M'Neile, at a public meeting in Preston to petition for the repeal of the Maynooth Act in 1852, put it like this: let the gentlemen of the press

tell how every corner of the hall was packed with men, with a few of those softer faces scattered here and there that we all delight to see in all our great achievements—(applause)—for we cannot get on in any of our great national movements without the countenance of the ladies—(renewed applause)—but let no sly radical press, trying to damage the movement, say, "There was a meeting a few nights ago in Preston, chiefly composed of ladies"—(laughter)—that is not the case; it is almost entirely composed of men—intelligent, well-dressed, animated, well-spoken-out men, who look for justice—(great applause).[60]

Serious and genteel women could only take an active public role in chapel and charity. Of the denominations that countenanced women playing a role of governance, only the Quakers were likely to attract some members of the bourgeoisie. Even here, women were strictly subordinate. As spelled out at the Marsden Yearly Meeting in 1792, women Friends' duties were to inspect and relieve the wants of poor women, but with money approved at the men's meeting; they were to join the men in visiting women applying for membership, reporting to the men's meeting; they were to report the delinquencies of women to the men's meeting, always bearing in mind that "No proceedings of the women only, are to be a sufficient ground for a testimony of disownment."[61] Decision making clearly lay with the men. The minutes of the

Women's Preparative Meeting for Edgworth and Bolton in the 1820s and 1830s report little activity beyond the appointment of representatives and the occasional reading and answering of queries. "There does not appear anything to notice" was the most frequent entry.[62]

Women did play an important role in the limited and deference-extracting redistribution of wealth through charity (see Chapter 8).[63] For example, the Preston Bible Association set up an auxiliary Ladies' Association in 1817 to promote the circulation of the Scriptures, especially among female servants.[64] This was a typical form of female voluntary association, bringing together diverse sectors of the female elite in a subsidiary capacity to promote an objective for the moral improvement of lesser members of their own sex. In this case it enabled ladies to step outside their own proper sphere only in order to advance an ideology of bourgeois domesticity (the decorative lady controlling a web of house-working women) which buttressed that sphere. Equally concerned with moralizing were the ladies' lying-in and clothing charities. The Bolton Ladies' Charity for poor expectant women, instituted in 1797 or 1798, confined relief to poor married women and widows whose husbands had died during their pregnancy.[65] A report for 1838 described the typical mechanism of operation: every subscriber of 5s. 6d. was entitled to a ticket for one woman. The ladies were reminded that they had the power to render the charity "not only a means of temporal and transitory relief, but also of permanent good, of moral and religious advantage both to rich and poor" by being discriminating in handing out tickets to the supplicants.[66] The same point was made for the Bolton Clothing Charity, established in 1816. The second report stressed that the charity

is careful that it may not be considered as the abettor of idleness or vice. The strict inquiry made into the character, as well as the necessities, of the objects relieved, with the visits of examination into the use made of the articles bestowed, prevent, as far as human prudence and diligence can prevent, the misapplication of the bounty of the Subscribers.

Female subscribers of ten shillings or more, of all denominations, formed the committee, and all female subscribers could attend the weekly meeting to make such articles of clothing as might be deemed necessary for the poor, while a lady read from a pleasing and instructive book. Visitors were appointed to inspect the poor and "to recommend industry, frugality, and cleanliness, with an attention to religious and moral duties."[67] Thus the ladies were bringing their practical skills to bear in the cause of social supervision. They were urged to participate or subscribe for the following reasons: the obligations of Christian duty; the compassionate attempt to remove the painful feeling ladies felt on seeing the inside of a poor weaver's home; the satisfaction arising from Christian benevolence, sure in the knowledge that it was more blessed to give than receive, and that the Lord was chalking it up in the credit balance; above all, "It is the appointment of an all wise Providence, that some should stand in need of the kindness of others; and scope is hereby afforded for the production of all those fruits which dignify and adorn the Christian character."[68]

Ladies usually organized only those societies that sought to cater to the physical and moral well-being of poor women. But there were exceptions, such as the Bolton Ladies' Auxiliary of the London Society for Promoting Christianity Amongst the Jews, formed at the instigation of the Rev. William Thistlethwaite of St. George's in 1813, which attracted many of the town's leading ladies.[69] Beyond these organizations, the public role of a lady, independent of her husband, was limited to being a ceremonial patroness of a charitable occasion, to selling her needlework at church, chapel, and charity bazaars, to visiting the destitute and sick, and to teaching in Sunday schools. Frequently these served purely denominational purposes; for example, the list of patronesses (mainly with their husbands) in a prospectus for raising a foundation for the Sisters of Charity in Preston in 1835,[70] or the ladies who manned the stalls at the bazaar for Holy Trinity Church, Blackburn, in 1840,[71] or the patronesses for a sale of useful and ornamental work to liquidate the debt on St. George's Schools, Bolton, in June 1849,[72] or the committee of females who visited the sick women of Mawdsley Street Independent Church, Blackburn.[73] Equally frequently they helped foster elite cohesion in pursuit of a common objective, be it the visiting of the poor and ill through the various relief committees, or a cultural event like a ball,[74] or a bazaar for a Mechanics' Institute. For example, a large number of ladies assisted at the stalls for the Preston Institution Bazaar in April 1849, while some of the aristocratic and elite patronesses made donations in money, and others contributed articles for sale. This was an occasion for fashionable display in exalted company, at which brightly attired ladies supposedly excelled. As one reporter described the event, "The appearance of the room was brilliant in the extreme. The splendid articles on the stalls, the gay attire of the ladies, and the élite of the beauty of our own town, presented such a scene as is seldom witnessed in Preston."[75]

A number of female roles either spanned the public and private spheres, or were essentially private but buttressed the public edifice. One such was fashion. Just as ladies were often the arbiters of taste or the unofficial commissioners for consumption in the home, the clothes they wore for public display signaled their refinement, rank, and respectability, at the same time as providing an important stimulus to the upper end of the textile market. This was also true of men, but as the cult of seriousness gradually stripped males of their brilliant plumage and replaced it with the dark, sober, and little-changing business suit, taste in dress, jewelry, accouterments, and hairstyle devolved ever more clearly onto women. The local press fastidiously reported the latest fashions from London.[76] On special occasions, such as the Preston Guilds (see Chapter 8), reporters described the ladies' clothes in detail.[77] Dress brought prestige and status snobbery, while incidentally broadcasting where one stood on the continuum between seriousness and gentility. It also gave a sense of the men showing off their wives: at the Preston Institution Bazaar quoted above, note that the male reporter considered that the genteel ladies, because of their attire, were comparable visual attractions to the wares on the stalls. After all, on public occasions the male assessment of women's public role was implicitly limited to their appearance: the standing toast to women at all-male dinners was to "the Lancashire witches," recalling the trials of witches from the Pendle Hill area in the early-seventeenth century but now transformed into a compliment to the county's women for their "bewitching beauty."[78]

Domestic Cages

Such were the extent and limitations of the public role of "the Lancashire witches." What of the private role? Central to the cult of domesticity was the Christian family, the beating heart of the home. Some historians of private life see the home as "seething with internal conflict," between male and female, parent and child, master and servant, a cauldron of low-level, individualized, gender, generational, and class warfare. Far from the home being the temple of virtue governed by its matriarchal high priestess, or the haven amid the swirling and tumultuous storm of the outside world battering upon the roof but not penetrating within, two of the standard metaphors of the cult of domesticity, it was the locus of childhood psychological torment, instilling terror of eternal damnation, and producing emotionally stunted individuals with warped notions of sexuality and the body.[79] Well, maybe. It all depends on which families one looks at. The picture needs to be balanced by looking at the positive role of the family, as providing ballast in an unstable society, an emotional center guarding against anomie, a psychological anchor. We do not have to accept the whole of bourgeois family ideology to acknowledge that some part of it had some basis in reality, nor reject as false consciousness those memoirs and diaries that dwell warmly upon their families, past and present. The succor has to be weighed alongside the terror.[80]

Less controversially, the middle-class home has been seen as a display cabinet of values and of patterns of consumption. It advertised its wares—sobriety, duty, thrift, self-help; or the moderated and rationalized consumption of luxury items, as the case may be—and it advertised its status, by the number of servants, the possession and size or type of carriage(s), the size and architecture of house and garden, and the internal furnishings and wall-hangings (all discussed in Chapter 11). All of this was consistent with being a bachelor or a spinster, but the standard supposition was that a wife or a husband would be present. Before the rise of the joint stock company, the economic importance of marriage in establishing networks of credit and resources, and also in recruiting junior members of the extended family to carry on the business, was significant. Kinship webs, largely denominationally based, festooned the cotton districts—bourgeois dynasties spanning new and old, landowning, manufacturing, and trading wealth. Women acted as the critical links in these chains of families, and therefore a woman's primary duty in her formative years was to prepare herself for marriage. It was virtually impossible for the bourgeois woman to survive outside the respectable home, so she had two basic choices: firstly, in a marriage pool that was restricted socially, geographically, and often denominationally and politically, she had limited scope for rejecting marriage proposals, and once she decided to marry she was to all intents and purposes stuck with her husband however companionable and fulfilling or utterly wretched the liaison might be; secondly, she could remain single, which usually meant continued residence in the parental home or with siblings, both of which options could be intolerably claustrophobic. If genteel but financially constrained, there was a third category, the option of living in another family's respectable dwelling as a governess, the most ambiguous position within the household, balancing on the boundary between respectability and servility; as Nelly Weeton discovered, it was not an enviable position.[81]

If a woman who wished to marry said no to a suitor she could easily end up a lifelong spinster, denied romance or sexual fulfillment, failing to carry out the marital and mothering duties by which society set most store. But some did say no, especially where the financial scaffolding propping up the alliance might appear too overt. Laurence Rawstorne, squire of Penwortham, returned from a Continental tour in 1817 and became engaged, which he intended as marking a new phase in his life compatible with a shift from worldly pleasure to sober responsibility.

After having had my full share of the vanities of the world & arrived at an age when these lose much of their novelty & delight as well as of their decency I settle in life with the advantage of having seen much of things & persons & I trust of having profited with what I have seen. The knowledge thus attained confirms me in the resolution of directing my thoughts & actions to those objects of public & private good which belong to the sphere in which I move. The connection which I am going to form not only gives me the hope of having one who will take a share & interest in these duties, but it will enable me to carry my wishes into effect by placing me in easy if not affluent circumstances. My first object is to pay off my incumbrances & to build at Penwortham.

For good measure he listed his fiancée's lands, stock, dividends, house rentals, and other assets. But then followed unpleasant wrangles with her family over who would receive her property if there were no issue from the marriage, and eventually she broke off the engagement because he seemed disappointed that he had yet to gain control of any of her money.[82]

Courting was a difficult business, conducted under the eye of relatives and society at home, at chapel, at marriage assemblies. A decision often had to be taken from brief glimpses and from repute rather than from intimate personal knowledge. First, after the initial sighting, came the decision whether to make overtures. Thomas Crouch Hincksman had his attention drawn to a certain lady in Chorley, and he asked the Lord whether to proceed further. He received no reply, so he decided against it; "It was providential, as he subsequently thought, that he thus decided, for the lady sickened and died a few years afterwards." After relocating to Preston, he decided to make his move early in 1832 with a formal note to his future wife:

Permit me to say, that during your stay in Preston, what I have had the pleasure of seeing and hearing of you, has been such as to produce an ardent wish to cultivate a more intimate acquaintance.

Should you kindly allow it, a few minutes of private conversation will be highly acceptable. I will take the liberty of calling this evening.[83]

Once the preliminaries were over, permission had to be gained from parents or guardians. John Horrocks Ainsworth proposed to Miss de Manneville in April 1824, apparently at a ball in honor of the king's birthday, after dancing with her many times before. She, it seems, said yes three days later, so he called on her mother for a "long" and "difficult" discussion. She in turn said yes three days later, but it was all to no avail as Miss de Manneville turned him down the following day, thinking that he was not in love with her.[84] Parents could simply refuse to give their consent or be difficult about it. So much economically and socially was at stake. Two of Henry Ashworth's daughters received marriage proposals in 1850. He made careful inquiries about the financial prospects of one—they were satisfactory, and the marriage took place—and about the health and lifestyle of the other, which he deemed unsatisfactory because of a slight paralysis attributed to dissipation. He declined the proposal on his distraught daughter's behalf, but she accepted someone else four months later.[85] A Captain Richardson proposed twice to Fanny, daughter of the Jacsons of Barton Lodge, before she accepted. He was a middle-aged widower with one child and uncertain prospects, and her parents only reluctantly agreed; the engagement was described as being oppressive. Fortunately, a few years after the marriage he succeeded to his cousin's property near Monaghan.[86] The Rev. John William Whittaker, vicar of Blackburn, proposed to Mary, daughter of William Feilden of Feniscowles Hall, in 1824. Love may well have ruled the match,[87] but the deal was not clinched without considerable opposition from Mary's parents. According to Whittaker, some of William Feilden's mercantile friends in Liverpool "had spoken of his daughter's match in no very flattering terms, expressing their surprise that she should think of sitting down as a Parson's wife & mending worsted stockings all her life!"[88] Whittaker was simply not sufficiently wealthy for the taste of a prosperous merchant: "Money matters are no *secondary* consideration at Feniscowles."[89] Then there was the question of social standing. His aunts had been engaged in school-keeping, one having been a private governess, another having married a music master. His mother considered that "all this must be grating to a family, who are desirous of being considered & ranked rather among the Squiralty, than the trading population of the County."[90] The summer months of 1824 were an anxious time for the vicar and Miss Feilden, and Whittaker had little complimentary to say about his future in-laws. In the end, the Feildens did consent to the marriage, which took place in 1825.[91]

Monetary concerns figured in Robert Heywood's courtship as well. At the end of 1847 he proposed to Elizabeth Shawcross by letter, remarking that she had deeply impressed him for three years, but he had held back because of the great disparity in ages—he was over sixty, she thirty-two. She, understandably, was taken completely by surprise and refused. He tried again, adding "another circumstance never intended to be alluded to though usually considered of much importance, I mean pecuniary affairs." He spoke of a plan to leave legacies to his nephews, who hitherto had stood to inherit, and that "If you knew the pecuniary sacrifices I felt willing to make to carry out the foolish wishes expressed in my last note I cannot but think your opposition would soften down." After a series of refusals, the couple married at the end of March 1848.[92]

Whether from mercenary or rational calculation, practical common sense, or status snobbery, money and social standing were of prime importance in nearly all marriages. Again this could create profound problems for a schizophrenic bourgeoisie. While gentility worshipped status, seriousness and rationalism lauded compatibility in marriage and financial soundness. But did not these tend to crowd out romantic love or the Christian ideal of the spiritual and mystical union of the flesh? The Rev. William Jones, Bolton Independent minister, thought so. Property should not be the determining cause for a connection for life. Often marriages were contracted

to secure a church living,—a fortune; to preserve a title;—to maintain great respectability!—or, to form a political alliance! Thus the ordinance of God is prostituted from its original design; and two are bound together by law, who have no regard for each other; the social order of society is broken, and a kind of legalized prostitution is practised without shame.[93]

Some marriages took place without the consent of parents or relatives. We have already seen the reaction to Edward Pedder's Gretna Green marriage to his dairymaid. Thomas Bancroft, before he entered the Church and became vicar of Bolton, eloped with his intended, Elizabeth Bennett. Her father, a wine merchant and alderman of Chester, in hot pursuit allegedly discharged his pistols into the carriage and managed to stab Bancroft in the leg. Bancroft received both damages and his bride, neither with the alderman's blessing.[94] Improper marriages could still rankle the particularly status-conscious a couple of generations later. Susan Maria ffarington of Worden Hall, writing her family history in 1876, described James, her grandfather, as a black sheep and "a low sporting and drinking sort of a fellow." He married a respectable innkeeper's widow, "who happily died soon and left no family," and then eloped to Scotland with the heiress of Roger Nowell of Altham.[95]

Once the lady had said yes in church or chapel, she was to all intents and purposes locked into marriage, at least if she wished to maintain any kind of respectability. One can argue about the dimensions of the cage, the latitude and liberties allowed in some cases, the degree of fulfillment discovered by some women, the influence they had in shaping the lives of their husbands and families, the scope for further encroachments from the semiprivate to the semipublic sphere. But it was still a cage, with only five keys to open it: death, by far the most common; desertion, rare indeed at this level of society; private separation; judicial separation in the church courts; and divorce, only attainable at great expense through act of Parliament, and entailing the washing of a great deal of very dirty linen in public, leaving its tidemark on the woman concerned.[96] In June 1848, Henry Hoghton, son and heir of Sir Henry Hoghton, brought an action against his wife of three years and Lieutenant Clarence Wigney of the East India Company, alleging that they had eloped together under assumed names. A sentence of divorce from bed, board, and mutual cohabitation was pronounced against her for adultery in February 1849. In July an act of Parliament annulled the marriage on the grounds that his wife "hath, by her adulterous and criminal conduct dissolved the bond of matrimony on her part, and your said subject stands deprived of the comforts of matrimony, and is liable to have a spurious issue imposed upon him." Hoghton could now remarry, and his ex-wife had no financial claim upon him.[97] The marriage of Ellen, daughter of William Turner of Shrigley Hall, Cheshire, Blackburn millowner and one of the town's first MPs, was also annulled in a bizarre and exceptional case. Four men, including Edward Gibbon Wakefield, conspired to get their hands on the Turner fortune. In 1826 they lured Ellen, aged fifteen, away from her governess on a pretext of her mother's serious illness, and while hastening northwards Wakefield managed to persuade her that her father was about to be arrested because of the state of his business affairs, and that the only way to save the Shrigley estates was for her to marry him, her father's friend. They were married at Gretna Green and then fled to France. Ellen's relatives caught up with them in Calais and rescued her. Wakefield and his brother William were subsequently imprisoned for three years, and the marriage, never consummated, was annulled. In 1829 she married Thomas Legh of Lyme. She died in childbirth two years later, at the age of nineteen. Wakefield made use of his time behind bars to reflect on the nature of punishment (he emerged as one of the foremost opponents of the death penalty) and to study the subject of colonization. He proceeded to an active colonial career—in particular his ideas propelled the foundation of South Australia—and ended up with a bust in the colonial office.[98]

Private separation, avoiding litigation, was more frequent than judicial separation and parliamentary divorce but still highly unusual.[99] One example is the indenture of separation between John Horrocks, MP for Preston, and his wife Mary in 1803, not long before his death. It read, "some unhappy differences have arisen between the said John Horrocks and Mary his Wife in consequence whereof they have mutually agreed to live separate and apart from each other." John agreed to settle £500 a year on Mary, his estate to be held by other parties in trust for payment to her.[100] Most other women trapped in unhappy unions were only released by their own or their spouse's death.

Much of what is known about plebeian marriages comes from court records which tend to accentuate the marital discord and male violence which brought unhappy couples before the law.[101] Conversely, few details of matrimonial discord form part of the bourgeois historical record: the need to maintain face and outward family dignity saw to that. There are a few instances of mistreatment: Edward Pedder striking his wife, shutting her out in the rain, or verbally abusing her; Lady Shelley's mother having to deal with two husbands inclined to drink, Thomas Winckley of Preston whom she dared not oppose when he had been at the bottle, and Major Barrington, who would beat her unless her daughter managed to fend off the blows.[102] There is the strange story of Leonard Thomas de Manneville, an aristocratic refugee from the French Revolution, who married (apparently clandestinely) Margaret Crompton of Bolton in 1800. By his own prolix account, the match failed because of the pernicious influence of his mother-in-law, and a prolonged bout of subterfuge, skullduggery, and legal proceedings before the King's Bench and in the Court of Chancery ensued for the custody of their daughter. The courts initially upheld the father's rights, but ultimately he lost the battle, maybe because his wife and her advisers were able to make great play of the fact—during a time of war—that he was French and Catholic.[103]

But much of what is known about bourgeois marriages comes from autobiographies and biographies which often tend toward the hagiographical, painting life stories with shiny gloss finishes, conforming to the strictures of the moral narrative, and piously repeating the refrains of domestic felicity. Letters, too, were couched in conventional form. But is that any reason to doubt the sentiments of Eliza Whitaker, for example, staying with her relatives the Horrockses at Edgworth in 1813 while her husband Charles went grouse shooting? She wrote to him, "I really seem quite an *unmarried Miss* having neither my husband to speak to nor my house to attend to—I adore my dependance [*sic*] & hope I ever shall . . . have reason to do so—for that will ever ensure the happiness of both." A few days later, she continued, "Charles love I can tell you that when once you get me home again I shall not stir from your side so you know what you have to expect. I have felt myself quite unmarried again since we have been absent & have had all the aches & pains I endured in our courtship when you were out of my sight." Her Aunt Robbins had the same feelings about her husband, sighing every now and again, "Oh my dear Robbins bless you I wish you were here." When Robbins died, his wife wrote to Sarah Horrocks of Lark Hill that these lines

will but ill express to you my feelings. The Lord above only knows how acute they are and as it is *his* will to afflict me so *deeply*, he will I fervently hope restore my mind to some degree of composure 'ere long. I ought to remember that thro' my *heavy & heart rending* trial, *he reared me up*, and that I cannot better recommend myself to his favour, than to submit with resignation and obedience to all his dispensations.[104]

Unless specific provisions had been made, a woman's property—including conjugal rights to her body—became her husband's on marriage.[105] As Dr. William St. Clare of Preston put it unambiguously in his will of 1812, the bequest of £1,000 that one Henry Townley Ward of London had made to his wife "does in Law belong to me."[106] This left a widow and children very much at the whim of a husband's will if he died first.[107] For example, Sir William Feilden, Blackburn cotton lord and gentleman-capitalist, died in 1850 having left a detailed will for the disposal of his property. Most of his estates went in trust for life-usage for his eldest surviving son, William Henry, and his mills and cottages in trust for his co-partners for the expiration of the term, and then to be offered for sale to one of the partners, his second surviving son, Montague Joseph. His wife was to receive all the household appurtenances at his residences at Feniscowles and in Hanover Square, London, Feniscowles Hall and part of the estate during her widowhood, £1,200 a year in lieu of the annuity of £300 provided by their marriage settlement and in full satisfaction of her dower, and the interest of all money arising from most of his property in Jamaica and from the property willed to her by her relatives. His daughters received £7,000 each on their marriages, half to be paid immediately, half following his decease. The moieties already advanced had been handed over to his daughters' husbands.[108] This was an unexceptionable document for a gentleman bridging the landowning and manufacturing elite. At this level of wealth the norm was that the prenuptial agreement guaranteed the lady a certain degree of financial independence.[109] Lady Feilden was very well provided for under the terms of the will, but this was not hers of right: in a sense it was a reward for good behavior during the course of the marriage, another token of female dependence in the marital state. And Feilden provided a heavy financial incentive, beyond all the other normative pressures, for his daughters to marry—that is, to move from a parental dependency to a dependence on their husbands.

Marrying the right husband was also, of course, important, and there could be additional pressures to make an acceptable choice. Robert Lowndes of Palterton, Northamptonshire, willed a legacy of £2,000 at interest to each of the daughters of Edward Gorst of Preston who married with the consent of her father or his trustees. In 1832 Dorothy Anne Gorst made an acceptable choice: she married William Adam Hulton with the full consent of the trustees.[110] Samuel Horrocks Sr. sought to influence his widow's movements beyond the grave. He left her the Lark Hill mansion during her lifetime, but if she was absent (except from illness) for more than two months at once or four months during the year, the house was to be offered to their daughters in turn.[111]

There were additional bars to the cage. Pregnancy, babies, and small children were the most obvious, the burden of reproduction being an important factor in keeping many women at home for a substantial portion of their third and fourth decades.[112] So were illness and doctors with few scientific credentials, making repeated childbirth hazardous and recovery from it often protracted and incomplete. It is much easier to find examples of incapacitated women than men. It comes as something of a shock after reading Catherine Jacson's feisty memoirs to be told that, following seven years of social, household, school, and parish activities after her marriage in 1846, she had spent the next forty years largely restricted to the invalid couch.[113] Bessy, wife of John Horrocks Ainsworth, bore a steady succession of children, but from 1847 his diary records that she spent lengthened periods confined through illness.[114] Mary Haughton Whittaker, wife of the vicar of Blackburn, bore ten children from the mid-1820s, but by 1836 she was suffering from some unspecified internal complaint, and her surgeon stipulated that she should no longer walk.[115] Were these exceptions or the tip of the iceberg? Incapacitating illness was clearly not gender-specific, but for physiological (childbearing) and cultural reasons it may have been more of a trial for more women. The languishing lady on the sofa as a stock figure of literary stereotype has her counterpart in the neurasthenic male; but the incapable male struck at the heart of the ideal of manliness and of man the producer and provider. John Horrocks Ainsworth was no more confined to the home from his failing eyesight and blindness by the late 1840s than was Albany Featherstonhaugh, Bolton surgeon, from his paraplegia.[116]

The sense of natural feminine fragility, compounded by restrictive and often voluminous, multilayered clothing, prevented ladies from participating in vigorous, "indecorous," and "masculine" activities, like grouse shooting, rowing, or cricket. When a party of ladies and gentlemen joined the Pedders to climb Fairfield, a Lakeland peak, in 1810, the ladies went in carts and all except two of the gentlemen on foot. "The other ladies," Nelly Weeton wrote, "screamed several times, expecting to be either overturned, or precipitated backwards." Only for the last stretch, when the carts could proceed no further, did the ladies actually do any exercise.[117]

This was conventional, another gender- and class-bound bar to full female expression. The education of girls imposed a further, fundamental limitation. At one extreme it could produce a polished intellectual vacuum to grace the drawing room, and at the other a highly accomplished musician, linguist, and literary sophisticate. It is not surprising that women excelled in writing, whether as novelists or local diarists, minutely and acutely noting the social milieux in which they moved, because a cultural curtain-wall prevented their access to public participation in other areas of endeavor and inquiry, like science, medicine, politics, history. The basis of the bourgeois lady's formal education in the small, private academies that multiplied in the early-nineteenth century was plain, fancy and ornamental needlework, and English grammar, care being taken that "the frequent Inaccuracies in common Conversation, and in Epistolary Correspondence, will be wholly corrected." It scarcely needed to be said that only "such School Books as have a Tendency to instil into their young Minds a Love for the Beauty of Moral Rectitude" would be selected. Beyond that, additional fees would secure the teaching of geography and the use of the globes, arithmetic, drawing, French, music, and dancing.[118] Few contested that these were the proper limits of instruction for a prospective wife and mother and that, as Peter Whittle put it, "We ought to regard all public and private schools as nurseries of men for the service of the church or state, and those for the softer sex as nurseries of piety and virtue."[119] When it came to teaching the lower strata, the very basics were deemed sufficient. The wife of the Rev. John Holland, the Bolton Unitarian minister, founded a girls' sewing school in 1810. The Rev. Franklin Baker could look back on this in 1853 and remark that it was continuing "its noiseless course of usefulness in training the gentler sex to those important duties which they may be called to fulfil!"[120]

The wealthiest bourgeois young ladies might be sent to London to be "finished." Louisa Potter was sent to a select ladies' school in Russell Square, which included among the usual items of instruction dancing lessons by a ballet master at the opera and an assiduous attention to deportment and carriage.[121] Catherine Formby was educated in Italian, German, and drawing in London, and then went on to a boarding school to learn "behavior"; as a parlor boarder she spent the evenings in the drawing room learning to be a true lady.[122] Frances Winckley spent two years from the age of fifteen with a Mrs. Olier in Portman Square, who received four young heiresses and charged £1,000 a piece per annum.[123] Duly finished, these ladies were ready to start— as wives, society ladies, and mothers.

These were some of the dimensions of the feminine and domestic cage. They did not preclude women from bringing a day-to-day influence within that apparently confining arena. There were several ways in which they could exert their domestic talents to have a considerable impact on the outside world: the raising of the children, the counseling of husbands and relatives, and the maintenance of social—and thus indirectly, economic and political— networks. According to her son, the life's task of Mrs. William Cross was in bringing up her offspring. Her husband died in 1827, leaving four sons and two daughters, all under eleven:

[S]he felt that the best way in which she could show her love and reverence for her husband was in educating his children. "Devotion to those children" will fully describe the remainder of her life. To her & to my aunts we all owe a lasting debt of gratitude.—She was allowed to live to accomplish her task. And no sooner was that over than she was called to rest.[124]

Wives and relatives acted as counselors, giving advice that their menfolk could heed or ignore. In the letters of Mrs. William Feilden concerning the building of Immanuel Church, Feniscowles, we have a good sense of the difference a pugnacious elite lady could make. As we shall see (Chapter 6), the vicar of Blackburn, Dr. Whittaker, had considerable problems with his in-laws over the patronage and design of the church. Mrs. Feilden played a full role in this. She wrote to the bishop of Chester in December 1833, somewhat disingenuously but conveying a sense of what was deemed appropriate for a woman, "My life has been passed in such entire seclusion, that I am scarcely conscious if the rules of etiquette established in the higher ranks, will [warrant?] my addressing myself personally to you, without an infringement upon them." She laid out her objections to the vicar's plans, but the Feildens backed down when the bishop sided with him. Then came trouble over the design, and an increasingly irritated correspondence culminating in Whittaker's allegation that all his suggestions had been "directly and rudely rejected" and that "in the course of correspondence, I have received letters containing vituperative language, such as no Lady ever before addressed to me." Mrs. Feilden made further suggestions and requested that he "send me a little darling, that every year out of my *butter money*, I shall be able to *put* and *do* something for." As for the earlier design, she told him to burn it "with the first auto de [sic] fee [sic] at the Priory," referring to the neighboring Catholic chapel in Pleasington. Finally he drew up a design that pleased her: "It will be lovely, and quite eclipse the one eyed Monster in the Vicinity," by which she meant the Priory with its large rose window. The church, she thought, could almost be considered a *"frontier garrison* of the Protestants."[125]

She was heavily involved in the preparations for the laying of the foundation stone at the end of January 1835. She wrote to Whittaker that she had set her heart on "'*God save the King*' in *full Chorus* as a finale, if you do not deem it incorrect" and explained in some detail the arrangements for the feast at the hall. In spite of her own pronounced anti-Catholicism, she implored him not to use his sermon on the occasion to antagonize the papists, as he had said he would. She wanted peace to reign on the day and preferred to win them over by the mild beams of the Sun of Righteousness than by thunder, lightning, and storm; or at least for him to postpone his ire until the cornerstone of Witton Church was laid, which he did. To make the day perfect, she requested that he arrange with the editor of the *Blackburn Standard* for there to be a good account of the proceedings, so that she could send copies to distant friends.[126] During the building, she gave precise directions for the family and the servants' pews, down to a little ledge for their umbrellas and parasols.[127]

All of this suggests Mrs. Feilden had a considerable voice of her own and influential input into the family decision making. There is no reason to suppose that this was unusual. Women played a significant role in both the organization of the household and the cementing of contacts. Dolly, wife of George Clayton of Lostock Hall, banker, meticulously noted in her diary her social round, an endless succession of dining, taking tea, receiving, calling, with and without her husband, linking anyone of any moment among the urban and rural gentry of Preston and its hinterland.[128] Louisa Potter describes how "Mrs. Weston" organized her household at Maudesleys. Visitors were allocated to bedrooms "according to the place they held in the hostess's estimation." Mrs. Weston slept in a bedroom with a view of the stableyard; opposite her bed there was a clock "by which she could regulate the rising of the maids and the punctuality of the men." She organized the dinner parties, decided which guests in her plans for upward mobility could be invited and which spurned. In some other respects she was not cut from the prescribed feminine cloth: "She rarely occupied herself with feminine accomplishments, such as embroidery or knitting. Her pleasures were a sound biological or historical work, especially approving those with a leaning to the Tory side; meddling with the farm, managing the house, or looking after the poor."[129]

How then did bachelor households or families without wife and mother fare? In terms of household management they relied on surrogate wives and mothers in the form of female housekeepers, cooks, and domestic servants. Sometimes spinster or widowed sisters or other relatives would act as housekeepers, particularly at the lower rungs of the bourgeoisie. At other times they had to be hired. After a dinner party he held at his Rivington house in May 1852, Charles James Darbishire, a bachelor, recorded in his diary:

The worst cooked & served dinner I ever had[.] Lamb cold—Salmon not fresh—cabbages short boiled no melted butter—Fowls brought in bare & miserably trussed—white sauce not thrown over them—mint sauce & parsley sauce too thin—ground rice pudding sour—Gooseberry dumplings & tart good & the only things that were except the browned potatoes—I had no new ones I thought them so bad—
I must change my housekeeper—I have no certainty that she will do anything right—& yet I consider her very honest & careful.

Two months later he gave Betsey notice and walked to Wigan to interview a potential replacement, acceptable except for "a provincial accent which I would rather have been without."[130] He thus relied on an efficient housekeeper for his socializing, and in making social contacts he like other bachelors had to depend partially on the social networks of relatives, friends, and business partners, bearing in mind that one of the prime functions of the social network—the provision of spouses or business and professional contacts for offspring—did not usually apply in their cases.

Darbishire's mother had died young, and the Darbishire household, five sons and two daughters, again as represented by Louisa Potter, is an interesting example of a motherless family. The children's father, Robert, usually only met the family at dinnertime, and there was a great sense of liberty. The girls received education from John Holland, the Unitarian minister, and their brothers, but mostly educated themselves. Even in this environment, the subjects learnt assumed a sexually segregated form, with Henry taking to Italian, Charles to the flute and entomology, Francis to chemistry, and the girls to cooking and the classics, ironing and the harp, clear-starching and Shakespeare. The girls became skilled needlewomen: "They would make workboxes, bind books, or sketch the solar system; excelled in nature printing, and carved intaglios in sulphate of lime," and Louisa, the eldest sister, would read aloud to them in bed romantic novels like *Guy Mannering* and *Sicilian Romance*. Louisa presided over the housekeeping from the age of sixteen as a surrogate mother, helped by a maid-of-all-work.[131]

Sexual Cages

The domestic cage had many bars; but for many it was attractive, marriages perfectly companionate, the bars to all intents and purposes invisible. It could seem no more restricting than for a man locked into patterns of relationships and conformity. There could also, perhaps, be a considerable latitude for the expression of conjugal bourgeois sexual pleasure, within the moralistic and ideological confines of religious and medical prescriptive norms.[132]

The local record is silent on this debate. What can be said with some confidence is that a husband could breech the bounds of holy wedlock more easily without causing the same scandal. There is no way of knowing how many bourgeois males had extramarital relationships or resorted to prostitutes, but there was the occasional offspring of illicit sex, and this meant ostracism neither for the father nor the child. James Barlow, who became one of Blackburn's leading medical men, married Elizabeth Winstanley in Chorley in 1795. The marriage was not a happy one, and they soon separated without issue, Barlow moving to Blackburn and passing himself off as a bachelor. In 1808 a child was born, christened James Barlow Stewardson Sturdy, "in whom Dr. Barlow took a paternal interest," as Abram delicately phrases it. The son became Barlow's heir, was educated as an attorney, became a prominent local solicitor, entered local politics as a town councillor and took his turn as mayor in 1862-63. He married a sister of Daniel Thwaites, the wealthy brewer of Woodfold Hall.[133] Thomas Clayton of Little Harwood Hall and Carr Hall, high sheriff of Lancashire in 1808, married in 1788 but his wife died within a year. In 1810 or 1811 Elizabeth was born, apparently his daughter by his twenty-year-old cook. He made her his heiress (over the claims of the child of a sister who had eloped with a Mr. Pickup of Church Street, Blackburn, by jumping out of a window at Little Harwood Hall), and she married Edward Every, second son of Sir Henry Every of Eggington Hall, Derbyshire.[134] In neither case were illegitimate sex or illegitimacy seriously damaging to status and reputation. In two other cases it is not clear whether many people knew about the natural children before the fathers' deaths. Samuel Horrocks Jr., Preston cotton lord and former mayor, died in 1846 and left £500 in his will to be invested for Alice Standing of Preston, spinster, and their natural daughter, Mary Standing.[135] Thomas Birchall Jr. of Ribbleton Hall, a senior Preston lawyer, had two children by different mistresses in the 1860s. His wife claimed that she knew nothing of these mistresses or children. Having improperly or fraudulently drawn up and executed the will of R. R. Rothwell, from which his wife received £45,000, this property passed to him in law as the husband. He then bequeathed the bulk of this to his illegitimate children, including his wife's jewelry after her death, and provided for his surviving mistress.[136] These were all prominent members of the elite, and in all four cases we know practically nothing about the women involved. The old double standard was very much in operation, as the Rev. Joseph Fletcher had lamented in 1811. What was, if not respectable, at least tolerable, for bourgeois men, was not so for bourgeois ladies.

This is not to claim that men necessarily had it easy. Much about this society—from the architecture of schools with their sexually segregated classrooms to the pronouncements of self-proclaimed experts to the masturbation taboo—indicates an extreme obsession with sex.[137] The number of newspaper advertisements promoting quack remedies for impotence and sexual malfunction suggests a ready market appealing to men anxious to measure up to the muscular Christian ideal of manliness and robust heterosexual identity and virility. Typical of the genre were advertisements for books in the *Bolton Free Press* in 1847, combining a curious mixture of commercial opportunism and moral censure. They came in sealed envelopes. One was

MANHOOD; the CAUSES of its PREMATURE DECLINE, with plain Directions for its PERFECT RESTORATION; a Medical Essay on those diseases of the Generative Organs emanating from solitary and sedentary habits, indiscriminate excesses, the effects of climate, and infection, &c.

Another commended

The Silent Friend . . . particularly addressed to those who are prevented from forming a Matrimonial Alliance, through fear of certain disqualifications for the discharge of the sacred obligations of marriage, and to the thoughtless youth, whose follies, (to speak mildly,) have entailed upon him debility, and disfiguring disease in their worst forms.[138]

Booksellers advertised a range of ready remedies, such as "Dr. Freeman's Never failing Ointment," which "cures the Itch by a single Application . . . without the Use of Mercury," or his celebrated drops of "Guttæ Salutaræ," good for all scorbutic and venereal complaints, gleets, seminal weaknesses, and strangury.[139]

A significant sexual cage for some men, bachelors or married, was the prohibition on same-sex sexual encounters. For those who were guilty of "unnatural" acts, there were ample reminders of the punishments meted out to offenders. For example, in 1810 the *Blackburn Mail* ran an extended account taken from the *Portsmouth Telegraph* of the execution of a navy surgeon on board the H. M. S. Jamaica. He was guilty of "an abominable crime." He confessed to the ship's chaplain that he had been practicing it frequently for a long time, and that "this crime is more general than you are aware of—*there is a society formed for the practice of it*! and, belonging to it, are some men whom the public look up to." He had seen the act committed in London, France, and the Mediterranean, and it was not considered a crime. Having read Voltaire and Bolingbroke, he had formed the opinion that he had a right to do with himself as he pleased, and that he was not accountable to God. Now he loathed himself and cried out for pardon.[140] To commit sodomy was to sin against God and nature, and the penalty death: by the 1840s, following the reduction in categories of capital crime over the previous two decades, no other offense after murder received as high a proportion of death sentences.[141] This was an indication of a sexually fearful and fragile society, and we can only speculate from silence as to the numbers of sexually tortured homosexuals forced into the strait-waistcoat of conformity.

Much of nineteenth-century thought on the subject of sexuality believed that gender identity, role, and orientation were determined unambiguously and permanently by the initial assignment of sex.[142] This may have allowed a privileged space for same-sex love before the scientific construction of homosexuality as a category of deviance and abnormality—the individual as biologically flawed rather than simply as prone to commit the sin of sodomy—toward the end of the century. After all, the Victorian ideal of "manliness" depicted a man's love for another man as being finer and nobler than that for a woman, because it was presumed to be innocent of carnal desire. A similar latitude may have been allowed to romantic love between women because given the contemporary mindset it was difficult to think in terms of female sexual activity or arousal that was not initiated by a man.[143]

So we return to the ladies of Llangollen and their romantic, transgressive love. Though thoroughly domesticated, they violated the gendered norms of the cult of domesticity. This ideology, an amalgam of competing discourses constantly being recreated in the nation and the industrializing milltowns, proved remarkably powerful, like the cult of seriousness one of the most potent organizing myths to which members of the bourgeoisie clung. But, again like that other cult, however hedged around with restrictions, censures, and Shalt Nots it might have been, there was at least some latitude for the negotiation of terms—and women could be transgressive and compliant simultaneously, rattling the bars of domestic, sexual, and gendered cages while seeking to reinforce them. There is not a great deal of evidence for the *increasing* separation of spheres, however much propagandists might have willed it, but as the bourgeoisie expanded, more and more families could afford to approximate separate-spheres ideals. Women were and continued to be excluded from the important public fora where questions of power were decided, be they the party committee room, the hustings, the boardroom, the council chamber, or the meeting of shareholders. Yet there were important areas of public life where women *did* find a role, and women's private influence on public activity and in network-building was often considerable. The culture the bourgeoisie constructed, the worldview that circumscribed its vision and limited its action, was filled with such contradictions, half-measures, and gaps between message and reality.

CHAPTER 5: POLICING AND PUNISHMENT

"When a condemned Criminal expostulated with his Judge, that it was hard he should be hanged for only *stealing a Horse!*" the Rev. Edward Whitehead, vicar of Bolton, preached in 1786, "—the Judge with great Propriety replied,—'You mistake, Man, you are not to be hanged *for stealing a Horse—* but *that Horses may not be stolen.*'" This was the essence of the Bloody Code. Whitehead was speaking the Sunday after the execution on Bolton Moor of one James Holland for croft-breaking—stealing cloth laid out for bleaching— and he used the occasion to call for vigorous justice:

[P]erhaps in no one Instance, and that particularly injurious to this Neighbourhood, has Mercy been so frequently and fatally extended as to CROFT-BREAKERS. . . . Had some hardened Offender (and many such I have known) been made to undergo the like exemplary Punishment Years ago,—how much valuable Property would have remained untouched in the Hands of its Owners?— What Numbers, that have been transported to foreign Climes, would have remained at Home,—their Country undeprived of their Labour, and their Families of their Support?[1]

This form of exemplary justice required maximum publicity for the hanging and the display of the "vile remains"[2] thereafter. As one small instance of the impact that this type of execution might have, Peter Whittle, early historian of Bolton, tells of a family Bible he had come across, with dates of birth inside corresponding to particular events, such as "Eawr Meary wur born in that great frost" (1776). Of the nine entries, two were as follows: "Eawr John wur born when Holland wur hung" (1786), and "Eawr Jenny wur born when Longworth wur gibbetted, an owd penny pieces wur made" (1796).[3]

More than six decades after "Holland wur hung," Laurence Rawstorne of Penwortham, after reading a description by Charles Dickens of the crowd at a London execution, concluded that capital punishment failed completely to act as a deterrent. Instead he advocated the American solution of life imprisonment. In an especially extreme version of the "throw away the key" mentality, he suggested that a "Murderer's Tower" be built in a central and conspicuous part of the kingdom, and that the prisoners be cut off forever from the outside world. Let them know when they entered that they would never retrace their steps.[4] Here the carceral institution was the highly visible and public deterrent;

punishment within was wholly private. Between these two dates there had been a significant transformation in ideas of how social order could best be maintained. The period witnessed a marked, but far from complete, shift away from the writing of the sentence of punishment upon the body (hanging, flogging) for full public impact, to the privatization of treatment for individual social dysfunction (incarceration to aid mental reformation); from inadequate and uncertain methods of detection and prosecution (rudimentary police forces, private prosecution) to the more systematic and certain (statistical investigation of crime, professional and disciplined police forces, public—i.e., police—prosecution); and—an aspiration in its infancy—from the military to the police as the principal means of maintaining public order.

Attempting to explain why has generated a fascinating body of conflicting interpretation. Whiggish optimists have seen police, prisons, asylums, and reformed workhouses as enlightened and humane, fitting for a liberal society progressing toward democratic maturity, a welcome movement away from an inglorious past of disorder, capricious justice, gibbets, and armed force. Radical pessimists, drawing their inspiration from the British civil-libertarian tradition and from thinkers as diverse as Marx, Weber, Nietzsche, and Foucault, disagree profoundly. They have variously seen the new institutions as sinister instruments of class power and of social control, or as steps along a counter-Whiggish highroad toward greater discipline, surveillance, and conformity. At its most extreme, in the writings of Foucault and his disciples, early-industrial society created a "carceral archipelago," the multiplication of monuments of domination resembling Jeremy Bentham's Panopticon, through which the objects of power, made visible, could be observed, labeled, dissected, and controlled, their deviance from prescribed norms measured and corrected. In this depiction of constraint, liberalism is nothing more than a guise for discipline, a power exercised by oppressive normalizers like teachers and doctors.[5] Ultimately, the end product would be—will be—the nightmare of the docile body, the gaze of surveillance sufficiently internalized to render overt coercion unnecessary.[6]

This is powerful material. As its critics point out, it is also deeply flawed, presenting an excessively gloomy portrayal of the entire process of modernization. It has little to say about human agents or about the partial, contingent implementation of conflicting agendas only after struggle and bargaining. The state and politics are curiously absent, as is any attempt to distinguish the benign from the illiberal features of a state.[7] Nevertheless, it is compelling to the extent that a whole new level of discipline *was* attempted in the early-nineteenth century, and there *were* disturbing or unsettling aspects to the advance of the "policeman state."[8] Much of the unequal accretion of power was used by, for, or with the approval of members of the local bourgeoisie.

Borough Police

The building of an ordered society increasingly came to depend upon policemen. The foundations were rudimentary. The rural townships had a constable apiece. Preston had three policemen, augmented by the 1815 Improvement Act to seven: a superintendent, an inspector, and five constables.[9] By 1835 there were eleven—a superintendent and ten policemen—the bulk of them appointed by the improvement commissioners but one or two (including, in practice, the superintendent) appointed by the court leet.[10] In Blackburn the part-time township constable was only superseded by a full-time constable appointed by the new select vestry, in 1818;[11] he subsequently had one or two paid deputies under him. In Bolton, policing was in the hands of the boroughreeves and constables (substantial inhabitants appointed annually at the court leet of the lords of the manor both for Great and Little Bolton) who delegated the task to deputies. In addition, the three towns made use of watchmen to walk around the streets at night. Those in Blackburn were authorized by the 1803 Improvement Act. In Great Bolton, ten watchmen were appointed in 1793 under the terms of the 1792 Bolton Enclosure and Improvement Act and were on duty from 10 p.m. to 5 a.m. These lasted only until March 1795 when the trustees decided that they were unnecessary.[12] The Great Bolton Special Constables' Society, a group of volunteers organized by the boroughreeve and constables into "classes," each "class" acting under the direction of a conductor, operated concurrently or began shortly afterwards.[13] These specials did the rounds of the town, patrolling the streets and the inns and keeping a log of any occurrences. Operating both at night and during the day, at various times the specials were deployed against Sabbath-breaking, to clear disorderly public houses, to report after-hours selling and to lock up the drunks. Much of this may have been more effective in terms of low-level harassment and minor vexation than intimidation: there are indications that their powers were both relatively limited and difficult to enforce. In the occurrence book for March 4, 1813, for example, the reporting special constables threatened not to attend to their duties any longer unless the landlord at the Royal Oak, brazenly refusing to restore order to his establishment, be taken before the magistrates. On December 15, 1819, they went to the Commercial Inn at 3 a.m., saw three people and told them to leave, only to be met by the retort from one of them that they had no business there, and God damn them if any lay a finger on him. They apparently obeyed his invitation to depart. Early in the new year, this entry was made: "We have endeavoured to attend to our duty, particularly in the search of public Houses where we heard quarelsome [sic] conduct, we were told we had no Bus^s in their Houses, if that be the case we consider the main purpose of the Watch and Ward is rendered fruitless."[14]

This body of volunteers apparently did not survive beyond the mid-1830s. By that time, the regular force had been somewhat strengthened, although its vicissitudes seem to have owed as much if not more to parish-pump politics than to overwhelming concerns about lawless Boltonians. Both the Great and Little Bolton trustees under their respective Improvement Acts had the power to appoint watchmen, but neither had done so; in the case of the Little Bolton trustees at least, this was because their watchmen would come under the jurisdiction of the boroughreeve. The police appointed by the boroughreeves and constables were paid out of the poor rates and therefore subject to the sanction of the vestry, a forum for factional politics and radical self-expression. Earlier in the decade, after two meetings and stiff opposition from the authorities, a vestry meeting was able to secure the replacement of a deputy constable called Barrett, accused of consorting with prostitutes and of doing rather well for himself through the practice of locking up many people and releasing some of them (without bringing them before a magistrate) on payment of seven or eight shillings. A meeting sanctioned the appointment of a new deputy constable and two assistants, fixing their salaries as an alternative to lockup perquisites. But this was only a limited victory for the reformers in the vestry, who claimed that vestry rights to refuse salaries had been disregarded by magistrates who enforced payment. Moreover, in 1836 a vestry meeting was called in response to the disorderly state of the streets and the molestation of respectable women; but the so-called "townspeople" present refused to appoint more officers unless the nomination and appointment were conceded to them. The authorities therefore appointed three more on their own. In retaliation, the following October a vestry meeting rejected the constables' accounts by a majority of 572. The boroughreeve and constables demanded a scrutiny, duly carried out by the vicar. Counting under the property-weighted terms of Sturges Bourne's Act, he returned a majority of 157 against the "townspeople."

By 1838, the year of the big battle for incorporation (Chapter 10), the Great Bolton police consisted of a deputy constable and six assistants, costing around £500, and the Little Bolton police a deputy constable and one assistant on Sundays, at around £100. The question of policing readily became an issue in the struggle. The constituted authorities, in opposing the incorporation of the borough, implied that the prevailing arrangements worked satisfactorily, that the police were accountable, and that they enjoyed the support of the majority of respectable ratepayers in the vestry meetings. The reformers complained that policing was to a considerable extent unaccountable, partisan (one assistant constable asserted that in general the only beersellers brought before the magistrates were reformers), and inadequate (fixed salaries had reduced the number of frivolous arrests, "but at the same time we are somewhat apprehensive that this system has been pursued to too great an avoidance of disorderly characters").[15]

The sole legal duty of the reformed councils was to organize a police force, and while this caused considerable ructions in Bolton, it had been much less traumatic in Preston, where the new council was imposed by the Municipal Corporations Act. The new corporation took control of the Preston Borough Police at the start of 1836. A superintendent, Samuel Banister, was appointed at £100 a year (plus fees and fines), along with ten uniformed constables, four for day duty, six for the night.[16] The payment of this force came from the council's limited funds, rather than from the prior watch rate, but in the summer of 1839, particularly after trouble with Irish navvies on the Lancaster Railway, Superintendent Banister reported that, given the uneasy state of the town, the police force should be doubled. Accordingly the council decided at the start of August to levy a watch rate of £500 and appointed an additional six constables. The force by 1847 had reached a strength of twenty-two—a superintendent, an inspector, a bookkeeper, five day duty men, three sergeants, ten night duty men, and a spare man—and the rate had climbed incrementally to £1,500 by 1848.[17]

This police force appears to have aroused little opposition in the ranks of the propertied. In contrast to Bolton, there was no sharp break with the old system, no political split over the control of policing, no functioning remnant of a rival force; although admonitions for intoxication and dereliction of duty were common,[18] there was apparently a lower rate of attrition; and the pressure seems to have been only for a moderate *increase* rather than a diminution of the numbers in the ranks.[19] The principle of local control was critical to the force's popularity. The council's opposition to certain proposed amendments to the County Constabulary Act in April 1840 stated this emphatically. It petitioned against clauses stipulating that the rules governing pay, clothing, and qualifications of the rural constables be enforced in every incorporated borough unless the borough could convince the home secretary that its own rules were more appropriate to local circumstances and that the boroughs should maintain at least as many constables per capita as the county JPs decided to appoint outside. This, the councillors argued, would result in needless expense, as fewer constables were required in boroughs with concentrated populations than in rural areas, and in "orderly and quiet" towns than in those that were "disorderly and easily excited." The councillors clearly believed that Preston slotted into the former category and that "the Watch Committee have from time to time appointed as many Constables as have been deemed or considered necessary, not only in their own judgment, but that of the Town at large, for the protection of the peace and property therein." Most important, "over this expence they will have no control, but must submit to an arbitrary rule, thereby repealing by a side wind the object and intention of the Municipal Reform Act, which was to give to Borough Towns the power of self government and the control over their expenditure."[20]

The new police in Bolton encountered considerably greater problems. At the end of 1838 the newly appointed watch committee began to organize a force of ten constables, headed by an inspector and a superintendent, and—as the committee scoured the region's forces for recruits, experience, and precedents—adopted the blue and white uniform of the Liverpool police, along with an amended rule book of the Stockport police.[21] Adapting the behavior of constables to those rules was not easily accomplished: most of the constables were, in the initial months, reprimanded, fined, or dismissed, above all for being intoxicated on duty and at the New Bailey Sessions, but also for insubordination and visiting brothels.[22] Superintendent Hiram Simpton himself did not enhance the image of the force when in September he committed suicide in Liverpool after rejection by a woman not his wife.[23] Nevertheless, the new police, like the old, could still fulfill their function of poking, prying, and harassing, and now in greater numbers. The Daily Memorandum Book catalogues the routinization of interference against gamblers and blacklegs (cheats at gambling), jerry shops and pubs, and prostitutes. On one occasion, Simpton visited the Man and Scythe and found fifty people dancing and drinking at 12:40 a.m. They were holding a wedding, the landlady said; but "adjoining the dancing room, up stairs, was an antichamber in wch I found a young man & two young women dressing! a bed was in the room!! the individuals in the room were *not* the Bride & Bridegroom." And so on through a steady stream of misdemeanors, disorderly conduct, and minor thefts.[24] The offenders could be hauled before the watch committee and then if need be before the magistrates.

While the borough force was beginning to assert its presence, party politics hacked at its roots. Initially the Tories did not accept the validity of the borough charter, and so the old police under the boroughreeve and constables remained in operation. The old authorities warned the new policemen of the serious consequences of their actions should their appointments be declared illegal by the courts.[25] The council found that it could not levy a rate while the Tory boycott continued and the legality of the charter remained in doubt, so the new police had to be sustained first by a private subscription from members of the council, then by bank loans. With the end of bank credit in sight, the reforming incorporators were left with the option of seeing their new police force collapse or of seeking government assistance. Charles James Darbishire, the Unitarian mayor, firmly hammering his colors to the law-and-order mast at a time of Chartist unrest, thought the police needed to be increased substantially rather than disbanded, so at the end of July he penned a request for an Exchequer loan on a mortgage of the rates, which would enable the continuation of a locally controlled force. When this was refused he formally asked in early August that Bolton be included alongside the proposed Police Bills for Birmingham and Manchester—measures pushed by incorporators fighting similar charter battles there and designed to provide both of them with temporary forces financed by government loans and under government-appointed commissioners.[26] After a skirmish in the Commons over the Manchester and Birmingham Bills, the Bolton Bill passed easily in their wake; it came under more attack in the Lords when Lyndhurst and Wellington used it as an opportunity to question the mayor's credentials because of his support for the principles of Chartism.[27]

The bill relieved the watch committee of control over the borough police, a substantial breach—if only for the duration—in the principle of local self-government. The *Bolton Free Press* grumbled about having to pay a large salary to a government commissioner to manage the police force of their own town, but saw it as a regrettable necessity saddled upon the people of Bolton by the obstinate and selfish opposition of a small knot of Tories. The Tory *Chronicle* also followed the party line, claiming that Bolton was as peaceable as any town in the country, that the "proper authorities" had ample means to put down any violence, and that there was no need of the "London Police."[28] The new commissioner, Lt. Col. E. A. Angelo, encountered a deeply unsatisfactory situation: a small force (now down to two senior officers and eight constables) acting as maids-of-all-work for the council (which was unable to appoint any other officials); a police station sharing part of a large room, formerly an Assembly Room attached to a hotel; and a lockup in a small and insecure house. (The old police for Great Bolton controlled a regular lockup of three cells (also insecure), and the Little Bolton old police had access to the more substantial cells in Little Bolton Town Hall, but neither of the old authorities allowed the new police to use their facilities.) With government money and mandate, Angelo could begin to organize a more formidable replacement force; but he did not stay even until its inception, resigning for public and private reasons.[29] He wrote to the mayor, "it would be a complete robbery upon the inhabitants of Bolton to receive from them the sum of £500 per annum for the fulfilment of an office no more important than the business of a common corporal in the regular service viz. the management of 20 men."[30] Darbishire suggested that he be replaced by Sir Charles Shaw, commissioner of the Manchester Police. If Shaw ran both forces, an addition of £200 to his salary would be sufficient, allowing more of the allocated Bolton rates to be spent on hiring additional constables.[31]

Shaw, duly appointed, added to Angelo's appointments and in November swore in the new force of superintendent, inspector, three or four sergeants, and thirty-six constables. The new police had, in effect, quadrupled overnight—ironically—because of the intense local factionalism as well as the Chartist challenge. Shaw reported no public hostility to the new force and suggested that the policemen's public standing had been reinforced by their zeal in tackling the blazes at two mills, presumed the work of arsonists, in the early hours of December 3. Like most senior policemen he wanted a bigger empire: "[T]he number of Constables to which I am restricted by the Amount of Funds at my disposal is by no means sufficient to guard effectively persons and property in a district so extensive and populous as Bolton." But he did concede that he had the advantage of novelty: "I should also remark that I am enabled to establish a smaller force than would otherwise be necessary in Bolton from the circumstance of there having been previously, hardly any police Establishment at all, and thus, I have an advantage which does not apply to Manchester, but quite the Contrary."[32]

The guards of persons and property were not an improvement on their predecessors. Of the initial intake of constables, only five were still on the force by the end of 1842. Seventeen had resigned to join other forces, particularly the new county force in 1840, or to work at their own trades. The rest had been dismissed for a variety of offenses: being drunk or drinking on duty, neglect of duty, absence from beat, going into a pub with two prostitutes while on duty, absence from court when attendance was essential, attempting to extort liquor by threatening a serving girl at the Wheatsheaf, appropriating money from a prisoner, "taking unbecoming liberties and otherwise assaulting" a married woman going to her work, and so on. One constable, Robert Hyslop, formerly a Dumfries laborer, was dismissed because of absence from duty all night, but reinstated at the request of the mayor; dismissed again "for assaulting with intent to commit a rape," but reinstated at two councillors' request until a position as a servant on the railway could be found; resigned to work at the Bolton and Manchester Railway Station; once more reappointed some time after and finally dismissed for being drunk and absent from his beat in August 1842.[33] There was something more than simple misconduct behind at least one firing. PC Stephen Hurley, born in Cork and recruited from the Manchester Police, wrote to Superintendent Boyd in November 1839 explaining his refusal to comply with the commissioner's order to attend and report on a public meeting in the Theatre. He said that he would rather resign than act as a spy; he would "Sooner be a dog and bay the Moon."[34] Shaw claimed in a letter to the Home Office that some of the Chartists had "got round" Hurley, inducing him to write the letter to provoke his dismissal so that the press could make him out as a martyr. Shaw refused to play into their hands. He had people watching Hurley, and he was acting so foolishly on other parts of his duty "that I shall soon get quit of him *quietly.*" Sure enough, he was dismissed on December 13, the stated reason being for absence from court when he was the principal witness.[35]

Alcohol, sex, insubordination, unfitness, and inefficiency continued to wreak carnage among the ranks of those subsequently appointed up to the summer of 1842. A number of constables were dismissed for more than one offense, but over thirty were fired for being under the influence, six for insubordination, ten for being absent from their duties, three for inefficiency, three as unfit, one each for striking a man with a truncheon, allowing a prisoner to escape, pilfering, and being discovered to be a convicted felon, and five for sexual misdemeanors (including one for taking indecent liberties with two women in a cellar in Stanley Street, one "For boasting of having had criminal connexion with a married woman," and one "for indecently exposing his person with a Prostitute when on duty"). This was a far from impressive record and at best only an incremental step up in the efficiency of the forces of order and surveillance.[36]

In September 1842, after the borough charter had been confirmed, the council's watch committee resumed its duties. With local control of the police restored, the emphasis was immediately on scaling back. A proposal in August to reduce the force to thirteen policemen, rejected only by thirteen to six, on the eve of the plug plotters arriving in town, did not betoken an overwhelming confidence in its crowd-control abilities. The watch committee decided instead, at the end of September, to dismiss twelve constables, reducing the force by a third. Although numbers gradually increased during the next few years, the watch committee employed a variety of parsimonious expedients to keep costs down. Five additional policemen were appointed in the agitated month of July 1848, but even then only after an application to Captain Woodford for the temporary loan of twenty of the county constabulary.[37] Crowd control was still primarily the military's province; the main tasks for the police were to enforce the new book of by-laws, to prevent "disorderly characters congregating" on Sundays, to stop "persons writing or useing [*sic*] obscene language," "to seize all Hoops from Boys found bowling the same in the Public Streets within the Borough," and to "apprehend all persons exhibiting wounds or deformities in the Public Streets within the Borough."[38] In short: to conduct a low-level campaign to enforce conformity to "respectable" norms.

County Police

They might complain about the cost, or the numbers, or which local groups should control it; but few bourgeois voices objected to the *principle* of a *local* police force. The *imposition* of police by the state was quite a different matter, however. Edwin Chadwick's craftily constructed report on the rural constabulary, apparently producing irrefutable evidence of the spiraling menace of rural crime and disorder, seemed to threaten a considerable degree of compulsion and centralization in the establishment of a county constabulary. Cross-party, local editorial opinion reacted with hostility to an expensive, unnecessary, foreign-sounding new police—a second standing army, "a band of promiscuous mercenaries . . . disciplined to military movements, distributed throughout the towns and villages of the country to perform professedly the ordinary functions of police constables," belonging to a system "hostile to the liberty of the subject and . . . abhorrent to the feelings of Englishmen." "[S]hould the 'centralization' policy fully succeed," declared the *Preston Chro-*

nicle, "our government will be all but despotic, and our governors all but absolute."[39] "The people are to be taxed for the support of an armed force to keep them quiet," thought the *Bolton Free Press*. "This is quite the old Tory, coercive system under a new garb. If the country really requires an improved constabulary force, why not allow it to be under the control of men chosen by the people, and, therefore, responsible to the people." The paper railed against the timidity of the middle classes, more concerned about the protection of property than an armed police at the disposal of the home secretary.[40] On the other hand, the rhetoric of constitutionality and of freeborn Englishmen emanating from the local prints does not suggest that the middling ranks felt overwhelmed by the threat to property and order—as long, that is, as both were underpinned by military force: the extent to which the occasional appearance of troops had been assimilated into the constitutional landscape by much of propertied England is striking.

It is not altogether surprising that the country gentlemen, supposedly the inheritors of Country ideology against executive encroachments, should be among the county constabulary's strongest supporters. They, after all, tended to support the New Poor Law, that other example of "centralizing despotism"; they were most concerned about rural crime; and it was they—the county's cream—who were to be in charge of implementing and directing the county-centered, permissive final measure.[41] At a meeting in the Court House in Preston in early February 1839, the county magistrates voted in favor of Lord John Russell's proposal. The resolution of Peter Hesketh Fleetwood, MP for Preston and government supporter, that a more efficient and well-regulated constabulary system would not only improve the protection of persons and property but also—addressing libertarian fears—enhance the liberty of the subject by placing less reliance on the military, was passed unanimously. The main objection, voiced by Laurence Rawstorne and William Marshall, was the expense of a new tax on the agricultural districts; but, lacking sufficient support, Rawstorne withdrew his amendment that the government foot half the bill.[42]

The Chartist challenge in 1839, combined with the alarmist statistics on rural crime, made the year particularly propitious for the extension of policing. But as the *Preston Chronicle* commented when the magistrates made their final decision to adopt the legislation in November, the "state of the times" could quite readily be made an excuse for any police expansion; in reality, there was nothing so desperate in the condition of society to justify this most expensive and obnoxious espionage system, this "semi-military surveillance." In the spring it was even more forthright: "we denounce, from beginning to end, the whole of this cumbersome, tyrannous, expensive, un-needed, and un-English system of police prowling and prying, by a band of blue-coated landsharks."[43]

The specific "state of the times" had little connection with the enthusiasm of some rural property owners, particularly those with concentrations of rural labor, for the new police. Henry Ashworth, for example, had argued in favor of the new force in giving evidence to the Royal Commission on the Constabulary, on the grounds that the neighboring township policemen had been useless when he attempted to introduce scabs into his mills during a strike in 1830.[44] In January 1841, the leading coalowners in the Bolton area called the attention of the magistrates to a strike of colliers for a wage rise and the determination of the masters "not to submit to such demand." Following their claim that "secret mischief" had already been done to the mines and that breaches of the peace were likely "by reason of the interference of the old men with the new," they requested "that the County Constabulary force may be considerably increased in such parts of the county as are thus threatened, & measures be taken to protect such men as may be induced to work in the Collieries."[45]

The new force was relatively expensive; cost therefore became the principal means of attack once the constables had made their appearance.[46] Unincorporated Blackburn was allocated twenty-five county constables, and a public meeting chaired by Banister Eccles in January 1841 protested about the expenditure: £870 had allegedly been spent on the force in the previous year, whereas the same work had been done under the old system for only about £100.[47] This was a common lament in townships across the region,[48] so much so that when the magistrates met at their Annual Sessions in Preston Court House in September 1841, Thomas Batty Addison, in the chair, reported that 203 petitions had been received for the total abolition of the new constabulary, with a further thirty-eight for modification. Another hundred or so were presented at the meeting. Peregrine Edward Towneley of Towneley Park moved and Col. Rawstorne seconded that the constabulary be discontinued as soon as possible on the grounds of inefficiency, unpopularity, and expense. This motion was carried by seventy-one to twenty-eight, in spite of the Rev. John Shepherd Birley's pleas for his colleagues to remember the vast amount of property at stake in the country, threatened by a large population, and that a reduction in size and the employment of more efficient people would be preferable.[49]

The resolution was reviewed at the end of six months, during which time the external opposition had continued apace, some still on the grounds of principle (the constabulary was either a force for keeping starving people quiet, or of little use except for spying on—and reporting to the clergy and squires—poachers and frequenters of country public houses),[50] most on the grounds of cost effectiveness. The magistrates encountered a mound of petitions. The language of the rights of freeborn Englishmen figured not at all in the JPs' deliberations. Towneley, again proposing abolition, thought that the constabulary was too expensive; the old constables, being locals, performed better; the new police had been utterly ineffective in a riot at Colne; and it would take the entire income of the county to maintain a civil force capable of quelling serious disturbances—that is, capable of replacing the military. Marshall complained that in Penwortham they had never paid more than two guineas for a constable, but in the past two years they had had to spend £93 and £88 respectively, and this for a worse service: there was never a policeman within four miles of his house. A chief constable (at £500) with an array of assistants and clerks was unnecessary, when some men might be found at a lesser cost, under the inspection of JPs, to keep the peace of their respective districts. Eighty-one voted in favor of abolition, fifty-five against; but as the act required a three-quarter's majority, the constabulary remained. Col. Austen therefore submitted resolutions for remodeling, unanimously agreed to, which created separate police districts, corresponding with the petty sessional divisions in each hundred; the number of police for each district was to be arranged by the JPs at their respective sessions. This in effect increased the powers of the county magistrates in their own localities, allowing them to reduce the force from 500 to 350, on the eve of the Plug Plot.[51]

This was an inauspicious start to a more policed society. Opposition from the ranks of the local elite and of opinion-formers was never going to be as strong again, though it certainly did not disappear. In 1845, for example, the *Preston Chronicle* in attacking expenditure on frivolous prosecutions—for assaults which would have been settled amicably and quickly but for the constables' interference, or for driving a cart on the wrong side of the road when no danger was likely to arise, or against vagrants—the paper took issue with one of the major functions of the police, the enforcing of conformity to an increasingly rule-bound and ordered society, with fewer spaces for the minor transgressions and peccadilloes of life.[52]

If, on the other hand, the police could prove themselves useful in time of riot or other threat to the sanctity of property, the reactions were somewhat different. The *Blackburn Standard* during the Plug Plot of 1842 had words of high praise for Superintendent Sheppard and his men, the Blackburn division of the county constabulary, for their spirited role in containing the riots.[53] Even the *Preston Chronicle*, in June 1848, commended the county and borough police in garlanded terms for their patient forbearance under provocation and for their courage and organization when called upon to act for the preservation of good order.[54]

More typical were the more mundane tasks of both the county and borough police where the military could not compete. A letter in the *Preston Guardian* in 1854 related that "very few beggars are to be seen" in the Winckley Square and Avenham area ever since a policeman had been patrolling it all day. As "my servant has other duties to perform than to be going to the bell every minute" to deal with vagrants, "I would suggest a continuance of this part of the town being properly watched, which is no more than the inhabitants are entitled to."[55] This is a classic instance of the usefulness of the police in deterring riffraff from disturbing the prosperous—one of the many ways in which resistance to the new forces died down as they became more familiar, the cost stabilized, the perceived threats to British liberties remained (for the majority) unrealized. The policeman state had notched up a further advance, and a new, incremental level of surveillance had been added. The constable, so recently seen as a despotic threat, could now embark on his representational journey toward his reincarnation as the benign British bobby, that beloved figure of propertied-class mythology, impartial, strictly just, a true guardian of civil liberties and individual rights.[56]

Magistrates

Behind many of the changes in policing and prisons stood the magistrates. The county bench broadly reflected the composition of the local notability. As David Foster has documented in detail, there was a certain amount of resistance to the admission of cotton manufacturers, however wealthy or prominent in local society, by elements in the county hierarchy. George Jacson of Barton Lodge, Preston, James Pilkington of Blackburn and, even as late as the early 1840s, Eccles Shorrock of Over Darwen were apparently initially rejected on the grounds that they were active manufacturers.[57] Nevertheless the precedent had been established and the walls breached in Lancashire as early as 1804 with the appointment of Samuel Horrocks in the same year as he was elected MP for Preston. Between 1833 and 1841, fifty manufacturers were appointed, in the following decade fifty-six, the names a virtual roll call of the manufacturing elite, with representatives from the families of Hornby, Birley, Pilkington, Dugdale, Bolling, Barnes, Horrocks, Miller, Kay, Ashworth, Lister, Feilden, Jacson, Heywood, Darbishire, and so on. They joined or were joined by other commercial men and industrialists, like Peter Rothwell, Bolton iron-founder, Charles Potter, Darwen papermaker, and Ridgway Bridson, Horwich bleacher; by bankers like James Pedder and Richard Newsham of Preston; by lawyers like Henry Brock Hollinshead of Tockholes, William Adam Hulton of Preston, and Thomas Batty Addison of Preston; and by Anglican clergymen like the Rev. Thomas Bancroft and Dr. T. D. Whitaker during the war and postwar years, and thereafter (though in declining numbers from the 1820s) the Revs. John Shepherd Birley of Bolton, Robert Hornby of Walton-le-Dale (both scions of the Kirkham manufacturing partnership), Robert Atherton Rawstorne of Penwortham (younger brother of Laurence of Penwortham), and John Owen Parr, vicar of Preston. Not surprisingly, given the high level of urbanization and the lack of suitable landed candidates at a time when the active magistracy was expanding at a faster rate than the population, industrial

JPs had begun to dominate in Salford Hundred by the late 1830s. But in Amounderness and Blackburn Hundreds, Foster still records a slight advantage to land and its allies in 1851.[58]

The borough magistracy did not carry the same cachet as the county bench, but it was still an honor, a government-stamped imprimatur on status achieved. In Preston, the transition from the old regime to the new in 1836 was relatively smooth, with considerable continuity in personnel. Cotton lords dominated over the next decade, with a lesser sprinkling of barristers, bankers, merchants, and substantial retailers.[59] In Bolton, the new borough bench immediately ran into the same political quicksands that had sucked in the new police. Immediately after the contested borough charter was issued and the new, Tory-boycotted council was formed at the end of 1838, the councillors petitioned for the appointment of borough magistrates and proposed a tentative list of six cotton men, one coal merchant, and three gentlemen, all "of Whig principles." The old authorities counterpetitioned to the effect that there were already enough county JPs in the vicinity; but this did not prevent a somewhat modified list—including three Tory county JPs, who declined to serve—from being appointed.[60]

The council followed this in February 1839 by appealing for a Court of Quarter Sessions in Bolton as an additional token of the town's civic dignity. Granted in May, John Addison, Preston barrister, was appointed recorder, John Taylor, Bolton attorney, was elected coroner, and John Gordon, Bolton attorney, clerk of the peace and registrar of the court of record. But then, while the Tories challenged the legitimacy of borough charter, bench, and quarter sessions, the situation swiftly degenerated into farce. For a time the county and the borough coroners operated concurrently, holding inquests on the same corpses, on occasions coming to different conclusions. The council's difficulty in collecting a rate meant that bills for prosecuting and conveying prisoners to gaol or the hulks could not be paid, while the Tory county JPs acted to ensure that the New Bailey in Salford could not be used for Bolton prisoners.[61] The animosity that had flooded over into the ranks of the county JPs was further revealed in a bizarre incident in March 1839. When the county magistrates met to appoint the overseers for Great Bolton, the liberal JPs present (in a majority) appointed one set of nominees (the list chosen by a large majority at a public meeting of ratepayers), while the Tory JPs appointed the rejected list. This left "two sets of conflicting overseers of the Town, each claiming authority to levy and collect rates &c. and the ratepayers are at fault which of them to recognize."[62] Legal challenges and attempted, but failed, compromises kept the party standoff bubbling and the legitimacy of borough justice unresolved until the legality of the charter was finally validated in the summer of 1842.[63] Thereafter a number of Tories were appointed as borough magistrates, but a substantial imbalance in favor of the liberals still remained at mid-century.[64]

Undignified squabbling aided the separation of parties but had little impact on the routine dispensation of justice. The law was a powerful weapon—and not only against radicals (see Chapter 3).[65] Justice was dispensed in a relatively rough and ready fashion. In Bolton, for example, a petty sessions was held twice a week in the "Sessions Room," the upper part of a pub;[66] the coroner, John Taylor, later recalled how Ralph Fletcher dealt out justice, in the few years before he died in 1832, on Friday nights at the Bowling Green Inn, Bradshawgate, sometimes alongside Major James Watkins, before retiring with other Bolton gentlemen to a private room upstairs for a supper of tripe. If any suspects were taken into custody after Monday's public court had finished, he would on occasions dispense justice on weekdays at his home, The Hollins.[67]

The early-industrial era saw a substantial increase in the number of summary offenses for magistrates to deal with in this manner, which multiplied prosecutions and acted as an important increment in the disciplining of the lower orders. These ranged from poaching, and embezzlement by outworkers, to most simple larcenies (the 1827 Larceny Act), and trespass (the 1827 Trespass Act). Most notably, the 1824 Vagrancy Act gave wide powers of arrest, detention, and summary conviction for being a "suspected Person and a reputed Thief"; and the Master and Servant Act of 1823 notoriously distinguished between breach of contract by an employee (a criminal offense, summarily tried) and by an employer (a civil offense: the "servant" could sue for damages).[68]

Robert Heywood took some minutes when he first became a county magistrate in 1835, serving at the Bolton sessions with Major Watkins of Bolton, Robert Lomax of Harwood, and Robert Darbishire of Rivington, and these give an interesting insight into the workings of the county bench. Justice depended much on magisterial or employer discretion. In a filiation case, a youthful miner, the father, was ordered to pay 1s. 6d. a week for the maintenance of his child, "as the girl could earn 6/ per week and appeared rather a loose character." A man from Longworth was brought up for being drunk on a Sunday, "but being the termination of Turton fair he was fined and admonished." A woman was cleared of a felony, but she was "a dirty idle looking creature" and "was sent to the tread mill for one month as a vagrant." Labor in particular lost out on a regular basis. A silk weaver refused to weave the work provided until his master paid him proper wages. "Mr. Lomax insisted of the work being done unconditionally as he had his remedy for the recovery of wages." The weaver still refused, so Lomax committed him for fourteen days' hard labor; but on the master stating that he had no desire for this, an arrangement was made, the weaver paying expenses. A young man employed by Blair, the bleacher, was found guilty of absenting himself without notice and sentenced to fourteen days, the usual committal for a first offense.

Soon after another still younger boy surrendered and pleaded guilty. Mr. L. observed that where more than one offender appeared at the same time it assumed a more serious aspect & the punishment of course was usually greater. But in consequence of the kind recommendation of their employer it was agreed that in this case he should undergo a similar punishment.

Six days later Blair called, wishing the youths to be liberated. One of Ridgway's men was summoned for leaving his service without due notice. Ridgway declined to take him back because of his frequent bad behavior, so he was sent to the treadmill for a month with the advice that if he behaved well perhaps his master might apply for an earlier liberation.[69]

Prisons

Punishment was the final stage in the penal process, after summary justice or trial by jury. At the end of the eighteenth century only a minority of people convicted were imprisoned; hanging, transportation, corporal punishment, or fines were the preferred sentences, and the wide variety of local cells, gaols, and houses of correction housed mainly debtors, those awaiting trial, vagrants, and petty offenders. There had been repeated experimentation with different types of punishment and incarceration before the late-eighteenth century, but the debate and innovations of that period marked a significant step in the emergence of the reformative prison as the primary means of punishment.[70]

In the few years before 1790, county magistrates rebuilt around forty-five prisons. They were reacting to a crime wave since the end of the American War, some serious outbreaks of gaol fever in prevailing unsanitary conditions, and to an effort to bring discipline and "civilization" to the lower orders, a campaign inspired by Evangelicals who found the laxity and disorder of most prisons—reported most influentially by John Howard—to be deeply troubling.[71] The Preston House of Correction, its name redolent of paternalistic chastisement belying its dour physical presence as a symbol of authority, was inaugurated in 1783 and opened in 1789 at the dawn of the era of the two revolutions.[72] A "very extensive and commodious building," conducted "on the Howardian plan," it "faces and commands Church Street, the principal thoroughfare"; in a town of few and small public buildings, its didactic message could not be misinterpreted. After the crowd attacked it in a postelection riot of November 1831, its resemblance to a feudal castle lording it over a cowering town was enhanced by the addition of four flanking towers, each supporting a cannon.[73]

In reality, the substance did not match the threatening façade. Militarily the defenses were futile, and there was a question mark over whether the rather flimsy brick towers "would tumble down if the guns were actually fired."[74] There was something of the same gap between threat and reality in the functioning of the regime within. Foucauldians see the new prisons as bricks in the edifice of enforced conformity, monuments of surveillance spawned by an urbanizing society and supported by the owners of property, landed and commercial. Revisionists quite rightly point out the distance between reforming ideas and their actual implementation, the contests between different factions about the purposes and policies of incarceration, and the continued chaos of much of the prison regime.[75] Nevertheless, the fact that Preston Gaol attempted a variety of reforms and that a number of leading inhabitants could come to put their faith, optimistically, in such an array of "Enlightened," "humanitarian," and "rational" measures gives us an insight into the nature of the bourgeoisie. There is some merit to Foucault's invitation to "Study the prison and understand bourgeois society."[76]

This was the great age of hope in the power of human institutions, through the grace of God, to alter human nature. Prominent visitors to the rebuilt Preston House of Correction approved of the efforts to reform the inmates and to inculcate the virtues of industry, especially through the widespread use of handlooms.[77] But as national prisoner numbers began to climb in the postwar era, the pressure for greater discipline and greater religious instruction mounted. The most active proponent of reform in Preston was the Rev. John Clay, prison chaplain from 1824. His annual reports made him a celebrity in prison-reform circles as he pondered the perennial question of whether the main objective was to punish, to deter, or to reform.[78] He became chaplain at a time when the county magistrates and governor were introducing a new, more disciplined regime: the construction of a treadmill, a greater emphasis on the religious and moral instruction of the prisoners, and, stipulated by Peel's acts of 1823 and 1824, the classification of prisoners, separating convicted felons, those awaiting trial on felony charges, misdemeanants, and vagrants.[79] The treadmill came into operation in September 1825 for grinding corn, nearly sixty men working the wheels at any one time. Clay was initially sanguine about its effects and credited it with a decline in committals: "[I]ts irksome and uninteresting labour has entirely destroyed that indifference to the restraints of a prison which formerly existed."[80] But he soon came to believe that the moral effect was being undermined by the fact that the conversation and behavior of the men on the wheels was largely beyond the control of the prison officers. The classification was, too, he thought, deficient. In each of the classes prisoners of every age and character associated together, meaning that boys were exposed to the bad example and conversation of the old lag, the hardened criminal.[81]

Clay's thoughts turned to other, improved measures of prison discipline. He read and approved of Capt. Basil Hall's description of Auburn Prison in New York state in his *Travels in North America in the years 1827 and 1828*. Auburn was organized on the silent system: communication between prisoners was prohibited. The great advantage of this was that "the whisperings of their awakened consciences" at divine worship might ripen into "complete reformation," if only they had the "opportunities for that solitary thought and reflection so essential to newly roused feelings of penitence," rather than being plunged back into the corrupting company of "the well read infidel, the daring blasphemer, the callous and ignorant creature." Such a degree of strictness was requisite and justifiable "in order to make prisons places of greater terror than they now are; and also as tending to enhance the value of religious instruction by making it's [sic] minister the only channel through which a prisoner can obtain anything like kindness or friendly advice."[82]

Locally, the chaplain did not at first meet with a receptive audience. The governor, Capt. Anthony, R. N., allegedly a firm believer in "Quarter-deck discipline," derided attempts at reformation. Clay did have an ally in Thomas Batty Addison, chairman of the Quarter Sessions, and through social intimacy with a number of other JPs in the Preston area he was apparently able to exert some leverage.[83] But it was not until 1834, after experiments by the West Riding and Cumberland JPs, that the Lancashire Quarter Sessions could be induced to consider "the system of silence and non-intercourse by and amongst prisoners which hath lately been adopted with great success in the gaols at Wakefield and Carlisle."[84] This was followed up in the spring of 1835 with the approval of a motion of Col. Rawstorne, seconded by Addison, to revise the prison rules with a view to enforcing the silent system.[85] The willingness to experiment with silence was based on the premise that the prevailing system of punishment and classification was failing to hinder the rise in the prison population. The recidivism rate remained high, and the gaol, it was suggested, had lost its terrors for a population that often had to suffer a worse diet and poorer health outside its walls; twelve or thirteen hours in a factory or fifteen hours at a handloom may not have appeared an especially appealing alternative; and the treadmill was not seen as a credible threat once increased numbers meant a lighter workload.[86] The number of convictions continued to climb in subsequent years, especially in Preston during the lockout of 1836-37, and in the prison's catchment area as a whole from the end of 1839, with the new rural constabulary achieving the time-honored equation of more police equals more crime detected equals more arrests equals more convicts.[87] The growing sentiment against capital punishment and the foreseeable end of transportation promised to swell the prison population yet further.[88] In this climate, with the merits of the American experimentation with the silent or separate (solitary confinement) systems being well discussed in Parliament and advocated by prison inspectors from the mid-1830s, competing discourses of crime and punishment came to the forefront of the public square.[89]

In spite of the vote for the silent system in 1835, radical reforms do not seem to have been implemented in Preston until the end of the decade. In October 1839, for the first time, some prisoners were sentenced to terms of solitary confinement during the initial month. The prisoner "is removed from the court of justice, while the solemnities and anxieties of his trial are still sobering and saddening his mind, into a solitary cell, where, left alone with his own thoughts, he may reflect upon his crime and its consequences, and weigh the pleasures of sin against the pains which follow, undisturbed by the jeers and scoffs of the hardened and irreclaimable." Some were also sentenced to a whipping as part of a joint strategy of correction, to bring pain to the body as well as anguish to the mind; flogging continued until the mid-1840s.[90]

In a manner increasingly familiar to an age of categorization, labeling, and dividing and ruling, the magistrates drew up a new set of rules in 1842 which classified the prisoners anew into eight groups in each sex, pending the restructuring of the prison for a yet more minute system of classification or for further individual separation. As they entered the gaol, all but remand prisoners and minor misdemeanants had their identities systematically stripped from them as they were bathed, inspected, dressed in uniform, and numbered. They could be visited and write a letter once every three months. They received clean linen at least once a week, had to wash their hands and faces every morning and their heads and feet on Saturdays; hair was to be as short as the keeper or surgeon thought necessary for cleanliness and health.[91]

This was a prelude to the building of seventy-two separate cells—the architect "was sent expressly to Pentonville Prison to take notes of what was executed there"[92]—opened in 1843 by a new governor, Col. Martin, "a hearty disciple of the new doctrines."[93] This extension of the separate system coincided with the abandonment of the treadmill and the application of the silent system to forty to forty-eight summarily convicted prisoners. They sat on forms about nine feet apart, all facing the officer's raised desk, picking cotton, except for a few undergoing the punishment of compulsory idleness. The same order was enforced at meals and in exercise, the inmates walking thirty feet apart. No sign or look was permitted.[94] The separation and the silence produced a very different list of minor offenses to that in the previous regime:

	July-Aug. 1839	*July-Aug. 1844*
Fighting	24	0
Riotous in yards	18	0
Refusing to tread wheel	3	0
Misbehavior in chapel	3	46
Cursing and swearing	2	7

Insolence to officers	6	2
Trading in tobacco, &c.	2	0
Stealing from prisoners	1	1
Gambling	1	0
Off wheel	32	0
Other offenses	21	0
Not completing tasks	0	655
Talking	0	99
Looking about	0	180
Other slight irregularities	<u>0</u>	<u>589</u>
Totals	113	1,579

The increase in misbehavior in chapel arose from notice being taken of such things as inmates looking around, which had previously been ignored. Most of the offenses were punished by deprivation of part of a meal. Now, Clay said, no irregularity, however slight, was passed over.[95] He could boldly conclude, "The enlightened and truly Christian views now entertained on the subject of prison discipline, which contemplate the criminal as a being whose dark mental and religious state has a strong claim upon our compassion and care, rather than as an object on whom society is bound to take vengeance for injuries done to it, are, I think, acted upon in this prison."[96] At the very least, vigorous prison discipline would deter those "incapable of mental and religious melioration"; at best it acted as a means of reformation "for all who can reason and feel." "Is it not then," he asked, "matter of rejoicing that the spirit of wisdom and the spirit of compassion at length pervade our prisons?"[97]

But he was not yet quite satisfied. To prevent the prison from continuing to be "a seminary of sin," even the untried needed to be separated; the JPs agreed and from June 1844 all boys committed for trial were separated, followed by the adults a year later. Clay agreed that this was of doubtful legality, but argued that this was a trifling matter when weighed against the immense moral benefits for prisoner and society. If the prisoner were guilty, no injustice had been done; if innocent, he had a *right* to be protected from criminal influences.[98] The rule of law could be undermined for the greater good. He was particularly proud of this: the authorities of Preston Gaol were, he thought, the first to take "the most momentous step ever yet taken in prison reform, by sanctioning *the individual separation of the UNTRIED*."[99]

The practice of "encellulement" worked, Clay thought. Except for "a sordid residue . . . whose moral state is so completely disordered that neither penal nor reformatory treatment can effect a cure," the process succeeded in breaking the spirit and crushing resistance in preparation for the stirrings of divinity. The dogged glance disappeared, the disposition became subdued, peaceful, and cheerful. "Few," he wrote, "can conceive the nature of those feelings which bring daily tears from eyes that never wept since childhood, and prompt the disturbed or penitent sinner to lay open to his minister a mind which it is almost awful to contemplate!" These sinners emerged contrite, penitent, and determined to sin no more, ready to be restored "to stations in which they may be useful, if not respectable."[100]

Although prison commissioners were reporting by 1848 cases of complete mental breakdown among those kept in solitary confinement for eighteen months at Pentonville, Clay was eager to stress that the Preston regime was not as psychologically trying as Pentonville or Reading, since the terms of separation were shorter and the inmates could see each other during exercise and in chapel.[101] Driven by the momentum of this relentless optimism, a new corridor of ninety-six cells was completed in 1849, pushing the total up to 168 and allowing the majority of the male prisoners to be kept in solitary confinement, still with communal, but silent, exercise and worship, and education in silent classes was added in 1850. The separate system was not applied to women: most of the recommitted women were of the hopeless class of prostitutes, Clay believed, and he consigned them to the category of lost causes.[102]

Happy as he professed to be with the reforms, the chaplain felt that there was yet more work to be done. He was exercised by the problem of former prisoners being plunged back into the maelstrom of corrupting influences, and the obvious solution was to extend the helping hand and the panoptical gaze beyond the prison walls. He advocated Houses of Refuge to provide shelter, food, clothing, and instruction for discharged boys, Prisoners' Relief Societies to help ex-convicts to find work, and the use of the constabulary to keep a check on them. He acknowledged that this implied "an amount of a *surveillance* unsanctioned by English law and feeling," but was satisfied that "watchfulness" was just, both for the punishment of evildoers and for the praise of those who did well.[103]

Clay's was the liberal-humanitarian voice of authority, the sound of a man determined to use chilling, "enlightened" measures for the greater good of the people in his care and therefore for the benefit of society as a whole. Confronted with the preponderance of evil around him in dancing rooms, singing rooms, beer houses, brothels, and pestiferous literature, libertarianism was misplaced: "[N]o law interposes. No voice of authority cries, 'Stay! The people shall not be destroyed!' No: our jealous notions of liberty protect every man's right—however poor or ignorant he may be—to degrade and ruin both himself and his family."[104] His analysis of society was essentially environmentalist: people did evil because of the conditions they lived in and their lack of access to education and the Word. By creating the ideal environment in the House of Correction—hygiene, a wholesome, alcohol-free diet, religious knowledge, an absence of distractions or corrupting influences—one could change the individual. Once his recalcitrant will had been broken, the individual could then breathe in the holy spirit; and from this point the chaplain trod very unstable ground indeed between free will and divine pleasure.[105] His fascination with phrenology was also problematic. In a letter to Lord Stanley in 1855 he explained that phrenological testing had not been applied to prisoners to any extent,

But any one who has an eye for form may perceive, at a glance, that the generality of these unfortunate persons have small, ill-shaped skulls, with (and among the Irish particularly) "foreheads villainous low." Not only are phrenological appearances unsatisfactory, but, physiognomically, the criminal class exhibit features belonging to the animal; they are truly "ill-favoured," and I am often greatly surprised that men of such unpromising aspect should be capable of the moral and religious improvement which—by God's blessing—is effected in no small number of them.[106]

If a man who dedicated so much of his time and attention to studying criminality could display such inconsistencies regarding nature, nurture, and the role of God, it is not surprising that there was a babel of voices in society at large. The significant question is to what extent the reforms pushed through in Preston went with or against the grain of informed opinion. This is not easy to judge. Prison experimentation did not provoke the same passions as the New Poor Law, the police, or a host of other issues; it had little direct impact on middle-class lives, clearly intended as it was to change the behavior of the divided-and-ruled residuum rather than the respectable working classes and all points north on the social scale. But to this degree it can be viewed as an integral part of the inculcation of hegemonic norms rather than a wayward aberration. Clay was clearly important as an apostle of the new regime, though the fact that most of our knowledge of his achievements is brought to us through his own reports and his son's hagiography should make us wary of exaggerating. To become policy, the reforms had to be adopted and promulgated by the county magistrates at the Quarter Sessions and relied to an extent on the zeal of the prison governors.[107] According to Walter Clay, Thomas Batty Addison, almost invariably chairman of the Sessions from the later 1820s, "shares almost equally with Mr. Clay himself the credit of raising the Preston Gaol to its fame and efficiency." He likewise pointed to a small knot of enthusiastic JPs in the Preston area who could be relied on to back the reform efforts,[108] in other words the very same group of landed and urban gentlemen who backed the classificatory measures of the New Poor Law and had few constitutional problems with the county constabulary. These were the people that mattered. Outside this group there was a good deal of apathy: "[T]here was hardly a place in England where the progress of the experiments in the Preston Gaol was less known and understood than in Preston itself," and at the Preston Lit. and Phil., "When he lectured on prison-discipline and public health, the topic thinned the audience, but on almost every other occasion, his lecture-room was crowded." Clay encountered a certain amount of ridicule in the press and from others for being overly sanguine about the possibility of reformation.[109] Charles Dickens's sneers at a regimen of facts and statistics was only the most prominent example; as Clay noted in a letter, "I see that Mr. Dickens, in *Hard Times*, has a laugh at my 'tabular statements,' and also at my credulity. He is not the only man I have met with who prefers to rely on his own theories and fancies rather than on well ascertained facts."[110]

The town newspapers, Tory and liberal, were the most solidly opposed to the reforms. The *Bolton Chronicle* targeted the state of the prisons in general, not focusing specifically on Preston, at the end of 1842. It found the cost-cutting of the "prison economists" repulsive, with which Clay would have agreed, but also frequent punishments like additional labor and the deprivation of food for petty offenses. Above all it condemned solitary confinement as revolting and barbarous, claiming that it ran counter to the grand objective of reformation.[111] The *Preston Chronicle* in 1840 had attacked all that was found wanting in the typical prison: "How utterly unfit for their object are our gaols. The air is contaminating; the system is not calculated to correct; and the child once taken to prison is a condemned thief."[112] Yet in 1848 it was no more favorable to the new prison discipline, welcoming the report on Preston of an inspector of prisons, particularly his strong opposition to the silent system, the more than six thousand prison punishments in the previous year, the separate system, the dark cells in which prisoners were frequently locked up, and the use of strait waistcoats.[113]

If Clay and the later governors found kindred spirits among the county magistrates, they also encountered some resistance even here. This was particularly true early on, but as late as 1851 he lamented the fact that there were insufficient separate cells, meaning that many were excluded from the benefits of that system by a shortsighted economy.[114] This economy, Clay thought, extended to the chaplain himself. In 1825, after the sessions resolved, following the 1823 Gaol Act, that the county chaplain should treat the post as a full-time job, his salary was raised from £100 to £250, considerably above the going rate for a local curate.[115] In 1839, against considerable opposition, his supporters managed to increase it to £350, Clay arguing that curates' salaries were "quite incommensurate with the services and station of the clergymen." Besides, ordinary clerical life was much more agreeable than his, he was barred from raising his income through additional employment like taking on pupils, and he was outside the patronage network, a stranger to the bishop and anyone else able to advance him along the path of preferment.[116] He was correct in this assessment that he would be overlooked locally, and it would not be far-fetched to see in his energetic production of reports and statistical series on a plethora of contemporary problems the activities of a talented man, profoundly concerned about his status and standing in society, who saw the usual channels of professional advancement blocked. Until near the end of his life he was sanguine that the government would recognize his diligence, but the only offer he ever received was in 1855 to the rectory of Castleford in Yorkshire from the chancellor of the Duchy of Lancaster. This he turned down because it was too large a task to undertake on his own and the income was insufficient to pay a curate.[117] He died in 1858, living long enough to see the widespread adoption of "encellulement" across the country and the creation of controlled environments beyond corrupting external influences. But the emphasis now was on punishment and deterrence, not reformation.[118] One of the few remaining voices of optimism and idealism expired with him.

Experiments in punishment and advances in policing blended fear and optimism: fear or disquiet about the pace of social and economic change, displaced onto the unknown hordes of masterless men and women, stewing in immorality, infidelity, and revolutionary notions; optimism that through a process of counting, dissecting, policing, and the separating out of "criminals" and other "deviants" for treatment, the *classes dangereuses* could be taught to internalize the moral values deemed proper for an ordered society. Divide and rule, discipline and teach self-restraint, and property and power might be maintained in the correct hands, without excessive recourse to those blunt instruments of state repression that could endanger liberties for the higher classes as well.[119]

Within this context, individual responses and decisions, in conjunction with state prompting, help explain the timing: the county magistrate eager for a rural police (if it were cheap, and he controlled it) to tackle poaching and those other country crimes lovingly detailed in Chadwick's report; the coalowner, anxious for the policing of his mines and the protection of blacklegs during strikes; the prison chaplain and the Christian moralist, believing that by manipulation of the carceral environment, the mind could be brought to that utter abasement before God necessary for salvation; the politician, who might think that a locally controlled police force was preferable to infantry and cavalry, or at least could provide a useful partner in the defense against popular radicalism.

Between them, these mingled desires produced a small-scale, inefficient, and unloved police, and partial prison reforms which did not generate much enthusiasm and which soon ran out of reformative zeal, all overseen by a local elite and a magistracy susceptible to party squabbling. Hardly, one might think, a massive step forward for the policeman state or the powers of conformity. For the comfortable and contented classes this was true. The new police and prisons were not designed to control *their* behavior; bourgeois crimes and misdemeanors—fraud, unsafe working practices, domestic violence, sexual abuse within the home, to name but a few—were not on the agenda. The bourgeoisie rarely came into contact with the law, except to implement it. In the dual conception of the state—controlling and enabling, surveilling and benign—the liberalizing features were initially of most benefit to the higher classes, whereas the lower orders felt first the weight of the disciplinary state and the powers of coercion deployed locally.[120] Defiance, deviance, nonconformity remained possible in such a lightly policed society and even under the new prison regimes as the failure of reformation attested. But as the parameters of acceptable behavior gradually became more effectively patrolled, the space for transgressions from propertied, respectable norms diminished. In that sense, police and punishment take their place in the armory of measures for the creation of a more ordered, more stable—more bourgeois—society.

CHAPTER 6: THE PEACE OF GOD

The Church was "greatly and grievously to blame," lamented the Rev. James Slade, vicar of Bolton, in 1836, for failing to keep pace with the population, and the consequences for the masses were dire:

Either they are driven to worship in places of dissent, or they worship not at all; live in the total neglect and profanation of the Lord's Day; and very naturally, and very soon, become, not only enemies of the Church, but the enemies of God; and thus, by a certain progress in the downward course of evil, enemies to the land, to the constitution, to good government and laws, to social order and peace, and safety. Of such persons the number in this town is awfully, tremendously great.[1]

Slade's cry of anguish signaled his continuing commitment to the last concerted effort in British history to reclaim the kingdom for God and thus good order. No study of the bourgeoisie can overlook this vast undertaking, nor the lives, ambitions, achievements, and failures of the clergymen, ministers, and priests who led the attack, the subjects of this chapter. These gentlemen, the principal ideologues of the bourgeoisie in the milltowns, deserve our attention for their conjoined efforts with other members of the elite to build a religio-paternalistic mosaic across the Lancashire landscape, attempting to incorporate the lower orders into a contented hierarchical community; and, not least, in their own right, as members of the bourgeoisie, but often as insecure members, their ministrations blighted by professional incoherence, rivalry, and status anxiety.

Church-Building and Patronage in Blackburn

In Blackburn, the Rev. John William Whittaker, vicar from 1822, was the man most responsible for the extension of the Church.[2] As we know a considerable amount about him—his methods, his beliefs, his ambitions—from his voluminous correspondence and other writings, we can trace his ministrations in some detail.[3] He took over a typically huge northern parish of over forty-five thousand acres, sixteen miles wide and six long, spanning twenty-six townships. A handful of small chapels, mostly of longstanding, served the needs of the scattered rural settlements, and three of these—Walton-le-Dale, Samlesbury, and Great Harwood—were more independent of the mother church than the others. Within the town the Church was in a sorry state. St.

John's—dating from 1789 and substantially financed by Henry Sudell of Woodfold Hall, cotton merchant, its classical style reflecting the town's growing wealth and pretensions to a polite and patrician gentility[4]—had for a time before Whittaker's arrival been the only church in use. But a new parish church was under construction to replace an ancient, venerable, but dangerously dilapidated, predecessor,[5] and the Church had at least begun to catch up with urban growth by the recent completion of the parliamentary church of St. Peter's out of the Waterloo Fund.[6] A fourth, anomalous church, St. Paul's, outside the Establishment, had resulted from an ill-documented feud in the early 1790s between the vicar, the Rev. Thomas Starkie, and the Rev. Samuel Dean, the master of the grammar school and a parish church curate; by 1829, via the Countess of Huntingdon's Connexion, it had crept into the fold.[7] But during Whittaker's incumbency the Church in Blackburn was transformed and—thanks to rapid urban growth within a preindustrial parochial structure—the vicar along with it. By mid-century his "minor bishopric"[8] of eighty-five thousand people was to boast more than a score of clergymen.

Whittaker was born in Manchester in 1790, the son of William Whittaker, a Manchester merchant, and Sarah Buck, who had property and land at Townhill Manor in Bradford. His father's business collapsed around 1793, and William Sr. then spent several years—including a time in America—evading his creditors before retiring to the Bradford property. After attending a variety of schools—private schools in Halifax and Bath, Bradford Grammar School, and Sedbergh School—William Jr. went up to St. John's College, Cambridge, in 1810, and subsequently became a fellow.[9] Clearly ambitious for promotion, in 1819 he applied unsuccessfully for the professorship in Arabic and entered at the same time into his first religious controversy, an attack on a new translation of the Hebrew Scriptures.[10] The work gained the attention of the High Church archbishop of Canterbury, Charles Manners-Sutton, and, passing up good prospects of heading a projected missionary and Bible-translation college in Calcutta, he became a domestic chaplain at Lambeth Palace in the spring of 1821. This post brought no emolument; "It is however a sure as well as a speedy step to most excellent preferment, & if that fruit ripens best on wh. the Sun always shines—Lambeth Palace must be a most admirable habitat for a young ecclesiastic."[11] In January 1822 the archbishop offered him the vacant living of Blackburn, which had a gross value of just short of £850 a year.[12] Even so, Whittaker thought he could do better: "I rather think it will not be possible for me to refuse this noble offer; though, if I could do so with propriety, I am inclined to think it would be for my ultimate advantage."[13] He accepted, and remained vicar of Blackburn until he died in 1854.

During his tenure his efforts in increasing church accommodation were remarkable.[14] The rigid parochial structure of the Established Church had failed completely to keep pace with the shifts and expansion of population in the manufacturing districts, and Whittaker was among the pioneers in remedying the Church's low standing.[15] There were five main elements in his attempt to build up a godly community in his parish: an effort to bring the poor into the fold by the provision of church accommodation together with active proselytizing ministers; the cajoling of the local elite into playing their part; an assault on all "error" and "untruth" propagated by religious competitors for the minds and souls of the people; an emphasis on maintaining the harmony of the clergy; and a denunciation of all radical doctrines that suggested an alternative view of society, class, and power.[16]

His procedure in building a new church followed a typical pattern: the identification of a "problem area," where the construction of mills had recently brought together an influx of working people; applications to various church-building bodies—principally the Church commissioners, the Incorporated Church Building Society, and the Chester Diocesan Building Society—for funds; the commencement of a subscription list to invite contributions from local inhabitants, the wealthy of the Blackburn neighborhood, and Church and political leaders; the hiring of an architect, chiefly the noted Gothic revivalist Thomas Rickman and Whittaker's cousin, the talented young Edmund Sharpe of Lancaster; and finally the process of contracting and building itself. Whittaker was expert at presenting a convincing case,[17] and all of his pleas for money stressed the plight of the poor. Take, for example, the projected chapel at Bamber Bridge. Prompted by the incumbent of Walton-le-Dale, Whittaker applied in 1824 to the Church commissioners for a donation, drawing attention to the four large cotton factories in the neighborhood, an area which "is almost wholly inhabited by persons in indigent circumstances, who have not the means of making any exertions in the cause of Religion & public morals by means of pecuniary contributions." Moreover—this was always a good scare tactic—"a Methodist Chapel has been erected at Bamber Bridge, to wh. the inhabitants *solely* resort because there is no church room for them, & . . . two Romish Chapels (*one* of very modern date) are within one and a half miles east & west."[18]

As the vicar pursued his strategy of following in the wake of the mills and their workers, seeking to enlighten dark and dense areas, he consistently gave a twofold rationale: to see to the spiritual and moral education of the people, and to do this before Dissenters and papists could beat him to it. The "Congregational Independents will anticipate me," he argued in 1837, if the building of All Saints' Church were not commenced forthwith in the Grimshaw Park neighborhood near the Leeds and Liverpool Canal. In 1835 he wished to take advantage of "a violent schism" in the Independents' ranks. He hoped that by building Trinity Church at Lark Hill he would attract malcontents and prevent seceders from constructing their own chapel.[19]

The most effective way of securing low-cost accommodation[20] and out-maneuvering the Dissenters simultaneously was to buy defunct Dissenting chapels: "We gain an additional place of worship, & produce the greatest dissatisfaction among the Dissenting laity who contributed to the building; wh. operates directly in the way of a 'caveat' against their engaging in similar speculations for the future."[21] A Wesleyan Methodist chapel at Daisyfield ran into financial difficulties in 1837 and was forced to sell at a fraction of the original building costs. The inhabitants of this new industrial suburb were "with very few exceptions singularly poor," being neither "Educated nor moral"[22] and "of a very disorderly character."[23] Many of them were "the lowest and most ignorant of the vagrant Irish & Scotch whom the manufacturers have attracted to settle here," having "the vaguest ideas of religion & scarcely any of the Church as a spiritually chartered community."[24] Whittaker believed that these people were sorely in need of the ministrations of the Church. He was building Trinity Church in the same vicinity, but already felt that the accommodation would be insufficient, and in any case the onset of a prolonged commercial depression substantially reduced the flow of subscriptions from the usual contributors, putting the construction on hold. Accordingly, the vicar bought the chapel with the intention of using it until Trinity was completed and then rebuilding it with the same materials in a more acceptable, church-like style.[25] He had another reason: it was in the midst of "a dense population of Irish Papists, low artisans, and weavers, who, being near the Romish Chapel & its priest, are almost entirely at his mercy." If it were to fall into the hands of the papists, their position would be "almost inexpugnable."[26] In appealing for aid in 1839 to refit the chapel, renamed St. Michael's, he identified yet another danger: "a society of Owenites are bestirring themselves in the vicinity with most alarming alacrity."[27]

The vicar had obtained a cut-price church at a time when he could not afford to build from scratch, and he felt that he had dealt a significant blow to the enemy. This explains the frustration he expressed in a letter to the bishop of Chester in 1844, at the refusal of the Incorporated Society to give aid for anything but a new church. The decision that they could build, but not purchase, places of worship "seems tantamount to an interdict against carrying on the war against the enemies of the church and taking possession of their 'high places'." The result was "that when we have *preached out* & *starved out* the Protestant Dissenting ministers, & their chapels are offered for sale, no religious body can purchase them but the Papists."[28]

Much of Whittaker's work brought him into contact with a select body of wealthy families on whom he depended for contributions and land for his chapels and to set an example to their flocks. But in return for land and a sizable donation toward a new chapel the donor almost invariably sought the patronage. Whittaker consistently refused, contending that the best interests of the Church required clerical unanimity in the parish, which depended on the power of appointment residing wholly with the vicar. There were to be no exceptions nor concessions to family interests—at least if he could help it.

This brought conflict. For example, after providing the land, a contribution, and a parsonage house for St. Mark's, Witton, Joseph Feilden insisted on having a say in the patronage. The vicar replied that, personally, he would prefer to be free from the burden: "But I feel & *know,* that the retention of the Vicar's patronage is the only mode in wh. cordial unanimity in the Parish can be secured. On this single point depends the prosperity of the Church in this extensive district." In a letter to the archbishop of Canterbury in 1836 he explained the position. The plans to build St. Mark's and another chapel, Immanuel, at Feniscowles, sponsored by the other branch of the Feilden family, had grown out of a project for one church halfway between the two, with Joseph of Witton and uncle William of Feniscowles alternately nominating the incumbent. The vicar had resisted this, partly because of its unfavorable location but mainly "because it was intended to build it under the act of the 1st. and 2nd. Gul. IV wh. would deprive the Vicar of his rights." Whittaker expressed his "utter disapprobation" for this, the 1831 Patronage Act, which allowed a bishop to give the right of nomination to generous donors if a chapel were more than two miles from an existing church, since "it is like asking a man to cut his own throat." Preoccupied in raising money for Trinity Church in the town, he had no immediate plans for Witton, but was forced into the scheme "by the importunity of Mr. Feilden." If he did nothing, he feared that Joseph Feilden would build a chapel at his own expense, "without the Vicar being a party to it."[29]

Whittaker failed to win out completely. Indeed, he said to one potential appointee to St. Mark's in 1839 that he was "the legal, but scarcely the actual patron of the living." That meant, it seems, that Feilden could recommend a candidate and the vicar could rubber-stamp or veto his choice. In 1839, for example, Whittaker was unenthusiastically prepared to accept Feilden's lackluster nominee ("mortals may be saved, I trust, without a constant excitement of imagination"), until he learned of the candidate's association with interdenominational societies ("with aliens from the Church"), and he rejected him. There was a similar arrangement at Feniscowles: the appointment rested with the vicar, but he "had always been good enough to submit the matter" to William Feilden, since the family not only had provided the land, the stone, and a contribution toward the building of the church, but later provided both a parsonage and a substantial endowment. Whittaker felt obliged to consult the family's wishes, and they in turn felt entitled to request that their choice of candidate be appointed. As Mrs. Feilden put it to him, "of course you must be the sole judge of the fitness on Doctrine & freedom from the Modern novelties, as well as Whig principles—for we have ever, & still wish to be so united with our future Pastor, that this can only be cemented by a similarity of feeling & thought, upon great leading matters."[30]

There were other tussles over patronage. Lord de Tabley agreed to surrender his right of patronage to Salesbury Church to the vicar in 1842, but not before making one last nomination. Whittaker considered the appointment of the Rev. T. R. Dickenson to be "a huge blunder," because he was "a man of great simplicity," "vapid," and "*considerably* vulgar."[31] In the case of the proposed St. Saviour's Chapel at Bamber Bridge the vicar came into conflict with Townley Parker of Cuerden Hall. The initial project of 1824 had stalled because of inadequate funds.[32] In 1831 Parker offered to give £200 for the building and £100 for the endowment if he could have the patronage, refusing to "consent by such endowment to augment the patronage of the present, or of any future Vicar of Blackburn even in so small a matter." Whittaker refused. In 1836, when building finally began, Parker again sought the nomination in return for the provision of a parsonage. Whittaker stood his ground and cited the example of the Feildens, their requests denied in spite of even more substantial donations; but he was prepared to allow Parker and other subscribers some *say* in the nomination. Parker apparently indicated his intention to appeal to the bishop for the right under the terms of the Patronage Act. Whittaker considered this threat "ungrateful & dishonourable," feared that all his country chapelries would be taken from him, trusted that the bishop of Chester would do no such thing, and asserted that he would never have recommended the construction of a church "on a footing of wh. I so thoroughly disapprove." The bishop was inclined to think that it would be better for the chapel to be in Parker's gift with a generous endowment than in the vicar's nomination with nothing and in "the miserable plight of Feniscowles." But Whittaker did not give way. He told the Rev. Henry McGrath, "my cession of the Patronage of Bamber Bridge Church was from the first improbable. But, let me see an attempt to extort it from me, and it shall be an impossibility."[33]

The patronage question was not the only problem Whittaker experienced with members of the local elite. Joseph Feilden's charity and good example—£200 toward building St. Mark's, a parsonage worth £700, and ten guineas for pew rents, even though he could easily drive to one of the two churches in town where he had pews—provided a model for the vicar in the building of a stable, hierarchical, Anglican community.[34] But the number of Joseph Feildens appeared to be in short supply, particularly with the onset of commercial depression from the late 1830s, and a hint of exasperation crept into some of the vicar's appeals: the millowners, responsible for bringing together the destitute masses, were not fulfilling their role in the theater of community solidarity and reciprocity. One problem was that the elite of a locality might be Nonconformist; as the Rev. Charles Hunt of Lower Darwen explained in 1837, "the leading manufacturers who are wealthy & influential are decided enemies to our venerable establishment."[35] Another problem was clerical respectability, often a struggle for low-income incumbents; Hunt's successor to Lower Darwen, the Rev. Charles Arnold, thought that clergymen had to be of a sufficiently high social standing—or monetary value—before the leading families would pull their weight: "[N]othing will give a minister so much weight with the 'soi disant' Church gentry as money."[36] The vicar reminded these Church gentry of their duty in 1851, in reference to the building of All Saints' Church—for which he had begun raising money as far back as 1837: "In Grimshaw Park and Nova Scotia there are densely populated streets, lanes, and alleys, filled with the unfortunate, the ignorant, and the vicious, from whom religious instruction cannot be withheld without great criminality on the part of those who are more prosperously situated and better instructed."[37]

The Pastoral Aid Society was similarly disappointed in the level of contributions from Blackburn. It had voted £4,860 in aid for the parish, but the wealthy of the parish had donated only £276 3s. 8d. in return.[38] The Rev. George Ashe of Witton received no response in 1854 "from those who can afford effectual assistance" to his suggestions for enlarging his church. The Rev. Christopher Robinson of Trinity in 1852 complained that he might have to resign because of "the little sympathy and encouragement afforded by the wealthy inhabitants of Blackburn."[39] The Rev. Henry Burgess, the curate employed in the All Saints' District pending the building of a church, attributed the widespread apathy toward religion among the lower orders to neglect by the respectable inhabitants, with only one person of any influence giving him the slightest assistance. With St. John's Church in mind he wrote, "it is scarcely to be expected that the lower orders will be much moved by religious considerations, when they see their masters & superiors leaving their neighbourhoods for a tranquil lounge at a fashionable Church." He put the point well in January 1852:

The subscribers [to the Curates' Society] have gone to the town in their carriages, to their pews at various Churches, leaving their depraved neighbourhoods, *created by themselves,* behind them; as though a single minister, by some talismanic power, could counteract the dismal effects of their neglect. This has been, and will be, a serious obstacle in the way of success. If Mr. Eccles or Mr. R. Hopwood had, about once a month, given me the support of their presence, I should have been encouraged, and their example would have done good, but it has been altogether wanting.[40]

The "Curates' Rebellion" and Parochial Subdivision

Burgess, a curate in Blackburn for four years, moved on to become the editor of *The Clerical Journal and Church and University Chronicle.* In 1855 he wrote a series of articles on "The History of an Overgrown Parish Statistical,

Pecuniary, and Moral."[41] His example was Blackburn, his message that, "If ever the hand of Reform was needed, it is in the case of an overgrown parish, rich in wealth, and yet neglected in its spiritualities." Blackburn, he claimed, was notorious for "its anomalies and moral evils," outstanding among a large class of similar parishes. Now, with a new clergyman in place after Whittaker's death, he hoped that there would be a change from "the selfish and perilous system which has so long reigned in the parish."

Burgess piled up a damning and impassioned indictment against Whittaker—unnamed, but evidently the intended posthumous target. He accused him of building up a regime that was "a reproach wherever its history is known," a sphere for his love of money and power, where he demanded servile obedience from the clergy, and the flock remained spiritually neglected and starved. The culmination of the attack was the startling assertion that, "It requires no great exercise of fancy to make such a parish as this a Popedom in miniature, and its vicar a Hildebrand in *bas relief*, bent upon making his domain productive and submissive to himself."

The indictment was multifaceted but the principal charge was that the vicar had failed to subdivide his parish. The increase in population had brought him an accretion of power and wealth. As a result of his heroic church-building and lock on the patronage, he appointed to nineteen livings (perpetual curacies), with additional stipendiary curates serving in the parish church. The vicarial glebe had become far more productive with the ground-renting of plots for building purposes. Surplice fees also increased vicarial revenue.[42] He had agreed to the creation of districts for the chapelries in the town in 1842 so that baptisms, marriages, and burials could take place within them, but only on condition that fees were still paid to the vicar as well as to the incumbents. This meant that most people continued to seek these services at the parish church. Burgess painted a picture of conveyor-belt ministrations, with the vicar or his curates baptizing forty children, marrying thirty couples, churching thirty women, and burying twenty to thirty people every week. In such circumstances, he thought, pastoral care was minimal, the people deprived of moral and spiritual instruction.

Burgess believed that Blackburn was only one parish among many, "though perhaps the *facile princeps* of the whole," subject "to the iron rule of this most anomalous and unchristian despotism." There was, he argued, something deeply flawed in the attempts of church-builders like Whittaker to create parochial communities based on large, undivided parishes with the vicar at the head commanding a squadron of subordinate clergymen. The deep irony is that, not only were the Church gentry failing to play their full role, and not only were the poor invalidating the prized notion that if accommodation were provided they would fill it, but that the men Whittaker had taken such pains to appoint rebelled against their subordinate status.[43] A combination of these factors, repeated across the country, precipitated the demise of the large industrial parish.

The confrontation in Blackburn came in 1849. Six incumbents of chapelries within Blackburn Parish called a meeting in Accrington on January 18— the main event of the "*Clerical Chartist conspiracy*," as Whittaker phrased it, equating insubordination in the ranks with radicalism in society, equally abhorrent—with the intention of petitioning the archbishop of York, the bishop of Manchester, and the prime minister to put in motion legislative measures for reform.[44] About fifty people attended, including nearly all the incumbents and curates of Blackburn, a number of clergymen from other parishes in the North West, and a deputation from the lay Manchester Church Reform Association. Most significantly, Dr. Whittaker turned up uninvited, determined to be heard and to vent his outrage at the subversion of authority. He declared that "It was a monstrous enormity that a meeting of the clergy of the archdeaconry should be called by six or seven curates of Blackburn . . . such an enormity as had never been heard of in our ecclesiastical annals, not from the days of Ethelbert." This set the tone for the meeting, plagued by interruptions and uproar. The incumbents complained about the iniquities of the parochial system, the fact that most of the parishioners went to the parish church for marriages, baptisms, churchings, and burials to avoid having to pay double fees and that the district system was the "most iniquitous anomaly that ever disgraced a Christian Church." The daughter churches were fettered by the mother church and, in sum, "the time was now come for a full revision of our parochial system."

In his vituperative response, Whittaker talked of the vested rights of the people in their parish church, secured to every Englishman by Magna Carta, the "charta de foresta," and the "*lex non scripta*," and property rights he held to be inviolable, especially when resting "upon a prescription older than the reformation." The Church, he believed, was prospering in Lancashire, and if individual ministers were unsuccessful in their labors, they had only themselves to blame:

[T]hese gentlemen thought that the weakness of their hands, the inefficiency of their ministrations and the want of regard paid to them by the laity, were to be all removed by these gentlemen being all made vicars.—(laughter.) Now, he did not see the connection between the two things—he did not think that if vicars were made as plentiful as blackberries they would be as much thought of as they were now. —(laughter.)

Napoleon had made the cross of the Legion of Honor a distinction, but Louis XVIII, by giving it to everybody, made it not worth a halfpenny.

There were some interesting exchanges as the antagonists wrestled to frame their arguments in current secular and political discourse. The Rev. Thomas

Sharples of St. Peter's Church referred to the twelve or fourteen church building acts, "all of which showed manifest symptoms of what, in the political
world, was called class legislation—(Hear, hear.)" Presumably he meant that
the acts maintained the rights of the incumbents of mother churches while
doing little for the benefit of subordinate clergymen, and therefore they cut
across the clerical leadership of the parochial community. But Whittaker
would have none of this. He objected strongly to the expression "'class legislation,' which originated with the chartists," since "There could be no legislation against a class that did not exist." He had built, rebuilt, or acquired
twelve new churches, not including the parish church, to add to the ten already in existence when he arrived in Blackburn:

When all these efforts were crowned with success, up comes some gentleman,
prates to him about "class legislation," and takes out of his hands Trinity Church,
or Feniscowles, or some other which he had built himself, and says, "you will have
nothing to do with it." He had built these churches, in many cases unaided, and
had given them to gentlemen who he thought would devote their energies to the
service of their Great Master, and not to running about the country agitating.

The Rev. Robert Hornby of Walton-le-Dale, backing up Whittaker's point
that the clergymen were all gentlemen, reverend gentlemen, whose duty it was
to impart to their flocks the doctrine of Christian obedience and not to act like
Chartists and agitators, focused on the concept of a class hierarchy within the
Church: "He wished the laymen who came there to instruct the clergy, to apply the same argument to a factory, and see how they would like all their
hands to divide the profits with them.—(Laughter.) He thought the way in
which the clergy had interfered with their vicar was setting a bad example to
their flocks." This unwittingly served the arguments of the malcontents. Were
they to be treated as gentlemen guiding the people or as factory hands under
the supervision of an employer? Interestingly, the Rev. Walter Chamberlain of
St. John's, Little Bolton, in an attack on local patronage the following year,
took up the same theme. He imagined how the working man must view the
relationship between vicar and subordinates: "The establishment of the
Church in his town is to our operative one vast mill. The Rector being the
master; the district Incumbents, spinners; the Curates, piecers."[45] The parish as
a factory was a new metaphor, the ties of hierarchy and subordination within
the Church being represented as a mirror image of the wage-relationship between millowners and workers in society at large. This was a logical extension
of calling the incumbents "clerical chartists," but it sat uneasily beside Whittaker's assertion that "class" divisions within the Church "did not exist," and
beside his attempt to endorse his parochial community. The meeting ended after four hours of "stormy" debate. Whittaker and his supporters walked out
before the end, and the resolution was carried unanimously.

The Blackburn reform movement was only one among many. The frustrations generated by the existing parochial structure were widespread, particularly in the large parishes of the North and Midlands, and it seems that a combination of economic and status pressures on the lower clergymen at the end of the 1840s provided the trigger.[46] The incumbents of Blackburn had contemplated forming a clerical association at the beginning of 1848, but the clergymen of Stone in Staffordshire had set the pace and held a meeting calling for reform in December 1848.[47] Their call found a receptive audience, in the press, in several other petitions and meetings, and in Parliament. Whittaker found himself out of step with majority opinion.[48] In a circular to the clergy and laity of the Archdeaconry of Manchester, he condemned the "hole and corner meeting" at Accrington and complained that the rebels "have done, in this one ill considered and rash escapade, more serious damage to the cause of the Church of England, than all its combined enemies within twenty miles of Blackburn could have accomplished."[49] The newspapers disagreed. The conservative *Blackburn Standard* supported reform and blamed Whittaker for the disreputable nature of the meeting.[50] The liberal *Manchester Guardian* called for a lay Church Reform Association to be established in every ecclesiastical district in Blackburn.[51] The *Manchester Courier* accused the requisitionists of factious agitation, insubordination, and having contempt for constituted authority; but it too supported the cause of reform.[52]

Lord Ashley, who saw the issue as promoting his evangelical and social agenda, inaugurated a series of parliamentary proceedings. He gained the cautious backing of the new Evangelical archbishop of Canterbury, J. B. Sumner, and at the last minute of Lord John Russell and the government.[53] His proposal for a commission to consider the subdivision of populous parishes so that the population in each should not exceed four thousand was introduced and debated in March 1849. His arguments followed closely the reasoning of the Blackburn rebels: that when an individual held a permanent cure of souls he should be free and independent, responsible only to the bishop, not accountable to the vicar of the mother church for fees. Only then could the Church carry out its true parochial function, and the populations of the huge parishes of the North and of London be subject to pastoral supervision. In an echo of Thomas Chalmers's famous experiment in St. John's Parish in Glasgow,[54] Ashley hoped that if the clergy could increase their knowledge of each individual parishioner, destitution could be wiped out, mendicancy and vagrancy virtually extinguished.

There was minimal opposition in the debate, with only the seasoned radicals Joseph Hume and John Bright raising objections. Both contended that the parochial vision could not work, Hume on the grounds that the overgrown parishes contained majorities of Dissenters, and Bright that the education, habits, and sympathies of the clergymen were much too distant from those of the people. But Bright also recognized that subdivision could strengthen the Church.[55] As Ashley recorded in his diary, "The truth is, [the Dissenters] see it as a heavy blow and great discouragement to Dissent and popular discontent; they see that, by this means, the Church can and will, God blessing us, recover her just position and 'conservatise' the kingdom."[56]

The most revealing insight into a range of views on the parish problem came in the Minutes of Evidence taken by the new commission between April and August 1849. Several rectors and vicars of large parishes raised serious objections to the proposals of subdivision. Their various concerns amounted to a fear that an ordered hierarchy within the Church and among the laity of a parish could be damaged or even dismantled. The Rev. John Garbett, rector of St. George's, Birmingham, thought that the city was so segregated by class that new parishes would sever the desirable ties between the poor and the respectable.[57] The Rev. Dr. J. Hume Spry, rector of Saint Marylebone, believed that "one superintending head will keep the whole arrangement in much better order than it would be kept by a number of independent persons. . . . The poor, and the rich too, do look up to a rector of a large parish in a way that they would not look up to a person having merely his small parish, with a very trifling income, and no means of assisting the poor."[58] The Hon. and Rev. Henry Montague Villiers, incumbent of St. George's, Bloomsbury, stated that a large number of people could be better managed by a single and central authority rather than from a number of smaller and separate centers. The country paid "considerable deference to what I may term the aristocracy of wealth. If the clergy are of a much poorer order than their parishioners you will find that they will lose their influence with the middle and upper classes."[59]

The contending vision of a parochial community took into account the considerable problems of the current arrangement. John Morley, a churchwarden of Manchester Parish Church, outlined one of the worst cases of an overgrown parish. The Parish of Manchester had a population that he estimated at 420,000, with fifty-four churches and chapels. In the mother church there were sometimes as many as sixty marriages on a Sunday, and in the previous year there had been 4,652 baptisms. At the same time, the average number of communicants out of a congregation of 1,500 to 1,800 oscillated between only forty and 120.[60] Such statistics led some vicars of large parishes to support the call for subdivision, even though this would hurt their status and pocketbooks. The Rev. Thomas Dale, vicar of St. Pancras, with a population of over 150,000, claimed that large parishes like his own were subversive of the very first principle of the Church. Subdivision was exceedingly desirable, if an adequate provision could be made for the ministers. But he too was concerned that this might result in a division into wealthy and poor parishes.[61] The Rev. Dr. Walter Hook, vicar of Leeds, had taken the unusual step of obtaining a private act in 1844 to subdivide his parish, so that his clergymen could convert their districts into vicarages entirely independent of the mother church. He argued that the primary duty of a parochial minister was to administer the sacraments and preach the Gospel, not to be immersed in administrative business like presiding over institutions and devising means for erecting new churches and schools. These duties belonged to a different order in the Church: to the episcopacy.[62]

The number of lower clergy giving evidence included the Rev. Frederick Wade, incumbent of the chapelry of Golden Hill in Staffordshire, who had been involved at the original reform meeting in Stone.[63] He objected to the people under his care having to pay double fees and two lots of church rates, and he claimed that there was an almost universal "strong sense of injury" among the clergy of district churches. He cited Whittaker as a prime example of a vicar who was opposed to subdivision, and commented,

One thing is quite certain, that the clergy of [Blackburn] conceive their position of dependence, whilst it has not promoted unity, has proved most injurious to their usefulness and the interests of their populous chapelries; and I most humbly conceive that their just cause of complaint should be removed, even at the loss of a little of Dr. Whittaker's estimate of vicarial importance, and the vested rights of mother churches.[64]

Archdeacon Rushton of Manchester, who was to succeed Whittaker to the Vicarage of Blackburn in 1854, raised the question of patronage, remarking, "Some few incumbents have secured the patronage to a considerable extent [in their parishes]: one I know to the extent of securing all the new churches in his parish." He was talking about the Church in Lancashire, and this was presumably a reference to Whittaker. Rushton, in contrast, believed in the virtues of private patronage, since it could cement the ties of substantial families and their circles of connections to a particular church, and it was especially useful if taken up by the employers of large numbers of operatives.[65] Here was a vision of a combined factory and Church community, knitting the ties of two forms of paternalism, but it could not find full expression in Whittaker's Blackburn.

The commissioners, who included leading Anglican clerics and laymen, produced three reports, recommending the complete subdivision of parishes, the assignment of fees arising within an ecclesiastical division to its incumbent, and compensation to the incumbent of the mother church. They further called for an extension of the Patronage Act of 1831 to encourage the erection and endowment of new churches by laymen, a consolidation of the powers of the church building commissioners, an equitable division of the church rate, and the building of six hundred new churches as a priority. They did, however, express misgivings as to whether most of the existing subdivisions of parishes could be made entirely independent before the means were found to provide sufficient endowments and to compensate the mother church incumbents.[66] Nevertheless, many of the findings of the commission were embodied in the New Parishes Act of 1856, introduced into the Commons the previous year by the marquess of Blandford, and into the Lords by Ashley, now the earl of Shaftesbury.[67] The intention of the act was to rationalize the eighteen Church Building Acts, to extend the Patronage Act, and above all to build on the highly praised 1843 District Churches Act of Sir Robert Peel.[68] This statute had provided for the creation of districts and the appointment of ministers in areas of populous parishes where there were no churches. On completion of a new church in the new district, the district was to become an independent new parish. The New Parishes Act stipulated that this principle of parish-creation could be extended to districts where a church already existed, but the incumbent of the mother church was to retain his rights of patronage and fees until the avoidance of the incumbency, unless he voluntarily relinquished them or received compensation.[69]

This was a substantial step in the direction that the rebels at Accrington had advocated. Whittaker had continued his opposition after the events of early 1849. In reply to a request from the Parish Subdivision Commission for details of his parish, he had replied that only something like the existing parochial system could have achieved as much in the way of church extension.[70] He had written to the secretary of the ecclesiastical commissioners in May 1849 that he had plans to build churches in the new industrial suburbs of All Saints' and St. Clement's, "and doubt not of success in both, unless some project respecting the utter dismemberment of this & similar parishes by some legislative enactment deprive me of my present ability to carry on such large designs."[71] In February 1850 he had commented to the archbishop of Canterbury that, "The Church, upon the whole, is prospering here, wh. is perhaps more than we deserve, for my attempts to restore union do not succeed;—& the 'disjecta membra,' to my mortification, still remain in a state of dislocation."[72]

The tide was against this miniature pope. The dissatisfaction of many of the lower clergymen with their status, their incomes, and their hampered ministrations met the drive for more efficiency and social order emanating from Westminster, jointly assailing the idea of the large parish with many clergymen marching to the tune of a powerful vicar. The most effective solution that both groups could devise was to eliminate the middle tier in the Church hierarchy, to have nothing between the incumbent in his small, individually manageable parish and the bishop in his diocese. This spelt the demise of a whole class of Whittakers and the attempt to create unified communities for the Church out of the new industrial towns. The division of the Parish of Blackburn into independent parishes was finally achieved on New Year's Day 1859.[73]

Throughout his vicariate, Whittaker had always attempted to ensure the unity and harmony of the clergy within the parish, and this formed one of the five main ingredients of his own vision of a parochial community. At the Accrington meeting he asserted that his appointees had promised on all occasions to act in friendly, perfect cooperation with himself and the rest of the clergy. To the archbishop of Canterbury's query as to whether there was any ambiguity in the language of the promise, he claimed to have replied, "'My lord bishop, I am prepared to bind what I have said to your lordship by the most solemn adjuration that can be couched in the strongest language which our vernacular tongue is capable of.'" The Rev. George Ashe of St. Mark's, Witton, took exception to this, saying that "if any clergyman had put himself in so contemptible a position as to put his judgment and conscience under the command of Dr. Whittaker, he . . . knew nothing of it."[74]

Nevertheless, it is clear from his letters that Whittaker was determined to admit no clergyman into his parish who was theologically unsound and who did not agree to certain preconditions, so that a united front could be presented to the laity and to "the enemies of the Church." He made this quite explicit to every applicant. For example, in July 1836 he set forth his requirements to the Rev. George Mingaye, an applicant for the parliamentary chapel of St. James, Lower Darwen. Whittaker would *not* receive into the parish anyone who made common cause with sectarians in interdenominational religious societies;[75] who denied the spiritual grace of baptism; who held *"ultra"* opinions on the doctrine of grace, especially high Calvinism; who failed to preach the great doctrines of Christianity—free grace, justification by faith, sanctification by the Spirit—but contented himself with ethical discourses to the people; and all "who are addicted to field sports, or make any kind of pleasure the business & not the recreation of life."[76]

In spite of all his precautions, the vicar obviously failed in his attempt to create a harmonious ministry. After the "curates' rebellion" he was even more insistent on only appointing clergymen acceptable to him, upon new and more stringent conditions as evidenced in a series of letters in 1850. The chapelry of Salesbury became vacant, and Whittaker wished to appoint the previous incumbent's curate to the post. But the curate, Dickens Haslewood, had to agree to "oppose to the utmost of his power any efforts to dismember the Parish of Blackburn, or to confiscate the temporalities of the vicarage, or to interfere directly or indirectly with the Vicar's right of nomination to the chapelries, or his free and unfettered exercise of that right." In the subsequent exchange of letters, Haslewood attempted to reply positively, but Whittaker remained unconvinced and suspicious, littering his remarks with references to "persons who are likely to join in a confederacy against me" and "the severe lesson taught me by the perfidy of others." All this was indicative of the extent to which he had been stung by the attempt to "plunder the Vicarage of Blackburn." As he explained to Lord de Tabley, "The effect of this conspiracy on me has been a resolution to bring into the Parish for the future a somewhat different class of clergymen, & to have a reasonable insurance that they will not join in any such nefarious schemes, but cooperate heartily with me for the welfare of the Church." As for Haslewood, he once more expressed his full desire to cooperate, but insisted that it be "a full, free, and unfettered cooperation: I say it with the fullest respect: it must be that or none." It was none. Whittaker appointed someone else to the incumbency.[77]

Church-Building and Patronage in Preston

Blackburn's contrasts and similarities with Preston, Bolton, and Deane parishes are instructive. Preston, a smaller parish, followed roughly the same trajectory of Church expansion. In 1789 there were two Anglican churches in town: the ancient parish church, which had limited accommodation for the poor, and St. George's, a proprietary chapel that catered almost exclusively to genteel tastes and where all the influential Anglican gentlemen in town owned a pew. Both of these brought together select and influential bodies of the Church bourgeoisie, meeting in weekly communion, in management, and in subscribing for occasional additions and improvements.[78]

A group of men outside the elite made the first attempt to shake the patrician torpor of the Establishment in 1813. In their project for Trinity Church they noted that "the poorer classes are completely excluded" from the existing churches, which were "divided into pews & allotted to Individuals as private property with the Exception of about 300 free sittings." Their design for a simple, economical building included at least a third of the sittings free for the poor. This was the plan, but the final product was very different. In a bid to attract the subscriptions of the wealthy, the original subscribers appointed a management committee of grandees (George Jacson, John Swainson, William Taylor, William Cross, Thomas Batty Addison, and William St. Clare—three cotton lords, two lawyers, and a physician) and planned a more elaborate structure. By November 1815 costs had spiraled to £7,200, more than double the original estimate. To recoup the expenditure, the 170 pews were sold for nearly £50 each, with an annual levy on each pew for the minister's salary, and the free sittings were fewer than anticipated.[79] The simple building providing for the poor had become the most respectable-looking church in town. "It was *a la mode*, in its most respectable sense," Hewitson wrote in the sixties, "it was Sabbatical *ton* in its genteelest form, to have and to hold a pew at Holy Trinity when George the Third was king. And for a considerable period afterwards this continued to be the case."[80]

The 1820s and 1830s, in Preston as in Blackburn, were particularly conducive to energetic church-building. A new vicar, the Rev. Roger Carus Wilson, drew on a pervasive evangelical sense of duty and accountability before God, coupled with the new readiness of local elites, Parliament, and national and diocesan bodies to spend money on palliating the fears of godless hordes. Before his early death in 1839, Wilson saw the building of six churches: two parliamentary churches, St. Peter's and St. Paul's, designed in simple Gothic by Thomas Rickman; four in the later 1830s to the designs of John Latham, an enthusiast for a rather curious variety of Norman architecture. A further church, obtained in 1838, took advantage of Nonconformist overreach: the Primitive Episcopalians had to sell their new chapel in Avenham Lane to pay off the building debt, and it was consecrated as St. James's in 1841.[81] The final church begun before mid-century (in 1846, though not consecrated for another decade) was All Saints' off Lancaster Road, which had an unusual history reminiscent of Trinity's. The Rev. W. Walling, a curate of St. James's, left for a living in Nottinghamshire around 1842. But he had attracted quite a following, for some workingmen began a subscription to build a new church for him in Preston, and gradually they raised £200. A number of wealthier men, in particular John Bairstow, stepped in to make up the £2,600 needed and, as at Trinity, assumed the management.[82]

The pattern of church-building may have been similar to that at Blackburn, but the vicars of Preston, though among the town's most powerful and influential men, did not achieve the same autonomy, salary, or accumulation of patronage as Whittaker. Lay influence was substantial. The patronage to the vicarage itself was in the hands of the rectors, the Hoghtons of Walton Hall, until Sir Henry Philip Hoghton in 1813 sold the next presentation to William Wilson Carus Wilson of Casterton Hall, Westmoreland, for £1,500 (Wilson appointed his son to the living) and then sold the advowson in 1828 to the Trustees of Hulme's Charity, Manchester (who appointed the Rev. John Owen Parr, the son of a London merchant, in 1839).[83] The Hoghtons retained legal custody of the chancel of the parish church, and in the late 1840s Parr discovered that the vicar was unable to make alterations in that part of his church without a written "plain denial" of any right by the vicar to interfere with it.[84]

Elsewhere, the patronage question for Trinity was hotly debated between proprietors, bishop, and vicar, before a decision was taken for the vicar and a select vestry of Church gentry to alternate the appointment.[85] Of the later churches, the bishop and the chancellor of Chester secured the nomination to Christ Church by virtue of a donation of £1,000 from the Diocesan Society;[86] St. Mary's, next to the new housing clustering around the Horrocks cotton mills, and St. James's were in the gift of trustees; St. Thomas's was funded out of the £50,000 bequest for church-building left by Miss Catherine Elizabeth

Hyndman, and the Hyndman Trustees assumed the patronage. This left only two of the churches in Preston township, St. Peter's and St. Paul's, with the vicar as sole patron. In addition there were four chapels in the parish outside the town, at Grimsargh (in the vicar's gift), Broughton (the Hoghton family), Barton (a donative belonging to the owners of Barton Lodge), and Ashton. This latter chapel, St. Andrew's, was completed in 1836 and came heavily under the influence of the Pedders, bankers, of Ashton Lodge. In the new church the Pedders had a box pew of squirearchical dimensions, and apparently the lesser children of the parish were expected to curtsey when the family processed in. But, initially at least, the patronage was vested in trustees, principally of the Rev. Wilson's family and connections.[87]

If they did not wish to or were unable to secure the entire control of appointment in their parishes, the vicars still remained insistent on the rights of the mother church. The Rev. James Penny, vicar at the time of the building of Trinity, was adamant that there be no marriages, christenings, or churchings at Trinity, no funerals without the vicar's consent, and that the vicar could require the assistance of the minister whenever the sacrament was administered at the parish church (or more specifically on Christmas Day, Good Friday, Easter Day, and Whitsunday).[88] During the 1840s, the Rev. John Owen Parr, like his colleagues, faced the problem of securing talented curates to minister to his unruly flock. "Churches situated and circumstanced as these are," he wrote in 1842, "require the very highest amount of qualification in the Ministers of them, and it is almost impossible to induce men so qualified to undertake so burthensome and ill requited a charge."[89] One way to augment the livings was to beg from the Church commissioners, who would only provide additional funding if separate districts were assigned to the chapels.[90] In applying, Parr insisted that no marriages be performed at the chapels:

In the first place, *the Patrons will not consent* to alienate any considerable portion of the revenues of the benefice, already inadequate to its importance & from their nature necessarily declining in value. A *considerable* portion of these revenues arises from Fees for Offices & copies of Registrations, and so serious a subtraction from their amount as the partition of the Rite of Marriage & general Registrations wd. occasion, wd. be directly a loss of income, & indirectly a loss of influence tending greatly to impair the usefulness of the Incumbent of such a Parish as this; while it wd. add in no important degree to the resources of the Chapels among which it wd. be distributed.[91]

His predecessor, Wilson, had estimated the income of the parish at £665 from disparate sources, with over £200 of this from surplice fees.[92] Beyond the question of fees, the maintenance of the parish pyramid of power was of considerable importance for Parr. He wrote that Wilson was strongly of the opinion that whatever shd. break the integrity & unity of this parish, circumstanced as it is, wd. prove greatly injurious to the real interests of religion. In this opinion, though my judgment is not entitled to the same weight, I fully concur; and I think it of the highest importance to those interests, that this town shd. continue to have, as an ecclesiastical body, a common Centre & a common head.

He threatened to withdraw the application if the district chapels were allowed to perform marriages. The commissioners duly assigned districts in October 1843 for five of the chapels in the town with only baptisms, churchings, and burials authorized.[93]

Church-Building and Patronage in Bolton and Deane

Church-building in Bolton Parish was a variation on a familiar theme. In 1789 the parish church of St. Peter presided over Great Bolton township, sharing the urban area with the early-eighteenth-century All Saints'—the "Chapel i'th' Fields"[94]—in Little Bolton, while a number of well-established chapels in the outer townships (Bradshaw, Turton, Walmsley, Rivington, and Blackrod in a detached portion of the parish) largely looked after themselves, sending only some of their fees and all of their brides and grooms (except, by ancient custom, Rivington) to the mother church. Little Lever Chapel, opened in 1791, was a new arrival in the country townships, but St. George's, Little Bolton, a proprietary chapel, was the first new church to take root in the expanding town. Like St. George's in Preston (expanded in the 1790s) and St. John's in Blackburn (built from 1789), St. George's was constructed to cater for the swelling polite society, for whatever taste and gentility the town could muster, for those who maybe found the parish church too uncomfortably close to a Christian ideal of brotherhood and spiritual equality, and who wished to put a greater distance between themselves and the common herd.[95] More than a quarter of a century of rapid urban growth then elapsed before the Church in Bolton began to try and catch up with it.[96] The parliamentary church of Holy Trinity, started in 1823, was an elaborate structure costing over £13,400.[97] Emmanuel Church, the first subscription "poor man's church," grew out of a collection of £500 in 1836 to provide a mark of respect for the vicar, the Rev. Slade, in the form of plate for his table, but he diverted the money into worthier channels.[98]

Fixing a lantern in one benighted neighborhood showed ever more starkly the contrasting grubby darkness of another. Slade himself was not a great church-builder in the Whittaker or Wilson mold, preferring to invest more of his energy in school-building. But by familiar means, the Church followed as the town inflated and fingered out to clasp surrounding settlements swollen by the impregnation of manufacturing and industry. The Methodist New

Connexion's Ebenezer Chapel became Christ Church in 1841 when the minister (embarked on an intellectual odyssey that would take him all the way to Tractarianism) and the bulk of his church joined the Establishment, partly as an escape from financial difficulties.[99] At Astley Bridge and in Little Bolton, chapels were planted in schools in the 1840s until sufficient funds could be raised for churches, which shortly followed. None of these had an outstanding patron or donor who could claim them as part of his church-paternalist sphere, the honors being shared among a number of local Church gentry.[100] The churches of St. Peter and St. Paul, Halliwell, in Deane Parish, were, as we shall see, more strictly church-paternalist ventures initiated, largely funded, and controlled by John Horrocks Ainsworth. The terra-cotta church of St. Stephen, Leverbridge, depended on the initiative, donations, and fire clay of John Fletcher, coalowner, and the land and money of Lord Bradford.[101] The cotton manufacturing family of Robert Lomax, JP, of Lomax Fold ("the only resident gentleman in the Township"), gave land and money for the building of Christ Church, Harwood, in the 1840s, plus endowments, schools, and an appended private family chapel and vault.[102]

This church-building and church-extension in the out townships largely followed a typical pattern whereby local wealth—landed or industrial, collectively or individually—sought to demonstrate its own piety and to inculcate an ordered Christianity by stringing up lanterns for the Lord.[103] But Bolton presented a more complicated picture and more uncertain distribution of power than Blackburn or even Preston: the town was expanding at the heart of not one but two "large and overgrown" parishes; and an array of vested proprietary interests—those of Lord Kenyon, patron of St. Paul's, Peel, for example; or George Matthew Hoare of Mordern Lodge, Mitcham, Surrey, patron of Turton Chapel; or William Hulton of Hulton Park, who had the biggest say at Deane Parish Church—presented greater scope for lay initiative.[104]

The pattern of power and patronage may have been different, but the debate over clerical rights was very similar. For instance, successive bishops of Chester in 1815 and 1830-31 mediated disputes between the incumbent of Peel chapelry, the Rev. William Allen, and successive vicars of Deane over the question of fees and attendance at the mother church on the great festivals. The bishop in 1831 evenhandedly thought it "quite as much incumbent upon" the vicar "to assert the rights of Dean" as it was a duty for Allen "to liberate Peel from any foreign obligations."[105] Peel seems by this time to have won on the question of fees, but as the income of the parish church was listed in the mid-twenties as being only around £200, the incumbent could be expected to fight his corner when it came to other chapelries. This was put to the test with the building of the parliamentary church of St. John, Farnworth with Kearsley, in the early 1820s, and the creation of a district for it in 1828—even though the vicar, the Rev. Thomas Brocklebank, pointed out that it would be "exceedingly hard" to deprive the parish church of any of its fees, unless the commissioners could provide compensation, given the size of the living. Double fees, he added, were always considered as a tax and a grievance, and often became a source of uneasiness and dispute between the incumbents of the mother churches and chapels. The vicar resigned in November 1829, and this meant that on the appointment of the Rev. Edward Girdlestone as the new vicar, Farnworth became a separate benefice, its incumbent a vicar. Girdlestone had no say in this, but he too asked if some compensation might be paid to the vicar of Deane, since the living was very poor, the duty laborious, and it could ill sustain even the most trifling loss. None was forthcoming, and the only continuing obligation of the District Parish and Vicarage of St. John to the older parish was in answering calls for repairs to the mother church.[106]

In Bolton Parish, the vicar noted in his diary in October 1829,

How grievous is the consideration that many of our parishes should have become so enormously overgrown as to render it impossible for the minister to have any adequate knowledge or superintendence of his flock. The people are increased and multiplied at the call of the interests of mammon, and no correspondent provision has been made for imparting unto them the true riches of life everlasting. The vineyard is grown so large and the labourers are so few! I fear there are portions of this populous parish overrun with ignorance almost heathen, and certainly with heathenish conduct and manners.[107]

But for him just as much as for his fellow vicars, by increasing the numbers of churches and laborers he did not mean to diminish the authority of the vicar. He opposed districts for the chapels, since a division of "this poor and laborious Vicarage" would deprive it of its principal source of emolument, parochial fees; the greater good of the parish should not be purchased at the sole expense of the vicarage.[108]

When districts were duly assigned in 1842 for the town chapels—Slade deferring to his patron and diocesan—the double-fee system remained in operation. As we have seen elsewhere, this was far from a solution to the vexed questions of increasingly unequal power, status, and income within the local Church. The proposition to carve out a new district in Little Bolton and license a day school for divine worship until a new church, to be called St. John's, was built, further aroused the ire of some established clergymen. The problem was that, under the terms of Peel's act, once the church had been constructed the new district would become a parish. The Rev. John Lyons of St. George's was especially bitter, since the new parish segmented from his own district would immediately be endowed, its minister could perform marriages and would not have to charge fees to be remitted to the mother church.

St. George's would still remain that Ecclesiastical delusion called a District for spiritual purposes, and the Incumbent would be placed, by comparison, in the odious position of demanding Baptismal registration fees from the inhabitants of one side of a street, whilst their opposite neighbours situated in the New Parish, would be triumphing in their immunity from all such fees.

Lyons was well aware that withholding his consent would only slightly delay the plan, but there was a principle at stake. "Very many of the Clergy feel deeply aggrieved that young men, some of them even without University Education, are elevated to privileges, and remunerated with Endowments, denied to those who have toiled for many years amidst difficulties and privations, that few are aware of." The Rev. John Leach of All Saints' consented to the new district for the good of church extension; but he too drew attention to the injustice against the old churches in not having at least equal privileges when it came to marrying, and in having to send fees to the parish church: "It is the general opinion of the Clergy in this neighbourhood, who are so situated, that something should be done, in order that we may no longer occupy the inferior position we at present do, with respect to the new district Churches."[109]

It was somewhat ironic that the Rev. Walter Chamberlain, the incumbent of St. John's, which was completed by the end of 1849, should be the one to take up the cudgel against parochial centralization, as we have seen. As the incumbent of a New Parish he had more freedom to speak out. But it is interesting that the primary focus of his argument was not fees but status. He saw local patronage as the chief evil: congregations viewed incumbents appointed by the vicar as dependent on his direction, while those installed by more distant patrons were able to command more respect.[110]

The conveyor-belt ministrations that the anti-centralizers described in Blackburn Parish Church were fully replicated in Bolton Parish Church. For example, the Rev. Thomas Loxham, curate of the parish church, recorded in his diary that in 1846 he conducted 966 baptisms, 450 marriages, and 1,003 funerals. His brother, Richard, also a parish church curate from 1849, recorded that on December 30 he married ten couples in the morning and baptized thirty-two individuals in the afternoon; and on New Year's Day 1850 he conducted ten weddings in the morning and five funerals in the afternoon, while the vicar performed a further fourteen weddings in the morning.[111]

The Rev. Slade lived out his time as vicar with his quasi-episcopal powers intact, except for the New Parishes separated out from the whole. But his successor was to have a much more limited sphere. The Rev. J. D. Cannon later recalled a conversation with Slade in the vicarage:

alluding to possible successors he pointed out through the windows the chimneys, the atmosphere, the crowd, and hovels, and added (having first said that such a successor would need, like him, resources apart from the Vicarage) "What successor with private means will live *here* in these days?" It was mentioned that all the district Churches would become independent of the new Vicar, who would be the poorer by the loss of the fees. I said, "The new Vicar will not really be the Vicar of Bolton." He answered, "He *will* in *name*."[112]

As in Blackburn so in Bolton: the name but not the substance.

Church Paternalism in Horwich and Halliwell

The Christian crusade did not only encounter friction between the clergy within each denomination or between local church leaders and influential members of the laity, as the tales of Horwich and Halliwell illustrate. Horwich, a manufacturing village on the western edge of the moors, owed much to its large bleachworks, especially to those of the Ridgway family. The Tory-Anglican Ridgways were the chief patrons of the Church in the village and assumed a traditional squirearchical role, assiduously milking their patronage—partially by default, the principal landowner, Thomas Stonor of Stonor, Oxfordshire, being nonresident and Catholic. When it came time to build a bigger church, the Church commissioners provided the bulk of the funding, and Stonor the land; but the Ridgways were still substantial subscribers, and donated the organ, bells, and clock.[113] Joseph Ridgway laid the foundation stone of the new Trinity Church in May 1830, and the family made use of the occasion to stage a show of good relations between masters and men. Around eight hundred workmen of Thomas Ridgway and Ridgway Bridson, his nephew and partner, marched in procession behind a band, pausing in turn at the houses of all three men, before being joined by clergy, magistrates, and gentry at the ceremony. While the workmen were treated to dinner at the Bull afterwards, the gentlemen dined at Thomas Ridgway's house and drank to toasts of a distinctly Tory flavor.[114]

This was typical behavior, as was the request—granted—for large blocks of pews on either side of the chapel for Thomas and Joseph Ridgway, their servants and tenants, following a similar pattern in the old chapel.[115] Where Joseph Ridgway differed somewhat in his patronage is revealed in his extraordinary will, proved in 1843, documenting both vainglory and a considerable, though unspecified, rift with the curate of the church. It reads,

I desire to be buried in my vault at the church in Horwich, and I direct my executors to erect a monument in the same church to my memory, to be executed by a London artist, at such expense as they, my executors, may think proper, but not less than £1,000 [*sic*]; also a tablet recording the benefactions which I have made by this my will or otherwise, to the said church, and the officers thereof, so that the said benefactions may not be lost for want of due notice of their proper application.

In addition, he provided for generous salaries for the church's officers and for the curate—but not for the present incumbent, the Rev. David Hewitt; and, after Hewitt's incumbency had ended, a service of communion plate, "the same to be massive and embossed with an inscription, and my armorial bearings thereon." Thomas Hampson, historian of Horwich in the 1880s, suggests that the rift might have had something to do with the fact that the church was "made to be more or less an heraldic monument of the Ridgway family, and [so]. . . the proscribed clergyman suffered through an unavoidable clash in defence of ecclesiastical rights and privileges."[116]

One of the best-documented examples of the workings and of the limitations of Church paternalism is that of another bleacher, John Horrocks Ainsworth, at Halliwell. He had already staked a claim to be the lay head of a Church community by contributing generously to the rebuilding of St. Peter's Church, Halliwell, in 1843-44, and securing the patronage under the Patronage Act. The church was consecrated in November 1844, followed by lunch for the bishop, thirty clergymen, and forty laymen at Moss Bank, buns for the Jubilee School children, and dinner for 150 at the works.[117]

Ainsworth decided to place himself at the head of a second Church-paternalist establishment centered on Moss Bank, largely catering for the workmen at the Temple Bleachworks. In 1847 he began building St. Paul's Church—the armorial bearings of himself, his father, and grandfather to be prominent in the lights of the nave—a school, and two rows of cottages in matching style.[118] It is clear from several of his diary entries that he was no laissez-faire paternalist. On March 19, 1847: "I spoke to several of my workmen who had neglected to go to Church and desired them to attend regular in the future." On December 7, 1848: "I . . . regretted to find that so few of the work men attended Church." On December 14: "Busy with the Churchwardens . . . in putting down names of persons to be requested to go to Church." On the sixteenth several men came to ask permission to go to their own places of worship, and "I gave my consent to nearly all of them." But on the eighteenth, "I sent for several of the persons who saw me on Saturday, & withdrew my consent that the[y] should attend their own places of worship as I found that they were not worthy of exception."[119]

The church was consecrated in June 1848. Ainsworth had already found a clergymen to his liking, the Rev. William Milton, a Londoner, a graduate of Exeter College, Oxford, and for two years curate in Holbeck, Leeds. Milton had been influenced by Tractarianism at Oxford, though this did not as yet seem to concern Ainsworth. It was of more concern to Prince Lee, bishop of Manchester, who declined to consecrate the church until Milton relented and agreed not to wear the surplice in preaching.[120] All was well for a while, until Ainsworth's belief in his rights as patron and master began to clash with Milton's conception of his own independence and the dignity of the Church and its ministers. Looking back in the spring of 1850, Milton explained that, "It was a new thing that a poor parish priest should resist a power hitherto popularly supposed in the township to be irresistable [*sic*]." Moreover,

I had uniformly shown a reluctance to be interfered with or dictated to in regard to my ministration at St. Paul's. I did not like being told, in a manner amounting to being ordered, to preach on such and such subjects. I did not like having six-penny books of the Christian Knowledge Society put into my hands, with a quasi-episcopal charge that *that* was the doctrine he expected me to preach. I did not like forms of doxology sent to me for use at the close of my sermons. These and many other things I did not like and did not comply with, being desirous to be the parish priest of my own parish. I had also the temerity to speak on some occasions in conversation with him on the subject of the overwork under which the people were suffering, and had so far taken an interest in the wellbeing of the people, as to be grieved to witness the hours of children and women's work, maintained at 18 hours a day, sometimes prolonged to 30, 40, and I have since learnt to 60 hours without rest.[121]

Ainsworth tried to rid himself of his turbulent priest by twice giving him notice to leave the parsonage and threatening to withdraw choir, organist, apparitor, and gas from the church. Twice he backed down because of strong feeling in support of Milton from the parishioners. Matters came to a head again in March 1850, after Ainsworth had drawn up a petition purporting to show that nearly the entire congregation objected to the form of the services, in particular the reading desk facing away from the people; after a couple of "violent" sermons against Ainsworth; and after Milton had spoken out at a Ten Hours meeting (chaired by Peter Ainsworth) against the excessive hours at the Ainsworth bleachworks (see Chapter 9). Ainsworth ordered Milton not to enter the school, whereupon Milton removed the books (a "gift," and therefore—unlike the parsonage and school—not Ainsworth's private property), intending to conduct the school in the church. On hearing this, Ainsworth went to Smithills Hall where two fellow magistrates, Darbishire and Ridgway, were dining with his brother, and they proceeded in the early hours of the morning to demand entrance to and search the houses of the schoolmaster and another teacher for the "stolen" books. Ainsworth, who had previously ordered his workmen to attend church, was now ordering them to stay away. To compound matters, the woman whom Milton had referred to at the Ten Hours meeting for working sixty hours at a stretch, died: at the funeral, Milton preached from Exodus 3:7-8: "And the Lord said, I have surely seen the affliction of my people which are in Egypt, and have heard their cry by reason of their taskmasters . . . And I am come down to deliver them out of the hands of the Egyptians." Ainsworth could draw only one conclusion: "Mr.

Milton compared himself to Moses, sent to deliver the people from slavery."
Milton spelled out his charge in his letter to the *Manchester Courier*:

[I]t is absurd in me to talk of British freedom and the liberty of the subject in Halliwell. An unchecked absolution [*sic*] has long ago driven these notions far from
the people's minds. They are mere serfs in the worst sense of the word. Driven into
Church, and then driven out of Church by the same arbitrary will; getting their
food at the master's shop, and their religion at the Church which their master shall
order them to attend.

Although Milton expressed his intention in March to stay on, the expenses of
the church had now fallen upon him, out of his income of £80-100. He conceded defeat in September by resigning and leaving Halliwell.[122]

The Church-paternalist model could therefore easily be destabilized, and in
quite dramatic fashion. Nevertheless, Church-paternalism did form the most
sustained effort by the bourgeoisie to anchor islands of hierarchical stability in
the milltowns and their hinterlands. It built on long-standing patterns of
Church extension; and was novel only in the intensity and vigor with which it
was pursued and in the extent of its incorporation of new wealth into the endeavor. Whatever its impact on the control and incorporation of the lower orders, its impact on the collective identities of the controllers themselves, clerical and lay, was profound.[123] Dr. Whittaker's was the most encompassing attempt, supervising (in theory) both the collective pooling of the resources of
the wealthy to fund churches in poor districts and the endeavors of individual
families to sustain their own local Church-paternalist ventures. In the other
parishes the structures of authority and patronage were more fragmented,
which tended to mean that the power of individual landowners or industrialists to create, sustain, or neglect their own religious communities was enhanced. As we shall see, voluntary associations (Chapter 8) sought collective
strategies in the battle for order; factory paternalism (Chapter 9) depended
upon the whim and means of the millowner; political parties (Chapter 12)
tried to bind individuals in a collective, but partisan, endeavor spanning the
nation; but religious paternalism to an extent bridged all three by attempting
to create a largely partisan, hierarchical structure with a series of individual
and collective remedies. Like voluntary societies, most of the churches represented a collective pooling of local landed, mercantile, manufacturing, and
professional wealth to achieve together what one individual rarely had the resources to accomplish alone; unlike them, they combined this wealth with
state resources and "national collective wealth" from the church-building societies. In this fashion the local wealthy bought themselves influence or shares
of influence in an interlocking jigsaw of power relationships across the country. Or perhaps a more telling image of bourgeois power is a series of superimposed transparencies projected on a screen, the churches and their support-

ers mapping one layer onto the cotton district, sometimes convergent with and sometimes divergent from other layers. But even that is too rigid, since this layer, like every other layer, was constantly being reworked in small and subtle ways, as the relationships of authority and subordination remained in a persistent state of flux and negotiation, challenge or reaffirmation.

Dissent

Only the Established Church had the structure, resources, and elite support to build pyramids of sectarianism across the landscape of the industrial town, either as subsets of larger clerical pyramids as in Blackburn, or as fragmented units of power and patronage as in Preston and Bolton. Roman Catholicism could to an extent rival this in rural areas in the immediate vicinity of a large Catholic family—Stonyhurst, Pleasington, and Osbaldeston being prime examples—but only in Preston did it have the numbers, and town-and-country elite support, for a clergy-led pyramid of anything like the same extent to be established. Because of their organization and—for some at least—limited elite support, few Nonconformist sects could attempt anything similar.

The sectarian returns of 1829 (see Appendix 2), though unreliable, give a rough indication of Nonconformist strength across the region.[124] A number of patterns are reasonably clear: the high levels of residual (that is, largely English, nonimmigrant) Catholicism in all three towns (in particular in Preston, though the figure given is almost certainly greatly inflated) and in the townships around Preston, to the southeast of the town, and up the Ribble valley; the almost complete lack of Catholics in the townships around Bolton and north to Darwen; and strong pockets of support for different Dissenting sects: Independents and Wesleyans in Blackburn, Independents, Presbyterians, Unitarians, and Methodists in Bolton, Independents in Horwich, Presbyterians in Rivington and Ainsworth, Unitarians in Harwood, and so on. My purpose here is not to analyze the historical and sociological reasons for such concentrations, but to examine what certain members of the clerical and lay bourgeoisie did with those concentrations in enhancing their own status and in establishing denominational communities.

There were three basic types of Dissenting community across these milltowns: the highly "respectable" chapels that made no serious attempt to proselytize or to attract a lower-order following; the chapels with little or no bourgeois presence; and the bourgeois-led sects that campaigned just as vigorously as the Church of England and the Catholic Church to create a visible pyramidal presence. Hewitson's survey of Preston churches in the 1860s brings out well the stratified patterns of churchgoing: the Primitive Methodist, Particular Baptist, Mormon, Wesley, and United Methodist Free Church (formerly Wesleyan Association) chapels were very largely composed of different gradations of the working classes and poor, including most of their ministers and preachers; the Swedenborgian (New Jerusalem) Chapel was maybe a notch higher on the social scale, and had a well-educated minister; Cannon Street Independent Chapel was "tolerably respectable" ("Not many poor peo ple join the charmed circle. A middle-class, shopkeeping halo largely environs the assemblage"); Lune Street Wesleyan Chapel was largely middle class, the most refined of the Wesleyan chapels; the Quaker Meeting House attracted small numbers of "very decorous, respectable, middle-class people"; and the Unitarian chapel boasted a small, wealthy congregation.[125] This was a fairly predictable configuration. No respectable bourgeois strayed near Mormonism or Primitive Methodism, though isolated individuals generously supported the Baptists and the Swedenborgians. Edward Burford and Peter and Ann Anstie—who migrated from London in the 1780s to become involved in the large Mosney Hall printworks on the river Darwen at Walton, before migrating back again when the business collapsed in 1788—partly founded Preston Baptism in 1782, but local Baptism apparently did not attract wealthy benefactors after their departure.[126] The Boardman family of Cherry Tree House supported Blackburn Baptism with bequests of at least £400, plus a house for the minister.[127] Hugh Becconsall, originally a grocer, became a convert to Swedenborgianism, began a short-lived society in Preston with Richard Parkinson, linen draper, in 1812, and built the New Jerusalem Chapel in 1843 at a cost of nearly £2,000;[128] while Samuel Crompton, inventor of the spinning mule, loomed large in Bolton Swedenborgianism.[129]

Unitarianism was rather different in its elitist appeal. In Preston the most prominent backers were the Ainsworth and Pilkington families, leading cotton manufacturers and attorneys respectively.[130] In Bolton, a significant portion of the liberal elite was Unitarian; Bank Street Chapel exerted a similarly disproportionate degree of influence to that of the Cross Street and Mosley Street Unitarian Chapels in Manchester[131]—and the kinship, friendship, and business connections between the Bolton and Manchester Unitarians were marked. A historian of the chapel related the following story in 1896:

A young man, who for a good many years had heard Unitarians spoken of with the usual horror as heretics, determined, after much screwing up of his mental courage, to go to the chapel and see what it was like. Selecting a quiet Sunday morning, he made his way, after service had begun, into the gallery, and found a place from which he had a good view. Looking down, he saw, sitting below, the leaders in every good movement in the town or in business, whose character and standing gave weight and authority to all they took in hand; who were acknowledged leaders in every liberal effort or institution for the general good.

The families were heavily intermarried and included the Dornings, Taylors, Darbishires, Pilkingtons, Heywoods, Mangnalls, Kays, Haslams, Deans, and Crooks. The Unitarians produced in Charles James Darbishire and Robert

Heywood the first two mayors of Bolton (partly a product of the temporary Tory-Anglican boycott), and they had vigorous polemicist ministers in the shape of the Revs. Phillip and John Holland and Franklin Baker (who married into the Crook family).[132]

The Quakers were not quite so elitist, but in the Ashworths of Turton and the Thomassons of Bolton they could boast wealthy millowners and Manchester-School liberals. Quakerism had a regional organization in the form of Monthly Meetings, which representatives from the different chapels attended, but no mass following. It was not easy to be or to remain a Quaker. Friends visited prospective members to decide whether to grant them clearance before membership could be conferred. After that, one could be disowned for intemperance, acting immorally, failing to attend chapel, marrying outside the church (yoking oneself "unequally . . . with such as differ from us in principles and profession, and also by that means recognizing the authority of the Priest"), or baptizing a child (an "empty Ceremony").[133]

The Methodists were well represented across the region but, except in Bolton, the numbers of prominent bourgeois Methodists were relatively small. John Wesley apparently first visited Blackburn in 1780 and claimed, implausibly, that "All the chief men of the town were there." Four years later he had a different tale to report: "I preached at five, to a numerous congregation, but not one well-dressed person among them, either morning or evening. Poor Blackburn!" According to the deed of 1785 of the Clayton Street Chapel, the only Blackburn trustees were a breadbaker and grocer, two weavers, and a yeoman. The Blackburn circuit was formed in 1787 and slowly developed a network of chapels in some of the neighboring villages, but the major contributions over the years came from individuals on middling incomes, in the retailing and craft sectors, with only one or two higher up like the Dall family, Samlesbury cotton manufacturers. In 1825 the Methodists built a school chapel at Daisyfield but, as we have seen, had to sell it to the vicar in 1837 because of financial difficulties. This was still causing pain to the Rev. John Ward forty years later:

When we have passed through that densely populated neighbourhood, and looked upon the character of its inhabitants, we have felt humiliated as we thought of the fact that there a Methodist Chapel and a flourishing Sabbath school once existed, but have both passed into other hands. A finer field for evangelical effort, and one in which Methodism would find a more suitable adaptation, we have never met with.

He admitted that Wesleyan Methodism was inferior in Blackburn to almost every other town in Lancashire of the same size, with only one moderate-sized chapel in the town center.[134]

In Preston early Methodism owed much to Roger Crane, ironmonger. He and his family hosted the early itinerant preachers, and when he inherited his portion of his father's money, he gave a quarter of it to building a chapel in the Orchard in 1787. Methodism did reasonably well over the years and gained the support of a number of prominent individuals, notably Thomas Crouch Hincksman, flax spinner, and the Parke family. John Parke of Longton founded Methodism in that village in 1790. His eldest son, Robert, laid the foundation stone of the Wesley Chapel in Preston in 1838.[135] Robert and his brother John established a rural factory colony in Withnell: Robert bought a substantial part of the Withnell estate in 1839 and built a cotton mill on Bury Lane; John the following year bought the rest of the manor and built the mill in Abbey Village. Robert's son, Thomas Blinkhorn Parke, began a paper mill in Withnell Fold in 1843 and set up a familiar paternalistic community around it. Methodist societies met in the warehouses of the mills until T. B. Parke built a chapel in 1852.[136]

Methodism in Bolton could count on substantial elite backing. Its most prominent adherents included the Peter Rothwell family, ironfounders, Roger Holland of Birch House, the builder of the Four Factories, the Knowles family of the Four Factories and Peel Mills, the Cannon family of Cannon and Haslam, manufacturers, the Taylors of Globe and Grecian Mills, Peter Crook, cotton spinner, the iron-founding Musgraves, and a number of other bourgeois names: Mrs. de Manneville, Fergus Ferguson, surgeon, Thomas Moscrop, oil merchant and druggist, and Richard Stockdale, draper.[137]

In Blackburn, with practically no Unitarian presence, Independency was by far the most successful vehicle for the Dissenting elite. The hub was Chapel Street Chapel, built in 1777 when the Rev. James McQuhae moved with part of his congregation from Tockholes, an old-established center of Nonconformity up on the moors. The church developed further under the vigorous leadership of the Rev. Joseph Fletcher, the son of a Chester goldsmith and a product of Hoxton Academy and Glasgow University. He became pastor in 1807 and took up residence with the prominent Blackburn banker, Roger Cunliffe and his wife at Lark Hill, before marrying Mary, daughter of John France of King Street, another leading Independent, in 1808. The chapel survived some early dissension. Disputes over the choice of minister nearly resulted in a schism in 1806. In 1808 Fletcher lamented a further bout of squabbling:

How will all the corps of Presbyterianism exult in such whirling and trifling, such religious Quixotism and windmill fighting,—instead of serious and dignified opposition to the world, the flesh, and the devil! It seems as debasing a prostitution of time and talents, as it would have been in our ministers quarrelling about the painting and colouring of the transports that were to convey the expedition to

Spain, when all their energy and influence should be employed in the great cause of patriotism and liberty.

In 1809 a small schism did take place, and a rival chapel became established at Mount Street which oscillated between Independency, Presbyterianism, and redundancy before being bought by the United Secession Church of Scotland in 1828. Still, Chapel Street flourished, attracting some notable elite backing, engaging in missionary activity, and spawning the Blackburn Independent Academy.[138]

One of the problems Independents faced was how to organize coordinated proselytizing activity without interfering with the basic tenet of their church government, that each separate chapel be independent as to rights and discipline. Their solution was the Lancashire Congregational Union, formed by a collection of Lancashire ministers in Mosley Street Chapel, Manchester, in 1806, who agreed to appoint annually a committee of thirteen to form plans and administer donations from member chapels to support itinerant ministers and new and outlying congregations. The union's historian describes these itinerant ministers performing heroic feats over the next thirty years in overlaying the county with a network of village stations and preaching in barns, in houses, and in the open. Many, he says, were rough and unlettered; they earned salaries of between £40 and £80, often with large families to maintain: a vast status difference indeed from the cultivated and gentlemanly Joseph Fletcher. Sir James Kay-Shuttleworth later evocatively described one such missionary endeavor:

I was fond of accompanying the deacons in their visits on Sundays to remote "folds" and hamlets in the hills of Blackstone Edge and Todmorden, or along the range from Knowl Hill to Rowley Moor. I remember long walks with the deacon, John Crabtree—his pious conversation on the way—our arrival at a weaver's cottage in some far distant "fold" on the edge of a wild moor—the simple breakfast of oatcake or oatmeal porridge and milk—the gathering of the neighbours, and the primitive Scriptural greetings sometimes uttered; the simple service and the quaint, rather dogmatic, discourse of my friend John; the mid-day meal of eggs, bacon, oatcake; then the walk home, and the arrival at Bamford in the twilight or night.[139]

At a relatively early date the Congregational Union wished to increase the educational caliber of its ministers—and thus the respectability of its mission—without having to rely on an inadequate supply from colleges in Yorkshire. Fletcher established his scholarly reputation with a published sermon in 1813 on the divine sovereignty and election, and a committee of the union fixed on him as president and theological tutor of a projected Theological Academy in Lancashire. A general meeting in Mosley Street Chapel in February 1816 accordingly decided to locate the new academy in Blackburn. Like an earlier, short-lived academy in Pendelton (1810-13), the aim was to combine a grammar-school-style education for young gentlemen alongside theological training for the ministry.[140]

Fletcher "found the interests of religion in the town and neighbourhood of Blackburn in a very low condition," his son wrote, "and left them in a state of comparative prosperity" by the time he moved on to London in 1822. Chapel, Sunday school, and academy were all prospering. But in a letter to Roger Cunliffe in the same year he sought to allay doubts about the location of the academy. He still believed Blackburn to be the best site, at least for the time being: it "is the most central situation in the county; . . . It is nearer the more destitute parts of the county than Manchester or Liverpool. . . . It presents a situation more free from temptations to the students, and exposure to mental dissipation, than larger places"; and many connections had already been formed in the neighborhood. He laid out what Cunliffe must do:

In Blackburn God has honoured you with large success. In Blackburn your influence is deservedly felt—and here you must in a great measure localize the institution, and erect, if I may so speak, a lasting monument to your Christian benevolence and zeal, by provisions that would form a solid basis for the future exertions of others.[141]

Cunliffe made an annual donation of £100 to the college and willed for this to continue after his death, but only on condition it remained in Blackburn. But in a letter in 1827 the students stated their dissatisfaction with the town:

Sincerely as we respect individuals in this town and neighbourhood, and highly as we appreciate the advantages wh. the Academy at present possesses, we cannot but regard Blackburn as destitute of those local facilities for improvement wh. some towns in the county present. Perhaps none but those who may be placed in circumstances similar to our own, can adequately feel their benumbing tendency.

They wished to move to a "town of greater importance," like Liverpool or Manchester, with scientific and literary resources.[142] Before this took place, a cohort of students (fifty-five in all) trained in Blackburn, and conducted Sunday schools and preached in the missions in neighboring villages. But the lack of sufficient regular contributions stymied the expansion of the academy, and it was probably this above all that influenced the decision in 1839 to leave Blackburn for Manchester, the hope of support from the Manchester wealthy being more than enough to counteract the loss of Cunliffe's legacy.[143]

The status of Independent ministers increased in proportion not only to their education but also to their salary, which depended on the respectability of the flock or financial aid from the union to the mission stations. "In old times the Lord did not 'call' so many parsons from one church to another as it is said He does now," Hewitson witheringly wrote in 1869, describing the linkages between upward mobility, reputation, and remuneration: "We have known multitudes of parsons, in our time, who have been 'called' to places where their salaries were increased; we know of but few who have gravitated to a church where the salary was less than the one left."[144]

At one end of the status scale was Fletcher who, according to a Birmingham minister, "Apart from his office, he would have passed current in well-bred society for a real, unaffected gentleman."[145] In the middle were those with pretensions to gentility, like the classical tutor at the academy, a man called Hayward. In 1841, the Rev. S. T. Porter of Darwen wrote to the Rev. Dr. Raffles of Liverpool that Hayward's salary of £110 a year was "scarcely sufficient to provide him with those means of mental furniture which he deems necessary to enable him to compete with the holders of similar chairs." Moreover, "He wishes to travel for a few months with a view to converse with foreign literati" and needed about £100 to do so and bring back a selection of books. (A correspondent, John Kelly, wrote, "The conceit of the letter is pro-di-gious. Mr. Hayward has extended the reputation of the Academy!!! and is going for about four months to Germany to converse with the literati that he might through the New College electrify the Country!!!! Bah. This is certainly modest.")[146] At the other end of the scale was John Harding Unwin, formerly master of the James Street day school, who became the unordained minister at the Belthorn Independent Chapel in 1846, apparently earning less than £40 a year until at least 1849.[147]

In spite of the fact that Independency was a demanding religion and membership not easy,[148] it was an important and expanding presence across the face of the three towns and in the outlying villages, particularly the settlements up on the moors.[149] For its institutional presence and pattern of strength it owed much to a handful of leading inhabitants, some of the most important figures in the social and political histories of Darwen and Blackburn in particular, including Roger Cunliffe, the extensive mill-owning Eccles clan of Blackburn and Darwen, the mill-owning Shorrocks of Darwen, the mill-owning Pilkingtons of Blackburn, and the paper-making Charles Potter of Darwen, who together constituted a formidable bloc of Independent wealth.[150] They funded the chapels as a means of demonstrating their piety, respectability, status and, like many of their Anglican colleagues, in an attempt to build up local paternalist communities. Joseph Eccles, for example, spent £1,300 on a school and chapel (opened in 1846) near his residence, Mill Hill House; at Grimshaw Park, William and James Pilkington of Park Place Mills opened their "handsome" schoolrooms in 1851, where a new church was established the following year; in Darwen, Eccles Shorrock built a similar British School costing upwards of £1,200.[151]

Preston Catholicism

In Preston, the Catholic Church under the leadership of Father Joseph Dunn of St. Wilfrid's made the most notable attempt to pursue a strategy of sectarian community-building, with occasional hostile forays or diplomatic initiatives into alien territory. Dunn (1746-1827), a Yorkshireman, was initiated into the Society of Jesus in 1764 at St. Omers, studied at Liège, and was teaching in Bruges (the new home of the College of St. Omers) when Pope Clement XIV suppressed the Jesuits there. The college and Dunn reestablished themselves at Liège, he leaving for a chaplaincy in Northumberland some time after, the college, harried by the French revolutionaries in 1794, finding a fourth refuge, this time at Stonyhurst, the somewhat dilapidated northern seat of Thomas Weld in the Ribble Valley. Dunn arrived in Preston in 1775 or 1776 as an assistant at St. Mary's Church on Friargate, the only Catholic chapel in town, becoming the superior in 1783. His brother, Dr. William Dunn (1749-1805), a secular priest educated at Douai, became a missionary in Blackburn, the priest of St. Alban's, the first Catholic chapel in town (built in 1773). During his long tenure at Preston, which became the foremost Catholic mission in the area, Fr. Joseph was instrumental in building St. Wilfrid's Church in 1793, restoring and reopening St. Mary's in 1815, initiating the Sunday schools in Friargate in 1787 and in Fox Street in 1814, and laying out a Catholic cemetery in 1823. He founded a Catholic Book Society, a Catholic Library, and a Society for the Defence of Catholic Principles; and on the secular level he was heavily involved in the Savings Bank, the Lit. and Phil., and the Gas Company. His links with his superiors at Stonyhurst remained strong, and it was he who introduced Samuel Clegg, pioneer gas engineer, to the college. Clegg used the scientific facilities at Stonyhurst to experiment with purification, and it became the first public institution to be lit by gas. Dunn, working through the Lit. and Phil., ensured that Preston was the first provincial town to have a gas works.[152]

This then was a kind of rationalist, improving Catholicism, hitching a ride on the wagon of progress and staking a claim for a share of the territory at the end of the trail. Dunn was a shrewd operator. Like many another successful clergyman, he was an intriguing mixture of piety and opportunism in extending the scope of his community, and it is not surprising that his arrogance and concern for his prerogatives generated friction along the way.

Dunn's best-documented attempt at paternalism was in the building of his schools in Fox Street. He had two stated aims: to train up the Catholic children in the fold and to indoctrinate subordination to king and country. To this end, and to pay off the school's debts, he solicited funds widely among Protestants as well as Catholics.[153] The bishop of Norwich, who favored Catholic Emancipation, donated £5, writing that, "With regard to the Catholic Sunday and Day School established at Preston every friend to Religion, every Man who has sincerely at heart the interest of social order and the welfare of Government must wish you success in so laudable an undertaking." Robert Peel Sr. donated £10, and his son donated twice. In a letter to the younger Peel, Dunn spoke of "the magnitude of my undertaking in order to instill the spirit of Loyalty & subordination into thousands of the Rising Generation & the adults in this Populous neighbourhood, where a great part of the people profess the Catholic Religion." To counter meetings critical of the government in 1817, he organized a loyal address to the Prince Regent, which over a thousand Catholics in the neighborhood signed, and which he presented to Peel, Sidmouth, and Castlereagh. Typically, he sought a dividend, as he wrote to Castlereagh: "We ask for no more in return for the Loyal Address which we presented last year to his Royal Highness than to obtain whatever Benefaction it may please his Royal Highness & the Government to bestow in order to enable us to pay the debt that we have contracted by erecting & maintaining an Establishment, which will contribute so much to preserve the loyalty & subordination of his Majesty's Catholic Subjects."

Referring to a subscription list, he wrote in the same letter, "Your Lordship will be glad to see that we are so much helped by our Protestant neighbours & that we live on such a good footing with them." While there was some truth in this, and there seems to have been a considerable lull in Protestant-Catholic tension, Protestant donations may simply have been an expression of duty, combined with a hope that it might do some good in the moralizing of the poor, rather than of any particular warmth toward Catholics. As the Rev. Charles Plowden of Stonyhurst wrote in 1818 after Dunn had painted the names of the subscribers on the school walls, he imagined that several of them would not be pleased to see their names there, "I mean all those, who subscribed from the motive, mentioned Luke 11.8."[154]

Dunn consistently fought to maintain the Preston mission under the control of himself and his fellow priests. This resulted in clashes with some of his wealthier parishioners. Between 1816 and at least the mid-1820s Dunn resisted the attempts of a party of laymen led by James Blanchard, attorney, and William Talbot, cotton merchant, to build a third chapel, which would be under lay rather than priestly control, and to replace the priests as trustees of St. Wilfrid's.[155] At the same time various members of the church hierarchy expressed concern at the independence and financial laxity of Dunn and his colleagues. Plowden of Stonyhurst upbraided him in February 1818 on the state of his finances, "I shall have a right to expect more economy, more frugality, than has been practised for the last thirty years." Although he acknowledged some improvement, he could still complain of "your frequent & expensive excursions of pleasure and amusement, frequent entertainments, parties &c[,] late hours[,] theatres &c. . . . Your friend abbé Mach, (Bp. of Trevers,) has often said, 'c'est une maison toute séculière.' You cannot be ignorant, that this has been the language of many other observers." He sent an emissary, Joseph Tristram, to examine the books. Dunn blocked this, leading Plowden to expostulate, "I must deplore the situation of Preston Mission, in the business of which, you allow me no influence, no control." Dunn scribbled a note at the top of this letter: "Most cynical & sarcastic. I am to disclose every thing relative to the Preston concern to him without the smallest assurance given to me that he will do any thing for us." In his reply, lamenting the fact that he had been asking for assistance for nearly three years without success, accusing Plowden of prevaricating, and partly blaming his fellow Preston priests for the mess at home, he threatened to resign:

[A]fter contributing much to make Preston the first Catholic Mission in England, with its Chapels, its Schools, its oratory, its cemetery, its garden, its chapel House & School furnished with Gas & its schools heated warmed [sic] with a Cockle or Hypocoust [sic] & after having got £10000 for other people & having received the title of the best beggar in England, when I found that no one would assist me, I had a right to retire & leave the management to others.[156]

Tristram in the summer of 1820 wrote to him, "What wounds me most, my Dear Sir, is to see an old missioner, after being the instrument in the hand of God for much good, sinking beneath the level of an ordinary Christian, in giving way to spleen and invective as your letters have been but too evident proof for a long time back." Early the following year he emphasized that Plowden was only asserting the same right he had exercised at other missions, the right of inspection into temporal concerns.[157]

After Dunn died in November 1827, it was left to his successor, Fr. Bird, to initiate in 1833 the building of a third chapel, St. Ignatius's, to try and keep pace with the expanding Catholic population. St. Augustine's followed in 1840, the first secular Catholic church in town, and by the mid-1840s both had new schools, run by the Irish Christian Brothers and the Irish Sisters of Charity.[158] Expansion into the northeast of town came toward mid-century in a manner familiar in the Anglican communion. William Talbot paid for the construction of the Talbot schools in the Maudlands, the first occasion in Preston that a single Catholic layman was so influential in a project, and his grandson, James Sidgreaves, banker, laid the first stone in May 1847. The school served as a chapel until the opening of St. Walburge's Church, built between 1850 and 1854 with money from donations, sermons, monthly collections from the working classes, lectures, tea parties, dances, bazaars, and a "Sale of Ladies' Fancy Work."[159]

In seeking to accommodate the growing population, which by now included sizable numbers of Irish immigrants,[160] Catholic priests had spearheaded the same kind of clerical revival that both the Evangelical and High Church church-builders were at once propelling and riding in the Established

Church. As John Bossy has pointed out, in 1770 the Catholic community was dominated by its secular aristocracy, but in 1850 by its clergy.[161] In Preston, Dunn, his fellow priests, and his successors were instrumental in making this happen, partly through their own insistence on the rights and dignities of the priesthood, partly because the leading laymen were not in a position to carve out their own individual territorial communities in partnership with a clergyman. Wealthy laymen were of course essential in financing the priests' buildings, but since the chapels tended to be built to accommodate a broad neighborhood, rarely did an individual's name or influence stand out.

Clerical Status Anxiety

Such were the attempts at church-building across the denominations, and it has become abundantly clear that many of the lower clergy, particularly within the Anglican Church, suffered acutely from a lack of money and of respect quite at odds with their exalted notions of the status of a reverend gentleman. We have already seen the insecurities in Blackburn Parish exploding into open confrontation, and that although there was nothing as dramatic elsewhere—possibly because the degree of impoverishment was not quite as marked, or the other vicars were not quite so tenacious of their rights as Whittaker, or the fractured patronage prevented one large and highly visible spider from dominating the web—the tensions between other vicars and incumbents, and between perpetual curacies or district chapelries with inadequate remuneration and the new, cushioned parishes could be considerable.

At the top of the pile, even Whittaker, with his ample income, worried how to maintain his own position as a gentleman, in order to interact correctly with the tiny, town-and-country-amphibious elite with wider connections who formed the corps of leading inhabitants (see Chapter 11). The lower clergy had more pressing concerns. By mid-century the augmentations from the ecclesiastical commissioners both to the district churches and the new Peel parishes had eased clerical poverty considerably. Where the patronage was private, under the Patronage Act, remunerations generally kept pace. No longer did clergymen depend so much upon fluctuating pew rents (under increasing pressure from grant-awarding bodies demanding an expansion of the numbers of free seats) nor did they feel quite so severely the loss of their fees. Even so, in most cases the income was only barely sufficient to maintain the status of a gentleman.[162] Many factors could make a difference between a "living" and a "starving": independent income; the number of children; whether or not the living had a parsonage, or whether rent had to be taken out of the salary;[163] whether repairs to the church fabric came out of the clergyman's own pocket; the amount of the almost unavoidable contributions for schools and other charities;[164] whether he had a second job, usually as a teacher.[165] Below the incumbents was a class of stipendiary curates, generally on even slimmer salaries (typically of £70-100) and on the whole supported by the Pastoral Aid Society or the Additional Curates' Society, who did the incumbents' bidding but at least had a steady income. These were usually younger men at the start of their careers and without heavy family or financial commitments who moved on relatively swiftly.

The archives are rich with examples of barely swimming, floundering, or sinking clerics. In Blackburn Parish, the Rev. Edward Ramsden of St. James's, Lower Darwen, received in 1830 £27 16s. 6d., arising solely from pew rents, and out of which the clerk had to be paid. He could only remain there because he had family property of his own. When the living became vacant six years later, and after an augmentation from Queen Anne's Bounty, it still only produced £56 a year. One applicant decided against the position, declining to take upon himself "a vow of poverty."[166] The living of Langho Chapel experienced a considerable decline in its tithe and a lengthy battle over the tithe's commutation. The Rev. Thomas Dent resigned in 1845 because the income had been less than £75 for some years, with no parsonage. His successor, the Rev. J. F. Coates, was caught up in the dispute in 1846 and received an income of only £11 in six months.[167] This had risen to £132 by 1851, but taxes reduced it to not much above £110.[168] The Rev. Edward Parker of Trinity claimed in 1849 that he had received no income in two years, since he had spent the annual £26 from pew rents on repairs to the building.[169] The 1851 religious census showed incomes varying between £74 for the incumbent of St. Peter's, Salesbury, and £179 for that of St. Mark's, Witton.[170] The Rev. Robert Hornby of Walton-le-Dale wrote that out of £153 he had paid a curate £80 a year for thirteen years, and I "shall feel obliged if parties requiring this return can render assistance towards getting the income of the living *increased*."[171] Only four years later the Rev. George Ashe of St. Mark's estimated that he needed nearly £300 a year to support and educate his family properly, at the standards expected of a gentleman.[172]

James Hardcastle of Firwood, bleacher, described the clergymen of Bolton Parish in 1847 as "miserably remunerated." He deplored the fact that part of the Lecturer's Closes, Church lands near the town center, had been lost to the building of the railway station rather than leased to support "the hardworking under paid Clergy of the Parish." Six years later he and a number of other influential Churchmen alleged that the twenty-three clergymen in the parish (sixteen incumbents, seven curates) only received an average annual income of £103 13s.[173] At St. George's, Little Bolton, the Rev. John Lyons changed benefices with the Rev. Neville Jones of London in 1847. This did not please the congregation nor, once he had arrived, the Rev. Jones. Lyons, he said, had told him that the benefice was worth over £330 a year, but he could only manage to scrape together £97. He wrote, "I am sorry to find, I have so sadly misunderstood Mr. Lyons in this matter," and that "all the affairs of St. George's seem to be in a sad state of Confusion."[174]

Many clergymen supplemented their income from other sources. For example, at All Saints', Little Bolton, the Revs. Francis Hodgson (incumbent 1768-1815) and Henry Crewe Boutflower (1828-34) served concurrently as headmasters of Bury Grammar School, a third, the Rev. Robert Bullock (1815-24) had a private school of his own in Tipping Place, and a fourth, the Rev. John Shepherd Birley (1834-43) was a landed gentleman and county magistrate holding the living in commendam for Francis Gartside Tipping, son of the patron of the living, Thomas Tipping of Davenport Hall near Congleton, Cheshire.[175] At Holy Trinity, Bolton, the first incumbent, the Rev. John Jenkins (1826-33), may have had a school at his home, Breightmet Hall, and his successor, the Rev. Alfred Hadfield, was an usher at Bolton Grammar School from 1834 to 1839.[176] The Rev. Robert Harris of St. George's, Preston, was headmaster of Preston Grammar School for forty-seven years.[177] The Rev. J. R. Alsop of Westhoughton augmented his income by taking in private pupils.[178] The Rev. Richard Bingham of Harwood claimed in 1851 that he could not do likewise since his parsonage was too small, both for clerical dignity and to accommodate pupils: it "is confessedly too small as a permanent residence for almost any Clergyman's family, and to the present Incumbent it is particularly inconvenient; precluding him also from augmenting his limited Clerical Income by such profits as might otherwise arise from a few Private Pupils."

Bingham was declared insolvent in the same year and resigned in 1852.[179] He was not alone in facing a financial crisis. The income of the Rev. T. R. Dickenson of Salesbury improved from £44 10s. in 1841 to £126 10s. in 1845, but during the years of low income he built up debts of nearly £300 and apparently had to move out of the area to escape his creditors.[180] Probably in 1855, when Immanuel, Feniscowles, was valued at £142 (minus £17 3s. in taxes and rates), a note in the Rushton volume comments, "Rev. Beilby is in difficulties & proposes to lay aside £50 per an: in liquidation of his debts."[181] The Rev. William Thistlethwaite of St. George's, Little Bolton, inherited a considerable sum from his mother in 1816 and became trustee for the part of the property left to her eldest son who lived in Upper Canada. He invested the two sums in John Cockshott's local manufacturing business, which collapsed in 1828 paying only a small dividend. Having to make good the sum for which he was in trust for his brother's heirs, he lost all his own property and had to fall back on a liberal subscription from his own congregation. In 1836, twenty-four of the congregation and friends paid for a curate to take on his duties because of the state of his health.[182] Then there was the sad case of the Rev. Henry Dunderdale, for thirty-four years curate of St. James's, Over Darwen, until a new incumbent in 1851, the Rev. Charles Greenway, had no more need of him. A year later, Archdeacon Rushton of Manchester, and the Revs. Parr of Preston, Sharples of St. Peter's, and Beilby of Immanuel, along with H. Haworth, solicitor, issued a private printed letter appealing on Dunderdale's behalf. He had received a very moderate salary during his curacy, had no private property, was now nearly sixty, had a wife and five children to support—and had contracted a debt of £604:

There is reason to believe that the fact of his being known to be embarrassed seriously militates against him in seeking preferment or clerical enjoyment; and now that he has lost the curacy by the appointment of an Incumbent who does not require his services, he has at present no means of subsistence but the kindness of a sister who is far from rich, or the loans of friends which he may never be able to repay. Were he set free from present anxiety and the prospect of ruin, he would gain confidence in renewed endeavours, aided by his growing family, to maintain his position as a clergyman, and head of a family who have no one to look to but himself for support.[183]

In 1855 the Rev. Henry Richardson, Bolton Parish Church Lecturer for nearly forty years, a man with a drink problem, was in deep financial difficulties. John Taylor and some other Churchmen bailed him out on condition he left town. He did so, paid back the money in installments and died around three years later.[184] The Rev. Gilmour Robinson wrote in 1854 about the dilapidated state of the buildings—the parsonage and a farm at Goosnargh—connected with the living of Tockholes: "I cannot see my friends, or purchase many things which I require, because all my spare cash is sunk in these buildings. Old benefices, it would appear, which have borne the heat & burthen of the day are, it seems quite overlooked, while the new ones like baby's toys are fondly regarded."[185] Financial worries, status anxieties, and an acute sense of grievance joined hands.

This clerical insecurity and marginality was significant for a number of reasons. It was rather less than edifying if the leadership of the parochial community was squabbling about status, rights, and money. If the incumbents had to spend a considerable portion of their time supplementing their income elsewhere their ministrations would inevitably suffer. If they were beholden for their limited incomes to particular individuals their independence of action was compromised; if curates were introduced into the parish by outside patrons or one of the two curates' societies a further space for contention and doctrinal difference was opened up. At these incomes the patrons could not expect the pick of the clerical litter; if the curates were competent, they had to suffer a great deal of snootiness from their betters, particularly if they were from Ireland or had been educated at St. Bees rather than Oxbridge: recall the comment that the Rev. Dickenson of Salesbury was "considerably vulgar"; or consider the remark of the Rev. R. N. Whitaker, vicar of Whalley, to Dr.

Whittaker in 1845 that he could suggest a candidate for the Feniscowles incumbency, one who was "not a member of that notorious body, whom we in the Parish of Whalley, call the Irish Brigade."[186] Until 1838, and in spite of persistent efforts, Whittaker could only raise the income for this chapel to £60, "a stipend upon wh. no clergyman who is a gentleman could subsist." Here as elsewhere, such a poor living promoted a high turnover of ministers, and the vicar had persistent problems in finding suitable replacements.[187]

Interdenominational Strife and Cooperation

We enter the realm of speculation in trying to establish a link between marginality and pontification; but it is not unreasonable to suggest that clerical preaching on thrift, temperance, and self-discipline was enhanced by the fact that many clergymen had no choice but to wrestle with these virtues in their own lives. Nor is it fanciful to suggest that much of the sound and fury of interdenominational invective lay in a calculated bid both for greater security through the benefits of membership of a broader communion and to draw borders against those who remained outside. This was well borne out in a series of letters between the Rev. John Bedford, Wesleyan minister, and the Rev. William Sutcliffe, curate of Farnworth, in 1842. Sutcliffe had been industriously visiting parishioners, including Wesleyans, and distributing tracts (among them the Rev. M. A. Gathercole's *Twenty-four Reasons why I dare not become a Dissenter*) that described Wesleyans as Dissenters and claimed that Wesley had taught immoral and licentious doctrines. Bedford, in his own exercise in boundary drawing, wished to distance Methodism from Dissent. The ensuing correspondence demonstrated clearly the contest for the same constituency, and both ministers' heightened sense of their own dignity and standing. Sutcliffe accused Wesleyans of circulating vituperative tracts against the Church. He quoted from one: "I cannot be a Churchman, because I am a follower of Jesus Christ"; and he threw in a quotation from an Independent tract for good measure: "*the mark of the beast is blazing on [the Church's] forehead . . . the* excellent *ministers and members of the Church of England, are an* unsightly *excrescence, growing upon it; and to esteem them, on this account, would be about as wise as the conduct of the Mahomedans in venerating idiots as saints.*" He denied the validity of Bedford's priesthood. Bedford, as a schismatic, could not be a reverend gentleman: he had to demonstrate gentlemanly status independently of occupational claims (Sutcliffe had treated him "with the courtesy which is due to a gentleman, such as you have shown yourself to be"). He patronizingly considered Bedford to be inexperienced in the tactics of controversy, or he would not have been so unwise as to challenge a minister of the Church of England. He implored the minister to

Cast away your prejudice, Sir, and let heaven's light beam upon your mind, and you will be painfully convinced that that reckless, impetuous man [Wesley], crossed the boundary line between *reformation and revolution*, and his followers, dissenting communities, are entangled by his false, unscriptural, and unhappy step in the difficulties which at present perplex them. Break up your class-meetings; those popish confessionals, which bind and fetter many a timid soul in worse "than Egyptian bondage," and hundreds and thousands will return to that holy church, who is the mother of us all.

Sutcliffe's vicar, the Rev. William Burns, weighed in with an insistence on the prerogatives of a clergyman of the Church: "His right to enter any house in this parish, as one of the lawfully appointed ministers, no man must dispute."[188]

Clerical gladiatorial combat aimed at defining territory, touting for proselytes, and establishing a voice or a claim to be heard for the individual minister as much as for the greater good of the denomination. These could be more-or-less courteous doctrinal debates conducted in the public prints. For example, in 1816, as a direct response to the zealous efforts of the Catholic priest in Blackburn, the Rev. Joseph Fletcher, Independent, published his *Lectures on the Principles and Institutions of the Roman Catholic Religion*. According to his son, Fletcher was a gentlemanly controversialist who managed the debate purely in religious terms.[189] Disputation at this temperature did not deeply rend asunder. But combat could be altogether more vicious. Unitarians, as deniers of the divinity of Christ, were favorite targets for "Christians" of all persuasions.[190] "While the Seraphim and the Cherubim before the throne of God, are sweeping their loudest, and most melodious strings to the praise and glory of Christ!," Independent ministers intoned in Bolton in 1796, "the proud socinian is degrading Him!" They vowed to form themselves into a gospel phalanx against the floodtide of the enemy.[191] Priestley and Price had "lived to see the death-blow given to their sentiments," the Rev. Thomas Macconnell of Grimshaw Street Chapel, Preston, preached in March 1824, "and I will not puzzle myself or trouble you with the uninteresting question, which rots the fastest, their sentiments in the land of the living, or their persons in the regions of the dead."[192] The prominence of certain Unitarians in the election politics of Bolton brought out streams of vitriol from the broadside scribblers in the early 1830s, while the attempt to establish a Unitarian congregation in Blackburn in 1833 provoked condemnation from an array of Anglican, Independent, Baptist, and Methodist pulpits.[193] In Preston, a Swedenborgian missionary from Manchester avoided the proffered use of the Unitarian chapel to give a lecture, the "public prejudice in this town being strong against Unitarians, and we being unwilling to identify ourselves with the people of that profession even in appearance." He engaged a room at the Bull Inn instead, but when some clergy and others put pressure on the landlord the Swedenborgians withdrew from the town. When a New Jerusalem chapel was eventually begun in 1843, the Rev. James Bonwell of Trinity Church took up the cudgel against this new "menace."[194]

What is noticeable in this range of examples is the extent to which any kind of movement provoked a response, while a certain tacit consensus on spheres of influence operated normally. The activities of a Catholic priest, the increase in the number of Catholic worshippers, the arrival of Unitarian or Swedenborgian or Methodist missionaries, the zeal of a new curate, the political involvement of Unitarians: all stimulated the defensive propping up of barricades. A settled pattern was rarely threatening. A visitor, approaching on foot the village of Rivington, described what he encountered:

On one side of the green was a deal table, from which a field preacher was holding forth with passionate, but fruitless energy; for, on the other side, and at the back of the crowd, was the parochial man of God, who had issued from his parsonage, armed with its largest tea-tray and the hall door key, and was battering the japan in the service of orthodoxy. No military music could more effectually neutralise the shrieks of battle. The more the Evangelist bellowed, the faster went the parish gong. It was impossible to confute the drum ecclesiastic, and the Methody's brass was fairly beaten out of the field by the Churchman's tin.[195]

But even in Rivington, the church and the Presbyterian/Unitarian chapel co-existed peacefully, the clergyman supporting the chapel library, and either church or chapel closing when an anniversary sermon was taking place at the other.[196]

The privileged position of the Established Church divided it from mainstream Dissent more than anything else. This became one of the major political issues of the 1830s,[197] given added bite by government reforms which left some Anglican clergymen feeling beleaguered and betrayed.[198] Dissenting clergymen led the local assault on the establishment and in favor of voluntarism. Their status was generally more precarious than the lower Anglican clergy's, as many of the latter did not scruple to tell them. Buoyed by the swelling prosperity of their own congregations, their voice of protest could be raised in volume while the barriers toward complete clerical-gentlemanly status seemed increasingly irksome. These were familiar milltown figures, part of an easily recognizable group that saw no conflict between Christian morality, political economy, and philosophical radicalism. In Blackburn the Rev. Francis Skinner, minister of Mount Street United Presbyterian Church, was the loudest of these propagandists in the 1830s, and it was his activity on the local political stage that transformed him from the unknown leader of a struggling, secessionist congregation to one of the town's foremost public figures. Central to his position was his belief in the independent, moral agent, unfettered in life's race, free to internalize the ordering values of Christian morality and to maximize his economic potential. He "saw that the dissemination of the knowledge and influence of the gospel was associated with just legislation, with cheap food, with unrestricted industry, with freedom everywhere of body and mind, of conscience and religious profession." Hence he was prominent in temperance, antislavery, and Repeal campaigns, and vehemently supported the "liberation" of the Church from state patronage and control.[199]

In 1836 Skinner crossed swords with Dr. Whittaker, after the vicar had appeared to categorize all the enemies of the Church as "a triple confederation of Superstition, Fanaticism, and Atheism,—an unholy alliance indeed!" Skinner took umbrage, and the two of them proceeded to trade insults in a public exchange of letters.[200] Whittaker decided to enlarge the controversy to embrace a consideration of the merits of the established as opposed to the voluntary system in a series of open letters addressed to a leading local Dissenter, William Eccles, attorney. Part I he provocatively entitled "The Blackburn Marsyas; or The Skinner Skinned."[201] He laid out very clearly his view that the Established Church was a substantial obstacle in the path of radicalism, that confiscation of Church property was a form of theft, and that allowing congregations to appoint their own ministers—making the choice of a minister dependent on "the voice of a multitude"—was loathsome.[202] But whether this level of invective did more harm than good to his cause is uncertain. The debate caused a stir in the town and provoked unfavorable editorial comment. One correspondent went so far as to claim that the vicar's writings "would do honour to the most accomplished *Fish-fag* of Billingsgate." Public indignation, we are told, pelted the vicar's notices on the walls around town with mud.[203] On the other hand, Whittaker gained some private support. The Rev. H. W. McGrath of Walton-le-Dale, for example, opined that Skinner had richly deserved his treatment, "and certainly you have pickled him."[204]

In Darwen, the Rev. Joseph Hague of Ebenezer Chapel and James Greenway, prominent Churchman and millowner, joined in battle in 1834. In defending the Established Church, Greenway saw as evidence of its divine sanctification the luminous cross that had appeared to Constantine, prompting him to raise Christianity from the dust and unite it to the state. He supported the exaction of a church rate on the grounds that Messrs. Hiltons, Eccles Shorrock, Potter, and Ross, Darwen Dissenting manufacturers and employers of large numbers, should not be exempted "from contributing to a rate or fund for the special instruction and spiritual consolation in sickness and in health of the poorer classes." Hague, in reply, brought out clearly the sense of grievance of second-class citizenship. The privileging of the members of one religious community, he said, degraded and stigmatized others who were equally good members of society. Giving a voluntary donation for the needs of another denomination was proper and good, a generous practice all sects followed; but a compulsory levy was altogether objectionable.[205]

The foremost polemicist for disestablishment in Bolton was the Rev. Franklin Baker of Bank Street Unitarian Chapel, radical reformer, Repealer, political economist, antislavery advocate, and a defender of factories. In May 1832, as the Reform crisis reached its climax, he lectured on the evils of church establishments: the Church of England displayed an unchristian inequality in gradations of rank, duty, and emolument, it imposed mental fetters (infant baptism, the catechism, the Thirty-Nine Articles) on clergy and laymen, and it was extravagant, wasteful, and a hindrance to good government.[206] Slade, the vicar, the loudest Boltonian voice in upholding a national religion, argued in contrast that Dissenters benefited from the charitable toleration and friendly shade of the Church establishment; if it should fall, the sects would fall with it. For a glimpse of a dreadful future without a National Church, one only needed to look at America: "nothing can be more unsatisfactory than the state of religion in that lax and latitudinarian country."[207] The Rev. Charles Wilbraham, formerly a Bolton curate, returned to the same theme in 1846. After a visit to the United States he felt he was in a position to extol the "beauty and wisdom of the Parochial System of England," where "*every* individual is in some measure placed under the spiritual superintendence of a Minister of Christ." Contrast this with America: "Religion is there a voluntary matter. Each man does what is right in his own eyes—some join one sect—some another—some none. The religion of a country should never be left, as it were, to chance. The souls of men should be cared for, whether they may desire it or not."[208] Parr, vicar of Preston, would not have dissented. In his Guild sermon in 1842, he stressed a further advantage for God's Own Nation of the establishment: "if we are an holy people unto the Lord, a special people unto him above all people that are on the face of the earth, it is owing *to the predominance of the Church of England.*"[209]

The Dissenters never won on the broader church-and-state question, and thus the status difference between the Church and Nonconformity remained intact—clergymen of the Church, however poor and insecure, were more readily given the benefit of the doubt in their claim to gentlemanly status. But on the more accessible issue of church rates, the Church conceded defeat relatively rapidly in the towns by making a tactical withdrawal. The vestry was a *locus classicus* for a radical voice in the unreformed towns, allowing in vestry meetings all ratepayers a vote and many non-ratepayers a say. The church rate was consequently vulnerable at the hands of working-class and Dissenting-middle-class attendees. In Blackburn a parish rate had built, expensively, the new parish church, consecrated in the autumn of 1827. The church-building trustees devolved the charge of the fabric onto the churchwardens, who signaled their intention to levy an additional rate to light and air the church. Following the example of other oppositions around the country, the radicals seized the opportunity, attended the vestry meeting in force and voted down the measure by a show of hands. Dixon Robinson, Anglican attorney, demanded a poll, and in the interim the broadsides and letters flew. Edward Hammond, an operative spinner and a leader of the opposition, addressed a crowd of five or six hundred on Blakeley Moor: "Consider, all England have their eyes upon you, and your triumph will be the signal for general opposition to clerical oppression." In the midst of misery and distress, he said, the vicar was demanding a tax "to support a church already bloated with wealth." The property-weighted voting under Sturges Bourne's Act pushed the rate through by a substantial margin after a five-day poll.[210] But it was something of a Pyrrhic victory. It was not the last church-rate clash in town—there were further protests over ordinary expenditure in at least 1832 and 1834—but there was increasingly a feeling in the Church party that if the only way to force through a rate was by way of a divisive poll that encouraged popular agitation and put the Church on the defensive, it might be better to abandon the practice.[211] When the roof of the parish church went up in flames in 1831, the £2,000 needed to replace it was raised by a voluntary subscription in order to avoid a new and "intolerably oppressive" rate.[212]

In the largely rural parish of Deane, the church rate continued in existence, but only apparently after the big landowners rallied their tenants to pack a vestry meeting in 1833.[213] In Preston, the vicar, the Rev. Roger Carus Wilson, in seeking to enlarge a gallery of the parish church in 1836, reported that it was "wholly out of the question to look for pecuniary aid for this object to the Church-rates, seeing that these rates have for some years past been most imperfectly raised & that during the present year none has even been laid."[214] In Bolton, compulsory church rates were not collected after 1833, following a brief campaign against them,[215] a leading example of a "negotiation" of a new forced consensus between Church and Dissent/radicalism as they eyed each other's strength cautiously. The perils awaiting any attempt to reintroduce the rates resurfaced as late as 1849. The churchwardens posted the usual notice of a vestry meeting to levy a church rate, as they had for the previous sixteen years, but a rumor circulated that they were going to attempt a compulsory levy. This prompted the pasting up of placards calling for those who valued their independence to be present. The consequent large crowd that crammed into the vestry retired only upon being reassured that there was no intention to change the voluntary subscription.[216]

The beast might have been caged at the local level, but the potential still remained. A principle was at stake, one which repeatedly prompted leading Dissenters and Catholics, clerical and lay, to attend public meetings in line with national campaigns against the rate.[217] But while the debate grumbled on, providing persistent arenas of contention, ironically the de facto ending of church rates in the towns as the solution to the problem compounded the incumbents' money problems. In 1843, the Rev. George Levy of Emmanuel,

Bolton, wrote to the Church Building Society for a grant toward a new floor in his church, on the grounds that the church was "situated in the poorest district of this town among a population composed chiefly of hand-loom-weavers, and their being no church-rates in the parish." The following year he pointed out the vulnerability of impecunious clergymen to wealthy parishioners with ideas of their own. The bill for the floor and re-pewing had been greater than estimated because one of the churchwardens (probably Peter Ormrod) had given orders to put a molding around the windows, which had cost £30 and necessitated a coloring of the church. As Levy could not raise this additional sum, the warden "will therefore have to pay it himself, which he can well afford to do—But I need not tell you that a wealthy manufacturer will not scruple to pay a large sum to gratify his own taste, when he will not do it to carry out the plans of the incorporated Society, except he himself approves them—However much I regret this—It is a fact—and I cannot help it."[218] Thus the tendrils of insecurity, denominational divisions, money, and patronage intertwined.

Such were the divisions and rivalries. On the other hand, "What a strong principle of attachment is religion!" exclaimed the Rev. Joseph Fletcher, the Blackburn Independent minister, after a conversation with strangers in Blackpool in 1810:

Two persons from parts of the globe which are antipodes to each other, may be as widely distant as their respective countries, in their civil habits, and modes, and customs; but if they be genuine believers in Christ, and can by any means understand each other, their hearts will be one, and an astonishing union of feelings will be inspired by those grand, sublime, and interesting truths of the precious gospel on which they build their hopes and expectations. If such be the effect of a transient intercourse and communion *here*, what will *heaven* be! Glorious, transporting thought! To sit down with Abraham and the patriarchs,—Isaiah and the prophets,—Christ and the apostles,—with all the noble army of confessors, martyrs, and ministers, and believers, who compose the general assembly and church of the first-born![219]

A glimpse of Heaven, perhaps; but how successful in fact were the attempts at cooperation? In Bolton the Rev. William Thistlethwaite, the Evangelical minister of St. George's, was an active bridge-builder as one of the joint secretaries of the Bolton Auxiliary of the British and Foreign Bible Society from its formation in 1813. This society, confined to those subscribing a guinea a year, was cross-denominational, only insisting that half the committee be Anglican.[220] Thistlethwaite labored strenuously for this and other societies, including the SPCK and the Bolton Ladies' Auxiliary to the Society for Promoting Christianity among the Jews (formed at his instigation), and he was the first treasurer of the Bolton Missionary Association, a joint auxiliary to the SPG and the CMS.[221] On his death in 1838, the Rev. William Jones, Independent minister of Mawdsley Street Chapel and joint secretary of the Bible Society with him for the previous seventeen years, preached that his passing was a public calamity. "May the Church of England," he said, "have all her pulpits filled with ministers of equal talents and equal piety." He took the opportunity to preach unity:

[W]hatever may be the diversity of religious opinions respecting the form of church government—whatever may be the rites and ceremonies introduced—whatever difference of judgement may exist about its discipline and order—the fundamental doctrines of the divinity and atonement of our Lord Jesus Christ, are held by all religious denominations, with the exception of one. . . . It would be absurd for the subordinate divisions of a great army to enter into a controversy about the varieties of their uniform, when the approach of an enemy called for united exertion and undaunted courage.[222]

A fellow enthusiast for the Bolton branch of the Bible Society was the Rev. T. A. Ashworth of St. John's, Farnworth. He and the Rev. Joseph Dyson of Market Street Congregational Church reportedly canvassed the parish jointly every Wednesday to see who needed Bibles. They started from each other's residence alternately, kneeling down together and offering up a short prayer, one after the other, on their united labors.[223] Peter Rothwell, ironfounder, large employer, conservative, prominent townsman and Wesleyan often presided at Bible Society meetings, as well as at Wesleyan Missionary Society meetings. His cross-denominationalism extended to being a churchwarden at St. George's for a number of years, and when he died in 1849 the funeral procession included the vicar and the Rev. Jones of St. George's.[224]

Whittaker of Blackburn preferred to keep the religious societies denominational and poured his energies into the SPG and the SPCK, strictly Anglican affairs.[225] Even before his arrival, denominational rivalries had postponed the formation of a Bible Society. Fletcher, an enthusiast for evangelical cooperation across boundaries, noted in 1814 on the formation of the Bolton Bible Society that, "Unhappily, ecclesiastical prejudices, and the *torpedo* touch of high church influence, have prevented us from establishing one here." When it was eventually launched, he played a key role.[226] The vicar's influence seemingly kept the Anglican clergy and Churchmen away from Bible Society meetings, though the Rev. Jackson Porter, Evangelical incumbent of St. John's, chaired at least one annual meeting, in 1835, and may have been an exception.[227]

During the first two decades of the century in Preston, where the Unitarian Rev. John Rudd and the Catholic priest Joseph Dunn were two of the most prominent players in elite society, and in the relative harmony created by coalition politics, a tradition of extensive cooperation across denominations developed. Founded in October 1812, the Preston Auxiliary Bible Society aimed, like the others, at "nothing less than an union of able Divines and Laymen associated for the purpose of promoting the moral improvement of the age," as John Grimshaw, JP, put it in 1815. Only *that*, given the inadequacy of the penal code, "could effectually establish morality and good order." The Rev. Thistlethwaite, visiting from the Bolton Bible Society, spoke to the purpose of the society in producing more efficient, collective action, and as a by-product promoting greater harmony:

Agreed in one point of far greater importance than all in which they differ, they have united, in order that they may act with much greater effect as a body, than they could hope to do as individuals. This society, therefore, has had an astonishing effect in uniting together the different denominations of Christians. Many attempts have been made with that view, but all have hitherto failed, because they attempted too much: compromises of principle were required which could not be made on this side or the other; but this institution requires no sacrifice of principle, no compromise of opinion; it only asks support in distributing to your fellow-creatures the sacred volume, in the authorized version, with out note or comment.

Fletcher of Blackburn agreed that "The Bible, The Bible Alone" was a standard behind which all soldiers of the cross had gathered, and asked, "Has [the Bible Society] not softened the asperities of party-feeling, and increased the facilities of friendly intercourse?"[228]

On his arrival in Preston in 1817 the Rev. Wilson became a vice president of the society—the president was Samuel Horrocks, MP—and at the annual meeting in October he suggested that there were few modes in which he could better promote the welfare of Christianity and the Church. Moreover, "Amongst the *collateral* benefits of the institution, it is no small one, that it has offered a closer approximation among Christians of various confessions, than the world has seen for many centuries."[229] But it is clear that this level of cooperation, only on very specific issues, could scarcely disguise fundamental tensions and differences. For example, in December 1833 a public meeting chaired by Thomas Batty Addison formed the Preston District Providence Society, a successor to the Ladies' Provident Society started the previous March. The Rev. John Clay explained the society's purpose: to unite the ranks of the wealthy so that they could establish friendly relations with their poorer brethren, teach them the value of domestic economy, sobriety, and forethought, and induce them to set aside small savings for the hour of need. The vicar was present and observed that most in attendance were of a different communion from him. There was certainly a need for such an institution, and he was willing to meet them on neutral ground to promote the same objectives, as he had done on every other possible occasion; but he protested that the meeting had been called without due notice to the clerical body, and in particular to him, his due as vicar of the town. The intention of the society "appeared to him to be nothing more nor less than to wrest the pastoral care of the community out of the hands of the established clergy of the place." Clay, apparently only one of two Establishment ministers involved in the venture, protested that he saw nothing in the resolution affecting the care of the town by the regular clergy and said that they had not approached the vicar because nine or ten months previously he had been firmly against the proposition.[230]

At the same time, Wilson was setting on foot the Preston District Visiting Society, planned he said before the beginning of the Ladies' Provident Society. This had very similar aims: to bring the wealthier classes into closer contact with the indigent, encouraging a better domestic management among the poor, and to aid the clergy in their pastoral care, strengthening the poor's sense of religious obligation. Members of the Church supervised by its ministers would conduct it, not with a sinister eye to proselytization—there was to be no interference with the religious beliefs of Dissenters—but so that the Church could fulfill its duty to its own people while manifesting a kind, catholic and beneficent spirit toward all. Wilson thought that most of these objectives were unattainable by Provident Societies, since they were governed by people of various religious denominations, and that could only result in painful conflict, injurious compromise, or religion being omitted.[231]

Wilson again made use of an outside stimulus in pursuit of his evangelical goals in April 1836 when, at a meeting chaired by Peter Hesketh Fleetwood, MP, he proposed the formation of a local society in association with the London Lord's Day Observance Society and inveighed against bathing carts, newsrooms, and the like in use on Sundays. One attendee tried to argue for the inclusion of Dissenters and Catholics on the committee as well as Churchmen, but Fleetwood explained that they were merely imitating the parent body in setting up an exclusive committee. The following week the Rev. R. Slate, the Independent minister, wrote an open letter to the vicar protesting against this exclusion, warning, "let us *all* take care that party zeal is not indulged so as to endanger the common interests of religion and of souls." He claimed that the vicar had it in his power to become the bond of union among all evangelical Christians in the parish, and that ministers of various denominations were willing to unite with him in everything calculated to promote the spiritual welfare of the people.[232]

Such were the dilemmas between constructing exclusive communities and in making common cause across a broader evangelical front. Many clergymen were willing to make Protestant alliances on at least some issues—the sharing of short-time platforms, for example (Chapter 9), or antislavery associations.[233] But the level of cooperation in religious societies varied significantly, depending to a large extent on the beliefs of the different vicars. Though it had its limitations, Preston's record of interdenominational cooperation was reasonably good, and this may be why there is apparently little evidence for major clashes on the church-and-state question in the town. The ways in which the different denominations sought to work together or against each other, to create broader evangelical or Christian communities or to achieve rigid sectarian exclusivity, to project a combined or a singular voice, presents us with a microcosm of bourgeois public life.

Anti-Popery and Anti-Tractarianism

There was one further area that might elicit a measure of cross-denominational support: Protestant unity against Roman Catholics. In the early part of the century, as the strength of anti-Catholicism seemed to diminish, this did not seem promising. Dr. Thomas Dunham Whitaker, Evangelical vicar of Whalley, wrote in 1801 of the way in which the Revolutionary War had made friends of enemies to tackle the greater evil:

[A]s we and they hold the fundamentals of Christianity in common, as both theirs and ours are true churches, claiming their respective rights in succession from the Apostles, during a contest like the present all memory of ancient wrongs ought, as far as possible, to be abolished; all subordinate distinctions of discipline and doctrine overlooked; and the ministers of religion, however separated in the exercise of their respective offices, cordially united in their efforts against the powers of earth and hell, which are leagued against them all.

The sight of "the distressed ecclesiastics of France" seeking refuge in Britain did not seem to indicate that Catholicism was a major threat.[234] "I think that from the frequency of their intermarriage of late years with Protestants, and from the appointment of Protestant trustees in Catholic families, which, as you know, has been the case in many instances, their influence has, upon the whole, been and is on the decline," the Evangelical Rev. Philip Nicholas Shuttleworth of Preston reassured the Speaker of the House of Commons in 1816.[235] It was this kind of atmosphere of semi-tolerance that enabled Fr. Joseph Dunn in Preston to swim with ease in Protestant genteel waters. The Rev. Mr. Shepherd, Catholic priest in Bolton during the same period, was equally tolerated, according to one witness. He was "a gentleman in every sense of the word—far above the class of Catholic clergy who succeeded him. He dressed well, wore powder, was highly educated and polished in his manner, and was respected by the whole community."[236] The Rev. Edward Kenyon, one of Blackburn's Catholic priests, was able to claim at the opening in 1819 of Pleasington Priory, a flamboyant Gothic chapel built by John Francis Butler on his estate, that a milder sun had dawned upon Catholics.[237]

But while this milder sun made Emancipation possible, anti-Catholicism had simultaneously by the 1820s come to be the primary organizing principle of the "Right."[238] For sections of the Church party, nurtured on a diet of nationalist Protestant constitutionality defined against Catholic and radical "others" within and without, allowing Catholics into public office would have been akin to permitting avowed communists a role in government in the United States of the 1950s. Bolton Churchmen began to ring the firebell when George Canning, pro-Emancipation, became prime minister. William Hulton warned at a Wellington Club anniversary in Stockport in 1827 that, "The gigantic strength of Protestant Ascendancy may lie dormant for a time, but let peril approach and we shall see it roused in such a manner that its enemies will quake at its approach."[239] In May he reported that there had been great stirrings in Pitt Clubs across the region.[240] The Rev. Slade prepared an address to the king, numerously signed by local elite Tories, praising his "protecting and maintaining, against every attempted innovation, the ancient barriers of our Established Church and our Protestant Faith."[241] But then Canning died, and three Bolton clergymen reportedly—though Slade strongly denied it—expressed their satisfaction "in the most indecent manner." For the Church party, the formation of a Wellington administration with Robert Peel in the Home Office was confirmation that the Church was safe.[242]

Peel had refused to serve under Canning. As he wrote to Hulton, "Could I with any regard to what is due to my own Character—and the Character of public men generally—acquiesce in an Arrangement by which the whole influence and Patronage of the Station of Prime Minister is to be transferred from the most marked Opponent to the most marked Advocate of the Catholic claims?"[243] He came to meet the local notability at Hulton Park in October 1828, and at a public breakfast in Bolton hosted by the boroughreeve he lauded Hulton, prominent at Peterloo, for his magisterial services. Hulton in return proclaimed his lasting political faith in Peel. Hence the sense of betrayal when Wellington and Peel pushed through Emancipation in response to the situation in Ireland. Hulton wrote to the Stockport Wellington Club that he could "no longer remain a member of a Club bearing the name of an individual who would rob his country of any part of that constitution to which our Protestant Church owes her only security."[244] Slade, at an anniversary dinner of the Bolton Church and King Club in March 1829, remarked that,

The country lay under vast obligations to the Duke of Wellington, but he would forfeit all claims to their gratitude if he allowed the fundamental principles of the Constitution to be destroyed. He had, however, always acted upon expediency, and when the moment arrived that he thought it expedient to give up our national bulwarks, rather than encounter the spirit of faction, he embraced it. But the conduct of Mr. Peel could admit of no such plea; no one, not even Mr. Peel himself, could answer the arguments which he (Mr. Peel), previous to his secession, had advanced against further concessions. When partaking of our hospitalities he was acting under a mask, and knew that he was about to break in upon the Constitution. His public character was sunk beyond the possibility of recovery, and he was more an object of pity than of indignation.[245]

A "Bolton Protestant Committee," chaired by Hulton, drew up a petition to the king; the Rev. George Marsden, Wesleyan minister, and Joseph Ridgway moved for its adoption. The more ardent Churchmen even boycotted a celebration of the king's birthday in April because he had eventually signed the Emancipation Act.[246]

In Blackburn, too, dormant anti-Catholicism flared up with the external stimulus of Emancipation, given greater momentum by the building of a new, enlarged St. Alban's Church at Larkhill, opened in 1826.[247] At the end of 1828 the Rev. James Sharples, the new priest, chaired a meeting at the New Inn of the "Friends of Civil and Religious Liberty"—reportedly attended by over twelve hundred people—to petition for Emancipation. "Bound as I am," the priest said, "in the chains of unmerited degradation, fettered in my liberties by bigotry and intolerance, I claim the privileges of a free born son of Britain.—(Loud Cheers.)" The meeting resolved on "the incontrovertible principle,—'that no Government has a right to deprive its subjects of the benefits of its constitution, merely on account of their strict and conscientious adherence to religious tenets, which are not incompatible with the allegiance of the subject, or the safety of the state.'"[248] Leading Churchmen, in contrast, responded to the Emancipation Bill in February 1829 with a petition: they feared that Parliament was about "to remove those substantial props and supports which have been erected by the foresight of our ancestors, to maintain and perpetuate our Protestant Constitution of these Realms." Roman Catholics could not be truly loyal when their consciences were under the dominion of a foreign prelate.[249]

Whittaker, never so virulent as when he was confronting the Papists, was at the forefront of this revived anti-Catholicism. He claimed for himself the privilege of being a Catholic priest,[250] belonging "to a pure, apostolic church, as nearly approaching to perfection in doctrine and government as any that has existed since the apostolic time."[251] The Romish Church had gone astray from the true path. As he explained to a meeting of the Blackburn Auxiliary of the British Society for Promoting the Religious Principles of the Reformation in 1829, "If the Romish church brands me with heresy, I hurl back the charge upon her, and will maintain not only that she is in error, but is infected with *heresy*—downright, palpable, and awful heresy. (This last sentence, pronounced with strong emphasis, and much animation, produced a deep impression on the meeting, and was answered by thunders of applause.)"[252] In his published sermons, his letters and in weightier tomes, Whittaker maintained his anti-Catholic momentum and unpacked all his prejudices against the Catholic Church. He accused it of tyranny over body and soul, and of being the "father and abettor of persecution and bloodshed."[253] The country was swarming with Jesuits, "actively employed in propagating the religious tenets of the dark ages."[254] In Samlesbury chapelry, "to combat a Jesuit priest, who has lately established himself in that neighbourhood," he appointed the Rev. Patrick Law, active against Catholics in Ireland, whose "chief forte is against Popery."[255] This competition for hearts and souls gained added impetus during the thirties in the town itself, where Catholicism and poor, illiterate Irish immigrants appeared to expand together, squashed into the new slums around the mills, the very areas where the vicar wished to extend the influence of the Anglican Church, and the sort of people he wished to capture as subordinate members of a loyal, controlled, hierarchical community.[256]

In Bolton, Slade was ever ready to raise the cry of the Church in danger, and in 1839 drew attention to the "gigantic" strides of Catholics to positions of power: numerous appointments in Ireland, a commissioner of education in England to assist in unchurching the young, a secretary at the Admiralty who had authority in the appointment of chaplains, a privy councillor who poured advice into the royal ear. He spoke of "the capital error of admitting Rome to a share in the executive government of Protestant people; of a people whose forefathers shed their best blood to cast off her yoke," and added, "I believe we shall never be easy or safe till the yoke is cast off again."[257] In the same month, the Rev. William Burdett, a curate of Deane, preached the anniversary sermon of the Gunpowder Plot in Deane Parish Church on the theme that not only was popery "*unchanged*, but its very *principle* is that it is unchangeable."[258] The 5th of November, that twofold anniversary of triumph over popery,[259] served as an annual public commemoration of anti-Catholicism, when people should, as the *Blackburn Standard* put it, "return thanks to the Great Disposer of all events for his merciful deliverance of the nation from the darkness and tyranny of Rome, and for the blessings of civil and religious freedom which have been vouchsafed to the people of England so abundantly and so permanently above all others."[260]

In this manner, sermons, tracts, and treatises kept alive the anti-Catholic tradition. Yet, because many of its proponents repeatedly deployed it as a primary means of self-definition for both the Church and the cause of Conservatism,[261] the prospects for a more all-embracing unity of Protestants proved weak, and bodies transcending party tended to be ephemeral. For example, Bolton established a presumably short-lived Protestant Association in November 1840. It probably owed more to peripatetic crusaders than to local initiative[262] and was open to all five-shilling annual subscribers (or a penny a week from the poorer classes) who were members of or friendly to the Church of England. It began in an evangelical "Great Protestant Meeting" in St. George's School, Little Bolton, chaired by Peter Rothwell, the Methodist ironfounder. The centerpieces were the tirades of the anti-Catholic firebrands, the Revs. Hugh Stowell and Hugh M'Neile. Stowell promised to strive until every popish mass-house was turned into a church, every popish priest into a Protestant clergyman, every poor papist into a good Protestant. His rant was overtly political:

[I]f we wished to get out the party at present in power, it was not simply because they were Whigs, but because they became the supple engines of Popery, the willing tools and slaves of O'Connell and the priesthood—(Prolonged Cheering). . . . Let them keep their places, if they will but say, "Down with Popery; up with Protestantism! No Popish aggression; Protestant ascendancy for ever!"—(Prolonged Cheering).

Local clergymen joined in. The Rev. Walter Gibbs of St. Peter's, Halliwell, who clearly believed that the end of the world was indeed nigh, inveighed comprehensively against the errors, delusions, frauds, abominations, unholy despotism, idolatry, degrading superstitions, blasphemous and revolting doctrines, and withering influence of popery. The Rev. J. Lyons of St. George's, who had convened the meeting, said of the opposition, "we of the Church of England profess to be Catholics in the real sense of the word, while they are only schismatics from the Catholic Church, adherents of the Pope, and, therefore, we give them their proper and distinctive appellation—Papists—(Loud Applause)."[263]

Meetings held in opposition to the Maynooth Endowment Act of 1845 looked more promising for the cause of interdenominational cooperation, but ended by demonstrating its limits. The first, in Blackburn in April 1845, met in the Assembly Room to petition against Peel's proposal to increase the grant to the college. The coroner, John Hargreaves, was in the chair, and at least fifteen Anglican clergymen and six Dissenting ministers joined him on the platform. As there were a large number of Catholics in the audience, the gathering was not a quiet one. The Revs. T. G. Walsh and T. Sharples moved that all support by the state for a superstitious and idolatrous system like the Church of Rome was calculated to bring down the judgment of God on this Protestant country. The Rev. S. Allen of Clayton Street Wesleyan Methodist Chapel thought that national support for popery would be a national sin, precipitating great national punishment. He was keen to stress Protestant unity. But then the united front began to disintegrate. The Rev. A. Fraser, Independent minister, proposed an amendment: that the permanent endowment of Maynooth was impolitic and unjust; and that grants or endowments to *any* sect or party, Protestant or Catholic, were manifestly unfair. The Rev. Francis Skinner seconded and drew attention to the discourteous treatment he and his Dissenting colleagues had received in regard to their prior requests whether the meeting was for the Established Church alone. The chairman lost all control of the meeting, and he and the Anglican clergy left the room. William Hoole, Independent schoolmaster, took the chair, proposed the amendment, and only five people voted against it.[264]

The second was a meeting of the Preston Protestant Association, chaired by the vicar as president. The Rev. Hugh M'Neile of Manchester gave the main address. Recycling a rhetoric of reaction familiar to many persecuted minorities on the receiving end, he insisted that he was a friend of religious liberty, including his own, which was under attack; he was merely acting in self-defense. The Rev. J. Priestley, Wesleyan, urged the meeting—which required little persuasion—to spare no effort until Protestant money was appropriated solely for the purpose of propagating Protestantism. The Rev. R. Slate, Independent, was present, he said, "to prove that there is more union amongst us Protestants than some imagine." Although he opposed *all* grants from government for religion, now was not the time to stress his Nonconformity. He delighted in the opportunity he occasionally had of uniting with his Christian brethren in accomplishing a good object, and he had been a member of the Bible Society for forty years and of the Religious Tract Society for twenty-five years in Preston. But he revealed the distance within the ranks of the profession when he said, addressing the vicar, "Sometimes, Sir, I have had the pleasure of exchanging pulpits with some of my friends with whom I differ on certain points; and happy shall I be if ever the day shall come when a minister of the Established Church and an humble Independent minister can exchange pulpits."[265]

The anti-Catholic crusade peaked in one of the most intriguing mid-century developments, redolent of both nationalist hubris and anxiety, the twin pillars of exclusivism and intolerance. The reaction to the "Papal Aggression"—the reestablishment of the territorial hierarchy of the Roman Catholic Church—in 1850 exhibited many of the characteristics of a moral panic: the displacement of real fears about an unstable social and economic structure, exacerbated by the influx of impoverished Irish into Lancashire towns and cities; a public primed by three centuries of anti-Catholic rhetoric that had no difficulty in identifying Rome as a principal public enemy; a government that had every incentive to divert attention from its own shortcomings, at home and abroad; a Church and other Protestant denominations that saw the advantage in cementing loyalties to themselves by defining themselves against the "anti-national Other"; and a largely compliant media, willing to inflate a trivial event into one of the passionate issues of the age.[266]

In an appeal for unity, the *Blackburn Standard* urged that minor differences be merged in a great drive to beat back tyrannous, body-and-soul-enslaving Rome.[267] A Protestant meeting in December, chaired by Joseph Feilden, allegedly attracted over sixteen hundred people. Feilden said that the resolutions had been framed to include Nonconformists, but although there were at least some prominent Dissenters present, most of them decided not to take part. The speakers put forward a variety of reasons for their ferocious denunciation of the aggression. The Rev. R. T. Wheeler of St. John's prepared a potent brew of nationalist rhetoric, arguments about the enemy within (Romanism had been spreading in the Church; "The premature and monstrous child, now brought to light, was conceived at Oxford, though delivered at Rome") and the thin end of the wedge ("'If you give them an inch they'll take an ell'"; Pio Nono might be succeeded by a Hildebrand). Capturing the apocalyptic mood of the moment, he outlined one of the principal myths of national consciousness—the unfolding of Protestantism and liberty in an incessant struggle against Rome—in a particularly vivid passage:

Europe is watching to see whether Protestant England will quail before the key and the triple crown. (Cheers, and "Never.") Many a Protestant state on the continent is anxiously looking for the result of our contest, as an index of its own fate. Shadows of the future seem gathering around us. Our country appeals to us with all its sympathies of hearth and home, of peace and liberty, its religion, and its God. (Loud cheers.) Our babes appeal to us; generations yet unborn seem to start into existence, and beseech you not to deliver them, bound hand and foot, to Roman despotism. (Renewed cheers.) And at this moment, if the dead can see us, "a noble army of martyrs" is watching over us; our own sainted Ridley, Latimer, Taylor, and Hooper, are looking down from their heavenly seats on that land which yet is warm with their spilt blood, white with their calcined bones, and lighted with the fire which slew them. (Enthusiastic cheering.)

Other speakers hammered home the same logic: they had nothing against Catholics, only against the principles of popery and the dominion of the pope; look at what this tyranny had already accomplished—the 1641 Irish massacre, the St. Bartholomew's Day massacre, and so forth; the glorious constitution was at stake; government was partly to blame by introducing Emancipation and by its pro-Catholic measures in Ireland. John Baynes, Anglican manufacturer, neatly linked the Bible, British liberty and greatness, and the preservation from revolution in 1848:

In those countries where the Bible is withheld from the people, we have seen thrones tottering, princes seeking safety by flight, nations trembling, the sense of security gone, civil war has done its desolating work, and one dynasty has been overthrown by the excited and lawless mob, whilst our own beloved country, the land of Bibles, has been comparatively at rest, and enjoying peace, happiness, and security unattained elsewhere. (Applause.) To what principle is this owing? It is to those principles which result from the sanctified perusal of the Bible, and the pure faith based upon it, which prepared Britain for the enjoyment of civil liberty, and in due time secured to her the possession of it; hence she has become the greatest of the nations, blessed above all in the possession of peace, wealth, influence, and power. (Applause.)

The meeting ended with the national anthem, three tremendous cheers for the queen, and three groans for the pope.[268]

In Bolton, the *Chronicle* considered the Aggression to be equally momentous, editorializing that "the one subject of the Pope's attempt to assume the sovereignty of this realm, will place the year 1850 among the most remarkable in the roll of time." A large meeting in the Temperance Hall at the end of November, chaired by Peter Ainsworth, attracted many of the Established clergy, plus two Methodist ministers and an Independent minister. The speakers once again brought out the linkage between the nation, its Church, and domesticity very strongly. William Ford Hulton, invoking the name of John Bull in opposition to the Italian Bull (which produced "loud and continued cheering"), recited a verse (itself productive of "great cheering"):

Our glorious institutions, and our good old English laws,
Have wrung from e'en our bitterest foes both rapture and applause:
O, his must be a coward's heart that could not make a stand,
For wife and child, and hearth and home, in such a native land:
Then let us give one hearty cheer—refuse it ye who dare—
God save old England's Church and Queen, be this our constant prayer.

The Rev. Edward Girdlestone exhorted the meeting to a messianic struggle "between darkness and light—between falsehood and truth,—between, on the one side, Popery, Anglo-Catholicism, and Infidelity; and on the other, the religion of the Word of God." Thomas Ridgway Bridson declared that he had been a lifelong advocate of civil and religious liberty and of Catholic Emancipation, but the present popish movement was monstrous; let them be staunch to their Protestantism, their Church, and their Queen.[269]

In Preston, editorial opinion was divided. While the *Pilot* protested against the outrage to the Protestant constitution, the *Chronicle* really could not see why the Catholic leaders should not call themselves the prelates of Westminster, Sheffield, Birmingham, and Liverpool, instead of the bishops of Melipotamus, Trachis, Hetalona, and Tioa, and vicars-apostolic in England. Let them. They were not dangerous. The agitation was injurious to the cause of civil and religious liberty, and could only be explained because the people of England were generally at a loss for some excitement and the Papal Bull acted as an antidote to the foggy, wet, and cold November weather. The editor of the *Guardian* commented, "Adhering to the principle which we have always recognised that every denomination of Christians has a perfect right to arrange its own ecclesiastical constitution as it thinks fit, providing that no encroachment is made upon the rights of others, we cannot but dissent from the proposal to bring our government into conflict with the pope on this question."[270] But a meeting of Nonconformists in the Corn Exchange at the start of December, chaired by the mayor, brought together the Revs. J. Spence (Independent), S. Kay (Wesleyan), R. Slate (Independent), Edward Shelton (Wesleyan), J. Jenkins (Countess of Huntingdon's Connexion), and J. Thompson (Wesleyan Association) with twelve hundred others in petitioning against the Aggression.[271]

The Rev. Parr made his own opinion clear in a sermon to the corporation in March of the following year. He called for legislation to defend liberty against "an aggressive power; a power in itself intolerant and oppressive; fatal to freedom of thought; fatal to freedom of conscience; fatal to freedom of action." His version of the island story was one of perpetual struggle against the triple-crowned tyrant until Parliament succeeded in casting him out of the kingdom. But Rome was always attempting to resume her power, first from above in the shape of Charles and James, now from below, "on the side of popular liberty," coming in "with the democratic spirit of the age." Thus popery, democracy, and misguided tolerance could be linked as equal manifestations of the same menace—a strikingly clear statement of displaced fear:

Having succeeded, through the rash liberality of the times, in getting all restraints of law cast off, she is again preparing to put her hook in the nose of the people, and her bridle in their mouth, by the establishment of a territorial hierarchy, and a summons to all baptized persons to surrender to its authority, at the peril of their souls! Is not the threat significant enough? Is not the danger manifest enough? Is Rome changed?

There could be no wavering in the face of this peril, and failure to act resolutely was in itself a sign of treachery. There was no via media; those who are not for us are against us: "We are either Protestants, or Romanists: if we decline to use every influence we can exercise to put legal restraints upon the increase of Romish error—to set up effectual barriers of law against its invasions—we are not real Protestants, but real Romanists."[272]

If the Papal Aggression stimulated a rallying of the ranks of Protestantism, however hesitantly, and with however many qualifications, it entailed deeper rifts in other directions. The division in the Church between Evangelicals (principally) and Tractarians became one of the starkest of the period as self-righteousness and that peculiar venom reserved for fifth columnists sparked against each other. The Rev. Neville Jones of St. George's, Little Bolton, indignant at the "open and insolent aggression on the part of Papal Rome," nevertheless pointed to "the much greater danger which threatens us from within."[273] Tractarianism's appeal to some insecure clergymen lay in the doctrine of apostolic succession, which—even if the state were to abandon the Church, as feared—confirmed clerical status against "unclerical" Dissenting ministers dependent on their congregations.[274] But for others it was only a tiny step from popery. Anyone who took that step was a pervert. A newspaper in

December 1851 referred to a curate who had apparently spent a short time at Emmanuel, Bolton:

PERVERSIONS.—More perverts are spoken of by a correspondent, who writes as follows:—'You will, probably, hear that the Rev. J. Scratton, A.M., of St. John's College, Cambridge, was on Sunday, Nov. 23, admitted a Papist at Hastings. He left his curacy in February last, and went to Bolton for a month or two as curate, and thence returned to unite himself to the Romanists. He had been in orders only two and a half years. His brother was a pervert (of Oxford) about a year and a half ago.[275]

Perverts could split families. Henry Formby, scion of the Formbys of Formby Hall and of the Peels of Accrington House, and his sister, Catherine, wife of Charles Jacson of Barton Lodge, the Preston cotton lord, were both attracted to the Oxford School, Henry during his studies at Brasenose College, Catherine through reading the Tracts of the Times, Newman, Froude, and Keble. But this tended to separate rather than unite them; "Already Henry was jealous of any approach to sharing ministerial interests, and was disposed to resent feminine intermeddling—'Women should mind their cookery books,' and so on." Henry became rector of Ruardean in the Forest of Dean, an impoverished living where he saw a field for transformation. As Catherine relates the story, under the effects of a blinding ideology his pleasant disposition gave way to a morbid condition of morose sanctity. On Newman's secession to the Catholic Church, he loyally followed. He had always been a dutiful son, but now, to the great distress of his mother, it was "'Come not near. Touch not the hem of the priestly robe.'"[276]

Some clergymen were accused of being Tractarians in Blackburn, but there appears to have been no open doctrinal rift in the clerical ranks, partly no doubt because of Dr. Whittaker's detailed vetting. As we have seen, the curates' revolt in 1849 was not a question of doctrine but of money and influence. Whittaker himself deprecated the attack on doctrinal purity from within the Church. In denying that the High Church doctrines he held—the grace of baptism, or the Real Presence in the Eucharist—were the exclusive property of the Oxford Movement, he wrote, "I would as soon introduce into the parish a clergyman who would deny the grace of one of the blessed sacraments as one whom I had reason to believe was tainted with errors contained in the Tracts of the Times."[277] Tractarianism was much more apparent in Preston, with its fragmented patronage. In 1843 the Rev. James Bonwell, a curate of the Rev. Thomas Raven at Trinity Church, began editing *The Preston Magazine and Christian's Miscellany*. He and fellow contributors rigorously defended themselves against charges of popery, but advocated Puseyite doctrines, pomp and circumstance in the conduct of services, a stress on authority, and a disdain both for Evangelicals and for collaboration with Dissenters.[278]

In Bolton and Deane the schisms were more publicly bitter, partly focusing on the Additional Curates' Aid Society, alleged by its critics to be a vehicle for the implanting of Tractarian clergymen. In 1849, the Evangelical Rev. Girdlestone, vicar of Deane, weighed into a dispute on this issue between the Tractarian vicar of Leigh and the new Evangelical bishop of Manchester, James Prince Lee, with his own condemnation of the Oxford Movement.[279] In early 1851, as Bishop Prince Lee continued to object to funds from the Additional Curates' Society, the Tractarian Rev. James Richard Alsop of St. Mary's, Westhoughton, confronted him in an acrimonious, public dispute. He accused the bishop of slandering him with the accusation that he preferred "'the wretched ceremonial of a past time to the vital essence of Christianity . . . clinging to the surplice in ministration, instead of clinging to the word and vital truths of God.'" Thomas Dickinson, Alsop's churchwarden, wrote to the *Manchester Courier* at the end of April that the congregation and Sunday school had dwindled to virtually nothing since Alsop arrived, because of his Tractarian practices. He claimed that the parishioners firmly supported the bishop's "bold and uncompromising opposition to Tractarianism" and insisted that, "Were the dismissal of Mr. Alsop from his incumbency dependent upon the votes of a majority of his parishioners, he would, as he is well aware, in a very few hours, have notice to quit."

So disgruntled were at least some of the parishioners that they undertook to build new schools, at Wingates, independently of the incumbent. At the laying of the first stone, by John Silvester of Atherton, in September 1851, Girdlestone spoke of his deep regret at the divisions in the chapelry and that "the bishop of the diocese has been set at defiance, and that the hearts of the people have been estranged from their minister by his own fault." But the schools would offer "first and foremost the Bible . . . no semi-popish additions or reservations: a good sound, scriptural, Protestant education in the principles of the Reformed Church of England," so that the young might grow up "not bigotted Papists or Puseyites, but enlightened Protestants and Bible Christians."[280]

Girdlestone registered his opposition to Tractarianism in two other ways. In April 1851 he attempted to rally support for acceptable candidates for the committee of the National Society against the alleged Puseyite tendencies of the sitting committee;[281] and at the time of the agitation against the Papal Aggression he was foremost in attacking the cankerous worm within. Slade of Bolton had convened a meeting of the clergy to draw up addresses to bishop and queen against the Aggression, but Girdlestone in addition proposed an address thanking Lord John Russell for his letter to the bishop of Durham, especially that part of it denouncing "unworthy sons of the Church" who had been leading their flocks step by step toward Rome. According to the *Times*, ten of the Bolton clergy voted in favor of this and ten against, Slade giving his casting vote against. The Evangelicals sponsored the public meeting that followed, and Slade and the High Churchmen were absent. Slade, in a letter to the *Times*, maintained that a convincing majority had rejected the proposed address and that his own vote was certainly not in favor of Puseyism, as the newspaper alleged, since "I have never belonged to any party in the Church, and by God's help I never will." The Rev. Thomas Berry of Christ Church, the local secretary of the Additional Curates' Aid Society and of the National School, wrote that committees of laymen acting without the clergy managed grants from the National Society, and J. M. Rodwell, secretary to the Curates' Society, argued that the charges of Romanizing activities within the society were totally unfounded. John Taylor of Silverwell House, on the other hand, pointed to Christ Church, Emmanuel, Leigh, and Westhoughton churches for evidence of Tractarianism and the stubbornness of curates furnished by the Curates' Society. He ended with a prayer: "May the Lord, in his great mercy, spare Britain for the sake of the many righteous found in her, and may they and all his faithful children stand by their God, their open Bibles, and their beloved Queen."[282]

Religious Education and the Rhetoric of Order

Most bourgeois ladies and gentlemen were quite willing to stand by their God, open Bibles, and queen. But they were not conspicuously good at doing it together or agreeing on how it should be done. While the thin fabric of unity was stretched taut over one division, a rent appeared elsewhere, or some religious agitator or polemicist set to work industriously with scissors, shears, or scythe. As clergymen, priests, and ministers, with lay support, sought to build their own sectarian communities and their own social status, it is not surprising that the fragmentation should have been more evident than the cohesion, that the great army of Christ squabbled bitterly over types of uniform and color-schemes of troopships.

In attempting to educate the people there were the same divisions. Sunday and day schools were prime elements in building the parochial, Catholic, or Dissenting community. In time the schools often became vehicles for independent, lower-class empowerment,[283] yet their intent was quite otherwise. They promised "such a Reformation of Manners among the lower Ranks of People, as will, in Time, dispel that Darkness which covers the Land"; to collect the "Children of the Poor . . . under proper Masters, to be instructed in what is right and good";[284] to teach the poor to "form early habits of industry and frugality, decency and order . . . to fear God, to honour and obey the king, to be respectful to their superiors."[285] As a Sunday school hymn explained,

Thy gracious hand, to different ranks,
Hath diff'rent tasks assign'd;

'Tis our's [*sic*], to tread the lower path,
And bear an humble mind.
'Tis our's, with industry and care
To earn our daily food:
We are not likely to be great,
But oh, may we be good.[286]

Not least, preached the Rev. William Thistlethwaite of St. George's, Little Bolton, "Is not [the poor's] moral and religious education the best security to a state? . . . surely he who obeys magistrates, because obedience is a Christian duty, is a character much more to be depended upon, than he who obeys through fear of punishment or expectation of favour and gain."[287] Peter Whittle, pithily summarizing the same point later on, had no need for a question mark: "It has been reserved for our time to make the discovery that the prevalence of ignorance among the working classes is incompatible with the peace of society, and the establishment of good order. Knowledge is tranquilizing."[288]

The agenda could not have been more unambiguous, and members of the bourgeoisie responded enthusiastically. Give me the child and I will give you the man it promised, and, alongside troops and charity, early on it took its place among the battery of measures intended to coerce, control, cajole, or conciliate the lower orders. After the initial Sunday schools in the 1780s and the first National Schools in the 1810s, supported by a rollcall of the local elite, much Anglican school-building followed closely the pattern of church-building, the schools being attached to existing structures or being built and licensed as temporary chapels, hopeful harbingers of future churches. Much of the initiative came from the vicars, some from other incumbents, and some from laymen, with money from the National Society and subscriptions.[289] The British and Foreign School Society—theoretically nondenominational but in practice often boycotted by Anglicans—performed a similar function to the National Society in the parallel process of Nonconformist school-building.[290] A number of individuals in town and country colonies—Hornby at Brookhouse, Feilden at Witton, Ainsworth at Halliwell, Horrocks at New Preston, to name but a few—provided a substantial portion of the funding for fabric and schoolteachers in schools largely for their own millhands or tenantry. They could carve their coats of arms above the entrances and be on hand with their wives and families on special occasions to distribute buns and bonhomie.

Henry Ashworth recalled in 1870 that his spinners used to prefer as piecers children who had been to school on the grounds that, "'If they have been to school they're obedient—they want less licking.'"[291] Others were less impressed with "the old, dull, dry, learn-nothing, drill-serjeant system of Bell and Lancaster,"[292] but local elites found it difficult to pass beyond the provision of a rudimentary level of sectarian education. Government schemes for national education repeatedly encountered a hostile response. Most Dissenters were as yet opposed on principle to state interference in education as a violation of the voluntarist ethic.[293] Churchmen feared that any plan acceptable to all denominations would leave religious instruction dangerously diluted—a position attacked by the Rev. Edward Girdlestone of Deane, who had no patience with "those who, in the retirement of their own studies, argue themselves into a persuasion that it is better not to educate the people at all than to give them an education deficient in one, even the least iota, of formulary and creed."[294] For example, at a meeting of Bolton Churchmen in July 1837 in response to a government plan to give grants to the National, British, and Catholic Schools, the Rev. J. S. Birley condemned a system of education that left religion an open question, and thought the proposed scheme would multiply Dissent, infidelity, and atheism. Slade argued for religious education, under the supervision of the Church; since the Chartists had been quoting Scripture for their own distorted purposes, merely reading the Bible was insufficient. William Hulton countered Lord John Russell's argument that the objectors to such a scheme of education were leaving eighty thousand children in Manchester and Salford alone without education. True, he said, such a godless system might be able to instruct these children—enough to enable them to write a forged bill of exchange.[295]

If state intervention proved problematic, perhaps the local elites could arrive at a collective solution themselves, in classic, bridge-building, voluntarist style. In Bolton in 1846, freshly released from years of party squabbling, this looked a distinct possibility.[296] The movement to establish an Athenæum in Bolton initially garnered all-party support from a broad band of leading inhabitants. At a meeting in November chaired by Peter Ainsworth, MP, the Tory-Anglican ironfounder John Hick summed up concisely the objectives of the proposed Athenæum: "The institution they desired to establish was proposed to proceed on neutral ground—a ground whereon all parties might meet to promote a good feeling between the employer and the employed; and this he conceived could not be better accomplished than by the education of the poor."[297] As the fund-raising handbill issued after the meeting put it,

We have no Institution of any kind at all commensurate to the intellectual wants of the town, or at all adapted to the extensive diffusion of useful knowledge amongst the bulk of the community. This defect it is desirable to remove, that our own town may become as distinguished for its intellectual and moral character as it is for wealth and population.[298]

The editor of *The Bolton Free Press* looked forward "to the establishment of an institution such as the growing wants of the town have long required, and to the happy blending together of parties, which in social matters is so essential to the mental progress of the people."[299]

As the subscriptions began to flow in, success seemed assured. But Robert Heywood, a leading subscriber, was expressing concern as early as the end of October that only a few conservatives had been induced to join the committee. A month later he was appealing for support outside the parish as "we meet with less encouragement in some quarters than we had a right to expect." Early in December John Butler, who subscribed a substantial sum, was able to read between the lines and conclude that, "I am sorry to see from the names of the subscribers there is something like party feeling in the affair certain parties keeping aloof or holding back." Heywood conceded this, but was still sanguine that the example of John Fletcher, Tory-Anglican coalowner, and one or two others might help in breaking down the strong political barriers. It was not to be. Near the end of December he admitted that the conservatives still had not been won over and were raising an active opposition, "with the Vicar as usual at its head and tail."[300] Slade, more than anyone, stymied the project. When a deputation asked for his endorsement of the institution he voiced his strong opposition on the grounds that no "educational institution could be suited to a Christian public, from the formation and framework of which religion should be of necessity excluded." Although he claimed that he would not take any active measures in opposition because some of the friends of the Church thought otherwise, he did take up the suggestion of a few of the clergy that a rival Church of England Educational Institution be established.[301] It was this institution that eventually won the battle for funding, while the Athenæum fell by the wayside.

A resolution pushed through at a public meeting toward the end of March 1847, that the institution's rules could be amended by a vote of 80 percent of a general meeting, applied the finishing touches to the collapse of the Athenæum. For Tories in particular this raised fears of a potentially high degree of popular control, which might allow a secular day school to be established—an idea previously vetoed to avoid religious dissension.[302] By April the scheme was clearly dead, and Heywood was engaged in trying to convince the subscribers to transfer their pledges to a new building for the Mechanics' Institute—a body long in bad odor because of its party squabbling, and which a nonpartisan Athenæum had been intended to supersede.[303]

Clearly a volatile mixture of party, class, and sect was involved in this demise, just as it was in another scheme immediately following—though the extent of denominational strife was more evident—to establish a system of secular education on a regional and then a national basis. The basic idea of the projectors of the Lancashire (later National) Public Schools Association was to introduce a denominationally neutral system of primary education for the lower orders. As they began campaigning in the milltowns in 1847 they elicited a response that to an extent cut across party and sectarian lines. For example, Thomas Ridgway Bridson, conservative bleacher, wrote in 1850,

I see no probability at the present time of any scheme including religious teaching being accepted with that degree of unanimity necessary to render it successful, and being strongly convinced that very many of the social evils that exist among us are entirely due to the prevalence of popular ignorance, I feel it my duty to give support to that scheme which, professing to impart secular education alone, occupies with respect to religion a position simply & strictly neutral. . . . It would in my opinion not only be unwise and impolitic, but criminal, longer to neglect the important subject of national education in deference to the religious animosities of the various religious denominations.[304]

But it seems that the scheme met with little support among the influential inhabitants. A slew of relatively prominent individuals—mainly liberals, mainly Dissenters—gave their blessing, while complaining of the difficulty of raising the enthusiasm of others in the area. Apparently the only Anglican minister to approve it—and even then with reservations—was the Rev. John Clay, reforming chaplain of Preston Gaol. Strong objections came in from a broad spectrum of Churchmen and voluntarists. Richard Fort of Read Hall, liberal-Anglican calico-printer, thought it impossible "in a Country like England where sectarian prejudices have from a variety of causes acquired a depth & prominence of a striking character, to produce such a state of unanimity & mutual confidence as may lead to the adoption of a Combined System of Education. . . . I doubt the possibility of conveying moral instruction to children, unaccompanied by religious instruction." The Rev. G. B. Johnson, Independent minister of Darwen, felt "ashamed that such a concoction should date from Lancashire . . . a people proud of their independence . . . and jealous of interference . . . with their civil and religious liberty." The Rev. William Probert of Walmsley feared that the committee and central board would be vested with a dangerous degree of power. The Rev. E. A. Verity of All Saints', Habergham, was the most vehement in his condemnation. "The most troublesome—rebellious—daring & refractory as well as iniquitous, peoples around me, are those who have a *secular*—but not a *religious* education—I speak from experience." Moreover, he doubted whether an amalgamation of creeds, proposed in the plan, could possibly work:

Would to God that nine different denominations *cd.* come together upon equal grounds of common respect for each other & agree . . . but my experience in human nature little as it is, tells me that yr. scheme is *impracticable in England*. It may do in America—in Caffirland—on the Continent—in India—but it can only provoke a smile on any man's face to think of it in Lancashire—When you can deprive the lion of his strength—the fox of his cunning—the hyæna of his malice—the tiger of his ferocity & the lamb of its fear—then *but not till then* will you get a committee of Churchmen (1)—Methodists (2) Unitarians (3) Romanists (4) Mormonites (5) Ranters (6) Independents (7) Baptists (8) Presbyterians (9)—to unite cordially upon *what* they shall teach of the Bible in public schools & *who* shall teach and expound it.[305]

The debate rumbled on, as men of God and laymen danced around the key issues of whether it was desirable to achieve collective action across sectarian divides, and to what extent the state should impinge upon the self-government of the localities. Sectarianism remained in the ascendant, and this tended to be confirmed when clergymen attempted another form of education: the preaching of the rhetoric of order from the pulpit. "GOD makes the rich for the poor, the poor for the rich, that each may bless the other," Parr of Preston reminded his audience in 1860 in a wide-ranging denunciation of combinations, strikes, secular education, and universal suffrage.

Let no class, as a class, demand an unnatural elevation of itself, or degradation of another. Subordination is an essential and profitable law of human association, having its type in all creation. The valleys are fertile; the mountain tops are sterile; and it is the streams and moulderings from the sides of the latter which enrich and make fruitful the bosom of the former. But what is true of the class, does not hold with the individual. Superior genius, pre-eminent usefulness, sagacious enterprise, determined frugality, have raised men from a lower to the highest stations in society, and have opened in them the fountains of the best blood of England.[306]

The preaching of strict political orthodoxy and antiradicalism by the towns' most prominent clergymen formed a major component of the building of parochial communities. But because this rhetoric conflated Dissent with radicalism, the thumping of the drumbeat of class proved to be profoundly partisan. Take, for example, the famous confrontations between vicars and Chartists in 1839, which formed a distinctive phase in the Chartist movement.[307] Large bodies of Chartists on Sunday, July 21, attended Stockport Parish Church, on the following Sunday and for two successive Sundays targeted Bolton Parish Church, and on August 4 crowded into Blackburn, Bury, Chorley, Preston, Leigh, and Manchester Parish Churches. The demonstrations were a calculated violation of the normal rules of propriety of an institution that they considered to be an integral part of a corrupt political order. In occupying pews they appeared to menace private property and transgress the boundaries of social hierarchy along the length of the nave from the best boxed pews to the free benches at the rear and in the galleries.[308] Yet in their good order, they exhibited a carefully contrived contempt for the notions of their "betters," the "respectable inhabitants." In many churches the Chartists proposed texts for the vicars' sermons: "Hear this, O ye that would swallow up the needy, and cause the poor of the land to fail"; or "If any will not work, neither shall he eat."[309]

In Blackburn, they challenged Dr. Whittaker to preach from James 5:1-16: "Go to now, *ye* rich men, weep and howl for your miseries that shall come upon *you*." He did so and inadvertently revealed the gulf separating his perceptions from those of his listeners, between the language of the Anglican community and the reality of class. The church was packed with a congregation of about four thousand, and Whittaker's wife and children had to sit on the altar steps. The *Blackburn Standard*, unwittingly reinforcing the Chartists' point, claimed that the Church "was filled with such a miscellaneous collection as its walls have seldom enclosed." Several of the congregation each held "a pike ornamented with the head of a Tory."[310] But Whittaker felt himself master of the situation. He contended that the stoning to death of James—"by a tumultuous assemblage of the poorer and lower classes"—was only one of tens of thousands of cases "which prove how fatal and how dreadful may be the consequences of unbridled passion, where discontented multitudes are encouraged to meet together for purposes which they do not distinctly understand, or to remove evils which they cannot control." The rich men James wrote about were oppressors of the poor; but *our* rich men, "the gentry of England," provided public institutions and charities for the relief of the distressed, in the "true spirit of genuine Christian charity." Blessed with plenty by the Lord, they freely imparted of that plenty, from love to God.

Whittaker broke off to comment on the motley nature of his congregation, their "not quite seemly" manner and guise, before insisting that he was not going to be intimidated by them. He informed them that they were "grossly deceived, most infamously and impudently deluded and practised upon by persons who have their own wicked and selfish ends to answer by your destruction." Equal property rights ultimately meant the seizure by force of their neighbors' goods. Universal manhood suffrage meant "that ignorance and numbers are the fullest qualifications for the high, difficult, delicate and intricate duties of legislation." He ended with an appeal: "Come, I repeat the invitation, come to your parish church; but come singly in humility, in penitence, in faith;—come not, as you have done this day, in ostentatious publicity and idle display." Whittaker was pleased with his sermon, even though it is unlikely that many of his congregation returned. He had it published, it sold well in several editions, and a bound, gold-lettered copy was presented to the Queen Dowager.[311] A myth, cultivated locally and still being propagated nearly twenty years after, held that the vicar had preached "with such effect that Chartism may be said to have been effectually put down in Blackburn, and sensibly diminished in the country."[312] The fact that the sermon had been listened to respectfully, and that the congregation had departed peacefully, had been badly misinterpreted. As Eileen Yeo remarks, Whittaker and other clergymen could not have played their parts better had they set out to prove the Chartist case that they were wolves in sheep's clothing, legitimizing op-pression.[313] There was mutual incomprehension.

Likewise in Preston. The Chartists invited the Rev. Wilson to preach from James 2:15-16, but he chose Job 34:29 instead.[314] His message was clear: "Dis-tinctions in classes there must always be; there always had been and always would be. The scriptures emphatically recognised such distinctions," and he quoted from 1 Samuel 2:7 —"'The Lord maketh poor, and maketh rich'"—to prove the point. Yet streams of kindness flowed from the opulent to the needy; in no other country was industry, forethought, and talent better rewarded; in no other country was there a better provision for the protection of personal property; here were to be found the most enlightened, pious, and industrious clergy, and most tolerant church, in the Christian world. In spite of these manifold advantages, "Recently there had sprung up among the people a spirit of murmuring and unthankfulness; of envy and of jealousy. Instead of ascribing the evils of their condition to their own misconduct, they were too apt to lay them at the door of the virtuous and the godly." Moreover, sharp-ening his Evangelical knife for a thrust at the organs of power, he complained of the signal lack of a decidedly Christian tone in the legislature and Whig government, witness the injury to the holy sacrament of baptism by the Regis-tration Act, the desecration of a sacred rite in the sanction of ungodly mar-riages, and the reluctance of Parliament to provide for the due observance of the Sabbath.[315]

Two contradictory elements here might be expected to upset bourgeois lib-erals and Dissenters. The first was the insistence on learning "in whatsoever state I am, *therewith* to be content," as any number of edited highlights from the Bible could demonstrate.[316] According to the *Bolton Free Press*, at the end of 1838 the Rev. John Lyons of St. George's, Little Bolton, preached that, "HE THAT RESISTETH THE POWERS THAT BE, SAITH THE HOLY GHOST, SHALL RECEIVE ETERNAL DAMNATION." The editor pointed out that this would have spelled trouble for Luther, Knox, and Milton, among others, and that the New Testament contained no warrant for such an outra-geous doctrine.[317] The second element was the undermining of this dogma of political quiescence by the clergymen themselves when they railed against the government of the day. When the Rev. James Slade lambasted the queen's ministers for being "greatly responsible for all the Royal acts, as they are for all the revolutionary outbreaks, by which this country, and I bitterly regret to add, this town, have been recently disgraced," he was evidently impaling him-self on the spikes of a contradiction: how to preach order and subordination while attacking the powers that be for allegedly bringing disorder and insub-ordination.[318]

What did the rhetoric of order achieve? It was essentially and intentionally divisive, a well-tried strategy of divide and rule in its attempt to incorporate a section of the lower orders into a deferential, hierarchical community while rigorously excluding all the radicals and unorthodox beyond the pale. It undoubtedly had some loyalist popular appeal, though it had more impact in consolidating an ideology of Conservatism among a section of the elite. But perhaps its most important and wholly paradoxical means of maintaining a relative stability was in generating and perpetuating a bourgeois opposition. Every time that a gentleman of the cloth rose in the political arena to defend the privileges of the Church, or to support Conservatism, or to preach the virtues of an undefiled constitution in Church and state, he was keeping the trench between him and many of the Dissenting and liberal middle classes clear from debris. We have seen that there were many bridges across that trench; but in so far as much of the political debate continued to be focused on the divisive issues within the higher ranks, the lack of a consolidated and class-conscious bourgeoisie meant to the radical lower orders (the divided and ruled) that the possibility existed of interclass, popular-liberal alliance, and rhetoric. It is from such divisions and fluidities of language and alliance that powerful hegemonies are constructed.

Chapter 7: Regulating Poverty

"There was a manufacturer at Darwen, of common calicoes; that man was giving 4s. a-piece for weaving those calicoes," related John Ashworth Jr., land agent, brother of the millowners Henry and Edmund. "If he went to market, and found he could not get for his calicoes as much as he had got on a previous day, he would go home and tell his weavers that they must do it for sixpence less," or cease production. "Well, the weavers would say, we might as well take the work out at so much as go to the parish quarrying and draining, we may as well take half-a-crown as go home and hunger; and by and by . . . those wages got quickly reduced from 4s. to 1s. 6d., and when reduced to the lowest point they begin to start up." The system was self-adjusting: low wages rendered trade profitable, inducing other manufacturers to start up, stimulating an increasing demand for labor and higher wages. The workhouse was a critical component in this process. Ashworth was describing the 1826 depression and the positive consequences of the introduction of the workhouse principle in the new establishment at Darwen: "[T]hey put over these paupers placed in the workhouse a sharp man—a man who understood how to manage them; and after the head of a family had been in a week or so, and found he must work before he ate, he found work for himself, and went out."[1]

The 1834 Poor Law Amendment Act built on this logic, and the Quaker Ashworth brothers, keen disciples of political economy, supported it strongly. Indeed, the Poor Law Report held up as a model the workhouse at Turton, reorganized by John Ashworth in the 1820s. Here, no sooner was the new system

put into full operation in the house than the able-bodied, hereditary paupers began to disappear; the discipline was new to them—they disliked the restraint; they soon found that by persevering industry and a little management, they could live above pauperism; and they left us with their habits improved, to make their way in the world without parochial assistance.[2]

The threat of the discipline and harsh conditions of the workhouse stimulated the able-bodied to self-reliance, which in turn helped reduce expenditure on poor relief—one fundamental advantage of the new system. A second advantage was that a New Poor Law, combined with the outlawing of trades unions, would reduce wages, which would induce people to marry later and have fewer children. As Henry Ashworth put it, "if an alteration in the poor laws and an overturning of Trades Unions were effected our manufacturing employments would then become fairly opened for general unrestricted competition,—the rate of wages would assimilate more nearly with those paid for the general labour of the Country and little or nothing would be heard again of superabundant population." A third advantage was that the anticipated breaking of the ties of laborer to parish would enable labor mobility within the country, so that "our native idlers" would not be encouraged to emigrate and manufacturers would not be forced to bring over "the outcasts and the discontented of the Sister Isle, a race of men greatly inferior in moral and frugal habits to those of our English peasantry who are thus exiled." These Irish, claimed Edmund Ashworth, were "ignorant discontented and turbulent people, who introducing and widely spreading their own habits, have a tendency gradually to demoralize our own native population."[3]

These apostles of free markets, free trade, and free labor, by whatever centralizing, coercive, and moralizing means might be necessary, illustrate well the "Janus-face of modern liberalism."[4] The greater uniformity, central regulation, and standardization that the New Poor Law promised addressed the Malthusian fear of overpopulation and the Ricardian prediction of a stationary state. Since the relatively generous provision of relief seemed to have been spiraling out of control during and since the war years, Poor Law Unions would reduce costs and the overindulging of the poor by raising the provision of poor relief to a plane above local and partial interests. The principle of less eligibility—that those supported by the ratepayers should, by virtue of their confinement to the workhouse, find themselves in less desirable circumstances than those who supported themselves and their families by their own labor— would stimulate workforce mobility while fostering individual independence, separating the poor, but hardworking, laborer from the pitiful pauperized residuum. This appealed both to political economists (eager to create a more disciplined and profitable labor force) and to Christian moralists (believing that only the independent individual could face the trial of faith alone before God).[5]

This was the theory. It played particularly well among the landed gentlemen of the south and their representatives in Parliament, an answer to high rates and rural unrest, and the capstone on their conversion to the values of the market economy.[6] But the old law was not in a state of crisis in the manufacturing districts, and the Poor Law commissioners were well aware that true believers like the Ashworths would not be readily available. Even so, they argued, Poor Law Unions could raise poor relief above sectional interests, and the contraction to one conspicuously large workhouse per union could achieve economies of scale and act as a deterrence. This was going to be a hard argu-

ment to sell: resistance in the north was formidable. For all those persuaded
by the beauty of a rational, accountable system, prodding the poor to help
themselves to the benefit of all, improving through rules and classifications the
squalor, demoralization, and brutality of many workhouses, there would be
others decrying the overriding of local interests, the apparent inhumanity, the
blaming of the poor for their poverty, the cowing of labor through the discipline of the "Bastile" (generally misspelt in protest literature), and the reduction in the power of the vestries, further crowding out and closing down the
lower-class voice. The commissioners in response to this opposition and to industrial business cycles were forced to bargain and make concessions. They
backtracked from their intention to allow only the necessitous poor (the children, the aged, the sick) "careful and liberal" relief in workhouses, with only a
Spartan workhouse regime for the able-bodied, and left it to the discretion of
the guardians in manufacturing districts whether to continue outdoor relief.[7]
This was the clearest indication that the Law could not be imposed without a
struggle, and only then in a milder form.

Bolton Union

In Bolton Union, where of the three towns the divisions over the New Poor
Law most nearly approximated party splits, some of the principal opponents
of the act were county magistrates and leading manufacturers, all Tories, and
they formed shifting opposition coalitions with urban-middling Tories and
lower-middle-class radicals. The government's strategy to rely on propertied
support and reduce the popular voice by introducing the multiple-votes system
and property qualifications for guardians, and making JPs ex officio guardians, proved unavailing.[8] The two aggressively partisan newspapers set the
tone. The Tory *Bolton Chronicle* called the act unnecessary and cruel, with its
vicious and degrading centralizing plan outraging every principle of humanity
and converting the necessitous into prisoners or desperadoes: "The ghosts of
Mill and Malthus shake hands with each other in their graves, and congratulate themselves that they have at last trampled over all human feeling, tenderness and compassion." This was one of many sustained attacks on the act,
presumably fueled by the personal pique of the editor, John Foster: he had
himself applied to be an assistant commissioner under the new act in 1834
and was still questioning his rejection two years later.[9] The liberal *Bolton Free
Press* did not wholeheartedly endorse the measure and may even have been
somewhat embarrassed by it, but felt compelled to come to its defense. Early
in 1837 the editor viewed opposition to it as a Tory ruse to divide Reformers
and to divert attention from the more important issues, the glaring corrup-
tions in church and state. The paper advised Reformers to give the measure a
fair trial and to "Leave the two great parties of the state to fight their own
battle. Look to your own interests: and know that you can never advance

them by a childish clamour about a few cases of real or apparent hardship in the operation of a new law."[10]

Opposition meetings called by the overseers in Great and Little Bolton in 1834 ("Factious meetings," Charles James Darbishire, Unitarian manufacturer, called them, "got up by the officials because there will now be a power above them which they cannot cajole")[11] were matched by a hostile meeting of leypayers in Little Bolton Town Hall early in 1837 when the commissioners decided to apply the New Poor Law to the manufacturing districts.[12] In the ensuing elections the liberals swept the board in Great Bolton and did well in Little Bolton, but there was still a conservative majority at the board: the four ex officio guardians for Horwich, Hulton, Harwood, and Tonge with Haulgh, together with the five elected guardians from their respective townships returned through their influence, alone were more than a match for the whole town of Bolton. In consequence the Tories picked up the key posts: Joseph Ridgway of Ridgmont (bleacher) was elected chairman, John Fletcher of The Hollins (of the coal-owning family) vice chairman, John Woodhouse (attorney) clerk, and James Kyrke Watkins (attorney) superintendent registrar.[13]

In March the anti-Poor Law guardians carried a resolution of John Smith Jr., bleacher and guardian for Great Lever, that

the intention of the poor Law Commissioners to carry into full operation in this Union the poor Law Amendment Act has occasioned great dissatisfaction throughout the Union and that such course is deemed uncalled for and highly inexpedient: uncalled for, inasmuch as the administration of the poor Laws has been well and sufficiently conducted with as much attention to economy as a due regard to the necessities of the poor permitted; and highly inexpedient as taking the management of the poor from those best able by reason of the Knowledge of the applicants to detect imposition and administer relief in a proper degree to the necessitous and is likely to produce an increase of the rates.[14]

This opposition failed to prevent the commissioners at length issuing an order for the guardians to take over the administration of poor relief in November 1838. But given the weight of the respective parties on the board, and the intense politicization of local government that Bolton was suffering during the battle over the borough charter, the transition to the new regime was chaotic and acrimonious. Despite Assistant Commissioner Charles Mott's assurances at a meeting in December that the guardians of manufacturing districts had discretion as to the distribution of relief, and that a petition would do no good since large majorities in both Houses had passed the act and it had the support of Wellington and Peel, the guardians voted to petition for its suspension.

Some guardians, Mott claimed, expressed the view at that meeting that "I should be piked."[15] Violence was also threatened the following February,

when Thomas Ridgway, bleacher, guardian for Horwich and staunch opponent, brandished a cudgel at Richard Nightingale, counterpane manufacturer,
during a board meeting, prompting James Winder, the town clerk, to wonder
whether the nine new borough magistrates—liberals—could serve as ex officio
guardians, as "it is quite time the party in favor of the Law were strengthened." Since this was denied and the opposition continued in the ascendant,
the board stumbled through a succession of adjournments, declarations of
noncompliance, or protests against commissioners' orders, refusals to pay
rates, disputed chairmanship elections, and the taking of important votes
when the opposing camps' numbers and guards were down.[16] John Ashworth
summed up all of these instances of party warfare and local-central tension in
a letter to Edwin Chadwick in July 1840:

There has been a strong party from the first who have done all they could to stop
the working of the new Law & if they can tire out a few more Guardians as they
have done some they will succeed, their conduct is most disgusting & remon-
strance is of no use & if it was not for the benefit of the Ratepayers & the Poor
upon a superior management under the new Law I would not go near them.[17]

Again in February 1841 the board petitioned Parliament to be relieved from
the operation of the New Poor Law, since its working "is not expedient in this
Union": the rates were heavier than before and the poor not better provided
for. The petitioners concluded, "That a virtuous and generous system of management and relief of the poor under the statute of Elizabeth with the additional protection to the Ratepayers of a public Auditor would in this Union be
a system preferable to the one now in practice."[18]

To say that the New Poor Law was "now in practice" would be to exag-
gerate. Mott outlined in the spring of 1841 how far short of the ideal the Bolton Union fell. Firstly, expenditure remained high because, he thought, the
conservative guardians had canvassed in the 1841 election as the true friends
of the poor, advocates of outdoor relief, opposed to the New Poor Law and
the "Bastile System": "So long as a Board of Guardians constituted like that
of Bolton is allowed to exercise an unlimited power to grant out door relief,
nothing can check or prevent the increase of it." Secondly, the guardians had
not suppressed demoralizing malpractices as the act intended. They paid cottage rents and granted relief on account of "insufficiency of earnings":

When the Weaver finds that if his shuttle move slowly, the same amount of money
will be produced (whether from the parish rates or from his employers pay) as if
his shuttle move quickly, we may expect more of such discoveries as that stated in
the evidence of the Relieving Officer of the Bolton Union who was asked Are you
aware of what has been the effect of relief in aid of wages on the industry of the
operatives relieved?—It has been to relax the industry.

He was adamant that at no time and in no district was it of greater importance to avoid this allowance system than in a manufacturing district during a period of commercial distress, because only then would the self-adjusting mechanism of market forces begin to operate. Thirdly, the guardians had not introduced a model workhouse. This question had produced much "angry" and "violent" debate. They had abandoned one of the union's establishments (Westhoughton) and retained two (Great Bolton and Turton); but beyond that there was little conformity to the act or to the wishes of the commissioners. Bolton workhouse, small and badly built, remained unclassified, inadequate, and improperly ventilated: there were only eighty-seven beds for 236 people: "One child is generally bedded with two adults and the usual care not being paid to children in the night the beds are damp and unhealthy in consequence of the children's evacuations." Mott concluded that there were few other examples where boards of guardians had exercised the flexibility conceded by the commissioners with such adverse effects.[19]

During much of the next year the chairman, John Bolling, a Tory gentleman of the cotton-spinning family, and many of the guardians continued to work to prevent the full implementation of the act. Contending that the old administration had been cheaper, they refused to pay higher salaries to the assistant overseers, in spite of commissioners' orders; they spoke repeatedly of setting aside the authority of the commissioners; they resisted the commissioners' medical orders; they drew up a petition for an amended Poor Law, which attracted nearly eighteen thousand signatures; they constantly agitated for an end to the subdivision of the union into five districts with an assistant overseer assigned to each and a reversion to the old system of a relieving officer appointed by each township, to be paid a salary agreed upon by the leypayers assembled in public vestry; and they illegally had two chairmen at every meeting, the one appointed at nine making way for Bolling at noon because, John Ashworth claimed, he "cannot rise so early as to meet the Board at 9 O Clock tho' he lives within 100 Yards of the Board Room." At the same time various townships attempted to go their own ways in the collection of rates and the dispersion of relief, and Ralph Shaw, farmer, guardian for Lostock, seems to have made a habit of this from the start of the union. Mott did however claim that the guardians became somewhat more tractable in the summer of 1842 when it became clear with the renewal of the commission that the Conservative government was not going to back away from the main points of the New Poor Law.[20]

The condition of the workhouse did not improve. In December 1842 James Flitcroft, a Chartist cart-sheet maker, oilcloth manufacturer, and a relentless ferreter-out of abuses, reported that a weak-minded cousin of his in the workhouse became so filthy that the inmates "scraped lice from his trowsers, frizzled them over the fire, and greased his clogs with the fat!" Flitcroft produced before the board about four hundred lice, picked off his cousin over a day or two, and said that he had considered forwarding them to the commissioners; the chairman "sneeringly observed that they would be a handsome present for you." The medical officer confirmed that many of the old inmates had lice on their bodies and clothes, and the children had lice in their hair.[21]

Even more shocking was the case of Ann Heywood. Assistant Commissioner Charles Clements concluded after an inquiry that she had been brutally dragged from her bed and downstairs on her mattress to be washed and laid out after a drunken nurse had proclaimed her dead, even though doubts had arisen. She was in fact still alive, but died later. Clements used this case as a prelude to a sustained attack on the management of the workhouse in January 1843. It was a "vile establishment . . . devoid of all the attributes which must be considered indispensable for an establishment of the kind by every well regulated mind": care for the sick, decent accommodation for the healthy, education for the young. There was no classification and nothing to prevent the unmarried from sleeping together. In the hospital, "I never saw two Wards in any public establishment where discomfort was more apparent." At the back of the workhouse, in a set of small cottages used as dormitories, in rooms sixteen feet square with four beds each, fourteen to sixteen people—including children with scarlet fever—slept in each room. Around twenty-two people had to share similar-sized dayrooms, where the linen had to be dried at the same time. "Such a state of things requires no comment. Nothing previous to the passing of the Amendment Act could be worse."[22]

The commissioners were appalled:

It is impossible to read the evidence . . . without feeling that a state of things more incompatible with Order, industry, good morals[,] health, or common decency cannot be imagined to exist. . . . The Comm^{rs} feel that the whole subject of this letter is a painful one—that it is such a Communication as they have rarely or never had occasion to address to any Board and such as must necessarily in all probability give rise to angry feelings—This result they cannot avoid—They feel it their duty not to shrink from stating every thing disclosed by the evidence before them in its full deformity.

The commissioners had exposed to the world "the doings of a workhouse upon the *old principle*," commented John Ashworth, "to the great disgrace of the Guardians . . . [and] if J. Bolling understands the English Language he has such a castigation as would drive him out of all respectable Society." The commissioners demanded to know what measures the board proposed to take, and whether they would now move toward the building of the new workhouse long urged upon them.[23]

The guardians continued to adhere to "the old principle" of workhouse management. They dismissed the master and matron, appointed a surveyor to look into altering and extending the building, but rejected "most unequivocally," seventeen to zero, the construction of any new workhouse.[24] Over the next few years they made gradual, piecemeal alterations, invariably voted down proposals for a new building, and took no steps toward classification.[25] The majority guardians' opposition to a new workhouse was presumably part principle, part economy. But it was difficult maintaining a principled stand against Malthusian economy when the condition of the workhouse was so poor that the commissioners could appear in the guise of humanitarians. This is why the guardians embraced the opportunity to reclaim the high ground in November 1845, when the commissioners issued an order against the pounding and grinding of bones in union workhouses in the wake of the scandal of famished inmates gnawing on such bones at the Andover Union workhouse. The guardians voted fourteen to five to the chairman's sanctimonious motion that "their Poor has never been degraded by an employment so disgusting and unhealthy," but that in any case there would be no danger of the Bolton inmates chewing putrid bones, since "The Inmates of the Bolton Workhouses have a sufficiency of good and wholesome food." They suggested that the commissioners amend their dietary tables, as the prescribed sustenance was "by *many degrees* deficient and inferior to that ordinarily allowed to *Convicted Felons*."[26] But given the state of the workhouse in recent memory, Bolling's protestation might have lacked conviction. The bounty of the workhouse is cast further into doubt by a report of Mott in the autumn of 1846 alleging that the governor of the workhouse was entirely ignorant of the duties required of him, had no knowledge of any rules for his guidance, had no diet table or prescribed allowances, "and he feeds the Paupers as cheaply as he could." In reacting, the board "wholly disclaims having given any directions either to the Master or any other person calculated or intended to make cheapness in the maintenance of the Poor a primary consideration."[27]

Alongside the reluctance to do the commissioners' bidding, the guardians repeatedly attempted to break up the union. In 1843 the guardians of the fourteen northern townships appealed to the commissioners to be able to split away and form a separate union, but this was vetoed. In May and June a number of townships attempted with the complicity of the board to have the district collectors deliver up their books to the overseers of the separate townships so that they could manage their own affairs—in other words, a reversion to the old system—but this too was apparently quashed by the commissioners.[28] In March 1844 a group of conservatives held a public meeting, chaired by Peter Rothwell, Methodist ironfounder, to petition Parliament against the New Poor Law. Speakers inveighed against the "'law-making triumvirate',", with their unconstitutional powers superseding local self-government, claimed that criminals in gaol were treated better than paupers in workhouses, and attacked the principle of separating man and wife, parent and child. Here again, the Tory attempt to appropriate anti-New Poor Law sentiment lacked conviction. As James Flitcroft protested, there were some gentlemen on the platform who professed to be friends of the poor, but whom he had never seen at a meeting for the extension of the suffrage; the New Poor Law at least gave household suffrage, and it was the commissioners who had stood up for the poor and forced the board to remedy the miserable state of the workhouse. A large Chartist presence apparently derailed the proposed petition. Isaac Barrow, timber merchant and builder, agreeing with the resolutions, moved an amendment—voted through by two-thirds of the meeting—that because Parliament was unrepresentative it was undeserving of public confidence, and so the meeting would not petition it.[29]

The passion generated by the New Poor Law subsided somewhat toward the end of the decade in parallel with the diminution of party tensions. But numerous areas of contention remained: between town and country guardians squabbling about the poor rate; between the Rev. J. S. Birley, though a Tory long an advocate of a new workhouse, blamed by his opponents for the overcrowded condition of the building in 1848 because he resisted patching up the existing structure; between Flitcroft and the governor and some Tory guardians, whom he accused of corruption and mismanagement; between liberals and Tories over the appointment of a politically partisan rate-collector; and between the guardians and the commissioners over yet another petition to divide the union in 1848. Only at mid-century was Ralph Shaw, guardian, overseer, constable, and rate-collector of Lostock, brought to heel and prevented from conducting the business of the township independently of the union.[30] Relics of the old regime resisted the imposition of the new, and across the fissured local elite imperfectly appealing to cross-class alliances, central government could only project its authority and ideas in a compromised, negotiated form.

Preston Union

The first steps of the Preston Union were scarcely less faltering, although the configuration pro and con was different. The press, helping to mold public opinion and keep it focused, was hostile to the New Poor Law: the *Preston Chronicle* was resolutely hostile at first (though somewhat more ambiguously when a partial change of ownership toward the end of the 1840s took it in a more liberal direction);[31] the *Preston Pilot* was a little less so, since it saw merit in some of the provisions;[32] and the *Preston Guardian* was emphatically so, adopting an anti-Poor Law position in its inaugural manifesto in 1844.[33] Two of the leading opponents of the act were Joseph Livesey, proprietor of the *Guardian*, and William Melville Lomas, editor of the *Chronicle*. For them, the New Poor Law was cruel, inhuman, un-English and un-Christian; in Livesey's words, "To suffer the poor to be thus insulted, punished like criminals, and sent broken hearted to a premature grave, to please the Malthusian economists, and to gratify the Scotch cold hearted philosophers, is what I cannot submit to without a struggle."[34] Peter Hesketh Fleetwood, MP, presented to the Commons in April 1837 a petition signed by twenty thousand Prestonians against the act.[35]

When the union was established regardless, the chief division that emerged was not on party lines but by and large between the cross-party, cross-denominational wealthy of the town and countryside and cross-party, cross-denominational town dwellers on middling incomes. This came out most clearly both toward the beginning and the end of the 1840s. The guardians unanimously elected Thomas Batty Addison, liberal barrister, as chairman in 1840, but his enthusiasm for the act and harsh attitude in administering relief provoked a fierce challenge in the 1841 election. Lomas, the *Chronicle* editor, a guardian for Preston, narrowly won, garnering all the votes of the Preston guardians, while the ex officio guardians, county JPs, voted en bloc for Addison. This entailed an almost immediate change in the granting of relief as the guardians agreed to divide the caseload by examining the Preston and the out-district paupers separately, in spite of Addison's protestation that such a proceeding was probably illegal. As the urban-middling group now had the upper hand on the board, cost-cutting became a priority. Only a mustering of the ex officio guardians, who were able to blunt the edge of the ax, averted swingeing cuts in administrative costs and union officers' salaries—in particular the halving of the salary of Joseph Thackeray, the clerk.[36]

A majority of the guardians resisted any pressure from the commissioners to create a new regime in the workhouses. Back in 1838 the union had retained five of the township workhouses and dispensed with four; Penwortham, one of those retained, was abandoned shortly after. This coincided with the rejection of the idea of transforming Preston workhouse (built in 1788) into a "Union workhouse." Briefly at the end of 1839 the modernizers managed to reverse this, voting seventeen to thirteen in favor of a motion of William Marshall of Penwortham Lodge to have one central workhouse instead of four. A committee drew up plans to enlarge the Preston establishment, but only six months later the board voted, twenty-one to five, that it was inexpedient to have only one workhouse at present—presumably because of the depression.[37] With Lomas as chairman the following year, the chances of change receded, in spite of Mott's protestations: "Without proper Classification, Discipline and Cleanliness," he informed the board after the guardians had applied to take on Penwortham workhouse once again until the economy improved, "Workhouses are worse than useless. Under the present arrangements of the workhouses of the Preston Union the Paupers live just the sort of life that suits them, and twenty Workhouses might be filled without lessening the demand for relief." He repeatedly held up Chorlton workhouse as a model ("the results are so different that one would hardly believe they are carrying out the same Law") and argued that to buy and enlarge Preston workhouse or to build a new one would actually be cheaper in the long run than renting and maintaining the various workhouses from the townships.[38] The guardians were not convinced. Addison and Marshall moved for a single, large work-house in December, but their opponents carried by twenty-three votes to six an amendment that the existing workhouses were well adapted for the needs of the union.[39]

When Mott reported on the state of Preston Union again the following February, the guardians were still "so determined in all matters in which they may be opposed to the opinions of the poor Law Commissioners. . . ." The workhouses were in "a most discreditable and unsatisfactory state," and the whole system of management "defective and inefficient." There were no re-ceiving or probationary wards and no bathrooms; there was no accommoda-tion for the sick (except in the House of Recovery at Preston workhouse) and no classification. The paupers mixed "promiscuously" in one yard during the day, all ages and sexes, and "all discipline is set at defiance." Able-bodied men slept with their wives. Mott concluded, "I despair of remedying the present state of the Workhouses by the present Board of Guardians, the majority of whom have shewn themselves determined to oppose the New Poor Law."[40]

This was the prelude to a particularly acrimonious year on the board as contending parties sought control. The opponents of the act, led by Lomas and Livesey, blocked an order of the commissioners in February that the workhouses and the paupers be classified, and attempted to prevent Thack-eray, the clerk, from being returning officer at the approaching election; they feared that he would use unfair influence to secure the return of pro-Poor Law candidates, and he feared the reverse.[41] "You cannot but be aware," Lomas and William Carr, vice chairman, reminded the commissioners, "that where there is a strong party feeling, in a large town like Preston, it is almost impos-sible for the Clerk to avoid making himself a partizan." This was not political partisanship, since the elected Preston guardians, including Livesey and Lomas themselves, split down the middle for the liberals and the conservatives in the 1841 parliamentary election. This anti-New Poor Law party believed "that unless poor law matters in this vicinity are conducted in a spirit of greater for-bearance & justice, an excitement will be aroused here, which all will have cause deeply to lament, and the consequences of which we tremble to contem-plate."[42] In an election manifesto the Preston guardians pointed out that the main issue was whether "the terrible expense" of a union workhouse and "the cruel system of separating husband and wife, parents and children" would be voted through—notions transcending political party and denominational lines. A Nonconformist radical like Livesey linked arms with a conservative like Lomas, whereas the liberal barrister Addison and the liberal clerk Thackeray could be linked with a swathe of wealthy Tory landowners like Marshall in more-or-less enthusiastically endorsing the provisions of the act. This confusion of parties did not prevent individuals couching their opinions in political terms. The opposition stance of Lomas—whose politics, as he described them himself, were "strictly and stringently conservative"—rested on a romantic Toryism. In his analysis, the "Somerset House dictators" were "the sordid instruments of the most cold-blooded code that ever disgraced the statute book of any country under heaven"; the object of the system was to lower laborers' wages so they could purchase less and farmers and shopkeepers would be ruined, the gentry and feudal aristocracy thereby being displaced by the commercial schemes of the Malthusian Whigs. The fact that Peel's government, in office after 1841, perpetuated the New Poor Law considerably disappointed him and made it even more difficult to sustain a convincing politically partisan opposition to the act.[43]

William Marshall of Penwortham Lodge, a no-nonsense, gruff-and-grim Tory and a long-standing county magistrate, projected an alternative voice of Conservatism, strongly supportive of the act. In the maneuverings for advantage by the contending parties he was repeatedly disappointed that the commissioners attempted to compromise with the majority guardians. When the commissioners backed down from their insistence that the clerk be the returning officer, he reprimanded them: "[I]f you, Gentlemen, *will not* support the ex officio Guardians, altho' in a minority, it will be in vain attempting to put the new poor law in operation."[44] He was even more chagrined when the commissioners declared the election of the majority of the guardians of the country townships (strongly influenced by county JPs) invalid, because the addresses of the nominators had not been included on the nomination papers (a printing error had omitted this instruction). "Gent[n]," he protested, "your decision has thrown me completely on my back, three years hard fighting I have had with Livesey & his party & our workhouses remain a disgrace to the country . . . preparatory schools, thro' the vices reigning there, for our prisons."[45]

The act's supporters now faced the prospect of losing the chairmanship again and of Livesey and his party wreaking maximum havoc before any new elections could be held in the voided townships. They tried to postpone the election for chairman, but without success since an order to that effect from the commissioners could not become operative in time. They then discovered that the nominees' addresses for the anti-Poor Law group had been filled in by an attorney acting for Livesey, meaning that these nominations too were invalid. The ex officio guardians mustered in strength at the first meeting of the new board in April, Marshall took the chair, and a motion that the five guardians for Preston and four others be struck off was voted through thirteen to six because the chairman refused to accept the votes of those who were being ousted. It was then a straightforward matter for Thomas Batty Addison to be elected chairman for the coming year. The commissioners then decided to investigate and in June ordered that fresh elections be carried out for three of the seats in Preston and for twenty-two of the out-townships—and this was in spite of the contention of Marshall, Addison, and Thackeray that the next three on the Preston list become guardians even though they had received fewer votes than the ousted three.[46]

For Marshall there were at least three impediments to the improved implementation of the act. One was the troublesome cheesemonger: "In Preston, I am convinced, we cannot advance so long as Livesey is a guardian." A second was the feebleness of the law and of its enforcers. In a letter to the commissioners he complained about the lack of classification, comparing the workhouses to brothels—citing among other things the example of two women who had conceived and given birth to the sons of one man, all while living in the workhouse—and asked, "Now Gent^m if we do not perform our duty, why do you not compel us? Is the New Poor Law powerless? If so, the sooner the unions are dissolved, the better."[47] The third was the prevailing voting eligibility. He objected to any person assessed at nearly £50 in rates only having the same vote as a "pauper" and called for a £10 minimum in the boroughs and £6 or preferably £8 in rural districts; for "believe me Gent^m, the higher you raise the standard of character for guardian, the less the opposition to the new poor law." The wealthy Bolton Tories who vehemently opposed the Act invalidated this as a general principle. But it held good for Preston. Assistant Commissioner W. Gilbert similarly pointed to the influence of a large constituency of artisans, customers at the shops of several of the guardians, who pressed for opposition to workhouse management and for generous out-relief. For both of these gentlemen, the popular voice that used to find some expression in the vestries had not been sufficiently crowded out. One further way of achieving this, Gilbert argued, would be to exclude the press from board meetings, which would diminish the number of angry speeches and allow the return of more "independent" guardians. At present, "In the papers of the Town the proceedings of the Guardians hold weekly a very conspicuous place; their speeches are reported at length and the names of the respective Guardians published as they vote."[48]

In the summer of 1842 the Preston Union was everything that the New Poor Law was not supposed to be. There were five unclassified, overcrowded workhouses, out-relief was profuse, and a sixth of the population was said to be receiving relief. Mott wrote of the "shockingly demoralised state of the inmates occasioned by being huddled together without classification or discipline, the aged and infirm, the worthless idle and abandoned characters and the innocent children, males and females of all ages mixed together presenting the most disgusting and disgraceful scenes that can be imagined."[49] He reported that the new board was somewhat more amenable.[50] A committee, after visiting Chorlton workhouse, even recommended classification, the retention of only two workhouses, and the granting of outdoor relief only in return for labor on an area of moss land. "Notwithstanding the report of the Committee," he noted, "I am satisfied that no efficient classification will be effected if the arrangements are left with the Guardians."[51] On his suggestion the commissioners issued an order setting out how the classification was going to take place. This the board refused to accept, in particular disapproving of the separation of spouses.[52] Thomas Walmsley proposed that aged and infirm spouses should be allowed to sleep together.[53] According to Marshall, Lomas, having denounced the classification as "*diabolical* & *cold blooded*'," (language which caused the Rev. R. A. Rawstorne to leave the room), thereupon "moved an amendment that the able bodied souls like wise [be allowed to sleep together] & a great deal of other foolery, of course he carried it & likewise that *the names* of the four individuals should be inserted in the newspapers who voted against him."[54]

The majority of guardians indicated their continuing hostility to much of the spirit of the act: by agreeing to proposals to divide the union into three separate unions (vetoed by the commissioners);[55] by reiterating their opposition to plans of the ex officio guardians to build a new workhouse ("as to carrying it," remarked Marshall, "the chances are just as great as that the world should stand still on the occasion");[56] and by the passage of a motion (with symbolic, but not practical, value and in a thinly attended meeting) to abolish the union and to revert to the old system of parochial management under the Vestry Act.[57] The board largely disregarded the prescribed scheme of classification, had an acrimonious dispute with the commissioners over the appointment of an assistant overseer, and one guardian fought a separate battle with the clerk over certain irregularities in the conduct of union affairs. Nevertheless, these middle years of the 1840s were as close as the Preston Union had come to acting in harmony since its inception. The removal of Lomas and Livesey from the board at the 1843 elections, and the reelection of Addison as chairman, presumably aided this process.[58]

Divisions broadened again with the onset of the slump in 1847. One split was on town and country lines. Livesey presented a memorial to the commissioners, signed by the mayor and borough magistrates, the vicar and some of the clergy, all the Preston guardians and many of the tradesmen, requesting a doubling of the guardians for Preston township to twelve. As the township had increased rapidly in population since the start of the union, and it paid half of the total funds but had only six out of the thirty-four guardians, an increase was in order. This was particularly true since relief was administered in a manner little different from the old vestry, with Preston guardians dealing with cases for Preston district in one room and the country guardians for the out-districts in another. Another memorial three months later, as the number of applications for relief mounted, restated the case.[59] On both occasions the board took a vote and the combined ex officio and country guardian numbers easily defeated the proposition.[60] The country guardians, said William Ainsworth, cotton spinner, guardian for Preston, "are naturally opposed to any change calculated to affect their power and influence."[61] Addison privately conceded that the request was reasonable, but requested that elections in Preston be by district, to prevent the popular excitement of an election of twelve in one list, which would only bring in an undesirable body of guardians. This, too, was the advice of Assistant Commissioner Alfred Austin, and the new Poor Law Board (the successor body to the commissioners) finally issued an order in March 1848 that six additional guardians be elected in future for Preston and that the township be divided into six wards for the purpose.[62]

A second division was a more familiar one, questioning again the whole ethos of the New Poor Law. In the prevailing distress of the spring of 1848, the flashpoint once more was the election of the chairman. The choice was between Thomas Batty Addison and Thomas Birchall of Ribbleton Hall, attorney, guardian for Ribbleton. Col. Rawstorne, in nominating Addison, admitted that he did not have a particularly high opinion of the New Poor Law but, since out-relief was being given indiscriminately, he saw the need for a tried and tested chairman.[63] John Livesey, Joseph's son, proposed Birchall, and in the *Guardian* Joseph was helping coordinate the opposition to what he saw as the dictatorial figure of Addison. "Mr. Addison's views and mine," he later wrote in his autobiography, "as to the character and merits of the poor, were so utterly at variance that it was impossible we could work well together. I knew their condition from actual visitation, and he did not. He was very severe, and I was lenient."[64] Most surprising of all was the stance of the vicar, the Rev. John Owen Parr, the only ex officio guardian to break ranks and vote against Addison. He launched a strongly worded attack on Addison's theory and practice of administering relief: "[I]f Mr. Addison's is to be the recognised theory, it is a board of guardians of the rich and not of the poor." Addison, he claimed, believing that idleness and vice were the parents of poverty, gave only the most meager relief on the severest scale, whereas Parr was not prepared to lay sole blame on the poor themselves: something had to be allowed for sickness, infirmities, age, and the hand of God. He continued,

it is with pain that I see him directing the relief of the poor. It is well known how very difficult it is when he is doing so to offer any difference of opinion with him on the subject, or to bring that difference of opinion to bear so as to obtain a more humane consideration for the poor. I have no doubt that Mr. Addison believes entirely that his is the principle of true humanity; and he has committed himself to what I think an inhuman humanity, or humane inhumanity.

The Rev. Robert Hornby regarded this speech as extraordinary and un-
charitable. The guardians had to stand between poor man and poor man; true
charity did not involve putting their hands into the ratepayers' pockets and
giving indiscriminately. Notwithstanding, the guardians voted twenty-five to
twenty in favor of Birchall, who declared that, "It is a triumph of the defenders of the true objects of benevolence and judicious humanity over cold-
hearted political economy."[65]

The new majority proceeded to resist certain Somerset House regulations
(including an order to cleanse inmates on entry and force them to wear workhouse dress), even passed a memorial by twenty-one votes to one (Addison's)
that the central control of the Poor Law Board be discontinued or diminished,
and presented themselves as champions of humane treatment.[66] But this laid
the board open to charges of profligate expenditure during the course of the
year. What for the vicar constituted a careful and attentive discharge of their
duties, and for Livesey was a necessary consequence of thousands being
thrown out of work as mills stood idle, was for cotton spinners like Thomas
Miller a great waste of public money. Relief, Rawstorne said in again proposing Addison for chairman in 1849, should only be given to the truly destitute applicant, in order to save him from starvation.[67]

This time Addison won by a narrow majority, and in 1850 he was elected
unopposed.[68] The heat and smoke of the height of the depression subsided as
expenditure stabilized; yet the picture in Preston still did not impress the Poor
Law Board. In the Preston workhouse during 1849, proper classification and
establishment clothing were still lacking, the inmates did not have a proper
weekly change of stockings, a pauper inmate taught the nearly one hundred
boys in the workhouse, and in one of the sleeping rooms eighteen boys slept in
three beds (which bed wetters saturated each night, urine running through the
bedding, straw, and wooden bottoms into large flat tin dishes beneath, sometimes not emptied for a week). A committee of guardians appointed to consider this report found the schooling satisfactory, the changes suggested in
classification expensive and unnecessary and recommended no alteration in
the practice of allowing the inmates to wear their own clothes, "more especially as but recently the Board of Guardians gave an expression of feeling on
the subject, which was opposed to this regulation." The following week the
board voted, twenty-eight to sixteen, against a motion to consider having one
union workhouse instead of five.[69] Such was the state of this union at mid-
century.

Blackburn Union

Blackburn Union was no more welcomed at its outset than neighboring
unions. The Tory *Blackburn Standard* strung the negative adjectives together:
brutal, unjust, illiberal, tyrannical, irreligious, infringing British liberty. At the

time of the implementation of the act at the start of 1838 the editor remarked sardonically,

the event was celebrated by a riot in the workhouse, the paupers declining to acknowledge the grateful blessing of that humane and interesting measure. The strange infatuation of persons who cannot perceive the benefits resulting from a separation from wife and child, cannot we apprehend be too deeply deplored. . . . There is no accounting for the thankless obduracy of some people.

The liberal *Blackburn Gazette* did not think the act needed to be applied to places like Blackburn, where— it claimed—the old poor law had been satisfactorily administered. But at the same time it attempted to undermine the local Tory venom displayed against the act, pointing out that the Tory leadership had supported the measure in Parliament, and that the clerk to the new union, Peter Ellingthorpe, was the secretary of the Blackburn Conservative Political Union. At the first board meeting, Banister Eccles, liberal Nonconformist millowner, argued that in Blackburn, where the rates were low and the poor well attended to, the act was unnecessary and disadvantageous. The guardians agreed on the motions of John Lister, Esq., JP (a conservative, retired manufacturer), Eccles, and James Pilkington (liberal Nonconformist cotton dealer) to draw up two petitions against the act, one from the board and one from the ratepayers.[70]

Still, in contrast to the major battles in Bolton and Preston, the organization of the union went ahead with apparently little friction. "[A]s to the satisfaction or dissatisfaction existing in this Union in reference to the new system of Poor Law Administration," Ellingthorpe wrote to Assistant Commissioner Alfred Power at the end of 1838, "I have great pleasure to inform you that if there is any manifestation of feeling at all on the subject in this Union such manifestation is decidedly favourable." This, he thought, derived from the fact that "a great deal has been accomplished towards redeeming the stigma which has attached to the new system in reference to its inapplicability to the necessities of a manufacturing population." The system would increase in popularity as long as it was left in control of the guardians but not, he warned, if the commissioners interfered to enforce a literal compliance with their rules and regulations.[71]

This notion, that all would be well if local leaders were left to deal with the poor as they saw fit and the commissioners kept out their inquisitive noses, was scarcely what the framers of the New Poor Law had in mind. But it was a working compromise that seemed to stave off a significant local-central conflict for several years—until August 1842, during the prolonged economic crisis. The guardians had long since reduced their five workhouses to two, at Blackburn and Over Darwen, and they even made moves toward classification by age and sex in the Blackburn establishment. But in 1842, Charles Mott, registering his characteristic distaste for everything that did not conform to the clean, Spartan, disciplined ideal, found able-bodied married couples and their families sleeping together. They had an abundance of good wholesome food. They worked at handlooms in the building and were allowed to retain part of their earnings, encouraging them to remain in the workhouse and destroying any notions of deterrence or self-reliance. There was no chaplain, hence no regular religious instruction. The governor or some proper person did not read prayers as directed by the commissioners, and it was left to the cook to call silence and say grace. There was no classification in the daytime and no instruction for the nearly three hundred children except from two aged paupers. There were no probationary wards and there was no uniformity of clothing, the paupers remaining in the filthy garments in which they arrived. Above all, economy in provisions and cooking was so lax that leftovers continuously fatted twenty to thirty hogs. Each year the inmates received at least £50-worth of tobacco and snuff, "a luxury which many small ratepayers cannot afford to indulge in." In the light of this laxity and blatant disregard for the rigors of the principle of less eligibility, Mott called on the commissioners to issue and enforce a set of workhouse regulations.[72]

Ellingthorpe defended the work of the union. Mott had visited at a particularly bad time because the workhouse had nearly two-thirds more inmates than usual. The guardians had kept the costs of indoor relief to a strict minimum, to general satisfaction: "No workhouse in this or any other County has maintained the paupers at so low a rate [1s. 9d. per head per week during the previous quarter] as since the commencement of the Union they have been supported here." Moreover, "In all the tumults and electioneering contests which have occurred in this Town, not a single voice has been raised against the Poor-law, or the generally obnoxious regulations of the Commissioners." Now, then, was not the time to introduce severe workhouse discipline, which would not only be impossible in the present disturbed times, it would not be of benefit in a large manufacturing district, and it would disrupt the good understanding that had hitherto existed among the guardians of the union:

Should the more respectable of the Guardians refuse to act in consequence of their measure and proceedings being as they might consider unduly interfered with by the Commissioners, a course which I am not without doubt they would adopt, we sho.d be left entirely without Guardians, or the management would fall into hands whose measures would defeat the objects of the enactment, and bring upon it a portion of the odium which attaches to the law in the neighbouring Unions.[73]

If the commissioners issued any orders, the clerk insisted in January 1843, the guardians would adopt "such a modification of them, as appeared adapted for the Local exigence of the Union." This was shortly after the board had reopened Livesey workhouse as a school for the pauper children. Charles

Clements visited both this and Blackburn workhouse in May. He discovered no order or regularity of any kind,

and the only object seems to be to stow away as many people as possible. It is really melancholy to think that anything bearing the name of Public Establishments should be permitted to remain in such a state. The sick are neglected, and the Able-bodied left in idleness. So little conception was there of proper management that the only persons at work were young boys breaking stones while great able men were doing nothing. All were in rags and filth.

Livesey workhouse "is in charge of a Pauper. I need say no more."[74]

At the end of the year the board unanimously rejected a plan for alterations in the workhouse on a large scale, to cost £1,830, and unanimously agreed instead not to spend more than £200 on alterations with a view to a better classification. Clements approved of the plans, while recognizing that full classification could not be achieved for such a small amount. Even those limited alterations were incompletely executed, and this, combined with the decanting of the children back into the workhouse after Livesey was again closed, destroyed the classification between the women, the children, and the sick of both sexes. In addition, the commissioners had recently censured the clerk because of irregularities in the fees he charged, and Clements was very unhappy with his inefficiency and the manner in which he conducted union affairs: "[D]oes not enter into his business, & keeps everything back as much as he can from the C^{rs}." Relations between the union and the commissioners descended to their nadir.[75]

At the same time the boasted respectability of the guardians seems to have dipped, or it was earlier exaggerated. Thomas Ainsworth of Showley, guardian for Clayton le Dale, considered resigning toward the end of 1843 because the board's public estimation was so low.[76] One anonymous ratepayer in October 1846 characterized most of the guardians as "illiterate Country men," and in December Richard Haworth, draper, a Blackburn guardian, called for more guardians for Blackburn township and complained that many guardians had "scarcely heard of" the commissioners' rules and regulations "and more that have not seen them at all."[77] This abuse was part of an escalating conflict between town and country. At a particularly charged board meeting in late January 1847, Oliver Roylance, another draper and Blackburn guardian, accused the country guardians of awarding union contracts only after being sweetened by a treat or a donation. John Rutherford, draper and tea dealer, a Blackburn guardian, accused Moses Cocker, farmer, guardian for Livesey, of having tea at the workhouse. "'Yigh, an aw'll do it agean'," replied Cocker, maintaining that "yo Blegburn Guerdians wants to talk an drive the country Guerdians." Rutherford further charged, "'All this eating and drinking cannot be out of your own pockets. Lancashire farmers have not much money to spend at public-houses; they cannot spend their own money that way.'" William Haworth, guardian for Church, "said they had never had this disturbance before, the old Blackburn Guardians never said nothing, but were quiet." But on being asked whether he would deny being treated by candidates for office he replied, "'Would you refuse a good dinner?'" Rutherford complained of being swamped by brute ignorance:

I am a supporter of the New Poor Law; I think it a good and humane law, if properly administered; but we experience, in such cases as this, that grievous abuses exist under it. . . . Blackburn sustains above a third of the expenses of the Union, maintains above a third of the paupers, but has absolutely no power in the settlement of the principal affairs of the Union.[78]

A rather different perspective is gleaned from the clerk after a vote in February by ten to nine in favor of an increase of four guardians for Blackburn, half of the affirmative votes coming from the Blackburn guardians. He wrote, "I regret to say there is an evident wish on the part of the Blackburn Guardians to swamp the Guardians of the Country Townships & that every advantage is taken of a thin attendance of Country Guardians to obtain an inimical decision." The combined poor-rate assessment of the five Blackburn guardians did not exceed £150, whereas the individual rating of several of the country guardians exceeded £2,000. If the qualifications for guardians for Blackburn township were increased, it would tend "to secure a class of guardians less likely to be influenced by party or sectarian purposes."[79]

In spite of the more promising early years, many of the same problems and tensions bedeviling the neighboring unions had risen to the surface. The onset of the late 1840s depression brought further overcrowding in the workhouse, renewed charges of defective management, of failure to keep it clean or to follow the rules or to have workhouse dress or to provide an adequate diet (miserliness and monotony now countering the previous allegations of extravagance).[80] And so it went. Clearly in neither Blackburn Union nor the other two was the Chadwickian vision being implemented by mid-century. The board meetings and elections did nothing so much as provide another venue for the contestation of public space and local power, and for the perpetual battle of wills ending in accommodation between centralists and localists. It is difficult to point to consistent patterns, and predicting an individual's opinion of the New Poor Law from his party, sect, or class was not possible. We find across the three towns a radical, free-trading cheesemonger, a conservative millowner, a conservative bleacher, a radical draper, a conservative vicar, and a conservative newspaper editor opposed to the Law; and a Unitarian manufacturer, a conservative clerical magistrate, a Quaker millowner, a Chartist cart-sheet maker, a conservative landowner, and a liberal barrister in favor. On the whole, the ex officio guardians—the local wealthy acting as county magistrates, still disproportionately conservative—tended to favor the act, and around Preston they were able to exert much influence in the election of favorable country guardians. The urban middling of Preston township joined forces in opposition. In Bolton some of the most prominent liberals were in favor, damaging the faltering popular alliance with the radicals, whereas some of the wealthiest Tory millowners were opposed. In Blackburn initial opposition came from liberal millowners as well as the Tory newspaper and the country farmers, though hostility was not as intense as elsewhere, perhaps indicating lower party tensions.

Did the New Poor Law work in the three unions? No: resting on a faulty diagnosis, it prescribed inappropriate remedies that were never fully implemented. The early years were therefore characterized by a continuity of practices, personnel, and attitudes between the old and new laws and a failure to implement a system of sufficient "less eligibility" for the reformers' tastes.[81] Too many people of necessity experienced the workhouse during depressions for the full stigmatizing impact to take effect, and the operation of the Law of Settlement may have been a more cogent deterrent against applying for relief than the workhouse.[82] Yes: after mid-century, as the economy stabilized and periodic unemployment became less devastating, and—from the late 1850s— all three unions at last built new workhouses, the majority of the laboring classes increasingly scrimped and scraped to avoid the shame of the Bastille and any form of parish relief.[83] Consider the testimony of Edwin Waugh, who reported for the *Manchester Examiner and Times* on the state of the Lancashire milltowns in 1862 during the cotton famine. He described attending the board of guardians in Blackburn: "'What; are you here, John?' said the chairman to a decent-looking man who stepped up in answer to his name. The poor fellow blushed with evident pain, and faltered out his story in few and simple words, as if ashamed that anything on earth should have driven him at last to such an extremity as this." An old man, given his relief ticket, looked hard at it "and, turning round, he said, 'Couldn't yo let me be a sweeper i'th streets, istid, Mr. Eccles?'" Waugh commented that there were some who willingly lived off the rates; "Such cases, however, are not numerous among the people of Lancashire." "[W]e know," wrote W. A. Abram in the 1890s, "that the most deserving of the humbler section of the community will not seek parish relief when misfortune overtakes them."[84] The New Poor Law was working.[85]

This was in the longer term. In the short term the most notable consequences of the New Poor Law were wholly unintended. Firstly, because it fueled Chartism and local-propertied dissent, the government's backpedaling and concessions helped promote the image of a responsible and responsive state, even during such an exercise in dividing and ruling. Secondly, the local bourgeoisie fragmented in new and unpredictable ways, further destabilizing any consolidation into blocs of class, sect, or party.

Medical Men

A final aspect of the New Poor Law merits attention. Of all the bourgeois groups, the medical men were the most directly and adversely affected. Doctors in this period faced the classic dilemmas of how to find and maintain status in a profession that stretched over a vast status-range, that had uncertain professional standards, anachronistic internal divisions, an ill-defined lower boundary, dubious effectiveness, and frequently did not have an adequate remuneration to compensate.[86] In his description of the state of Bolton in 1837, Dr. James Black outlined the condition and the problems of the medical profession. There were sixteen medical practitioners in town, or about one to every three thousand people.

A division to this extent may be thought a fair, if not an ample field for a medical man; but when the kind and circumstances of the mass of the inhabitants are considered, it will be found that the field for professional income by no means corresponds with the extent of the sphere of practice. Deducting the practice engrossed by a host of low empirics, *irregulars*, and the whole body of druggists, along with the relief afforded at the Dispensary to dozens who are well able to pay a small remuneration to a regular surgeon, there remain comparatively, but a few thousands out of the whole population, as an available field of remunerating practice.[87]

The competing "unhonoured dabblers in physic" ranged from quacks, propagandizing their pills, worm medicines, and healing powers through the advertising pages of the local newspapers, to bonesetters. There were two osteologists in Bolton who had never seen a body dissected but who treated more cases of fracture and dislocation than the whole of the regular faculty combined.[88] As Dr. Charles Rothwell pointed out in a later retrospective on the profession in Bolton, it was not surprising that "the heroic system" of orthodox treatment—including salts, senna, opium, calomel, and antimony used "*ad nauseam, ad libitum*, and *ad absurdum*"—should have given birth to milder alternatives such as homeopathy:[89] for a time there were two "high priests" of this "apostasy" in Bolton. More traditional competition came from the pharmacists, true partisans of the heroic: "In the name of treatment, first came the venesection, then the emetic, then the Plummer's Pill, and lastly, the Black Draught—all within the 24 hours—all to clean out the primoe vioe, as if they were a veritable Augean stable of peccant matter."[90]

As the *Preston Chronicle* unkindly noted at the time of the cholera outbreak of 1832, one of the major problems for medical men was that they were "as little skilled, if we judge from their contradictory opinions on cholera, in the cure of some of the ills that flesh is heir to, as were their great grandfathers a hundred years ago."[91] It was about this time, according to Black, that surgeons' status and pocketbooks—inextricably linked—came under particular pressure. As clergymen were discovering, the expansion of opportunities for professional endeavor in the burgeoning towns did not automatically translate into enhanced power, honor, and profit. Doctors had to compete ruinously to become the medical attendants of various sick clubs and friendly societies. Some took contracts for as low as 2s. 2d. per head per annum—not sufficient for a single visit and a bottle of medicine. This lowered the public esteem of the profession, so the Bolton practitioners unanimously decided only to charge each member of a sick club separately and not to attend any births below the class of respectable shopkeeper without payment on the nail. The practitioners now "prefer to charge where they can, in a fair manner, and when objects of charity throw themselves in the way of their practice, to let the honor and feeling of the practitioner bestow that aid, which has ever been held to be the characteristic of a learned and humane profession."[92]

Even so, at the time of the introduction of the New Poor Law, milltown doctors did not impress James Barlow, an eminent Blackburn surgeon, in *An Address to Medical and Surgical Pupils, on the Studies and Duties of their Profession.* His complaints were various: there were many young men of limited education in the ranks of the profession; the study of medicine was "most miserably conducted," producing students "either not sufficiently versed in the pharmaceutical part of their profession, or not able to conduct the minor departments of Surgery with safety to the patient"; the profession was in a degraded state, riven by the "vile evil" of "envy, selfishness, and the mammon of this world," the "arbitrary and unfounded distinction between Physician and Surgeon" being only one source of tension; places of preferment and honor were filled through influence, partiality, and flattery instead of merit; and it was "an overstocked profession, where the avenues to public patronage, favour, and support, are grouped with anxious expectants." The medical provisions of the New Poor Law made a sorry situation worse, since they were "calculated to sacrifice life to a niggardly economy." Indeed, the "vile and contemptible" system of tender tempted young practitioners "'to practice by chance, and grow wise by murder'; or I would rather say, to practice by chance, and murder without growing wise."[93]

The guardians of their own and of the public's purse were notoriously economical when it came to paying the salaries of their servants, be they clerks, relieving officers, assistant overseers, or medical officers; in a buyer's market, they could generally keep costs down. For example, in 1843 the guardians divided Blackburn township into two medical districts (the population warranted three, but they considered two quite sufficient), appointing Robert Wilding to one at £70 a year, including attendance at the workhouse, and Richard Brownlow Barlow to the second at £35 a year. In response to the commissioners' comment that the salaries were fixed at a very low rate, the guardians retorted that these salaries combined with per capita midwifery fees were ample and nearly twice the amount paid to former medical officers. "The fact that the medical officers make no complaint as to the insufficiency of the remuneration," the clerk wrote, "is in the opinion of the guardians strong evidence of its sufficiency."[94]

The medical officers did make a complaint and apply for pay rises in March 1847, at a time when the editor of the *Blackburn Standard* described them as "shamefully over-worked, and pitifully under-paid." In 1843 Wilding had received £110 10s., which included ten shillings for every midwifery case. But three years later, because of a reduction in the number of midwifery cases and a considerable rise in general cases, he earned only £95 10s. Barlow had earned £57 10s. in the previous year, or 8³/4d. for every non-midwifery case; "Think of paying a medical man *eightpence three farthings*," the editor demanded, "for attending and furnishing medicine in any case of sickness the Board may think fit!" Even though Barlow pointed out that nothing of his fixed salary remained after he had administered medicine, and Wilding that the substantial increase in population in his district was not reflected in his pay, the guardians were largely unimpressed. They were confident that other medical men could be found for the asking price. Put like that, Wilding and Barlow agreed to stay on at the same rate of pay.[95]

In Preston Union the guardians followed similar policies of resisting pressure from doctors and commissioners to increase salaries.[96] The Bolton guardians, most obstreperous of all in their dealings with the commissioners, proved more devious. First of all, the board, chaired by John Bolling, denounced the commissioners' new medical orders in 1843—designed to improve both the administration of medical provision and the remuneration of medical officers—as uncalled for and very expensive. Once the orders had been enforced, the guardians stated their belief that respectable, qualified men would undertake the duties without any additional fees for surgical and midwifery calls. In spite of the commissioners' refusal to accept this, and of a meeting of seventeen Bolton medical practitioners to denounce the board, the guardians forced the candidates to renounce their rights to the fees. The commissioners declared the contracts between the guardians and their MOs void after several months of noncompliance with their instructions.[97] Albany Featherstonhaugh, twenty-three, one of the new MOs for Great Bolton, wrote to Chadwick that this refusal of the commissioners to sanction the surgeons' appointments did not inconvenience the guardians "but presses heavily on the poor, unfortunate Medici." The medical officers did not dare resign their nominal appointments since others would be found to replace them. To resolve the impasse, the guardians proposed to lower the fixed salary paid to the MOs and allow them fees, "whilst the Chairman proposes as an excellent trick, to *extort* from the '*satisfied* Surgeons' a private agreement to receive no more of the fees mentioned in the Medical Order than will raise the lowered payment to the original amount for which they agreed."[98] Presumably this again was unacceptable to the commissioners because shortly afterwards the guardians resolved to reappoint the MOs at the same fixed salaries plus fees. But that was not the end of the saga. A year later Featherstonhaugh gave the real story behind the apparent back-down on fees. He told the commissioners that the guardians had advertised for new elections for surgeons, holding out the threat of nonelection to the current medical officers if they did not enter into a private arrangement to forfeit the additional fees: "I may add in explanation, that through this private arrangement we have felt ourselves bound to forfeit the fees mentioned, and I am not aware of any Surgeon who has received anything in this form."[99]

None of this scramble for poorly remunerated posts treating union paupers enhanced doctors' status and self-esteem. If union duties served as a means of building a reputation and contacts for more lucrative work, all well and good; but as Frederick William Marshall, medical officer for Westhoughton, explained this could only function in one of two ways: either the district had to be sufficiently small so "that I could myself attend without unavoidable loss of more remunerative practice," or the salary had to be large enough for him to be able to employ an assistant to take charge of the Poor Law work. Both of these were doubtful.[100] In addition, practitioners had to face other occupational hazards because of their union duties: the prospect of premature death, professional rivalries, and being hauled up in front of a court.

During the typhus epidemic of 1847-48, known locally as the "Irish fever" because of its prevalence among recent Irish immigrants, Richard Robinson, medical officer of the Great Bolton eastern district, William Hatton of the western district, William Harrison, master of the temporary fever ward, John Kean Colman, relieving officer for the western district, and Barlow, medical officer of a Blackburn district, all contracted the disease and died. Thomas B. Garstang, medical officer of the Bolton fever hospital, also fell ill but survived. The guardians had a collection for the widows and children of Robinson and Hatton but raised only £22, whereupon they appealed to the Poor Law Board to solicit an additional sum from the government, as it was essential to secure attendance on the sick poor "and to stimulate others to the like exertions that the services of those who face the danger and die in the discharge of their duty should not pass unnoticed or unrewarded." The Treasury, the board replied, would not oblige.[101]

Less drastic were professional jealousies regarding the treatment of the poor. For example, F. W. Marshall, MB (London), MRCS, LSA, was passed over in three applications—by the factory inspector, Leonard Horner, for a factory appointment, and by the Bolton guardians for both a vaccination and a medical officer appointment—in favor of people with inferior qualifications, the latter two rejections a reminder of James Barlow's complaint that lobbying, influence, and economy would prevail over qualifications when appointments depended on election by guardians. Marshall felt that his honor was at stake: "I have studied very hard for the Qualifications which I possess . . . and should be jealous of any slight cast upon them, not only for the sake of my own feelings, but for the sake of the School where I studied and the University where I graduated."[102] Alternatively, the regulation that the medical man reside in his district often meant that the guardians were severely constricted in their choice; the appointment of individuals without the right qualifications provoked a number of challenges from the commissioners or left MOs vulnerable to sniping from colleagues.[103] When Samuel Hope Wraith, a Darwen surgeon, complained that he had to attend a woman in labor because the MO, William Gaulter, was unavailable, unwilling, or intoxicated, he slipped in the gratuitous aside that Gaulter "has neither a license or Diploma of any kind."[104]

On occasions medical officers found themselves in trouble with the law after one of their patients had died. In 1843 a coroner's jury, investigating the death of Joseph Wilson, an inmate of Bolton workhouse, accused Albany Featherstonhaugh of negligence, and Assistant Commissioner W. H. S. Hawley was sent to investigate. Featherstonhaugh saw Wilson four times and concluded that, apart from a chronic constriction of the urethra, he was exaggerating his ailments in order to obtain extra food. The following day the patient died. The surgeon who performed the postmortem stated that the lungs were so acutely inflamed that it was impossible for any medical man of ordinary abilities and common care and attention not to have detected it. Two other medical men disputed this, and Hawley decided to exonerate Featherstonhaugh. He was cautioned but not, as the jurors demanded, dismissed.[105]

Joseph Lomax Heap, medical officer for Bolton workhouse, applied to the board in October 1841 for permission to install an apparatus for fumigating and cleansing "such of the Inmates as were in a state of filth and uncleanness." The board agreed, if he held himself responsible for any of the consequences, being rather uneasy about any proceedings that had the appearance "of being mere experiments on the Inmates." On the first trial of the "stoving system," Margaret Heywood, a pauper afflicted with "the lousy evil," was placed naked on a chair in an air-proof oil-case buttoned up to the neck. Brimstone was fired under her and the fumes covered her body for a minute and a half. She died over a fortnight later from inflammation of the lungs. John Marshall Robinson, conducting the postmortem, maintained that such sulfur baths were common for diseases of the skin among all classes, and that the apparatus had been properly constructed, but the borough coroner's jury charged Heap with manslaughter and he was committed for trial at Liverpool.

At this period of divided jurisdiction the county coroner's jury returned a verdict of death from natural causes. Heap was supported by the guardians and nearly all the medical men in Bolton, the prosecution did not offer any evidence at the Liverpool Assizes, and the Grand Jury threw out the indictment against him. The question of who was going to pay the £25 12s. 6d. then became a major point of contention between the guardians, who charged it to the poor rate, and the commissioners who took it all the way to Chancery before John Bolling and four other guardians, the defendants, agreed to repay the sum at interest, plus costs.[106]

Thus, in its impact on medical men, as in so many other matters, the New Poor Law was akin to a firecracker ignited in the manufacturing districts, flailing around in different directions, creating sparks, and kindling small fires. It helped increase tensions between status-conscious medical gentlemen struggling to establish their individual and collective credentials, and between them and other gentlemen acting as guardians: further twists to the bourgeois kaleidoscope.

CHAPTER 8: VOLUNTARY ASSOCIATIONS

"N.B. The Subscriptions will be published," the Rev. Thomas Jones, minister of St. George's, Little Bolton, candidly appended to an appeal for money for his schools in 1797.[1] The advertising of an individual's donation broadcast his or her social standing in the finely calibrated social hierarchy.[2] Conspicuous contribution rivaled conspicuous consumption as a means of establishing status. Donations to a range of selected causes demonstrated a proper degree of duty; too small a contribution denoted meanness or an anemic sense of responsibility or financial difficulties; too large a contribution signified a certain uppitiness, a bid to bat above one's wealth and station.

The subscription list was an important component of the voluntary association, which was a ubiquitous presence on the middle-class civic landscape, a form of organization that fragmented the bourgeoisie into a profusion of interlocking economic, political, social, and cultural subsets across each milltown and beyond. Sympathy, social responsibility, religious zeal, and civic pride jostle alongside self-interest and fear of social unrest in explaining the rise of voluntary associations. They had many possible purposes. The first was to provide the financial and organizational basis for collective action, since few coketown individuals had the power or resources to proceed alone, and since the only other alternative—state action—was only deemed desirable in certain circumstances, and then but hesitatingly. The second was to act as a means for the limited redistribution of resources within the community while exacting maximum deference, thus inserting a finger into the dike of the current socioeconomic system and avoiding far-reaching structural change. The third was the attempt to percolate ideological messages further down the social scale, by persuasion or by coercion. The fourth was to forge links across party and sectarian divides and to draw the shopkeeper class into a shaky fraternal embrace calculated to draw its radical sting. The fifth was to reaffirm certain bourgeois moral and ethical values by contrasting them with the lack thereof in the masses: there was a sense that the vices, failures, and poverty of the poor were all too convenient in shoring up the collective identities of respectability.[3] The sixth was to build up a network of essential contacts and to facilitate the flow of information upon which decisions at the business, professional, and civic level could be based; it thus followed that *all* forms of voluntary association, above party or not, formal or informal, could facilitate the construction of both a market and a civic culture, even those that were most disruptive and dysfunctional as far as ideological cohesion was concerned.[4] As enthusiasts for and theorists of civil society from Tocqueville to Habermas have argued, the voluntary association was a critical factor in the emergence of liberal democracy, both in maintaining a vibrant public sphere not directly controlled by the state and in creating an accountable and responsible forum for organization, discussion, and debate.[5]

Any student of this subject is clearly indebted to R. J. Morris's masterly analysis of the growth of voluntarism in Leeds. He argues that the increasing density of the organizational undergrowth belies the expectations of the theorists of anomie and alienation in the urban environment. The associations were part of the search for order and stability, the prime desiderata of the propertied, and he charts their progression from the straightforwardly coercive to more subtle forms of ideological and cultural domination. Perhaps less convincingly he maintains that the voluntary association was one of the primary means by which divisions within the middle class were overcome and that a limited degree of class action was essential in the 1830s and 1840s if the privileges of property and power were to be stabilized and extended independently of the state.[6] But my emphasis throughout this study has been on the vast and fluctuating range of measures of coercion, concession, and incorporation as various members of the bourgeoisie and fractions of capital in conjunction with the state devised their own halting, conflicting, cross-cutting, and incomplete solutions. A powerful hegemony, relationships of authority within the broader cultural framework of the dominance of capitalism, and a pulsating civic and market culture do not *need* united class action, and the hunt for the class-conscious middleclass might best be dispensed with. The variety of semi-contradictory organizational endeavors and conflicting ideological messages was a sign of *strength*, not of weakness.[7]

Among the main types of voluntary association, some of which we have already encountered, the commonest, involving the largest numbers of people, were those promoting profit or professional cohesion. As such they were completely divorced from any attempts to seduce the lower orders. In bringing together individuals as shareholders and directors with divergent ideological perspectives they superimposed a further layer of conflicting identities and interests on the map of kinship networks, party affiliations, sectarian allegiances, and town-and-country alliances.[8] Secondly, among the earliest, the coercive and the patriotic associations were designed respectively for the defense of property and of the nation. A third tier consisted of religious societies, either seeking interdenominational cooperation or shoring up exclusive denominational identities. From the 1830s a fourth cluster of associations were the local political societies or pressure groups like the Anti-Corn Law League with particular axes to grind (see Chapter 12). The two main outstanding forms of organization, the foci of this chapter, spoke equally candidly of bourgeois ideological commitment and generally sought to bridge the internal divisions within the middle classes: the charitable and the cultural.

Alleviating Distress

Charitable organizations sought in some way to impact upon the lower orders: by the alleviation of distress, by the provision of basic medical facilities, and by indoctrination or—increasingly—through more subtle attempts to incorporate the lower orders into a "civilized" rather than a "controlling" civic culture.[9] Collective bourgeois action to alleviate distress was a staple of the cotton towns throughout the period. It indicated clearly who perceived themselves or wished to be perceived as members of an active elite, joining together in subscription lists, believing that an alternative to ratepayer aid was necessary and/or desirable. Repeated bouts of distress throughout the war and postwar years prompted a typical pattern of response.[10] The 1826 crisis, a particularly dire example, strained the system to its limits, and the fabric was only reknit with sabers, poor rates, and charity. Widespread unemployment brought its usual disastrous consequences: the poor selling or pawning their clothes and household goods, crowding ever more closely, and eating starvation rations; shopkeepers and craftsmen, having lost much of their custom, descending toward a state of penury; poor rates shooting up; the breaking up of the sick clubs and friendly societies, and the exhaustion of small deposits in savings banks.[11] In Lower Darwen, for example, every family depended or relied heavily on the loom, directly or—as farmers paying rack rents and producing milk and butter for the poor weavers—indirectly. Three quarters of the weavers were unemployed, and poor rates were so high that they were almost impossible to collect. The weavers had behaved peacefully;

At the same time we must not dissemble that a spirit hostile to all possessors of property is rapidly spreading among them. Starving themselves for the want of the necessaries of life they begin to think that no one else should enjoy the means of subsistence. Circumstanced as they are & with little or no religious principle to restrain them there seems to be no security against their going to the greatest extremes.[12]

In response, local elites set up committees to organize charitable relief on the understanding that they could distribute aid more systematically and more fairly than the wealthy individually. First they raised as much as they could locally and then appealed further afield, in particular to the Manufacturers' Relief Committee in London and to the government. In these appeals there were two main approaches, beyond the distressing descriptions: one was to stress how quiescent the poor were under almost unimaginable privations and therefore how truly deserving of succor as a reward; the other was to underline how restless the indigent were becoming and hence how essential relief was, and quickly. The vicar, J. W. Whittaker, chaired the Blackburn relief committee which, by the start of April, was undertaking its third subscription and was appealing to both a local and a wider audience. He urged the cotton masters, out of a sense of duty and self-interest, to do more:

I hope that it will be superfluous to remind the master manufacturers, and proprietors of factories, how particularly they are called upon by existing circumstances, to exert unusual liberality on this occasion—Should they stand aloof, they cannot expect that the whole burden of relieving the poor, whom they encouraged to settle here, should fall on those unconnected with trade.—This class is manifestly unable to bear it: and the consequence would be a frightful increase of the poor's rates, which would chiefly fall on those who withhold gratuitous contributions.[13]

George IV donated £1,000; "It will probably have the effect of counteracting any tendency to riot," Whittaker wrote, "wh. existing distress and a few factious agitators may have produced in the populace." James Slade, the vicar of Bolton, leading the Bolton relief effort, appealed to the same source because the £1,200 local subscription was nearly exhausted. "It is my duty & my pride to add, that our suffering poor are not altogether unworthy of the Royal compassion & bounty; inasmuch as they have hitherto endured their privations with most exemplary patience & submission." The £500 that duly arrived elicited "unbounded satisfaction & joy. . . . [T]ho' our Poor have already suffered with wonderful fortitude, I am confident they will now be still more reconciled to their miserable privations." William Hulton agreed, "confident that every endeavor will be used to make it a new bond of union between the lower orders and the Government"; and if not, the arrival of a regular military force into Bolton at the same time would perform the task instead.[14]

Distress of this magnitude thus drew upon the resources of government (armed force, subventions disguised as monarchical donations but administered locally), the ratepayer, individual face-to-face largesse,[15] and the charitable organization, all weaving a web of restraint and support across the mill-town landscape. Having so many arrows in the quiver of containment did not necessarily produce gratitude. John McAdam, the celebrated road builder, sent as an emissary of the London Relief Committee to put the unemployed to work repairing the roads, reported in August that the populace seemed very quiet and congratulated itself for this. He was pointing to the fact that even quiescence was a form of negotiation, a calculated bid for the reallocation of resources, an appeal for a social compact that sprang from an exaggeratedly weak and unequal bargaining position, but one to which the elite had to respond nonetheless. But there was always the threat of disorder as a second string to the poor's bow. McAdam thought that the people could explode into lawlessness if the distress were allowed to continue, in all its severity, much longer. In September he wrote, "this part of the Country is in a most distressed situation, irritable, *seditious*, perfectly unthankful to the superior Class who have exerted themselves so meritoriously in their behalf."[16]

Relief committees were frequently employed in subsequent years, but not until 1840-41 did the bourgeoisie have to placate and succor the distressed poor on a similarly large scale. This was most heavily publicized in Bolton, where suffering could be kicked around in battles over the New Poor Law and the Corn Laws, and between political parties. William Pearce, a weaver in Howell's Croft, ineligible for relief because he did not belong to the parish, died in February 1840 after apparently eating nothing more than a basin of gruel a day for three or four weeks. He lived with his family in a cellar containing a broken table, a stool, a chair, and a sacking bed with no covering. The back cellar was awash with sewage from a midden channel that ran through it, and soon after his death the corpse was covered in hundreds of maggots. A coroner's jury allegedly returned a verdict of "Died for want of food," though the coroner failed to record it. This and many other cases convinced William Naisby, radical draper, "whilst I was a guardian, from what I saw at the board, and by visiting the poor, that deaths were occurring nearly every week in Bolton for want of the necessities of life, or, perhaps, more properly speaking, from sickness produced by want, and ending in death, which amounts to the same thing." The *Free Press* agreed, contending that hundreds had perished where a just verdict would have been "'died from lingering disease produced by want.'" Naisby passed on the cases in 1841 to Dr. Bowring, the town's new MP, who spoke in Parliament of the suffering in Bolton and referred to deaths from starvation. Assistant Poor Law Commissioner Charles Mott, sent to investigate, found the charges unsubstantiated. He did not deny that there was genuine distress, but refused to accept that it was as bad as some individuals were trying to make out. In addition, a group of Little Bolton liberal gentlemen had undertaken an inquiry into the condition of the poor the previous December, made known their findings at an Anti-Corn Law League meeting and presented the cases of 309 families to the board of guardians. This resulted in a series of charges and countercharges between the guardians, the Leaguers, and Mott about the true state of the poor and the politicization of poverty.[17]

The distress was real enough, but the partisans of the League determined to make the most of it and to attribute it directly to the Corn Laws. Perronet Thompson, prominent Leaguer, wrote in *The Sun* at the end of 1841, after a visit to Bolton, anything like the squalid misery, the slow, moulding, putrefying death by which the weak and the feeble of the working classes are perishing here, it never befell my eyes to behold, nor my imagination to conceive. And the creatures seem to have no idea of resisting, or even repining. They sit down with oriental submission, as if it was God and not the landlords that was laying his hand upon them. And when their honourable representative in Parliament gave description of their sufferings, "liar" was the best word applied to him by the organs of tyranny.[18]

Bowring, imitating Shelley, put his passion into poetry:

"'DIED OF STARVATION'—CORONERS' INQUESTS"

"I met Famine on my way,
Prowling for human prey,
Clogg'd with filth, and clad in rags,
Ugliest of all ugly hags.
Lo! a sceptre wreathed with snakes
In her wither'd hand she shakes;
And I heard the hag proclaim—
'*Bread Tax*, is my sceptre's name!'
On remorseless mission sent,
Maiming, murdering as she went,
Spreading death from street to street,
O! I heard the hag repeat,
(Shuddering while I heard and saw,)
'Mine is RIGHT and MIGHT and LAW;'
Then to solitude I flew—
'Gracious Heaven can this be true?'
On my trembling knees I fell:
God! thou God of mercy tell,
Can the very fiends of hell
In thy name their pandects draw,
And declare their license—*law*?
Dare they in thy holy sight
To proclaim their robbery—*right*?
Rouse thee! raise thine awful rod!
Lord how long, how long, O God?'"[19]

Where poverty was being used to score partisan points, the voluntary association could be particularly useful. The Bolton Society for the Protection of the Poor, founded in July 1840, brought together all sections of the elite in its aim to provide relief in cases of extreme and temporary distress and to suppress mendacity and fraud. Such an organization was a necessary adjunct for the values being instilled by the New Poor Law. William Cooke Taylor was just one of the many commentators who spoke of the horror that most of the lower orders felt at being forced to receive parish relief: "They may have been talked into a hatred of the New Poor Law, but from their souls they loathed pauperism, as being odious to that sturdy pride of independence which no race of mankind ever possessed in such superabundance as the men of Lancashire."[20] Whether it was as yet true that many of the poor agreed to play by the rules of social stigma laid down by their betters, or merely wishful thinking, the quid pro quo was a charitable organization to give non-stigmatic, temporary relief in a time of crisis.

The Bolton society followed the well-established custom of attempting to winnow the deserving wheat from the undeserving chaff: "[I]t has given encouragement to the honest poor, and put down the clamorous pretensions of the idle and deceitful," noted the first report.[21] In February 1841 it merged with the District Provident Society, established to "encourage habits of prudence and economy amongst the industrious poor, and to promote a friendly intercourse between the different classes of society": in other words, the regulation of the behavior of the poor and the strapping of ties across the class divide. Ladies and gentlemen visited the homes of the working classes, collecting small sums of money and investing them at 5 percent interest. The 1840 report commented that, after initial suspicion that the wealthy were trying to discover on how small a pittance life could be sustained, there was now "increased good feeling," the consequence "of a greater intercourse between the higher and lower classes of the community."[22]

In good times, one branch of the society afforded opportunities of laying up provision against the day of adversity. In bad times, especially during the lowest point of the depression in 1841-42, the other branch collected and distributed subscriptions, set up a soup kitchen, handed out £1,100 from the London Distressed Manufacturers' Relief Committee, and sought work for the able-bodied male applicants—particularly, in cooperation with the Great Bolton trustees, in the construction of a large reservoir.[23] The society took its task of separating between the worthy and the rest seriously, making it known that immorality and impropriety would be taken into consideration when the cases were heard, and that any of those working on the reservoir who swore, used improper language, or struck a fellow workman, would be discharged. According to Charles Mott in December 1841, of 776 recent applicants, only 218 were granted relief; the rest were denied on various grounds, including telling deliberate falsehoods, being professional mendicants, vagrants, females of disorderly character, or confirmed drunkards, refusing to work, or being unworthy of private charity.[24] The boasted success in promoting "a friendly intercourse" between the classes is much less certain; the enfolding of the lower orders under the wings of charity, one marked comfort, the other coercion, was less encompassing than the bourgeoisie wished to believe. But the new society once again acted to bring together disparate sectors of the middle classes,[25] and once again it played a role in the full panoply of measures to keep the portcullis manned against discontent and to maintain the structure of society substantially unchanged.

Mechanics' Institutes

Charity was one way to attempt this, education another. Shortly after the founding of Bolton's Mechanics' Institute in 1825, J. H. Arrowsmith spelled out the philosophy behind it. The principal objective was "to afford the Mechanic an opportunity of improving himself in the first principles of his art," by reading scientific works, hearing lectures, and witnessing experiments. Only in that way could English technological superiority be maintained. Secondary objectives flowed rather more apologetically. In spite of much criticism, there was no religious instruction, because no one form would suit all parties: "No party spirit is so vehement and intolerant, as that arising from religion; no feeling so overwhelming as religious enthusiasm." He hoped that the mingling of Christians of every denomination at the institute would promote greater understanding. Would the institute damage domesticity? No, since fathers would be lured away from the alehouses where they spent their leisure hours, their wages would go not on drink but on contributing to family comforts, and they would take their sons to the institute with them, supervising them more closely. Intemperance would diminish; as the mechanics "become more interested in scientific pursuits, they will become less addicted to sensual gratification. Pleasures of so opposite a nature cannot be combined." But would it not be better "to persuade the mechanics to spend their evening in reading the Bible at home, and in other devotional exercises"? No doubt; but this was unrealistic:

It will generally be allowed, that, if the mechanic devotes half an hour every evening to his religious duties, he devotes as much as he can be expected to do, or as much as religion requires. Those already in the habit will not be deterred from continuing so good a practice by too great a fondness for scientific research.

But was not a little learning dangerous? Since no political works were allowed, the safety of the state could not be endangered. Besides, "We ought to have such confidence in the excellence of our Constitution, as to think that the more thoroughly it is known, the more it will be appreciated and admired." Would, then, education disrupt the social hierarchy? No:

It is not to be apprehended that the Mechanics will become less satisfied with their situation, or that they will become more intelligent than their masters. The Mechanic, who frequents the Institute, and renders himself a superior workman, by uniting theoretical with practical information, will deserve, and will expect, a higher remuneration than his fellow-workmen, who do or do not attend it. The masters, observing the improvement of their men, will naturally be led to make a corresponding improvement in their own talents; and thus the same distance will still be kept up between servant and master as at present, and society will be constantly advancing in the scale of human improvement.[26]

The first annual report expected that the Bolton institute would "have a powerful influence on the happiness and temperance of individuals, and on the good order of society; and is eminently calculated to uphold our superiority, as a great manufacturing and trading nation, in these times of national competition."[27] Whether it achieved this is doubtful, given limited mechanic enrollment, which peaked at 276 in the first year but dropped to fifty in the third and thereafter rose only to 146 in 1830-31.[28] "Mr. Black, a Bolton doctor, tried to give a series of free lectures on anatomy," reported a visiting Frenchman, Gustave d'Eichthal, in 1828; "no one turned up to them. Someone told me that to attract English workers into the Mechanics' Institution it was necessary to give them a few pints of ale every evening."[29] Did the institute help foster elite cohesion, the purpose behind Rule XII: "The Committee shall not admit into the Library, either by donation or purchase, any Books of a Political or Theological nature, nor any novels or plays"? Yes, in that anyone with pretensions was included in the list of honorary members and donors, those who had donated and/or subscribed at least a guinea. In that very act they were acquiring prestige by demonstrating largesse (and the closer to the top of the list the greater the kudos), as well as in some sense subscribing to a common ideology that viewed the Mechanics' Institute as a desirable phenomenon, a commonsensical approach to the problem of the lower orders. No, in the sense that it was very easy to send off a guinea each year, or to cease to do so when trade was depressed, or when it became less fashionable, or when the subscription lists were no longer accorded such prominence, with little or no further involvement or thought, the nineteenth-century equivalent of buying a plastic-and-paper poppy once a year. This level of commitment certainly did nothing for face-to-face elite group-cohesion; only at the level of committee organization can this have been significant—that is, among a handful of people.

Throughout the thirties the committee repeated the various messages the institute was attempting to inculcate: "[T]hat education is the best preservative of order and the surest guarantee for a sober and blameless life"; that reading and similar calm intellectual pursuits would "safeguard against the disastrous excesses of intemperance" and were a "sure guarantee for a quiet and happy fireside"; that "rational and innocent recreations" would "wean the mechanic from those amusements which are obnoxious to good morals," and to this end "No game has yet been introduced . . . but CHESS." But the lack of numbers was worrying, particularly within the lower-middle class. The committee reported at the start of 1837 that the shopmen and clerks in mercantile and professional concerns, who frequently constituted a great majority of the membership in other towns, had largely remained aloof. Perhaps, they surmised, this was because the rooms in Acres Field were dark, inconvenient, badly ventilated, and unsightly. They moved to larger premises in Bridge Street in June 1838, and the attendance picked up to an average of 320 in the following year, though this was not as big an increase as they had anticipated.[30]

At some stage around 1840 many of the conservatives withdrew their support,[31] another casualty of the intense political ructions of those years, and the institute could be said to be failing in all three of its main functions: the education of the mechanics, the incorporation of the petite bourgeoisie in an extended category of respectability, and the banishment of party politics so as to promote bourgeois cohesion for united action. The 1847 report noted that it had been a matter of regret to the friends and managers of the institute for many years "that a large portion of our townsmen should stand aloof and thus give it the appearance of being devoted to party purposes." Several influential gentlemen thought the promotion of the Athenæum offered an opportunity for a coalition of all parties, and so they laid aside a plan to expand the institute. With the Athenæum's collapse on sectarian grounds, the institute's plans were revived, but had to be suspended again at the onset of the depression. The membership was continuing to decline in 1850, when trade had revived, and even with a conservative, T. R. Bridson, as president. "Why this town, with its numerous and industrious population," the report of November 1851 lamented, "should be so far behind our neighbours who boast separate institutions and public libraries in ones and twos and threes, has long been a matter of surprise to all who have visited it." Only new, more extensive, more agreeable premises would excite sufficient interest to bring forward the means necessary for the support of such an institute "as Bolton can and should maintain."[32]

The Preston Institution for the Diffusion of Knowledge, the town's equivalent of a Mechanics' Institute, was founded in October 1828.[33] Thomas Batty Addison, presiding at the opening meeting, talked enthusiastically about the new London University and claimed that Preston on a proportionate scale might emulate the metropolitan example.[34] The institution apparently prospered initially, but then numbers dwindled, especially of working-class men both on the committee and as members, slumping to only an eighth of total membership by 1837. In 1841 the membership list demonstrated that, in a circumscribed manner, the institution was helping foster ties principally among members of the upper-middle and lower-middle class: on the books were six ladies, fourteen gentlemen, three bankers, ninety-six professional men, forty manufacturers, seventy-six tradesmen, eighty-five clerks and shopmen, seventeen mechanics, thirty-four joiners and other operatives, six youths at school, six factory hands, and twenty-nine miscellaneous.[35]

The library maintained a taboo on deistical, atheistical, party political, and polemical theological works, but it seems that fiction was allowed from 1837 (subject to the president's judgment of its propriety), presumably in a bid to attract members. One of the problems was that, while the institution's objective was to promote the diffusion of scientific, useful, and general knowledge, above all among the operative classes, subscriptions at 6s. 6d. a year or life membership at five guineas were stiff prices for most of the lower orders.[36] Still, it survived, and a successful exhibition in 1840 boosted funds; but then the committee split over whether to move premises from Cannon Street. The majority seceded to form an alternative Lit. and Phil. Institution, which paradoxically helped revive the older institution with an infusion of new blood. In June 1846 the mayor, Thomas German, laid the foundation stone for an imposing colonnaded structure in a prime location opposite Avenham Walks, and in April 1849 a bazaar raised money to complete it. A bazaar was one of those occasions that could bring together a diverse array of individuals to focus resources on a particular objective. It put the elite on display as patrons (names and contributions prominent in the printed program) and as ostentatious consumers (since it was, after all, in a good cause, one need feel no guilt about damaging one's standing by sinning against the commandments of thrift and frugality). The ladies demonstrated their active involvement in charity; dressed in their finery, they played at being tradespeople for a few hours while genteelly manning the stalls. If not quite so ubiquitous as the public dinner, the bazaar was more representative of the bourgeois elite (often with a sprinkling of aristocratic and gentry patrons and patronesses) in that it encompassed women as well as men. For this particular event the catalogue rhapsodized,

Whatever work wants doing, a Bazaar is held; if a church is to be finished, there is a Bazaar; or a peal of bells wants renewing, there is a Bazaar; a missionary society is destitute of funds, there is a Bazaar; a soup kitchen wants its boilers at work, a Bazaar; a Sunday school is incomplete, there is a Bazaar; and, finally, here in Preston, when the most elegant and most classical—yea, and one of the most useful buildings in North Lancashire is to be completed, one of the most splendid Bazaars, for a local purpose, that ever graced the provinces, is held with a success proportionate to the worthiness of the object in favour of which it was instituted.

The editor of the *Chronicle* remarked that the occasion was receiving the support of every class, sect, and party, amounting to a more general spirit of cooperation than he could remember. The Avenham Institute, costing £6,000, opened in October 1849.[37]

The Blackburn Mechanics' Institute, predictably slower off the mark than its neighbors, was founded at a meeting chaired by John Abbott, cotton manufacturer, in March 1844, with the usual proviso that "the introduction of party politics, controversial theology or sentiment having an infidel or immoral tendency" be "strictly prohibited." Although the first rule of the institute laid out that the humblest member was eligible for the highest position, the founding was a resolutely elite affair: Joseph Feilden, the first president, and the Rev. Thomas Rutherford Dickenson, Frederick Adolphe Margraf, Ph.D., professor of languages, John Spencer Birch, surgeon, and James Pilkington, the vice presidents, neatly encompassed representatives of landed, commercial, professional, and intellectual property and of more than one denomination and party. The objectives of the institute were true to form:

[T]o interest the operative in the principles of his employment, and teach him to understand them *at the least possible expense,* that he may be enabled to acquire a greater degree of skill in the practice of his business, and thus secure more domestic comfort and natural enjoyment, while he will learn to pity those who spend their time in idleness and debauchery: and to encourage the acquisition of general knowledge, and the study of literature and science among all classes of the community.

In the appeal for money the traditional refrain that this particular town was more spectacularly ignorant than any other bulked large:

The Directors would especially call the attention of the Public to the fact proved by the last Parliamentary returns, that *Blackburn,* with its teeming population, *is at the present time behind every other town in England in intelligence,* for it appears that out of every 100 men only 39 can write their own name; and out of 100 women only 11 are able to do so![38]

There are indications that the institute did not fulfill its promise. A correspondent remarked in January 1848 that it "has failed to elicit that degree of public patronage which has been lavished upon similar associations in the neighbouring towns," for which he blamed the management.[39] Peter Whittle in 1852 lamented the lack of receptivity of the lower orders to higher-class moralizing:

The short time bill has liberated the factory workers in the evenings to some extent; but how do they spend them? Not in Mechanics' Institutes; not at cheap concerts; not much in dancing; not at home in reading, writing, or in music. . . . They run to foolish singing rooms in Shorrock fold and Darwen street, where depravity prevails and morality is at a low ebb; after which both parents and children retire to the beer shop, and thus spend their hard earned weekly wages. Their very bodies are poisoned with smoke and drink, ribaldry and obscenity.[40]

Medical Charities

A third type of charitable organization sought to bring basic medical care to the poor. A public meeting in Preston in 1809 decided to launch a subscription for a dispensary to commemorate George III's golden jubilee. Its purpose was couched in terms of religious self-interest and duty:

Our Blessed Redeemer, and future Judge, has graciously forewarned us that the Terms on which we must meet the final Sentence of Approbation or Condemnation, will be, the Performance or neglect of those Christian Duties among which he has expressly enumerated the "Visiting of the Sick"—And having adopted and adorned the Station of the Poor when he came to visit us in great Humility, he has solemnly assured us that he will take to himself our attention to or neglect of the Poor, at his second and glorious Coming to Judgement—"In as much as ye have done it, *or have not done it*, to one of the least of these my Brethren, ye have done it, *or have not done it*, unto me."[41]

With the earl of Derby as patron, the town's mercantile and professional elite—Anglican, largely Tory, members of the municipal corporation—dominated the Dispensary. Fr. Joseph Dunn, the Catholic priest, president in 1815-16, was the most notable exception.

The Tory-Anglican supremacy apparently lasted a quarter of a century; Meg Whittle suggests that a change of committee in 1835 was analogous to the end of the old regime in the corporation.[42] Like most other such institutions, it was not immune from politicking and status squabbles. One such dispute was between the medical men, who had a particularly well-developed sense of honor, status, and the pecking order within the ranks. On the founding of the dispensary, the two senior physicians of the town were given honorary appointments as "a compliment to w^h a fair and legitimate claim had been established," and "w^h gave but little interruption to private professional engagements." These were the "Extraordinary Physicians"; the "Ordinary Physicians" did the bulk of the work. In November 1814 Dr. James Chew was appointed Extraordinary Physician in the place of the late Dr. Lowe. Chew claimed seniority because he had taken his MD back in 1795, but the Ordinary Physicians, while promising to work cordially with him if the committee and subscribers were going to appoint him, regarded him as junior since he had only recently arrived in town, and were clearly irritated that he was being promoted over their heads.[43]

A second squabble arose over the infirmary. From 1813 the corporation provided a house of recovery, run in conjunction with the dispensary and designed to be a container of disease; "what Individual in this Town," the report of 1816 asked, "may not attribute his present health and safety to it?" But it had to close down in 1823 because of a wrangle over the overseers' accounts, part of a struggle for control of the select vestry after 1820. Thomas Birchall gave notice of an appeal to the Quarter Sessions against several items in the accounts, including the annual sum of £80 paid to the dispensary, and the overseers announced that, to protect themselves, this payment would be discontinued and the house of recovery, partly funded from the poor rates, would have to close. They did this reluctantly, being "fully convinced that this institution has been the cause of saving the lives of hundreds, not only of the Poor but the higher classes of the inhabitants of this populous Town by putting an effectual check to Fever and preventing its being spread (which was formerly the case) in a manner too lamentable to be contemplated without feelings of pain." It apparently remained closed until reestablished under the care of the overseers and the select vestry in July 1824 on a more permanent footing; and in 1829 the annual report noted that a commodious building was being constructed for a new house of recovery. After further delays because of disputes over the control of the select vestry, this opened in 1832.[44]

Jealousies between physicians, and strife over the question of local government expenditure, were joined by a third and fourth level of conflict: between medical men and the dispensary committee, and between physicians and surgeons. The committee appointed three honorary surgeons in 1830, and the two "senior physicians" restricted their activities accordingly. But the "junior physician," Dr. Alexander Moore, maintained his share of surgical cases and continued to act as a general practitioner. So did the senior physicians' successors, meaning that in practice there were six general practitioners; the formal distinction between medical and surgical accounted for little. Nevertheless, harmony apparently prevailed until the end of 1834, when a dispensary subcommittee made inquiries about allegations of irregular attendance by some of the honorary medical officers and insisted that they should record their names and attendance times in a book whenever they visited the dispensary. The medical gentlemen, seeing this as an insult to their professional status, protested against such a "species of Surveillance" and against a modified proposal that the house surgeon insert their names in the attendance book. All six of them tendered their resignations, while promising to continue their services until replacements had been found. But the united front of the medical men against the committee and subscribers fell apart in May when the physicians agreed to stay on, resulting in the surgeons penning an angry letter to *The Lancet* accusing Dr. Moore and his colleagues of sacrificing their word. The surgeons, "for the honour of the profession," withdrew from the dispensary, and three replacements were elected the following January.[45]

The Bolton Dispensary, established in December 1813, drew on all sectors of the elite.[46] The committee appealed to self-interest: the poor man, struggling to make ends meet, frequently neglected to seek medical aid, and infection could quickly spread through a crowded district;

nor let the rich imagine, that they, in such a case, are personally unconcerned: If contagion once prevail, who shall say, "hitherto shalt thou go and no further?" The mansions of the great, as well as the abodes of poverty and wretchedness, are open to "the pestilence that walketh in darkness, and the destruction that wasteth at noon-day."

But self-interest alone was insufficient; it was

not the principle to which, on this occasion, we are most anxious to appeal. An enlightened and a Christian community will be influenced by far other motives and views, will cordially unite in the prosecution of this benevolent design, for the sake of evincing that faith which "worketh by love," for the sake of HIM.

Each guinea subscriber to the dispensary could have a patient on the books. In return for treatment, every ounce of deference was to be milked: "Patients, when cured, are to return their tickets of admission at the Dispensary, and receive a letter of thanks, which they are immediately to present to the Subscribers who recommended them; and also to return public thanks to Almighty God, in the place of worship which they may usually attend."[47] The Lord God, of course, had created the poor as a trial for the rich so as to give the rich the opportunity to demonstrate their charity or lack thereof; but it was always gratifying to receive one's due meed of praise and flattery in the here and now.[48]

True to the pattern that doctors could be relied on to fight over whatever territory opened up to their endeavors, Dr. James Black's application to become physician to the dispensary in 1823 resulted in an exchange of printed letters and addresses with the dispensary surgeons. The surgeons attempted to block his election, accusing him of practicing surgery, pharmacy, and midwifery, contrary to fair medical practice. They had only discovered that the previous incumbent had practiced pharmacy while he was physician to the dispensary during their attendance on him in his final illness and—"in order to preserve the honour and respectability of the Profession, and to guard themselves from the like encroachments in future"—they determined to prevent it from happening again. Black countered that except in emergencies, and on very rare occasions gratuitously to the poor, he had not practiced surgery for a long time; that he did not practice pharmacy; but that, in common with many physicians, he did keep a lying-in hospital. From his "situation in life" and his "rank or character in the profession," he objected to having "the fairness of my Medical practice, frittered away or impugned." The surgeons disputed much of this. But the full force of status tension came out clearly when they wrote,

This Physician effects an air of disdain towards the Surgeons, but when it is recollected that the long and extensive experience of which he boasts was acquired principally as Surgeon's-mate and Surgeon on board a man of war—that when he was proposed as Physician to the Dispensary at the Annual Meeting in March 1820, his assumed title of M.D. was fictitious, being at that time *only a Surgeon*; and that he endeavoured to gain notoriety by advertisements posted in the public streets, a practice to which "*these Surgeons*" would not condescend; does not this boasted superiority of rank and character in the profession evaporate into an "airy nothing?"[49]

A new building, also constructed in 1823, put the dispensary into debt in 1825. "The income of the Dispensary derived from the contributions of annual subscribers," the committee complained in 1828, "does not, we presume, bear that honourable proportion to the wealth and population of the neighbourhood, which we should be proud to record." It reminded those who preferred to bestow charity in their own way, individually, that the dispensary was a surer channel for the distribution of income to deserving causes and was better able to detect impostors. But the following year's report noted with regret "that the powerful appeal in the address of last year to the liberality of a Christian Public has been so little attended to." It emphasized again that the dispensary did "the greatest degree of good at the least possible expense." A bazaar, a fancy dress ball, and the appointment of the earl of Bradford as president in place of the late John Pilkington, merchant (presumably partly to acknowledge his contribution of land for the building, partly so that the dispensary could shine from the vicarious luster of a—non-participating—aristocratic figurehead): the committee resorted to them all in an attempt to increase revenue.[50]

For much of the next two decades income stubbornly refused to rise above expenditure and sometimes fell short, in spite of urgent appeals and in spite of the assurance that those whom the dispensary had failed to restore to health "have died abounding with expressions of gratitude for what has been done for them, satisfied that all that *man* could do, has been done for their recovery." The original plan for the new dispensary included wards for inpatients, but the committee did not have the funds for these additions until 1838, boosted by an exhibition of paintings which raised nearly £530; and even then they only had enough money for seven beds, though there was space for thirty. The debt grew, the income declined,[51] the stream of appeals continued unabated. At one time, these appeals stressed the divide-bridging function (the dispensary was "one of the few purposes, for which people of all descriptions may unite together harmoniously and happily, in one common bond of benevolence and love"),[52] at another, the way in which the voluntary redistribution of income bolstered laboring-poor respectability and kept them off the parish (those who benefited from the institution "are the *industrious* poor; those who, in an honest spirit of independence, are supporting themselves and their families by their own exertions; and who, while they have the power to do without, are unwilling to apply for parochial relief. Surely, for such objects, a humane and Christian public cannot long be appealed to in vain!").[53] The Lord "has been pleased to make kindness shown to the poor and destitute, the test of love to Himself," and thus "Surely it is not too much to expect that, with the increasing wealth of the town and neighbourhood, there should be an increase of contributions to charitable purposes."[54]

After a series of donations and bequests and the proceeds of a public concert, the committee discharged the debt by the mid-forties, but the annual receipts were still inadequate, and now only six partially furnished beds were operative. With the onset of depression in 1847 and the arrival of the wretched, fever-bearing Irish poor, whom "it has pleased Almighty God to afflict with the more awful visitations of a famine," the committee once again brought self-preservation back into play as a more powerful persuasive device, "if the higher feelings of Christian Charity fail to exert a sufficient influence."[55] Gratitude for working-class passivity provided an additional reason for contributing to the dispensary after the Year of Revolutions. "That 'the poor shall never cease out of the land,' is an ordinance, which, because it is of God, cannot be overthrown by man." It therefore followed that it was a Christian duty to use this poverty as "a sphere for the exercise of Christian benevolence and love." That being the case,

As contrasted with those of continental Europe, the poor of this country, and of this neighbourhood in particular, have during the last twelve months, exhibited a most striking example of keeping aloof from the unhallowed agitation for causing the poor to cease out of the land; and, therefore, it would be but right for the rich to show that they acknowledge and are ready to discharge the obligation which this ordinance of God imposes upon them.[56]

Many of the wealthy did not appear to be listening. Donations and the proceeds from an exhibition of paintings for the joint benefit of the baths and the dispensary in 1850 helped restore a "legacy fund," intended to be put out at interest but broken into the previous year, yet steady income still remained "lamentable" and "reproachful." The committee in particular accused heads of large manufacturing establishments, even though they were prospering, of too often leaving their workmen and families to the care of the overworked medical officers of the union. The cholera epidemic had fallen only lightly on Bolton, but this was a motive for all to acknowledge a sense of His mercy by increased liberality (and indeed whatever God might or might not throw at any town was, following this flexible line of argument, cause to contribute more in His name). As late as 1852, only a portion of the infirmary was in use, the other part being let out as a house.[57] In short, the Bolton Dispensary was a typical milltown venture: well-intentioned, underfunded, and partially successful. Where it did better than much else in Bolton was in rising above faction. The vicar, the Rev. James Slade, usually chaired the meetings, and the Unitarian Robert Heywood was the long-standing secretary. In 1848, Heywood said that, while he regretted to see so much apathy prevailing, "he had taken great pleasure in the institution's operations since its commencement; particularly so, because, while in many other things in the town, party spirit existed, there they met together on mutual grounds, to promote a common good."[58]

"No Institute can be so essential to the welfare of a large town," claimed the first report of the Blackburn General Dispensary, opened in February 1824.[59] But the trustees—the coroner, John Hargreaves, the vicar, J.W. Whittaker, John Hornby and Dixon Robinson—immediately wanted to go further and construct a general infirmary for Blackburn and the surrounding area, on the grounds that the town was in a central location and the nearest infirmaries in Newcastle, Leeds, Liverpool, and Manchester.[60] "We trust," they wrote, "that this fair monument of charitable piety may, ere many years have elapsed, adorn our town, and gladden the hearts of those to whom the work of active benevolence is dear."[61]

Not until the sixties did this come to pass. Fund raising began, and nine of the great and good subscribed £2,150[62] before the advent of the 1826 depression suspended the project. By 1829 the infirmary fund, made up of benefactions and surplus income, amounted to £1,250, in addition to the sums pledged; but the estimated cost was more than £4,220. In spite of the expansion of the appeal to the entire Hundred of Blackburn and beyond, and the repetition of familiar arguments—particularly the notion that an infirmary was in everyone's best interest, since contagion could not be confined to the close, overcrowded, and dirty homes of the poor—not enough support could be generated for the project to go ahead. In the early 1830s the dispensary was not flourishing either, the victim of increased demand pressing on dwindling resources. The township of Blackburn still paid a fixed sum of £235 from the poor rates even though the number of poor had greatly increased. The annual subscription in 1825 had amounted to £227 11s.; in 1834 it stood at £133 8s. 6d. which, with the money from Blackburn township, fell below the average annual expenditure of £430.

While so much money lay in the infirmary account, the governors feared that this deterred some people from contributing toward ordinary expenses. They launched another attempt to put the infirmary plan into operation in 1834, with a decision to collect the sums promised in 1826 and to obtain others of not less than £100 each—an unusual example of restricting donations to the very wealthy and a marked contrast to the period when the infirmary was actually built and workmen in different mills were invited to compete in the amount of their pooled contributions.[63] A committee earmarked a site, but its applications for money were either ignored or answered unfavorably. The governors considered going ahead with a more limited project which could be expanded in due course, in the hope that many would contribute liberally as soon as the work had begun. But at the same time money had to be transferred from the permanent fund to meet ordinary expenditure,[64] and the scheme did not get off the ground. In 1838, with the imposition of the New Poor Law, Blackburn township withdrew its grant and the dispensary was forced to close. From then until the 1860s the poor of the town had three options if they required medical treatment: they could pay for it if they could afford it; they could depend on individual charity; or they could receive treatment as parish paupers. Blackburn's attempts at collective charitable medical provision had ended ignominiously.

Temperance

The messages from the temperance movements were far more convoluted and less amenable to elite control than those already described. The British and Foreign Temperance Society promised to be an inspiration for a typical, elite-led, nonsectarian, local voluntary association. The Blackburn society, founded in April 1831 at a crowded meeting in the Music Hall, pledged abstinence from spirits and the imbibing of other liquors only in great moderation. "Would that English ladies," said the Rev. Francis Skinner, a leading figure in the local movement, "so fond of imitating French ladies in dress, were to imitate them also in hospitality, and instead of providing their guests with loads of strong spirits, and strong wines, give them an abundance of coffee and a moderate quantity of light wine. We invite the influence of the fair sex." Skinner made the classic case for the voluntary association—the need to set sectarian differences aside in the collective tackling of social problems—later in the year, when he stated that religious or political party spirit was unknown to the committee:

Why cannot men agree to differ upon some points, and cordially combine their energies for the accomplishment of that in which they are agreed? Let them bury suspicion and distrust in oblivion, and go forth, in one firm phalanx, against every common foe. Such is the conduct of those who compose the Committee of the Blackburn Association for the Suppression of Intemperance, in reference to one of the most formidable enemies of our land.

In his report at the second annual meeting in June 1833, he revealed that the vicar was president of the society (the BFTS tended to work through a network of local vicars), an Anglican clergyman, a Quaker, and two Independents were vice presidents, and there was a committee of Episcopalians, Presbyterians, Independents, Baptists, Methodists, and Quakers.[65]

The Bolton Temperance Society, founded in July 1831, likewise headed by the vicar, with the Rev. William Thistlethwaite as secretary, maintained an ecumenical appeal by planning monthly district meetings at the Sunday schools of the parish church, Dukes Alley Chapel, Ebenezer Chapel, and All Saints' Church.[66] But in both towns rival organizations developed, associated with the liberal-radical popular front and constituting a deliberate break from the Anglican-led organization. The Bolton New Temperance Society was formed in July 1833, after a missionary visit from Joseph Livesey and Thomas Swindlehurst of Preston. This was teetotal, it met in a former Primitive Methodist chapel and was led by a non-bourgeois committee. On the opening of its new Temperance Hall in 1840, William Hodson, the secretary, commented,

The subscribers included men of all shades of belief in religion and politics, and it was at once determined to exclude politics altogether, and to build the principles by which they should be guided on the basis of our common Christianity,— (cheers);—they should advocate the one with the other, and when they were forbidden to ally total abstinence with Christian principle, then would they cease to advocate it altogether.

The venture had some bourgeois patrons, largely liberal and Nonconformist, though they clearly were not in charge of the day-to-day running of the society. Peter Ainsworth, MP, also put in an appearance and spoke at a meeting, confessing that he had hesitated to do so because he did not agree with the somewhat severe code of morals to which the members subscribed. His brand of conservative-liberal Anglicanism defined the outer limits of elite support for petit-bourgeois teetotalism.[67]

In Blackburn, a teetotal society was founded during a week of meetings staged by the Preston missionaries at the Theatre, Easter 1835. The total abstinence men refused to come to any arrangement with the Temperance Society; as a correspondent later put it, "Since the teetotal societies were thus established to supersede the original temperance societies, and a cry has been raised 'away with these moderation men,' the original temperance societies all over the country have been held in abeyance." The Rev. Skinner, who had exchanged his "glass of toddy after the fatigue of the day" for "a dish of good porridge and sweet milk" back in 1830, with the determination "to extend the advantages not of partial, but of entire abstinence," gave his support to the teetotalers. So did a Northgate chemist and druggist, Benjamin Barton, a Quaker philanthropist. Beyond that, the local leading men seem to have kept their distance.[68]

The sequence of events was somewhat different in Preston. At a meeting in the Theatre in March 1832 chaired by Moses Holden, astronomer and Methodist preacher, a deputation from the Blackburn society—the Rev. Skinner and George Edmondson, Quaker schoolmaster of Lower Bank Academy—

moved the formation of a similar venture in Preston. This was seconded by the Rev. Richard Slate, Independent minister, and all the local clergy and ministers were declared ex officio members of the committee of the Preston Temperance Society.[69] However, it was soon clear that the temperance question in Preston was being politicized beyond the usual boundaries of the non-sectarian voluntary society. It quickly became associated with the kind of Nonconformist shopkeeper-radicalism represented by Joseph Livesey and his *Moral Reformer*, which viewed as the prime enemy the aristocratic interest and the groups that clung to its tail, such as the Church and the big London brewers. Clinging fiercely to local and individual independence, this radicalism sought answers to social ills in two places: corrupt oligarchical government and personal failings; hence the attraction of temperance as part of a radical-individualist moral assault on the old order. It may have helped unify a Nonconformist interest across a huge status spectrum: it tended to wear its hostility to the Church on its sleeve, and wealthier Nonconformists could feel comfortable with such a radical reformist issue because it sought to displace the sociopolitical onto the personal dysfunctional. Men in Livesey's circle were the first, publicly, to go beyond simple anti-spirits and take the teetotal pledge at a temperance meeting in September 1832. They believed that moderation was not enough to inspire missionary zeal and that the drinking of beer was as much of a problem as gin. Traveling in a cart around the local towns, the Preston teetotalers spread the word in the manufacturing district, while Livesey's press pumped out tracts and periodicals, including the influential *Preston Temperance Advocate*, begun in 1834. The Preston Temperance Society, in contrast to its neighbors, voted in favor of total abstinence in 1835.

This was a long way indeed from the evangelical paternalism of the British and Foreign Temperance Society. While the Preston Temperance Society attracted influential bourgeois support at the start, how many of these stayed on after the commitment to teetotalism is unclear. For example, Charles Swainson, cotton spinner, was a warm advocate of temperance and presided at the first annual meeting in 1833. James Harrison, surgeon, was a zealous visitor and writer of pamphlets. Peter Hesketh Fleetwood, MP, was still lending the society his support in 1835, but in 1838 his fellow MP, Robert Townley Parker, curtly refused to take any part in it.[70] The Rev. John Clay was an important asset because of the wide repute of his annual prison chaplain's reports. He was an active promoter of the temperance society, but not a convert to teetotalism, disapproving of the taking or imposing of vows involved in the pledge and arguing that, "'To deprive the people of their chief means of animal gratification, while they are still incapable of any gratification which is not animal, would be a dangerous experiment.'"[71] But his reports beat away at the need to tackle drunkenness. He traced the beginnings of crime "to habits of intoxication and the Distress produced thereby and in very few Cases to

Poverty not occasioned by the Parties' own Misconduct."[72] He railed against the licensing of places that tempted the laborer and the artisan into excess and ruin,[73] in particular the singing rooms, festering dens of drink, smoke, ribaldry, and immorality. Often he feared that his message was not percolating through to the wealthier inhabitants. If, he noted in 1845, the influential were too busy to learn the real nature and extent of the horrors of drink, "it is to be wondered at that they are not more sensible—(a low argument, but, I fear, the most likely to be listened to) of the ENORMOUS EXPENCE which it fixes on the community."[74]

While moral entrepreneurs like Clay saw a smorgasbord of vices, of poisoned minds and bodies ripe for decontamination, he had to persuade the leading inhabitants of this and to look beyond the confines of their privileged and protected circles. While most of the bourgeoisie took part at least in some degree in measures of containment, persuasion, or instruction—discovering a variety of negative self-definitions by gingerly prodding what they found distasteful—going the whole hog or adopting a united strategy in the manner that Clay advocated was never achieved. There was no consensus on intemperance as first among evils, and hence no coordinated attempt to quash it.

Self-Improvement

A final major category of voluntary associations is the cultural, under whose broad rubric can be included the educational, the political-convivial, the frivolous, and the recreational, all in some ways aiming at group cohesion of sections of the male bourgeoisie rather than attempting to regulate the lives of others. Typical of the genre was the Preston Literary and Philosophical Society, founded in 1810 at the instigation of the Rev. John Rudd, the Unitarian minister. This kind of society was a product of a polite, Enlightenment culture—interdenominational, professional, and commercial—dedicated to the notion that "the enlargement of the mind is that which constitutes the dignity of human nature."[75] It was *de facto* limited to the elite by the annual fee of one guinea, plus a guinea on election, and, as further safeguards against undesirable elements, all new members had to be elected by two-thirds of the membership at a general meeting, having been proposed by at least three members who had signed a certificate that the candidate was a fit person to be admitted. To attract a broad swathe of the elite, the tenth rule was crucial: "The President shall enforce the observance of order, in all discussions that may take place: and in particular shall put a stop to all observations upon different sects or forms of Religion, or upon modern politics." Men of all parties and sects subscribed. Rudd was the first president, succeeded by Thomas Batty Addison, and Fr. Joseph Dunn served as vice president.

The society spent considerable sums on books and philosophical and scientific apparatus, and in the ensuing years the members heard papers on topics ranging from steam engines to fuel economy, radiation, magnetism, a Roman inscription at Ribchester, and the differences between ancient and modern tragedy. They discussed questions like "How are we to account for the remains of Marine Animals being found on very elevated situations, in different parts of the globe?" But the society spent beyond its means and by 1816 was not prospering. In spite of loans from the membership, indebtedness continued to mount with no probability of it being paid off by annual subscriptions. Even so a meeting in November decided against dissolution and to meet regularly every fortnight.[76] It presumably did not survive much longer. A hiatus of nearly a quarter century followed before a new Lit. and Phil. venture was begun in 1840 in the Corn Exchange, originating in what Hardwick describes as "a slight misunderstanding" with the committee and some of the members of the Institution for the Diffusion of Knowledge, apparently over the question of moving premises. This breakaway organization amalgamated with the Preston Society of Arts in 1841, and together they opened in 1846 in Winckley Square an ornate new building boasting a library, reading room, museum, and lecture theater.[77]

The Bolton Lit. and Phil. was established in 1813 along similar lines following a similar cardinal rule, as outlined by John Rainforth, one of the secretaries: "We contemplate not the scheme as furnishing an arena for disputation, but rather a refuge or an asylum from the contests of sects and parties, from political wranglings, from political controversies, and from all those unprofitable debates, in which those, who indulge, often find 'no end, in wandering mazes lost.'" The first objective was edifying conversation.[78] A select group of young men apparently founded in 1823 the Blackburn Lit. and Phil., which met in the Music Hall in Market Street Lane. By 1844 it had a library of almost two thousand volumes, and the trustees launched a project to provide a museum, a newsroom, and series of lectures and entertainments.[79] Blackburn also had a Scientific Society or Institution, begun in 1831, apparently through the efforts of Benjamin Barton, Quaker chemist and druggist.[80]

Few bourgeois gentlemen could afford an extensive library of their own.[81] Subscriptions to libraries and newsrooms were the middle-class way to collective knowledge and information. There were many different varieties, as Tom Dunne has demonstrated in his extensive study of Bolton's libraries: libraries attached to chapels, particularly Unitarian, from at least as early as 1789; circulating libraries attached to bookshops; subscription libraries associated with inns and appealing to different sections of the literate public; libraries connected with institutions like the Lit. and Phil. or the Mechanics' Institute; and mill libraries at the paternalistic showcases on the fringes of the town.[82] Some of them were aggressively partisan. On January 10, 1793, Thomas Paine was hanged and burned in effigy in Bolton marketplace, the "Wrongs of Man" pinned to his breast. On the same day the subscribers to a certain "Bolton

Public Library" voted that the whole of Paine's works, among others, be thrown out and likewise burned in the market place.[83] The Church and King Club, Tory almost to a man, founded in 1790, at some stage developed a politically correct library of its own, which was not sold off until 1855, after the public library had been established.[84] In March 1829, according to a draft letter of Robert Heywood, the subscribers to the library resolved, on a motion of the vicar, not to admit any Dissenters in the future. Heywood explained that, in spite of its name and nature, a few Dissenters had joined because "the virulence of party spirit for which this place has long been distinguished" had prevented the establishment of any good library in the town for many years. The Church and King excluded the works of Dissenting authors from the library, and "in fact no english [*sic*] literature seemed to be approved unless it proceeded from persons educated either at Oxford or Cambridge."[85]

The library of the Exchange newsroom seems to have been a rival to the Church and King library. At a newsroom set up in the Commercial Hotel in 1813, readers paid annual subscriptions for the London, Manchester, Liverpool, and local newspapers. Around 1823-24 the committee began raising money for a separate building, to include a newsroom, a library, and a general meeting place to discuss the markets and do business. This may have resulted from a schism from the committee of the old newsroom after one group had succeeded in excluding *The Times* because of its condemnation of Peterloo.[86] But if it started out as partisan, a list of proprietors from 1827 includes a fair sprinkling of the cross-denominational elite, as does a subscription list from 1848.[87] By then the library had ceased, and there are repeated references to the fact that the newsroom was attracting only just enough subscribers to keep it open at all.[88]

Blackburn had a similar range of libraries—commercial, subscription, connected with chapels—but the most extensive seems to have been more successful at papering over the cracks in the elite than its Bolton counterparts. This was the Blackburn Subscription Library, founded in or before 1787, reputedly by the vicar, the Rev. Thomas Starkie. Membership cost seven and a half guineas, plus an annual subscription of fifteen shillings, with a ballot for prospective members. In 1825 at least, the leading professional, manufacturing, mercantile, and retail inhabitants were enrolled. But for some reason it collapsed in debt at mid-century, with the more than three thousand volumes being sold off to a Northgate bookseller in 1851 for £60.[89] The Exchange newsroom, apparently founded in 1834 with James Pickup as chairman, met in the premises of W. H. Morrice, printer and bookseller, who acted as treasurer and secretary. With an annual fee of thirty shillings and a membership limited to sixty, the newsroom evidently aimed at—and achieved—social exclusivity. It was also a largely Tory affair.[90]

Preston had a subscription library of unknown vintage in Church Street, but this dissolved in 1819; another one took off in 1825. The Lit. and Phil.'s library contained four thousand volumes by the mid-1850s, with additional books for circulation obtained from a London library to which the directors subscribed. The only significantly different features in the town were Dr. Shepherd's Library, bequeathed by a physician in 1761 and growing to 5,700 volumes by 1852, and its Law Library, dating from 1833, a form of professional association appropriate to a town with such a preponderance of lawyers and courts. In the mid-forties, when the president was Robert Segar, all shareholders had to subscribe £6 in money or books, plus £1 10s. a year. Attorney's clerks were admitted as well on payment of ten shillings a year, but they could only take out one book at a time. A library that might be expected to enhance professional cohesion and access to professional knowledge also marked out the internal status structure.[91]

After mid-century, outside intervention in the form of the Public Libraries Act nudged the way forward in the three towns to more permanent, rate-supported institutions truly transcending sect or party. In Bolton, for example, following a motion of James Greenhalgh and P. R. Arrowsmith for a poll, ratepayers voted heavily in favor of adopting the act in March 1852, and fund-raising and building occupied the course of the next year. There was little recorded opposition; the arguments in favor ranged from Christian duty to the need to ensure that the working classes were sufficiently educated to use their votes.[92] The public library represented the blending of the middle-class means to collective knowledge with the middle-class wish to instruct inferiors.

Convivial and Recreational Societies

Some of the frivolous organizations had something of a political purpose, and they acted in the same way as their more serious brethren to reinforce party or wider-elite loyalties. Most of them finally succumbed to the call to seriousness and the tightening of moralistic sensibilities in the first decades of the nineteenth century. One such was the Preston Oyster and Parched Pea Club, the records for which begin in 1773. The membership was initially limited to twelve, all apparently leading Tories, mostly from Preston's urban gentry. They met weekly, dined together annually on oysters, peas, and port, and acted with all the mock solemnity of a sophomoric dining society. The Rev. Thomas Wilson, incumbent of Clitheroe and Downham and headmaster of Clitheroe Grammar School, which many of the local mercantile-gentry elite had attended, was an honorary member and sometimes acted as deputy "rhymesmith" in the first decade of the century. The editors of the *Preston Chronicle* published the records of the society in 1861, remarking of one of his poems in particular, "the humour is a little too broad for publication in an age that is somewhat more refined than its predecessors."[93]

The main purpose of the society was convivial:

Dear Brethren, to what shall I liken our Club?
We're *Pipe-staves hoop'd* firmly and forming a *Tub*.
In fraternity thus when so closely we link,
We're qualify'd better for holding *more drink*.

But there was also an ideological message too, even from gentlemen in their cups. Wilson's rhymes were naturally patriotic and anti-French, and the one at the beginning of this book managed to marry a hierarchical quiescence to an encomium for the virtues of the middle ranks.

A resolution of February 1815 facetiously censured married men for their irregular attendance and for preferring the society of their families at their own firesides; it directed a petition to their wives, praying them to allow their husbands to attend the club. Under the impact of this cultural revolution, the club seems to have become more lackluster in later years. It folded in 1841.[94]

Pitt Clubs and Church and King Clubs were overtly political-convivial, arenas for male bonding and the confirmation of prejudices among friends. The Bolton Pitt Club, established in 1810, attracted a formidable body of elite Tory support.[95] The Blackburn Hundred Pitt Club met for an annual binge "to commemorate the birth of the immortal and invaluable Statesman the late Right Hon. WILLIAM PITT."[96] The Bolton Church and King Club also harked back to an era of bitterly divided loyalties. It was founded in 1790 to celebrate the defeat in the Commons of Charles James Fox's motion for the repeal of the Test and Corporation Acts, and still in 1828 one of its standing toasts was to the "virtuous majority of 294 members of the House of Commons who voted against the repeal of the Corporation and Test Acts on the 2 March 1790." As it prepared to celebrate its thirty-fifth anniversary in 1825, the Rev. George Harris, Unitarian minister, pondered, "is its real object to rejoice that the reign of bigotry is prolonged, that intolerance is successful, and that its members may congratulate each other that their virtuous and enlightened fellow subjects are branded as aliens from the commonwealth, and degraded in consequence of the religious sentiments they entertain?" Apparently so; as "A Dissenter" put it in 1829, "Experience has taught me, that whenever just and enlightened principles are advancing in other parts of the world, it is only necessary to pay a visit to the good town of Bolton in the Moors, to see a steady front opposed to their progress."[97] Still, the Church and King Club seems to have lost ground. The *Free Press*, admittedly a hostile source, claimed that its gathering in September 1845 was but a ghost of former festivities, and only the remnant of an electioneering clique participated. It commented,

Ample justice we need not say, in such a company, was done to fish, flesh, fowl, and accompaniments. However, but meagre fare followed the withdrawal of the cloth, for instead of
"The feast of reason and the flow of soul,"
there was only
The bile of bigotry and drain of bowl.[98]

The drink-sodden emotionalism of this sort of occasion, lighting up at the sound of key words and figures in the loyalist pantheon, was brought out well by the editor of the *Bolton Chronicle*, quoting from the *Blackburn Mail*, concerning a public dinner in October 1827 to celebrate the success of the vote on the airing and lighting of Blackburn Parish Church (see Chapter 6). Le Gendre Starkie gave a toast for the Protestant Ascendancy in church and state.

"These words," says the Mail, "had barely escaped the lips of the worthy president, when a scene commenced which baffles all description—We know not how many cheers were given. A shout for ten times ten was heard, but cheer followed upon cheer with increasing vigour, till all regard to numerical order was lost. Nor was this all. After the seats were resumed—an *incessant thunder* of applause was kept up, heart and hand, by every one present, till the whole company again simultaneously rose on their feet,—mounted the chairs, and with handkerchiefs waving, renewed their cheers with redoubled ardour. Finally, one of the most *glorious bursts* of enthusiasm we ever had the pleasure of witnessing, concluded with a general round of *thundering* applause."

The *Chronicle* laconically attributed this to the number of bumpers already drunk.[99]

Central to many voluntary associations, and to the celebration of many events, was the all-male, well-liquored dinner. Peter Whittle was only exaggerating mildly in the 1850s when he wrote,

It is true that the first rule observed of our religious, moral, civil, and literary institutions, is a dinner. A church is built, or consecrated; a railroad opened; the vestry accounts inspected; a revolution or victory takes; a subscription is made; a death is celebrated; a friend to be supported; all alike by a dinner. . . . An Englishman talks of Magna Charta, and the Bill of Rights, and of roast beef in a breath; his own glorious constitution and that of the country are indissolubly united. The security of the laws, the sanctity of the church, the bonds of society, the cement of our religious, political and moral obligations, and the actual existence of the country and its vital interests, all, all depend upon a good dinner, and plenty of choice wines and spirits.[100]

One social club intended to be nonpolitical and nonsectarian was the Union Club in Blackburn, founded in October 1849 with William Henry Hornby as first chairman and apparently modeled on the cigar-and-brandy variety of

London club: a place to meet, to read, to socialize, to make contacts among other gentlemen of the elite.[101] A second was the Bolton Delta Society, formed at a meeting at the house of Dr. Haworth in February 1844, and soon attracting many of the cross-denominational, cross-party elite. The society met once a month in each others' houses for conversation and discussion, excluding subjects of local or party politics and controversial divinity.[102] Another, a nightly informal gathering rather than a club, took place in the 1830s in a room of the George and Dragon, Bolton. According to the coroner, John Taylor, twenty or thirty gentlemen of various characters, opinions, tastes, and politics, of many religions and none, tradesmen and professional men, used to meet to dispute on every question likely to arise between California and Chowbent. Here many future members of the town council cultivated their oratorical skills.[103] The Winckley Club in Preston, opened in 1846 alongside and in architectural harmony with the new Lit. and Phil.—a successor both to a "Gentleman's Coffee Room" built in the 1820s on Lancaster Road, and a "Gentleman's News Room" at the Guild Hall—contained a newsroom and rooms for billiards, cards, and refreshments for its elite clientele.[104]

Other clubs for recreational purposes required at least a modicum of activity as they brought together gentlemen for the pursuit of pleasure and the cementing of contacts. The Bolton Billiard Club, apparently founded in 1840, was one such exclusive venture. Proprietors (not to exceed thirty in number) paid £13 on admission and an annual subscription, while an additional ten members paid a five guinea entrance fee.[105] Another was the Blackburn Subscription Bowling Club, reputedly established some time before 1749, and bringing together a healthy sample of upper tradesmen and above.[106] The Blackburn Cricket Club was patronized and led by the town's MPs—William Feilden, John Hornby, and James Pilkington—and various members of their families.[107] On a piece of ground near The Hollins, home of the Fletchers, a club of Bolton ladies and gentlemen practiced archery and occasionally had tournaments, the gentlemen fetchingly dressed in green with wide-brimmed hats and plumes.[108]

Yet more societies cultivated other pastimes. A Preston Botanic Society commenced as early as 1804 at the Butchers' Arms, and another subsequently at the Lamb and Packet, clientele unknown; the Preston Natural History Society, instituted in 1824, with a two guinea initial fee and a one guinea annual subscription, attracted a cross-party and cross-denominational segment of the elite; the Preston Floral and Horticultural Society, dating from 1821, was patronized by the earl of Derby and had Nicholas Grimshaw as its president in 1826.[109] Presumably these did not have the same commercial improving intent as the various agricultural societies, which brought together farmers and landowners of all stripes, or the Bolton Cattle Fair Society, presided over by Thomas Ridgway in 1834, and attracting the support of the industrialists in the big houses on the town's outskirts.[110] The Preston Phrenological Society, founded in 1838, was open to all ladies and gentlemen who could afford ten shillings a year and induce two-thirds of the members at a meeting to endorse them.[111] The Blackburn Chess Club, presided over by John Fowden Hindle, met in the Music Hall from 1844.[112] The glee clubs[113] and the choral societies, which kept up a steady diet of oratorios, catered for those with singing talents. For example, in 1823 the Bolton Choral Society sang Haydn's *The Creation* and Handel's *Grand Coronation Anthem*.[114] The Blackburn Choral Society, founded in 1829, performed Handel's *Deborah* in 1850 in the parish church, at a time when William Kenworthy was president, and the clergy, millowners, and professional men of all parties turned out for the occasion.[115] The Bolton Harmonic Society assayed Mendelssohn's *Elijah* in the same year; a correspondent noted, "There was a lamentable lack of H.'s in the chorus of the priests[.] 'Baal, *ear* and answer,' may be in the true style of Lancashire patois, but such mistakes should be checked at rehearsals, and must be voted an infliction upon an audience." Nevertheless, the editor of the *Bolton Chronicle* was pleased to see the formation of this new society after a pause of some years, and he rather ambitiously looked to it to diffuse intellectual pleasures, relieve the town of dullness and monotony, promote social feelings, and prevent the spread of vice.[116]

The Masonic lodge was a final type of male voluntary association, the most prestigious of all friendly societies. The membership, predominantly Tory and Anglican, could stretch from royal or aristocratic patrons down through the bourgeoisie and Anglican clergymen to tradesmen and craftsmen, some lodges covering a wider status range than others.[117] They blended elements of a social club and of a hierarchical, patriotic, conservative, incorporativist organization. Stephen Blair, Bolton bleacher, explained in 1846, on the occasion of his promotion to Deputy Provincial Grand Master, some of the loyalist and moralist philosophy behind Freemasonry:

Genuine Masonry disapproves and abhors every immoral action. It abhors all disorder, intemperance, and profaneness. It enjoins you to be quiet and peaceable subjects, true to your Prince, just to your country, and faithful to its laws. Keep the sacred lamp of brotherly love well-trimmed, and burning brightly among you. In all your labours make the Word of God your safe guide.[118]

Freemasons were accorded all due honor in ceremonial parades. For example, on the funeral day of George III, the Freemasons from the Lodge of Perseverance in Blackburn joined the solemn procession to St. John's Church. Dressed in black, with black sashes, white aprons bound with black crepe, decorated with three crepe roses, they were headed by a band, two tylers with drawn swords, one of the fraternity carrying a transparency representing the king and the late duke of Kent, and an emblematic painting of some ancient, august personage receiving a scroll from an invisible deity's hand, guarded by three angels, one with a trumpet, the other two with a scroll bearing the words, "The secrets that here are shown, / Are only to a Mason known." The duly impressed editor of the *Mail* wrote of the "awful sublimity" of their institution.[119]

Occasional Associationism

In addition to the voluntary associations, occasional happenings required a measure of elite cohesion for success. These forms of occasional associationism included royal events, public funerals, the Preston Guild, assemblies, and exhibitions. Events following the royal family's life-cycle needed to be planned by a cross-section of the bourgeoisie, and the proper response put into operation for the wake, the wedding, the coronation, the jubilee. More surely than an election procession (where lower order participation was considered legitimizing and thus necessary, if regrettable; where the elites encouraged the plebs to divide along party lines; and which could go dreadfully wrong), royal celebrations could be choreographed. Moreover, they could be "read" by any observer as clearly as a denominational status hierarchy could be decoded by walking down the nave of a church: who was where in the pecking order, who was present, who was not. They strove to suggest that in spite of their differences, the elite could at least agree to resolve them at a higher level, in the shape of members of the royal family, the embodiment of the nation; at least they could give a reminder of collective power, at least for a day. For example the celebrations for Victoria's coronation in Bolton were absolutely typical. A grand procession was headed by the Sunday school children of all denominations, followed by the Odd Fellows, Freemasons and assorted friendly societies, the yeomanry cavalry, representatives of the trades, the band, the deputy constables, the overseers, the clergy of all denominations, the councillors, the magistrates, the gentlemen of the town and neighborhood, the Eighty-eighth Infantry, and the special constables, with the cavalry bringing up the rear. The day provided opportunities for expansive paternalistic gestures connected with the workplace, the church, or the chapel, and also for the inevitable dinner for the bigwigs of the town, imbibing to a studiedly party-neutral succession of toasts. Likewise at Preston, where at the mayor's dinner at the Red Lion "All political or party feeling appeared on this occasion to be absorbed in the highly interesting event."[120]

But things did not always go so smoothly. In 1829 in Bolton at the Commercial Inn the boroughreeves of Great and Little Bolton presided over the standard dinner to celebrate the king's birthday. But this was shortly after George IV had acceded to Catholic Emancipation, and was not in good odor with the Tories. The Orangemen and other Ultras pointedly absented themselves from the dinner, and the editor of the *Chronicle* did not see a single magistrate and only very few clergymen present; one reverend gentleman apparently had said that he would as soon acknowledge allegiance to the emperor of Morocco as to the king. The vicar was present, on the grounds that "Whatever changes may have taken place in the political world, I trust we shall never be found deficient in honour to our King." To ease the tension on the occasion, James Crompton, presiding, said that in selecting the toasts, "it had been the intention of the parties who had arranged them, to avoid all unpleasantness, and to promote cheerfulness and good company. He wished to preserve unanimity and good order, and he hoped that no gentleman would propose any toast out of the list."[121]

Another occasion that was not fully successful, and hence received bad press, was the celebration of Princess Victoria's birthday in 1837. A number of gentlemen of various political opinions met to plan a holiday and treat for the children of the factories and the schools. But once it became clear that Thomas Miller, of Horrocks, Miller and Co., was opposed on the grounds that neither the children nor the masters could afford to sacrifice the wages, the plan was abandoned, and a dinner at five shillings a head agreed upon. As the *Chronicle* noted sardonically,

the gentlemen have been good enough to arrange, that all persons, *who have five shillings to spend, may be permitted to commemorate this happy event by eating a good dinner at the Bull Inn.* Such as have not 5s. must, forsooth, leave the happy event un-commemorated, or rather, some will have to commemorate it, at the loom, others, at the spinning-wheel, in the card room, &c.!

Nevertheless, as it was understood in advance that there would be no political toasts or discussion, the dinner was successful in bringing together the fragmented elite.[122] This contrasted with the celebration of the queen's birthday in 1839 in Bolton, during the town's phase of divided institutions. Two elite dinners took place, the liberal gathering presided over by the mayor, the Tory festivities by the boroughreeve.[123]

While members of the bourgeoisie died quietly, preferably serenely, resigned, and contented, they were buried with considerable ostentation. Again, the funeral could be turned into a display by the power-elite of an ordered hierarchy, or it could be—less frequently—a largely party affair. Take the funeral of John Lister of Blackburn, a Tory Anglican, who had retired a wealthy man from a cotton-merchant partnership with the elder James Pilkington in 1821 and subsequently became a magistrate and a deputy lieutenant. He died in Cheltenham in 1844 aged 63; his body arrived in Preston on the mail train, where it was met by the mourning coach and his two brothers from Liverpool. As the cortege approached Blackburn along Preston New Road, John Fowden Hindle joined it in his carriage at Woodfold Hall, followed by Joseph Feilden of Witton and James Simpson of Foxhill Bank in their carriages and James and William Pilkington and others in their chaises about a mile from town. At Limefield sixty or seventy of the respectable inhabitants of various parties and denominations formed a procession in front of the hearse to St. John's Church. The shops were closed along the streets the procession passed, and a large crowd had gathered near the church, where Lister was laid to rest in the family vault, "there to mingle with its kindred dust until the voice of the Archangel and the trump of God shall call all men to the last dread tribunal," as the *Standard* put it. Here were all the elements of a milltown patrician burial: representatives of local landed, mercantile, and manufacturing wealth across party and sectarian divisions on conspicuous display, their status confirmed by type of carriage and position in the procession; the closed shops; a large and deferential crowd; a pious eulogy in the newspaper.[124]

Even those funerals which aimed to be "private" could make a strong public statement. Samuel Horrocks of Preston left word that his interment, in 1842, be private; but the crowds turned out to line the streets and the shops closed nonetheless, "a mark of respect which can only be purchased by a long life of meritorious exertions in promoting a community's welfare—and this envied acknowledgement, so well deserved by the deceased, was tendered so universally as fully to compensate for the absence of the most gorgeous pageant." The cortege from his house, Lark Hill, to St. George's Church included the carriages of his nearest relatives, the clergy, and his immediate friends, with a long train of people in his employ (which cannot have been spontaneous).[125]

Some funerals were true public spectacles, as grandiose on the local level as a royal burial on the national. Such was the dispatching of William Bolling, MP for Bolton, in September 1848. More than five hundred gentlemen and tradesmen, "representing a vast amount of the property and influence of the borough, irrespective of religious or political opinions," joined the procession. The police, the churchwardens, the legal and medical gentlemen, the county and borough magistrates, the councillors, and about 260 of Bolling's workmen all had their allotted places. The hearse and two mourning coaches, each drawn by four horses, preceded the closed, private carriage of the deceased and eleven other private carriages bearing local notables. Nearly all the shops and inns were closed, and the streets were thronged with an estimated 15-20,000 people. Muffled peals, funeral dirges on the organ in the parish church, and the Dead March from Handel's oratorio *Saul*, completed the interment in the family vault.[126]

But there were other, politically charged occasions when the elite did not pull together, when a death could exacerbate tensions and be used to make political capital. Ralph Fletcher, zealous warrior against radicals and infidels, died in February 1832. Far from providing the customary respectful tribute,

the *Chronicle* launched into an attack on him as the uncompromising supporter of a corrupt government, the prime mover of the spy system in the area,
and as an inveterate Orangeman, illiberal in his religious beliefs. At least a section of his peers accorded him a ceremonial send-off, but in terms of a coherent ideological message, since the amplifier of the message was pulling in a
contrary direction, the public death of Col. Fletcher was not a triumph.[127]

Preston had one further way of parading its pecking order of power. Every
twenty years the town celebrated the Preston Guild, originally an occasion to
enroll tradesmen into all the privileges of burgesses of the borough, but since
the late-eighteenth century purely of social significance. The guild was a
sprawling series of events capable of making a range of cultural statements,
but all in some sense stressing harmony, good order, a stable hierarchy. The
succession of guilds maps both the transformation of the town and the attempt to incorporate mill-gotten wealth into the older structure of authority.
The guild, as it evolved during the polite-and-proud-Preston years of the
eighteenth century, involved processions led by the corporate body, including
a procession of the trades as a reminder of its origins, and a host of patrician-
led festivities ranging from the socially exclusive (balls, assemblies) for the local aristocracy, gentry, and urban patriciate, to the socially incorporative
(races) for everyone, plus a medley of plebeian activities. The 1802 guild
marked a departure. Cotton manufacturing was represented for the first time
in the procession, which included one of John Horrocks's new spinning mules
being worked by a boy and girl with powdered hair and dressed in white cotton (this was well before "child slavery" had raised much of an outcry). Then
came twenty-four young women from different factories, dressed in cloth
manufactured in the town, each carrying an artificial cotton tree in full bloom,
entirely made from cotton by Mrs. Horrocks and members of her family.
They were headed by two men who superintended the women's work in the
factories, a public indication, perhaps, that sexual hierarchies were not being
transgressed behind mill walls. Next, "Mr. Horrocks and Mr. Watson, in
whose employ the women are, followed arm in arm, carrying white wands. A
number of proprietors of manufactories followed, two and two, with white
wands in their hands."[128] The bystander could read this not only as a recognition by the authorities of the importance of cotton manufacturing in the
town—they had done this ever since they adopted Horrocks as their candidate
in the 1796 election—but also as a visual representation of the compact between land and industry as coequals signified by the new electoral coalition.
Watson, as a partisan of Lord Derby, had represented the subordination of
manufacturing to land, whereas a section of the professional and mercantile
elite had supported Horrocks as a realistic assessment of how best to secure
independence from the hegemony of the Stanleys. Now these two erstwhile an-

tagonists marched arm in arm through the streets of Preston, emblems of a new hegemony of wealth and power—or such was the didactic message if not yet the fact.

Thomas Erskine, KC, future lord chancellor, remarked that he was "proud to take a place in a procession which so strikingly exhibited the happy effects of civil order and industry in the wealth and prosperity of the Town and the surrounding Country."[129] This was a recurrent theme in the successive guilds. They provided considerable scope for the minute ordering of status relationships; but there was always the risk in any incorporating enterprise that those being invited and coerced into playing their allotted role would fail to do so. In 1822 the journeyman tailors refused to walk in the procession because they had not been placed at the head, which offended their sense of craft hierarchy. More important, the mayor had to decide what the likelihood of popular unrest would be during the weeks of festivities. In 1822 he was apparently urged to have a detachment of the military in town but decided not to, which proved an accurate judgment: even the members of the Liverpool police in attendance were not required.[130]

The 1842 guild was potentially much more dangerous. The guild, which always began on the Monday after the Feast of the Decollation of John the Baptist, was going to commence only a fortnight after the army had killed a number of Plug Plot turnouts in Preston. The mayor, Samuel Horrocks, at the center of this suppression, was to head the guild. Some councillors had already questioned the holding of a guild at all, since it no longer fulfilled any function beyond the social, and since it was tainted by association with the old, unreformed, Tory-Anglican corporation. But the council decided to proceed, and the guild became an opportunity to reknit the social fabric. Although the weavers apparently did not take part in the procession, most of the mills were closed for an average of four days, and nearly all in Blackburn were closed for at least two days. One commentator noted the gaiety and good humor of the celebrations, in spite of the inauspicious circumstances, and drew the moral "that the comforts of the workpeople were not overlooked in providing for the convenience of the masters, and that while catering for the amusements of those who have derived their gratification from the exertions of the humble ranks in the community, these latter have been cared for in turn by the higher."[131]

The celebrations were once more shot through with consensual and conflictual messages. In terms of the social elite, the established families of the urban and local rural gentries, made up variously of propertied, mercantile, and professional wealth, predominated, underlining the extent to which continuity and incorporation or absorption were the prime modes of elite formation in Preston. In spite of the reformed corporation, new, liberal, Nonconformist manufacturing wealth was much less visible. Due deference was accorded to the influx of the nobility and gentry, who had long since ceased to show up for the annual "Preston season."[132] While the processions suggested consensual hierarchy, and the ladies' procession—with soberly dressed elite males escorting and displaying their plumed and primped possessions in a parade to church—suggested sexual hierarchy, at other times the celebrants dissolved into their social and denominational parts or sought to inculcate a sectarian message. The guild sermon of the vicar, John Owen Parr, for example, on "The duty and advantage of National Union in the National Church," cannot have had universal appeal. Although all the schoolchildren took part in the celebrations, they did so in a segregated fashion: the Church schoolchildren mustered in the marketplace to cheer the queen and the mayor and mayoress, to wave flags and banners, before being "marched off to their schools to be regaled"; many of the Dissenting children went on a trip by rail to Fleetwood; for the Catholic children, a tour of a bazaar at Fox Street school preceded refreshments and a visit to Pablo Fanque's circus. Then of course there was the traditional contrast between festivities for the people and those for the people of position (including *The Messiah* in the parish church, and the costume ball, where one could dress as a Tyrolean peasant, a Medieval craftsman, or a Spanish forester, if one so chose).[133]

John Horrocks Ainsworth of the Bolton bleaching family attended the Preston Guild in 1822. Between September 2 and 13 he graced five balls, three oratorios, two concerts, one masquerade, one play, a public breakfast and quadrille, went to the races four times, shot birds at Goosnargh, and dined with his relatives—the Samuel Horrockses at Lark Hill and the Peter Horrockses at Penwortham Lodge. This was unusually concentrated, but throughout his twenties he devoted a lot of energy to going to balls, dinners, quadrille parties, masquerades, and the theater, often in private houses, often in London, Liverpool, and other Lancashire towns on his social circuit. In November 1822 he was present at the Bolton Assembly, in April 1824 at the Bachelors' Ball and a ball in honor of the king's birthday, in January 1825 at the Dispensary Ball in Blackburn, in January 1833 at the Election Ball in Bolton, and so on.[134] Some of these were patriotic occasions, some fund-raising events, some marriage markets, some presumably attempts to reproduce civilized gentility in dirty Bolton. They were a central feature of bourgeois life. The ladies and gentlemen of Blackburn attended a public ball in the Commercial Room on the fall of Napoleon, and "Never did greater pleasantness and unanimity prevail upon any public affair in this populous town."[135] The Bolton Assemblies seem to have been a regular feature: four were planned for the winter season of 1816-17, for example, at a guinea for gentlemen and 15s. for ladies, and four more during the winter of 1827-28, at £1 11s. 6d. for gentlemen and a guinea for ladies. Others were more ad hoc, such as the ball to commemorate the opening of Little Bolton Town Hall in 1828. On this occasion, the patronesses, patrons, and stewards were largely but not exclusively representatives of the Anglican mill-owning cream.[136]

The ladies and gentlemen of Preston had always enjoyed dressing up at the guild fancy dress ball in a broad array of historical and regional costumes, and they chose to do so again for a costume ball organized by the mayor, John Paley Jr., in 1845; this allegedly formed the principal topic of conversation of this social set for weeks beforehand. The editor of the *Chronicle* felt that he had to defend "the real object, character, and use of a fancy ball" against cold and calculating utilitarian detractors. It betokened a "revival of the old taste for pageantry" and therefore, he hoped, "a degree of charity and of consideration for other classes, and particularly for the poor," among the wealthier classes. There was the employment of many artisans in the fabrication of costumes and the staging of the event to be considered. Above all, perhaps, a costume ball

prevents the growth of the unfeeling, calculating, money-grubbing, but tasteless and unsympathizing, utilitarian desire, of amassing mere money wealth. With the moderate exercise of a different spirit, we should also encourage the revival of a taste for the beautiful decorations in tapestry, paintings, statues, and other articles of *vertu*, rich costume, and splendidly illuminated books, in which our ancestors delighted in the sixteenth and seventeenth centuries.[137]

Thus a fancy dress ball could be seen as much more significant than a mere social event, but part of the Young England, return-to-chivalry, Gothic revivalist, golden age, gentry-and-monastery charitability that was being posited in the troubled forties as a solution to the "Condition of England" question. Something similar can be seen in the coming-of-age celebrations of John Turner Hopwood, only son of Robert Hopwood Jr., in Blackburn in 1850. Here was a richly symbolic mingling of cultures, a kind of embourgeoised gentrification. First came the father's paternalistic gestures: the liberal treat to the hands, the laying of the foundation stone for a new girls' charity school in Grimshaw Park, close to the family mills and on family land. Then the grand ball for nearly 220 ladies and gentlemen of all denominations and parties in the locality, with no expense spared ("one of the most liberal and sumptuous entertainments recorded in the county"), a caterer from Liverpool, a full-length portrait of the young man by a London artist prominent above the mantelpiece, the family arms emblazoned over the fireplace in the dining room. All the elements were present for a meeting of *noblesse* and *fabricant oblige*: charity, lavish hospitality, the launching into the world of the heir. Did this betoken any lessening of entrepreneurial vigor on the part of Robert Hopwood and Son? Far from it. The fact that the ball was held in the Bolton, Blackburn, Clitheroe and West Yorkshire Railway Company station, fitted out like a gentleman's mansion for the evening by an upholsterer from Manchester, speaks volumes about the gap between new and old elites, however heavily cultural symbols might have been appropriated.[138]

"High" culture posed a problem for the milltown bourgeoisie. The Bounderbian and Gradgrindian stereotypes imagined by southerners weighed heavily with at least some of the local industrialists, particularly those who had extensive art collections of their own. The bipartisan committee managing the Bolton Dispensary attempted to remedy this and to make a cultural statement in 1838 when it chose to raise money to pay off the debt of nearly £500 on the wings of the infirmary by holding an art exhibition. The exhibition served a double purpose by opening, along with the new additions, on coronation day. The 537 ancient and modern masters, collected largely from members of the local elite, had been seldom equaled in that part of the country (so the catalogue claimed) for beauty, diversity, and local interest.[139]

Toward the end of 1837 the editor of the *Preston Chronicle* stated that a great number of townsmen had been complaining for years about the low esteem of the fine arts in Preston. This was not simply a question of some highcultural icing on the material cake: a "school of design" to improve the design of cloth would be profitable for manufacturers; a large exhibition of works by local artists, with free admission, would draw the operative classes from their "more groveling pursuits." In short, "The present state of the arts in this town may be considered a blot upon its beauty and a disgrace to its character, while a different course, would increase the wealth of our merchants, correct the morals of all classes,—counteract a vitiated, and engender a refined taste, and qualify this local community to confer a great benefit on mankind at large."[140]

He was not alone in his faith in the redemptive power of art, though how many would have followed him in his belief in the full range of practical and moral benefits is a moot point. A Society of Arts, formed in September 1834 to purchase works of eminent artists and to circulate them among members, held its second annual exhibition at the county court in the middle of December 1837. Here, seventy or eighty ladies and gentlemen of the urban gentry, in full dress, attended the first of two select "*converzationes*" [*sic*]; "lively conversation, polished critique, and refined witticisms, together with a little tea, coffee, and biscuit, were the staple enjoyments of the evening." At the second meeting, much was apparently said about how such gatherings would tend to enliven and polish the social spirit of the town, promoting a greater taste for the fine arts and hence an improved tone of thought among the middling and higher classes.[141]

This, then, was seen as the refining function of art among the bourgeoisie themselves, the answer to the grubby coketown stigma, and notably before any real attempts had been made to make the coketowns less grubby. The function of art to reach down to the lower orders and pull them up by the straps of their clogs was partially implemented on this occasion, when at the end of the exhibition nearly three hundred operatives were let in free of charge, but more fully in November 1839 with a decision to form a public exhibition of works of art and manufactures. Following the success of similar events in Manchester, Sheffield, Leeds, and Derby, the intention was, as the committee chairman, the Rev. John Clay, explained it, to form a collection of everything calculated to instruct the working classes and to draw their thoughts into a profitable channel. With this in mind, the admission price should be low—perhaps sixpence at first, reduced to threepence later—and the exhibition open until late in the evening. Then it would be up to the poor to make the most of the liberal opportunities. Thomas Batty Addison spelled this out with characteristic bluntness:

That there should be distinctions in society there could be no doubt; but poverty and misery were generally the consequence of talents misapplied, and opportunities neglected. He wished the lower classes to look upon prosperity not as a lottery prize bestowed upon one or two, but as a prize which all might obtain. It was the reward of good conduct, and it was in their power to obtain it.

The exhibition opened in January 1840, displaying a large collection of paintings, sculptures, antiques, and geological specimens contributed by a diverse array of owners, and the proceeds were to go toward a new building for the Institution for the Diffusion of Knowledge.[142]

While Thomas Miller, Richard Newsham, Thomas Birchall, and others continued to add to their private collections, the public spirit for art waned rapidly. After two or three years the Society of Arts merged into the Lit. and Phil., and its few pictures and books were therein entombed. The fine arts stepped out of the limelight again, just as they had in Bolton, which saw no exhibition of paintings between the coronation and a fund-raising event for the baths and the dispensary at the Baths Assembly Rooms starting in December 1849. This exhibition was patronized by the mayor, the earls of Bradford and of Ellesmere, the town's MPs, the vicar as president of the dispensary committee, and John Horrocks Ainsworth as chairman of the baths committee. With party-neutrality apparently being observed, the elite could once more attempt a collective display of high culture for a charitable purpose.[143] In Preston toward the end of 1850 the *Chronicle* was similarly hopeful of a fresh start. The new Avenham Institute had space for the building up of a respectable permanent collection of paintings. And there was one particularly significant indicator of the taste of the town: "The feeling of the public meeting which unanimously resolved upon the erection of a statue to the memory of the late illustrious Sir Robert Peel, must be regarded as the most significant mark of our progress in this respect."[144]

Peel, who split his party but whose death briefly united the milltown bourgeoisie behind tributes aimed at utilitarian or cultural improvement, perhaps is a fitting figure with whom to end this discussion of voluntary associations and occasional associationism. Each of these societies and events, covering a considerable spectrum of bourgeois public life, brought together segments of bourgeois wealth, organization, and presence in a tangle of relationships and alliances to communicate a variety of ideological messages. While enriching different individuals, financially and culturally, they acted as means of imparting sustenance and values to the lower orders. If they brought members of the bourgeoisie together for one reason or for one event, membership of a different organization could just as easily rupture that alliance, and so cohesion and disunity kept power relationships in perpetual flux, constantly reworking and reordering the warp and weft of authority, moving with or against the state and the institutions in the public sphere. A coherent bourgeoisie cannot be discovered; but the culture of voluntarism was perpetually and persistently re-creating the culture of market values and civil society, reinforcing the ideological hegemony of the liberal-capitalist system.

CHAPTER 9: DEALING WITH LABOR

In 1859, Gilbert James French, a Bolton church-furniture and clerical-robe maker, wrote a celebration of the life of one of the town's most famous sons, Samuel Crompton, the inventor of the spinning mule. In it, he acknowledged that Crompton "disliked the factory system"; but, he went on, this was because "he did not live to see its development in the lofty rooms of modern mills kept scrupulously clean, in which a single spinner watches the fairy-like work of *mules* bearing from one to four thousand spindles, moving with marvellous precision and with a celerity and silence which appear the work of enchantment."[1]

This was positioning the factory on an ethereal plane some distance beyond the looking glass. It is unlikely that those who worked amidst the humid, cotton-dusty, oily and—if in a weaving mill—deafening conditions of the various aspects of cotton manufacture would have been quite so lyrical. Nor those subjected to the tyranny of the bell, to the rules of "Order, Promptitude, and Perseverance,"[2] to "a discipline that a hand-loom weaver can never submit to."[3] But French's statement was not so much a factual description as an intervention in a vigorous debate that had been raging for more than half a century. The factory and the manufacturing system became rhetorical devices in this struggle, touchstones for defenders and detractors of the startling new age of the machine, territory upon which conflicting bourgeois agendas for dealing with labor could be worked out.

The increasingly rude and obtrusive presence of the factory on the landscape, coupled with the burgeoning weaving populations in towns, villages, and on the moors, provoked aghast reactions from those who unfavorably compared the new and the old in Lancashire. John Byng, later Viscount Torrington, touring the cotton district in 1792, lamented that the valleys now teemed with cotton mills, which "Have chosen the Old Abbey situations; in the abbies [sic] there was religion, and decency; in the cotton mills, blasphemy and immorality."[4] The Rev. Dr. Thomas Dunham Whitaker, vicar of Whalley and of Blackburn, in his histories of the region published at intervals between 1801 and 1823, contrasted a settled past of resident, gentry families inculcating "civility and respect to superiors," with an uncivilized present of "pernicious independence."[5] In Preston, for example, the manufactories were "hotbeds of insubordination and sedition . . . which have debased the manners of the lower orders more rapidly than they have increased the population of the place." This he attributed to "the dreadful visitation of Providence which for our sins has fallen upon this age and country."[6] John Corry, historian of Lancashire, was impressed in 1825 with the commercial prosperity, booming population, and disseminated wealth of the region; but he also had reservations about cotton manufacturing: "the numerous concomitant evils which this traffick has introduced among us, have by the deterioration of the health and morals of tens of thousands of God's rational creatures, most awfully contributed to the predominance of vice over virtue in our crowded factories."[7]

Detractors provoked defenders. Dr. James Black, a Bolton Tory, in a measured defense of the factory system in 1837 argued that, "whatever evils may attend the system, many of which have been exaggerated or misunderstood, the majority of them are necessary ones, and are, in many instances, compensated by the benefits which could not otherwise be supplied": food and clothing, constant employment, good wages, and habits of industry.[8] The Rev. John Shepherd Birley, a scion of the Birley mill-owning dynasty with a web of connections to the Tory landed gentry, said in 1850, "There were persons who attributed nothing but evil to the manufacturing system, but with them he had no sympathy. He was aware that it had its evils, but it tended much to increase the comforts of life, while, it also awakened the fertility of intellect and grasp of understanding, and roused the powers of the mind."[9]

This was qualified praise from those who believed that, on the whole, the benefits outweighed the costs. Other defenders of the factory system enthusiastically subverted the notion that mills could be equated with disorder. The Rev. Franklin Baker, Bolton's radical Unitarian minister, contributed a pamphlet in 1850 in response to an open letter from a Suffolk rector who depicted the cotton mill as a scene of moral and physical chaos. On the contrary, he noted:

There is no industrial employment in which the employer is more directly interested in preventing all dissipation of thought and time, and in securing order and attention on the part of his workpeople . . . in proportion as he makes his mill the scene of attention, order, and propriety of behaviour; he succeeds in raising the character of the article which he manufactures, and obtains for it a better price in the general market.[10]

The Rev. John Clay of Preston Gaol, who had strong links to the mill-owning Swainson family, also saw the mill as enhancing rather than undermining discipline. In his report of 1827 he observed that the regularity, superintendence, and control of a factory tended to prevent rather than increase crime, a theme he emphatically reiterated in 1849:

We can now understand the reason of the small ratio of crime to population in Preston. No commital *for any offence,*—no summons to the Town-Hall,—of Messrs. Horrocks' and Miller's hands, numbering about 2000,—or of Messrs. Catteralls', numbering about 800—has taken place within a period of more than two years. How strongly do these facts negative the assumption which imputes crime to the "manufacturing system." The cotton factory permits few opportunities for the growth and practice of dishonesty; and in the hands of wise and good masters, not only provides regular and remunerative labour, but also promotes the mental and spiritual cultivation of the labourers with a regularity and success unattainable where employment is less systematic, and where the workers are more scattered.[11]

Factory Paternalism

Clay was highlighting two factors: that the cash nexus, the need to earn a living, was the most pervasive form of discipline, and that the factory formed a controlled environment in which free time was limited. But "wise and good masters" could go a step further in attempting to demonstrate the merits of the factory system: they could seek to extend the influence of the employer beyond the workplace. Either to entice a workforce or to pacify it, these masters proffered a range of benefits outside mill-time, increasing their scope for sermonizing and for a moralizing surveillance. This involved the—theoretically—contradictory deployment of authoritarian measures to prop up a laissez-faire ideology of free labor and free men.[12] Edward Baines Jr., apostle of political economy and philosophical radicalism, believed that the evils of the factory could be overcome by the spread of the coercion and comfort of factory paternalism. Some millowners already enforced cleanliness and neatness, regulated morality, provided schools, libraries, and benefit societies, and brought in doctors to inspect the workpeople. If each millowner were to adopt such a course, "by an apparatus of means like those above mentioned, by the appointment of steady overlookers, and by his own vigilant superintendence, much, very much, might be done to make a factory rather a school of virtue than of vice." Benevolence, emulation, shame, a sense of duty: these were all good reasons for the outlay of a trifling expenditure; "and we believe the conviction is strengthening and spreading, that it is eminently the *interest* of a manufacturer, to have a moral, sober, well-informed, healthy, and comfortable body of workmen."[13]

Paternalism was grounded in an attempt to reforge relationships between masters and men on a more stable, more durable footing. Given that liberal millowners, Owenites, and local vicars each experimented with versions of paternalism (which is to stretch the sense of the word to its capacious limits, but each of the phenomena have elective affinities), and that corporate paternalism in the twentieth century became a standard model for muted workplace class-antagonisms in advanced industrial societies, there was nothing intrinsically anachronistic about it.[14] Factory paternalism constituted an individual effort at reconciliation, not as a substitute for collective endeavors but to act concurrently with them, recognizing that while the one was appropriate to a master's immediate sphere, the others alone were capable of managing relationships on a town-wide scale.

Millowner paternalism graduated from the attempts by nouveaux-riches merchants to establish themselves as gentlemen. If old money like Le Gendre Pierce Starkie of Huntroyd could regale the poor of Padiham in 1805 with beef and ale to celebrate Trafalgar and in memory of Nelson, on the grounds that "it behoved the rich, on that day, particularly, to make the hearts of ALL rejoice," new money could pick auspicious occasions to do likewise, just as ostentatiously. Henry Sudell of Woodfold Hall, mercantile prince of the Blackburn putters-out, distributed beef and money to the poor of Mellor each Christmas. John Horrocks of Preston slaughtered five fat beasts for his workpeople, Christmas 1798, and dished out other rewards to salute previous conduct and as an incentive for future good behavior. To celebrate George III's golden jubilee in 1809, Richard Ainsworth of Smithills Hall, Halliwell, bleacher, treated his workforce of five hundred to a "plentiful repast," and the poor of the neighborhood to soup and cold meat.[15] But, without fully subscribing to the prior golden age myth being pedaled by the Rev. Dr. Whitaker, there is some force to the argument that this largesse was little more than tokenism at a time when gentry and gentleman-capitalists between them were dismantling a more extensive paternalism and undermining the moral economy in Parliament.[16]

Far more substantial were the examples of whole-hog factory paternalism of the kind advocated by Baines and a flood of prescriptive literature in response to the "Condition of England" question in the thirties and forties. The Ashworth brothers of Egerton and Turton built one of the most notable model communities of houses, schools, and a reading room. The site of their mills, on the streams running off the moors to the north of Bolton, required them to build cottages to attract a workforce. But they only began regular inspections around 1830 after fever—blamed on tenants' filthy habits—had broken out in some new houses. From this they gathered that for large families small dwellings made for indelicate living arrangements, and so they began to build larger, three-bedroomed cottages.[17]

There were sound economic reasons why the brothers and others similarly circumstanced in country mills might choose to play the paternalist hand. They rented out the cottages for between 1s. 6d. and 3s. 6d. a week, rates included, securing a return on the investment of 7 or 8 percent a year, or only marginally less than what was considered a fair rate of profit for manufacturing capital.[18] Being both employer and landlord, the Ashworths had more than the usual opportunities for disciplining their workers and workers' families, molding better, more diligent millhands from the resistant plebeian clay. If the people had moved directly from country districts, this sculpting could take time, as Henry Ashworth explained in 1846: "[I]f you are attracted into a Country Place where there is Water Power as an Inducement, it requires a Generation or Two before you have made the People apt enough to work profitably, as compared with those who are in Towns." The brothers made every effort to train them correctly. Henry Ashworth described in 1833 with evident pride the way in which they exercised a superintendence over all those—the majority—who lived in their houses. They visited the houses, examined the state and cleanliness of the rooms, bedding, and furniture "very minutely," and carefully inquired into the condition of the tenants' children, income, and habits of life.[19] As considerable landowners in the area the Ashworths were able to exclude pubs from the two villages, and there were only two beer-shops in the neighborhood; heavy drinking or immorality could lead to dismissal or at least eviction from a cottage.[20]

Visitors to the Ashworth colony were impressed by "the order, the regularity, and the cleanliness of both the machinery and work-people,"[21] with the well-furnished, tidy cottages and their small collections of morally improving books, by the newsroom and small library, by the absence of dramshops, pawnbrokers, trades unions, and poaching in the neighborhood, by the apparent healthiness of the people, and by the discouragement of married women with young families from working in the mills. William Dodd in 1842 approved of the custom, "which I think it would be well to imitate elsewhere, of inspecting the cottages of the work-people once a quarter, or oftener, if found necessary; and should anything be wanting to make them comfortable (such articles as blankets, sheets, &c.), money is instantly advanced by the masters, the necessary articles procured, and the money paid back by installments, as they can afford it." He believed that the women employees behaved in a more becoming manner than in large cotton mills in towns, partly because of the absence of a great many temptations, partly because of the vigilant eye of the masters. The women "seem to be as much afraid of the masters, as of their fathers and husbands. Hence the families are kept more comfortable than in most towns."[22] W. Cooke Taylor, visiting in the same year to collect material for a disguised propaganda piece for the Anti-Corn Law League, discovered that surveillance was becoming internalized:

I was informed by the operatives that permission to rent one of the cottages was regarded as a privilege and a favour, that it was in fact a reward reserved for honesty, industry and sobriety, and that a tenant guilty of any vice or immorality would at once be dismissed. Mr. Ashworth was said to be very strict in enforcing attention to cleanliness, both of house and person, and in requiring the use of separate sleeping apartments for the children of different sexes. It was sufficiently obvious, from the gossip I heard, that public opinion had established a very stringent form of moral police in the village, which superseded the necessity of any other.

He spoke to a woman from the Midlands who complained that the rules of cleanliness and decency added hugely to her work. But, he concluded, her standard of morality did not appear to be very high, as she spoke very bitterly of a millowner who dismissed a girl for bearing an illegitimate child.[23]

In sum, the Ashworths strictly regulated whom they employed, barred trades unions, attempted to enforce a moralistic code—and paid slightly lower wages than in the town, on the grounds that their rents and provisions were cheaper.[24] Cooke Taylor believed that all this helped cement good relations between masters and men, especially as in times of distress the manufacturer in a factory colony tended to keep his mills running so that there was at least some return on capital invested in the cottages.[25] But, in spite of this optimism, there are a number of indications that the experiment in authoritarian amelioration was only partially successful. Although the only strike occurred in 1830, Henry Ashworth complained in 1833 that "the contentment and good order of the work-people has been seriously disturbed, chiefly by the interference of mischievous agitators." He displaced blame on to these convenient external agitators again in 1834:

The pretended friends of the working classes, not inaptly called the agitators, have for several years kept up a continual strife betwixt our workpeople (who support them) and ourselves; causing serious interruptions to our business; sometimes by disagreements on the subject of wages, at other times by their intermeddling with our authority, or the regulations of our trading concerns, and latterly by their concocting of time bills.

In the downturn of 1839-40 the hands became Chartists and denounced their employers both for the distress and for being oppressive. The lowering of the radical temperature apparently only came about in the prosperity of the mid-forties, when the workers took advantage of cheap excursions and could afford to buy good clothes; at that point, "The Harmony and Goodwill that prevailed betwixt Masters and Workpeople was of the most satisfactory Nature."[26]

The results of moral regulation were equally mixed. Ashworth stated categorically in 1833, furthering an agenda of domesticity, that "I am happy to say that there is no married female employed by us . . . nor do I know that we have any married workman who finds it necessary or is desirous that his wife should follow any employment but that of her domestic duties."[27] But Leon Faucher noted that some work, such as winding and repairing, was distributed to married women in their homes. He also cast doubt on the reality of juvenile sexual segregation:

[T]he benevolent intention of the proprietor has, in this instance, been too much in advance of the habits of his work-people. They have not the sentiment of modesty sufficiently developed to separate their children of both sexes, during the night. There are never more than two chambers occupied, and it is even a mark of attention to decency if they draw a curtain, or put a partition between themselves and their children.

He further alleged that, in spite of the severe discipline, there had been twenty-four illegitimate births in one of the mills in three and a half years. All but one of the seducers, claimed Ashworth, were from neighboring establishments.[28]

A second conspicuous example of extensive paternalism was the sewing-cotton and smallware-manufacturing enterprise of James and Robert Chadwick at Eagley Mills, a branch of J. and N. Philips of Manchester, closely related to the Gregs of Styal and part of the Cross Street Unitarian Chapel nexus. A bowling green, a cricket pitch, a library and reading room, a brass band and a park followed the building of model cottages.[29] A third major example could be found at the Dean Mills, Barrowbridge, Halliwell, in another wooded site by a stream on the edge of the moors north of Bolton. The millowners, Robert Gardner, his son Richard, and Thomas Bazley, extensive manufacturers across the region, built terraces of model cottages with gardens for around three hundred of their hands and later added a bathhouse and a large building containing a boys' school, library, newsroom, lecture room, and "hall of science." The workmen established a cooperative provision store. When the Prince Consort paid a visit in 1851, the *Illustrated London News* enthused that the "community of interest between the employer and the employed" was "perfectly illustrated by the good-will and thoughtful attention of the former to the interest and welfare of their subordinates, and the contentment, steadiness, and affectionate zeal of the latter." All told, the general harmony indicated "a well organised community never equalled by the utopias of philosophy."[30]

The Turton and Egerton Mills, the Dean Mills, and Eagley Mills between them made a clear ideological statement. With the exception of Robert Gardner, the proprietors were prominent Manchester School men, liberal political activists and Leaguers, propagators of a coherent middle-class identity and consciousness in battle with the landed interest.[31] Their assumption of a paternalistic role was not only born of necessity (the need to attract workers) and of self-interest (healthier, more disciplined hands), but also of a desire to demonstrate to the naysayers that this was a civilization that worked, and that a working relationship between capital and labor could reestablish a stable society on a higher, more affluent, more moralistic plane.

These model communities received so much attention because there were so few of them.[32] The great majority of mills were located in the towns, releasing the millowners from the obligation of building houses;[33] though these

masters might own some housing,[34] individual inspection of morals was unusual. Spheres of influence—around, say, the Pilkington Factories at Grimshaw Park or the Hopwood factories at Nova Scotia, Blackburn—were not in
the same league. Hornbyism came closer. The Hornby family, with its power
base in the Brookhouse Mills, Blackburn, went on to establish a formidable
Tory electoral interest in the second half of the century on the back of a muscular Christian populism.[35] This was the conservative response to liberal-
political-economist paternalism; its message was more one of squirearchical
bonhomie than moralistic regulation. William Henry Hornby and William
Kenworthy supplemented their fostering of Operative Conservative Associations and support for Ten Hours with a school (attached to St. Michael's
Church but largely constructed with Hornby's money, and bearing his coat of
arms), and a gymnasium, which opened in 1841. Cooke Taylor remarked on
this the following year, "glad are we to know that a feeling is spreading
among the opulent manufacturers and others, in favor of making suitable
provision to enable those who are engaged in mills and factories to take those
manly exercises, and enjoy those pleasing recreations, which are required by a
regard as much to their health as to their morals."[36]

Such was whole-hog paternalism. It was supplemented by a far more
common—but rather less convincing—variety following more nearly in the
tradition of the roasted beast at Christmas. Treats or day-trips multiplied in
number in the 1840s. Previously they had tended to be confined to special occasions, like the laying of foundation stones, the completion of buildings, or
coronations. At Victoria's coronation in 1838, for example, after a grand procession, groups of workmen were regaled in "good old English" style (roast
beef, plum pudding, and ale, the *table d'hôte* for patriotic occasions) by their
respective employers at foundry or mill.[37] But toward mid-century the masters
began to divorce treats from special events, putting into operation a quite
clear agenda for class conciliation, a conciliation spelled out so loudly precisely because it was lacking in practice. Take, for example, a treat of tea and
sandwiches given by Thomas Taylor of the Grecian Mills, Bolton, to his
workmen and their wives in the autumn of 1850. One speaker, surveying the
decorated room, asked that "the flowers be taken to represent the beauty and
loveliness of the union, as he trusted it existed—and he thought there was
good evidence that it did exist—between employers and employed," and that
the evergreens be considered "as emblematic of the lively and enduring nature
of that union." In return the workmen gave an address thanking Taylor for
the party, for keeping his mills running during the late distress, and for erecting a new mill. The editor of the *Chronicle* then dutifully played his role by
broadcasting the proceedings while commenting on "the general good feeling
evinced and expressed between employers and employed."[38]

Similar ideological statements greeted the rash of railway excursions, which became a popular method of trying to express employer goodwill. For example, in early July 1849, six hundred hands and their families from Bashall's Wellfield Mill, Preston, marched to the station, traveled on a special train to Fleetwood, processed at the other end to the Mount for "rural" sports (sack races and the like), before being divided by age and gender (the men dined at the Victoria Inn, the women and the younger folk had refreshments on the beach or at private houses). More sports followed and then a trip on the steamer around the lighthouse. Later in the month John Paley and Company treated their workpeople to many of the same elements on a trip to Fleetwood: a band, a procession, decorated railway carriages, races, a steamer ride, coffee, and buns. True to the intent of reciprocity, the workers gave three cheers for Paley and Company, and the band played the national anthem. On the first Saturday in August, three or four thousand workers from Preston mills were sardined into trains and despatched to Fleetwood. On a Saturday toward the end of the month, the hands from William Taylor's Tulketh Factory, of H. A. and W. Dawson, of Horrocks, Miller and Company, and from Paul Catterall's Park Place Mills could be found at Fleetwood, those of Swainson, Birley and Company along with the Catholic schoolchildren at Lytham, of Shaw and Company in the Lake District, and of Riley's Bank Top Mill, Fishwick, and Hawkins's Adelphi Street Mill at Poulton-le-Sands.[39]

So what were the capitalists attempting to buy with this annual display of mayfly paternalism? Harmony, social stability, good order; a consensus behind the legitimacy of their authority and of the social structure; "Masters and men, men and masters, all enjoying themselves together in one boat,—no differences, no contentions, no jealousies," as a correspondent described an outing of Grundy and Company's hands. The master showed his respect for his men "by associating with them, and joining in all their sports;" they showed "their love and respect for good masters, by greeting Mr. Grundy, . . . on his every appearance, with such joyous rounds of applauding shouts, the like of which can be heard only in 'Merry England.'" What a contrast to "the misery and despair" reigning over most of Europe! What an answer, by the "contented, happy, satisfied, intelligent, and loyal" English mechanic to "the base and foolish trials made by the Socialist or concealed Republican, to change with violence that constitution which guarantees his freedom."[40]

Critics remained unmoved by millowners' feeble attempts at paternalist amelioration. Peter Whittle, comparing factories with baronial castles and manufacturers with feudal lords entrusted by Providence to rule, thought that, "With some noble exceptions, . . . the capitalists and manufacturers of England have not only, not fulfilled the trust committed to them in any tolerable degree, but have rather acted with a deep unconsciousness that they had any trust or duty to fulfil, beyond that of getting rich as fast as they could."[41] At a grand "Factory Workers' Bazaar" held in Bolton in 1852, one of those occasions that brought together the elite in an attempt to elevate the moral, social, and spiritual condition of the workers, the Rev. Edward Girdlestone, vicar of Deane, remarked that "the kind of feeling existing between the mechanics and those who employed them" did not compare favorably with the bonds of affection between feudal or contemporary landlords and their tenants. He appealed for "the masters of the mechanics [to] take an interest in their spiritual and religious welfare," and for "the people [to] learn their duty"; then "there would be a stronger bond of affection between employer and those employed, and, under the divine blessing, a greater measure of love to that God who made, and redeemed, and sanctified, both master and man."[42] Some Bolton manufacturers, thought the Rev. E. A. Verity, indeed treated their operatives as "brothers and members of the great family of mankind"; but "the majority were the grasping, greedy, ambitious and selfish sham manufacturers . . . who by abatements of every description, by all kinds of fines, by hard rules which if man were a piece of clockwork he could not keep exactly, by every kind of ill treatment and chicanery, sought to reduce the wages of the operatives."[43]

Short Time

Like Church paternalists, moaning that the urban gentry in new working-class areas were not pulling their weight, or the managers of collective projects of supervision and redistribution, complaining that the opulent were not subscribing enough of their mite for their projects to function properly, writers and assorted moralists protested that the cotton barons were rather less noble than the genuine article. But if individual, voluntarist initiatives remained sporadic, superficial, and unconvincing, an alternative strategy was to confront or conciliate labor collectively.

Confrontation predominated; concessions were screwed out of reluctant millowners. At the end of the wars, when most Preston mills worked thirteen-and-a-half hours a day, John Swainson was struck by how the male adult spinners in his mill looked older than their actual ages. He tried and failed to get all hours reduced in the town and neighborhood, and for a while his and another mill shortened their hours unilaterally, before abandoning the experiment. Swainson's testimony was among the evidence presented to a Select Committee on Children in Manufactories in 1816, painting a grim picture of the state of the textile factories in the town. Children "in a wretched condition from being overworked," and of "a sickly and emaciated appearance," failed to dent the employers' conviction that a curtailment of hours would be injurious, that legislation reducing the employment of children would force families on to the parish, and that the children were better off and as healthy as those employed in handloom weaving.[44]

In response to Sir Robert Peel's bill to regulate the hours of child labor, the Bolton master cotton spinners attempted a compromise in the spring of 1818, resolving that work should not exceed twelve hours a day, should be within the hours 5 a.m. to 9 p.m., that children under nine should not work in such mills, but that all those employed should work the same hours.[45] After the passage of the 1819 Factory Act,[46] visiting magistrates discovered frequent noncompliance: poor working conditions, the employment of considerable numbers of children under nine, and a continued determination by millowners to milk as many minutes as possible from their operatives.[47] Two JPs visiting Banister Eccles and Company's Jubilee Mill in Blackburn in 1824 came across a particularly fraudulent example of the employers' control of time. The firm professed to work seventy-two hours a week, but their working time was calculated not by "the Common Time piece" but by "the *Engine Clock*," an instrument worked by the steam engine. Ordinarily the engine would make twenty-three strokes a minute and the dial travel a twelfth of the circumference of the plate in one hour. But because the engine was overloaded with machinery it could make only twenty-one strokes, and the dial took six minutes longer to travel the same distance. That meant that the hands worked thirteen hours a day but were paid only for twelve.[48]

Forced into a slow retreat by incremental "legislative interference," millowners fought for every square inch of territory. The Bolton master spinners petitioned in 1825 against the further restrictions on child labor proposed by Sir John Cam Hobhouse.[49] He succeeded only in limiting night work (in 1825) and in a minor reduction of child working-hours (in 1831), but for the masters these measures acted as new benchmarks beyond which state interference was unwarranted.[50] The arguments marshaled against the 1833 Factory Bill were predictable. Firstly, reduced hours would diminish profits and stimulate foreign competition. "Does your Lordship really think you can mend the condition of the workman by ruining the employer?" Henry Ashworth asked of Lord Ashley, a principal proponent of the bill. "Pause my Lord:—have you forgot the Fable of killing the goose which laid the golden eggs?" Secondly, the adult workers were free agents who could always seek alternative employment; and they had freely and deliberately chosen for their children a more remunerative employment than they might obtain elsewhere.[51] Thirdly, long hours in factories neither damaged health nor morals; a number of local surgeons agreed that mill children did not compare badly with domestic drudges and the children of miners, weavers, dressmakers, and so on, and certainly "The health of factory people is much better than their pallid appearance would indicate."[52] Fourthly, self-regulation was acceptable, but state regulation was coercive and un-English. This logic of voluntary concession— designed to maximize profits while appearing conciliatory, to prevent overproduction, and to ensure against unfair advantage—in July 1833 lay behind a meeting of Bolton spinners resolving to limit hours to sixty-nine (twelve on weekdays and nine on Saturdays), to employ no children under eleven in the mills, to appoint a warden in each district to enforce the act, and to abolish night-working.[53]

The new act, excluding the under nines and limiting the under thirteens to nine hours and the under eighteens to twelve hours, became the millowners' *ne plus ultra*. They fabricated the redoubt behind which they sheltered out of a familiar rhetoric of immobility. Sixty-nine hours a week might be sensible, to avoid glutting the market, and because operatives became "languid and exhausted" and unprofitable after twelve hours a day. But "any time of working less than the present must be ruinous to our business," claimed Banister Eccles and Company. This was the "killing-the-golden-goose" argument. A variant of it, explaining the need for young children, held that operatives employed from infancy grew up to be quicker and more skillful at their work.[54] The "misguided humanity" argument purported to have the best interests of the workers at heart. A "Ten Hours Bill will tend to decrease instead of increasing the comforts of the working class," claimed John Sparrow of Blackburn, "by causing a reduction of wages, to meet foreigners in their own market." "Without cheaper bread," observed Thomas Thomasson of Bolton, making the same point by linking it to an attack on the Corn Laws, "I should consider a reduction of hours of working an act very unwise; with it, a measure of unspeakable advantage to the moral and physical condition of the operatives." Most sardonically of all, Robert Lund of Blackburn commented:

The foreigner, fettered by no restrictions, and possessing many advantages not attainable by us, would be able to compete with us in our own markets; an impetus would thus be given to the improvement of foreign machinery (which has already attained a fearful state of perfection), the wages of our workpeople must be reduced, and the brawlers for the miscalled "Cause of Humanity" would have the consolation of reflecting that their ignorant exertions had occasioned the misery and absolute beggary which would universally prevail from want of employment and low wages.

The "impossible to enforce" argument worried that, as Horrocks, Miller and Company of Preston put it, if the hours were restricted to fifty-eight under a Ten Hours Act, "no moral power on earth could prevent in many instances a contravention of such restriction"; the most respectable and best-managed concerns, which adhered to the law, would be ruined. This same fear, that some businesses would undercut others, had ironically convinced some masters of the merits of regulation. For Livesey and Rodgett of Blackburn, "We think the Act now in force (if strictly enforced) sufficient." William Garnett Taylor of Astley Bridge advocated "An effective enactment, stopping night work altogether, heavy penalties, a sworn warden or surveyor to each district, to see the law strictly observed, thereby preventing one concern working his people more than another, which at this time most seriously affects the trade."[55]

Only a very small number of masters were prepared to move even a yard or two beyond these entrenched positions.[56] Although there was some expression of the status divisions between "respectable" and unscrupulous mills, the more prosperous and the more marginal,[57] there were as yet no discernible joints along sectarian lines, or any encouraging signs that the master manufacturers were going to undertake an active, collective program of class amelioration. The state and other sectors of the bourgeoisie were going to have to do their duty for them.

"I do not think work-people, of late, care much about their masters," wrote Daniel Haughton, Blackburn millowner, in 1834,[58] and, during much of the decade, masters gave little indication of caring much for their workpeople either. In the considerable labor unrest of those years, the capitalists showed a largely successful determination to resist worker demands and the spread of unionism. Typically the disputes were over hours of labor, wage rates, technological innovation and de-skilling, and trades union rights. In Bolton, as R. A. Sykes has cataloged, the Ashworths had a violent dispute with their hands in 1830, as did the machine makers at Dobson's in 1831, while the miners on the southeast Lancashire coalfield struck intermittently between 1830 and 1832, the sawyers at Heaton's yard in 1832, the tailors in 1834 and 1836, and the shoemakers and builders repeatedly in 1835-36.[59] The Ashworths broke the strike at Egerton through a vigorous combination of the Master and Servants Law, the use of blacklegs, and forcing workers to sign a declaration that they would not join a union.[60] William Hulton, confronting his colliers at Hulton early in 1831 during the coal strike (a dispute over wages and unionization), pledged *"that I will never again engage"* a collier who was a union member.[61]

Trades unionism sinned against a key nostrum of political economy, the unfettered right of every individual—employer and employee—to strike a bargain to hire or be hired. Parliamentary suggestions that handloom weavers receive government assistance—the death throes of the moral economy—were equally distasteful in liberal-economic eyes. Peter Hesketh Fleetwood, MP for Preston, and William Bolling, Col. Torrens, and Peter Ainsworth, MPs for Bolton, all supported parliamentary inquiries into the condition of the weavers, and some Bolton clergymen, gentry, and manufacturers signed a petition in 1834 to establish local boards of trade to arbitrate wages.[62] A select committee, skillfully manipulated by John Fielden and John Maxwell, did report in favor of wage regulation, but this made no impact on a Parliament—albeit predominantly of landowners—that had recently voted through the New Poor

Law. The subsequent royal commission on handloom weavers ultimately reported against a minimum wage.[63] As Dr. Bowring, radical candidate for
Blackburn and later MP for Bolton, explained in the Commons in 1835, no
advance was ever made in manufactures but at some cost to those in the rear;
his best advice to handloom weavers was to abandon their trade and adopt
another.[64]

There was one area, however, where employers readily and rapidly abandoned free market tenets. Masters' combinations were, theoretically, taboo;
but in response to the Preston strike of the winter of 1836-37, the most traumatic of the decade in the three towns, they established the Preston Master
Spinners' Association.[65] The Bolton Spinners' Union had, through a number of
strikes, achieved a 5 percent wage rise in 1836, and spinners in Preston,
Blackburn, and Chorley began to demand the Bolton list.[66] The turnout began
in Preston at the start of November when the spinners' union, growing in
strength and resolution since the summer, refused to abandon the union in return for a 10 percent wage increase. Repeated attempts at mediation by individuals unconnected with cotton, such as Alderman John Noble, maltster, and
Joseph Livesey, cheesemonger and printer, proved unavailing. The spinners
clung to the union and the masters to the position that—as the Tory *Preston
Pilot* expressed it—"there can be no tyranny exceed that in injustice and ab-
surdity, which would arrogantly dictate to another the price at which he may
and may only exercise an unalienable right—to dispose of his own labour on
his own terms."[67] The union funds ran out in mid-December. By the time the
masters had won their point, through a combination of far greater resources,
collective organization, and the military standing by, a number of people had
reportedly died from starvation, some young women had turned to prostitution, most families had pawned much of their clothes and furniture, and many
small shopkeepers had suffered severely from the knock-on effects. The masters reopened the mills in early January and slowly filled them with two hundred new hands and a reluctant trickle-back of strikers, forced to agree to the
nonunion terms outlined by the Preston Master Spinners' Association.[68]

At the end of the dispute, Swainson, Birley and Company ("Your affectionate Masters") penned a statement of the Divine Right of Masters at its
most extreme to the workers of the Fishwick Mills. They stressed that the outcome of the contest had not been in doubt, since they had been determined,
"however great the pecuniary sacrifice," to break the union. But, "We do not
forget that we are placed by the Almighty in the situation of masters, not that
we should oppress you, but that we should do all we possibly can, to render
your lives happy and comfortable." They lamented that they were unable to
take back many old hands; but "if we can in any way afford assistance to
them or their families, it will be to us a source of great gratification." Clearly
believing that they themselves were "actuated by Christian principles," they

urged that servants as well as masters "be under the guidance of religion, for rest assured there is no motive like a religious motive to insure the performance of a right action, there is no law equal to the law of God, as a guide to what is good, and a check to what is evil." The response from the "United Trades of Preston" was forthright: "They [the "Cotton Tyrants"] say they consider the Almighty placed them in the situation of masters. . . . What solemn mockery,—what a gross insult to common sense,—what a perfect libel on Christianity!" Citing this as evidence, Charles Swainson wrote to Lord John Russell at the Home Office that "unless some Means are used to check the bad & increasing Spirit that prevails, the Consequences ere long will be most serious."[69] The question was, what means? The military could not be used indefinitely. Prolonged lockouts, while securing short-term compliance, were expensive and evidently did little to cow the workers' "bad and increasing Spirit." The onset of a depression, and the forcing down of wage advances secured in the more prosperous years, could hardly be expected to quell discontent.[70] One, limited, individualist answer at the rock face of class relations was factory paternalism. Short time was another such concession to unionism and Chartism.

Short time was not an initiative seized swiftly. The high level of labor unrest in the thirties, combined with the political and labor crisis of 1838-42, did not translate into a reflexive bourgeois response on the question of hours. It is notable that only in the mill-building boom of the mid-forties, and maybe as much from the promptings of a cult of domesticity as from working-class pressure, did local members of the bourgeoisie board the short-time omnibus publicly and in force. Even then, millowners across the political spectrum, by and large, remained reluctant, spinning imaginative permutations on the rhetoric of immobility. Long hours and a "high" family income, they maintained, generated order, morality, and prosperity, all of which would be jeopardized by reckless tampering.[71] Only one local cotton lord came out as a leading advocate of short time. William Kenworthy, junior partner in the Hornby mills at Brookhouse, Blackburn, in an open letter in November 1842, reversing his fellow industrialists' logic, argued for a sixty-hour week on practical and moral grounds. Practically, daily fluctuations in the market often made a greater difference in the cost of goods than would be caused by a reduction in hours, and fewer hours would increase the numbers employed which would boost domestic consumption. Morally, shorter hours would restore "cheerfulness and contentment . . . to the domestic hearth" and bring about "a decided moral and intellectual improvement." He entreated the textile masters "to lend an active and energetic helping hand to snatch from the vortex of disease, immorality, and crime, in which they are engulphed, the major part of the manufacturing artizans—the wealth of Great Britain."[72]

Hornby and Kenworthy had already begun their experiments in limited paternalism, so could be credited with doing their bit "to lend an active and energetic helping hand." Kenworthy was also actively and energetically making a political statement, offering short time as a better remedy than free trade. For this, Richard Cobden, Edmund Ashworth, and Joseph Livesey, leading Anti-Corn Law Leaguers, immediately attacked his letter. In his spirited reply Kenworthy contended that a restriction of hours would help reduce the overproduction caused by improvements in machinery. Repeal would not. The "spouters of the League are even less disposed to minister to the physical wants of the labouring classes, than the slave-owners of any country in the world." They might "cry out for a cheap loaf," but their main objective was purely self-interested, "to extend trade, and for their own sordid purposes they would work the poor operative to the last extremity of human endurance." Having risen from the ranks himself and worked in a cotton mill from the age of eight, he spoke from experience and was no recent convert to short time.[73]

This attempt to politicize the issue, and even to appropriate it for the Tory cause, made little headway.[74] Independent of party or sect, local medical men and men of God, with some support from lawyers and non-cotton industrialists, played the biggest bourgeois part. The question of Ten Hours came to the forefront of the national agenda in the mid-1840s, local meetings often being generated by the crusading zeal of Lord Ashley, Richard Oastler, and other itinerant short-timers. For example, in one such meeting in Bolton in the spring of 1846, the local worthies joining Ashley on the platform included Anglican, Unitarian, Baptist, New Jerusalem, and Wesleyan Methodist Association ministers, a surgeon, a Methodist ironfounder (Peter Rothwell, in the chair), an Anglican bleacher (Peter Ainsworth, Liberal MP for Bolton), and a Unitarian counterpane manufacturer and bleacher (Robert Heywood). Millowners were conspicuously absent. In their speeches both Heywood and the Rev. Franklin Baker, the Unitarian minister and staunch defender of the factory system, stated that they had hoped masters and men could resolve the question without parliamentary intervention; but this had not happened, and they convey a clear sense of taking on the burden of duty and leadership because the millowners had abdicated their responsibilities.[75]

Yet Bolton and Blackburn textile masters seem to have shed their diehard opposition of the previous decade. The majority remained aloof, but some at least attended the meetings, though apparently playing little or no role.[76] Some—especially in combination with the Repeal of the Corn Laws—stated their willingness to compromise on eleven hours.[77] Oastler and Kenworthy claimed at a meeting in Blackburn Theatre in the spring of 1844 that Lancashire and Yorkshire millowners in general, and Blackburn manufacturers in particular, had softened their stance.[78] At a meeting in Accrington in May

1844 Robert Hargreaves, who employed nearly two thousand workers, even moved the resolution in favor of a Ten Hours Bill, saying that he had long been in favor of the measure.[79]

Preston was a different matter; "I am truly sorry that I cannot speak so favourably of the Preston masters," said Kenworthy in 1844.[80] They retained the Master Spinners' Association after the 1836-37 strike, levying a subscription of one shilling per horsepower to defray expenses and in September 1843 remodeling it as the Millowners Association of Preston and the Neighbourhood. This and imitation societies were to become fora for the negotiation of agreed lists of prices and earnings with workers' associations;[81] but in the shorter term the cohesion and resolution that this organization provided may well have sustained the Preston millowners' firm hostility to a Ten Hours Bill. In early 1846—and again in early 1847—the association resolved "That in the opinion of this meeting any further interference with a view to a reduction of the hours of Labor in Factories would be impolitic and dangerous."

A tea party of the Preston operative cotton spinners in the Corn Exchange in late 1845 is a good indication of the tensions existing. Two millowners, John Paley Jr. and William Ainsworth, Samuel Riding Grimshaw, attorney, Joseph Livesey, and about seven hundred operatives attended the meeting, ostensibly called to cement a good feeling between masters and men. Emblems like "May nothing separate the interests of employer and employed" draped the room. John Sergeant in the chair regretted that a good feeling did not fully exist and that such meetings were necessary. But Paley was suspicious of the intention of the gathering, as apparently were many other masters who had stayed away and, suspecting that it was a front for unionist attempts to introduce Bolton wages, he failed to play his choreographed role in the dance of harmonic class relations. He complained about the unions:

If he was paying a man 20s. per week, and he could procure another person to do it for 15s., that man had no right to be tyrranized [sic] over by his fellow-workmen. . . . He did not approve of their combinations, but if the men would combine, they might depend upon it that the masters would combine likewise, and they might take it for granted that the masters would be strongest.[83]

Opposition to state enforcement did not necessarily translate into a complete refusal to introduce a shorter working week. In 1844-45 Robert Gardner, a member of the Master Spinners' Association, experimented successfully with eleven hours. The *Preston Chronicle* wished this kind of voluntary agreement to be extended, rather than compulsory interference with the rights of labor and capital which would bring the millowners no compensatory gratitude.[84] But John Bright in Parliament in 1846, true to Manchester School principles, tried to discredit the experiment and claimed that Gardner had only nominally reduced hours while increasing the engine speed and shortening mealtimes, a charge condemned as untrue by a meeting of Gardner's hands.[85] Horrocks, Miller and Company tried eleven hours at their Moss Factory during March. They concluded at the end of the trial period that there had been a slight gain in productivity per hour on the hand mules and a slight proportionate loss on the self-acting mules and throstles (because the machinery required the same daily cleaning, regardless of hours worked, and because, being self-acting, the machines could not be accelerated by harder work). They insisted that the experiment had been scrupulously fair:

We feel justified in remarking that during this experiment, the workpeople have had every inducement to make the result as favorable as possible to the 64 Hours system. They were informed that the intended Trial of 64 Hours, was only to continue for 4 Weeks and we are aware that every effort was made by the Advocates of Short-time, to stimulate them to extra exertion so as to shew a result favorable to their views.

The bottom line seems to have been the only consideration, and the mill reverted to twelve hours.[86]

Similar to the reasoning of the Rev. Baker and Robert Heywood in Bolton, this failure of self-regulation now convinced the *Chronicle* that millowners in favor of short time would only introduce it if legislation forced their neighbors to do likewise.[87] Here too, clergymen and doctors led the way. A speaker at a public meeting in March 1846 in Preston Theatre revealed that fourteen out of sixteen of the clergy of the Church were favorable to the cause, that all the Dissenting ministers but three in Preston had signed a petition, and that nineteen of the medical men thought the prevailing hours too long. With Ashley again in attendance, the vicar, the Rev. John Owen Parr, made his position abundantly clear. He praised the Preston millowners for their benevolence, integrity, and intelligence; he had not come to give any support "to any feeling which may be inconsistent with the due subordination which ought to animate a Christian servant towards a Christian master." But in comparison to the people in agricultural counties, where he had lived until five years previously, the factory hands looked very unhealthy:

You cannot take a human being at a very early period of life, and consign it, when growing to maturity,—and confine such a being, I say, within the walls of a factory, for twelve hours a day—however clear, however well ventilated and well regulated such a place may be at the best—when every possible precaution has been taken, and the system is conducted in the best manner—you cannot, I say, do this, and expect that an infant, so confined for years, will not dwindle and fade, and lose part of its natural health and vigour. (Cheers.)

Just as manufacturers had said to the agriculturalists that they must do without protection, the manufacturers had to be told they must do without their last two hours.[88] Here was a resounding answer to the long-timers, aiming a particular swipe at the factory paternalists of the Manchester School. He reiterated the message to the textile masters from different sectors of the bourgeoisie: If you do not act, the state—with our blessing—will act for you.

The 1847 Ten Hours Act, limiting "unfree agents"—women and young children—to ten hours a day, with the understanding that adult males would be equally restricted in consequence, failed to anticipate that some millowners might employ their women and young in relays, enabling them to work the men longer. This, and the attempts emanating from Manchester to bring in a compromise act, drew out the old campaigners during 1849 and 1850, the spectacle once again of a segment of the elite leading a worker-encompassing battle against another segment of the elite. All three towns, and smaller mill settlements like Farnworth, held one or more meetings with a heavy clerical and medical presence—several of them with Oastler, the Rev. J. R. Stephens, and Samuel or Joshua Fielden as guest speakers. None of the speakers reported that *local* millowners were running relays or otherwise violating the spirit of the act. Their gaze was directed further afield, and in excoriating those who failed to accept that the long-time argument had been lost, they took the opportunity to restate the short-time case. For William Henry Hornby in Blackburn, the act protected capital by cutting down on overproduction. He called for heavy fines to counter the relay system, since "I cannot conceive how a man can call himself a gentleman and a Christian, and adopt such a system of fraud on the working classes."[89] The Rev. John Shepherd Birley in Bolton, giving a very clear exposition of the ideology of domesticity that motivated many adherents to short time, argued that, "the very greatest evil incident to the manufacturing system has been the long confinement of females in factories." He believed that "all the comforts of a well-regulated household, which lead to make a contented fireside and a happy home, are mainly dependent on female management" and therefore wished to see "such a limitation of the hours of labour as may enable them to *return early* to their homes."[90] In Preston, the *Chronicle* commented in March 1850 that Ten Hours had not proved prejudicial to capital while already the benefits to the operatives could be seen.[91] For John Cooper, manufacturer, those benefits included another welcome variant on the domesticity theme: a father in the center of his family, his children gamboling around him, walking in the summer evenings around the beautiful environs of the town.[92] William Kenworthy agreed on the principle: "There is a time to work and a time to play;—a time to learn and admire the wonders of the Creator, in a natural world, and a time to pray for the attainment of a better." Critically, all this sharpened the perception that Ten Hours had slung a rope bridge across the capital-labor chasm: "The cheerfulness, contentment, and happiness manifested in the operatives during the time of working, afford ample proof that a step has been taken in the right direction towards social improvement, and for establishing a better understanding between the employer and the employed."[93] The Ten Hours Act "has been greatly instrumental in correcting the evils both physical and social which have been deemed to be incidental to factory employment," explained a memorial from Bolton Corporation to Parliament in May 1850. It had created a feeling of such general satisfaction among the factory workers that any deviation from it "will revive agitation and spread a distrust in the Government as well as animosity towards Employers."[94]

The Limits to Concession

Some of the millowners, putting their faith in factory paternalism, looked to purely homegrown, voluntarist solutions for the reduction of lower-order discontent and for the inculcation of the mores of an ordered society. At the same time a cross-denominational, cross-party segment of the elite, including a large proportion of doctors, clergymen, and ministers, together with a smattering of industrialists, joined together with workingmen in fluctuating coalitions to press for short time. The timing of the agitation depended crucially on outside intervention in the form of peripatetic crusaders and legislation. Both sets of rhetoric drew on notions of happy hearths and homes, rational and improving recreation for the working classes, and the need to concede something to labor to decrease societal and workplace discontent.

But there were severe limits to the extent and success of these endeavors. Labor-capital relations remained frequently knife-edged and confrontational. For example, Joseph Eccles, Blackburn millowner, wrote in 1849 that he had supported eleven hours and had experimented on those lines in 1846, but that he might not have started building his new mill in 1844, costing nearly £50,000, if he had known Parliament was going to reduce the hours to ten. This drew a biting response, combined with an attack on the League, from the Committee of Operative Cotton Spinners and Self-acting Minders of Blackburn, claiming that Eccles had twice refused to restore the 10 percent wage reduction he had made in his mill:

If, to support such a mercenary faction as that of which Mr. Cobden formed a part—if, to prop up and encourage a system, the chief elements of which were fraud, falsehood, and intolerant bigotry—if, to keep in exercise a band of morbid agitators, whose only aim was to gull the ears and empty the pockets of the gaping multitude—if, to establish and promote such a giant humbug as that, *Mr. Eccles could contribute one thousand pounds,* it is "wondrous pitiful" if he cannot afford to *give back* to his workpeople the percentage he so "quietly" took from them![95]

The fierce Preston strike over wages of 1852-53 demonstrated that the politics of economic consensus still had a considerable distance to travel. This was a time when, as one pamphleteer memorably described a masters' meeting, "Thirty or forty well-clad men, every one of whom almost had come in a carriage, or vehicle of some description, were meeting to discuss the question of how little they could pay."[96] Only in the aftermath of this dispute, combined with the greater economic stability of the decade, did the Preston cotton lords become convinced of the virtues of negotiated, regional piece-rate lists.[97]

The paternalism and paternalist legislation of the 1840s also needs to be assessed against evidence of the evasion of regulations. For example, Leonard Horner, factory inspector, reported checking on overworking during the dinner hour at a Bolton mill in 1842. The millowner told him, "'You may save yourself the trouble, we have been expecting you here for a week, and you will find all right; besides, the young people are well tutored what to answer when the Inspector asks them questions about their hours of work.'" Even if masters were caught out, local magistrates set the penalties. In early 1842 Messrs. Goodbrand, Baxter and Company were prosecuted for overworking on three sample days. The magistrates, Charles James Darbishire and Robert Walsh, both textile masters, fined them £2. The superintendent protested that a penalty should be given for each of the three charges. The magistrates agreed, and split the £2 fine in three. In another case, Samuel and Thomas Taylor of Bolton were fined £4 for overworking, leading Horner to comment, "Mill owners will be able to judge whether the balance of pecuniary loss was in favour of working contrary to law."

Theft of time and labor did not equate to theft of property. Beyond the time infringements, neglect of workers' safety was commonplace. In the mill of John Tong in Bolton, crowded with machinery, the buckle of the driving belt caught John Taylor, aged twelve, and crushed him to death between the drum of the main shaft and the ceiling. But when a superintendent, Joseph Ewings, visited the mill, "I found that no alteration had been made in the situation of the machinery, and that everything was going on just as before the accident took place."[98] Although such instances, which can be readily multiplied, helped bring about the fencing of machinery in the 1844 Factory Act, all the shortcuts and dishonesty of unscrupulous masters further served to undermine the limited paternalism of the 1840s.[99]

This was in the cotton industry. The battle over time and conditions centered on the cotton mill because of its appropriation as a symbol of all that was best or worst about industrial progress. But equally poor—or worse— conditions of labor pertained in other branches of extractive and manufacturing industry, and because less public attention was focused upon them and the workforces tended to be less well organized, attempts at amelioration were more protracted.

Conditions in the collieries received prominence in the parliamentary inquiry of 1842, when graphic descriptions of barbarous savages and of half-naked women and children working long hours in brutal conditions raised horrified fears of rampant immorality and masterless men. Betty Harris, thirty-seven, a drawer in Andrew Knowles's coal pit in Little Bolton, described how she worked eleven hours a day for no more than seven shillings a week, a belt around her waist—even when pregnant—and a chain between her legs, her clothes drenched, pulling coal trucks on her hands and knees. Her husband beat her frequently for not being ready: "I have known many a man beat his drawer. I have known men take liberty with the drawers, and some of the women have bastards." She was once off work for twenty-three weeks after her hips were crushed. Her story was typical. John Kennedy, who investigated the mines in the area, depicted the children and young people employed in the pits in the mining villages to the south and east of Bolton as stunted in growth, ignorant, "deteriorated as workmen and dangerous as subjects." The legislature's interference was "necessary for the protection of the children who were not able to protect themselves; and also for the protection of the state from the growth of an ignorant, depraved, and dangerous population."[100] In the small pits working thin seams in the coal belt from Oswaldtwistle and Little Harwood to the Darwen moors, miners took in young children as fillers and drawers because the mines were so low, and although the miners themselves worked horizontally, larger children dragging the trucks out would have required more space. By the time the boys became men, claimed Thomas Whalley, relieving officer of Over Darwen, they were old men.[101]

After a case of brutality came before Burnley magistrates, Assistant Poor Law Commissioner Charles Mott investigated the employment of children in the mines within Blackburn Union, including some sent from the workhouse. He discovered that employing boys aged seven to nine was very common, that the jobs were considered good because they paid better than handloom weaving, and that, all told, "the practice of allowing Children to work in the Coal Mines at so young an age is so common and is considered so advantageous that the Guardians expressed surprize [sic] that any doubt should have been expressed as to the propriety of it."[102]

Peter Ainsworth, Liberal MP for Bolton, a coalowner, a man who later set himself up as a leading friend of short time in cotton mills (of which he owned none), was rather less in favor of regulating the mines. In fact he was a leader of the opposition to Ashley's Coal Mines Act of 1842. He claimed that the mining children were much better off and healthier than factory children, and that if Parliament prohibited boys under nine from working and limited boys aged ten to twelve to three days a week, hundreds of children would be thrown out of work and hundreds of families driven into the workhouse. "The noble Lord had already interfered with the cotton-spinners, and gone such great lengths as to cause great privation amongst them, and the result of this measure would be the same with regard to the mining population."[103] Once again the state stepped in where local self-interest proved unwilling to act; the 1842 Mines Act banned females from working underground and the employment of boys under ten.

A parliamentary inquiry into other industries in 1843 highlighted the dire conditions elsewhere. At William Yates's calico printing works at Blackrod, Hannah Berry had been working a twelve-hour day—and often more at night when an order was due in a hurry—since the age of nine. In Accrington, on many occasions Simpson's kept the children at work for sixteen to eighteen hours. In the region's foundries, the operatives labored for twenty-four or even thirty-six successive hours usually at least twice a year when "breakdowns" occurred. Until recently Messrs. Hilton's paper works at Darwen had continued in relays, day and night, the nightworkers not stopping for meals but eating while they worked. In Preston, Richard Whiteside, aged eleven, twisted tobacco by turning a wheel, earning 1s. 6d. per week, while at home a maker-up of hats employed two of his sisters, eleven and fourteen, working from 6 a.m. to 9 p.m. for 2s. 6d. a week for the pair of them. And so on in an archipelago of fragmented exploitation across the manufacturing districts.[104]

Short time came later to industries beyond the cotton mill. In bleaching, as we have seen (Chapter 6), John Horrocks Ainsworth of Halliwell had a bitter public squabble about excessive hours at the end of the forties with the Rev. Milton, incumbent of his church. The operatives began mobilizing in 1853, and Ashley introduced a bill to regulate the hours in bleachworks in June 1854. This sent some of the big Bolton bleachers—Ainsworth, Thomas Ridgway Bridson, one of the Blair brothers, one of the Howarths, and James Hardcastle—scurrying to London to lobby for a committee of inquiry instead. Palmerston agreed to this in the form of the Tremenheere Commission. The bleachers made a series of arguments familiar to the manufacturers of the previous decade: legislation would be an unwarranted interference and would compel trade to move to Europe; bleaching was a healthy occupation; bleachers had to work irregular hours to fulfill irregular orders and to keep up with the other branches of the industry. Of the Bolton bleachmasters giving evidence, only Robert Heywood, consistent with his support for Ten Hours in the cotton mills, spoke in favor of a reduction in hours. Tremenheere concluded that fourteen to sixteen hours' work was common in the industry for months at a time, that many of the workers were sickly and stunted, and that the masters had failed to prove their case regarding the flow of trade. He suggested that the hours of the Factory Act be applied. But, in spite of the fact that nearly all the Bolton medical men and clergymen signed petitions in favor of regulation, the bleachers had a formidable lobbying machine and demonstrated that the profit motive could remain a more powerful argument than domesticity and social cohesion. Parliament did not vote through legislation until 1860 and even then allowed "over work" for up to two hours a day.[105]

Regulation and paternalism scarcely touched another group of workers, the hordes of railway navvies that were a prominent feature on the Lancashire landscape. The *Preston Chronicle* commented that railways were advancing the great cause of civilization, but this *"classe dangereuse"* was neglected and subject to much oppression and injustice, the target of nothing more philanthropic than the coercive vengeance of the law.[106] This was not wholly true, as moralizers and proselytizers did try and reach at least some of them. For example, it was brought to the attention of the Lancashire Congregational Union, date unspecified, that navvies

were often located in numerous groups for a considerable period in remote parts of the country, far away from church, chapel, or school, and from the restraints imposed by the presence of civilised society; and that the consequence too generally was that they sought relief from their laborious and dangerous employments in sensual enjoyments of the lowest and most degrading kinds.

In 1846, during the construction of the Bolton and Blackburn line, the Congregational Union gave money to the Revs. S. T. Porter of Darwin and William Roaf of Wigan to evangelize these laborers, with services, tracts, and Bibles, in the villages and hamlets along the moors. One of the missionaries reported on a visit to Blacksnape:

I did not enter more than four houses where there was not drinking; and at one or two I found, from the fiendish yells and horrid imprecations proceeding from them, that it would be prudent not to enter at all. This is a wretched place. It has fallen to my lot when in London to visit some of the vicious purlieus and dens of the metropolis, but never did I behold such scenes of degradation, ignorance, and vice as I have witnessed at Blacksnape.[107]

Many workers, therefore, remained beyond the protection of the state, and even where Parliament or local capitalists did make attempts at amelioration, reality often fell far short of rhetoric. In any case, the critics of the concept of "social control" have warned us to beware of exaggerating the impact of moralizing and conditioning messages and measures. The working classes were not a blank wall for the inscription of bourgeois doctrine, and each aspect of imposed norms—paternalism, education, rational recreation, organized celebrations—could quite easily be rejected or contentiously filter down into an independent working-class culture.[108] Even so, paternalism and short time joined that spectrum of measures of coercion, concession, and incorporation employed by different elements among the local elites and by the state to stabilize a social system in flux. They also helped reinforce part competing, part overlapping bourgeois ideals, between those who favored the quasi-squirearchical role of the gentleman capitalist, those who used paternalism as a means of broadcasting the wonders of factory civilization, and those who looked to or rejected the aid of the state in attempting to impose norms of domesticity. At their best these aspirations proclaimed a responsible bourgeoisie, beyond rapacious money-grubbing; but, as was the bourgeois way, while some diligently knotted the rope bridge together, others hacked at the cables, many endeavors ending up dangling pointlessly down the rock face.

CHAPTER 10: ORDERING THE TOWN

On approaching the manufacturing district from the south by rail in 1849, Angus Bethune Reach, a *Morning Chronicle* journalist, first became aware of the dull, smoke-laden sky squatting over the distance. Then small manufacturing villages, canals, turbid and thick rivers; the first tall chimneys; stunted and smutty foliage; coal-dust-blackened footpaths across fields.

You shoot by town after town—the outlying satellites of the great cotton metropolis. They have all similar features—they are all little Manchesters. Huge, shapeless, unsightly mills, with their countless rows of windows, their towering shafts, their jets of waste steam continually puffing in panting gushes from the brown, grimy wall. Between these vast establishments, a network of mean but regular streets, unpicturesque and unadorned—just the sort of private houses you would expect in the vicinity of such public edifices; and around all this, and here and there scattered amongst all this, great irregular muddy spaces of waste ground, studded with black pools and swarming with dirty children.[1]

This was a common representation of deterioration, the descent into a heart of darkness: the narrator is sucked "into the dark and troubled vortex of manufactures," as William Cooke Taylor described his arrival in Blackburn in the early 1840s. In these unnatural, sunlight-deprived surroundings, "the poorer sort of people" exhibited "pale and emaciated features"; those who had migrated from rural areas had struck a Faustian pact, "bartering away health, perhaps character, for higher wages and low animal gratifications."[2]

It is a straightforward task to quote selectively and describe an alien landscape crawling over Lancashire's moors and valleys in the course of a generation or two. Dr. John Aikin described Preston as a handsome, well-built, and genteel county town in the 1790s;[3] by about 1820, "an elegant and economical town, the resort of well-born but ill-portioned and ill-endowed old maids and widows, has," complained Dr. T. D. Whitaker, vicar of Blackburn, "by the fatal genius of modern commerce, been converted into a smoky, dirty, populous, expensive town."[4] Polite, powdered, and preened Preston was well on the way to becoming a dingy, desolate model for Charles Dickens's Coketown in *Hard Times*.[5]

Yet, just as mills, industry, and factory civilization had both detractors and promoters, it was possible to project a quite different image. Sir George Head, visiting Preston in 1835, chose to make no mention of urban deterioration; his comments instead focused on "the suburbs of the southern extremity, where ample space has been allotted to the streets and houses, many of which, of a superior description, have been erected within a few years." Here, "the eye is refreshed by handsome elevations of bright red brick, embellished by healthy young trees; and from hence a public walk and raised terrace form a commanding eminence . . . over a charming valley."[6] Alternatively, from a distant vantage point, an optimist could still see the packed and concentrated, but yet-small, towns as specks on a rural canvas. Charles Hardwick, historian of Preston in the 1850s, described the view from Naze Point on the Ribble estuary: "Preston is seen to advantage from this spot. Its numerous tall chimneys uprear their heads in the midst of a lovely pastoral landscape; which, at this distance, receives but slight blemish from the heavy cloud of coal smoke that crawls leisurely through the morning mist into the clearer upper atmosphere. Beautiful nature and human enterprise, ingenuity, and industry, are here presented in harmonious conjunction."[7] Amidst this ambivalence, these alternate voices of revulsion and wonder at what they had created, how, when, and why did members of the bourgeoisie set about putting their towns in order?

Municipal Reform

First they had to build the appropriate organs of local government. During the initial "Age of Improvement" around the turn of the century, each town supplemented its manorial courts and parish vestries with improvement commissioners.[8] In Bolton, an Improvement Act of 1792 appointed trustees to use the proceeds from the selling off of Bolton Moor.[9] Both the manorial and improvement arms of government were substantially Tory and Anglican, the first reflecting the predilections of the lords of the manor, the second the result of a co-opting body formed at a time when the wealth of the town consisted of a preponderance of one particular political hue and one particular denominational stripe. The trustees proceeded to lay down some common sewers in the principal streets, to organize the watch, to see to the condition of the streets, and to construct a new butchers' shambles. They approved plans for a new marketplace and a town hall in 1797 and paid rent to Lord Bradford for earmarked land from 1799; but in spite of repeated attempts to resurrect the project, they did not begin the New Market Place until 1820, and the trustees never did build the town hall. Fresh moves in the early twenties were stymied by doubts about whether the trustees had the necessary powers, and more important by the quagmire of local politics.[10] The radical middling-order assault on Old Corruption, peaking between 1827 and 1832, was expressed in attempts through the vestry—the one institution of local government to which broader ratepayer access was available—to fix the salaries of the town's officers, and in contests over the appointment of the overseer, churchwardens, and sidesmen.[11] This was paralleled by at least three attempts to make the trustees more responsible, particularly when the trustees invoked their power to levy a rate to meet increased expenditure. The first, a Chancery suit mounted by an opposition party in 1824-25, ended in a compromise: the trustees agreed that whenever there was a vacancy in their ranks, the churchwarden or sidesman, the boroughreeve and constables, and the overseers of Great Bolton should have the privilege of recommending between three and five people qualified to serve.[12] The second, notice by an opposition group at the end of 1829 to apply for a new act, also seemed to be heading toward a compromise in the summer of 1830 to avoid the expense of a legal contest: a toned-down bill, prepared by a joint committee, with due regard paid to the qualifications of trustees and electors, "for the purpose of keeping the Trust respectable."[13] This was similar to a reform measure pushed through in Little Bolton in the same year. There the trust had not achieved the same level of exclusivity, and as one party did not stand to lose by reform, the move toward an expansion of powers was apparently uncontroversial. Although embodied under the same statute as the Great Bolton trust, the Little Bolton trustees did not share in the proceeds from Bolton Moor; a rate was essential, and with it a large measure of ratepayer consent. The new act fixed the qualification for voters at £10 and for trustees at £30.[14] But the haggling continued in Great Bolton, no joint bill emerged, and both parties finally came to an agreement in November: when any vacancy occurred it would be filled by a selection from four names nominated at a vestry meeting.[15] This apparently lasted for three years, but since it operated against the Tories, they took the opportunity while still in a majority to rescind the resolution. The trust reverted to being self-elected, perpetuating a grievance that would work itself out in the municipal reform controversy. Two trustees, William Simpson, cotton spinner, and Robert Heywood, proposed in 1837 a third attempt at reform—the suggestion that vacancies be filled from a selection nominated at a vestry meeting by those qualified to vote in general elections—but this was swiftly voted down.[16]

Blackburn gained its first Improvement Act in 1803 with twelve named trustees—the Rev. Thomas Starkie (the vicar), Richard Birley, Samuel Bower, Richard Cardwell, Thomas Clayton, Henry Feilden, William Feilden, Isaac Glover, John Hornby, John Fowden Hindle, James De la Pryme, and Henry Sudell—mostly cotton merchants, Anglicans, and Tories, the town's leading inhabitants at the turn of the century. The act gave powers to regulate the market, to enforce bylaws and to raise a rate of up to 1s. 6d. in the pound for the watch, for street cleaning, and for the provision of a scavenger.[17] Henry Feilden, joint lord of the manor with the archbishop of Canterbury, had initially opposed the bill because it questioned his and the archbishop's rights, especially with regard to the Town's Moor. His son and successor, Joseph, demonstrated in 1824-25 that the power of the lords of the manor still remained considerable, if only as an obstacle in the way of change. The trustees gave notice that they were going to apply for an amended act to obtain further powers, including the control of markets and the establishment of a new marketplace if necessary, and the right to dispose of the Town's Moor for building or other purposes. Feilden's reassertion of his and the archbishop's rights over wastelands and the markets may have been sufficient in itself to waylay the proposition, and it fizzled out.[18]

Preston had to wait until 1815 for its Improvement Act, a measure that made commissioners of the mayor and aldermen ex officio, the owners of property worth at least £100, and all occupiers paying £50 rent per year (£100 for victuallers): around two hundred men in total by the mid-1830s.[19] The impetus for this partly came from members of the Lit. and Phil., who met in the premises of Isaac Wilcockson of the *Preston Chronicle*; he had announced in his opening editorial in 1812 that civic affairs were going to be one of his priorities. The gas company—owing much to the enthusiasm of Fr. Joseph Dunn, showing considerable overlap in membership with the Lit. and Phil., and also meeting at Wilcockson's—began to light the streets and Horrocks and Jacson's mill in February 1816, after negotiations with the new improvement commissioners.[20] The town also had its municipal corporation, a self-elected body drawing from a narrow segment of the elite, with the mayor annually appointed from among the aldermen in rotation. It lacked popular legitimacy but (beyond its judicial role)[21] exercised only limited functions, above all the management of the market and a certain amount of property, the whole bringing in the meager sum of £2,620 in 1836. It also nursed a substantial debt—£16,300 by the mid-1830s—mainly incurred in building a corn exchange in 1822-24. Nearly all of this money was borrowed from members of the corporation at 4 or 5 percent interest. Such instances—of questionable practices, not of glaring corruption—made the task of the royal commissioners on municipal corporations relatively straightforward. These gentlemen, appointed by the Whig government to ferret out abuses in predominantly Tory-Anglican corporations so as to justify its reforming agenda, outlined all the anomalies, privileges, and problems, concluding to no one's surprise that Preston should be included in the list of corporations to be abolished and replaced by an elected town council; "a decided opinion was expressed, both by members of the corporation, and others," they reported with suggestive vagueness, "that it would be beneficial to introduce a more open and popular form of election, and that inhabitants, occupiers of houses of a certain value in the town, should be allowed to participate in elections and other privileges now enjoyed by burgesses only."[22]

Municipal reform was intended to improve the efficiency of local government and to strengthen the national-local alliance between Whigs, liberals, radicals, and Dissenters.[23] At least two public meetings addressed by prominent liberal-radicals in the summer of 1835 supported the government's aim.[24]

The Tory *Preston Pilot* predictably opposed the bill, but was reconciled by the various property-weighting amendments imposed by the House of Lords.[25] Hence the bill passed relatively quietly in Preston, with party emotions only simmering. The elite tried to take advantage of this in an intriguing attempt— a vestigial reminder of the old parliamentary election coalition (Chapters 1 and 12)—to apoliticize this renovated arena of local government. "The arrangement of a matter of so much moment" as the setting of taxation levels and the security of persons and property, "ought not to be left to chance, or to any one's own opinion of self," declared Thomas Batty Addison, chairing an all-party gathering of the respectable at the Bull Inn in October; "nor should it be decided by political feeling (hear, hear.) In the choice of adequate councillors, it was desirable that they should be such as should include all the interests and feelings of the town; and to gain this object all canvas [*sic*], or intrigue, or underhand means ought to be avoided." Robert Segar, the radical barrister, objected to what looked like a higher-class plot to dictate to the electorate and advocated at least the inclusion of a few workingmen in the council, "men who, thus elevated to civic honours, by their intercourse with the more polished members of the body, might carry into their own circle the honourable and high minded feelings, and manners of, and at the same time thus increase their respect for, those of the higher orders." Regardless, the meeting agreed to establish a cross-party, cross-denominational general committee, with a chairman and secretary for each ward, to secure the election of a respectable council.[26]

This promising exercise in elite cooperation rapidly folded as separate parties in the wards drew up their own partisan—"Tory" and "Reform"—lists of preferred candidates.[27] Not that party labels were, as yet, firmly adhesive. The editor of the *Preston Chronicle* judged that twenty-four of the newly elected favored Melbourne (ranging from old Whigs to radical reformers) and twelve preferred Peel ("Conservative Reformers"). But, in the aftermath of the election, and particularly in the nomination of aldermen, the editor decided that the two parties could be more easily distinguished on religious than political grounds, and he took to calling them the "Church" and the "Anti-Church" parties, twenty-one Anglicans in the former, five Catholics, four Methodists, and six Dissenters in the latter.[28] By the following election he reluctantly described the new councillors as five "Liberals" and seven "Conservatives"— reluctantly because, "what has the election of a dozen individuals, selected professedly for the purpose of assisting in the domestic management—in the police regulations,—or in the appropriation of the borough finances of a large manufacturing town . . . to do with Whigism [*sic*], Conservatism, Liberalism, or any other system of political creed or catechism however defined?"[29]

TABLE 5

Occupations of Preston Councillors, 1835-50

Ward	Textile employers	Other manu-facturers	Gentle-men	Profes-sionals	Retailers & whole-salers	Others
St. John's	2	6	3	7	17	4
Trinity	0	11	0	13	13	3
Fishwick	23	0	5	7	3	2
Christ Church	4	2	12	17	4	1
St. George's	9	2	6	1	18	3
St. Peter's	27	2	0	1	6	2
Totals	65	23	26	46	61	15

SOURCE: LRO, Borough of Preston, Council Minutes, CBP/1/1. The table is inclusive of all elections and byelections until the end of 1850. It records the occupation at each election and not individual councillors, many of whom were repeatedly reelected and thus will have been counted several times. (For a year-by-year breakdown employing rather different criteria and indicating a slight shift away from retailers and wholesalers in favor of textile employers and professionals over the period, see H. N. B. Morgan, "Social and Political Leadership in Preston 1820-1860" (M.Litt thesis, Lancaster University, 1980), 184.) The categories are as follows:

Textile employers: cotton spinners, flax spinners, manufacturers, calico printers.
Other manufacturers: ironfounders, coachmakers, machine makers, leather manufacturers, tobacco manufacturers, spindle makers, rollermakers, maltsters.
Gentlemen: gentlemen and esquires.
Professionals: attorneys, barristers, surgeons, physicians, bankers (though not strictly "professional," they occur seven times).
Retailers & wholesalers: coal agents, chemists and druggists, hotelkeepers, "merchants," timber, wine, spirit, corn and coal merchants/dealers, grocers, cheese factors, tobacconists, booksellers, hosiers, drapers.
Others: land surveyors, stationers/publishers/newspaper proprietors, commission agents, plumbers, artists, engineers.

It was a valid question. But it did not receive a considered response, since municipal reform had opened up a new space within which rival factions of the elite could contend for power on an equal footing.[30] And, in spite of a substantial "shopkeeper" presence, Preston council *was* an elite affair up to mid-century[31] (Table 5)—even more so at the aldermanic level: of the twenty-five men serving in that capacity in the first fifteen years, twelve were textile masters, six lawyers, three bankers, two surgeons, one a corn merchant, and one a maltster, fifteen of them serving as mayor.[32] The fate of Alderman John Noble, maltster—who, "barring his politics, is a very respectable man"—marked out the political boundaries acceptable to the majority of the elite. He attended the monster meeting of North Lancashire Chartists chaired by Richard Marsden in November 1838, and consequently at the election of aldermen shortly afterwards he was voted out—one of only two aldermen before mid-century to fail in their bid for reelection. This was purely political: "[W]e do think that if any man can so far forget the respect that is due to his own character, as to become an actor in such proceedings as are carried on at Demonstration Meetings," noted the *Pilot*, "from that time he forfeits every claim to become a member of any body that is composed of gentlemen."[33]

A body of gentlemen: a reminder that members of the bourgeoisie sought municipal office not only to further their own and municipal interests but also for prestige and status. This was always vulnerable to a bad press at legislators' efforts[34] or to well-aimed, deflating satire: "Amongst our town councillors we have some of the sharpest, some of the most independent and clear-headed, some of the shallowest minded and most illiterate men that can be found in a fair day's journey," Anthony Hewitson reminded his readers at a later date. "The Wind Whistle Islanders who haven't sense enough to stand back from the fire when they get too hot, could beat a few of them in wisdom."[35] Party rancor, relatively tepid in Preston,[36] could also strip away respect for councillors. Moreover, it could even create a crisis of legitimacy in the competing organs of local government, as the Bolton elite discovered.

The Bolton reformers had taken a keen interest in the passage of the Municipal Corporations Bill in the summer of 1835.[37] The act provided that if a majority of assessed property in an unincorporated town were to petition in favor of a borough charter, it would be granted. Bolton, Manchester, Birmingham, and Sheffield were the first towns to petition.[38] Bolton's movement for incorporation began among the Nonconformist-dominated, liberal-radical elite, close to the Manchester School and to the developing momentum for the Anti-Corn Law League. The same group owned the *Bolton Free Press*, which was enthusiastic in its support for Richard Cobden's pamphlet advice to the citizens of Manchester: *Incorporate Your Borough!*[39] An initial tea party at Silverwell House, the home of John Dean, cotton merchant and manufacturer, was followed by a public meeting in Little Bolton Town Hall in January 1838.[40] The motivation was quite explicit: Tories ran the governing bodies—court leets of the lords of the manor and the improvement trustees of Great Bolton—to the almost total exclusion of Dissenters and liberals, and the policy of proscription percolated down to the lowliest position that patronage reached.[41] "If the Trustees had only kept faith with regard to their appointments," Robert Heywood maintained, "—the Court Leet been more moderate in their proceedings and the Boroughreeves had not frequently rejected the most respectable and numerously signed requisitions to call public meetings I am persuaded no efforts would have been made to have the Town incorporated."[42]

The Tories vigorously resisted the threatened loss of their entrenched power-base by means of a counter-petitioning campaign.[43] The lords of the manor of Great and Little Bolton petitioned for their rights and interests to be preserved inviolate. The principal petition from Great Bolton, deploying the truth with considerable economy, argued not only that policing arrangements were fair and sufficient (a major point of contention, as we have seen in Chapter 5), but that a jury appointed the boroughreeve and constables from among the most intelligent and respectable class of inhabitants—so they were not mere nominees of the lords of the manor, they had invariably discharged their duties "with impartiality and effect," no competent person had been excluded from municipal office by political bias, and the authorities had enjoyed a very high degree of confidence and support from their townsmen.[44] A petition from the ratepayers of Little Bolton was more convincing. It pointed out that under the terms of their Improvement Act of 1830, the trustees were ratepayer-elected, already formed a body corporate, and that incorporation would bring nothing but heavier taxation. They already had a town hall, recently built for £3,000, and policing was cheaper than in Great Bolton. Incorporation could be seen as a way for Great Bolton to spread the burden of paying for its deficiencies across its own boundaries into Little Bolton and Haulgh (which also sent an anti-charter petition).[45]

The Privy Council dispatched an emissary, Capt. Joshua Jebb, to report on the competing claims and to test the assessed property thrown into each side of the balance. He found the government of Great Bolton—its "irresponsible" officials, its policing, and administration of justice—to be deeply unsatisfactory. There was also a pending problem of municipal expenditure. The trustees funded their limited improvements out of a budget of £2,850, mostly the rents from the selling off of Bolton Moor. Incorporation would not directly affect this: a council would have no jurisdiction over the sanitary state of the town. But the co-opted trustees had no popular mandate for the collection of a rate, necessary if their functions were to be expanded, and it was therefore likely that at some point in the future an elected council would seek to take over the trustees' powers.[46] So building a case for Great Bolton's incorporation was not difficult; for Little Bolton and Haulgh it was more problematic. Jebb acknowledged the fear that, if incorporated, Little Bolton would have only a third of the councillors, whereas any question concerning the township would be decided by a majority in the council: they would lose the power of self-government and control over their own expenditure. But he argued that under the Municipal Reform Act the only power directly affected would be that of the boroughreeve and constables; the trustees would retain their powers until they considered it advantageous to resign them. As for Haulgh, whose annual expenditure on the police was £5, he recognized that the rates would increase; but since the township was being laid out by Lord Bradford for building ground, further expenditure on such things as lighting and paving would be incurred in any case.

Jebb's dilemma was how to make the voting figures fit the desired outcome. His initial scrutiny revealed 3,213 male ratepayers[47] in favor of incorporation and 2,956 against; but—partly because of the opposition of the large Tory millowners—property assessments came out to £57,472 against, compared with only £40,530 in favor. He therefore decided to exclude the Little Bolton petitioners altogether, on the grounds that they were not arguing against municipal reform *per se*, but against incorporation with the other two townships, which did not involve the same general principle of government. The new figures looked like this:[48]

	Ratepayers	Assessments
For:	3,213	£40,530
Against:	1,886	£33,681
Difference:	1,327	£6,849

These numbers proved sufficient, after some delay, for a borough charter to be granted. But the reformed government's mandate was sufficiently dubious for the Tories to begin a boycott,[49] creating—as we have seen—a gridlock in the realm of policing and justice, the areas for which the council was as yet most heavily responsible. During the next three years of Tory litigation and obstruction, the council was a wholly liberal concern, with no Tories standing. The old and rival authorities continued to run concurrently, the orchestrated tactic of nonpayment frustrated the levying of a rate, and the functions of policing had to be handed over to a government-appointed commissioner for the duration. The council could do little more than issue partisan petitions or civic addresses regarding events in the queen's life. The electors of Little Bolton further exacerbated the divisions between authorities by retaliating in the annual elections for a third of the trustees. The trust had been predominantly liberal since the 1830 act, but now, swelled by the Tory multi-voters mustering in force, all ten new trustees were conservative.[50]

With the resolution of the standoff in September 1842, the onset of party politics in the council chamber could begin. Their monopoly about to end, the liberals hatched in Little Bolton a most illiberal piece of electoral maneuvering known as the "Fifteen Plot." The council had laid a rate in March 1842 but made no attempt to collect it. On the last day of the qualifying period for the 1843 election, August 31, fifteen leading liberals including the mayor, Robert Walsh, manufacturer, paid up. As only those who had paid their rates were entitled to vote, these fifteen gentlemen were attempting to monopolize the suffrage for the township. The ruse failed, because during the Court of Revisions in October, limited by law to ten days, the conservatives objected to 1,980 names on the Great Bolton voting list, effectively consuming the time,

TABLE 6
Occupations of Bolton Councillors, 1843-50

	1843-45		1846-50	
	No.	Pct (%)	No.	Pct (%)
Manufacturers	66	50.8	96	53.0
Merchants	0	0.0	3	1.7
Shopkeepers/dealers	37	28.5	45	24.9
Building trades	2	1.5	3	1.7
Named merchants	3	2.3	4	2.2
Other businessmen	1	0.8	5	2.8
"Gentlemen"	19	14.6	14	7.7
Professionals	2	1.5	11	6.1
Totals	130	100.0	181	100.0

SOURCE: John Garrard, *Leadership and Power in Victorian Industrial Towns 1830-80* (Manchester: Manchester University Press, 1983), 16. His categories are as follows:
Manufacturers: manufacturers, cotton spinners, sizers, dyers, ironfounders, machine makers, brewers, brickmakers, quarry masters, colliery proprietors, mill furnishers, and manufacturing chemists.
Merchants: "merchants" and bankers.
Named merchants: iron, timber, wine and spirit, coal, and tea merchants.
Building trades: builders, joiners, carpenters, plumbers.
Professionals: solicitors, barristers, Drs., surgeons, vets, surveyors, sheriff's officers, engineers, journalists, editors.
Shopkeepers/dealers: shopkeepers, dealers, tea dealers, drapers, grocers, corn merchants, pawnbrokers, stationers, butchers, bakers, chandlers, chemists, druggists, cordwainers, licensed victuallers, and beersellers.

invalidating the franchise list for the year and forcing the use of the previous year's list.[51] The conservatives in fact gained their first majority in November 1844 and promptly used it to replace the town clerk, James Winder, with a conservative, James Kyrke Watkins. They kept their majority until 1853.[52]

John Garrard has analyzed the composition of the council in some detail (Table 6). While one might debate his categorization of some of the occupations, the overall picture seems clear: the industrial masters predominated in the council—especially given that many of the "gentlemen" would have been retired manufacturers—and their majority seemed to be gradually increasing at the expense of the shop-keeping and dealing element. This reflected a similar predominance in the trusts of Great and Little Bolton. But as we have seen and shall see again repeatedly, the ability of these big men to get what they wanted depended on a multilayered process of filtration through competing and divisive interests and ideologies.[53]

The Sanitary Question

With imperfect, divided instruments of municipal power and imperfect, divided notions of what needed to be done and why, local elites set about the ordering of the urban environment. This process has attracted considerable scholarly attention. Why did leading inhabitants begin to take urban decay seriously, when they did? The obvious answer is that, as conditions deteriorated in each town, the accumulations of filth and foul air amidst haphazard, shoddily constructed, cramped dwellings reached a saturation point of intolerability, some time in the 1840s.[54] Statistical investigation and "Condition of England" writings merely broadcast the truth.[55] The less obvious answer sees alarm at the state of the environment as an ideological construction, not a simple reflection of "reality." Leading inhabitants, whether they extolled a town's beauties or lamented its blemishes, could buy better air, water, housing, and prospects for themselves, escape into the countryside when need be, persuade themselves that the living conditions of the poor were a product of moral flaccidity and individual fecklessness, and insulate themselves with a layer of political-economy rhetoric.[56] The fact that escapism and intellectual absolution became less comfortable in the 1840s than in the 1830s had less to do with creeping decline than with a confluence of agendas looking to urban renewal for solutions.[57]

During the cholera scare of 1832, the perceived necessity for widespread sanitary reform had not yet arrived. Medical officers warned the public "to prepare themselves for the visitation of this awful scourge," but makeshift measures left no permanent residue.[58] When the *Bolton Free Press* began publication in 1835, sanitation did not figure in its opening manifesto.[59] Dr. James Black, in his study of living conditions in Bolton in 1837, provided an upbeat assessment, befitting his task of discovering "at what rate we, as a nation, are progressing in the grand path of improving our species, in sound knowledge, in religious and moral habits, and in social happiness." Granted, there was some dilapidated housing, "inhabited by Irish families, or by destitute widows, aged work people, and the dissolute, which form a part of every community." But overall, "Bolton may be considered a healthy town and situation; and though it may be said to consist wholly of a manufacturing population, yet, from the diversity of employments, the open and dispersed state of the streets and dwellings, and the plentiful supply of good water, it has, of late years, been visited with fewer epidemics of a serious nature, with the exception of dysentery, than most other towns of a similar character."[60]

In such another town, Preston, there was equally little sense of impending crisis. Beyond a steady stream of loyal addresses to mark propitious moments in the royal family's life-cycle or to condemn attacks upon the royal person, practically everything that the revamped corporation proposed during its early years was intended to further the interests of capital and its necessary con-comitant, good order, rather than to tackle—or cajole the improvement com-missioners into tackling—poor living conditions. The corporation's primary concerns were a more commodious and covered market; the widening and scouring of the Ribble to allow oceangoing vessels to come right up to the town, transforming it into a port; memorials to the postmaster general or the Commons for a better delivery of the mail; the maintenance of the borough police force; and the business of the grammar school.[61]

One man who found this complacency unacceptable was the Rev. John Clay, prison chaplain, statistician, and moral reformer, the quintessential bourgeois crusader against proletarian vice and ignorance. As his son ex-plained it, "His hopes for the future rested almost entirely upon the possibility of rousing, not merely a few here and there, but the general public, to a knowledge of the true state of the country." When the higher classes appreci-ated the enormity of the task, sectarian and partisan conflicts could be over-come so that drunkenness, ignorance, and miserable dwellings—all powerful causes of crime—could be tackled.[62] For Clay, the advocacy of sanitary reform was thus part of a broader strategy that passed along the whole gamut of re-formist initiatives from penal reform through religious instruction to temper-ance. This was a quite different strategy to any attempt at incorporation into a populist alliance or a conservative bulwark (Chapter 12), or the redirection of animosities between capital and labor onto the landed interest, or the reliance on saber and sermon to cow the discontented. Clay believed that individual reformation and regeneration could only come about through radical trans-formation of the individual's environment, be it the separate cell for the crimi-nal or improved living conditions for the lower classes, both of which required collective action from above.

Clay was given his cue by a nudge from outside, Edwin Chadwick's 1842 "Report on the Sanitary Condition of the Labouring Population," which gave powerful backing to an environmental over a flawed-character analysis.[63] The ensuing Commission on the State of Towns called for local reports, and a committee in Preston deputed the town's principal statistician, Clay. His lurid description of working-class squalor skillfully appealed to the fear, self-interest, and humanity of the comfortable classes. Why should the elite, the governing classes, care about the muck and misery of the masses when they could buy a cleaner, spacious, attractive environment for themselves? What was it to them that unregulated, penny-pinching building had failed so cata-strophically and that a considerable proportion of the population lived amidst piles of excrement and choked, open sewers? Did it really matter that the av-erage age of death for workers and their families was 18.28 years, if members of gentry and professional families lived on average to 47.39 years?[64] Clay stated three reasons why it *did* matter. Firstly, the argument of moralizing humanity: what was happening in parts of Preston was deeply offensive to bourgeois sensibility: "[F]ilthiness of person and sordidness of mind are usually united . . . Amidst the dirt and disease of filthy back courts and alleys and yards, vices and crimes are lurking altogether unimagined by those who have never visited such abodes." Secondly, the argument of self-interest: the amount spent on sewers, drains, water closets, and ventilation would be offset in little over a year from the savings: sickness would be less and therefore fewer workdays lost; sewage would be used as productive manure; smoke consumed by mills would cut down on the expense of laundry, house-painting, and fruit and vegetable washing. Thirdly, the argument of fear: the reservoirs of contagion might overflow their boundaries and the pent-up rage of the multitude might explode unless the elite made a conscious effort to bridge the distance and ameliorate the ills: "[T]he moral and intellectual extremes of society are as far asunder as if separated by untrodden deserts or untried seas. . . . [T]he great mass is yet chaotic; and unless, by God's blessing, breathed upon by the spirit of intelligence, and of order, and of religion, it may be hurled upon all that is fair and good among us, with a momentum as sudden as irresistible."[65]

Preston did have some countervailing advantages, referred to by most commentators: its elevated site, its open spaces and promenades for recreation (Avenham Walks, Moor Park, the Marsh), its relatively good water supply from the Longridge reservoirs of the Preston Waterworks Company, statutorily established from 1832.[66] Bolton, according to the report on its sanitary condition compiled in 1845 for the Health of Towns Commission by an outsider, Dr. Lyon Playfair, had fewer. Little Bolton was not too badly provided: its Improvement Act had compulsory powers and its sewerage system, though unscientific, was reasonable. Great Bolton, on the other hand, "can be compared in filthiness only to the poorer districts of Liverpool, and to those of Wigan and Rochdale." Playfair discovered an Improvement Act that appeared to be inoperative, trustees with wholly inadequate powers to preserve cleanliness or to regulate buildings, the sewerage in a deplorable state—many streets had no sewers, some of the sewers had right-angled junctions, all emptied into small rivers that wound sluggishly and stinkingly through the town—and the privies were pitiful in number and disgusting. All this was sound evidence for his preconceived conclusion: "Sound political economy cannot be in any way opposed to true humanity," and true humanity called for the intervention of a paternalistic legislature, just as Clay advocated. The improvement of the sanitary condition of the population was conducive to the good order and prosperity of the state.[67]

Investigations thereafter tended to confirm Engels's opinion that "Even on a really fine day Bolton is a gloomy, unattractive hole."[68] John Entwisle, secretary to the Mechanics' Institute, prepared a report in 1848 at the instigation of the mayor, Thomas Ridgway Bridson, who was acting in his private capacity but using his authority as a way of publicizing the findings. Like Clay, Engels, and Playfair, Entwisle deliberately built a shocking case, offensive to the deepest convictions of bourgeois morality, before suggesting that self-interest and Christian duty urgently demanded remedies. The average member of the working class in Great Bolton lived for nineteen years and six months, of the tradesman class for twenty-seven years and two months, and of the professional and gentleman class for fifty-one years. More than a fifth of the population died within their first year, 35 percent by age five. Great Bolton was in a terrible state, the paving bad (where it existed), the streets unswept for months, the sewers small, square, choked up, rat-infested, and prone to flooding the cellars (where 7,090 people lived, on average five to a cellar). The worst housing—"Hidden from public view by the front houses of the street"—was in the old and filthy courts and yards behind Deansgate, Churchgate, Bradshawgate, and a portion of Old Acres. A court with ten dwellings at the end of Gaffer Ginnel contained about seventy people, one large fly-infested privy, a malodorous tallow-chandler's works, and a tobacco manufactory. Around Wigan Lane there were ten reeking slaughterhouses, stables, pig sties, and dung heaps in a space thirty yards by twenty, but the inspector of nuisances had not been able to impress the magistrates that this was actionable: "Thus private interest wages a successful war with the public good, outrages with impunity every claim of public decency and public health, and maintains in the heart of the town a vile pestiferous laboratory of disease and death." Sixteen necessaries in Andrew Street, mostly without doors, for nine hundred people; eighty-four mendicant lodging houses, often the foci of fever, with both sexes sleeping in the same room; the graveyards crammed full of corpses, generally higher than the level of the streets; no successful attempts to abolish the smoke nuisance: the remorseless cataloging of evils continued. There were only two positive things to be said: the water supply was reasonably good, and the newly opened public baths were well patronized.[69]

So what was to be done? "We may declaim as long and as loud as we please against the coarseness and indelicacy of the labouring classes, but while these things remain, it is hopeless to expect they should be otherwise," Entwisle wrote. "A delicate perception of the proprieties and decencies of life, refinement of manners, and high moral feeling, cannot exist long under such conditions, even if they be already formed, much less develope [*sic*] themselves *ab initio*." He fervently hoped that a local government could be created possessing sufficient powers, under a central supervision, to protect the public health. Sanitary reform would be economical, in savings from the poor rates and in the scientific application of manure to agriculture; it was imperative for the sake of decency and compassion; above all, it would enable a cult of domesticity to percolate down to the lower orders, children to be kept off the streets and men away from pubs and dissolute habits. He called for "a thorough reform in the construction of workmen's dwellings: they should be so constructed that the domestic duties of the household may be discharged, without subjecting the husband, when he returns from his labour, to any annoyance that may induce him to quit his home for a walk in the street."[70]

Cleaning Up Preston

If a number of crusaders, with external prompting, had begun to pump out the message of environmental amelioration as a solution to societal ills, local elites still needed convincing; their response tended to be as sluggish as the flow of the towns' drains, the obstacles as constricting as a right-angled sewer. In Preston, the *Chronicle*, joining the national-level chorus of voices in the mid-1840s and reporting the increasing concern expressed in speeches and lectures locally, commented toward the end of 1844 that "The dwellings, the cleanliness, the recreations, the economy, and the religion of the occupants of cottages, and back streets, and cellars, have been seen to be things requiring attention,"[71] since "a large portion of the collective community of this country is radically bad and vicious, and ought to be promptly amended."[72] Yet, in spite of the copious literature and statistical information, initially little was achieved. Before parliamentary pressure galvanized the local elite, a consensus on the necessity for urgent action in the environmental sphere was lacking. The revelation or reminder of poor living conditions was merely one further ingredient in a fuzzy notion of the *classes dangereuses*, at once fearsome and offensive to bourgeois values; and whether coercion, indoctrination, incorporation, or environmental engineering would work best, singly or in combination, were still moot points.[73] Division of authority between commissioners and councillors compounded the problem. The commissioners, by definition the wealthiest inhabitants, attended meetings in small numbers, except when it came to the allocation of the rate,[74] were not accountable to any constituency, and lacked legitimacy in raising money or direct incentives to spend it on the districts of the poor. The councillors, dependent on voter approval (which could tell for or against sanitary reform), had a limited budget and, as we have seen, a remit confined to policing, controlling the markets, managing corporate property, and being the public and civic face of the town on state occasions.

Their sole item of adventurous expenditure, the Ribble Navigation Company—a further demonstration of the way in which they perceived their own self-interest and the town's prosperity as proceeding in tandem—was an interesting exercise in wishful thinking. The landowners bordering the Ribble from Preston to Lytham formed the first company in 1806 in order to reclaim rich farmland along the banks by straightening the river. This they failed to accomplish, and the income from river traffic did not live up to expectations.

The scheme languished. Greater traffic in the twenties and an increasing mercantile desire to bring larger vessels as close to Preston as possible stimulated more activity: new quays, opened in 1831, built by the improvement commissioners; £2,300 spent on removing rocks from the riverbed and in building more groynes between 1825 and 1832; the purchasing of a steamer to tow vessels in and out of the river and to carry goods and passengers to Liverpool. The results were, once again, disappointing. The mercantile and manufacturing community looked for better ways of expediting the transit of their products and raw materials. A plan for a ship canal to extend from the docks at Marsh Lane to Lytham foundered because of its excessive estimated cost of £105,000. Peter Hesketh Fleetwood, MP engaged in his scheme to open up Fleetwood as a resort town and the Wyre estuary as Preston's principal port, connecting port and Preston with a fast railway over the flatlands of the Fylde; his interests were always in actual or potential conflict with those of the town he was representing in Parliament.[75]

But some of the influential men of Preston had not yet given up on the Ribble.[76] Peter Haydock, an alderman in the reformed corporation, began to push for active involvement by the corporation in a scheme intended to double the size of Preston in a decade. "The Ribble might," he said, "for the purposes of navigation be made equal to the Mersey, and Preston be formed into a port like Liverpool for the reception of large vessels."[77] Positive surveys for the Admiralty and from Robert Stevenson and Son, civil engineers from Edinburgh, impressed the corporation.[78] When a new Navigation Company, with new statutory powers and Haydock as chairman, commenced operations in 1837, councillors across sect and party bought into it, individually and on behalf of the town.[79] Twenty-six of the forty-eight councillors already had Navigation Company shares; forty-eight of the original subscribers were councillors at some stage—a large number of people besides Alderman Haydock who had a very heavy and direct interest in the public promotion of their private commercial venture and who might be tempted to gamble with public money on a risky undertaking.[80]

The Treasury denied an application by the council to raise £12,500 at interest for shares and the extension of the quays, so the councillors paid the first calls on the shares—£7,490—by advances from bankers and by applying the surplus of the corporation's annual income. Thus began a spiral of greater involvement. By 1842 the council's surplus had run out; plans for the long-meditated covered market had to be postponed, "considering the state of the Corporation finances." This time the Treasury allowed the borrowing of up to £12,000 because the council was so deeply committed and its projections of the Ribble's future prosperity so bullish.[81]

In the quarter century after 1838 the corporation poured in more than £20,000 for new quays and their road and rail connections, and it invested

£21,800 as shareholders. The improvements increased tolls, but these failed to match the expenditure on excavation, dredging, training-walls, a branch railway, a lighthouse, and a new dock at Lytham. In 1846 the Irish famine considerably reduced grain imports into Preston and a corresponding flow of coal outwards. To curtail spending the dredging was ceased, and only a minimum maintenance of the incomplete walls was carried out. Even so, the corporation continued to take up shares; as Peter Catterall, a long-standing opponent of the scheme commented, "'it appeared that there were a number of gentlemen so bound up with the . . . Company that they would not listen to contrary views.'" Only in 1860 did trade reach the 1845 level again. By the time the corporation took over the entire venture in 1883 and undertook a vast expansion, it had received dividends amounting to £4,470 on its investment.[82] Although rental income and wharfage rates from property on and near the docks on the Marsh estate increased to £600-£700 a year by 1850,[83] and even the partial development of the river's resources had helped keep railway rates down between Preston and Liverpool,[84] this was very far from the lofty dreams of the investors in 1837. A new Mersey or Clyde, the Ribble was not.

Not everyone had been enticed by the venture. Catterall recalled in 1867 "'that the late Mr. S. Horrocks, who was as sound a thinking man and had as good a judgement as anyone, once, when asked about subscribing to the Ribble scheme, said that if he had any money to put into the Ribble he would go up on Penwortham bridge and throw it in.'"[85] Still, while giving a good indication of the elite's municipal priorities, there is little indication—beyond the covered market, eventually constructed in 1875—that this siphoning off of funds to throw into the river thwarted alternative schemes.[86] Besides, the most urgent improvements—the housing and sanitation of the working classes—did not fall within the jurisdiction of the corporation.

Avenham Walks provides another indication of elite priorities. The reformed corporation adopted a policy of preventing building on the land below the walks stretching down to the Ribble, with the intention of preserving the view and buying parcels of land piecemeal for the extension of the gardens and pleasure grounds. This "will contribute greatly to the health, rational enjoyment, kindly intercourse, and good morals of all classes of the people."[87] The motivation was no doubt genuine, and the provision of controlled spaces for rational recreation and *de haut en bas* class mingling needs to take its place alongside all the other tension-reducing, displacement stratagems, as a later report of the Health and Recreation Committee made clear: "[A]mongst the many efforts now making for the amelioration of the moral and physical state of our deserving and industrious population, none is more fraught with unmixed good than that which, in providing them with the means of rational and healthful recreation, offers them a powerful inducement to forsake those more alluring though more dangerous and demoralizing pleasures which have hitherto so frequently formed the amusement of our working population."[88] But it is also notable that the preservation of the prospect and the laying out of walks would, at least in the short term, most benefit the local wealthy. Whose view was it? Most noticeably that of the propertied whose gardens and houses jutted onto West Cliffe and were strung along Ribblesdale Place, the town's most elegant neighborhood. Who promenaded and displayed along the walks? Largely, it seems, the tone of the town, just as they had in the days of polite and proud Georgian Preston. When Edwin Waugh visited Preston in 1862—a time of unusual distress, but probably only an exaggeration of a normal pattern—he found that on Avenham Walks "the nursemaids and children, and dainty folk, are wandering as usual, airing their curls in the fresh breeze," whereas "within a few yards of plenty" there was destitution, "cowering in squalid corners," in courts, and in alleys swarming with people.[89]

Many of the ambiguities of private and public concern emerged strongly in a dispute between two rival railway companies, the corporation, and a number of property owners. Capital investment, commercial expansion, the rights of property, and the need for "urban lungs" were all at stake. In approaching Preston, the North Union Railway from Wigan had been the first to bridge the Ribble. The corporation objected to a second bridge for the Blackburn and Preston Railway, and so Parliament sanctioned a circuitous route that joined the NUR line at Farington, thus using the same bridge to enter the town. This proved to be scarcely satisfactory, especially when the East Lancashire Railway took over the Blackburn line in 1845. The ELR claimed that its traffic was impeded by the NUR and that the arrangements for its passengers at the NUR's station in Preston were generally chaotic. The directors placed two bids for a separate line and station; these entailed a second crossing of the Ribble and an embankment across the Avenham pleasure grounds, slicing them in two.

The divergent viewpoints came out during the Commons' and Lords' Select Committee inquiries in 1847 on the occasion of the second application. Many interests were involved, including those of shareholders from competing companies, individual landowners, householders, and wharf owners. The corporation petitioned against the new line, and a parade of witnesses testified that it would damage the corporation's landscaping plans, important for the general health of the town.[90] The ELR's proposed embankment would be "a great loss to the Public and the working classes in particular," Peter Haydock affirmed during questioning, especially as "the design of placing the Mechanics Institute there [at the top of Avenham Walks] was to render the locality more attractive to the working classes."[91]

But other concerns cut across the desire for public improvements. Several members of the corporation were shareholders in the Fleetwood, Preston and West Riding Railway, a rival line to the ELR. Thomas Miller, proposer of the corporation petition against the ELR line, was brother-in-law to William Marshall, a director of the Manchester and Leeds Railway, the lessees of the NUR. Marshall had been active in promoting a petition against the ELR scheme. Haydock feared that his own house would be spoiled because of its proximity to the projected line, and commented, "I think it is exceedingly wrong that parties should be forced out of their houses and that a great public improvement should be spoiled merely because two Companies were wrangling about their Charges."[92] A large number of influential inhabitants who lived within three hundred yards of the projected works recorded their opposition in two petitions. Thomas German protested that his house and ornamental grounds would fall between the two lines, the Rev. Clay and the Rev. John Owen Parr that the new line would interfere with their privacy and with the views from their houses.[93]

The ELR in the end won its bill, but with a number of clauses favorable to the corporation: the railway company had to landscape its embankment, make an ornamental archway for carriages and pedestrians underneath it, and construct a footbridge on top. This is merely one instance of a highly complex web of competing claims. The point to notice is that while the provision of a green space may have been on the agenda for a number of years, even by the late 1840s it was hardly a rallying cry for united action to mollify the lower classes. As for sanitary reform, the improvement commissioners had appointed a special committee in November 1844 to consider applying for an amended Improvement Act with more extensive and better-defined powers, especially concerning house and street drainage, sewerage, and the removal of nuisances, but nothing came of it. When the government moved toward its own measures of sanitary intervention, the local authorities shadowed its movements. Both the commissioners and the councillors agreed in principle on the merits of Lord Morpeth's Public Health Bill in 1847-48; the council recognized "to its fullest extent the urgent necessity which exists for the introduction of a general measure of sanatory reform, and highly approve of several of the details of the Bill which have for their object the promotion of health in large and populous towns by means of improved and scientific systems of drainage, purification, and ventilation." But then came the predictable localist caveat: the bill should be modified so "that the local boards of health may have the power of free and discretionary action, unfettered by such odious and inquisitorial interference as would be imposed upon them by the Bill as it now stands."[94] This stipulation frustrated some of the reformers, most vociferously the editor of the *Chronicle*. "To leave the health of the population to local powers, such as our 'Nuisance Committee,' alone," he wrote, "—the members thereof being interested in preventing compulsory expenditure on their own part, and on the part of their neighbours, and in permitting the continuance of the smoke nuisance, and letting cellars for inhabitants—often on the truck system—would be little better than leaving the poor to die by slow poison, without making an effort to save them; endangering at the same time the health and lives of the whole community."[95] In a substantial departure from the *Chronicle*'s earlier anti-centralization stance, he argued that the most valuable part of the bill was precisely the control by the General Board of Health, which after all was responsible to Parliament. "We are prepared to sympathise deeply with those corporate bodies which are to be coerced," he added facetiously. "It will be something new to them. They are proverbially tortoise or turtle-like in all their movements, and it cannot fail to be painful to them to be spurred to activity."[96]

Parliament accepted the movement of the government toward state intervention in the guise of the 1848 Public Health Act—a product of the belief of key figures that permissive legislation permitted local inactivity—partly because of the accumulated weight upon the mind of Chadwickian and Health of Towns Association propaganda, and partly because of the timely stimulus of disease—typhoid and cholera—in 1847-49.[97] The same chronology, two steps behind, is discernible in Preston. Clay's reports, newspaper indictments, the setting up of a branch of the Health of Towns Association in May 1847[98] all helped build a certain momentum. Some scholars have seen local elites' adoption of sanitary reforms as antirevolutionary measures, diverting attention from the dysfunctional socioeconomic system by the application of a soothing balm of improvements.[99] In Preston, although the *Chronicle* and the Rev. Clay had pointed out the relationship between better living conditions and social stabilization, and this was no doubt at the front or back of many other people's minds during 1848, it is not easy to make many such linkages. The tardiness of sanitary improvement suggests that environmentalist intervention was never particularly to the forefront as a strategy for co-option, incorporation, or displacement. After the frisson of fear in the spring of 1848, the council sent a loyal address to the queen, rather complacently congratulating the nation with a version of the concessionist "myth." It approved this address on the same day as it renewed its intention to build a covered market.[100] If the idea was to tone down social unrest, this could be counted among the more oblique strategies.

The reason why in October the council appointed a committee to consider the sanitary condition of the borough, with authority to take all necessary measures under the Nuisances Removal and Diseases Prevention Act, and to consider the adoption of the Public Health Act, is much clearer: as the mayor said at the council meeting, cholera had arrived on the country's shores, and it was time to take measures.[101] The improvement commissioners and the Poor Law guardians also bestirred themselves against the same threat,[102] and in November the council and the commissioners requested that the General Board of Health send an inspector, the next step in the adoption of the Public Health

Act.[103] This inspector, George Thomas Clark, conducted his inquiry in May 1849 and, like so many before him, commented favorably on the town's natural advantages of position, water, and drainage. In spite of this, "the condition of the dwellings of the lower classes has been but little attended to, and in consequence of the inefficient sewerage, the scanty supply of water (or rather the scanty application of a very copious supply) the unremoved collections of putrid animal and vegetable matter, and the general absence of the means of ordinary cleanliness, disease is engendered or aggravated, and the mortality materially increased." The annual death rate, 29.24/1,000, made Preston the seventh worst among Lancashire's twenty-one districts and was well above the national average of 21/1,000. Clark therefore advocated the application of the Public Health Act to the entire municipal borough (including Fishwick, outside the improvement commissioners' jurisdiction), which would lead to a compulsory water supply to every house, a complete system of main sewerage, and the regulation of the thirty-one filthy slaughter houses and of the forty-three lodging houses ("receptacles for vagabonds, vicious, dishonest, idle and drunken persons"). From the brief time he spent conducting his inquiry, his admiration for Clay's reports, and his conversations with John James Myres (the commissioners' surveyor and clerk) and Philip Park (the corporation's treasurer and steward), he gained an impression contrary to that persistently purveyed by the *Chronicle*: "Among the numerous towns, into the sanitary condition of which I have been called upon to inquire, with a view to the application of the Public Health Act, I have found none in which there was a more generally expressed conviction of the absolute necessity for the measures rendered practicable by the Act, or, as far as I could judge, a better disposition to ameliorate the condition of the poor."[104]

Poor Law medical officers' reports of disease throughout 1849 may have further focused attention.[105] Whatever the individual reasoning, there does not appear to have been significant opposition to the council's request, in the wake of Clark's report, for the Public Health Act to be applied to Preston, nor the improvement commissioners' request that the provisions of the Preston Improvement Act of 1815 be transferred to the new Local Board of Health.[106] Anti-centralists were not vocal nor party differences visible. The Tory *Pilot*, like the *Chronicle*, welcomed the transfer of the commissioners' powers to the council so as to simplify government and taxation, end the possibility of collision, and ensure accountability to the ratepayers.[107] Only the ratepayers of Fishwick registered strenuous objections, on economic grounds, when they realized in the summer of 1850 that their township was to be included under the Local Board of Health. Their appeals were unavailing,[108] but they do illustrate quite strikingly the economistic strain against which the environmental interventionists and social ameliorationists always had to do battle, whether under improvement commissioners or boards of health. Nevertheless, these years saw the opening of public baths and washhouses in Saul Street in 1850, the appointment of a surveyor, an inspector of nuisances, and attendant officers for the new board in the autumn, and moves during 1849 and 1850 toward the construction of a public cemetery to counteract the evils of foul-smelling, mass, pauper graves in churchyards across town.[109] It was apparent that the leading inhabitants of Preston, goaded, cajoled, and assisted by the state, had equipped themselves with most of the necessary powers and some of the necessary will to begin cleansing the nest they had fouled.

Cleaning Up Bolton

Bolton greeted its environmental deterioration in similar ways to Preston: with an institutionally fractured local governmental system, a degree of hesitation and reluctance, pressure from without, and the prodding of a number of concerned environmentalist "moral statisticians" from within. The council was hobbled from the start by the fierce Tory opposition to its existence and its inability to enforce payment of a rate. Loyal and political addresses to the queen, petitions to the Post Office for the better delivery of the mail, concerns of the police and the courts, the fight for the legality of the borough charter: these were the stuff of council business during its first, insecure years. The Great Bolton trustees (nearly all conservative) stoutly resisted any encroachments on their powers by the town council while it was monopolized by the liberals or—once the boycott ended—while the Tories remained in a minority.[110] But the extent to which environmental improvement was stymied by partisan gridlock is doubtful: the chronology of the council's incremental improvement plans followed rather closely the pattern in Preston, which was distinctly less handicapped by party politicking, and by the time the issue was being taken seriously the council was working together more cohesively and the atmosphere was less politically charged. The *Bolton Free Press* had called for sanitary reform in 1842 in the wake of Chadwick's report, seizing upon one his key points, that the home rather than the workplace was to blame for unhealthiness; but only after Playfair's report did the council establish, in September 1845, a committee to give serious consideration to the various measures before Parliament.[111] "The evil is proclaimed," the *Free Press* reported on this occasion, "the remedy is within reach, and, we trust that, having put their hands to the good work of improvement, they will not hesitate nor look back." "Those who have read the report of the Health of Towns commission upon the state of this borough must feel ashamed that the inhabitants have not evinced more regard for its healthy condition, and creditable appearance," stated P. R. Arrowsmith in the council chamber, capturing a sense of deflated civic pride: "It was high time the council should have powers to put this borough in an improved sanatory state, in the state in which a place of so much importance ought to be seen." From the conservative side, George Piggot and

John Bolling, veteran campaigner against Somerset House centralization, joined Arrowsmith in pragmatically arguing that if they themselves did not take the matter in hand the government would do it for them.[112] Since Tory councillors were now in a majority, moves toward an application to Parliament for greater improvement powers to be vested in the council met with the approval of the Great Bolton trustees.[113]

The *Free Press* noted in August 1846 that there was unusual unanimity of opinion in the council on the need for an Improvement Act.[114] But unity across institutional boundaries proved more problematic: in the autumn the Little Bolton ratepayers and trustees, led by prominent liberals, voted heavily against vesting the powers of the trust in the Tory-dominated council and against the plans for an Improvement Act for the entire borough. The problems in Little Bolton were not as severe as those in its larger neighbor, partly because it was a less dense, more peripheral settlement, and partly because its Improvement Act was more effective. The Little Bolton Trust became the major stumbling block in the way of a united front to tackle urban decay until the end of the decade, and the radical-liberal Thomas Thomasson emerged as the foremost opponent of council-led sanitary reform.[115] This opposition threatened an expensive challenge; by way of compromise it allowed the passage of the Improvement Act in 1847 in return for the dropping of the attempt to absorb the trusts.[116] The final measure, concerned above all with enabling the council to lease the waterworks so as to provide a cheaper supply of water,[117] gave the council only limited improvement powers; a sanitary committee, established in November, discovered that its powers to take all lawful measures relating to the health and sanitary condition of the borough were illusory. The committee members ruefully noted in February 1848 that, because they were not legally authorized to spend money from the borough fund for general sanitary improvements, they "are unable at present to direct the adoption of any effectual means to carry out the object proposed by the appointment of this Committee."[118]

Clearly, little progress had been made in the consolidation of powers or to preempt state pressure. Local opinion-formers therefore faced the prospect of having measures forced on them with the publication of Morpeth's bill in the spring of 1848. The *Chronicle*, an advocate of improvements for a number of years, railed against the arbitrary powers to be given to "the *central board of five*"—a continuation of the tradition of opprobrium first tested out on the Somerset House Triumvirate. "If this act, or anything like it, passes into a law," charged the editor, "it will have to be recorded in history that the Court of Star Chamber was abolished in 17 Car. 1, A.D. 1641, but was reestablished, with greatly increased powers, in 11 Victoria, A.D. 1848." The councillors passed a motion objecting to the centralization on the grounds that they themselves could spend their own money and improve the town much more effectively than parties in London—an assertion lacking corroborative evidence. But the council's sanitary committee, commenting on the status of the modified bill in April, was relieved "That the Bill as amended in Committee is much improved inasmuch as it deprives the General Board of much of their control over the Local Boards whilst retaining a general superintendence to secure the carrying out of the objects of the Bill."[119]

The timely publication of John Entwisle's Report, given extensive publicity by the *Chronicle,* was one factor refocusing attention on Bolton's "foul eminence": "for abundant dirt and lack of drainage, for crowded and disgusting homes or holes, for the numbers sweltering amidst most noxious airs and poisonous gases, for pestilential nuisances, defective sewarage [*sic*] and complete absence of all sanitary arrangements, properly so called, we can justly claim, if we do not bear away, the palm." The editor outlined the consequences: intemperance (attributable to poor living conditions, immorality ("We assure our readers who have not visited the places described in the *Report,* that the most active imagination cannot conceive the horrors there narrated with all the circumstantiality of literal truth"); expense (wise to the strategy of the environmental reformers that the path to the ratepayer's heart lay through the pocketbook); disease (a terrible epidemic was only a month's journey from the nation's shores); *something* must be done, and *quickly*. But was the message getting through? When Entwisle gave two lectures in the Temperance Hall in August on the health of towns he attracted a fair attendance of the working classes but not of the occupiers of the gallery and the reserved seats. In October, as the cholera crept closer, the *Chronicle* bemoaned the lack of enforcement of sanitary measures, contrasting the "wonderful" excitement of the era of revolutions with the "astounding" apathy displayed about the approach of the epidemic.[120] The Report of the Bolton Society for the Protection of the Poor at the end of 1848 made a rare explicit link between the year of revolutions, social stability, and the perceived need to do something about it:

The past has been an eventful year. The disorders of Continental Europe have caused much misery amongst ourselves. Still we have had much for which we ought to be thankful. Our manufacturing system, on which the comforts of this district at least so much depend, has been severely tested, and its stability proved. Matters look brighter: and it is hoped that a return of commercial prosperity will soon bring a return of their comforts to our deserving workmen. Their patient endurance of distress and general good conduct, amidst evil example abroad, and incendiary harangues at home, have been eminently conspicuous, and have won for them the admiration of society. It is universally acknowledged that their moral and social condition has not been cared for as it ought to have been. Able men both within and without the walls of the Parliament-house have turned their attention to the amelioration of the condition of the poor. And the committee earnestly hope that this general effort of the community will be crowned with success, and we shall exhibit to the world the picture of a paternal Government and a contented and happy people.[121]

Still the institutional and legislative confusion continued. The council could *watch* the inhabitants, but not clean, repair, or light the streets; its sanitary committee might have a general superintendence over these matters, but they were primarily the province of the trustees, who lacked the necessary powers and funds to do a decent job. The application of the Nuisances Removal and Diseases Prevention Act at the end of the year added further complications, because the expense of dealing with nuisances came out of Poor Law Union coffers, putting the guardians in charge. The guardians, in turn, had to rely on the borough police (back to the council) to deal with offenders and bring them before the borough magistrates if need be. Although members of the Bolton public received 553 notices of nuisances in the next five and a half months, the *Chronicle* pointed out that the board was chiefly composed of *country* guardians who could neither be expected to be deeply concerned about the condition of the town nor willing to contribute toward the expense of remedies. The upshot was that one body of councillors, two sets of trustees, and a board of guardians, assisted by the borough police, succeeded poorly in achieving what one suitably empowered body might do well. A complete and systematic sewerage, the enclosure of the river Croal, the regulation of cellar dwellings, the provision of a covered market—all remained untackled.[122]

A new, zealous mayor, Thomas Lever Rushton, Tory attorney, pressed matters forward in the summer of 1849, aided—as in Preston—by the apprehension felt at the approach of cholera[123] (by the end of October, 190 people had contracted the disease and ninety-two of these had died).[124] Rushton was concerned not only about sanitation but even more so about the moral state of the "low lodging houses," where "the practice prevailed therein to a very great extent of both sexes sleeping indiscriminately together without any Clothing whatsoever only one Bedcover for any number in one room." To remedy the evil, the Home Office and the Poor Law Board recommended that the borough be brought under the provisions of the Public Health Act; this "is calculated in the opinion of many to subject us to large expense and to a centralised control," Rushton wrote to the trustees, "both of which it is thought may be spared by the adoption of another course." He repeated the old refrain: "Unless some such measures be taken by us, they will be taken for us."[125]

The Great Bolton trustees reconfirmed their willingness to transfer their powers,[126] and the council resolved in August to apply to Parliament in the next session for a consolidation and enlargement of its jurisdiction and for the ability to build a town hall, market houses, and slaughterhouses, to purchase the gasworks, to extend the waterworks, to purchase and demolish buildings in densely populated districts so as to improve the ventilation and widen the streets, to incorporate many of the provisions of the multiple clauses acts, and to levy rates and borrow on a mortgage. The only real debate in council came between supporters of a private act, who hoped this would preserve a greater degree of local independence, and those who preferred the application of the Public Health Act. In spite of Rushton's own conversion to the merits of the latter during correspondence with the General Board of Health, the former group prevailed. A debate in mid-October revealed only three dissentient voices: Richard Stockdale, linen draper, objected to the expense and greater regulation that purification entailed, George Piggot saw nothing especially offensive about the sewerage system, and Thomas Thomasson saw no pressing necessity for doing anything at all.[127] His objections at the start of 1850 to the cost, earmarked site, and necessity of the projected market house, which were extensions of a deeper argument that private companies could manage public undertakings better than public bodies, struck no chord. Evidently, the majority of the cross-party political elite in Great Bolton by this stage required no further persuasion of the necessity of more coordinated and extended measures. Thomasson had been the sole member of the council not to sign a requisition requesting Rushton, the most capable and enthusiastic proponent of improvements, to be mayor for a second year.[128]

Little Bolton still remained opposed to the bill. The township's sanitary condition was *not* essentially better than that of its neighbor, Rushton claimed at a meeting of ratepayers and property owners convened by the trustees. Neither the trustees nor the council had sufficient powers for the regulation of cellar residences, pestilential lodging houses, brothels, or mass graves. The pauper grave at the Catholic chapel was sixteen feet deep and well below the water table, meaning that the percolation from the coffins collected in a pool in the clay at the bottom; on a new vault being dug three feet away much decomposed matter flowed in, and the gravediggers had to hoist it out in buckets. The local authorities were powerless to interfere. Still, the meeting, led by Thomasson and the clerk to the trustees, John Gordon, voted to petition against the bill, on the grounds that the 1830 act was quite sufficient, that only a third of the councillors were elected by Little Bolton inhabitants so they would always be in a minority, that Little Bolton would be unfairly burdened with Great Bolton's much greater expenses, that Little Bolton would be injured by a market house in Great Bolton, and that the sanitary condition, lighting, watch, and water supply for the township were satisfactory.[129]

The opposition proved unavailing, but it did protract the passage of the bill, cause considerable expense, and necessitate the insertion of a number of diluting amendments before it was finally enacted in the summer of 1850.[130] The Bolton Improvement Act incorporated provisions both from the 1847 Town Improvement Clauses Act and the Public Health Act and empowered the council to act as a Board of Health for an area stretching over Great and

Little Bolton and nine other townships. The trusts ceased to exist.[131] In November the Treasury sanctioned the borrowing of £40,000 to build a market house and to extend the waterworks to the Farnworth area.[132] Like Preston, Bolton now had the consolidated power to make progress.

Reform in Blackburn

Catherine Jacson remembered the Blackburn of the 1820s as "a black dirty place where all the more unlovely features of an altogether manufacturing town everywhere displayed themselves,"[133] and we have seen how Cooke Taylor in the early 1840s was equally unimpressed. But, if sanitation was scarcely a galvanizing issue in Bolton and Preston, it was even less so in Blackburn. Blackburn did not have a town council in the 1840s or a strong crusading voice for sanitary reform from a moral statistician or the local newspaper—no publicist of the stamp of Clay or Entwisle. Discontent with the state of the town was largely left to indignant letters and occasional editorials in the pages of the *Standard*.[134] For example, one problem received particular attention in the 1840s: the state of the river Blakewater, the common sewer of the town. Weirs and dams blocked its fall, turning it for much of the time into a series of elongated cesspools. A correspondent, Isaac Lloyd, gave a particularly colorful description in 1846:

With all its natural advantages of soil and position, and notwithstanding its happy exemption from many of the evils by which other places are afflicted, the town of Blackburn possesses *one monster nuisance*, which more than neutralizes all the benefits to which I have alluded. Your readers will perceive by anticipation, that I now refer to that black, murky, slimy, filthy, sink of abomination, egregiously misnamed a *brook*, that, like a poisonous serpent, seems to envelope the town in its sinuous and deadly folds. Well is the town called *Blackburn*, if the etymology of its name is to be traced to that foul and fetid agglomeration of nastiness—that lethiferous, stygian *burn*, on whose gloomy margin so many of its inhabitants have the misfortune to be domiciled.[135]

In the spring of 1843, the editor praised the paternalist language of Peel's government and the suggestion that a wholesale cleansing of the poor's environment was necessary if the workingman's home were to supersede the beer house. Then, "parents and children will discover that the greatest happiness is to be secured in their own society, and we shall speedily have a population not given to dissipation, discontent, and insubordination, but ever ready to maintain, in their moral integrity, the laws which govern society."[136] But this was not an agenda the paper pursued with vigor.

During the 1830s and 1840s the local elite took uncertain steps toward building up the civic infrastructure. In the summer of 1833 it clearly and erroneously believed that the government would soon grant corporate status to the newly enfranchised parliamentary boroughs. Cross-party maneuvers in the same year and in 1835 to build a town hall, either through shares or the poor rate, for the sake of civic dignity and the administration of law and order, proved no more successful; presumably inadequate funding and maybe difficulties in the negotiations with Joseph Feilden, who owned the most desirable sites for such a building, stymied the project.[137] The Feildens tenaciously continued to maintain their rights as joint lords of the manor and won a legal victory in 1839 over the improvement trustees (the case revolved around a circus set up on Blakeley Moor which Feilden approved but the trustees demolished). When the trustees initiated fresh moves for an amended act, this could not be obtained without considerable bargaining with Feilden, and careful specification of the manorial rights. Feilden agreed to allow the continuance of the Blakeley Moor cattle market on payment of a small acknowledgment, to appropriate land in the Tackets for a new marketplace, and to donate land for a town hall.[138]

The 1841 Improvement Act was significant because it replaced a small, nominated, conservative trust with an improvement commission consisting of any male over twenty-one who was rated at more than £30 annually and chose to attend meetings (making it similar to the Preston and Little Bolton trusts, less party-riven than the Tory vehicle of Great Bolton trust).[139] This body made progress, though not especially rapid, with the new market. The commissioners haggled over the price of land, ultimately agreeing to the Feildens' final offer because of the cramped state of the existing marketplace, the dangers of crowding it posed on market days, the eligibility of the new site, and the promised adjacent free space for a town hall (which would follow later, subject to the Feildens' approval of the plans). Joseph Feilden consented to end the old markets (except for the Blakeley Moor cattle market) when the new market house opened, and to obtain the archbishop's agreement.[140]

A second measure the commissioners contemplated, in 1844, was to improve on the inadequate supply of water, which came from wells and two small reservoirs leased by William Townley on Feilden-owned and -leased land at Pemberton Clough. They declined to take the matter on board themselves on the grounds of cost, but encouraged a private undertaking to do so; it would be fair to speculate that as the provisional committee of the new Blackburn Waterworks Company contained many prominent commissioners, the opportunity to reap an individual profit was an important consideration. The company, established at the end of August, still had to circumnavigate the obstacles and interests of the Feildens, who petitioned against the bill in Parliament, claiming that the existing waterworks were quite sufficient, provided water at reasonable rates, and could be expanded if need be. They further maintained that the new company's projected reservoirs at Yate and Pickup Bank and at Guide could not be built for the estimated £40,000 and that the

quality of the water was, according to Henry Hough Watson, a Bolton consulting chemist, deficient. The Feildens invited the company to pay them full
compensation for their waterworks (after all, they did not want to stand in the
way of public improvements); if not, they threatened to push their claim in
Parliament and to apply for powers to extend their works.[141] It seems that the
Feildens' commitment to the quality of the water was rather less than that to
their own interests. While the act went through, the company was forced to
buy them out merely to discontinue their works and proceed with its own
project.

None of this addressed the piles of filth at the cottage door,[142] nor did the
commissioners' flagging of new footpaths along the main streets, given due
praise by the *Standard*.[143] An inquiry by two commissioners of HM Woods,
Forests, Land Revenues, Works and Buildings in February 1847—the necessary preliminary to an intention of the improvement commissioners to apply
for another Improvement Act, mainly for power to borrow a larger sum of
money (up to £50,000) on the credit of the rates—revealed how concentrated
these activities had been. Their report gives the most detailed account before
mid-century of the state of the town. The Blackburn commissioners had spent
£600-£700 in new paving since the 1841 act, but all of it in laying out the new
marketplace; they had repaired old drains, but not built new ones, all of which
still emptied into the still-obstructed Blakewater; they cleansed the streets, but
largely with water taken from the river, which was not always fit for use.
They contemplated arching over the river and removing the main obstructing
weir, building a new slaughterhouse away from dwelling houses, going ahead
with the town hall (estimated at £10,000), and widening certain streets (entailing some compulsory purchasing and demolition of property). This, the
visitors concluded, plus completing and fitting out the market house, required
far more than the £6,000 that the local commissioners could currently raise on
the rates. Following the report, the 1847 Improvement Act passed without
opposition.[144]

The ceremonial opening of the market house and celebratory dinner in the
Hotel at the end of January 1848, gave the elite the opportunity in a nonpartisan spirit to process, to preen, and to reflect upon the condition of Blackburn. This was the town's first substantial public building, and the general
tenor of speakers' remarks was that until very recently so little had been done,
so much remained to be done, but that a certain momentum had gathered.
"Hitherto the chief care of the inhabitants seemed to be how they could best
promote their pecuniary interests," said the architect, Terence Flanagan, "but
they had recently changed their minds, and determined to progress with those
around them." "He knew Blackburn was behindhand in many important improvements," William Yates, the contractor, concurred, "but he hoped that
the dark cloud which now hung over it would be removed, and a brighter one

come in its place. (Applause.) The town ought to have come out before; but now that it had 'come out,' what with railways, water companies, and market places, it had taken one very long step all at once. (Applause.)" "For a long time Blackburn had been stationary," thought James Pilkington, MP, but advantages could now be derived from this "patience": "[I]f they began to move now they would have the experience of sister towns, and by so much could excel them." Specifically, he, like William Hoole, the proprietor of the Independent boarding school on King Street and chairman of the market committee, placed sanitary improvements at the top of the agenda. Blackburn may have been healthier than its neighbors, he stated, "but at the same time no one could go from one end to the other of the streets and shut his eyes to the want of improvement"; Parliament was about to pass a compulsory law, but Blackburnians could improve the drainage of their own accord.

But could they? Even amidst the convivial harmony of the occasion, Hoole and John Hargreaves, clerk to the commissioners, made it plain that the elite was not pulling its full weight—an allegation, as we have seen (Chapter 6), that various clergymen leveled against it at the same time—thus hampering the work of the commissioners. "The Commissioners regretted exceedingly," Hoole said, "that more gentlemen of large property, influence, and ability, did not assemble with them from time to time and take part in their deliberations."[145] This was a potential problem with a "self-elected and irresponsible"[146] body: if the town's chief men were insufficiently convinced of the case for change, and electoral accountability and calculation were not spurring factors, then no one was going to build a town hall and a proper sewerage system with unseemly haste. The case for sanitation, green lungs, public walks, baths, and washhouses was, as one correspondent put it in 1849, "to supply a course of discipline which cannot fail to have the most beneficial and salutary operation on the appearance of the town, in imparting a more refined tone of moral feeling and conduct; and improving the health and condition of the people."[147] The case for a town hall rested principally on the grounds of the administration of justice; "It was a reproach to the town that there was neither Police-office nor Sessions'-room in it," as James Pilkington expressed it. "It was disreputable to a town of 40,000 inhabitants that it could find no better room for the administration of justice than one which was some 12 or 14 feet square." The main case against both was the expense—the timidity the commissioners felt in raising the rates without popular consent, from small and large ratepayers, particularly during a time of high relief expenditure (and it is notable that Hoole assured his listeners that the building of the market house had not only provided employment in a period of distress, but the income from market tolls was expected to pay the interest on money borrowed without recourse to increased rates).[148] The case for incorporation was that taxation with representation might free the necessary funds for improvements, that sanitary powers vested in commissioners and guardians could be consolidated in one body responsible to townsmen (avoiding the Poor Law Union's preponderance of countrymen), and that a resident, borough bench would improve the efficiency of justice.[149] The case against: increased rates, electiontime turmoil, party conflict.[150]

As reformers pointed out, Blackburn was one of the largest unincorporated towns in the country, and the spirit of civic emulation was a major factor in a renewed focus on obtaining a charter. So too was the recognition or hope that incorporation would ease open the sluice gates, allowing greater improvements; although the commissioners moved forward with plans—but nothing more—for the town hall during 1849 and 1850, they shelved sanitary improvements pending the settling of the issue of incorporation. This had to wait until the end of 1850, but by then the improvers were pushing at an open door. They began petitions in the autumn, and at the end of November a public meeting of ratepayers, chaired by Christopher Parkinson, wholesale grocer, took place at the behest of some of Blackburn's biggest employers. The elite had decided the question must be resolved. There were no party divisions. Thomas Dugdale, surgeon, proposed a petition for a charter; Hoole of the commissioners spoke in favor, as did the old radicals George Dewhurst and William Durham. W. H. Hornby was apparently the only prominent opponent, fearing that the rates would be doubled under a corporation; but even he promised not to throw obstacles in the way if the majority were in favor. Two-thirds of the borough's householders had allegedly already signed the petition, and no one voted against it at this meeting. The committee appointed to carry it forward reflected the consensus: nonsectarian, nonpartisan, spanning the professions, manufactures, and trades and the full spectrum of middle-class wealth and property.[151] By the time the petition was submitted, the wealth, weight, and vast majority of the town's ratepayers had signed it, and the editor of the *Standard*—initially rather dubious—had given his blessing.[152] The borough charter was granted without complications in 1851 and, ironically, W. H. Hornby became the first mayor.

The council did not assume the functions of the commissioners until 1854, and it was as a surveyor to the commissioners that John Withers drew up a report in 1852, detailing how much needed to be done. The rather complacent assumption of many Blackburnians that the town, give or take the odd problem like the river, had not experienced the environmental deterioration of its neighbors—and even the cholera epidemic of 1849, apparently causing somewhat fewer deaths in Blackburn than in some other towns, appeared to confirm this[153]—could scarcely survive his report, which concentrated on the worst neighborhoods. "The neglected parts of the town," he wrote, "the parts without sewers or conveniences, unpaved, rarely scavenged, and where the laws of decency and propriety are set at defiance by over-crowded dwellings, generally indicate the localities of Typhus, &c., which will be found co-existant with uncleanliness and filth." He described cellars, "principally occupied by the lower class of Irish," that were "exceedingly unwholesome: cooking, sleeping, sick and healthy, male and female beds, &c., all being in one apartment," and privies, few in number, mostly filthy, which, "being common property, no one considers themselves responsible for their cleanliness." The Blakewater remained untouched, the very few street sewers were built on the worst possible principles, allowing seepage, blockage, and flooding, and the streets—two-thirds of them too narrow for the commissioners' powers—were in a poor state. The town's annual mortality rate was a dismal 33.14 per thousand.[154] Blackburn, like its neighbors, had enriched itself on the cheap.[155]

The great Victorian cleanup, moving into a higher gear around mid-century, fitted admirably bourgeois notions of order. If working-class homes could be sanitized the working classes might be induced to spend more time in them. Pernicious, teeming, alcohol-fueled street life; gangs of disorderly, dissolute, thieving youths; crowds and combinations of collectivized, politicized, threatening men: all could be eradicated if only the poor could be corralled into contented and contained families.[156] This was the song of a growing number of sanitary reformers, statisticians, doctors, newspaper editors, and politicians in the 1840s, the assertion that the well-being of the poor was vital to the stability and good order of the nation: "If the poor are badly fed and badly lodged, it is now found that they generate fevers and pestilence; grow vicious and demoralised, and become dangerous to the peace, order, and safety of the country."[157] It is therefore quite legitimate to see sanitary reform primarily as a means of social and moral discipline, closer to the ideology behind the New Poor Law, the new police, and the new carceral regimes than complacent Whiggish accounts once suggested.

Tackling the piles of ordure could, potentially, foster good relations between classes by projecting a benevolent image of local- and national-elite paternalism, and yet be relatively nonpartisan and uncontroversial. It would take a special talent to be actively *against* cleaner air, water, streets, and houses, which is why opponents of reform based their objections on denial (things really are not that bad), cost (things may be bad, but the expense of rectifying them is prohibitive; or—the lament of small property-owners—the expense falls disproportionately on struggling people like ourselves), and anti-centralization (whatever good may be effected, it will be more than offset by the erosion of local liberties). These objections did not disappear, but Chadwick and his fellow reformers minimized the range of opposition by deliberately circumscribing the terms of debate. Working conditions, wages, the quality and quantity of food, political rights, the existing power structure: none of these inflammatory questions were on the sanitary agenda; all of them

could be reduced to the much less combustible topic of environmental policing.[158]

Stated thus, sanitary reform is evidently a leading contender in the avoid-
ance-of-revolution sweepstakes, a galvanizer of local elites and of a responsive
and responsible state behind a mollifying, power-maintaining agenda. It is
plausible that the vast expenditure on urban improvement in the second half
of the nineteenth century—impressive or inadequate and tardy, according to
taste[159]—did impress the discontented with the scope for change under the existing structure and did enable the greater penetration of (filtered and modified) bourgeois values of happy hearths and homes. Yet caution is in order lest
we impose too much explanatory weight on slim shoulders. Who supported
environmental reform? Active campaigners and supporters were few.[160] Clay
and Entwisle played to thinly attended houses when they lectured on sanitation. Their reports were so graphic and lurid precisely because most bourgeois
ladies and gentlemen accorded minimal weight to the problems and fears expressed—and there is little indication of a dramatic shift in opinion. Even
when local elites at length came to see the merits of overcoming governmental
fragmentation, there were so many competing, colliding motivations—to improve efficiency, to end gridlock, to enhance profits, to preempt government
imposition, to promote the spirit of civic pride and emulation,[161] to build imposing municipal edifices, to respond to the cholera outbreak[162]—that it would
be rash to place the desire for improved social order (let alone a direct response to the threat of revolution) at the head of the list.

Besides, just because local authorities now had new powers did not necessarily mean that they would deploy them swiftly and smoothly. In Blackburn,
the face of the town undoubtedly improved in the fifties, with the development
of the lands of the See of Canterbury, the construction of the town hall at last,
the opening of Corporation Park, the building of villas along Preston New
Road, the beginnings of better working-class housing[163]—and the drainage
improved too, but at a pace belying its supposedly high priority at the time of
incorporation. Blackburn did not (though Over Darwen did)[164] create a Board
of Health. The council took over from the improvement commission in 1854,
obtained additional powers in the 1854 Blackburn Improvement Act, began
drainage works in 1856, and completed the main outlet sewer in 1861—a full
decade after incorporation. Preston's Board of Health apparently did little, if
anything, during the first three years of its existence. It purchased the Preston
Waterworks Company in 1853, but did not begin an obligatory survey of the
town's drainage until 1856.[165] Bolton took to improvements with more gusto
under the influence of Thomas Lever Rushton. But the large and costly undertakings of the new united authority soon aroused the ire of the economist element. At a meeting in October 1852 Thomas Thomasson and Richard Stockdale accused the council and Rushton of reckless and extravagant expenditure.

The ratepayers apparently agreed—and the liberals exploited the issue—because Rushton lost his seat in the 1852 election. The liberals rejoiced, overlooking their previous bipartisan support for his initiatives, but at the opening of the market hall in 1855, P. R. Arrowsmith, radical liberal, regretted that party spirit had deprived the town of his friend's eminent services. Rushton himself sniped at the economists: "In promoting the sanitary improvement of the borough, in doing away with those places of filth, misery, and vice which still existed let them not look entirely to the pounds, shillings, and pence, but seek to promote the health by lengthening the lives of the people committed to their care."[166]

Doing away with filth, misery, and vice—an unstable trinity of the objective, the subjective, and the judgmental—thus met many obstacles as members of the bourgeoisie differed in their interpretation of their duties and self-interests or came up against the limitations of their powers. Sanitary reform as a means of engineering social norms attracted more diffuse, less strident bourgeois support than political parties, the churches, the Anti-Corn Law League, the short-time movement, the military, the police, and a rash of voluntary associations. It was but one—and not the most significant—of the competing, partially overlapping solutions in the bourgeois quest for social order.

CHAPTER 11: BOURGEOIS TIME AND SPACE

Around mid-century, Henry Ashworth retired from active oversight of his mills and took to foreign travel. He visited Egypt, Syria, Germany, Switzerland, and the United States.[1] While in Massachusetts, he noted the progressive social and intellectual condition of the people, the devotion to industry, the inventive genius, and the healthy manufacturing and commercial activity. It seemed to him that there was no other country in the world in which the elements of human happiness were more amply diffused. He commented on the highly creditable array of mansions, villas, and genteel residences in Brookline, Cambridge, and Dorchester. But overall this was his verdict on the United States: "The people are generally intelligent, but they appear to possess no recognised standard of cultivation or refinement. There is great freedom, and but little etiquette; an independence which borders on rudeness amongst the inferior class: and it may be said the states have made only a beginning in the cultivation of a taste for the fine arts."[2] And this from a Bolton Quaker cotton manufacturer! But then, as his obituarist would put it in 1880, "Mr. Ashworth was a most honourable representative of those different social elements which have been thought to be so hard of combination in an individual—the gentry, the trading interest, and Nonconformity; and the union was none the less successful in him for being so entirely unobtrusive."[3]

This chapter, a further exploration of the culture that the bourgeoisie built, shaped, and shared in their quest for an ordered society, is about consumption and its meanings, and the organization of private time and space—how the Henry Ashworths of Lancashire spent their expanding wealth on their homes and gardens, furnishings and art, leisure and travel. We have already seen (Chapter 2) the potential tension between the material and celestial worlds, and how a number of individuals reconciled the two. As the obituary indicates, upwardly mobile bourgeois males seeking to enhance their social standing could discover that their attempts to clothe their material worth with the wrappings of gentility were equally challenging.

Upward Mobility

A number of scholars have pointed out that very few industrialists vaulted the legendary distance up the social hierarchy from rags to riches.[4] There are sporadic examples of men from humble backgrounds—a handloom weaver, an apprentice hairdresser, an operative molder (the son of a rank-and-file soldier)[5]—who made fortunes; but more typical was a less spectacular, yet still considerable, mobility within the broad ranks of the middle classes, from families possessing a modest amount of capital. Still, wealthy, powerful men whose fathers had been small farmers, innkeepers, craftsmen, or retailers could with some legitimacy label themselves as "self-made."[6]

Men who had opened up a large gap between their past and present could take pride in the didactic message of their life stories. For example, on the opening of Corporation Park in Blackburn in 1857, Alderman John Baynes, manufacturer, pointed out some of the largest mill complexes in town: in the distance to his right, a leviathan establishment built by William Eccles, who as a boy had worked in a warehouse, but by industry and perseverance entered the legal profession, and then invested his earned capital in cotton; in the center, the largest mills in town, belonging to Robert Hopwood who, "(to his honour be it spoken)," told the council when he became mayor that he had worked in a humble capacity in a cotton mill; and the large building to his left, built by the Pilkington brothers, James and William, sometime MP and mayor respectively, whose father had been a Blackburn bookkeeper. "All these are worthy examples of what knowledge, aided by perseverance, industry, and good conduct, could accomplish, and the same path was open to all. (Hear.)"[7] John Mercer (1791-1866), a leading industrial chemist, a partner in the Forts' Oakenshaw printworks and a Fellow of the Royal Society, began work as a handloom weaver after the early death of his father (previously a small millowner and then a farmer). Sir James Kay-Shuttleworth later held him up to an audience at the Oldham School of Science and Art as an example worthy of imitation:

The son of a handloom weaver [he] lived in a wild part of this county in so rude a condition that in his childhood and youth he was literally clad in the half-tanned skins of calves with the hair innermost. His only school was that of nature among the cloughs and torrents, and along the hills and moors around his home. Steeped in poverty, he lost his father, but there awoke in him the desire for knowledge. . . . There is nothing in his life which is not at least a subject of laudable emulation to you. He was simple, sober, pious, and genial in his personal intercourse; a native gentleman, speaking our Lancashire dialect; full of intellectual activity, and living a happy life, illuminated by the light which science shed upon his humble home.[8]

Such individuals, whether they chose to dwell on their lowly origins or to forget them, faced considerable difficulties in cultivating the proper bearing of a gentleman. W. A. Abram, at the end of the century, distinguished three types of gentleman: the ancient usage, denoting the son of an esquire or the possessor of a freehold estate smaller than an esquire's and larger than a yeoman's;[9] the more recent term for a man who had retired from business and was living by his own means; and the "'born gentleman'" (or, like John Mercer, "native gentleman"), who did not necessarily have the means for supporting his status (unlike many who *had* amassed wealth but who could never be mistaken for real gentlemen), but readily distinguishable because "in his outward manifestation, his demeanour, address and style, there is an indefinable yet visible gentility."[10]

Abram pointed to an ambiguous and flexible set of objective and subjective characteristics, without precise definition.[11] Note that the man who was merely wealthy still had to earn the right to be a "natural" gentleman through a certain "demeanour, address and style" before he could transcend the barriers of status snobbery. Frances, Lady Shelley tells a tale of her father, Thomas Winckley, attorney, a well-connected member of the Preston urban gentry, presumably in the early 1790s:

One day my father, in a towering passion, left his old house never to return. He had gone as usual in the morning to select his fish for dinner. On his arrival at the fishmonger's, he found himself forestalled in the purchase of the finest turbot by a Mr. Horrocks, a cotton spinner! This was too much for my father's sense of dignity. He pronounced Preston no longer a fit place for a gentleman to live in.[12]

For some, a mere manufacturer could not be a proper gentleman. Then again, money could go a long way to buying the requisite veneer of gentility, as the fishmonger recognized.[13] John Horrocks, who farmed a plot of land and owned a small quarry north of Bolton, came to Preston in the late 1780s with little but ambition. With the assistance of local bankers, he and his brother Samuel built up one of the largest spinning and manufacturing concerns in the country.[14] Both became MPs for Preston after the turn of the century and established themselves as fixtures of local polite society in spite of their broad accents and lack of polished education. One of Samuel's daughters married Charles Whitaker of Roefield, a branch of an old-established East Lancashire landed family; a second married Dr. William St. Clare, a Preston physician well connected to the leading local families; a third married the Rev. James Streynsham Master, rector of Chorley, part of a web of minor gentry, professional, military, and East India Company families.[15] Lowly origins and rustic enunciation clearly did not prevent widespread marital and social alliances between lesser gentry and old and new members of the bourgeoisie—although the transition to gentility became easier with a move away from the day-to-day running of the enterprise and the cultivation of those activities that greater leisure allowed, often in the second generation. Peter Rothwell, Bolton Methodist ironfounder and engineer, reputedly rose at five each morning and breakfasted on toasted cheese and a pint of ale before he set off for the works. His son, Peter (1792-1849), JP, who built up a choice art collection and library, presumably did not.[16]

Accent was an evident problem and liability for those on the rise. Every time a newspaper editor ridiculed a person's broad Lancashire vowels and phrases he was making an implicit claim to the superiority of a more "correct" and refined mode of expression. But again, for some the roughness of accent could be a source of pride. For example, when James Hardcastle of Bolton stood for election in Wigan in 1831, he made much of his accent as well as his origins in appealing to the constituents. His father, "'in his youth, was personally acquainted with poverty, and he knows what it is to feel poor. Now we pay £80,000 in "money wages" annually.'" As for his own accent, "'If there be any gentleman, with those nice ears, that he cannot understand my imperfect intonation, I beg he will excuse me. I have been accustomed to mingle with workmen, and I naturally love their phrases, and above all things, as a Lancashire man, I must say that I admire Tim Bobbin!'"[17] But with the rise in refinement came a decline in regional distinctions among the wealthy and educated across the nation and a consequential accentuation of linguistic differences *within* local society. More than ever, dialect came to denote class.[18] Abram claimed in 1894 that fifty to seventy years previously one heard the Lancashire dialect spoken broadly everywhere, from the inn parlor to the commercial room to the exchange, but this was no longer the case.[19]

Dress and style formed essential components of deportment and bearing. Particularly in rapidly expanding, anonymous towns where the local elite could no longer expect to be recognized automatically, or where an individual was claiming membership for the first time, dress was one of the most important material manifestations of social standing.[20] Portraits of Peter and John Horrocks Ainsworth, for example, in dark, double-breasted suits and high collars, hair brushed forward at the sides and with long sideburns, aim to communicate the refinement, sobriety, and masculinity of the early-Victorian paterfamilias—conventional representations of class and gender.[21] The dramatic transformation in male clothing from the powdered flamboyance of an earlier generation is well known; but this did not prevent some mid-century males from dressing with a certain panache and, within circumscribed limits, using clothing as a status-enhancer. Consider, for instance, Abram's pen portrait of Peter Ellingthorp, attorney, clerk to the Blackburn Union, who dressed around 1850 like a wealthy cotton magnate and apparently surpassed in dress and deportment all of the town's principal cotton spinners:

The silk hat somewhat jauntily poised on the head; the elaborate coloured silk scarf round the neck, sustaining the upright starched linen collars, and with its gold pin stuck in front; the coat of glossy dark brown cloth, buttoned across the breast, but cut away below, displaying the white or flowered vest beneath; the light cloth trousers kept straight and tight by straps passing under the polished boots; the gloves; the "nobby" walking-stick; and the unfailing flower, crimson carnation or rose, or perhaps camelia, fixed in the button-hole of the coat.[22]

All of the attempts at speaking properly, acting in a gentlemanly fashion, and clothing oneself aright could be jeopardized by a fundamental problem for the bourgeoisie and the minor gentry: the Lord's bounty might be withdrawn. Since one's worldly goods and position in respectable society were dependent on people buying one's product or services, they were vulnerable to the vagaries of the market.[23] Bankruptcies were common, and while the more fortunate might be able to start up again in another enterprise, apparently rapidly regaining face if they managed to pay off their creditors in full, others collapsed permanently. The directory of bankrupts lists a large number of prominent casualties.[24] After Henry Sudell failed in 1827, he seems to have lived quite comfortably at a country house near Chippenham rather than reconciling himself to a lesser status and influence in the Blackburn area. He apparently never came back even to visit.[25] Robert Andrews of Rivington Hall put a great deal of money into a Manchester business, which failed shortly after he died in 1793, leaving the estates heavily encumbered and a narrow income for the heir, Robert. But with the rise in land values and the letting of a particularly productive coal mine, Robert was able to maintain his rank and station as a country gentleman and a JP.[26] Although he did not fail, William Hulton's income from the Hulton collieries diminished considerably during the 1837-42 slump. He wrote to Peel in May 1842 from Leamington, explaining that because he was experiencing great difficulties and was apprehending even greater ones, he had left Hulton Park, resolved for the sake of his younger sons to abandon the comforts he had so long enjoyed and to live in London. Could Peel nominate him "to any employment with *very hard work*, and *very little pay*?" Peel regretted that he was not able to do so.[27] Hulton's eldest son, William Ford Hulton, continued to live in the family home. In 1846 he explained that, "His father felt the panic some years ago and he did not feel justified in keeping up his external establishments and lavishing upon himself those comforts which under more fortunate circumstances a country squire would have been justified in doing."[28]

Bourgeois Housing

Above all, one staked a claim for the comforts and status of gentility by the house one built, bought, or occupied, the number of domestic servants one kept, the consumer items with which one graced the interior, and the extent and cultivation of the garden, all of which could be displayed to fellow members of the same band of society at tea parties and dinners. There were three main varieties of bourgeois housing.[29] Firstly, the wealthiest could buy country estates not too far distant from their warehouses in town. Notable early examples in the Blackburn vicinity included Henry Sudell, merchant, who built Woodfold Hall between 1796 and 1800 to a design of James Wyatt,[30] and also

Richard Fort, calico printer, who rebuilt Read Hall in a fashionable style and surrounded it with six hundred thousand trees on his fourteen-hundred-acre estate.[31] Or—especially later in the period—they could purchase estates further afield but still maintain their local business interests and maybe a house as well. Peter Ormrod was one such example. His father, James, came to Bolton in the 1790s and went into cotton spinning, then into bleaching with Thomas Hardcastle of Firwood, and finally into banking with Hardcastle, Cross, Barlow and Rushton. In typical fashion he bought a big house, Chamber Hall, in the neighborhood. Peter married Eliza, daughter of Hardcastle, renovated Chamber Hall, then moved into Halliwell Hall, and finally bought the seventhousand-acre Wyresdale Park estate near Garstang from the duke of Hamilton for £199,000 in 1853, where he began building a mansion in 1856. He resided at Halliwell and Wyresdale alternately. His brother and partner, James, remained in residence in Halliwell Lodge.[32] It was very likely that the second or third generation in this sector would renounce the family business and spin off into the ranks of the gentry. The sons of John Horrocks of Preston, for example, fled the town: John Jr. bought and lived at Tullichewan Castle in Dumbartonshire, and Peter moved to Beomond, Surrey.[33]

The second type of bourgeois housing consisted of mansions—either newly constructed "villas" or refurbished old halls—scattered in the peripheral countryside but lacking any substantial farmland. These were very often adjacent to an industrial concern; in towns as small as Blackburn or Bolton at the turn of the century, with relatively ill-developed and unattractive urban centers, and where much of early industry—printing, bleaching, spinning, mining, and so on—was rural, the tendency was for industrialists to build their houses next to their works and to travel into town to do business.

Studies of the bourgeoisie that have concentrated on the town and plotted the chromatographic separation out of classes with the spread of suburbanization, particularly in the middle of the nineteenth century, have tended to underplay these first two categories of bourgeois housing; a large proportion of the bourgeois elite was to be found in the semi-industrialized countryside surrounding the towns from a very early date. John Holt, in his description of agriculture in Lancashire in 1795, gave one description of this prototypical suburbanization:

The buildings of the merchants and tradesmen dispersed over many parts of the country, and particularly in the vicinities of large towns, certainly merit notice.— Considerable expence having been laid out of late years in the erection, finishing, and embellishing many of them in a superior style—many of which are furnished with hot walls, green-houses, the rarest plants and finest fruits: the adjoining grounds have been improved, laid out in various styles, and fringed with plantations.

A taste for the fine arts has also gone forth, and a great number of expensive paintings have been purchased to ornament the walls, and engravings to fill their port-folios.[34]

R. W. Dickson in 1815 wrote of the neat, well-constructed houses in the villa style in the vicinity of most of the large manufacturing and trading towns.[35] A perusal of the six-inch Ordnance Survey maps of the mid-1840s[36] reveals in quite striking fashion how this pattern had developed and persisted: across the parishes, the villas or "gentlemen's seats" of the owners of rural industry mingled with the houses of members of the bourgeoisie who had urban businesses. These dwellings had substantial "demesnes" of garden and other land, though they paled in comparison to the private parks at Cuerden, Woodfold, Huntroyde, Read Hall, and so on. In the 1850s, Whittle, standing near Hall-i'th-Wood outside Bolton, described how "the whole vicinity [was] interspersed with neat mansions, the domiciles of commercial gentlemen." He conceded that the smoke of hundreds of mills polluted the air and fields, but this scarcely dampened his enthusiasm:

There are now fine, tall, and elegant houses, of brick and stone, neat and well finished, abounding in elegant window beys [sic], rich porticoes, unique gateways, open lawns, pretty gardens, and other domestic appendages, entirely befitting the abode of noblemen of the first rank. [That] [t]hese are not so ancient and picturesque as the halls, mansions, manor-houses, towers, &c. of our ancestors, must be allowed; yet the whole is cheering and pleasing, as giving a pre-eminence to the present nineteenth century, as the residence of men who are actuated by commerce and manufacture.[37]

The third category of bourgeois housing comprised sizable houses within town, either alone or clustered in terraces and squares. In the small nucleus of Blackburn town center in the eighteenth century, the local wealthy began to establish themselves along King Street. The Feilden, Sudell, Cardwell, Livesey, Glover, Markland, and Leyland families—the leading lights of the putting-out mercantile elite—all built or occupied King Street residences and the street continued to be the town's most desirable into the second half of the nineteenth century.[38] A few strands of more-or-less exclusivity joined it from early in the century, though the extent of bourgeois housing remained small. A square of good houses—St. John's Place, Garden Street, and James Street— rose up around St. John's Church, Blackburn's most fashionable place of worship.[39] The smartest street constructed in the period was Richmond Terrace, completed in 1838 on Feilden property, its dignity imposed by strict building regulations.[40] The only other terraces of note were at Strawberry Bank on Preston New Road, described by Whittle in 1851 as "the Avenham of Blackburn for salubrity."[41] Besides these rows or clusters of high-tone residence, the best bourgeois housing tended to present itself singly—in splendid isolation from anything comparable. For example, William Carr, attorney, lived in Shadsworth House, his partner, the coroner John Hargreaves, in Larkhill House (built by Christopher Baron, excise officer, in 1762). William Turner, MP, lived in Mill Hill House close to his works when in Blackburn and otherwise at Shrigley Hall, his Cheshire estate. The Pickups, spirit merchants, built Galligreaves, which Joseph Harrison, ironfounder, bought in the late 1840s. James and William Pilkington, cotton spinners, each had a house at Park Place, surrounded by four or five acres of garden, next door to their mills. James also bought Swinethwaite Hall, Bedale, Yorkshire, while William later moved to Wilpshire Grange. Robert Hopwood Sr., cotton spinner, built Highfield at Nova Scotia, and Thomas Dugdale, a surgeon who went into cotton manufacturing, later built Griffin Lodge, both alongside their mills.

Suburbanization as we know it—villas with relatively little land, at the edge of the urban spread, alongside similar housing and often strung out along or close to major highways—was only just beginning to take hold by mid-century with the first shoots of the development of Preston New Road as a prosperous western neighborhood. James Barlow, surgeon, built Spring Mount, the first such villa on the side of the road, and William Eccles, attorney and cotton spinner, lived there after him. William Dickinson, ironfounder and cotton manufacturer, built Ouzehead House in Grecian style further along the road in the early 1850s. The mill-owning Lewis brothers soon followed suit with neighboring houses at Billinge End.[42] These were all strictly suburban: large houses with gardens, no pretense at agricultural pursuits, and close to a major connecting road for rapid access into the town. But they were also, at this date, few and far between.

Darwen, a dispersed collection of manufactories and settlements partially hemmed in by the moors and taking the Blackburn-Bolton road as its chief organizing principle, was only beginning to take shape as a small town with a nucleus toward mid-century. The big employers' residences were as scattered as their works,[43] and only very gradually was anything approaching a bourgeois suburb consolidated. By the time Abram was writing in 1877, "Chiefly on the south-west side of the town, the mansions and villas of the gentry of Darwen occupy admirable situations on the knolls and slopes overlooking the glades and dingles at the base of the Darwen Moor, which form beautiful secluded shrubberies and plantations enlivened by natural cascades."[44]

Bolton town housing replicated the pattern in Blackburn. Acresfield, a mansion built by Thomas Bolling, surgeon, in 1776, and Silverwell House, built by John Pilkington, dimity manufacturer, in 1790, both on what were then the fringes of the town, were early examples of solitary big houses constructed outside the town center by mercantile, manufacturing, and professional wealth.[45] A second phase of bourgeois house-building saw the development of terraces. The regular and respectable housing in and around three new squares built in the 1820s—New Market Square, Nelson Square, and Bradford Square[46]—apparently largely attracted only a lower-middle-class presence, but the 1851 census data reveal that, amidst the same kind of fragmented bourgeois presence as in Blackburn, Newport Terrace and St. George's Street attracted relatively high bourgeois numbers.[47] The development of a string of smart houses along Chorley New Road, under way by mid-century, inaugurated a third phase, that of mid-Victorian suburbanization and with it a greater degree of class segregation.[48] Dr. Samuel Chadwick, a prominent Bolton philanthropist and sanitary reformer, described this process in a speech to the corporation around 1860:

to those who are *au fait* in our street geography, it must be pretty evident that a member of the Town Council is not to be looked for about the Old Acres (a laugh); on the contrary, he is a *rara avis* in that locality. The exodus from Manchester-road set in some time ago, and immigration is incessantly going on (laughter). The affluent and the influential are removing to the favorite and invigorating clime at the other side of the town, while the occupants of Manchester-road will soon be left alone in their glory; and should these gentlemen, at some future time, with gracious condescension revisit their former *habitat*, there will be nothing to be seen or heard but second-class people and the railway whistle. (Renewed laughter.)[49]

Near Preston, on the south bank of the Ribble, John Horrocks built his spacious mansion, Penwortham Lodge, in 1799-1801, and his brother Samuel built Lark Hill on the Preston side. Upstream, in Walton-le-Dale, a number of gentlemen's seats crowned the banks of the river Darwen.[50] This pattern expanded with many "active citizens," as the *Preston Chronicle* put it in the mid-1830s, building elegant mansions or handsome villas on airy sites, "wherein, after a life of successful devotion to business, they may enjoy rural quiet and amusement."[51] But as befitted a surrogate county town with a plethora of professional men, an "urban renaissance" past, and a favorable location overlooking the Ribble, the built-up area of Preston developed a greater proportion of bourgeois housing than either Blackburn or Bolton when it began to flesh out from its three straggling main streets. The most significant step came when William Cross, attorney, bought Town End Field from Thomas Winckley, put up the first house on it for himself in 1799, and then the second for Col. Nicholas Grimshaw.[52] In 1805 Cross (and subsequently a committee of the inhabitants of the square, he and his heirs maintaining the casting vote) precisely regulated the development of Winckley Square and its enclosed, locked-to-outsiders garden-cum-pleasure ground in the middle. The specifications required three-story houses with uniform frontages, worth at least £40 a year.[53] Various members of the Aspden, Gorst, Dalton, Addison, Wilson, Miller, and Horrocks families subsequently built or bought houses in the square. Other streets of terraced and detached housing grew up in the same vicinity, around Avenham Walks and at East and West Cliff, with views over the Ribble valley.[54] This area, and particularly Winckley Square itself, housed a hefty proportion of Preston's leading families, retaining them in the core well into the second half of the nineteenth century. In the 1850s Hardwick thought that, "In point of extent and picturesque beauty, this provincial *'rus in urbe'* might successfully compete with many in the metropolis."[55] As late as the 1880s, Hewitson commented that the center "has a beautifully-umbrageous, pleasantly-floral appearance—has an emerald charm and propriety of culture about it suggestive of select country ground rather than of sub-divided town land, within a good stone-throw of a busy, tram-wayed street, in the heart of a large borough."[56]

Part of the secret of this neighborhood's longevity lay in keeping plebeian Preston at bay, preserving the approaches and views of the best property. In 1836, for example, the *Preston Chronicle* boasted of the signs of improvement and enlargement in the town, including the building of new mills and the laying out of new streets in compact manufacturing districts on the north side of the town. This close proximity of workers' housing and mills was admirable, the editor thought, since it would probably supersede any notions of building such streets to the south and southwest sides of the borough, "where their erection would be detrimental to the property in those quarters, and destroy the beauty of the finest part of the town—Ribblesdale place and Avenham."[57]

Other pockets of salubrious housing in Preston grew up toward mid-century, especially around Moor Park—Philip Park's plan of the new park in 1835 shows that surrounding plots of land in strips were to be sold off for detached villas, a specific intention to create an upmarket neighborhood[58]—and along the river at Ashton and Penwortham. Hardwick took a walk from the Ribble estuary toward Preston in 1857. He described the "suburban villas" gracing the heights in Ashton, built on the property of James Pedder of Ashton Lodge and of Joseph Bray, attorney; the first-class mansions on the opposite bank in Penwortham—The Oaks (built in 1843 for John Cooper, cotton manufacturer), Hurst Grange (in the late 1840s, for William Adam Hulton, County Court judge), the Hall (the home of the Marshalls); and the handsome houses with less land, occupying the high ground on the Preston side closer to town.[59]

Brian Bristow has analyzed residential patterning in mid-nineteenth century Preston in detail. He demonstrates that in such a compact town, with many of the wealthy still remaining in the core, the residential proximity and intermingling of socioeconomic groups was marked, and fine houses were never far from shops, workshops, cellar dwellings, and crowded courts. But the mixing was not promiscuous: the wealthier tended to be concentrated in the areas already discussed, with further islands of fair prosperity in the squares around

St. Paul's, St. Peter's, and St. Ignatius's Churches. The most prestigious groups were the most exclusive: lawyers and clergymen, for example, were somewhat more concentrated in the best areas than doctors, who were more widely dispersed. Ground landlords were also planting the seeds of a much greater segregation: in the mill districts near the canals and railways, land for whole swathes of working-class terraced housing; on the Tulketh estate and on the Freehold Land Movement's Fulwood estate in the early 1850s, the beginnings of desirable suburbs of spaced housing, wide streets, and interspersed trees, following basic rules and specifications.[60]

This accords well with the findings of other historical geographers who suggest that, while by no means randomly mixed, English towns and cities were segregated only at street level until quite late—more like mosaics of small pieces of class presence, as F. M. L. Thompson puts it, than bold patterns.[61] Two considerations flow from this. The first is that the perception of increasing residential segregation in the 1830s and 1840s, fostered by investigators like James Philips Kay in Manchester, Robert Baker in Leeds, and John Clay in Preston, is exaggerated. There was, evidently, *some* foundation to the widespread belief among moralists and alarmists in the separation out of the classes and the masses into brazenly exclusive residential quarters and hidden, festering ghettoes[62]—but the early-Victorian patchwork quilt was only a pallid precursor to the bolder class patterns of the later nineteenth and twentieth centuries. In any case, although Clay's sanitary report paid due homage to this idea, some of his rhetoric actually stressed *proximity*, and social rather than physical apartheid: "Breathing the same air, daily in our sight," he wrote in 1844, "we know them [the poor] little better than we know the people of the opposite hemisphere."[63]

Friedrich Engels famously described the "hypocritical" town-planning of Manchester: the reflection of class stratifications in residential zoning, with rows of decent shops screening the working-class quarters from the respectable as they rode into the city center to do business.[64] He supposed that segregation allowed the rich to ignore the poor and the reality of urban squalor and deterioration; and full segregation, of the type that was beginning to develop in Birmingham's Edgbaston or Glasgow's Kelvingrove (or in the plutocratic enclaves carved out by mid-century in New York's Brooklyn Heights or Boston's Beacon Hill) *could* have this effect, since environmental concerns and fears of crime and immorality were no longer as threatening.[65] But in Manchester and the milltowns, the rhetorical flights of Engels and his fellow commentators aimed at reconstructing imagined maps of urban space to suit their own agendas. Standing Engels on his head, it may be nearer the truth that exaggerated perceptions of segregation planted the fears—without the *cordon sanitaire* of distance—that helped nudge forward elite intervention.

A second point worth pondering is what the patterning of bourgeois housing can reveal about the cult of domesticity. Attempts to suggest a greater separation of workplace from home, or suburbanization as the fruits of an ideology of domesticity, do not carry conviction in the area covered in this study.[66] The cult of domesticity was, as we have seen (Chapter 4), widespread across bourgeois society, the gentry, and the broader middle classes. It flourished in the doctor's house in Winckley Square, the master bleacher's mansion cheek by jowl with his bleachworks in Horwich, and in the vicarage at Blackburn. In no real sense was work separated from home in any of these instances. Of course, the bleachworks, printworks, or cotton mill were not actually a part of the home, but then they never had been, and for the bulk of manufacturers who maintained a managing interest in their concerns there was no discernible attempt to move away from the sites of their rural or semi-urban industries until later in the century, when congestion and pollution forced them to do so. Domesticity and the separation of spheres could operate, whether or not the source of income came from the consulting room on the ground floor, the mill within walking distance or the printworks miles away, wherever there was sufficient space within the home, wherever there were enough servants, and—preferably—wherever a garden could be cultivated. Second-phase suburbanization in the milltowns, when it finally arrived in any quantity, can readily be explained by the desire of those on middling incomes who could afford to escape the chimneys to keep one step ahead of the urban sprawl, close to lines of transportation, emulating the process begun in the big cities.

Inside the Bourgeois Home

We have been inside the bourgeois house a number of times before in pursuit of notions of seriousness and domesticity, but have not lingered on the furnishings or on the ordering of everyday life. At the most opulent end of the bourgeois scale, Henry Sudell was forced to allow the world—or anyone who could read a sale catalog—a glimpse of his home in 1828 when he sold off Woodfold Hall and its contents following his bankruptcy. Among its other attractions, the hall boasted twenty bedrooms, a music room, a billiard room, and a shooters' room, a wine cellar with 6,164 bottles of vintage wine, and a selection of household goods that took over sixty pages to itemize, ranging from sixty-eight damask tablecloths to thirty-two cut wine decanters.[67] On nearly the same level of magnificence was John Horrocks Ainsworth's Moss Bank, a splendid house with equally splendid furniture and paintings and a large library. The extensive gardens boasted a canal or moat, ponds, walks and parterres, hothouses, greenhouses, an aviary (for foreign birds of golden plumage), and—an added attraction at a short distance from the hall—a four-tiered brick tower with stained-glass windows and a flagstaff where one could admire the fine prospect from the parapet or study astronomy on a clear night.[68]

The 1851 census lists eleven servants and a governess in residence at Moss Bank and six servants at Woodfold Park (then rented by Henry Paul Fleetwood, a Preston banker). Most bourgeois families had either one or two domestic servants (see Appendix 3). Samuel Leach (1829-1923) describes what it was like growing up in a two-servant,[69] six-bedroomed, Winckley Square house built by his father, Thomas, a hosier and draper with a warehouse in Manchester. The maids (who shared one of the bedrooms) were all-purpose domestic servants; his first experience of specialized-function servants—butlers and ladies' maids—came when he was in his mid-teens on a visit to the Samuel Martins in Liverpool, family friends, prosperous merchants in the South American trade, and several notches higher in the social hierarchy. When Leach was about twelve his father began to keep a gig, partly for his mother's health, partly to travel for orders in the wholesale business. This meant the family had clambered onto the lowest rung of the carriage-owning classes. They stabled their gray mare at the Castle Hotel in the marketplace. Most afternoons they would drive into the country for air—to Broughton or round Moor Park—or take a day off and drive to Garstang to visit his mother's cousins. In socializing, the family drank tea in the houses of neighbors and friends ("our private friendships were quite free from any political bias, and we took in both papers," the *Pilot* and the *Chronicle*) and entertained themselves with games, the piano, and singing. They frequently hosted small gatherings of a few amateurs for song and accompaniment. Samuel's main form of entertainment came in playing with his schoolfriends and competitors at the grammar school; he describes walking along the Ribble and the Darwen with the son of Philip Park, the borough treasurer, turning out objects on Dr. Robert Brown's son's lathe, and dancing on top of the unfilled gasometers with the son of John Rofe, the gas engineer—all fellow residents of Winckley Square.[70]

Dr. Brown's household in Winckley Square was a few status-degrees higher than that of the Leaches. Brown rode in a four-wheeled carriage in wet weather and a two-wheeled gig (later replaced by a phaeton, a four-wheeled open carriage, because of the dangers of injury from the gig shafts breaking) on fine days. A coachman drove these and tended to the three horses. A cook, a parlormaid, and a housemaid served the house in the 1840s, and there was a governess and a nurse for the seven children. In this social stratum the servants—all four of whom shared the same bedroom—each performed a number of duties. The parlormaid waited on the family, answered the door and helped the housemaid with making the beds. All of them, including the cook, joined forces to tackle the washing; the night watchman called them up at 1 a.m. on a Monday.[71] This was also true at the Leach household, and it was an indication of the hidden labor on which scrubbed and starched respectability depended: the watchman would knock with his stick on the wall just under the maids' bedroom on Monday mornings at half past two for the wash, "so that by the time we came down to breakfast we often saw the clothes, already dried, being brought in from the grass plot at the bottom of our garden."[72]

The Brown and Leach households were gravitating gently upwards in prosperity and status. The household of the vicar of Blackburn provides an interesting example of a clash of upward and downward mobility. J. W. Whittaker, as we have seen (Chapter 6), came from a relatively modest background and had to be careful in his expenditure when he first arrived in Blackburn in 1822. His mother was concerned that his income even with the strictest economy would be little enough to make ends meet. He would need two female servants—the vicarage was large—but a footman, requiring board, wages, and liveries amounting to £70 a year, could be dispensed with:

[T]he appearance of being without one can have nothing shabby in it or at all impeach your *respectability* as Vicar of Blackburne [*sic*] (using the word in its worldly acceptation). No one can suppose or expect a young man on his first preferment & not in the enjoyment of a private fortune to set out in a style as if already in independent circumstances.[73]

His wife, Mary, was the daughter of William Feilden and used to the luxuries of Feniscowles Hall. When they first married, Mary wrote to her mother-in-law for advice on how to divide the household work of the vicarage between only two servants—especially as her maid (presumably transplanted from the Hall) refused to take any part in the household work because she had always lived in good families. The servants they chose did not always please. "I have had such atrociously bad servants," Whittaker wrote in 1834, "that all the horses I have hitherto had, have been ruined by them, & I have been obliged to sell them at a dead loss"; the cook, Agnes, hardly paid any attention to directions, "She boils potatoes villainously,—as bad as a Yorkshire woman, & is extremely wasteful of every thing," and the christening of their latest child had been delayed "till we could have an artiste in the kitchen who can dress an eatable dinner."[74] The vicar's correspondence with his family was filled with such concerns about the ordering of the domestic world and about the status symbols being transmitted. As the possession of a carriage carried so much freight in bourgeois circles, it is not surprising to find him worrying about whether he should borrow money at interest from his mother to buy a horse and four-wheeled carriage—for the sake of his wife and growing family, and because he confessed to being unskilled, shortsighted, and accident-prone in handling an unstable gig—rather than from Blackburn lenders, since borrowing for such a "luxury" item might cause comment.[75]

Bourgeois families spent a good deal of time negotiating for the comforts of daily life and establishing and enhancing the status symbols fitting for their particular stratum in the bourgeois pyramid. One of the best examples is provided by Louisa Potter, who portrayed characters from her youth under disguised names. She described the movement toward gentility at "Maudesleys," a brick-fronted house cladding a black and white structure, set in a garden of immaculate gravel walks, flower beds, and a pond. "Mr. Weston" had a gig to travel to his warehouse in town, and the only other conveyance for the family was a heavy gig with a hood, drawn by old Smiler, who also carted coals. But with the advancement of prosperity, the gig was exchanged for an inside car, which made way for a green chariot, "and then the boundary was passed between respectability and gentility." Mrs. Weston had

a strong love for the genteel . . . and the old teas and suppers were put down with the gig, and dinner parties succeeded at the fashionable hour of five; and besides all this, there was a fire in the drawing-room every day, instead of only on Sundays. The first effort in the dinner line was rewarded by Mrs. Philips remarking loudly, when oyster-sauce was offered with her boiled turkey, "Well, I did not expect to have met with this here!" But Mrs. P. was a sour old widow, that would not have been asked, only she was related to the Philipses of the Park; so what she said did not signify. And Mrs. Weston lived all that down, for her dinners were capital. And as years went on, she in turn began to wonder who was visitable and who ought not to be noticed; and became so very difficult, that though the Bilberrys purchased silver corner-dishes for the purpose of conciliating her and getting her to dine with them, they could never accomplish it. I remember the drawing-room re-furnished three times—damask succeeding chintz, and satin, all the way from Paris, taking the place of damask; and in her old age, the best bed of brown and yellow print, with lions' heads at the corners, that had been a marvel of grandeur in its youth, was put aside for a piece of blue-and-white modern upholstery, for the very efficient reason, that at the sale of the furniture that must follow her death, "the old bed would look so shabby."

On the death of Mr. Weston—John the manservant was ever thereafter clothed in black, with a tuft on his shoulder—Mrs. Weston, because of reduced income, decided to leave Maudesleys. She took a house not far away, "and in a rather more genteel neighbourhood—a gentility that amply compensated for any grief she might feel at leaving the home of her life."[76]

Such conspicuous consumption in the pursuit of gentility created a world of meanings for the individual and broadcast a claim for the true worth of oneself and one's family to be acknowledged. Tea parties, card-leaving, and dinners at home marked out boundaries, established and reaffirmed circles of connections and put on show domestic interiors to other members of the same class. The architecture of the home (such as the encasing of the old black and white with fashionable brick) made a public statement, while the private works of art decorating the interior could be used to impress guests, by advertising the collector's taste and refinement. We have observed (Chapter 8) the sporadic uses of art in public; these exhibitions were largely made up of the collections—often quite extensive—of the local elite. A partial listing of "valuable" and "fine" collections includes those of Henry Paul Fleetwood of Woodfold Park, banker (antiques, prints, and books, as well as paintings),[77] John Hargreaves of Broad Oak, calico printer, Frederick Steiner of Hyndburn House, calico printer and dyer,[78] Richard Newsham of Preston, banker, Thomas Birchall Jr. of Ribbleton Hall, attorney, the Pedders of Ashton Lodge, bankers, Col. Rawstorne of Penwortham Priory (noted for his modern statues from the studio of Canova),[79] and William and Joseph Feilden, who had art galleries at Feniscowles Hall and Witton House.[80] Three other industrialists ranked among Lancashire's foremost collectors and patrons of modern British art. *The Art Union* described Benjamin Hick, Bolton ironfounder, on his death in 1842, as "a patron of Art in the true sense of the word; encouraging genius and artistic worth wherever he found it; and his loss will be much felt by a number of artists of the present day, with whom he was on terms of intimacy."[81] He especially supported Henry Liverseege: he "not only bought his pictures himself, but induced his friends to do the same"—including fellow Boltonian ironfounders Peter Rothwell and Benjamin Dobson. "'He is my best friend', said the grateful Artist with emotion. . . . Give honour where honour is due, and Bolton has the undoubted honour of supporting the genius of Liverseege and of rendering the path towards fame comparatively an easy and pleasant one."[82] The two other noted British-art collectors and patrons were William Bashall of Farington, a partner in Bashall and Boardman, manufacturers, and Thomas Miller Jr., Preston cotton lord.[83] Miller's "gallery of paintings by modern artists," his obituarist wrote in 1865, "is one of the best selected and most valuable in the kingdom."[84] This included seven works by William Powell Frith (one of which, "The Old Woman Accused of Witchcraft," cost him five hundred guineas in 1848). Frith recorded in his autobiography, "An intimacy such as frequently exists between artist and patron, arose between Mr. Miller and me. I spent many happy hours with him at Preston. He was one of the truest gentlemen and the warmest friend of art for art's sake, that I have ever known."[85]

It would be unfair to say that art was simply a vehicle to impress the neighbors, or a good investment, or a thin veneer over rough-edged philistinism. It could be all of these, but it also could involve an expression or a search for a personal identity. The depictions of the British landscape, of English history, of pathos, sentimentality, and religiosity often couched in wildly idealized medieval-chivalric forms, the dominant themes in the collections of Hick, Bashall, and Miller, point clearly enough to a saccharine sense of pride in the nation's moral superiority.[86] The same might be said of the much more mundane paintings gracing the walls of Red Scar, the home of William Cross, Preston attorney—a farmhouse that he bought in 1803 because of its beauty and converted into a fine mansion. A list of the pictures, date unspecified, details over a hundred paintings or prints, largely portraits (of family and friends, George III and IV, eminent judges like Lord Eldon), landscapes (cattle, cottages, Wales, Red Scar, and Browsholme being among the items), and religious themes (The Last Supper, The Crucifixion, and two prints of Gloucester Cathedral bringing together religion, Gothic architecture, and the scenic).[87] He loved scenery. "He had a thorough love for whatever was *Beautiful*. For example he could not help loving pure Gothic Architecture because it comes nearer to *Beauty* than any other style."[88] Here was one ordering of a personal world around the familiar icons of a religious romanticism; he incorporated into his home reminders of all that he felt important to him: family, leaders he admired, the beauties of the divine and of nature—nature trapped on canvas and tamed in domestic space.

There is a more significant sense in which the home "tamed": the process of silent socialization—the muted messages and the trivial routines ingraining a particular patterning of private life and making it seem entirely natural, commonsensical, and incontrovertible.[89] Different color schemes and furniture in boys' and girls' rooms; gender-specific toys; the segregation of masculine space—the study, with its muted colors, ordered rows of books, and distinctly masculine air of mahogany and leather; mirrors dotted around the house to observe better the dignity and decorum of one's posture; dinner tables with their straight-backed chairs and elaborate rules of seating and of etiquette: all contributed to that sense of disciplined identity, presence, standing, rank, and class. This internalization of self-control of the body—of gestures, posture, speech-patterns—was inculcated during the first few years of life, which made it very much more difficult for those clambering a considerable distance up the social scale to adapt their comportment to suit their new station.

Catherine Jacson addressed one aspect of this domestic socialization in describing her transition from childhood to young girlhood at about the age of thirteen:

It is no longer the wondering, all believing, all revering little unit of a pigmy size to be lifted up and kissed, to be tormented with puzzles, teazed [*sic*] or petted, to be led by the hand, and seated on the knee; it is the little girl to be shaken hands with, to be addressed with a few patronizing words, and passed over. Romps are no longer quite legitimate. The three children are no longer to be classed together as "the boys." It is a question now of carriage and demeanour.

Though she claimed that her case was somewhat different, because she was the youngest, was brought up with boys, and came from a life of travels, this is how she described children brought up in "Society":

The girls are dressed as little women, and are admitted to the evening drawing-room, where they hear "Society" conversation—of "parentage and birth, who danced with whom, and who are like to wed"—if not of things worse, scandals and disgraces. It commonly becomes their ambition to take their part in the drama, and win their share of the social prizes.[90]

Another aspect was the management of time in the bourgeois household. There is a paradox here. Increased wealth promised more free time, even in the more rigidly time-bound society that is the fruit of urbanization and industrialization:[91] time for the pursuit of leisure and travel, as we shall see; time to languish through "delicious do-nothing days"[92] or indulge in undemanding self-cultivation. "Bolton is proverbially dull just now," wrote Alice Ainsworth in May 1816, describing life at Moss Bank, "but it affords us plenty of time for all our country employments of walking & gardening and reading. We are abundantly supplied with books from our french [sic] and English clubs & I have been fortunate in procuring drawings to copy so that our time is fully occupied."[93] And time for a mélange of gardening (or at least enjoying the fruits of the garden), entertaining, study, and the pursuit of public duty, as the mayor of Bolton, Robert Heywood, described it in 1840 in a letter to a relative living in the United States:

I continue to live in the same house one that we built on the Manch[r] road near top of the Heights about 15 years ago large enough you will think for a bachelor when I tell you there are seven bed rooms. I have also the garden well stocked with fruit trees, a stream flowing through it with a fountain and fish ponds, also a hot and green house furnishing me with grapes and flowers, the latter occasionally brought down and placed in my parlour windows. There is a cottage for the gardener and also a room where I have occasionally tea parties during the summer. This with a good library, organ &c. and a good deal of public business which has latterly been considerably augmented by the appointment to the office of Mayor you will readily suppose fill up my time pretty well.[94]

Yet the clock punctuated the bourgeois day.[95] Fixed times for household prayers and family meals complemented the silent socialization, the inculcation of orderly norms of self-rule. The timing of the dinner hour and the very frequent dinner parties broadcast social messages: each family tended to fix a regular hour, generally in the middle of the afternoon, distinct from the workers' noon dinner hour and the aristocratic early-evening meal. But there were many different shadings depending on claims to gentility—as we have seen with the "Westons"—and increasingly from the 1840s both middle and upper classes imitated Queen Victoria's preference for eating later in the evening, which tended to suit middle-class business or professional schedules better.[96] The Heywood and Ainsworth Papers have repeated instances of experimentation with different dining hours as the families sought to balance between practicality and fashion. In the quest for self-order, self-regulation, self-policing, the siren call of genteel status once again played in counterpoint to the call to seriousness and strict accountability for one's time before the world and before God.

Bourgeois Leisure and Travel

Beyond domestic time and space, free time and surplus income allowed members of the bourgeoisie to travel and to go on vacation. The late-eighteenth century was the first time that they began to take to the seaside in any numbers. At the turn of the century the *Blackburn Mail* regularly indicated in the summer months the names of the fashionable families who had, that week, arrived in Blackpool. The names included various members of the Peel, Potter, Birley, Cardwell, Sudell, Rawstorne, Clayton, Parker, Markland, and Clifton families, representatives of all forms of bourgeois and lesser-gentry money.[97] The mixed society at the fashionable resort was another means for status to be claimed and contacts to be made. While Blackpool was the smartest—Whittle explained in 1831 that the company at Lytham was usually very select and respectable, if not as fashionable as at Blackpool—members of the Lancashire bourgeoisie patronized a number of embryo resorts along the shoreline. Some built for themselves. Edward Pedder of the Preston banking family built Bispham Lodge as a holiday home in 1790. Whittle in 1831 wrote of the pretty cottage of William Rawstorne, Preston attorney, and of Hornby's Chinese cottage at Lytham, as well as the cottage near Mount Pleasant, Blackpool, of John Greenwood of Preston.[98] William Henry Hornby took over the family mills in Blackburn while still young because his father, John, retired to the seaside home at Raikes, Blackpool.[99] James Eden, partner with Joseph Thwaites at Waters Meeting bleachworks, Sharples, built Fair Lawn, Lytham, in the late 1840s.[100] Others just came and rented for vacations. To give but a few prominent examples, the Formbys spent summers as tenants of Rawstorne at Lytham Cottage in the thirties, and there Catherine Formby met Charles Roger Jacson, her future husband, the Jacsons of Barton renting the next house.[101] William Cross and his family used to spend a week or two at a time at Southport.[102] In 1820 the Whitakers of Roe Field rented, through Dr. William St. Clare, a cottage at Lytham for a month, and they apparently stayed there again the following year.[103] In June 1834 Mary Whittaker went to Blackpool with the children and took a cottage on the beach, while the vicar remained at home working.[104] The intermarried Fletcher-Watkins-Langshaw family, coalowners, landowners, and lawyers from the southwest of Bolton, from time to time vacationed in Poulton-le-Sands.[105]

The countryside was a popular alternative to the sea air. For some the attraction was less the wonders of nature than the pleasure of killing sentient creatures. Thomas Bonsor Crompton, for example, Farnworth papermaker, cotton spinner, and London newspaper proprietor, unwound by shooting grouse on his own moors in the Highlands and at Saddleworth.[106] On occasion male members of the Hornby, Whitaker, Ridgway, Peel, and Fort families, among other local notables, joined James Lomax of Clayton Hall and his pack of otter-hounds along north and east Lancashire rivers—and displayed considerable cruelty in the process: "[T]he hounds worried [the otter] to the great pleasure and satisfaction of a number of sportsmen," runs a typical entry in Lomax's diary.[107] But these were minority and exclusively male tastes. Sojourns in the countryside more frequently sought out "the scenic"—Catherine Formby's description of the new world she discovered in the summer of 1836 during a long vacation at a house of some relatives in the hills near Penmaenmawr, North Wales.[108] Nelly Weeton described her feelings on ascending the Lakeland peak of Fairfield in 1810 in conventional terms of awe. "A fine, noble, lofty, rugged mountain," she explained, "has far more charms for me than a fine, formal, artificial walk in a garden or pleasure-ground."[109] Alice Ainsworth of the bleaching family, around 1821, enjoyed both a very happy stay at Blackpool and a five-week vacation exploring the beautiful countryside around Leamington, the romantic beauties of Hawkstone, and so on.[110]

Excursions—slow and winding journeys through scenic countryside connecting places of cultural interest—were increasingly favored during this period. Descriptions of these were similarly nearly always couched in a fashionable language lifted from the romantic writers, theorists of the picturesque, and marvelers at the poetry and power of nature. The romantic idiom captured, in varying degrees, an emotional freedom from the greater organization of town and country, combined with the Christian reminder of the impermanence of human life.[111] The Rev. James Slade, vicar of Bolton, traveled down the Wye valley in May 1824. He found Ludlow castle "majestic," the view of the Wye at Ross "enchanting," the setting sun between Newnham and Gloucester a sight of "greater beauty and sublimity than can possibly be imagined": "We were quite overcome with the splendid and awful spectacle." But Tintern Abbey was disappointing, not rising to the expectations of its advance publicity: "Upon the whole it may certainly be called a fine ruin, but there is nothing about it of the splendid, the awful, or the sublime."[112]

During his tour of North Wales in 1790 with his father and a friend, William Cross reveled in the "romantic," "picturesque" scenery and the "noble" ruins and admired the mansions of gentlemen. But like many another reflective tourist, he compared and contrasted and found much wanting. The people were civil, deferential, and attended church regularly; but they were poor because there was no trade except in Denbigh and Holywell; and few could speak English. Yet there was room for optimism. English was gaining ground, and "the People appeared to us to have lost their ancient Spirit together with their Indepency [*sic*] A happy Circumstance for all Parties."[113]

The early-nineteenth century was the first time members of the bourgeoisie traveled abroad in any numbers,[114] and they did so for any combination of stated reasons: rest and relaxation, predominantly; to stir the emotions by an encounter with sublime scenery; as a cultural odyssey through the layers of the history of civilization; for the sake of their health (Samuel Horrocks planned to travel to France in September 1814, for example, apparently to escape from London to improve his health[115]); to cut down on expenditure without losing face at home (the Formbys stayed in France from 1826 to 1829, mainly so that they could save enough to give Catherine's brothers a college education, as well as a knowledge of French[116]); and to gather whatever information might be useful for a businessman. In one case at least, commercial depression at home provided the leisure to travel: as a letter of introduction for Robert Heywood put it in 1826, "[I]l profite de l'état d'inactivité de notre place pour faire un voyage de plaisir."[117]

Laurence Rawstorne of Penwortham went on a grand tour of France, Italy, Switzerland, Germany, and the Netherlands in 1816-17, describing in his diary the "sublime" scenery, and the antiquities, statues, and pictures he visited en route. He was introduced at the French court, had an audience with the pope, visited Ferney (Voltaire's house) and Gibbon's house at Lausanne, took in Pompeii, traced recent battle sites from the Napoleonic Wars and classical battle sites and other scenery from descriptions in Livy, Virgil, and Pliny. His jottings reflected a typical medley of insight and prejudice, praise and denigration. On February 13, 1817, for example, he found the people of Rome "so much changed that one can scarcely suppose them to belong to the same soil as those of whom we read in the pages of Livy." This was the product, he noted three days earlier of the poor of Loreto, "of a bad government and the tyranny of the priesthood over a blind and bigoted race of people." In France he bemoaned the lack of gentlemen's seats similar to his own in Lancashire: "In France there is no intermediate class between the Lord and the peasant. There are consequently none of those villas with ornamented grounds which gives such a cheerfulness to an English scene."[118]

In 1819 the Rev. John William Whittaker, then a fellow at St. John's College, Cambridge, visited Paris and found much to admire (for example, "I find French cookery not amiss, and do not find their light wines disagree with me") and some to criticize, particularly aspects of Roman Catholicism and baroque architecture, both of which he despised. He traveled south toward Marseilles. In Tours he heard some excellent music in the noble Gothic cathedral, but found the priests "a wretched miserable people, too poor to support them-selves creditably in society, debarred from domestic enjoyments, unrespected by the mass of the people, & too ignorant to preserve the dignity & self-respect which the clerical character requires." In Nîmes he found the *maison carrée* exquisite, but the celebrated fountain nothing more than a huge piece of masonry "in the most despicable taste of the age of Louis 14th."[119] The Whittakers traveled to Paris on their honeymoon in 1825, and Mary, too, took very well to French cooking. They toured the sights and collections, Mary bought some hats, they visited the opera and the theater and went out to Père Lachaise cemetery, which they found sentimental and affected, but at least the view of Paris was superb, the atmosphere not polluted "with one particle of smoke:—very unlike my bishoprick at Blackburn!"[120]

Robert Heywood was among the best traveled of all the local bourgeoisie,[121] and from his diaries we can derive a detailed, day-by-day account of the delights and travails of overseas travel. The travails consisted of seasickness, slow and jostling journeys in diligences, poor-quality inns and bed bugs, fleas, mosquitoes, lengthened quarantine in a lazaretto near Constantinople, delays and obstructions at border crossings, problems with passports, and unfamiliar food (Avallon, May 7, 1826: "[M]ade a good supper of milk & bread boiled instead of a dinner of all sorts of rubbish. When I asked what to pay she said 10 sous but finding me english [*sic*] she doubled it still it was the cheapest and best meal I got in France"). None of these could detract significantly from the delights of social, cultural, and topographical exploration. In 1823 he visited Ireland, toured the sights of Dublin, Belfast, the Giant's Causeway and went hill-climbing near Killarney. In 1826 his grand Continental tour encompassed Paris, Switzerland, Italy, Germany, and Belgium. He was entranced by the grand, romantic scenery of the Alps and visited Lausanne and Ferney, as well as Waterloo. When he traveled to America in 1834, according to another letter of introduction, it was "with the view of making himself more intimately acquainted with the valuable social and scientific institutions of the United states [*sic*] as well as to visit the more remarkable scenery of your country."[122] True to his intention he visited not only the principal sights and scenery between Washington, Cincinnati, Toronto, and New York, but also penitentiaries, cotton and carpet factories at Lowell, and dry docks and prisons in Boston. He met President Andrew Jackson, and as a good Unitarian and liberal visited Dr. Channing, the celebrated Boston Unitarian writer and preacher, and made pilgrimages to the graves of Joseph Priestley and Benjamin Franklin.[123] With Charles James Darbishire in 1845 he traveled to Spain, Cairo (where they met Mehemet Ali), Constantinople, Venice, Vienna, Prague, Berlin, and Hamburg. For his honeymoon in the spring of 1848 he and his wife nonchalantly traveled through revolutionary Europe. This time his wife, Elizabeth, kept the travel record and was enthralled by Alpine scenery. Their trip included Paris, Rome, Pompeii, Vesuvius, Waterloo, and yet again Gibbon's house in Lausanne.[124]

This eclectic visual dipping into culture, scenery, and the practical (mills and penitentiaries), as well as seeking audiences with the high and mighty, was typical, following a well-trodden path crowded with historical and literary references but also throwing in a few items of interest to a Lancashire manufacturer, magistrate, and local politician. When Peter Horrocks recorded a trip to Scotland in his diary in 1810, he described both the scenery and a tour of the New Lanark Mills.[125] John Horrocks Ainsworth traveled in France, Switzerland, and Italy in 1820-21, noting literary reminders, toured the romantic scenery of Scotland with his family in 1819 (drawing on scenic references from Scott's novels) and of Wales in 1823, was back in France in 1824, went to Ireland in 1826 and to the Low Countries, Germany, and France in 1827 and honeymooned in Scotland in 1833. Like other British travelers, he was not interested solely in the scenery, arts, and architecture, but also in aspects of modern industrial, urban, or social infrastructure, in a sense combining the cultural pseudosophistication of the High Tourist with the inquisitiveness of a bleacher from Bolton. For example, in Paris in 1824 he visited water-purifying establishments, the Savonnerie carpet factory, and the Paris morgue, describing them all in his travel diary. On his way to Scotland for his honeymoon in 1833, he and his wife visited the gaol at Lancaster Castle, and he jotted in his diary details of the treadmill, looms, and cells.[126]

The Rev. Charles P. Wilbraham, a curate at Bolton Parish Church, derived from his travels confirmation of his faith and of the need of God's chosen people to spread it. After a visit to Palestine he delivered two lectures to point out how completely prophecies had been fulfilled and how wonderfully the present topography and state of the country corresponded with Biblical accounts (for instance, he and his companions pitched their tent next to the sweet fountain of the miracle of Elisha (II Kings 2:19)). He considered that the melancholy fate of the Jews (in Moses' words—Deuteronomy 28:66—"thy life shall hang in doubt before thee, and thou shalt fear day and night and shalt have none assurance of thy life") bore testimony to the truth of Christianity.[127] Around 1839, while in the army, he traveled throughout North America. In spite of a certain admiration for the native peoples ("Degraded though they be, yet they possess some of the virtues of savage life, and are in many points not unlike the Arabs of the Desert"), his travels revealed to him the distance between civilization and savagery, and the critical work that needed to be done for Christ and commerce to triumph:

Our own island has been, during so many thousand years, the abode of man, industry and ingenuity have been so busy in creating an artificial existence, that we turn with interest to those widely different scenes in the West, where yet the Indian savage hunts his prey—where yet the bark canoe glides over the waters of the great Lakes,—where yet the boundless trackless forest offers future homes for the overpeopled cities of Great Britain. . . . England has a great work to do, as a

Christian nation, to carry her Church and its ordinances to her remotest Colonies. Wherever she plants her flag, there also should she plant the Cross! Let her religion go hand-in-hand with her commerce, to spread civilization and happiness over the Western World.[128]

For all of these ladies and gentlemen, for whom money and leisure had opened up the opportunity to explore beyond domestic and local space (or, like Wilbraham, who traveled in their line of work) and to encounter different peoples and cultures, travel involved a statement or a subtle reordering of a congeries of forms of identity. They all, in their own way and across different shades of perception, explicitly or implicitly positioned themselves in relation to forms of national identity and historical time. Whether individuals toured Graeco-Roman relics, sought Biblical sites in Palestine, visited noble Gothic architecture or made pilgrimages to the homes or graves of Enlightenment figures like Voltaire, Gibbon, Franklin, and Priestley, they were appealing to the people and artifacts of the past as a way of anchoring a claim to a form of understanding of an unstable present. Combined with observations on favored or disfavored aspects of the culture of others, such as religious observance, technological progress, or domestic ideals, they were prescribing semi-contradictory visions of the future of the British nation: as the proud inheritor and expositor of a classical or a Gothic tradition, as a crusading state spreading the Word, as an industrial nation rapidly traversing the grooves of progress, as a democratic and rational polity, or as an exemplar of a country of contented, pious, and orderly families, hearths, and homes. Some of these were compatible, some not, jostling in confused and contradictory mixtures within the same individuals in that spectrum of tastes, ideals, and expressions that we call the bourgeoisie. They point to a diffuse and elusive form of Britishness measured against a broad variety of "otherness," and they hint that *all* forms of national or other identity, when examined closely, are much more diverse, contested, and fluid than outsiders or committed insiders might imagine or pretend.[129]

Let us end as we began, with Henry Ashworth, rural millowner and householder in the periphery of Bolton; liberal, Leaguer, and bourgeois crusader; proponent of the New Poor Law, opponent of short time; factory paternalist and disciplinarian, regulator of the morals, work time and domestic space of his operatives; a Quaker imbued with the cults of seriousness and domesticity who indulged in a genteel lifestyle at The Oaks and enjoyed shooting; pacifist and magistrate and foreign traveler. We have seen or shall see him in each of these guises and heard him marry quite happily progress, commerce, and industry with cultivation, refinement, and a taste for the fine arts. He had a clear vision of the nation that he wished to see, one reflective of the competing strands—all typical of different aspects of bourgeois ideologies—within his own character and worldview, and which he was able to compare with other nations in his foreign travels. Ashworth was a typical bourgeois in that he adhered to many of the different aspects of the patterning of bourgeois time and space that we have discussed in this chapter. He was also typical in harboring many of the contradictions within his own person. In ordering themselves, in grappling with a medley of cultures, the bourgeoisie displayed all the heterogeneity of approach and clash of solutions that they displayed in the ordering of others and of society at large.

CHAPTER 12: PEACETIME

During the campaign for the repeal of the Corn Laws, John Talbot Clifton of Clifton Hall, Lytham, who became Conservative MP for North Lancashire in 1844, wrote, "I think those who suppose, that on the settlement of this question [Repeal], agitation is to cease, are quite mistaken as Mr. Bright told me the other night (*Bless* him!!!!)—'We *will* have this and then go on for the rest.' What he means by the rest I don't know, except a republic of Quakers."[1] "The rest" for the radical-liberals who attended a tea party in Preston Corn Exchange in June 1848, chaired by John Goodair, millowner, and patronized by the town's two Liberal MPs, Sir George Strickland and Charles Pascoe Grenfell, meant representation for "the people"—a decisive refutation of Lord John Russell's declaration that the middle classes had no desire for reform—and support for the projected motion of Joseph Hume for franchise extension, the ballot, triennial parliaments, equal electoral districts, and retrenchment.[2] "The rest" for the *Preston Chronicle* in a New Year's editorial in 1850 signified a new party to institute a thorough revision of the whole system of national government; to uproot the remaining obnoxious feudal laws—primogeniture and entail, copyholds and absurd tenures, game laws, naval and military chieftainships, dishonest sinecures; to complete the reformation of the Church; to reduce the army and navy; and to promote science, trade, commerce, industry, and education without waiting to be coerced by outside agitation.[3]

This was to be a wholesale onslaught on the aristocratic state and the apparatus of Old Corruption. Such an agenda can be sewn together very neatly with the messianic vision of triumphant middle-class ideology in the statements of a number of local millowners in the late 1840s and 1850s. Alderman John Baynes, for example, a Blackburn manufacturer, liberal, and Evangelical Churchman, believed that,

THE MISSION OF THE COTTON TRADE is, to develop the resources of this nation—to multiply the springs of industry—to stimulate inventive genius—to encourage art and science—to increase profitably the employment of labour—to improve agriculture—to create large towns—to promote education—to elevate the moral and social status of the working population—to secure civil liberty—to confer political privileges—to check immorality—to encourage religion—to destroy monopolies—to give freedom to all—to enkindle a spirit of loyalty—to foster probity and honour—to discountenance war—to extinguish slavery—to promote peace—and to raise Britain to be the protector of the weak, the friend of the strong, a bright example to all nations, and the grand instrument for promoting the evangelization of the world.

In the missionary vanguard of God's Own Nation were the middle classes. Their rapid advance in wealth, power, and influence had brought about repeal of the Test and Corporation Acts, Catholic Emancipation, parliamentary reform, abolition of the slave trade, and municipal reform. During the rise of manufactures, when great immorality pervaded the upper strata and social and moral degradation the lower, the middle classes "were the salt which preserved society from falling to decay." They had created the large towns, necessary for the establishment of representative municipal government which kept centralizing national governments at bay, and allowed opportunities for the better municipal regulation and improved living conditions of concentrated populations. Towns and factories helped inculcate discipline, order, and regularity, all essential attributes of progress, civilization, and intellectual superiority: "No one need be reminded, how much more amenable to public opinion men are in cities than in remote hamlets; how much more easily are they brought under civilizing influences; and what superior advantages they possess for the improvement of their minds, and the acquisition of useful knowledge."[4]

Here was a classic statement of urban-industrial-bourgeois self-confidence, assured and didactic rather than defensive. But in spite of his sense of the middle class as "the salt which preserved society," Baynes did not advocate the full radical program. His attachment to the Church was later to take him into Tory ranks in protest at Gladstone's disestablishment of the Church of Ireland.[5] Nor were many others persuaded: after Repeal, the Manchester School radicals failed to mobilize the middle classes as an independent political force against the aristocratic-military complex. Support was sporadic for free trade in land, disestablishment of the Church, national nonsectarian education, further parliamentary reform, the Peace Society, and the abolition of the East India Company.[6] These items did not rank high on the local middle-class agenda.

On incorporation in 1851, the borough of Blackburn married peace and trade by adopting a coat of arms surmounted by a dove clasping the thread of a shuttle in its beak—a statement and a cliché of manufacturing pride and intent.[7] Baynes likewise trumpeted this familiar refrain that the two were an obvious match. But he had come to terms with the state and its military machine as the means to that end. In breaking up the feudal system in Russia, in bringing religious freedom to Turkey, and in producing considerable commercial advantages for Britain, the Crimean War had been utterly righteous.[8] In an ongoing, readily reversible process, other radical-liberals[9] had made their accommodation much sooner; for some the moment of truth came only with the bombing open of the port of Canton in 1857 by Sir John Bowring, formerly radical MP for Bolton. Alderman Henry Marriott Richardson, a Bolton attorney, argued in 1852 that he and his liberal colleagues "did not believe in the system which sent missionaries on deck and the implements of death in the hold; they believed that commerce, free and unrestricted trade, was the great harbinger of peace and civilization"; but, in supporting Bowring five years later, he was not for having England's flag insulted or disgraced.[10]

Back in 1849, Henry Ashworth wrote to Richard Cobden, "I think we have good and practical grounds for believing, that enlightened self interest, and the social reforms which proceed from the use of the steam Engine whether Stationary or Locomotive, will one day be found to overpower the vainglory of the red coated freebooter." Having said that, he recognized with disgust how even members of the radical-liberal bourgeoisie were discovering what their more conservative brethren had known all along: that the military-aristocratic state was perfectly compatible with the progress of capital.[11] As soon as foreigners threatened trading interests, "the first thing that crosses men's minds here is to set our 'Bull dogs' upon them. This reliance upon the Military has associated the Army & Navy with our industry;—a sort of wedlock has been recognised, and the unhallowed alliance has received too manifest a recognition by Manufacturers toasting, as Jno Potter [mayor of Manchester] did the other day The 'Army & Navy'!!" Again in 1852 he blushed for Manchester after a proposal for a commemorative horseback statue of the Duke of Wellington: "It is a desecration of Mill-got-money to subscribe it for any such unhallowed purpose."[12]

So much for a republic of radical Quakers. An alternative, perhaps more typical, image of the bourgeoisie in this period might instead be taken from the ceiling of Trinity Church in Blackburn. In 1846 Dr. Whittaker invited the local Anglican nobility, gentry, and gentlemen to pay for their shields to be painted onto ceiling panels down the nave, at the crossing, and in the transepts. Mingled with Church leaders, local baronets, local MPs, and the older families of gentry are the families of relatively new wealth from commerce, manufacturing, and the professions, inserted seamlessly into a timeless hierarchy, just as surely as their houses and halls slotted smoothly into the countryside without causing a rupture.[13]

Now, this might lend itself easily to a co-option thesis: the bourgeoisie was bought out—"feudalized"—and therefore failed to develop and to implement an independent bourgeois politics.[14] But this would be misleading. What is more interesting and important is not to suggest the victory of one image over the other, one depiction of the bourgeoisie over the next, but to stress the building of contrasting narratives, elaborated as we have seen (Chapter 1) during the war years: a narrative of accommodation under the broad mantle of Church, state, and the prevailing power structure, and a narrative defining itself in opposition to and seeking to supersede that power structure.

Postwar Politics

In the peacetime years after 1815, an insistent bourgeois oppositional voice continued to be heard. For example, the high sheriff, Robert Townley Parker of Cuerden Hall, chaired a county meeting at Preston court house in February 1817. Dr. Peter Crompton of Liverpool, a member of the Liverpool Concentric Society of gentlemen reformers,[15] and Dr. Taylor of Bolton, the radical Unitarian physician who was prominent in exposing the blackfaces in 1812, effectively hijacked proceedings by carrying (on a show of hands) an alternative address: "[T]he Administration of Affairs by your present Councellors [*sic*], has diffused through this Country a degree of Misery never before experienced."[16] This was the liberal-radical, dissenting (and disproportionately Dissenting), alternative face of the bourgeoisie.

It is difficult to tell how radical this opposition was. Home Office records in these years point to a number of committed reformers from the wealthier strata who were apparently prepared to go some distance in the risky business of supporting the radicals. For instance, a spy ("Mr. J. W.") sent Ralph Fletcher, the Bolton magistrate, the following information in January 1817:

Rigby afterwards met with Mr. Cunliff [*sic*] Banker of Blackburn and Mr. Turner Manufacturer, at his Brother-in-law's Mr. King's . . . Mr. Cunliff strongly advocated the Cause of Reform and Mr. Turner approved it—Mr. Cunliff said if all the Manufacturers would be of his Mind He would shut up his Banking House the Morning following—if they [*sic*] Manufacturers would shut up their warehouses and others would follow their Example they could bring things to a point before six weeks were over.[17]

In 1820 another of Fletcher's spies, "Alpha," infiltrated two small-scale gatherings of Bolton manufacturers and shopkeepers who had met to discuss the principles of reform. John Brandreth—presumably the same man whom Fletcher had kept under surveillance back in 1808 because of his antiwar activities—was present at both. So was his fellow Unitarian, Robert Heywood, quilting manufacturer and future mayor, who allegedly spoke of living "in a generation that would be as remarkable for its Political Changes as it had been for a false spirit of Military and Naval Glory."[18]

Fletcher's paranoia no doubt took refuge in the argument that a revolution was only likely to occur after an irreparable breach in the ranks of the propertied, and therefore it made sense to keep tabs on the potentially disaffected. But even if the reports were accurate, they were scarcely frightening enough to raise goose pimples on the flesh of the most zealous warrior among the forces of order. The alleged comments were no more seditious or subversive than the public expressions in the county meeting in Preston, or at a public meeting in Bolton Sessions Room in September 1816 to protest against crushing taxation and to call for parliamentary reform,[19] or at a post-Peterloo meeting in Bolton to express admiration for Henry Hunt and to denounce "those infamous ruffians" who had stamped on constitutional rights of assembly.[20] All this is clear evidence of links in personnel and ideas between wartime and peacetime liberal-radicals. But the bourgeois names are few, and W. A. Abram, a later Blackburn newspaper editor and local historian, was probably near the mark when he wrote that, during the postwar agitation, "The moderate reformers held rigidly aloof, foreseeing the evil and danger. The Pilkingtons, Eccles's, Turners, Haughtons, and a few other respectable families who were not reckoned as Pittites or Tories, were too cautious and cool to think of joining hands with the admirers of Harry Hunt."[21]

Across the political divide, the party of order found a rallying post in William Hulton of Hulton Park, whose stock rose precisely because he was one of the magistrates at Peterloo. In the election of 1820 there was a possibility that John Blackburne, one of the long-standing MPs for Lancashire, would retire, and Hulton seems to have been the principal Tory choice as a replacement. One requisition, signed by many of the big Tory names—the Fletchers (coal-owners) and Bollings (millowners) of Bolton, John Hornby (merchant) and Dixon Robinson (attorney) of Blackburn, James Greenway (millowner) of Darwen, and so on—appealed to him to offer himself, "In Times unexampled in the History of this Country," against candidates who "are hostile to the best Interests of Society and the great Safeguard of our Liberties, the British Constitution unimpaired." As it turned out, Blackburne continued to sit, but Hulton, in agreeing to stand whenever Blackburne retired, acknowledged how recent events had burnished his image as a defender of Toryism: "A period of national disquietude and alarm has made us intimately acquainted with each other. An identity of feeling has establish'd our mutual regard."[22]

Clearly this was a fractured local elite, building on the contrasting narratives molded during the wars. The Queen Caroline Affair of 1820 further pointed up the divisions. In Preston, the friends of the queen greeted the rejection of the Bill of Pains and Penalties by ringing bells, holding dinners, setting off fireworks, exhibiting transparencies, and staging a procession. The backstreets lit up en masse in a celebratory illumination, as did most dwellings in the Market Place, Church Street, Friargate, and Lord Street. But in Fishergate, Chapel Street, and Winckley Square the lighted houses were thinly scattered. It seems that while the majority of the shopkeepers—whether from conviction or sound business sense—lit up, the bulk of the most respectable inhabitants did not feel like celebrating. The mayor, aldermen, and capital burgesses of Preston sent loyal addresses of support to the king, as did some inhabitants of Blackburn.[23] The editor of the *Blackburn Mail* could not disguise the extensive nature of the celebrations and illumination in the town, but he took solace in the fact that "The whole of the respectable private houses with few exceptions, remained in total darkness."[24]

Preston poll-books give the best indication of how the bourgeoisie divided in the pre-Reform period. The Derby/corporation coalition held firm for over a decade after Waterloo, but Preston's wide franchise acted as a magnate for radicals and reformers seeking to break it and into Parliament, just as the Hanson brothers had tried in 1807 and 1812. Dr. Peter Crompton of Liverpool, the man who proposed the amended address to the Prince Regent, made the attempt in 1818. The sitting candidates, Samuel Horrocks and Edmund Hornby, saw off Crompton's challenge—but at a cost of £6,017 2s. in election expenses.[25]

The price tag in 1820 was considerably more inflated—£11,559 12s. 8d.— because of the severity of the struggle against two opposition candidates, John Williams, a reforming Whig barrister who successfully defended Queen Caroline against George IV's divorce attempt later in the year, and Henry Hunt. Williams, standing on a platform of triennial parliaments, seat redistribution, press freedom, and for an inquiry into the Peterloo Massacre, garnered influential support.[26] After a lengthy, disorderly, drink-sodden poll, and after cohorts of voters had been convinced, bribed, pressurized, or threatened with the sack, the coalition again emerged victorious.[27] An imperfect assessment of elite voting gives 97 votes for Horrocks, 82 for Hornby (81 voting a Horrocks-Hornby ticket), 43 for Williams, and 9 for Hunt.[28] This probably overestimates the opposition's share, since elite votes tended to be concentrated toward the end of the poll to increase the respectability of a candidate in the critical final days, meaning that if the losing candidate conceded defeat many gentlemen might go unpolled.[29] As one coalition supporter wrote just before the close, "a friend sent me word, *we* had Eleven Tallies of Staunch Votes in the Guild Hall, and that we had as yet little occasion for Broad Cloth, not the case with the Radicals."[30] Nevertheless, this was a substantial inroad into coalition strength.

If the coalition were failing to curb contests, expenditure, and turmoil, then its *raison d'être* had substantially diminished. The Derbyites apparently concluded during the 1820 election that it no longer benefited them, and so they abandoned it; at the 1826 election the Hon. Edward Geoffrey Smith Stanley, son of the thirteenth earl, future fourteenth earl and prime minister, nephew of Hornby, stood independently.[31] With Samuel Horrocks deciding to stand down and his son declining to take his place, the corporation gave up overt interference in electioneering. Capt. Robert Barrie, RN, put up for the Tories, John Wood, a Liverpool barrister and a scion of Cross Street Unitarian Chapel in Manchester, with influential support from John Edward Taylor of the *Manchester Guardian*, for the "independent and reforming" Whigs, and

William Cobbett for the radicals. Freed from the coalition's restraints, Stanley's committee favored Wood over Barrie (despite protests from Horrocks), presumably because of a greater ideological convergence between Whiggery and moderate reform. Barrie's committee took aim mostly at Wood, finding a ready target in his Unitarianism ("a man who denies his Saviour," claimed one Barrie supporter, "is . . . no better than a Jew"). Barrie's refusal to pledge greater civil rights for Nonconformists prompted Dissenting ministers to issue an address urging their coreligionists to support Stanley or Wood.[32] Cobbett reserved most of his withering scorn for those who supported the cockfighting, horse-racing Stanleys; they were like the slaves of "haughty and insolent" Roman nobles, "who, while they fed them, like dogs, on offal and on garbage, instituted shows and games to amuse them."[33] Stanley and Wood won, even though the urban gentry and professional elite and much of the mercantile elite supported Stanley and Barrie as the unofficial heirs of the old coalition factions: 128 of them voted for Stanley, 91 for Barrie, 41 for Wood, 5 for Cobbett (including 86 splits for Barrie and Stanley, and 39 for Wood and Stanley).[34]

The election had been expensive and violent, the unpleasant price for such a periodic display of popular legitimation. While different factions of the elite needed, sanctioned, and attempted to choreograph crowd activities—for elections, loyal demonstrations, Reform rallies—crowds could act independently from the start or acquire lives of their own or work to the advantage of other elite interests. Then a crowd became "the mob" or "the rabble," its violence perverse and unacceptable.[35] Claims and counterclaims for urban space, necessary permissions balanced by attempted curtailments and restrictions, found particular expression in Preston after the 1826 election. Since their candidate had lost, Barrie's supporters considered petitioning for the election to be set aside, claiming that the partisans and bludgeon men of Wood and Cobbett had conspired to prevent his voters having access to the poll. Legal opinion was discouraging: since in populous places elections were always accompanied by great excitement and generally by tumult—an acceptable level of violence—the Tories would have to demonstrate that violence was so excessive that men of firmness and courage were deterred from voting. This was difficult to prove.[36] Attempts to regulate the mode of conducting the election were more successful. Both sides favored this as a way to curb disorder, and so Stanley and Wood drew up a bill. But then the corporation opposed it in an attempt to revisit the controversy of 1768: whether Preston's franchise should include the inhabitants generally or only those householders who paid Scot and Lot (see Chapter 1). In dropping the bill, Stanley wrote, "With regard . . . to the only principle upon which the Corporation seem inclined to give their assistance, or withdraw their opposition, namely that of restricting the Elective Franchise, I must state at once, that, whatever I may think of the right of voting as an abstract question, I consider it one which is finally settled as respects Preston, and cannot consent to any Bill which has for its object to deprive the Voters of their rights."[37] In the event a general statute (9 Geo. IV c. 59), prescribing polling in compartments by voting district and reducing the maximum length of the poll from fifteen to eight days, accomplished the main objectives of the Stanley-Wood measure. William Cross of Red Scar, a Barrie supporter, did however caution against the possible consequences of this: "In providing for voting by Booths &c, care must be taken not thereby to lessen the expense so much as to make it easy for every Demagogue to try the experiment of a Contest—In the present constitution of Preston, the Expense of an Election is one great Bar to such attempts—almost the only one."[38]

Members of the elite, if they moved carefully, and if they kept their internal divisions in check, almost always had the upper hand, whether in the interpretation of the franchise, in influencing their workers' voting patterns, in using their power as consumers to patronize selectively and punitively,[39] or in having the financial resources to sustain a long and expensive electoral contest. But things could go awry, as happened in the by-election of 1830. Stanley and Wood had been elected in the summer with the usual measure of largesse displayed at Derby-owned hostelries about town and with at least a measure of collusion between the two parties. Henry Hunt trailed in third. But Stanley was appointed chief secretary for Ireland by the Grey administration and so stood for reelection. Hunt stood against him but did not put in an appearance before the polling began, and therefore the Whigs overconfidently failed to canvass, to rally the factory votes or to resort to the customary bacchanalian bribery. The Tories, including the editor of the *Preston Pilot*, were apparently sufficiently disgruntled at Stanley's pro-Reform stance to deny him their support and may even have given covert financial assistance to the Huntites. The radical vote was better organized than in the general election, the radical committee had the active backing of a spinners' union seeking revenge for those of its members sacked for voting for Hunt, and the entire cause was buoyed by enthusiasm for the July Revolution in France.[40] In addition there was considerable electoral malpractice—the final vote tally came to more than the entire eligible electorate for the borough—and anecdotal evidence suggests this favored Hunt over Stanley.[41] Hunt won by 3,730 votes to 3,392. The elite was trounced: voters in leading occupations polled 255 for Stanley and only 21 for Hunt, demonstrating that even voting together for a single favored candidate was not enough to ward off danger.[42] The radical potential of such a wide-electorate borough was finally achieved at the eleventh hour before the Great Reform Act attempted to legislate against such possibilities and to restrict the legitimate national public sphere to responsible ten-pounders.[43]

Parliamentary Reform

The Reform Bill was by no means carried on a wave of bourgeois demand. Radical Unitarians and "reforming Whigs" had certainly pressed their claims; postwar events, electoral contests (in Preston), vestry battles against Church rates, the repeal of the Test and Corporation Acts, and Catholic Emancipation—all had kept partisan and sectarian rivalries charged: but still bourgeois expressions of conservatism in the three towns preponderated over reformist statements. Only after political conjuncture and contingency—the split in Tory ranks over Emancipation, the aftershocks of the July Revolution, and the Swing riots—generated a crisis of governability and enabled a Whig government to place moderate Reform on the agenda did it garner widespread bourgeois support.[44]

"Gods! what a change!!" was one correspondent's reaction to a Reform meeting in Blackburn in February 1831. "The Catholic Priest, the Protestant Vicar, and Dissenting Minister, and Doctors and Lawyers, with their late-iron-bound, treason-charged, gaol-imprisoned neighbours, join in harmonious hosannas to the GENIUS of REFORM!!!" He was referring to the Tory vicar, Dr. Whittaker (who favored Reform "as a means of doing away with those abuses which a lapse of time had introduced into our institutions, and of restoring them to their pristine beauty") teaming up with Banister Eccles, Congregationalist millowner, William Eccles, Methodist attorney, and the Rev. J. Sharples, Catholic priest, behind a pro-Reform petition—and then agreeing to a resolution for the ballot as a way of heading off a radical challenge from George Dewhurst, reedmaker, once imprisoned for sedition.[45] Here elite orchestration, seeking to incorporate a wider constituency into a controlled and moderate measure of Reform, worked, but only because of an element of flexibility.

Similar meetings in Bolton and Preston were not quite so successful. In Bolton, Peter Ainsworth, Anglican bleacher, stated that the organizers had framed the resolutions to accommodate the wishes of gentlemen of different opinions. William Naisby, radical draper, "felt proud to be placed by the side of so many respectable gentlemen, who never were reformers before," and the meeting voted unanimously for the advertised resolutions: that the Commons did not fairly represent the people, property, or intelligence of the nation, and that Bolton ought to have MPs. But Naisby, the Unitarian minister Franklin Baker, and others, pushed the meeting further and carried majorities for the ballot and to extend the suffrage to all those liable for militia service.[46] In the meeting at Preston, chaired by Thomas Batty Addison, the radicals Joseph Livesey and Robert Segar sought to hold the line behind the limited reform on offer, in spite of their own wish for something more advanced. But Joseph Mitchell, Liverpool draper and radical journalist, and John Johnston, a once-imprisoned radical tailor, the leading members of Henry Hunt's committee, won a vote for "'such reform as would secure to the labouring classes the full wages of their labour for the use of themselves and their families'."[47]

The debates revealed that the milltowns broadly favored Reform, whether moderate or radical. At the cautious end of the spectrum, Reform promised a greater say to manufacturing industry: "[I]f there be a body of men in the Empire," said James Hardcastle, bleacher, at the Bolton meeting, "who have a right more than any other to demand the right of representation, that body is the manufacturers."[48] As William Bolling, Bolton Tory-Anglican cotton lord, put it more fully the following year,

The members for manufacturing towns would all go as a body, and upon a very different footing to that of all former members of Parliament. He hoped that all towns would send at least one person in trade, such persons, representatives from Manchester, Bolton, Glasgow, and all other important towns, would meet from time to time, and would deliberate upon matters of trade, and co-operate with each other. They would be such a body as were never known in Parliament before:—but if a gentleman had to represent manufacturing interests, who was not himself connected with trade, and was unacquainted with manufactures, the probability was, that he would do more harm than good, from his ignorance of the subject; but if persons connected with trade and manufactures were sent, one would get up after another when matters of that nature were under discussion, and the subject would be rendered so clear and there would be such a powerful combination of practical knowledge, that no ministers could successfully resist it.[49]

Even the *Preston Pilot*, the most conservative editorial voice, while aghast at the bills proposed by the government, advocated representation for large towns "ever since the fatal breaking in upon the constitution"—the ultra-Tory response to a boroughmongering system that had delivered up Catholic Emancipation in defiance of public opinion.[50] The *Preston Chronicle* claimed in October 1831 that three of the four barristers in town, a large number of the (Tory-Anglican) corporation, one or more partners in all the large manufacturing establishments, and a great number of the higher ranks of society had signed a petition to the Lords to pass the bill. The town, it said, was divided between supporters of the bill and partisans of a more extensive measure; the "no-reformers" were too small to merit consideration.[51]

The problem for Reform leaders was how to restrain the eager without losing the timid and to mobilize popular opinion to the minimum necessary to persuade the recalcitrant at Westminster. This was especially difficult in Preston because its new MP, Henry Hunt, and his supporters opposed any half-measured reform. One solution was to raise the specter of civil war if the Lords did not back down or if "the people" were divided. For example, at a public meeting in October 1831 Thomas Batty Addison and Richard Arrowsmith, banker, appealed to the top, in moving that the king take energetic measures to indicate his firm commitment to Reform, so that all occasion for violence could be removed. Robert Segar appealed to the crowd:

> If they had wives and children whom they loved, at such an awful crisis they might see them destroyed before their eyes;—the industrious shuttle would be silenced,—their houses would be levelled with the dust,—their fields laid waste—the whole country whelmed [*sic*] in misery and ruin—and the end would be the utter loss of all our liberties, and the establishment of a despotism which those degraded by its operation would struggle in vain to overcome. (Cheers). This would not occur if the people were determined to be unanimous.

But a large majority rejected the motion for the creation of peers in favor of a resolution for annual parliaments, universal suffrage, and the ballot. A Huntite leader named Taylor called the moderate reformers' bluff:

> What the ten-pounders said about bloodshed and riot, if the Bill did not pass, was nothing but a pack of heaped-up lies and faction. (Cheers.) Would the lower orders favour such a measure? When they had nothing to defend by supporting it, was it likely they would run the risk of being shot, or hung, or transported, all for another man's gain? (Cheers.) The ten-pound system might do some good in Liverpool, but in Preston, and in small towns where rents were low, it would not do. It might destroy the boroughmongering faction, but it would create another. (Cheers.)[52]

This prefigured later divisions and attempts at reconciliation in the ranks of a "popular front" of liberal and radical reformers. The rhetoric of "the people" used by the bourgeois reformers propelled them, logically, to a more dramatic stance than they anticipated. Having whipped up the crowd pressure for Reform, having defined themselves as the people against the boroughmongers, having scythed through the propertied strata, when Grey's ministry fell and Wellington tried to form an administration in the heady "Days of May," 1832, they stared at a choice between ignominious retreat into the safety of property and order, or stepping into uncharted revolutionary terrain.

"The news in every part of the town was as the shock of an unexpected thunderbolt, and business became totally suspended," wrote one correspondent in Blackburn when news arrived of Grey's government's resignation; "looks of despondency in some, and desperation in others, were visible everywhere." John Trevor, the editor of the *Bolton Chronicle* called on "the people" to resist paying taxes; the king—one of a long line of "Fools, knaves, idiots, dotards" who had led the nation and led it badly—had betrayed them. Sending for Wellington, he had perhaps thrown himself into the arms of a military ruler, and "we now pray God that it may not produce results of the most direful description, probably involving a civil war, a total dissolution of society, anarchy, and all its attendant evils." During the following week

Trevor chaired a meeting to petition for the withholding of supplies; this allegedly gathered 20,304 signatures in two days.[53]

At another rally in Blackburn, a large crowd of the middle and working classes, reportedly headed by William Eccles and William Feilden, accompanied by a band and the Blackburn Political Union, converged on Blakeley Moor waving the tricolor and other flags.[54] In Preston, at a meeting in the Corn Exchange, Joseph Livesey moved an agreed resolution for household suffrage, the ballot, and short parliaments—an indication of a significant radicalization of the moderate position in the wake of the Lords' repudiation. This was still not far enough for the radicals, and Taylor successfully moved to substitute "universal suffrage" for "household suffrage."[55] The center ground seemed to be collapsing. When the meeting resumed the following evening in Chadwick's Orchard, Segar proclaimed that only agitation could prevent a mock reform, the Tory abolition of a handful of rotten boroughs, and the enfranchisement of some of the largest towns so as to "draw from the cause of reform the people of those places. They will then weaken the reformers—they will then act upon their old plans of dividing and conquering." To prevent that, "It is essentially necessary that men should know, see, and feel that their interests are bound together, the highest and the lowest, the rich and the poor, there ought to be no distinction of interest or of classes, but tax-eaters and tax-payers."[56]

By this stage the crisis was passing; the great strength of public opinion, as the *Bolton Chronicle* expressed it, had beaten the "Polignac Wellington."[57] As one small indication of the extent to which the government was drawing back from a precipice, Segar, a leading bourgeois, a barrister, said at this meeting in the Orchard, with Henry Hetherington of the *Poor Man's Guardian* on the same platform, that "if circumstances had not fortunately taken a turn, the country would have been thrown into such a state, that he himself, (as well as others,) would have in all probability by this time been with arms in their hands."[58]

The Great Reform Act instantly opened up a new political space in Blackburn and Bolton, and a spectrum of candidates who had supported Reform tried to exploit the lack of firm party constituencies, organization, or clear-cut local agendas. In Bolton, William Bolling, posing as an honest townsman above party, stood on a gradualist-reformist platform: economy in public expenditure, the lessening of restrictions on commerce, a revision in the Corn Laws, reforms in Church property and finances, the gradual abolition of slavery, and a parliamentary inquiry into the condition of handloom weavers.[59] But leading liberals were not deceived. Charles James Darbishire described a meeting in the Theatre where James Hardcastle "to our great entertainment" appeared as a friend and advocate of Bolling, "(who has issued a *reforming* address accepting the invitation)," and offered to answer any questions. To "his great horror I am sure," the Rev. Franklin Baker, the Unitarian minister, kept him on the rack for two hours. Hardcastle maintained that Bolling was a liberal reformer, "but he was so shuffling & lengthy in proving this that everybody was satisfied & when it was put to the meeting after this display whether Bolling was a fit person to represent us in parliament not one hand was held up for him but a storm of hisses & groans was raised which was with difficulty quelled—I never groan'd so heartily in my life."[60] Robert Heywood, in the draft of a letter, further pricked Bolling's pretensions. Bolling had a large commercial establishment and would of course exert himself "in promoting such measures as he thought likely to benefit *his order* as for instance repealing the duty upon raw cotton &c."; but what about interests other than those pertaining to "the cotton lords"? Would he support humane measures like the abolition of slavery, or Sadler's Time Bill, or any future Truck Bill? In his private character, Bolling dispensed alms freely; but as a preacher once put it, "Some of you (addressing his congregation) set yourselves up as being very good charitable sort of folks . . . while all the time you are busy screwing and screwing thousands of pounds out of the very heart's blood of the poor wretches in your employ." Heywood added, "How far this applies to the 'Townsman' I shall leave to be decided by those who have not yet forgotten the numerous altercations that have taken place between him and his work people."[61]

Standing against Bolling were three more credible reformers. The main moderate-liberal contender, Col. Robert Torrens, an officer in the marines, had developed a reputation as a leading political economist through his publications, his proprietorship of *The Globe* newspaper in London, and debate in Parliament. Although a frequent target of William Cobbett because of his military office, his pension, and his support for emigration ("the *transportation of the people*") as a means of economic relief, he was an enthusiast for political reform and advocated repeal of the Corn Laws, the abolition of tithes, and Poor Law reform.[62] John Ashton Yates, a Unitarian, favored a more radical program: an enlarged suffrage, the ballot, short parliaments, Repeal, reform of the Church to allow for the election of ministers, the abolition of all places and pensions, a reduction of the armed forces to pre-American War strength, the abolition of all monopolies, the opening of trade to India and China, impartial and free justice, the abolition of slavery, equitable taxation, repeal of the law of primogeniture, and a tax on absentee landlords. He was vulnerable to anti-"Unit" jibes in Bollingite broadsides: "The greatest objection to Mr. Yates," Darbishire regretted, "is his religious creed." William Eagle, a barrister and a Suffolk landowner, supported many similar radical policies. He had the active support of Cobbett but few local backers.[63]

Leading liberal-radicals rallied behind Torrens and Yates, while Bolling was clearly the preferred candidate of the wealthy, the conservative, and the Anglican. Any doubts must have been dispelled by his grand public entry into town a fortnight before the election. His open landau drawn by four grays was accompanied by fourteen carriages of gentlemen, a hundred gentlemen on horseback, Bolton's biggest industrialists—including James Hardcastle, Stephen Blair, and Thomas Ridgway, bleachers, John Cross and William Garnett Taylor, manufacturers, and John Fletcher, coalowner—along with their dragooned workforces, the Chelsea Pensioners, assorted handloom weavers, and the band of the Local Militia, all sporting more than six hundred flags and banners. When they had arrived at the Swan Hotel, 205 gentlemen, including the boroughreeves and constables of Great and Little Bolton and several clergymen and magistrates, tucked into a two hundred-pound baron of beef. Here, truly, was the united face of Bolton loyalism, anxious to secure a seat for their man and to control as much as possible of the new local political arena.[64]

Bolling and Torrens won the election. Even with the shopkeeper vote, the reformers had insufficient strength to gain both seats, and the conservatives were not prepared to put up two candidates and risk losing both. But, with the uncertainty over party labels and only one conservative candidate standing, "mixed" voting was substantial: 109 in leading occupations split for Torrens and Bolling, 42 plumped for Bolling, and 93 voted for some combination of Torrens, Yates, and Eagle (Table 7).

In Blackburn, radicals vested their hopes in Dr. John Bowring of London, Unitarian, philosophical radical and political economist, friend and onetime secretary of Jeremy Bentham, and editor of the *Westminster Review*. He stood for free trade, popular education, law reform, new modes of prison discipline, reform of the Poor Laws, universal suffrage, shortened parliaments and the ballot, the separation of church and state, antislavery, and economical government—a rigorously Benthamite program.[65] Bowring was the candidate of the *Blackburn Gazette*, of the crowd, of lower-middle-class radicals including George Dewhurst, reedmaker, Samuel Slater, chairmaker, and George Meikle, bookseller, and of bourgeois liberal-radicals like James Pilkington, Joseph Eccles (his Congregationalist nominators), and the Rev. James Sharples, the Catholic priest.[66] He faced three men who held home advantage. William Feilden of Feniscowles Hall, landowner and one of the town's most extensive millowners, had indicated his intention to stand as early as March 1831.[67] Like Bolling in Bolton he was Anglican and essentially conservative, but he pitched himself as a liberal reformer, for Repeal, against monopolies and lavish expenditure, for the abolition of slavery with compensation (his father-in-law had estates in Jamaica and was presumably a slaveowner), for the modification of tithes, for the extension of the suffrage as education increased,

TABLE 7

Bourgeois Voting in Bolton, 1832

	TB	TY	BY	BE	YE	T	B	Y	E
Attorney	12	1			1		4		
Banker	1						1		
Bleacher	8	2		1			4		
Boroughreeve							1		
Carrier[a]	1						1		
Clergyman	1	1					2		
Coalmaster	1						1		
Gentleman	13	16		1	2	3	8	4	
Ironfounder	7		2			2	2		
Land surveyor							1		
Machinemaker	1						1		
Manufacturer	21	35	2		6		5		1
Mfrg. chemist	2								
Minister		3							
Papermaker	1								
Physician	1								
Spinner	15	7	5	1	1	4	10		
Surgeon	10	4	1				1		
Totals	95	69	10	3	10	9	42	4	1

SOURCE: Brimelow, *Political and Parliamentary*, 156-92.

Key: T = Torrens; B = Bolling; Y = Yates; E = Eagle

[a] These were no ordinary "carriers" but members of the Hargreaves family, who in the firm of Hick Hargreaves were building up a railway-rolling-stock, cotton-spinning, iron-founding empire.

and even maybe for the ballot.[68] *The Globe* newspaper characterized him as "a man of considerable local influence, who has been much improved by the times and declares himself a vigorous reformer in state affairs, though he appears rather backward in denouncing the abuses of the church with which he is pretty intimately connected by family ties"[69]—his son-in-law was the vicar of Blackburn and his nephew the co-lessee with the archbishop of Canterbury of the rectory. In him, the Church, land, trade, and industry were conjoined. The second wealthy millowner to stand was William Turner of Mill Hill and Shrigley Hall in Cheshire, former high sheriff of Cheshire. His broadly Whiggish platform provoked a High-Church-and-Tory response in the guise of a third local candidate, John Fowden Hindle of Woodfold Hall, who had the backing of the *Blackburn Alfred* (an edition of the London *Alfred* spiced with a smattering of local news, begun in the summer of 1832 specifically to rally conservative opinion).[70]

The show of hands at the hustings favored Bowring and Turner, prompting Hindle to withdraw before the poll to increase Feilden's chances; as in Bolton, the conservatives did not have sufficient strength to return two candidates. The first day's polling put Feilden and Bowring ahead, but after a night of alleged furious vote-buying and collusion in the Feilden and Turner camps, the millowners emerged victorious by the end of the poll—Feilden 376, Turner 347, Bowring 334—precipitating a riot directed against the Old Bull, the conservative headquarters. Once elected, Feilden "never took any active part in any parliamentary measures," claimed Bowring, "or did anything to distinguish himself from the mass of mediocrities who, from local influence, or the possession of money, make their way into parliament," but at least "he was quite entitled to rank among respectable M.P.'s." Not so Turner, who "had absolutely NO recommendation whatever, but that he had wealth and was willing to spend it to obtain the HONOUR of a position which he was about as fitted to fill as to quadrate the circle, to calculate an eclipse, or to give a lecture on Plato."[71]

In Preston the election was rather different. The electorate was comparatively very large: only 736 ten-pounders, but 6,291 voters by ancient right, that is those who had the vote prior to the Reform Act and would retain it until they moved or died. This number would dwindle relatively rapidly in the following years, but until then lower-class voters needed to be "managed" by the elite as effectively as possible to avoid a repetition of the shocking election of Henry Hunt. Anecdotal evidence suggests that the pressurizing of workers was substantial. For example, one anonymous correspondent wrote in November of the previous year, "Sopose [sic] some of us had to ask work of Mr. Miller (who came to preston [sic] as a fancy weaver) he would if not too proud to give a civil answer, look in his book and find that we had voted for Hunt, which would be quite sufficient to settle the business; for no one was ever more tyranical [sic] in this respect than Miller."[72] The radicals could reply with intimidation, but the extravagance of their threats hints at a very unequal contest. A Huntite address to shopkeepers in the summer warned:

Beware how you insult the majesty of the people of Proud Preston. Think ye we shall suffer it with impunity? no, no. We will mark you by not dealing with you— we will mark you by publishing you, so that all may see your perverse folly, and laugh at your calamities, for your merchandize [sic] shall rot—your hands delicately withered for want of employ—your boasted privilege of being a ten-pounder will be exchanged for a parish pauper—your children vagabonds and beggars. Then beware. I say beware—the men of Preston have the power—depend upon it they will use it.

In the aftermath of the election, an address urging the ostracism of working-class voters who voted the wrong way reached extraordinarily vitriolic verbal heights:

[N]ever disgrace yourselves by ever sitting in the same company, avoid them as you would wild beasts, yea, laugh at their misery and rejoice if starvation was to separate their souls from their bodies: in all your unions and societies never let one of these vipers creep in, whatever their plea may be, either conscience, interest, or intimidation; they are a cowardly, beastly, grovelling set of bipeds, a disgrace to the name of man, and a curse to the country.[73]

Henry Hunt and a naval officer, Capt. John Forbes, acting in concert, led the radical forces in the election. A third candidate, Dr. Charles Crompton, son of the man who had tried to break the coalition in 1818, advocated a liberal-radical ticket of short parliaments, further franchise extension, free trade, and the separation of church and state. But the successful candidates were Henry Thomas Stanley, younger brother of Edward who had lost to Hunt in 1830, and another extensive local landowner, Peter Hesketh Fleetwood. Stanley, in the family Whig interest, and Fleetwood, nominally an independent but relying on conservative support, in some senses recreated the old coalition, and they won the election by a substantial margin, with Hunt and Forbes coming third and fourth. Crompton, the bourgeois-radical candidate, withdrew after trailing on the first day, which only served to polarize the electorate further.[74] Leading inhabitants voted overwhelmingly for the landowners: 235 for Fleetwood, 237 for Stanley—225 split for Stanley and Fleetwood—8 for Hunt, 8 for Crompton, and 5 for Forbes.[75]

Party Building

By keeping out the more radical candidates and electing a medley of leading landowners and millowners, conservatives and moderate liberals in all three boroughs could be relatively satisfied. Still, the candidates' rhetoric had been notably fluid, a number of them had stressed their "independence," and a generous proportion of voters had split their votes in a nonpartisan fashion. Independent voting by MPs and the electorate, however, was set to diminish.[76] The Reform Act accelerated the process of party building in two significant ways: by mandating uniform electoral registers and reducing the length of the poll, forcing parties to maintain a coherent organization between elections, rather than simply coming together shortly before the hustings; and, by increasing the element of "popular" election, reducing the ability of the executive to manipulate a band of loyal placemen behind any policy. Parties, to a greater extent, had to appeal to the people and, as John Phillips puts it, all this tended to substitute national political issues for the local and idiosyncratic, simplifying political choices and enhancing partisan behavior.[77] This process can be traced, in Appendix 4, by a sketch of party fortunes and election results in the three towns before mid-century and, here, by a consideration of the meaning and significance of party ideology.

In a bid to broaden their bases and to build their constituencies, what did the parties stand for, and how were the contrasting bourgeois narratives elaborated? The Tories, weak and demoralized in the aftermath of Reform, were the first to see the need to regroup around a resurrected and coherent ideology. As spelt out by the *Blackburn Alfred* early in 1833 this involved a few basic principles: an upholding of the legitimate prerogatives of the Crown; the protection of the Protestant religion against all innovation; the support of the rights of the aristocracy; strenuous opposition to universal suffrage, the ballot, annual parliaments, and repeal of the Corn Laws; a firm commitment to the union with Ireland; the backing of legislation designed to increase trade and commerce; and the preservation of England's honor.[78]

This was a clear enough agenda around which an elite-led party and institutional apparatus could mobilize, bolstered by the organs of the Tory press. As further electoral reform was not on the mainstream agenda, and the prerogatives of the Crown and of the Lords were not noticeably under siege, the initial focus could be quite heavily on the Church and in particular upon its nemesis, Irish Catholicism. Early in the reformed Parliament the *Blackburn Alfred* greeted the proposed reform of the Church of Ireland as a measure of spoliation, pregnant with danger for the Protestant cause: "We assert—and we take history as our guide—that the measure submitted to Parliament paves the way for the establishment of Popery in these realms; in fine, it is in substance, principle, and detail, nothing short of the policy of the Stuarts."[79] During the election campaign at the end of 1834, Lord Kenyon of Peel thought it time "to declare for real vital Christianity, or to let infidelity sweep away all moral restraints, every social tie, every domestic comfort. The battle is to be fought in and for Ireland." The king, "like his sainted father," had said "'I WILL DIE FIRST'," rather than sanction a partial extinction of Protestantism in Ireland: "WE WILL STAND BY OUR KING. We will not desert our GOD."[80]

One of the principal organizers of a coherent local conservative identity after 1832 was William Hulton. He was indelibly marked with the notoriety of August 16, 1819—"there goes old Peterloo," cried a hostile election crowd as late as 1841 as it spied him in the streets of Bolton[81]—and for Tories this continued to be one of his chief distinguishing features. Lord Althorp in the Commons unintentionally highlighted it in 1831 when, opposing an investigation into the conduct of magistrates during a riot in Winchester, he claimed that it was not comparable to the "unjustifiable" actions of the Peterloo magistrates. Hulton promptly resigned from the bench and engaged in a public exchange of letters with Althorp. He claimed he would do again the same as he had done in 1819; "If I neglected thus to act, I should have to witness a conflagration of the great manufacturing establishments I was bound by my oath to guard"; "What benefit may result to the Government from driving the friends of order from the Commission of the Peace remains to be proved." This martyrdom to the cause could only enhance Hulton's reputation with the party of order.[82]

Hulton, reconciled to Robert Peel following the betrayal over Catholic Emancipation, expressed at the end of 1834 his "fervent prayer, that you may be destined by the Almighty to save the country at the moment of peril." He also advised Peel to "Peep into the house at Knowsley," convinced that if Peel headed an administration Edward Stanley could be persuaded to desert the Whig cause and join him. This was an early indication of "the Derby dilly," the most important political defection of the decade, and Peel was not slow to solicit Stanley's support for his government.[83]

It was Hulton who initiated the South Lancashire Conservative Association in February 1833, partly in reaction to the radical political unions, and partly to provide a base for the Tories to bid for the county representation, lost in 1832.[84] This was the first in Lancashire, and others followed: a Conservative Society for the Northern Division, for example, formed in June 1835 at a very well-attended meeting of gentry and bourgeois notables chaired by Sir T. D. Hesketh of Rufford in the Assembly Room of the Bull Inn, Preston;[85] and the Blackburn Conservative Association, founded in February 1835 to unite the area's urban and rural Tory elites, with John Fowden Hindle as president and William Henry Hornby as vice president.[86]

This was at the elite level, and this was where conservative associationism was at its most effective. But to protect Protestant nation and constitution required more than elite support in the new era of institutionalized parties: it necessitated a reaching down the social scale to incorporate as large a following as possible, not only to forestall a Whig-liberal-radical monopolization of the electorate and those below, but also because of a genuine fear that the lower orders were being radicalized beyond redemption, lost to all notion of morality and subordination. This radical threat tied in directly with the threat of popery, since—as the *Bolton Chronicle* put it in November 1835—the Whigs and Irish demagogues had joined forces in a grand alliance of Irish papists and renegade Protestants in an attack on the Church at home and across the water. The formation of Operative Conservative Associations would help inoculate the masses against Whig and radical eloquence: "The fact is, that reason is resuming its sway, and the nobility, gentry, and other influential persons, are happily rousing their energies, and making common cause with the people, who have too long been left sacrifices to the pernicious and insidious unction poured upon them by rambling Demagogues."[87]

Blackburn and Bolton each established an OCA in November 1835, Preston in February 1836.[88] The Bolton OCA's first public dinner in June 1836, allegedly for 450 members, gave a fair indication of the kind of rhetoric and symbolism that induced an enthusiastic, alcohol-assisted response. Local notables graced the platform, exemplifying the message of a stable hierarchy. The dinner comprised, inevitably, roast beef and plum pudding. The royal arms and slogans like "Loyalty in the People" decorated the room. Amidst the toasts for the glorious constitution, members of the royal family, Tory leaders in church and state, and such illustrious local names as William Hulton, "'the father of Conservatism in South Lancashire'—(tremendous cheering)," there was a reiterated appeal to a certain reading of and appropriation of English history, an epic tale of struggle to prevent malign, disruptive forces toppling the marvelous edifice of the Protestant constitution.[89] "The conservative operative association was nothing more than a remodelling, a renewal of the old constitutional associations" of the 1790s, claimed the chairman, William Holt, "which were instituted to preserve the altar and the throne from the attacks of anarchists and revolutionists (*loud cheers*)." Then the danger came from radicals, now the powers of evil—Irish papists, supported by the treacherous handmaids of ruin, Dissenters and Whigs—were seeking to perform their task by way of an attack on the Church. The demon leading the charge could be personified in the figure of Daniel O'Connell. Philip Halliwell, a weaver, weaving together myth-history, racism, and anti-Catholicism, reached back to the persecution of the Lollards as proof that O'Connell, as a papist, could not be a friend to civil and religious liberty. O'Connell was laboring to destroy a constitution that conferred such inestimable benefits as a division of powers, a Church Establishment, trial by jury, and liberty of the press and of speech. But "was it, he asked, to be borne that the descendants of the heroes of Cressy, Agincourt, and Waterloo—the men who had conquered all Europe, was it to be tolerated, he repeated, that they should be insulted by a *pettifogging, bog-trotting beggar*—(tremendous cheering for some time)."[90]

Joseph Ridgway of Ridgmont, the Horwich bleacher, founded two OCAs at Blackrod and Horwich, closely associated with his family's works, in the summer of 1835. On the first anniversary of the Horwich OCA in August 1836, three hundred operatives led by a band processed to and from his mansion, cheered for Church, King, and Mrs. Ridgway, and sang the national anthem twice. At the ensuing dinner, which he chaired, Ridgway proclaimed, "I am a Conservative to the heart's core! . . . for a deep feeling of loyalty to my King—my Church—and my Country—(added Mr. Ridgway, with emotion and emphasis,) I will yield to no man breathing!" The toasts were interspersed with renditions of "O! the Roast of Old England," "When good King Arthur ruled this land," and—following a eulogy to William Hulton ("the truly staunch friend of Conservatism," and the "saviour of Manchester")—"The Fine Old English Gentleman."[91]

Crown, Church, Nation, and Constitution: the four points of the compass of conservatism: Pope, Roman Catholicism, Ireland, and Anarchy its antitheses. This was genuinely reactionary, accepting innovation and reform only insofar as they buttressed and strengthened the established institutions of the realm. "Liberal" economic nostrums were, of course, important elements in conservative administrations from Pitt through Liverpool to Peel;[92] but these did not have the same emotional and rhetorical power as the distinctly more "Tory" aspects of "liberal Toryism." As soon as the threat posed by papists and Church reformers receded in the late 1830s it was readily replaced in a hierarchy of horrors by a fear of revolution, and the rhetoric of reaction shifted emphasis. Take, for example, the speech of the Rev. John Bidgood Bennett, headmaster of Blackburn Grammar School, at the Blackburn OCA dinner in November 1839:

It is my opinion that a great portion of the lower classes of operatives in our manufacturing districts are democratic . . . Now sir if we take into view the constant flux of new population . . . the breaking up of the old framework of society, the dispersion of domestic circles, everyone left to his own resources, the consequent overflow of operatives, the reduction in wages, the poverty and discontent, the innumerable temptations to improvidence and vice with which they are beset, we need seek no further for the present condition of reckless desire for change and for the facility of political excitement presented to every agitator among these classes . . . Now sir for improving the perilous situation of this class it is the duty of every wealthy Conservative to contribute by his wealth and influence to the diffusion of Conservative principles . . . It is the duty of every operative Conservative to invite and encourage his poorer neighbour to become a member of our Association, to attend our reading room, and thereby learn to be content in that station of life to which providence has pleased to call him; he would thereby arm himself against the poisonous principles which are promulgated by those rabid and fanatical revolutionists who would raise themselves on the ruin of our altars and our houses.[93]

The vicar, Dr. Whittaker, on the same occasion thought—or hoped—that with the spread of Conservative Societies and OCAs, old English maxims, habits, morals, and wisdom were once more resuming their sway.[94] But just how many operatives this brand of rhetoric actually reached, and how consistently, are interesting questions. R. A. Sykes notes the unpromising material available in Bolton and southeast Lancashire for a Tory and radical rapprochement: the lack of conservative support for Ten Hours before the mid-1840s, the dominance of conservative mills with poor labor-relations records, and the memory of Tory anti-populism. Working-class support for the OCAs was consequently limited.[95] David Walsh has pointed out that operative conservatism was as susceptible to divisions over such issues as the Poor Law and

Repeal as elite conservatism. Elite-led, -managed, and -financed, it performed
the role of partisan elite cohesion just like any other party-based voluntary association, and if it incorporated any substantial numbers further down, it was
at the lower-middle-class level, those who clustered around the £10 divide and
who generally formed the major constituency of electoral radicalism. For the
registration this was significant; as a means of lowering the temperature of
Chartism, much less so.[96]

In the face of considerable local-elite support for Toryism, bourgeois-
radical crusaders were frequently discouraged by the "sad, uphill work" facing them (see Appendix 4) or the "desecration of Mill-got-money"—the selling out by members of the bourgeoisie to the aristocratic state, a betrayal of
class interests. Nevertheless, these gentlemen possessed an inner conviction
born of rational and Dissenting Christianity and a history of dissenting politics that they were on the side of Progress and History. They needed only to
cast their minds back a few years to remind themselves of this. As the Bolton
millowner Thomas Thomasson put it at the annual meeting of the Bolton Reform Association in August 1838, referring to the Peterloo massacre, "At that
time had a meeting like the present taken place, legal though their proceedings
were, they might have been dispersed by the military, hounded on by Tory
magistrates. The more active members might have been incarcerated in a Tory
dungeon, tried by a Tory jury, and sentenced to imprisonment or transportation by a Tory judge."[97] In the opinion of George Dewhurst at a municipal reform meeting in Blackburn in August 1835,

if the spirits of those departed Reformers who agitated in 1819, 1826, and 1830,
could be called from their graves they could not credit that this is the same country in which they then lived, amidst the terrors and oppression of Tory misrule.
(Cheers.) . . . It had been the fate of other nations to fight for their freedom, and
to lose it in the struggle; but happily the people of England have found out a different way. (Cheers.) They had a better weapon than the sword, and that weapon
was—public opinion. (Continued cheering.)[98]

The bourgeois radicals had relied on "public opinion" during the Reform
crisis, had defined the struggle as between taxeaters and taxpayers, idle drones
and workers, had rejected insinuations that once enfranchised they would
leave the lower classes behind.[99] After 1832 they sought to deliver on their
debts, ideals, and promises. The most sustained attempt to maintain the
popular front came in Bolton, largely through the agency of the small circle of
committed Dissenting bourgeois radicals and the *Bolton Free Press*. The
newspaper's first issue at the end of 1835 set out its stall in favor of further reform, the ballot, triennial parliaments, repeal of the Corn Laws, the reduction
of the standing army, reform of the Church and the Lords, and an all-round

reduction of aristocratic corruption and power: a full radical agenda. Aristocrats, it claimed—part of a sustained effort to displace a labor-capital confrontation and to reimagine the major faultline running between a popular front and the aristocracy—were "men born to consume and not to produce," men "who fatten in idleness on the hard earnings of industry."[100] These radicals founded the Bolton Reform Association in 1837 in order to organize the reform interest in a campaign for household suffrage, triennial parliaments, the ballot, national education, Repeal, and incorporation of the borough. Some of these prominent reformers—people like Thomas Thomasson and Charles James Darbishire—even came out in support of the Charter in the autumn of 1838.[101]

In Blackburn and Preston, with a smaller bourgeois-Nonconformist presence (particularly Unitarian and Quaker) and a stronger conservative predominance, the level of cooperation between popular radicals and bourgeois liberal-radicals was rather less. Still, "the people" were not unceremoniously dumped as soon as the union was consummated in 1832. The liberal-radical candidates in both towns attracted some bourgeois support; both towns achieved popular fronts over the question of municipal reform in 1835 (see Chapter 10). But overt bourgeois support for Chartism was apparently lacking. The papers were hostile. In Preston, only John Noble, the prosperous Catholic maltster, seems to have spoken out in favor of the Charter. Though he expressed some doubts about part of the program, he addressed the great Chartist demonstration on the moor in November 1838[102]—and we have noted (Chapter 10) that his colleagues tipped him off the aldermanic bench as a consequence.

In spite of the attempts at building a popular front, the alliance was noticeable as much for its ruptures as its cohesion. It confronted several problems and incompatibilities, some of which we have already encountered. One was the question of political economy. The *Bolton Free Press* recognized clearly enough in 1838 the mutual hostility of most workers and masters—the laborers seeing the capitalists reaping their rewards from the face-grinding toil of the poor, employers lumping the working classes as ignorant malcontents, least troublesome when wages were lowest. The paper's editor defended trades unions, but only as "great evils produced by that disordered state of the manufacturing and commercial system which has its origins in an aristocratic taxation." He insisted that

master and workmen unite together in order to get that load of bread taxes, and other enormous taxes from off their shoulders, and combinations would cease to present so alarming an appearance as they have lately done. . . . It is evident that the wider the breach between labour and capital, the greater is the strength of the Landowners' Union—the monster mother of all Trades Combinations.[103]

In the autumn of the following year he reaffirmed that "There is only one interest opposed to that of the people—the interest of the aristocracy"; but

Mr. Oastler and Mr. O'Connor have laboured most assiduously to make those men who live by the labour of their hands believe that their interests are opposed to those of the men who live by shopkeeping and manufacturing. Mr. O'Brien, with equal diligence and with equal success, has inculcated the mischievous doctrine, that the worst enemies of the men who live by wages are the men who live by profits.[104]

The radical-liberals who lived by profits also tended to back the New Poor Law, and the New Poor Law was a major tributary feeding Chartism. This factor did not make it any easier to negotiate a compromise between Chartist and bourgeois-reforming agendas.

The popular alliance also split over the question of tactics. Local liberals in power—even those who came closest to embracing Chartism—had little compunction in enforcing law and order by all the means they deemed necessary. In the Chartist meeting in the Bolton Theatre in September 1838, Charles James Darbishire voiced his support for extension of the suffrage, explicitly in fulfillment of the promise to the people at the time of the Reform Bill.[105] Within a year, as mayor, he had arrested two of his fellow speakers on that occasion, the working-class leaders George Lloyd and John Warden. The popular alliance was that fragile. After the rioting was put down, the *Bolton Free Press* wrote: "We believe that the Mayor, in common with the great majority of sincere and earnest Reformers, is of opinion that the suffrage ought to be extended to the labouring classes; but does it therefore follow, that he would not be as active and vigilant in repressing outrage and disturbance, as the most rabid Conservative?"[106]

If the arms of "the people" tended to point in different directions, who was to blame? Not only the "deluded multitudes," thought the *Bolton Free Press*, but also the indifferent middle classes: "What are Socialism and Physical-force Chartism but the antagonism which this indifference has engendered in the labouring masses, who, finding all hope from co-operation with those above them cut off, have commenced a determined course of action for themselves."[107] The bourgeois-radical solution was to try and resuscitate a semicomatose class-cooperation. Thomas Cullen, the mayor of Bolton, presided over one attempt to reunite the middle and working classes in a meeting in the Temperance Hall in February 1842, with resolutions intended to meet the Repealers and the Chartists halfway. In spite of speeches by a number of Chartists opposed to the Anti-Corn Law League, the audience fell into line behind those Chartist leaders who had helped to organize the event. One of them, J. Gillaspie, argued, "It was thought that the people were opposed to the capitalists. They were not so. All they wanted was, that the labour of the working man should be as sacred as the capital of the rich man." P. R. Arrowsmith, regretting that divisions had sprung up between the middle and working classes, now hoped "that they might make a common attack on the common enemy," the aristocracy, and that they would "meet again and again, and agitate, agitate, until every vestige of class legislation was erased from the statute book."[108]

Again the united front proved ephemeral. Again the ship foundered on the question of means. Such a delicate vessel could scarcely survive the Plug Plot unholed: many liberals sought the safety of the forces of order at the first signs of upheaval ("Men of property," the *Bolton Free Press* reminded its readers, "are of a timid disposition");[109] members of the middle classes sworn in as special constables could find themselves actively confronting their erstwhile allies; and the League, susceptible to charges of incitement, found itself on the defensive. Yet the *Free Press* was anxious that the timid should not retreat behind their mental moats but refortify their efforts:

The insurrection may be put down by the great physical force powers which the Government possesses: but a forced tranquillity of this description—a tranquillity, which on the approach of winter might again be broken—is a species of calm which no man who loves his country, and who cares one jot for the happiness of his fellow men, would wish to be the characteristic tranquillity of England. The condition of the people must be improved, and then all apprehension of further disturbances will naturally subside. A repeal of the Corn Laws, accompanied by an immediate rise of wages, of from 15 to 20 per cent, would tranquillise the country more effectually, than all the bayonets and bullets of all the soldiers in the British empire.[110]

Bourgeois Crusaders

Repeal of the Corn Laws ranked first in this prescription for tranquilizing the country. The Anti-Corn Law League framed its rhetoric in popular-front terms, positing a bourgeois-led, people-incorporating crusade against the "class legislation" of the aristocratic state. Protection was designed "for the selfish interests of a class against the great interests of society," John Bowring put it to the electors of Bolton in 1841; "WE DEMAND FREE TRADE, THE MAGNA CHARTA OF LABOUR."[111] The Repeal campaign mingled self-interest with political partisanship and moral fervor: self-interest in that the large millowners considered cheaper bread and extended markets economically beneficial; partisan rivalry in that it served as a rallying cry for the Nonconformist and liberal interest, discomfited and divided Tory manufacturers,[112] and aimed at incorporating swathes of the lower orders. And moral fervor in that many of the campaigners saw the League as part of a moral-reformist, evangelizing mission, akin to the antislavery movement.[113] For some, like

David Whitehead, Methodist cotton manufacturer of Rawtenstall, this was overtly religious. He and his brothers joined the League

from a thorough conviction that free trade was a great movement in the right direction to help on the Ark of our God. It appeared to us impossible for war and bloodshed ever to cease while we had such an abominable system of class legislation. We viewed the Corn Law as the keystone of the arch of tyrannical monopoly; and we thought, if this stone were once drawn, it would be a fine introduction to free trade in this country, and would have its effect through all the world. It would tend very much towards establishing universal peace, hasten on the "millenium" [sic], "when war and bloodshed shall come to an end, and righteousness and peace be established in the earth."[114]

This was not the language of a rational Dissenter like Bowring, but he too linked Repeal to the cause of peace in a way that was to become a central part of the message: "Do you believe that war would be possible when we had universal trade?. . . Who would seek to quarrel with those who were perpetually communicating to them benefits and blessings?"[115] Still less was it the language of many supporters who, as Henry Ashworth recognized, might be mobilized more effectively by "a modified appeal to the *Self Interest*, though less amiable," than by moral conviction.[116]

The League was strongest in Bolton, thanks to a core of prominent liberals who, from the summer of 1838 to the achievement of Repeal in 1846, lobbied hard for their objective via meetings, tours, petitions, propaganda through the *Bolton Free Press*, delegations to London, and speeches—especially those of A. W. Paulton, former medical student and subsequently editor of the *Manchester Examiner and Times*.[117] The League's biggest Bolton bankrollers were the Ashworths and Thomas Thomasson, who pitched in £1,000 to the £250,000 fund in 1845.[118] Thomasson supported Cobden personally with over £10,000, apparently regarding him as "'the greatest benefactor of mankind since the invention of printing'."[119] In Blackburn and Darwen the League's stalwarts included members of the Eccles, Shorrock, and Pilkington families, Independent manufacturers, all £1,000 donors to the 1845 fund.[120] In Preston, after the formation of the Preston Anti-Corn Law Association in January 1839, with William Ainsworth, Unitarian millowner, as the first president, the ubiquitous Joseph Livesey provided local backbone with his campaigning press, and a number of leading liberal manufacturers and cotton spinners headed the delegations, manned the podiums, and footed the bills.[121] In all three towns, Dissenting ministers formed a reliable supporting cast.[122]

The concept of "the people" proved rather less reliable, oscillating between fledgling reality and imaginative promise. One of the first Repeal meetings staged by the Bolton branch of the Anti-Corn Law Association in 1839 gave an early indication of how difficult it would be to cajole Chartists and Repealers to sing from the same hymn-sheet. Two working-class Chartists carried an amendment by an "immense majority" that it was useless to petition Parliament since it would never repeal the Corn Laws, and that the agitation had been manufactured to divert the minds of the people from the only true remedy for political grievances.[123]

The Complete Suffrage Union—the attempt by the Birmingham radical Quaker Joseph Sturge to effect a reconciliation between Repealers and Chartists—promised to reforge the popular front in the wake of the Plug Plot in 1842. Yet here again such concerted marriage-guidance counseling enjoyed only limited success. In Preston, for example, the liberals won Chartist backing for their pro-Reform, pro-Repeal stance during the 1841 election after they pledged to support the release of Chartist prisoners. But there was no lasting relationship. In December 1842 the Chartists hijacked a meeting of the League and packed a meeting to choose a delegate for the CSU, electing their leading local figure, the handloom weaver Richard Marsden.[124] In Bolton, at a large meeting in the Temperance Hall of the Bolton Complete Suffrage Association in early 1844, James Lord, a Chartist, cautioned the Chartists against being led astray by the rich, and moved "That it is the opinion of this meeting that the source of all the people's grievances arise out of class legislation, and that the means of remedying the evil can only be obtained by the enactment of a bill entitled the people's charter." But on this occasion the meeting by a solid majority adopted the original motion of Isaac Barrow, builder, to request the borough MPs to vote against the granting of supplies.[125] With Sturge and a delegation from Birmingham in attendance, Chartists and Repealers could be persuaded to entertain thoughts of romance.

Shortly thereafter, however, confronting the renewed vigor of the short-time movement, many of the bourgeois radicals found themselves on the opposite bench on the question of Ten Hours. For Thomas Thomasson, short time was only feasible if accompanied by Repeal, and yet the working classes were opposing Repeal. "Can there be anything equal to the folly of complaining of your long hours of labour," he asked in March 1844, "and yet heaping abuse continually upon those who are seeking to remove the causes of the necessity of working those long hours?" He too found the spectacle of children torn from their beds and driven to the factories to "fatten the coach horses of the landowners" objectionable. Thomas Brindle, secretary of the operative cotton spinners, found such arguments risible. Our children, he said, only fatten the coach horses of the "Cotton Masters."[126]

This, then, was a frequently interrupted dialogue, the pulse of the popular alliance often weak and erratic. And, although many single-issue campaigners and the more ambitious continued to push the bourgeois-radical narrative, ensuring that it would become an important plank in the liberal platform from Gladstone to Lloyd George,[127] the optimistic vision of a "republic of Quakers"

or its equivalent soon evaporated after Repeal in 1846. At the final meeting of
the League in July 1846, Henry Ashworth had indicated that the famous victory was but one step along the road: "Gentlemen, it is now seen that business
industry, with a good cause, can beat titled power with a bad one. (Cheers.)
We now know our strength—it behoves us not to use it heedlessly and improperly, but, at the same time, not to hesitate to use it on all proper occasions."[128] But even in Bolton, a League stronghold, that strength was severely
compromised. The conservatives had achieved a majority in the council; the
Bolton Free Press, apparently never a strong concern and more recently undercut by wide circulation of local news in the Manchester papers, folded
early in 1847, with two short-lived resuscitations following;[129] and the liberals
lost one of their seats in the 1847 election.

The tale of the Parliamentary and Reform Association illustrates how the
bourgeois radicals kept alive the reforming impetus and endeavored to keep
the communication channels to plebeian radicals open, but were left stranded
by the ebbing enthusiasm of a broader constituency. In the aftermath of the
Chartist failure at Kennington Common in April 1848, Joseph Hume, Richard
Cobden, and other bourgeois radicals attempted to resurrect the popular front
behind the "Little Charter" and its four points: household suffrage, the ballot,
triennial parliaments, and more equal electoral districts. After an initial burst
of energy, this failed to make much headway in Parliament or the country.
Leading radicals and regional associations—the Liverpool Financial Reform
Association, the Peace Society, the Freehold Land Movement[130]—pursued their
pet agendas and their preferred remedies, fragmenting the movement. The
man who did most to draw the threads together again and to keep the primary
focus on extension of the suffrage was Sir Joshua Walmsley, a Liverpudlian
merchant who had earned his radical-liberal credentials in Liverpool municipal politics (he was mayor at the time of Queen Victoria's marriage, hence his
knighthood) and in the League. Briefly MP for Leicester in 1847 before being
unseated on a charge of bribery, he became MP for Bolton in 1849. Shortly afterwards, in May 1849, he became the first president of the Metropolitan
(later National) Parliamentary and Financial Reform Association, an organization dedicated to an amalgam of reforms, including the principles of the Little Charter.[131]

In tours, speeches, rallies, and tracts Walmsley and his colleagues tried to
recapture the momentum of the League. The effort flagged during 1850, was
rejuvenated early in 1851 when Lord John Russell announced his intention to
introduce a Reform Bill, and limped along after the government's defeat. In
1854 the failure of another bill and the onset of the Crimean War finally in-
terred it. The association was, on one level, a success: it was a factor forcing
the government to revive the reform question in order to retain the support of
radical MPs, and it perpetuated the (albeit difficult) dialogue across the class

divide. But it did not achieve its immediate goals, for a number of reasons. Firstly, the association failed to supersede the diverse regional efforts, meaning that energy was dissipated. Secondly, tours and speeches often left little residue—no effectively developed local organizational infrastructure. Thirdly, "the hardly disguised Chartism of Walmsley," as Bright expressed it,[132] ran the risk of alienating timid middle-class supporters, while his public adherence to the Little Charter was not enough to bring the Chartists on board.[133] *Some* Chartist leaders—William Lovett, George Jacob Holyoake, even Feargus O'Connor for a time—endorsed the association's policy of class cooperation, but the movement as a whole did not, and figures like G. J. Harney and Ernest Jones remained hostile.[134] Walmsley later recalled a debate at an association meeting between himself and Jones, who moved a counterresolution for the Charter, and it illuminates clearly one of the major fault lines that the popular front had long struggled to bridge:

"Little discussion, I showed, was necessary on this point, for on the Charter as a declaration of principles, there was no difference amongst us. The real object of Mr. Jones's speech was to bring into antagonism, instead of into co-operation of mutual interests, the working classes and their employers. 'This cry of capital as being opposed to labour,' I said, 'is a miserable fallacy, and an unworthy attempt to create ill-will and inflame the passions rather than to convince the reason of the masses. I shall dispose of it by asking this simple question of the working-men around me: What would be the position of labour in the present state of society without capital?'"[135]

The fourth and most compelling reason for the association's failure was economic. As Cobden reminded Walmsley in September 1851, "There never was much enthusiasm in favour of political reform in the manufacturing districts whilst trade was prosperous, employment good, and bread cheap, which you will be glad to find is the case now."[136] If the state were fiscally responsible, if economic growth enabled it to cut taxes and duties while maintaining expenditure on the military scaffolding of the commercial empire, and if the stables of Old Corruption looked increasingly well scrubbed—then what need was there for financial reform?[137] If it was not necessary to lever the right type of people into Parliament, what need was there for political reform?

The association's failure merely confirmed that various bourgeois radicals or liberals had come to accept more and more facets of the state, not because of acquiescence in aristocratic values, but either on solid grounds of self-interest or because of successive governments' undermining of anti-aristocratic-state rhetoric.[138] Even at its height, during the Repeal campaign, the radical vision in the three milltowns was a creed only for the few, a militant bourgeois minority grouped around a whole class-conscious agenda confronting and sometimes making contact with a much larger bloc of intertwined commercial, landed, and professional opinion. But if the bourgeois radicals, like the Chartists, did not manage to storm the Establishment ramparts and plant their flags firmly on the top turrets, this did not betoken defeat so much as that push and pull of arm-twisting and accommodation characterizing the response of the state and its propertied classes to the long-drawn-out process of British industrialization.[139] Put another way, if property rallied when the Chartists came over the bridge and marched up the hill, it was because the state had previously shown itself responsive to bourgeois interests and to be an evolving form worth fighting for, better than anything that might replace it. Without Reform, municipal reform, and Repeal; without the gradual dismantling of the apparatus of Old Corruption; without a liberalizing state; without concessions to the Nonconformist and Catholic conscience; without a restrained military after the warning given by the outcry over Peterloo: one can speculate that members of the radical bourgeois minority would have found themselves on the popular side of the barricade in the event of a serious challenge to authority.

The bourgeois majority seemed happy enough with the Reformed, Repealed, ordered, "liberal" state, allowing spheres of influence in the localities while providing laws, trade routes, and military power at the center.[140] Two symbolic moments in 1850 and 1851 can be seen as an acknowledgment of widespread bourgeois accommodation with the state, at least in the short term: the Great Exhibition and the death of Sir Robert Peel. An exhibition of industry and commerce under the patronage of a prince to bring nations together in a spirit of camaraderie elicited almost universal expressions of bourgeois praise. In Blackburn, practically everyone of note signed a requisition for a public meeting in early 1850 to promote the Exhibition. The *Blackburn Standard* commented,

we believe we are secure in saying that there is scarcely a political party, religious body, profession, manufacture, or trade, that is not directly or indirectly represented . . . Such a requisition we believe to be a perfect novelty to the town, and in its comprehensiveness, freedom from all signs of political, sectarian, or professional difference, and complete unanimity of sentiment, may be regarded as no less honourable to the inhabitants, than it is in strict accordance with the project and purpose of the Prince Consort.[141]

Peel's untimely death enabled the liberals to acknowledge him as a symbol of a benign and responsive state—an improbable bourgeois hero like Pitt half a century earlier, but one who was less divisive and more inclusive. The mill-town elites mobilized to memorialize him in the form of parks, baths, or statues, and to incorporate working-class contributions.[142] Peel was a man who, "with a patriotism rarely equalled," as Alderman Baynes of Blackburn later put it, "sacrificed his own comfort and peace, his friends and connections, and by his consummate tact and ability, succeeded in carrying the repeal of the corn laws, and so saving the nation."[143] His iconic usefulness could extend further as the meeting point of the Establishment and Lancashire cotton within one body, but as one who had not sold out: "Sprung from the order of industry, he manifested no puerile disposition for aristocratic distinction."[144] Baynes pointed out the lesson to his lower-class listeners: "In him and his predecessors you have an excellent example of what may be achieved by talent, industry, good conduct, and perseverance: a proof that the highest offices of state are open to all. His grandfather was born in Fish-lane, a back street, in this town."[145]

The didactic message from these collective celebrations of national pride and of national mourning was clear enough: there was no need for a radical overhaul of the system of government. The humblest could rise from a Blackburn backstreet all the way to Downing Street: "[I]t is one of the best and happiest elements of the constitution of this country that merit and genius are almost sure to attain their proper ascendancy," as the vicar of Bolton claimed before the local Great Exhibition committee.[146] In addition, Providence had beamed astonishingly brightly on this small corner of the country, assigning it the task of clothing mankind—a critical part of the grand design for Great Britain to civilize, emancipate, and Christianize peoples and nations.[147] If all this were true—and who could doubt it?—then much seemed to be right with the world. The Lord's ways were no longer mysterious but really rather transparent.

CONCLUSION

The remarkable rhetorical sense of calm and well-being surrounding the Great Exhibition reflected not only economic good times but also the ways in which successive governments had drawn much of the working- and middle-class radical sting by responding to the radical challenge. Even Henry Ashworth signaled this. In 1850 he expressed a certain softening of his uncompromising opposition to the ruling class and all its attributes. He saw the approaching Exhibition as a sign that the court was no longer going to confine its favors to Acres and noted the ennoblement of a cotton manufacturer and the creation of some "cotton knights." On the one hand he felt that this might result in a lessening of individual titled-entrepreneurial drive and evidently remained wary of expressions of loyalty. On the other, when Lord Granville (accompanying Queen Victoria on a visit to Manchester and vicinity in 1851) asked him why extravagant manifestations of loyalty had replaced the discontent of earlier years,

My reply was, that *Class interests* had been at the bottom of it—Her Majesty had been identified with measures which were based upon justice and which were in harmony with the spirit of Com^{ce} . Favouritism & Class interests were done with, the people of Manch^r were now reaping the benefits, and they had shewn Her Majesty that she could rely as safely upon those who were identified with Shuttles and spindles, as upon those who had to do with Turnips and Tup Sheep.[1]

One of my aims in this book has been to describe the building of a bourgeois-radical narrative in opposition to an aristocratic state at the national level and to a developing Toryism at the local level—a loyalist Toryism that was itself not unconditional but dependent on an accommodating state—and how the flexibility of a reforming state steadily undermined the bourgeois-radical message. But for those who prefer their history to be ragged at the edges, Ashworth's quotation and my conclusion to the last chapter are almost too neat and tidy. They give a false sense of closure, an unrealistic feeling of poststorm tranquillity and of postclimb repose on a new plateau of stability and consensus. The concurrent hysterical reaction to the "Papal Aggression" hardly suggests a nation at ease.[2] At the dawn of the age of equipoise many of the material and political factors feeding the anger and revolutionary potential of recent decades had scarcely abated. Military power still underpinned the whole system of authority. And although increasing numbers of the bourgeoisie had made their peace with the state, a bourgeois oppositional voice of fluctuating intensity still remained, still eager to forge cross-class alliances, later finding a home in Gladstonian Liberalism.

Nevertheless, the major crisis years had indeed passed by 1851, and the prospects for a revolution (or a military dictatorship) had receded. A brief summary of my take on the bourgeois role in this is in order. In the light of the full-scale retreat from the reductionist class interpretation of modern British history, I have put forward an argument in the radical tradition that sets a relatively high value on the role of the state (and not only in relation to evolving bourgeois narratives) and that plays down middle-class solidarity. It can be boiled down to four main suggestions. First of all, the vast majority of the propertied classes rallied behind the flag of order and applauded the government's web of containment at key moments. This depended critically on the relative discipline of the armed forces and on state appeasement of bourgeois interests (or at least the radical-liberal bourgeois hope and belief that governments could be induced to move in the right direction). Secondly, members of the bourgeoisie (however indecisively and with however many reservations) supported and implemented the gradual advances of the policeman state—a mesh of measures designed to create a more disciplined and orderly society. Thirdly, different bourgeois individuals and segments devised a broad array of ameliorative and palliative solutions. These ranged from simple charity, through factory paternalism, to diverse forms of education and indoctrination, to support for short-time legislation, to attempts at incorporation of the working classes into hierarchies of party, sect, and association. The fourth suggestion emphasizes the importance of the unconscious, unintended consequences of the manifold divisions within bourgeois ranks. The absence of bourgeois rigidity or solidarity, the existence of divergent, religious-based narratives or traditions grounded in arguments about the powers and scope of the state and the rights of citizenship, and the willingness of certain fractions of the bourgeoisie to argue causes repugnant to other bourgeois sectors, generated the potential for the workings of cross-class alliances and rhetoric.

I have been at pains to document the full range of bourgeois attempts—which I have labeled coercion, concession, incorporation, and indoctrination—to bring stability to the urban-industrial environment they were creating and to stave off revolutionary pressures. I have also indicated the lack of success of many of these measures in reaching their intended targets and that they frequently contradicted and undermined each other. But the various forms of bourgeois association and organization—whether aimed at the working classes or not—worked in another sense, by building the infrastructure of the towns (however slowly and inefficiently) and by creating and perpetuating a vibrant market and civic culture. And the sheer combined weight of the soldier, the policeman, the parson, the millowner, the overseer, the visitor, and the schoolmaster did have a considerable impact. This is not in any vulgar sense of social control. The liberal-capitalist hegemony was hammered out during a long period of conflict and concession. Working-class "consent" to the prevailing power structure—the acquiescence in a relatively oppressive, exploitative, but liberalizing, society—depended not only on a tempered and filtered acceptance of bourgeois messages and values, but also on material conditions, a realistic appraisal of the strength of the forces of order, and an assessment of the viable alternatives.

This will scarcely satisfy those readers who are searching for a more coherent hegemonic project, nor those who prefer a stronger (and more uniform) theoretical taste than that produced by the flavorful mélange of theorists with whom I have chosen to spice my broth. But the evidence from these three towns points to a degree of incoherence and unpredictability as to who was supporting which strategy and why, and my contention is that all four of the above grouped suggestions were essential, in varying degrees at different periods and in diverse places, in ensuring stability. More light would be shed on these questions by a more thorough engagement with lower-class receptivity to these strategies; but that would be another, very different book.

Beyond advancing an argument about class, power, and social stability, I have attempted in this study to capture as many of the public and private angles of this important body of Lancastrians as possible. I have reveled in the kaleidoscopic complexities of bourgeois thought, culture, and action, in the glorious messiness of people's lives. Positive alignments, negative barricading, and a medley of snippets of received wisdom, ideological statements, and disparate discourses made up the multiple identities of each individual bourgeois. Many of these people had to wrestle with status anxieties and financial insecurity in their lives, and often responded by throwing up fences and defining themselves against "inferior" others: the clergyman against the Nonconformist minister and the priest, the doctor against the apothecary or the quack, the well-spoken against the dialect-speaker, the polite against the plebeian, the rational recreationist against indulgers in "traditional" popular culture, the Sabbatarian against the defilers of Sundays, the lady against the working wife, the Manchester Man against the idle aristocrat, and so on. Each of them sought to reconcile to his or her own satisfaction a puritanically and evangelically inspired seriousness with the pleasures and status-enhancing claims of gentility, frugality with consumption, the work ethic with the extended vacation, the strict ordering of household time with wealth-generated opportunities for leisure. The prescriptive ideals, constantly being reworked to keep pace with a rapidly evolving nation, rarely matched mundane reality. Navigating a passage through the currents of the outside world was just as challenging. Was the town a locus of civilized living, or a Sodom and Gomorrah of festering masses divorced from God and decency? Was factory industry the purveyor of progress and a new discipline or the destroyer of social ties, health, and good order?

The imperfect, human personas these people created, the muddled answers they gave, the confused solutions they engineered, were to have a profound impact on their and future generations. Love them or loathe them, for good and ill, the bourgeoisie in the Age of the Two Revolutions cast a long shadow.

APPENDIX 1: THE BOURGEOISIE
FROM THE 1851 CENSUS

Given that the bourgeoisie is largely an invented and imposed category, with very imprecise transitional bands marking the boundaries above and below, any attempt to define it numerically can only be impressionistic and unscientific. But it is possible and necessary to give some sense of the numbers involved and of the distribution of the bourgeoisie across occupations. Table 3 (p. 12) provides a comprehensive summary of the bourgeois town-and-country presence from the tip of Deane Parish in the south to the northern end of Preston Parish. Each of the three place categories includes the town and the surrounding area. For example, "Blackburn" includes Darwen and much of the parish, Bolton includes Farnworth and both Bolton and Deane Parishes, and so on.

At the top end of the scale I have included the handful of landowners and minor gentry who lived within the area of study: their marriage links, social alliances and business involvement with the bourgeoisie make teasing them out and setting them to one side difficult and artificial. For the "core" membership of the bourgeois club and in drawing a boundary at the lower end, I have relied on a modified version of the schemata of Richard Trainor, *Black Country Elites: The Exercise of Authority in an Industrialized Area 1830-1900* (Oxford: Clarendon Press, 1993), appendix 1, and Theodore Koditschek, *Class Formation and Urban-Industrial Society: Bradford, 1750-1850* (Cambridge: Cambridge University Press, 1990), appendix. I have estimated membership based on a flexible combination of wealth, status, and qualification. I have included all those in the established professions (lawyers, Anglican clergymen, medical men); all industrial and commercial men and women employing more than ten people outside the family (where numbers of employees are not specified and a guess has to be made as to whether, say, the "cotton spinner" is a master or an operative, I have used other criteria like residential location and whether younger family members are employed); all those in the dealing sector employing at least five people outside the family and having at least one domestic servant; and all employing two or more domestic servants. Thus any individuals in typically lower-middle-class or managerial occupations or the "new professions" who do not meet these criteria have been excluded, except in a few instances where residential location seems to warrant inclusion. I have, secondly, excluded farmers, which is unsatisfactory, but advisable (quite apart from the difficulties of determining criteria of gentility from acreage, or a dairymaid from a "true" domestic servant), since the farmers only rarely involved themselves in the political, social, and cultural organization of the towns (except as Poor Law guardians) and therefore cannot be viewed in any meaningful sense as part of the same elite. I have also excluded people of independent means who did not have two or more servants (because of the possibility that the "annuitant" or "proprietor of houses" might be surviving off only a very small income), but not those labeled "ladies" or "gentlemen." Again this is unsatisfactory, as the middling grocer who made enough to retire could well call himself a gentleman. On the other hand it is highly likely that, say, a well-educated, genteel lady with a single retainer, but only described as an "annuitant," has been kept out of my sample, whereas the builder with fifty laborers but no domestic servants and (so far as we know) no pretensions to gentility, has been included. Servant-holding as a criterion is problematic in other ways: it is impossible to tell whether the grocer, for example, included in the sample because he had two teenage domestic servants (assuming that they *were* domestic servants and not simply shopgirls improperly described by the enumerator)—to which he would only pay a pittance—is not substantially smaller scale than the upmarket draper down the street employing (at much higher wages) a single mature housekeeper. Moreover, the sample is likely to overrepresent families (especially families with small children hiring nurses), who might employ greater numbers of servants than a wealthier but single individual; and to overrepresent families with a paucity of female relatives (since female relatives might otherwise act as housekeepers in lieu of domestic servants). Such examples of problems can be readily multiplied and merely reinforce the point: the figures give a useful order of magnitude, and the higher up one progresses in the mercantile, manufacturing, and professional world (the main focus of this study), away from all but the most prosperous of wholesalers and retailers, the more accurate they become. There are three final qualifications to the sample: I have only included a handful of the most extensive hotel- and innkeepers, given that the large numbers of "domestic servants" at most inns would have been to serve the clientele rather than the family; but I have included Catholic priests and Nonconformist ministers of all stripes, regardless of their eligibility from other criteria, because of their "intellectual capital" and their recurrent and disproportionate role in relation to their wealth in the affairs of the towns; and there are a small number of cases, which I have included, where the head of the household does not meet the criteria for inclusion but has a near relative living in the household who does.

Categories Employed

Where one individual held more than one occupation, I have listed him or her under the leading or most significant occupation (e.g., "cotton spinner and banker" is included under "Textile manufacturing," "army officer and chief constable" is included under "Other professional" rather than under "Armed forces"). I have included those listed as "retired . . ." or "gentleman," and so on, under their previous occupations if listed (thus "retired bleacher" under "Textile finishing").

Industrial
Textile manufacturing: (cotton) spinner or (cotton) spinner and manufacturer or (cotton) manufacturer, counterpane or quilting manufacturer, cotton merchant, flax spinner, gold thread manufacturer.
Textile finishing: calico printer, bleacher.
Other industrial: ironfounder, millwright, machine maker, roller maker, tobacco manufacturer, vitriol manufacturer, manufacturing chemist, bobbin and shuttle maker, spindle and fly maker, sizer, loom merchant, rope maker, papermaker, boilermaker, brassfounder, coalowner, brewer.

Banking: banker, bank manager.

Managerial: manager, agent, cashier, steward, clerk, bookkeeper.

Professional
Armed forces: army officer, R. N. officer, "army militia."
Law: attorney or solicitor, barrister, judge.
Medicine: physician, MD, surgeon, dentist.
Church: Anglican clergyman, clerical schoolmaster (of the grammar schools).
Other "professional": police officer, governor of the House of Correction, inspector of factories, inspector of schools, county treasurer, civil engineer/engineer, auctioneer and sheriff's officer, accountant, commissioner of taxes, registrar of births and deaths, newspaper proprietor, land agent or land surveyor, articled clerk, professor of music, music teacher, boarding schoolmaster, veterinary surgeon.

Retail and Wholesale: bookseller/stationer/printer, boot and shoe dealer, chemist, druggist, china and glass dealer, coal merchant, corn merchant/miller, draper, general merchant, grocer, tea dealer, hosier and glover, hotel/innkeeper, ironmonger, leather cutter/dealer, licensed victualler, tailor, upholsterer, provision dealer, butcher, commission agent, coach proprietor, oyster dealer, traveller, saddler, shopowner, silk mercer, tobacconist, wine merchant, pawnbroker, warehouseman.

Craft: builder, cabinetmaker, hat manufacturer, joiner and builder, shoemaker, stonemason, quarrymaster, shipwright, painter, coachmaker, soap manufacturer, brush manufacturer, pipe manufacturer, coppersmith, tanner and currier, biscuit maker, combmaker, organ builder, wheelwright and smith, manufacturer of church furniture, engraver.

Independent means: widow, no specification, gentleman, lady, Esq., annuitant, fundholder, gentlewoman, house proprietor, personal property, proprietor of railway shares.

APPENDIX 2: CATHOLIC AND DISSENTING STRENGTH

TABLE A1

*Catholic and Dissenting Strength in Preston
and Surrounding Townships, 1829*

Township	RC	Ind	Meth	Bap	Pres	CH	PM	Uni	Q
Amounderness Hundred									
Broughton	144	5[a]							
Fishwick	173		8	24		20			
Freckleton	31	20	49						
Fulwood	248			13					
Goosnargh with Newsham	469	61	10						
Grimsargh with Brockhole	116		3						
Lea, Ashton, Ingol and Cottam	341	10	7				7	4	
Preston	10,900	1,130[b]	1,065	289		800	80	164	82
Ribbleton	45		12						
Woodplumpton	556		268[c]						
Leyland Hundred									
Brindle	626								
Clayton le Woods	450								
Cuerden	169	1[a]	9						
Hoghton			51						
Penwortham	178	57[d]	97	6			1		
Wheelton	300		118	2	2	[+17 "Moralists"]			
Whittle le Woods	669	27	79						
Withnell			50						

SOURCE: LRO, QDV/9/1-412, Sectarian Returns, 1829.
KEY: RC = Roman Catholic; Ind = Independent; Meth = Methodist ("Methodist," "Wesleyan," "Wesleyan Protestant Methodist"); Bap = Baptist ("Baptist," "Particular Baptist," "Dipper"); Pres = Presbyterian; CH = Countess of Huntingdon's Connexion; PM = Primitive Methodist (and "Ranters"); Uni = Unitarian; Q = Quaker.

[a] Calvinist.
[b] Including 30 Scotch Independents.
[c] "Methodists and Ranters"
[d] Including 17 Calvinists.

TABLE A2

*Catholic and Dissenting Strength in Blackburn
and Surrounding Townships, 1829*

Township	RC	Ind	Meth	Bap	Pres	PM	Uni	Q	Swe
Balderstone	120	66[a]							
Billington	54		25						
Blackburn	3,400	1,500	800	260	240	80		46	
Church	89		44	92					
Clayton le Dale	84					[+4 "Dissenters"]			
Clayton le Moors	204		72	111					
Cuerdale	30								
Lower Darwen			34						
Over Darwen			250		950	70			30
Dilworth			40						
Dinkley	76								
Dutton	240								
Eccleshill	5	321[a]	18	7					
Great Harwood	95	27	144						
Little Harwood	22					[+6 "Dissenters"]			
Livesey	25	126	350						
Mellor			300						
Osbaldeston	74		11						
Oswaldtwistle			450		100				
Pleasington	68	12	50						
Ramsgreave	27					[+30 "Dissenters"]			
Rishton	41		5						
Salesbury	30								
Samlesbury	838		79			[+1,064 "protestants"]			
Tockholes		370							
Walton le Dale	1,500		200[b]						
Wilpshire	15					[+13 "Dissenters"]			
Witton	72					[+157 "Dissenters"]			

SOURCE: As for Table A1.

KEY: As for Table A1; Swe = Swedenborgian.

[a] Calvinist.

[b] 50 "Class Methodists" and 150 "Methodists and other professions."

TABLE A3
Catholic and Dissenting Strength in Bolton and Surrounding Townships, 1829

Township	RC	Ind	Meth	Bap	Pres	PM	Uni	Q	Swe
Great Bolton	3,000	1,370	300	110[a]	750	750[b]	200		
Little Bolton	100		1,800[c]					60	120
Edgworth			300		200				
Entwisle							[326 "Dissenters"]		
Farnworth	14	500	150						
Halliwell	58	149[d]	313	22		56	41		
Harwood		38	166				241		
Horwich		650	550						
Little Hulton		60[d]	130						
Middle Hulton			44						
Over Hulton	9								
Great Lever			[no useful figures]						
Little Lever	2		41				[+16 "Dissenters"]		
Longworth		42[d]					74		
Lostock	9		20					2	
Quarlton			[no Dissenters]						
Rivington					306				
Rumworth	6		18				5		
Tonge			40						
Tonge with Haulgh		40	50				50		20
Turton		200			250				
Westhoughton		120	65					75	

SOURCE: As for Tables A1 and A2.
KEY: As for Tables A1 and A2.
   [a] Includes 10 "Baptist Gadsbyites."
   [b] 450 "Kilhamite Methodists" and 300 "Ranters."
   [c] 400 Independent Methodists and 1,400 "Old Established Methodists."
   [d] Calvinists.

APPENDIX 3: SERVANT-KEEPING, 1851

These are the numbers of servants for each of the households in the bourgeois sample (Table 3, p. 12) drawn from the 1851 census. At the higher end the numbers are often underestimates, since they include only household servants and not coachmen and others living in the lodge or elsewhere on the property.

Number of Servants	Blackburn area	Bolton area	Preston area
>4	9	10	18
4	4	20	25
3	27	41	58
2	89	160	154
1	126	147	103
0	48	62	10

It is worth noting the names and residences of those heads of household with four or more servants, a mixed-wealth elite-within-an-elite. Note the extent to which only Preston of the three towns contained a number of its truly rich within the town itself.

Blackburn area
Joseph Feilden, Witton Hall (14 servants); Thomas Bright Crosse, Shaw Hill (10); Lady Feilden, Feniscowles Hall (9); Thomas Eastwood, Brindle Lodge (7); James Lomax, Clayton Hall (7); John Butler, Pleasington Hall (6); Henry Paul Fleetwood, Woodfold Park (6); Henry Hargreaves, solicitor, Beardwood (5); William Mosley Perfect, solicitor, Ainsworth St. (5); and 4 each: Helen Neville, attorney's widow, Beardwood House; Henry Brock Hollinshead, attorney, Billinge Scar; Henry Hoyle, solicitor, Little Harwood Hall; Charles Potter, papermaker, Earnsdale.

Bolton area
Anne Maria Ridgway, bleacher's widow, Ridgmont (10); Mary Chisonhale, widow, Arley Hall (9); Jacob Fletcher Fletcher, New Peel Hall (7); William Ford Hulton, New Brook House (6); Charles Howarth, bleacher, Moor Platt (6); James Hardcastle, bleacher, Firwood House (6); the Rev. John Richardson, Walmsley Parsonage (6); John Hick, master engineer, Highfield House (6); a Royal Navy Captain, Darley Hall (6); the Rev. Edward Girdlestone of Deane (5); and 4 each: Thomas Bonsor Crompton, papermaker, cot-

ton manufacturer, and newspaper proprietor, Farnworth Vale; James Sylvester, annuitant, Chorley Road; George Knowles, cotton spinner, Tudor Villa; Thomas Cross, bleacher, spinner, and banker, Mortfield; the Rev. John Shepherd Birley, Halliwell; Peter Ainsworth, Smithills Hall [this might be 9 servants, but is unclear]; James Kyrke Watkins, solicitor, Haulgh Cottage; Thomas Ridgway Bridson, bleacher, Vale Bank; John Fletcher, land- and coalowner, The Hollins; John Ashworth, land agent, Turton; Henry Ashworth, Great Oak [*sic*]; James Kay, Turton Tower; Edmund Ashworth, Egerton Hall; the Rev. Charles Wright, Hill Topp; Elizabeth Bolling, cotton spinner's widow, New Hall; the Rev. James Slade, vicarage; George Mallett, surgeon, Mawdsley St.; Elizabeth Rothwell, Sunning Hill; Thomas Lever Rushton, banker, ironmaster, solicitor, West Bank; George Hargraves, cotton spinner, Birch House.

Preston area
Robert Townley Parker, Cuerden Hall (14); William Assheton Cross, Red Scar (12); William Marshall, Penwortham Hall (8); John Frederick Chadwick, landowner, Hermitage (8); Dr. William Winstanley, West Cliff (7); Horrocks, Lark Hill House (6, presumably not the full complement, the family being absent); John Paley, cotton spinner, Fishergate Hill (6); Charles Roger Jacson, Barton Lodge (6); Wilson (absent), Broughton House (6); Lt. Gen. Sir Thomas Whitehead, Uplands (6); 5 each: Charles Swainson, calico printer, Frenchwood; John Catterall, cotton spinner, Bushell Place; Thomas Miller, cotton manufacturer, Winckley Square; Henry Miller, cotton manufacturer, Winckley Square; Thomas Ashton, JP, Winckley Square; Edward Chaddock Gorst, lawyer, West Cliff; William Adam Hulton, judge, Hurst Grange; Charles Swainson, retired cotton spinner, Cooper Hill; and 4 each: Edward Hollins, cotton spinner, Avenham Cottage; the Rev. William J. Kennedy, HM inspector of schools, Bank Parade; John Addison, county judge, Winckley Square; Elizabeth Gorst, fundholder, Chapel St.; Margaret Gorst, lady, Winckley Square; Thomas Ainsworth, cotton spinner, Winckley Square; Paul Catterall, cotton manufacturer, Winckley Square; Peter Catterall, attorney, Winckley Square; Hugh Dawson, cotton manufacturer, West Cliff; Joseph B. Dickson, solicitor, West Cliff; John Winstanley, attorney, Fishergate; Robert Ascroft, solicitor, Charles St.; Lt. James Chapman, R. N., Railway House; the Rev. John Owen Parr, vicarage; the Rev. John Clay, prison chaplain, East Cliff; William Taylor, Moss Cottage; Henry N. Pedder, banker, Ashton Lodge; Capt. T. B. Ward, 85th Regt., Ivy Cottage, Deepdale Rd.; Thomas Norris, retired landed proprietor, Howick House; John Cooper, cotton spinner, The Oaks; William Bashall, cotton manufacturer, Farington Lodge; William Calrow, Walton Lodge; John Rooper, army militia, High Wood House; Miles Rodgett, landed proprietor, Darwen Bank House; James F. Anderton, landowner, Wood Bottom, Haighton.

APPENDIX 4: PARTY FORTUNES AND ELECTION RESULTS AFTER 1832

"Toryism unfortunately prevails here," Robert Heywood of Bolton wrote in 1836; "The liberals are by no means wealthy or influential."[1] "The cause of reform is sad up-hill work but we must do the best we can," he added in 1838;[2] "almost all the large spinning and bleaching concerns in this neighbourhood are owned by conservatives."[3] The cause of conservatism was indeed formidable in Bolton, as in the other two towns, and occasioned some surprise among outsiders. "I can only regret," wrote one to Heywood, "that a population such as yours, and a new Boro' cannot steadily send up two liberal Members."[4] But Heywood's pessimism seems exaggerated. William Bolling regained his seat in 1835 and 1837, but the conservatives did not risk a second candidate. Peter Ainsworth, Anglican bleacher from Halliwell, won both times for the liberals, beating out a much-chagrined Col. Torrens on the first occasion and Andrew Knowles, Bolton coalowner, on the second.[5] A greater tendency toward party voting, even though Bolling remained the only conservative candidate, was noticeable during both elections after the relative confusion of 1832. In 1835, 74 leading inhabitants voted liberal (plumping or splitting for Ainsworth and Torrens), 63 conservative (plumping for Bolling), and 93 voted across parties. In 1837, 106 voted liberal (Ainsworth and Knowles), 127 conservative (Bolling), and only 44 mixed their votes.

During the 1830s the elected liberals disappointed the more radical elements. William Naisby, the radical draper, publicly attacked Torrens for his less-than-wholehearted adherence to radical reform once he was in the Commons and for his commitment to political economy, including support for the New Poor Law.[6] The only reason Heywood's "Unitarian" circle did not put up a more radical candidate in 1835 was tactical: "it was not deemed advisable to bring Mr. Yates forward lest we should divide the liberals and ultimately let in two tories."[7] Ainsworth's voting record in Parliament repeatedly attracted the public censure of reformers, but again they rallied behind him during the 1841 election to avoid a split in the ranks. This time two conservatives stood, Bolling and Peter Rothwell, and they both lost to a duo of liberals, Ainsworth and Dr. John Bowring, a man the bourgeois radicals could trust.[8] Bourgeois voters were evenly divided between liberals and conservatives (126 votes apiece), with the bulk in each category voting a party ticket (112 splitting

TABLE A4
Bourgeois Voting in Bolton, 1835

	BA	AT	TB	B	T	A
Attorney	1	1	3	8	1	4
Banker					1	
Bleacher	2		1	4	2	3
Carrier					1	
Clergyman	2			1		
Coalmaster				8		
Gentleman	10	7	7	7	2	5
Ironfounder	8		1	4		1
Land surveyor					1	
Machinemaker	1			1		
Manufacturer	18	22	12	9	8	4
Mfrg. chemist	1					
Minister				4		
Papermaker	1	1				
Physician			1			
Spinner	7	2	7	16	1	4
Surgeon	7	2	3	2		
Totals	58	35	35	64	17	21

SOURCE: *A List of Persons Who Voted* (Bolton, 1835).
KEY: B = Bolling; A = Ainsworth; T = Torrens.

TABLE A5
Bourgeois Voting in Bolton, 1837

	KB	AK	BA	B	A	K
Attorney	1	5		14	1	
Banker				1		
Bleacher		3	3	7	1	
Carrier			1	2		
Clergyman				4		
Coalmaster		1		6		
Gentleman	1	16	7	16	1	
Ironfounder	2	3	7	6		
Land surveyor				1		
Machinemaker		1		3		
Manufacturer	4	41	9	20		1
Mfrg. chemist			1	1		
Minister		5				
Papermaker		1		1		
Physician		1				
Spinner	1	20	3	39	2	
Surgeon		3	4	6		
Totals	9	100	35	127	5	1

SOURCE: *A List of Persons Who Voted* (Bolton, 1837).
KEY: K = Knowles; B = Bolling; A = Ainsworth.

TABLE A6
Bourgeois Voting in Bolton, 1841

	ABw	BR	RA	BBw	BA	BwR	A	Bw	B	R
Attorney	3	16	2				2			
Banker		3								
Barrister		1								
Bleacher	4	8	1							
Carrier		1								
Clergyman		4								
Gentleman	15	22				1		2		1
Ironfounder	2	6	4	1			1	1		1
Manufacturer	32	19	3				1	1		2
Mfrg. chemist	1									
Minister	3							1		
Papermaker	1									
Physician	1									
Spinner	49	36	6		1		1	2		
Surgeon	2	6	1		2	1	1			
Totals	113	122	17	1	3	2	6	7	0	4

SOURCE: Brimelow, *Political and Parliamentary*, 417-44.
KEY: A = Ainsworth; B = Bolling; R = Rothwell; Bw = Bowring.

TABLE A7
Sample of Bourgeois Voting in Bolton, 1847

	B	BwBr	BBw	BBr
Attorney/solicitor	6	1		
Banker	1			
Bleacher	3	3		1
Carrier	1			
Clergyman	3			
Coalmaster	3			
Cotton spinner	10	18		
Gentleman	11	6	2	
Ironfounder	3	2		
Land surveyor	1			
Machinemaker			1	
Manufacturer	9	18		1
Minister		1		
Papermaker			1	
Surgeon	4	1		
Totals	55	50	4	2

SOURCE: *A List of the Persons Who Voted* (Bolton, 1847).[a]

KEY: B = Bolling; Br = Brooks; Bw = Bowring.

[a] As the poll book does not list occupations, I have matched up names and addresses with the 1837 and 1841 poll books to produce this sample: 49 voted liberal both in 1841 (of, if they did not vote in 1841, in 1837) and 1847, and 49 voted conservative; only 11 voted differently. The voting of the full electorate in 1847 was as follows. Plumpers: Bolling, 597; Bowring, 7; Brooks, 4. Splitters: Bolling and Bowring, 61; Bolling and Brooks, 57; Brooks and Bowring, 584. Total votes: Bolling, 714; Bowring, 652; Brooks, 645.

for Ainsworth and Bowring, 122 for Bolling and Rothwell). Only 23 divided their votes across parties (Table A6). This consolidation of party voting was partly a product of the party organization over the previous few years, partly the fact that Bolling supporters now had a conservative candidate for their second votes.[9]

Once re-elected, Peter Ainsworth continued to think and act too independently for his reformer friends, particularly incensing them over his refusal to support total repeal of the Corn Laws.[10] "The judgment of your Member is in a strange and bewildered state," John Bright said at an Anti-Corn Law League meeting in January 1843. "I think his head is more to blame than his heart. He is evidently not a man of firm purpose; he has a longing after lords and aristocratic association, and he has been unable to withstand the blandishments which are so abundantly lavished upon all who appear likely to be drawn within the web of aristocratic dependence."[11] Before the 1847 election the disgruntled Reform Association at last withdrew its backing for him, threatening a schism in liberal ranks and raising the fear that the supporters of Ainsworth and Bolling, though scarcely compatible, might nevertheless unite to deprive Bowring of his seat, especially as Ainsworth was a Churchman.[12] The danger was averted when Ainsworth stepped down, expressly because of the "violent and uncalled for opposition."[13] Bolling now recaptured a seat for the conservatives, keeping out John Brooks, the second liberal candidate.[14] Voting was again largely on party lines, with a great deal of continuity from 1841 (Table A7). But the liberals still had a strong voice in Bowring, and when he resigned to do government service in the Far East in 1849, Sir Joshua Walmsley, a fellow bourgeois radical, was elected in his stead, beating T. R. Bridson, Tory bleacher. Stephen Blair, another bleacher, maintained the balance for the conservatives by replacing Bolling, who died in August 1848.[15]

Throughout the 1840s, professional men and certain industrialists—bleachers, ironfounders—favored the conservatives, but manufacturers and spinners were more liberal, partially at least because of the free trade question. Religious affiliation, however, continued to be one of the clearest indicators of voting patterns. Table A8 shows the denominational breakdown of the voting in 1847 as far as the *Bolton Free Press* could judge. Aside from the Wesleyans, Nonconformists and Catholics cast 438 votes for the two liberals, and 31 votes for the conservative. The Wesleyans were evenly divided, and the Churchmen heavily favored the conservative, though with a substantial liberal minority.

In Blackburn, the *Blackburn Standard*'s analysis after the 1835 election presented a similar picture. Feilden, Turner, and Bowring stood again: Anglicans voted for Feilden and/or Turner by a ratio of 3:1 over Bowring; Independents, Methodists, and Catholics gave the bulk of their support to Bowring, with Turner polling reasonably well among them, and Feilden picking up

TABLE A8
Voting by Religious Affiliation, Bolton, 1847

	Bowring	Brooks	Bolling
Churchmen	95	97	376
Wesleyans	71	79	82
Independents	92	93	19
Unitarians	55	55	2
Baptists	6	6	0
Catholics	31	25	7
Quakers	12	13	0
Independent and other Methodists	7	7	0
Cowardites	1	1	0
Swedenborgians	7	9	2
Scotch Kirk	9	9	1

SOURCE: *BFP*, Aug.14, p. 3.

less than a quarter of their votes; Baptists, Quakers, and Unitarians sided heavily with Bowring (36 votes, as against 8 for Turner and 1 for Feilden).[16] The wealthier were also significantly more likely to vote for Feilden or Turner. As the 1835 poll book indicates (Table A9), listing voters by rateable value rather than occupation, support for Bowring was bunched at the lower-middle-class end of the voting scale. Bowringites were somewhat more likely to plump for their man than to split for Turner, indicating radical dissatisfaction with the latter's reforming zeal.[17] He posed once more as an independent reformer, but the *Blackburn Gazette* accused him of again colluding with Feilden, and the two held a joint victory dinner at which Turner promised to support Peel's administration when at all possible. Feilden, who also expressed himself a Peelite,[18] was clearly the Tory-Anglican candidate—"That the names of few Dissenters are found in the list of my supporters during the late contest," he acknowledged, "is to me a matter of deep regret"[19]—and the radicals had not taken his reformist credentials seriously for long. He became a reformer that he might become an MP, was how Bowring described it, and having accomplished that, he "returned like a dog [to his] vomit."[20]

TABLE A9
Voting in Blackburn, 1835

	Voters' rateable value					
	≤£10	≤£20	≤£50	≤£100	>£100	Total
Plumpers						
Feilden	1	2	2	0	1	6
Turner	6	2	8	2	0	18
Bowring	61	64	30	4	3	162
Splitters						
Feilden/Turner	63	63	103	44	19	292
Feilden/Bowring	4	5	6	2	1	18
Bowring/Turner	48	37	29	8	1	123
Total votes received						
Feilden	68	70	111	46	21	316
Turner	117	102	140	54	20	433
Bowring	113	106	65	14	4	302

SOURCE: LRO, DDPr 50/4a, *List of Persons Who Voted* (Blackburn, 1835).

The 1837 election was no better for the liberal-radicals. Although Turner's voting record during the 1836 session damned him in the eyes of the *Blackburn Standard* as a "Whig-Radical supporter of the O'Connell Cabinet,"[21] his firm commitment as a Churchman to church and state and his pattern of independent voting ensured that the radicals had no more confidence in him as a bearer of the reform interest than the Bolton radicals had in Peter Ainsworth. They turned to John Benjamin Smith of Manchester, county magistrate, retired cotton merchant, and another of the ubiquitous band of liberal-radicals from Cross Street Unitarian Chapel.[22] Introduced to the electorate by Joseph Eccles, he stood on the populist platform of the ballot, shorter parliaments, reduction of expenditure on the army and navy, abolition of sinecures and unmerited pensions, Church reform, and Repeal.[23] "I knew that I had no chance of success," he later wrote, "& was induced to offer myself only because our reform friends thought the interest at Bkburn [sic] might droop if not kept alive by a contest however hopeless."[24] He withdrew before the poll: "finding I could only get in by bribery I retired after having been elected by a shew of hands";[25] "we lost all but our honour; that we preserved unstained—I could have won the election by swilling the electors."[26]

Feilden reported to Peel the following year that "our Borough is becoming more Conservative daily . . . The Registration has just passed off *most satisfactorily* to our Cause; and I feel great confidence in the future."[27] This confidence induced the conservatives to put up two candidates in 1841: Feilden ("the firm supporter," he wrote to Peel, "of those principles you so ably, and so conscientiously advocate")[28] and John Hornby of the Brookhouse manufacturing family, brother of the local conservative chairman, William Henry Hornby. The liberals could only muster Turner in reply, now standing as an unequivocal liberal and free trader. The two Tories traded pledged votes on polling day to shut out Turner by one vote; he petitioned, but to no avail.[29] In the electorate as a whole, voting was largely along party lines but, following the norm in a three-cornered contest, bipartisan voting was substantial: 310 voted liberal (Turner), 387 conservative (Hornby and Feilden), and 114 voted across parties.[30] The liberals partially reversed this disappointing result in 1847, when Feilden retired. Hornby, the sole Tory candidate, headed the poll (649), James Pilkington, the Congregationalist, liberal-radical millowner came in second (602), leaving a second liberal-radical, William Hargreaves of the Broad Oak printworks, and William Prowting Roberts, Chartist lawyer, trailing (392 and 68 respectively).[31]

In Blackburn, as in Bolton, the period after 1832 had seen the elaboration of the two broad-churched parties, both possessing considerable strength, and the Tories holding up their vote even more firmly than in Bolton. Preston was, again, different, but a pattern of political convergence paralleled its increasing physical resemblance to its neighbors. The influence of the Stanleys still remained large in the town, and this was to continue for the rest of the century and beyond; but industrializing Preston was becoming a very different type of town from its polite and patrician forerunner. The Stanleys reduced their cultural patronage, ending their horse races in 1833, and pulling down their stately townhouse, Patten House, in 1835.[32] Henry Thomas Stanley stood again in the 1835 election and was re-elected alongside Hesketh Fleetwood, but retired in 1837. The liberal-radicals managed only the absentee candidacy of Perronet Thompson, the prominent radical political economist, and the popular radicals brought forward a Cobbettite, Thomas Smith of Liverpool.[33] Bourgeois voting remained remarkably loyal to the Fleetwood-Stanley "coalition," resolutely bipartisan: 168 plumped or split for Fleetwood and Stanley and only 23 voted differently (Table A10).

TABLE A10
Bourgeois Voting in Preston, 1835

	FS	ST	FT	TSm	F	S	T
Attorney	47	2			3	6	3
Banker	4				1		
Barrister	1						1
Clergyman	2						
Cotton spinner	20	1			1		
Esquire	7						
Gentleman	42	2		1		3	
Governor (House of Correction)	1						
Manufacturer	17	2	1	3	1		3
Minister		3					1
Physician	2						
Surgeon	5				2	1	
Surveyor	2						
Totals	150	10	1	4	8	10	8

SOURCE: LRO, DDPr 131/24, *A List of Persons Who Voted at the Election* (Preston, 1835).
KEY: F = Fleetwood; S = Stanley; T = Thompson; Sm = Smith.

Bourgeois Voting in Preston, 1837

	FP	FC	PC	P	F	C
Army officer	1					
Attorney	40	8	1	11	1	
Banker	2	2		2		
Barrister	1	1				
Clergyman	1			3		
Cotton spinner	13	5		7	1	
Esquire	4	1				
Flax spinner	2	2		1		
Gentleman	32	14	1	3		1
Governor (House of Correction)	1					
Manufacturer	11	5		3	4	1
Minister		3				
Physician	2	1				
Surgeon	4	3		3		
Surveyor	3					
Totals	117	45	2	33	6	2

SOURCE: *A List of Persons Who Voted* (Preston, 1838).
  KEY: P = Parker; F = Fleetwood; C = Crawfurd.

Fleetwood, still supported by the conservatives, was beginning to cause doubts and dissension in the ranks. By the 1837 election, when he again stood as an independent but stressed that there was only one issue, the New Poor Law, on which he had disagreed with the Whig government during the previous session, many local conservative leaders had deserted him. They adopted another landed gentleman, Robert Townley Parker of Cuerden Hall. On the hustings Parker was greeted with loud cheering "from all that were respectable," claimed the *Pilot*, "and by as hearty a disapprobation as any truly independent gentleman could desire, by the gaping crowds who had in reality no more to do with the Preston election, than they have in determining who shall be the next emperor of Morocco." The radical-liberal challenge came from John Crawfurd, previously governor of Singapore, and an active associate of John Bowring and Perronet Thompson at the *Westminster Review*. His platform proposed Repeal, "peace, retrenchment and reform," "Justice to Ireland," shorter parliaments, and universal suffrage. The Chartist leader, Feargus O'Connor, was the fourth candidate, but stood down in favor of Crawfurd without going to the poll.[34] Parker and Fleetwood won, and the town's tradition of hitching to the parliamentary wagon two oxen pulling in different directions continued.

The 1841 election, by contrast, was a straightforwardly two-party race, Fleetwood and Sir George Strickland (a former MP for Yorkshire) on the liberal ticket and Parker and Charles Swainson (of Swainson, Birley and Co.) for the conservatives. The local liberals made free trade the key issue. Because Fleetwood advocated Repeal, Peel presented him with a seal of the Fleetwood crest, a wheat sheaf, surrounded by the words "You deserve a good thrashing."[35] One liberal supporter claimed, "It is a struggle between the Landed Interest and the Commercial Interest"[36]—but as there were commercial and landed interests on both sides, and as the national Whig leadership was equivocal on the issue, such decisive rhetorical clarification was scarcely compelling. Yet the Repeal question troubled local Tories. In an attempt to square the circle of protecting his own commercial interests, appealing to the electorate, and bowing to the expressed will of his party, Swainson came out for an "alteration" in the Corn Laws, just as Feilden and Hornby in Blackburn talked about a need for a "revision" in the Corn Laws without damaging agriculture for the sake of trade and industry. Parker expressed considerable unease in private at toeing the party line, which he knew would be unpopular in Preston; his abstention from voting on the reduction of sugar duties, for example, earned him the sobriquet "Sour Pie Parker."[37]

On nomination day, leading inhabitants escorted Parker and Swainson into town from Walton Bridge; "We have never," observed the *Chronicle*, "witnessed a more magnificent gathering of the 'broad cloth' of Preston." Nevertheless the liberals won both seats for their platform of free trade, extension of

TABLE A12
Bourgeois Voting in Preston, 1841

	PSw	FSt	PF	FSw	F	St
Attorney	41	11				
Banker	6	3				
Barrister	1	2				
Clergyman	3					
Cotton spinner	23	4	1			
Editor	1					
Esquire	4					
Flax spinner	3	2				
Gentleman	38	22		1	2	
Governor (House of Correction)		1				
Ironfounder	1			2		
Manufacturer	12	12				
Merchant	1					
Minister		3				1
Physician	1	1	1			
Surgeon	8	3				
Surveyor	2					
Totals	145	64	2	3	2	1

SOURCE: *List of Persons Who Voted* (Preston, 1841).
  KEY: P = Parker; Sw = Swainson; F = Fleetwood; St = Strickland.

the suffrage, and the ballot.[38] As in Bolton, a four-cornered contest reduced bipartisan bourgeois voting drastically, only five men voting across party lines; unlike in Bolton, bourgeois voters recorded a more than two-to-one verdict in favor of the conservatives (145 for Parker and Swainson, 67 for Fleetwood and Strickland) (Table A12). The conservatives picked up the vast majority of the votes of those who had voted Fleetwood/Stanley in 1835.[39]

This pattern was repeated in 1847 (when Fleetwood retired), another notable triumph for the Preston free traders. The electorate returned the liberal Leaguers Strickland and Charles Pascoe Grenfell, a well-connected London and Liverpool merchant and a director of the Bank of England. In spite of the liberals' victory, the bourgeois votes once more heavily favored Parker, standing alone for the conservatives, and displayed a high degree of continuity from the 1841 election.[40]

NOTES

Abbreviations Used in the Notes

Newspapers
BA	*Blackburn Alfred*
BC	*Bolton Chronicle*
BFP	*Bolton Free Press*
BG	*Blackburn Gazette*
BM	*Blackburn Mail*
BS	*Blackburn Standard*
BT	*Blackburn Times*
MC	*Manchester Courier*
MG	*Manchester Guardian*
PC	*Preston Chronicle*
PG	*Preston Guardian*
PP	*Preston Pilot*

Archives
ASJ	Archives of the Society of Jesus, London
BALS	Bolton Archives and Local Studies
BL	British Library
BM	Blackburn Museum
BRL	Blackburn Reference Library
CERC	Church of England Record Centre
CMA	City of Manchester Archives
CUL	Cambridge University Library
LPL	Lambeth Palace Library
LRO	Lancashire Record Office, Preston
MCL	Manchester Central Library
PRL	Preston Reference Library
PRO	Public Record Office, Kew
SJC	St. John's College Library, Cambridge
WRO	Wigan Record Office

Journals
AHR	American Historical Review
BIHR	Bulletin of the Institute of Historical Research
Econ HR	Economic History Review
EHR	English Historical Review
HJ	Historical Journal
HW(J)	History Workshop (Journal)
IRSH	International Review of Social History
JBS	Journal of British Studies

JHG	Journal of Historical Geography
JMH	Journal of Modern History
JSH	Journal of Social History
JUH	Journal of Urban History
P&P	Past and Present
SH	Social History
THSLC	Transactions of the Historic Society of Lancashire and Cheshire
TIBG	Transactions of the Institute of British Geographers
TLCAS	Transactions of the Lancashire and Cheshire Antiquarian Society
UH(Y)	Urban History (Yearbook)

Notes to Introduction

[1] *Records of the Preston Oyster and Parched Pea Club 1773-1841* (Preston, 1861).

[2] The "bourgeoisie" was a term used only occasionally in Britain (see Penelope J. Corfield, "Concepts of the Urban Middle Class in Theory and Practice: England 1750-1850," in *Die Wiederkehr des Stadtbürgers: Städtereformen im europäischen Vergleich 1750 bis 1850,* ed. Brigitte Meier and Helga Schultz (Berlin: Berlin-Verlag A. Spitz, 1994), 239-42), but there is something to be said for using the same expression to describe a similar layer of society across the whole of Europe. My use of it is purely descriptive, presupposing no particular socioeconomic model. For a useful discussion of the distinctions between the "middle class" and the French *bourgeoisie,* the Italian *borghesia,* and the German *Bürgertum* (subdivided into the *Wirtschaftsbürgertum* (businessmen) and *Bildungsbürgertum* (professional men), and distinct from the *Kleinbürgertum* or *petite bourgeoisie*), see Jürgen Kocka, introduction to *Bourgeois Society in Nineteenth-Century Europe,* ed. Kocka and Allen Mitchell (Oxford and Providence, Rhode Island: Berg, 1993), x. For an alternative usage, see Alan Kidd and David Nicholls, "Introduction: The Making of the British Middle Class?" in *The Making of the British Middle Class? Studies of Regional and Cultural Diversity Since the Eighteenth Century,* ed. idem (Stroud, Gloucestershire: Sutton, 1998), xxiv.

[3] See Jürgen Kocka, "The Middle Classes in Europe," *JMH* 67, 4 (Dec. 1995): 804.

[4] See Frank O'Gorman's thoughts on the "much-vaunted, yet poorly understood, avoidance of serious social dislocation between 1800 and 1832. . . ." ("Eighteenth-Century England as an *Ancien Régime,*" in *Hanoverian Britain and Empire,* ed. Stephen Taylor, Richard Connors, and Clyve Jones (Woodbridge, Suffolk: Boydell Press, 1998), 36).

[5] See, e.g., Roderick Floud and Donald McCloskey, eds., *The Economic History of Britain Since 1700,* vol. I (Cambridge: Cambridge University Press, 1981); Maxine Berg, *The Age of Manufactures: Industry, Innovation and Work in Britain 1700-1820* (Oxford: Blackwell, 1985); N. F. R. Crafts, *British Economic Growth During the Industrial Revolution* (Oxford: Clarendon Press, 1985); V. A. C. Gatrell, "Labour, Power, and the Size of Firms in Lancashire Cotton in the Second Quarter of the Nineteenth Century," *Econ HR* 2nd ser., XXX, i (Feb. 1977): 95-139; Patrick Joyce, "Work," in *The Cambridge Social History of Britain 1750-1950,* vol. 2, ed. F. M. L. Thompson (Cambridge: Cambridge University Press, 1990); S. D. Chapman, "Financial Restraints on the Growth of Firms in the Cotton Industry, 1790-1850," *Econ HR* 2nd ser., XXXII, 1 (Feb. 1979): 50-69; idem, *The Cotton Industry in the Industrial Revolution,* 2nd ed. (1987; reprinted in L. A. Clarkson, ed., *The Industrial Revolution: A Compendium* (Basingstoke: Macmillan, 1990)); David Cannadine, "The Past and the Present in the English Industrial Revolution 1880-1980," *P&P* 103 (May 1984): 131-72. But for recent challenges to the slow-growth thesis, see Patrick O'Brien, "Introduc-

tion: Modern Conceptions of the Industrial Revolution," in *The Industrial Revolution and British Society*, ed. O'Brien and Roland Quinault (Cambridge: Cambridge University Press, 1993); David S. Landes, "The Fable of the Dead Horse; or, The Industrial Revolution Revisited," in *The British Industrial Revolution: An Economic Perspective*, ed. Joel Mokyr (Boulder, Colo.: Westview Press, 1993); Donald McCloskey, "1780-1860: a survey," in *The Economic History of Britain Since 1700*, ed. Roderick Floud and McCloskey, 2nd ed. (Cambridge: Cambridge University Press, 1994), I: 242-43; Geoffrey Timmins, *Made in Lancashire: A History of Regional Industrialisation* (Manchester: Manchester University Press, 1998), chap. 6.

[6.] Notably Jonathan C. D. Clark, *English Society, 1688-1832: Ideology, Social Structure and Political Practice During the Ancien Regime* (Cambridge: Cambridge University Press, 1985).

[7.] See, e.g., John Stevenson, "Social Aspects of the Industrial Revolution," in *Industrial Revolution*, ed. O'Brien and Quinault, 248-49.

[8.] Notably Tom Nairn, "The British Political Elite," and Perry Anderson, "Origins of the Present Crisis," *New Left Review*, 23 (1964); Nairn "The English Working Class," *New Left Review*, 24 (1964); idem, *The Enchanted Glass: Britain and its Monarchy* (London: Radius, 1988).

[9.] Famously, Elie Halévy, *Histoire du peuple anglais au XIXe siècle*, vol. I (Paris, 1912); Eric J. Hobsbawm, "The Labour Aristocracy in Nineteenth-century Britain," in his *Labouring Men: Studies in the History of Labour* (New York: Basic Books, 1964), 272-315.

[10.] John Saville, *1848: The British State and the Chartist Movement* (Cambridge: Cambridge University Press, 1987).

[11.] V. I. Lenin, *The Collapse of the Second International* (1915), in vol. 21 of his *Collected Works* (Moscow: Progress Publishers, 1964), 213-14. I owe this reference to V. A. C. Gatrell.

[12.] Michael Mann, *The Sources of Social Power*, vol. II, *The Rise of Classes and Nation-States, 1760-1914* (Cambridge: Cambridge University Press, 1993), 529-31, 541, 724.

[13.] Gareth Stedman Jones, "Rethinking Chartism," in his *Languages of Class: Studies in English Working Class History 1832-1982* (Cambridge: Cambridge University Press, 1983); J. R. Dinwiddy, "Chartism," in his *Radicalism and Reform in Britain, 1780-1850* (London: Hambledon Press, 1992), 416-20.

[14.] Charles Tilly, *Popular Contention in Great Britain 1758-1834* (Cambridge, Mass.: Harvard University Press, 1995), 12-19, 23-24.

[15.] E. P. Thompson, "The Peculiarities of the English," in his *The Poverty of Theory and Other Essays* (New York: Monthly Review Press, 1978), 257-66; Robert Gray, "Bourgeois Hegemony in Victorian Britain," in *Papers on Class, Hegemony and Party*, ed. Jonathan Bloomfield (London: Lawrence and Wishart, 1977); David Blackbourn and Geoff Eley, *The Peculiarities of German History: Bourgeois Society and Politics in Nineteenth-Century Germany* (Oxford: Oxford University Press, 1984), 16-18.

[16.] Patrick Joyce, introduction to *Oxford Readers: Class*, ed. idem (Oxford: Oxford University Press, 1995), 3-16; David Cannadine, *The Rise and Fall of Class in Britain* (New York: Columbia University Press, 1999), chap. 1; William M. Reddy, "The Concept of Class," in *Social Orders and Social Classes in Europe Since 1500: Studies in Social Stratification*, ed. M. L. Bush (London: Longman, 1992).

[17.] Attempts to date the achievement of class consciousness include Harold Perkin, *The Origins of Modern English Society 1780-1880* (London: Routledge and Kegan Paul, 1969), 209; Edward Royle, *Modern Britain: A Social History 1750-1985* (London: Edward Arnold, 1987), 96-98; Clive Emsley, *British Society and the French Wars 1793-1815* (London: Macmillan, 1979), 177; Michael E. Rose, "Social Change and the Industrial Revolution," in *Economic History of Britain,* ed. Floud and McCloskey, 1st ed., 1: 256-58; E. P. Thompson, *The Making of the English Working Class,* rev. ed. (London: Victor Gollancz, 1980), 887-88; Dorothy Thompson, *The Chartists* (London: Temple Smith, 1984), 5; Stedman Jones, "Rethinking Chartism," 105, 173; Clark, *English Society,* 92; F. M. L. Thompson, *The Rise of Respectable Society: A Social History of Victorian Britain, 1830-1900* (London: Fontana, 1988), 16; R. S. Neale, "The Bourgeoisie, Historically, has Played a Most Revolutionary Part," in his *Writing Marxist History: British Society, Economy and Culture since 1700* (Oxford: Blackwell, 1985); Craig Calhoun, "Class, Place and Industrial Revolution," in *Class and Space: The Making of Urban Society,* ed. Nigel Thrift and Peter Williams (London: Routledge and Kegan Paul, 1987), 54. For skepticism, see Tom Nossiter, "The Middle Class and Nineteenth Century Politics: Notes on the Literature," and Keith Robbins, "John Bright and the Middle Class in Politics," in *The Middle Class in Politics,* ed. John Garrard et al. (Farnborough: Saxon House, 1978), 28, 32, 80-81; Norman McCord, "Adding a Touch of Class," *History* 70, 230 (Oct. 1985): 410-19; Nicholas Rogers, introduction to "Making the English Middle Class, ca. 1700-1850," *JBS* 32, 4 (Oct. 1993): 299-304; David Cannadine, introduction to *Patricians, Power and Politics in Nineteenth-Century Towns,* ed. idem (Leicester: Leicester University Press, 1982), 8-10.

[18.] Peter Earle, *The Making of the English Middle Class: Business, Society and Family Life in London, 1660-1730* (London: Methuen, 1989); Peter Borsay, *The English Urban Renaissance: Culture and Society in the Provincial Town, 1660-1770* (Oxford: Clarendon Press, 1989); Penelope J. Corfield, *The Impact of English Towns, 1700-1800* (Oxford: Oxford University Press, 1982); idem, "Class by Name and Number in Eighteenth-Century Britain," *History* 72 (1987): 38-61; idem, *Power and the Professions in Britain 1700-1850* (London: Routledge, 1995); Paul Langford, *A Polite and Commercial People: England 1727-1783* (Oxford: Clarendon Press, 1989); John Brewer, *Party Ideology and Popular Politics at the Accession of George III* (Cambridge: Cambridge University Press, 1976); Neil McKendrick, John Brewer, and J. H. Plumb, eds., *The Birth of a Consumer Society: The Commercialization of Eighteenth-Century England* (London: Europa Publications, 1982); John Brewer and Roy Porter, eds., *Consumption and the World of Goods* (London: Routledge, 1993); Hoh-Cheung Mui and Lorna H. Mui, *Shops and Shopkeeping in Eighteenth-Century England* (Kingston and Montreal: McGill-Queen's University Press, 1989); John Smail, *The Origins of Middle Class Culture: Halifax, Yorkshire, 1660-1780* (Ithaca: Cornell University Press, 1994); Kathleen Wilson, *The Sense of the People: Politics, Culture and Imperialism in England, 1715-1785* (Cambridge: Cambridge University Press, 1995); Jonathan Barry and Christopher Brooks, eds., *The Middling Sort of People: Culture, Society and Politics in England, 1550-1800* (New York: St. Martin's Press, 1994); Margaret R. Hunt, *The Middling Sort: Commerce, Gender, and the Family in England, 1680-1780* (Berkeley and Los Angeles: University of California Press, 1996); H. R. French, "The Search for the 'Middle Sort of People' in England, 1600-1800," *HJ* 43, 1 (2000): 277-93. These depictions are very far from Jonathan Clark's Ancien Régime society or Edward Thompson's fields of force around patrician and plebeian poles (see his "Patrician Society, Plebeian Culture," *JSH* 7 (1974): 381-405, and his considered reply to his critics, "The Patricians and the Plebs," in his *Customs in Common* (New York: The New Press, 1991), 18-32, 87-90, 95-96).

[19.] Jürgen Habermas, *The Structural Transformation of the Public Sphere: An Inquiry into a Category of Bourgeois Society*, trans. Thomas Burger (Cambridge, Mass.: MIT Press, 1989); Geoff Eley, "Nations, Publics, and Political Cultures: Placing Habermas in the Nineteenth Century," in *Habermas and the Public Sphere*, ed. Craig Calhoun (Cambridge, Mass.: MIT Press, 1992); Steve Pincus, "'Coffee Politicians Does Create': Coffeehouses and Restoration Political Culture," *JMH* 67, 4 (Dec. 1995): 807-34.

[20.] See, e.g., William Reddy, *Money and Liberty in Modern Europe: A Critique of Historical Understanding* (Cambridge: Cambridge University Press, 1987); Michelle Perrot, introduction to *From the Fires of Revolution to the Great War*, ed. idem, vol. IV, *A History of Private Life*, ed. Philippe Ariès and Georges Duby (Cambridge, Mass.: Harvard University Press, 1990), 1-2; Patrick Joyce, *Visions of the People: Industrial England and the Question of Class 1848-1914* (Cambridge: Cambridge University Press, 1991), 27-29; Keith Michael Baker, *Inventing the French Revolution: Essays on French Political Culture in the Eighteenth Century* (Cambridge: Cambridge University Press, 1990), 5-9, 19; Terry Eagleton, *Ideology: An Introduction* (London: Verso, 1991), 206ff.; Charles Tilly, "Citizenship, Identity and Social History," *IRSH* 40, supplement 3 (1995): 3-5; Erik Olin Wright, *Classes* (London: Verso, 1985), 56ff., for a critique; Ernest Gellner, *Plough, Sword and Book: The Structure of Human History* (London: Paladin, 1991), 34-35.

[21.] Asa Briggs, "The Language of 'Class' in Early Nineteenth-Century England," and "The Language of 'Mass' and 'Masses' in Nineteenth-Century England," in *The Collected Essays of Asa Briggs*, vol.1 (Brighton: Harvester Press, 1985).

[22.] Cannadine, *Rise and Fall*, chap. 3.

[23.] Dror Wahrman, *Imagining the Middle Class: The Political Representation of Class in Britain, c.1780-1840* (Cambridge: Cambridge University Press, 1995); idem, "Virtual Representation: Parliamentary Reporting and Languages of Class in the 1790s," *P&P* 136 (Aug. 1992): 83-113; idem, "'Middle-Class' Domesticity Goes Public: Gender, Class, and Politics from Queen Caroline to Queen Victoria," *JBS* 32, 4 (Oct. 1993): 396-432. Also Geoffrey Crossick, "From Gentlemen to the Residuum: Languages of Social Description in Victorian Britain," in *Language, History and Class*, ed. Corfield, 158, 177; Raymond Williams, *Keywords: A Vocabulary of Culture and Society* (Oxford: Oxford University Press, 1985), 61-69; Patrick Joyce, *Democratic Subjects: The Self and the Social in Nineteenth-century England* (Cambridge: Cambridge University Press, 1994), chap. 13.

[24.] See, variously, Philip Hills, "Division and Cohesion in the Nineteenth-Century Middle Class: the Case of Ipswich 1830-1870," *UHY* (1987): 42-50; John L. Field, "Bourgeois Portsmouth: Social Relations in a Victorian Dockyard Town, 1815-75" (Ph.D. diss., Warwick University, 1979), 348, 488; P. Jones, "Perspective, Sources and Methodology in a Comparative Study of the Middle Class in Nineteenth-Century Leicester and Peterborough," *UHY* (1987): 22-32; Richard Trainor, "Authority and Social Structure in an Industrialized Area: A Study of Three Black Country Towns, 1840-1890" (D.Phil. diss., Oxford University, 1981), 57-61; Corfield, *Power and the Professions*, chap. 10; M. J. Daunton, "'Gentlemanly Capitalism' and British Industry 1820-1914," *P&P* 122 (Feb. 1989): 156; David W. Bebbington, *Evangelicalism in Modern Britain: A History from the 1730s to the 1980s* (London: Unwin Hyman, 1989), 136; David Blackbourn, "The German Bourgeoisie: an Introduction," in *The German Bourgeoisie: Essays on the Social History of the German Middle Class from the Late Eighteenth to the Early Twentieth Century*, ed. Blackbourn and Richard J. Evans (London: Routledge, 1991), 8-12; Patrick Joyce, *Work, Society and Politics: The*

Culture of the Factory in Later Victorian England (Brighton: Harvester Press, 1980), chap. 1; James Obelkevich, "Religion," in *The Cambridge Social History*, ed. Thompson, 3: 322, 333-34; John Seed, "Theologies of Power: Unitarianism and the Social Relations of Religious Discourse, 1800-50," in *Class, Power and Social Structure in British Nineteenth-Century Towns*, ed. R. J. Morris (Leicester: Leicester University Press, 1986), 130-31, 146; Simon Gunn, "The Ministry, the Middle Class and the 'Civilizing Mission' in Manchester, 1850-80," *SH* 21, 1 (Jan. 1996): 23, 35-36; Leonore Davidoff and Catherine Hall, *Family Fortunes: Men and Women of the English Middle Class, 1780-1850* (London: Hutchinson, 1987); Kidd and Nicholls, introduction to *Making of the British Middle Class*, ed. idem, xxv-xxvii; Phillida Ballard, "A Commercial and Industrial Elite: Upper-Middle Classes of Birmingham, 1780-1914" (Ph.D. diss., Reading University, 1984).

[25.] Notably Davidoff and Hall, *Family Fortunes*; Theodore Koditschek, *Class Formation and Urban-Industrial Society: Bradford, 1750-1850* (Cambridge: Cambridge University Press, 1990); R. J. Morris, *Class, Sect and Party: The Making of the British Middle Class, Leeds 1820-1850* (Manchester: Manchester University Press, 1990).

[26.] For a critique of the exclusion of the state and politics from a number of notable studies, see Adrian Wilson, "A Critical Portrait of Social History," in *Rethinking Social History: English Society 1570-1920 and its Interpretation*, ed. idem (Manchester: Manchester University Press, 1993), 19, 26-27; John Seed, "Capital and Class Formation in Early Industrial England," *SH* 18, 1 (Jan. 1993): 17-30.

[27.] See, e.g., Leslie G. Mitchell, *Charles James Fox* (London: Penguin, 1997); Peter Mandler, *Aristocratic Government in the Age of Reform: Whigs and Liberals, 1830-1852* (Oxford: Clarendon Press, 1990); T. A. Jenkins, *The Liberal Ascendancy, 1830-1886* (New York: St. Martin's Press, 1994), 7.

[28.] Roger Wells, *Wretched Faces: Famine in Wartime England 1793-1801* (Gloucester: Sutton, 1988), 324.

[29.] Robert Gray, *The Factory Question and Industrial England, 1830-1860* (Cambridge: Cambridge University Press, 1996), 48, 129, 209-10.

[30.] See, e.g., Anthony Giddens, *A Contemporary Critique of Historical Materialism*, vol. I, *Power, Property and the State* (Berkeley and Los Angeles: University of California Press, 1981), vol. II, *The Nation-State and Violence* (Cambridge: Polity Press, 1987); Charles Tilly, *Coercion, Capital, and European States, AD 990-1990* (Oxford: Blackwell, 1990); Ernest Gellner, *Nations and Nationalism* (Oxford: Blackwell, 1983), 55-57.

[31.] See, e.g., Michel Foucault, *Discipline and Punish: The Birth of the Prison* (New York: Pantheon Books, 1977); Giddens, *Nation-State and Violence*; Michael Ignatieff, "Total Institutions and Working Classes: A Review Essay," *HW(J)* 15 (Spring 1983).

[32.] See Brian Harrison, *Peaceable Kingdom: Stability and Change in Modern Britain* (Oxford: Clarendon Press, 1982), 3-4.

[33.] E. P. Thompson, *Witness Against the Beast: William Blake and the Moral Law* (Cambridge: Cambridge University Press, 1993), 108-109.

[34.] See Philip Corrigan and Derek Sayer, *The Great Arch: English State Formation as Cultural Revolution* (Oxford: Blackwell, 1985), 130, 189-95, 201-202, 207-208; Antonio Gramsci, *Selections from the Prison Notebooks*, ed. and trans. Quintin Hoare and Geoffrey Nowell-Smith (New York: International Publishers, 1971); Ernesto Laclau and Chantal Mouffe, introduction to *Hegemony & Socialist Strategy: Towards a Radical Democratic Politics* (London: Verso, 1985).

[35.] See Patrick Curry, "Towards a Post-Marxist Social History: Thompson, Clark and Beyond," in *Rethinking Social History*, ed. Wilson, 165-87; Raymond Williams,

"Selections from *Marxism and Literature*," in *Culture/Power/History: A Reader in Contemporary Social Theory*, ed. Nicholas B. Dirks, Geoff Eley, and Sherry B. Ortner (Princeton: Princeton University Press, 1994), 596-98; and contrast Stephen Hill, "Britain: The Dominant Ideology Thesis after a Decade," and Bryan S. Turner, "Conclusion: Peroration on Ideology," in *Dominant Ideologies*, ed. Nicholas Abercrombie, Hill, and Turner (London: Unwin Hyman, 1990).

[36.] See Geoff Eley, "Edward Thompson, Social History and Political Culture: The Making of a Working-Class Public, 1780-1850," in *E. P. Thompson: Critical Perspectives*, ed. Harvey J. Kaye and Keith McClelland (Philadelphia: Temple University Press, 1990), 29, 36-39.

[37.] Marc W. Steinberg, "Culturally Speaking: Finding a Commons Between Post-Structuralism and the Thompsonian Perspective," *SH* 21, 2 (May 1996): 205.

[38.] According to *Census of Great Britain, 1851: Population Tables, Division VIII* (London, 1852): Blackburn Parish: 45,269 acres; Bolton Parish: 30,062 acres; Preston Parish: 15,659 acres; Deane Parish: 19,340 acres. The area of study includes two enclaves: Fulwood, a detached part of Lancaster Parish to the north of the town of Preston and surrounded by Preston Parish; and Great Lever, a detached part of Middleton Parish to the south of the town of Bolton and sandwiched between Bolton and Deane Parishes.

[39.] This needs particular emphasis in light of attempts to devalue the importance of the northern bourgeoisie. See W. D. Rubinstein, *Elites and the Wealthy in Modern British History: Essays in Social and Economic History* (Brighton: Harvester Press, 1987); idem, *Men of Property: The Very Wealthy in Britain Since the Industrial Revolution* (London: Croom Helm, 1981); P. J. Cain and A. G. Hopkins, *British Imperialism*, vol. 1, *Innovation and Expansion 1688-1914* (London and New York: Longman, 1993). For perceptive critiques see Daunton, "'Gentlemanly Capitalism'," 119-58; Geoffrey Ingham, "British Capitalism: Empire, Merchants and Decline," *SH* 20, 3 (Oct. 1995): 339-54.

[40.] LRO, Derby Papers, DDK 27/11, annual income for 1797; 1549/1, Preston survey 1774; /9, Preston survey 1819.

[41.] LRO, Bradford Papers, DDBm 1/34, "Survey of Estates belonging to the Rt. Hon. Lord Bradford," 1810; BALS, ZBR/4/5, "A Plan of Estates belonging to the Right Honble. Orlando Lord Bradford" (Chorlton and Piggot, 1815).

[42.] As pointed out by G. Rogers, "Social and Economic Change on Lancashire Landed Estates During the Nineteenth Century with Special Reference to the Clifton Estate 1832-1916" (Ph.D. diss., Lancaster University, 1981), 326-27. For details of local landownership see Brian Lewis, "Bourgeois Ideology and Order: Middle-Class Culture and Politics in Lancashire, 1789-1851" (Ph.D. diss., Harvard University, 1994), 25-30.

[43.] There is much valuable information about local calico printers in S. D. Chapman and S. Chassagne, *European Textile Printers in the Eighteenth Century: A Study of Peel and Oberkampf* (London: Heinemann, 1981); John Graham, "The Chemistry of Calico Printing from 1790 to 1835 and History of Printworks in the Manchester District from 1760-1846" (MS in MCL, Reference Library, 1846); Sydney H. Pavière, "History of Cotton Printing: New Light on Early Days," *Texture* (Mar. 1957): 7-14.

[44.] For bleachers and papermakers, see Sir Alan John Sykes et al., *Concerning the Bleaching Industry* (Manchester, 1925); Denis Lyddon and Peter Marshall, *Paper in Bolton: A Papermaker's Tale* (Altrincham, 1975); Ian A. Hughes, *Hughes—A Family of Papermakers* (Northcote, Victoria, Australia, 1978); Cyril G. Hampson, *150th Anniversary History of Robert Fletcher and Son Ltd.* (Manchester, 1973); James J. Francis, *History of Bradshaw, Part two: Bradshaw Works* (Turton, 1979); A. V. Sugden and E. A. Entwisle, *Potters of Darwen, 1839-1939: A Century of Wallpaper Printing by Machinery* (Manchester, 1939).

[45.] All aspects of the local cotton industry are discussed in the general local histories repeatedly cited throughout the book, and in Stanley Chapman, *Merchant Enterprise in Britain: From the Industrial Revolution to World War I* (Cambridge: Cambridge University Press, 1992), especially 63, 89-92, 101-102; Mary B. Rose, ed., *The Lancashire Cotton Industry: A History Since 1700* (Preston: Lancashire County Books, 1996); Timmins, *Made in Lancashire*, chaps. 4-6; R. S. Crossley, *Accrington Captains of Industry* (Accrington, 1930); *Industries of Lancashire 1889-90* (London, 1889-90); CMA, MS f310.6 MS, "1837: Bolton District: Presented to the Manchester Statistical Society by H. and E. Ashworth, Turton April 11 1837"; MCL, Local History Library, MS 942.72 S154, Giles Shaw MSS, vol. XIV: Edwin Butterworth, "MS History of Bolton-le-Moors," 142-56; James H. Longworth, *The Cotton Mills of Bolton 1780-1985: A Historical Directory* (Bolton, 1987); Michael Rothwell, "The Oswaldtwistle Cotton Industry 1760-1960" (typescript in BRL, 1966-74); idem, *Industrial Heritage: A Guide to the Industrial Archaeology of Blackburn*, vol. I, "The Textile Industry" (Hyndburn Local History Society, 1985); Rhodes Boyson, *The Ashworth Cotton Enterprise: The Rise and Fall of a Family Firm* (Oxford: Clarendon Press, 1970); Brian Hall, *Lowerhouse and the Dugdales: The Story of a Lancashire Mill Community* (Burnley and District Historical Society, 1976); Sir Charles Brown, *Origins and Progress of Horrockses, Crewdson and Co.* (Preston, n.d.); Various Writers, *Fortunes Made in Business* (London, 1887), vol. III (on Horrocks, Miller and Co.); W. P. Crankshaw and Alfred Blackburn, *A Century and a Half of Cotton Spinning 1797-1947: The History of Knowles, Ltd. of Bolton* (Bolton, n.d.); H. N. Davies, *Moscow Mill and its People* (n.p., n.d.); LRO, DDHs, Horrocks, Crewdson and Co. Papers. Other industries are treated in Michael Rothwell, "Industrial Oswaldtwistle 1760-1960: The History and Industrial Archaeology of Coal, Chemicals and Other Industries in Oswaldtwistle" (typescript in BRL, 1980); idem, *Industrial Heritage: A Guide to the Industrial Archaeology of Blackburn*, vol. II, "Other Industries" (1986); Lesley Richmond and Alison Turton, eds., *The Brewing Industry: A Guide to Historical Records* (Manchester: Manchester University Press, 1990); Arthur Noel Walker, *The Walker Family 1681 to 1946* (printed for private circulation, 1947), of Rose Hill Tannery, Bolton; James J. Francis, *History of Bradshaw, part one: Lords of the Manor of Bradshaw* (Turton Local History Society, 1977); idem, *Bradshaw and Harwood Collieries* (Turton, 1982); Philip W. Pilling, "Hick Hargreaves and Co.: The History of an Engineering Firm c.1833-1939: A Study with Special Reference to Technological Change and Markets" (Ph.D. diss., Liverpool University, 1985); anon., *Samuel Crompton [and] a Short History of Messrs. Dobson and Barlow Ltd.* (Bolton, 1927), engineers and iron-founders; David Brownlie, "John George Bodmer, His Life and Work, Particularly in Relation to the Evolution of Mechanical Stoking," *Newcomen Society Transactions* VI (1925-26), 86-110; J. G. Shaw, *History of Thomas Hart's Rope-Works Blackburn* (reprinted from *BT*, 1930).

Notes to Chapter 1

[1.] LRO, Hoghton Papers, DDHo/454, E. Wilbraham Bootle to Sir Henry Philip Hoghton, June 4, 1811; /459, obituaries in *London Gazette* and *Preston Journal*, June 15; /452, Maj. Gen. Stewart to Hoghton, May 29; /456, George Ramsden, aide-de-camp, to Hoghton, June 13. See also /449, Ramsden to Hoghton, n.d.; /450, Thomas

Coffin to Hoghton, May 18; /451, Wellington to Wellesley, May 22 (enclosed in /453, Wellesley to Wilbraham Bootle).

2. Sir Lees Knowles, ed., *The War in the Peninsula: Some Letters of Lieutenant Robert Knowles, a Bolton Officer* (Bolton, 1909; reprinted from *Bolton Journal and Guardian*), 28-29 (Knowles to father, Oct. 7, 1811), 31, 40 (to father, Dec. 31, 1811), 61-62 (to father, Feb. 7, 1813; here the tone is different: "the miseries I have witnessed and partially endured in this country have in some measure hardened my feelings"), 65.

3. LRO, Hoghton Papers, DDHo/448, May 3, 1811.

4. For the strength of loyalism, see H. T. Dickinson, *Liberty and Property: Political Ideology in Eighteenth-Century Britain* (London: Weidenfeld and Nicolson, 1977), chap. 8; David Eastwood, "Patriotism and the English State in the 1790s," and John Dinwiddy, "Interpretations of Anti-Jacobinism," in *The French Revolution and British Popular Politics*, ed. Mark Philp (Cambridge: Cambridge University Press, 1991), 38-49, 146-48.

5. See introduction to Nicholas B. Dirks, Geoff Eley, and Sherry B. Ortner, eds., *Culture/Power/History: A Reader in Contemporary Social Theory* (Princeton: Princeton University Press, 1994), 3-16: The construction of narratives advanced a "set of discursive claims about the social world," allowing individuals to make sense of themselves in time and space and to mobilize behind active political agendas.

6. On these competing visions of state and society, and their early manifestation during the American War, see James E. Bradley, *Religion, Revolution, and English Radicalism: Nonconformity in Eighteenth-Century Politics and Society* (Cambridge: Cambridge University Press, 1990), 419, 422, and passim.

7. See Jan Albers, "'Papist Traitors' and 'Presbyterian Rogues': Religious Identities in Eighteenth-century Lancashire," in *The Church of England c.1689-c.1833: From Toleration to Tractarianism*, ed. John Walsh, Colin Haydon, and Stephen Taylor (Cambridge: Cambridge University Press, 1993), 319-20; Michael R. Watts, *The Dissenters*, vol. I, *From the Reformation to the French Revolution* (Oxford: Clarendon Press, 1978), 3-5.

8. See John Brewer, "English Radicalism in the Age of George III," in *Three British Revolutions: 1641, 1688, 1776*, ed. J. G. A. Pocock (Princeton: Princeton University Press, 1980), 323-67; John Seed, "Gentlemen Dissenters: The Social and Political Meanings of Rational Dissent in the 1770s and 1780s," *HJ* 28, 2 (1985): 299.

9. Paul Langford, *Public Life and the Propertied Englishman 1689-1798* (Oxford: Clarendon Press, 1991), 73-76; Bradley, *Religion, Revolution, and English Radicalism*, 36-37.

10. A Dissenter [Holland], *An Address to the Members of the Establishment, in the Town and Neighbourhood of Bolton* (1790), 13-14.

11. Jan M. Albers, "Seeds of Contention: Society, Politics and the Church of England in Lancashire, 1689-1790" (Ph.D. diss., Yale University, 1988), 297, 377, 496-97; Albert Goodwin, *The Friends of Liberty: The English Democratic Movement in the Age of the French Revolution* (London: Hutchinson, 1979), 81-85, 89-93; Frank O'Gorman, "Pitt and the 'Tory' Reaction to the French Revolution 1789-1815," in *Britain and the French Revolution, 1789-1815*, ed. H. T. Dickinson (Basingstoke: Macmillan, 1989), 114-15.

12. Dumas Malone, *The Public Life of Thomas Cooper 1783-1839* (New Haven: Yale University Press, 1926), 3-9, 17.

13. BALS, B 274.2 FLE. PB, *Letter of Samuel Fletcher, Little Lever*, to Thomas Plumbe, chairman of the Bolton Meeting, Feb. 27, 1790; MCL, Broadsides, f1790/2/A,

quoted by Albers, "Seeds of Contention," 464-65; Archibald Prentice, *Historical Sketches and Personal Recollections of Manchester. Intended to Illustrate the Progress of Public Opinion From 1792 to 1832*, 2nd ed. (1851; reprint, London: Cass, 1970), 4; G. M. Ditchfield, "The Campaign in Lancashire and Cheshire for the Repeal of the Test and Corporation Acts, 1787-1790," *THSLC* 126 (1976): 118-19.

[14] MCL, Broadsides, f1790/2/B, quoted by Albers, "Seeds of Contention," 466.

[15] Goodwin, *Friends of Liberty*, 96-98, 145-47.

[16] Malone, *Cooper*, 71-72, 75.

[17] W. Brimelow, *Political and Parliamentary History of Bolton* (Bolton, 1882), 7-10; *BC*, Sept. 9, 1837, p. 2; Maureen Price, "Bolton and the Effects of the French Revolution and Napoleonic Wars 1789-1815" (Cert. Ed. thesis, Chorley College, 1972), 11-12.

[18] Franklin Baker, *The Rise and Progress of Nonconformity in Bolton* (London, 1854), 68.

[19] See Robert R. Dozier, *For King, Constitution, and Country: The English Loyalists and the French Revolution* (Lexington: University Press of Kentucky, 1983), 54-55, 59, 62; H. T. Dickinson, "Popular Conservatism and Militant Loyalism 1789-1815," in *Britain and the French Revolution*, ed. idem, 114-15.

[20] See, e.g., poem in *BM*, June 19, 1793, p. 4.

[21] *BM*, Mar. 19, 1794, p. 3 (taken from a published Fast Day sermon in St. John's Church, Leeds).

[22] Thomas Starkie, *A Sermon, Occasioned by the Present Times* (Blackburn, 1793), 5-12.

[23] Thomas Bancroft, *The Chain of Duty; or, An Exhortation to Civil and Religious Obedience* (Bolton, 1797), 3-12, 20.

[24] Thomas Bancroft, *A Sermon Preached Before the Officers and Privates of the Loyal Bolton Volunteer Corps of Infantry, on Thursday, May 6th, 1802, Being the Day on which they were Disembodied, and their Colours Deposited in the Parish Church of Bolton* (Bolton, 1802), 10-11.

[25] *BM*, June 12, 1793, p. 3.

[26] Joseph Barrett, *Candour and Mutual Forbearance: A Sermon, Preached to a Congregation of Dissenters at Darwen, Lancashire, and Applicable to the Present State of Parties in this Kingdom* (Blackburn, 1795), 5, 8, 10, 12-13.

[27] *BM*, e.g., June 12, 1793, p. 1; July 10, p. 4; July 17, p. 1; Sept. 4, p. 1; Sept. 11, p. 4; Sept. 25, 1793, p. 4; Feb. 26, 1794, p. 4.

[28] *BM*, July 24, 1793.

[29] *BM*, Feb. 12, 1794, p. 3. See also Jan. 4, 1809, p. 3; and the Rev. T. Stevenson, *A Sermon, Preached at St. John's Church, Blackburn, Lancashire, on Thursday, December 5, 1805, being the day appointed for a General Thanksgiving to Almighty God, for the glorious and important Victories, obtained by his Majesty's arms over the United Fleets of France and Spain, on the 21st of October, and 4th of November last* (Blackburn, 1805), 14. For instances of largesse, see *BM*, Dec. 25, 1793, p. 3 (Henry Sudell and others); Apr. 19, 1797 (Cross of Preston); Jan. 9, 1799, p. 3 (Sudell and Horrocks); Dec. 11, 1805, p. 3 (Le Gendre Pierce Starkie of Huntroyd); Nov. 2, 1808, p. 3 (Hulton of Hulton Park); Apr. 5, 1809, p. 3 (William Assheton of Downham); Nov. 1, 1809, p. 3 (Sudell, and Joseph Hornby of Ribby House); Nov. 8, 1809, p. 3 (Richard Ainsworth of Halliwell); Aug. 21, 1811, p. 3 (Le Gendre Starkie of Huntroyd).

[30] *BM*, June 4, 1794, p. 3. But note that in 1797 (*BM*, May 31, p. 3), the editor reported that there were fewer oak boughs than usual, and he did not know whether to blame the wet weather or disloyalty to the monarchy.

[31.] *BM*, June 18, 1794, p. 3; Oct. 25, 1797, p. 3.

[32.] Quoted by William Alexander Abram, "Sketches in Local History," vol. 7, p. 159 (cuttings from *PG*, 1877-84, in PRL).

[33.] E.g., *BM*, Mar. 1, 1797, p. 3 (quotation); Mar. 7, 1810, p. 3.

[34.] *BM*, Nov. 20, 1793, p. 3; Dec. 4, p. 3; Dec. 11, p. 3; Jan. 8, 1794, p. 3; Jan. 22, p. 3; Jan. 29, p. 3; Feb. 5, p. 3; Nov. 1, 1797, p. 3; Nov. 8, p. 3.

[35.] *BM*, Apr. 25, 1798, p. 2.

[36.] *BM*, Mar. 14, 1798, p. 3.

[37.] *BM*, Mar. 7, p. 2.

[38.] *BM*, Apr. 4, p. 3; Apr. 11, p. 3; Apr. 18, p. 3; Apr. 25, p. 2. For subscriptions in Lower Darwen, see J. G. Shaw, *History and Traditions of Darwen and its People* (Blackburn, 1889), 138-39.

[39.] See J. E. Cookson, *The Friends of Peace: Anti-War Liberalism in England, 1793-1815* (Cambridge: Cambridge University Press, 1982), 163, 184-85; idem, *The British Armed Nation 1793-1815* (Oxford: Clarendon Press, 1997), v, 244, and passim.

[40.] J. R. Western, "The Volunteer Movement as an Anti-revolutionary Force, 1793-1801," *EHR* LXXI (Oct. 1956): 605-607; Austin Gee, "The British Volunteer Movement 1793-1807" (D.Phil. diss., Oxford University, 1989), xiii-xiv, 30, 48, 179, and passim; Linda Colley, *Britons: Forging the Nation 1707-1837* (New Haven: Yale University Press, 1992), chaps. 6-7; idem, "Whose Nation? Class and National Consciousness in Britain 1750-1830," *P&P* 113 (Nov. 1986): 109-17; idem, "The Apotheosis of George III: Loyalty, Royalty and the British Nation 1760-1820," *P&P* 102 (Feb. 1984): 96-97; J. W. Fortescue, *The British Army 1783-1802: Four Lectures Delivered at the Staff College and Cavalry School* (London, 1905), 49-50; Dickinson, "Popular Conservatism," and Clive Emsley, "The Social Impact of the French Wars," in *Britain and the French Revolution*, ed. Dickinson, 117-18, 213, 219.

[41.] Lt. Col. B. Palin Dobson, *History of the Bolton Artillery 1860-1928* (Bolton, 1929), 2-3.

[42.] *BM*, Apr. 25, p. 3; May 2, p. 3; June 27, 1798, p. 3; William Alexander Abram, *A History of Blackburn, Town and Parish* (Blackburn, 1877), 412.

[43.] Bancroft, *Sermon . . . May 6th 1802*, 13; *BM*, Mar. 15, 1797, p. 4.

[44.] *BM*, Apr. 25, 1798, p. 3.

[45.] See *BM*, May 16, 1798, p. 3; Sept. 24, 1800.

[46.] *BM*, May 2, 1798, p. 3; May 9, p. 3.

[47.] Alan Booth, "Reform, Repression and Revolution: Radicalism and Loyalism in the North-West of England, 1789-1803" (Ph.D. diss., Lancaster University, 1979), 237, 241.

[48.] PRO, HO 42/53, anon., Bolton, to Portland, Nov. 3, 1800 (postmark); Bancroft to J. King, undersecretary of state, Nov. 18.

[49.] Bancroft, *A Sermon . . . May 6th, 1802*, 4, 13.

[50.] "Autobiography of the late Mr Singleton Cooper" (typescript in BALS, n.d.), 1-2.

[51.] The painting is now prominently displayed in the county museum in Preston.

[52.] *BM*, July 16, 1800, p. 3.

[53.] T. Wood, *A Sermon, Preached on the Death of Mr. N. Aspden, Surgeon, before a respectable Audience, in the Methodist Chapel, Blackburn, on Sunday, September 30th, 1798* (Blackburn, 1798), 44.

[54.] *BM*, Oct. 3, 1798, p. 3.

[55.] Contrast, for example, Roger Wells, *Insurrection: The British Experience, 1795-1803* (Gloucester: Sutton, 1983), and idem, *Wretched Faces: Famine in War-time England, 1793-1801* (Gloucester: Sutton, 1988), with Ian R. Christie, *Stress and Sta-*

bility in Late Eighteenth Century England (Oxford: Clarendon Press, 1984). And see Colley, *Britons,* 289 n. 15; E. P. Thompson, "Which Britons?," *Dissent* (Summer 1993), reprinted in his *Persons & Polemics* (London: Merlin Press, 1994), 324-26; Frank O'Gorman, *The Long Eighteenth Century: British Political and Social History 1688-1832* (London: Arnold, 1997), 266-73; Douglas Hay and Nicholas Rogers, *Eighteenth-Century English Society: Shuttles and Swords* (Oxford: Oxford University Press, 1997), 183-85.

⁵⁶· See E. P. Thompson, *The Making of the English Working Class,* rev. ed. (London: Victor Gollancz, 1980), 536: "From the Public Record Office, Bolton appears to have been the most insurrectionary centre in England, from the late 1790s until 1820. But it is by no means clear whether this was because Boltonians *were* exceptionally revolutionary in disposition; or because Bolton suffered from two unusually zealous magistrates—the Rev. Thomas Bancroft and Colonel Fletcher—both of whom employed spies (or 'missionaries') on an exceptional scale." For an assessment of the value of the Home Office information and details of the spies, see Booth, "Reform, Repression and Revolution," passim, and idem, "The United Englishmen and Radical Politics in the Industrial North-West of England, 1795-1803," *IRSH* xxxi, 3 (1986): 272.

⁵⁷· E.g., PRO, HO 42/61, Bancroft to King, Feb. 9, 12, 1801.

⁵⁸· PRO, HO 42/53, Bancroft to King, Nov. 19, 1801.

⁵⁹· PRO, HO 42/61, Bancroft to Portland, Mar. 14, 18, 1801; HO 42/61, Fletcher to Portland, Apr. 6; Thomas Ainsworth to Sir Robert Peel, Mar. 12; "A. B.," Bolton, to Bancroft, Mar. 22.

⁶⁰· *BC,* Mar. 15, 1831, open letter of Moor to Fletcher, reprinted in *The Blackfaces of 1812, Consisting of Dr. Taylor's Letter Regarding the Disturbances in Bolton, in 1812; William Moor's Letter to the Late Col. Fletcher; With an Introduction Containing Some Notice of the Spy System in 1812, 1817, and 1819* (Bolton, 1839), 18-20, reprinted in Kenneth E. Carpenter, ed., *British Labour Struggles: Contemporary Pamphlets 1727-1850: The Luddites* (New York: Arno Press, 1972).

⁶¹· Booth, "Reform, Repression and Revolution," 329, 335-38.

⁶²· PRO, HO 42/61, Fletcher to Portland, June 6, 1801, quoted by Booth, "Reform, Repression and Revolution," 379.

⁶³· *BM,* Oct. 1, 1800, p. 3.

⁶⁴· PRO, HO 50/40, Peter Rasbotham to Derby, Feb. 22, 1798, quoted by David Eastwood, "Patriotism and the English State in the 1790s," in *The French Revolution and British Popular Politics,* ed. Mark Philp (Cambridge: Cambridge University Press, 1991), 159.

⁶⁵· PRO, HO 50/338, Feilden to Derby, July 10, 1802.

⁶⁶· *BM,* Aug. 3, 1803, p. 3.

⁶⁷· PRO, HO 50/75, Cardwell to Derby, July 30, 1803.

⁶⁸· PRO, HO 50/137, ffarington (also signed by Cornet Septimus Gorst, manufacturer, and Thomas Low, surgeon) to Brig. Gen. Bulwer, May 7, 1805. For the composition of the Bolton Light Horse Volunteers at the start of the Napoleonic War, see Bt. Lt. Col. J. G. Rawstorne, *An Account of the Regiments of Royal Lancashire Militia, 1759-1870* (Lancaster, 1874), 232.

⁶⁹· PRO, HO 50/75, Watson to Derby, July 23, 1803; Derby to ?, July 26, 1803.

⁷⁰· LRO, DDPR 132/1, [illegible], Whitehall, to Grimshaw, 19 Nov., 1803; ? to [Grimshaw?], 25 June, 1804; *BM,* Jan. 9, 1805, p.1; Nicholas Grimshaw, *Observations on the Reply to a Statement of the Question, Respecting the Comparative Rank of the Two Corps of Preston Volunteer Infantry* (Preston, 1805), 3-7, dated Jan. 17, 1805.

[71.] PRO, HO 50/172, Markland to Lord Hawkesbury, Oct. 25, 1807; Thomas Wilson (clerk to the General Meetings of the Lancashire Lieutenancy) to Derby, Nov. 5; Major John Walton Jr. to Derby, Nov. 21; Capt. Charles Ambler to Derby, Nov. 28; HO 50/196, Ambler to Derby, Jan. 20, 1808; Derby to ?, June 1, 6.

[72.] Cookson, *British Armed Nation*, 92-93, 185-88; J. W. Fortescue, *The County Lieutenancies and the Army 1803-1814* (London, 1909), 211-13, 285-86; Gee, "British Volunteer Movement," 65-66.

[73.] HO 50/196, Derby to Hawkesbury, Nov. 29, 1808; HO 50/224, "List of gentlemen desirous of holding commissions in Blackburn Hundred Local Militia, Lower Division," Apr. And see HO 50/224, Henry Hulton to Lord Liverpool, May 27, 1809, aggrieved that his years of army service did not give him precedence over the other Lt. Cols. of the Local Militia and Yeomanry. For the composition of three of the volunteer corps just prior to their amalgamation in the Local Militia, see HO 50/196, Grimshaw to Derby, return of those enrolled in the Preston Volunteer Infantry, July 11, 1808; Capt. William Brade to Derby, July 19, 1808 (Preston Rifle Corps); Ralph Fletcher to Derby, July 11, 1808 (Bolton Volunteers). The Bolton Light Horse Volunteers continued embodied until 1816, were re-raised in 1819 as the Bolton Yeomanry Cavalry under Capt. James Kearsley, amalgamated with the Wigan and Furness cavalry units in 1828, and became known as the Duke of Lancaster's Own Corps of Yeomanry Cavalry in 1834, a regiment of three troops with approximately 170 men. See Fergus Read, *The Duke of Lancaster's Own Yeomanry* (Preston: Lancashire County Books, 1992), 6-7, 10-11.

[74.] Cookson, *British Armed Nation*, 188.

[75.] J. R. Western, *The English Militia in the Eighteenth Century: The Story of a Political Issue 1660-1802* (London: Routledge and Kegan Paul, 1965), chap. 9 (on the militia's expansion), p. 282 (on the augmentation of the Lancashire militia from one regiment to five in 1796, reduced to three in 1799), p. 340 (on property qualifications for officers).

[76.] See J. Lawson Whalley, *Roll of Officers of the Old County Regiment of Lancashire Militia 1642-1889* (London, 1889), 109 and passim; Rawstorne, *Royal Lancashire Militia*, 17-19; *BM*, July 5, 1797, p. 3 (on the first muster of the Supplementary Cavalry for Blackburn Hundred). But note Western, *English Militia*, chap. 12, on the difficulties of finding competent and qualified officers.

[77.] This universal male suffrage was later modified by a clause in 26 Geo. 3, c. 100 (1786) that required six months' residence. See Edward Baines, *The History of the County Palatine and Duchy of Lancaster*, 4th ed., revised, enlarged, and edited by James Croston (Manchester, 1888), IV: 333.

[78.] H. W. Clemesha, *A History of Preston in Amounderness* (Manchester, 1912), 198, 201-202, 208, 231; Stephen W. Urbanski, "Parliamentary Politics, 1796-1832, in an Industrializing Borough: Preston, Lancashire" (Ph.D. diss., Emory University, 1976), 45-51; William Dobson, *History of the Parliamentary Representation of Preston*, 2nd ed. (Preston, 1868), 48-54; R. G. Thorne, *The History of Parliament: The House of Commons 1790-1820* (London: Secker and Warburg, 1986), II: 236; LRO, Derby Papers, DDK 1683/3, Watson to David Stevenson, Dec. 11, 1788.

[79.] Horrocks's address, May 30, in *An Entire and Impartial Collection of all the Papers, Squibs and Songs* (Preston, 1796), contained in LRO collection, *Preston Election Squibs 1796-1841*, 8; LRO, DDK 1683/5, "W. B." to Derby, Dec. 25, 1794; /8, W.? Cunliffe to Mr. Alty, May 30, 1796.

[80.] "A Freeman of Preston," *A Letter to A Noble Lord, on the Conduct of Himself and his Committee in the Borough of Preston 1796*, 3-4, 7, 11.

[81.] "Marmaduke Tulketh" [Peter Whittle], *History of Preston*, vol. I, *A Topographical, Statistical, and Historical Account of the Borough of Preston* (Preston, 1821), 255-56.

[82.] DDK 1683/9-13, election correspondence; /14, Wilson to Derby (copy), Jan. 12, 1797; /33, final poll tally; /35, itemized expenditure. For the poll figures, see LRO, DDPr 131/11, Preston Poll Book, No. 2, 1796: I have included as "leading occupations" at this stage gentlemen, esquires, clerks [i.e. clergymen], bankers, manufacturers and machine makers, corn factors, linen drapers, chapmen, merchants, medical men, and the governor of the House of Correction. See also *BM*, Apr. 27, 1796, quoted by Abram, "Sketches" (*PG*, Aug. 27, 1881), for an account of Stanley's coming of age at Preston: Two thousand staunch supporters dined on roast beef and stout ale, and the toasts included "May the Houses of Stanley and Hoghton ever ride triumphant over Corporation Influence," with twelve huzzas.

[83.] See n. 86.

[84.] Urbanski, "Parliamentary Politics," 58-60; Michael J. Turner, *Reform and Respectability: The Making of a Middle-Class Liberalism in Early Nineteenth-Century Manchester* (Manchester: Chetham Society, 1995), 48-50; Dobson, *Parliamentary Representation*, 54, 64-65; H. W. Clemesha, "'The Weaver's Friend.' A Short Account of a Former Parliamentary Candidate for Preston" (MS in LRO, [1927?]); *Preston Election Squibs*, 1804, especially p. 5, Horrocks's address; pp. 3-4, 8, the offer of Thomas D. Hesketh of Rufford Hall to stand, but only if Horrocks did not stand, so that harmony could be preserved; p. 16, "An Independent Elector to Fellow Townsmen," Mar. 14; *Preston Election Squibs*, 1807, pp. 4, 9, "To the Independent Electors"; pp. 23-24, "An Impartial Observer," May 12; p. 45, "SOUND REASONS!—A DIALOGUE"; p. 48, "The Green Sight"; p. 50, "*The interesting Speech*"; Hanson to Independent Electors, May 18. For the polling figures see *An Alphabetical List of the Electors Polled* (Preston, 1807). Judging status from occupation as listed in poll books is always imperfect but can be helpful in indicating an order of magnitude. By my calculation, forty-three men in leading occupations voted for Hanson. This includes clerks, gentlemen, attorneys, land surveyors, surgeons, manufacturers, timber merchants, ironfounders, spinning masters, machine makers, and calico printers, and so might incorporate a number of operatives in some of these categories. It does not include retailers. Eleven of the forty-three split their votes with either Horrocks or Stanley. Hanson polled 1,002 votes, and in total 2,582 people voted.

[85.] Turner, *Reform and Respectability*, 49-52; Prentice, *Historical Sketches*, 31-33; PP (1811), II, "Report on Petition of Several Weavers: Evidence of Joseph Hanson, Esq.," 2-3, 13.

[86.] *PC*, Oct. 10, 1812; Nov. 7, pp. 2-3; Thorne, *Parliament*, II: 237. Hornby was son of the rector of Winwick and the Hon. Lucy Stanley, and husband to his cousin, Lady Charlotte Stanley, daughter of the 12th earl of Derby. Note that although the coalition candidates represented different interests in Preston, when it came to voting in parliament the distinctions were far from clear-cut. Samuel Horrocks seems to have generally supported the government of the day from Pitt onwards, with more fluctuating support for Perceval and Liverpool. He voted against the Corn Bill in 1815 and Catholic Relief in 1813. Both of the Hoghtons also voted with Pitt. Hornby followed the Derby Whig line and voted consistently for Catholic Relief. See Thorne, *Parliament*, III: 318-19 (Burgoyne), IV: 212-13 (the Hoghtons), 233-35 (Hornby), 248 (Horrocks), V: 138 (Cunliffe Shawe), 215-17 (Stanley).

[87.] The assessment of Turner, *Reform and Respectability*, 1-3, 52, 317.

88. François Crouzet, "The Impact of the French Wars on the British Economy," in *Britain and the French Revolution*, ed. Dickinson, 192-94; *BM*, Dec. 23, 1807, p. 4; June 1, 1808, p. 3; June 8, p. 3; June 15, p. 3; July 6, 1808, p. 3; Charles Hardwick, *History of the Borough of Preston and its Environs* (Preston, 1857), 375; PRO, HO 137/224, Ralph Fletcher, J. S. Lawson, Thomas Bancroft, JPs, to ?, Jan. 9, 1809; Bolton weavers' handbill of Jan. 29, 1808, in Abram, "Sketches," vol. 2, Jan. 24, 1880; J. L. Hammond and Barbara Hammond, *The Skilled Labourer 1760-1832*, 2nd ed. (London: Longmans, Green, 1920), 73-79; John K. Walton, *Lancashire: A Social History, 1558-1939* (Manchester: Manchester University Press, 1987), 145.

89. Cookson, *Friends of Peace*, 187, 192, 209-12; *Manchester Gazette*, Feb. 13, 20, 1808, cited by Cookson, 211; HO 42/95, Fletcher to Lord Hawkesbury, Feb. 1808, quoted by Cookson, 209.

90. Brimelow, *Bolton*, 17-19.

91. Colley, *Britons*, 222-25.

92. PRO, HO 40/1, Fletcher to John Beckett, undersecretary of state, Apr. 6, 7, 30, 11, 22, 26, 1812; HO 50/285, William Hulton, Richard Ainsworth, Ralph Fletcher, and William [Hampson?] to Major Pilkington, Apr. 20, 1812; Thompson, *The Making*, 621.

93. PRO, HO 50/285, General Meeting of Lieutenancy, May 1, 1812.

94. PRO, HO 50/285, Maitland to Sidmouth, June 22; to Richard Ryder, May 6, 9.

95. *The Blackfaces of 1812*, 8-18. For support of the allegations that the mill was burnt at the instigation of spies, and for the activities of John Stones, a spy/agent provocateur supplying information to Adjutant Warr of the Bolton Local Militia, who was working for Ralph Fletcher, see Prentice, *Historical Sketches*, 54-56; Hammond and Hammond, *Skilled Labourer*, 277-85; Frank Ongley Darvall, *Popular Disturbances and Public Order in Regency England* (1934; reprint, New York: A M. Kelley, 1969), 196-97, 287-90.

96. Dinwiddy, "Luddism and Politics," 58, has discovered only one Lancashire middle-class radical implicated in dubious activities: Thomas Hulme, a partner in the extensive Bolton-area bleaching firm of Cooke and Hulme. According to Fletcher (PRO, HO 40/1, Fletcher to ?, May 15, 1812), Hulme had chaired a Reform meeting and "is a most violent Character and appears as likely as any Person in this neighbourhood to commit himself by some illegal act." There is one other possible candidate to add to Dinwiddy's very short list: Davis, the Presbyterian or Socinian clergyman of Chowbent, another whom Fletcher thought should by his rank in life and education know better than to encourage sedition (HO 40/1, Fletcher to Beckett, June 16; Joseph Rowley (chaplain of Lancaster Castle) to Fletcher, with information against Davis, June 15).

97. BALS, Heywood papers, ZHE/18-27, Mar. 15, 1828.

98. *BFP*, Nov. 28, 1835, p. 7; Aug. 18, 1838, p. 2.

99. Grimshaw, *The Cogitations and Opinions of Timothy Grimshaw Esq.* (Bolton, 1839), 7. Note also that the editors of the 1839 edition of Taylor's letter (*The Blackfaces of 1812*, 3) were using it for a didactic purpose and drawing a contemporary parallel: "How much of the present lamentable and distracted state of public feeling owes its origin to Government agency, it would, as yet, be difficult to ascertain; but it will be an easy task to shew, that in former years Ministers deemed it their duty to foment treasonable plots and conspiracies, for the very laudable purpose of throwing odium on the cause of Reform, and of making the more wealthy and timid portion of the middle classes call for a strong government."

100. *BM*, Mar. 13, 1811, p. 3.

101. *BM*, Mar. 4, 1812, p. 1.

102. Cookson, *Friends of Peace*, 215-19, 228-29.

103. *BM*, Mar. 18, p. 3; Mar. 25, p. 3.

104. *BM*, Apr. 1, p. 2.

105. François Crouzet, *L'Économie Britannique et le Blocus Continental (1806-1813)*, (Paris: Presses Universitaires de France, 1958) II: 793ff., 809-29; Cookson, *Friends of Peace*, 216-17.

106. See Miles Taylor, "John Bull and the Iconography of Public Opinion in England c.1712-1929," *P&P* 134 (Feb. 1992): 93-128.

107. 1 Peter 2:17 and Proverbs 24:21. See, e.g., the Rev. Samuel Johnson in a general Thanksgiving Day sermon, July 1814, quoted by Thomas Hampson, *Horwich: Its History, Legends, and Church* (Wigan, 1883), 209-14.

108. On the appropriation of Pitt, see James J. Sack, *From Jacobite to Conservative: Reaction and Orthodoxy in Britain, c.1760-1832* (Cambridge: Cambridge University Press, 1993), 85, 88-90. He was relatively liberal regarding reform, religion, and Catholic Emancipation, and held a Whiggish outlook on history, philosophy, and theology. But his press turned him into something quite different. As such he may have been a more important icon in an evolving conservatism than the royal family, which attracted the censure of some of the right-wing press over, for example, the Duke of York's affair in 1809 and the Queen Caroline Affair (134ff.).

Notes to Chapter 2

1. CMA, MS. F 929/2/W126, Whittaker Family Letters 1783-1837, vol. I, William to Sarah Whittaker, Jan. 24, 1795.

2. For an example of the widespread claims made for the impact of the Evangelical Revival, see W. Pilkington, *The Makers of Wesleyan Methodism in Preston* (London and Preston, 1890), 238-39.

3. Peter Borsay, *The English Urban Renaissance: Culture and Society in the Provincial Town 1660-1770* (Oxford: Clarendon Press, 1989), 284-86. Richard L. Bushman, *The Refinement of America: Persons, Houses, Cities* (New York: Knopf, 1992), 193, 278-79, 402-403, 411, argues a similar case for the United States.

4. Frank M. Turner, *Contesting Cultural Authority: Essays in Victorian Intellectual Life* (Cambridge: Cambridge University Press, 1993), 75-78. He attributes the crusade to the evangelical revival, the political reaction to the French Revolution, and inter-denominational competition.

5. E. Whitehead, *A Sermon Preached in the Parish Church of Bolton, on Sunday the 24th of September, 1786; Being the Next Lord's Day After the Execution of James Holland, on Bolton Moor, for Croft-Breaking* (Bolton, 1786), 7-9, 11-12, 15-16.

6. *BM*, Nov. 1, 1797, p. 4.

7. LRO, DDHu/53/82/96, Rev. Thomas Jones, "Address to Inhabitants," Oct. 1, 1797; idem, *Radical Reform, addressed to all particularly to the Magistrates, Clergy, Traders and others in Great Britain* (Manchester, 1798); idem, *Radical Reform, addressed to the Inhabitants of Great Britain* (Manchester, 1798), quoted by Maureen Price, "Bolton and the Effect of the French Revolution and Napoleonic Wars 1789-1815" (Cert. Ed. thesis, Chorley College, 1972), 53-54.

8. Rev. Thomas Stevenson, *A Sermon Preached at St. John's Church, Blackburn, Lancashire, on Wednesday, February 25, 1807, Being the day Appointed by His Majesty, for a Public Fast* (Blackburn, 1807), 5, 15-16, 22-24, 29-33.

9. John Gough Nichols, "Biographical Memoirs," in Whitaker, *An History of the Original Parish of Whalley*, 4th ed. (London, 1872), I: xiv-vi, xlviii-l.

[10.] Ibid., xxxiv, letter to Rev. Thomas Wilson, 1806.

[11.] Ibid., lix, 249-53 (long footnote, also revealing his antipathy to Methodists).

[12.] Whitaker, *Loidis et Elmete* (Leeds, 1816), 22, 86-87.

[13.] Joseph Fletcher Jr., *The Select Works and Memoirs of the Late Rev. Joseph Fletcher, D.D.*, vol. I, *Memoirs of the Life and Correspondence of the late Rev. Joseph Fletcher, D.D.* (London, 1846), 5, 14, 33, 44, 64, 131-32, 179-81 (letter to Mrs. C., Jan. 15, 1813), 299-300 (letter of Joseph France, May 1846).

[14.] George Thistlethwaite, *Memoirs of the Life of the Rev. W. Thistlethwaite, M.A., By his Son* (London, 1838), 1, 82-83, 97.

[15.] *Fragments of the Experience of the late John M'Kenzie, Minister of the Gospel, Preston, Lancashire. Selected From His Own Papers* (London, 1850), 21, 33, 69, 73-75.

[16.] Roger Carus Wilson, *The Life of Peter Houghton, B.A., Late assistant Curate of Walton-le-Dale* (London, 1832), 1-8, 15, 19, 24-25, 41-54, 139, 141.

[17.] J. A. Atkinson, *Memoir of the Rev. Canon Slade* (Bolton, 1892), 10, 13-15, 16 (Thynne quotation), 17-18 (Hick quotation), 35-36 (quotation from *Passages in the Life of Luke Boardman*), 50 (diary, Oct. 29, 1825), 61-62 (diary, Jan. 1, 1827), 294-95 (letter of Feb. 21, 1860, found after his death on May 15).

[18.] Edward Girdlestone, *Home; or, The Friend of His Family The Friend of God* (London, n.d.), 14-15, 20, 29, 40-41, 65-69.

[19.] Joseph Dodson Greenhalgh, *Sayings and Doings of the Rev. James Folds, otherwise Parson Folds, Lecturer of Bolton Parish Church from 1755 to 1820* (Bolton, 1879), 72-73; for Wilson, see below, chap. 8, and the Rev. F. R. Raines, *Miscellanies: Being A Selection from the Poems and Correspondence of the Rev. Thomas Wilson, B.D.* (Manchester, 1857), lxxvii-lxxviii, 183-85 (letter of Wilson to T. D. Whitaker, Feb. 1806, using extensive scatological humor).

[20.] Thomas Wood, *A Sermon, Preached on the Death of Mr. N. Aspden, Surgeon, before a respectable Audience, in the Methodist Chapel, Blackburn, on Sunday, September 30th, 1798* (Blackburn, 1798), 42-48; idem, *A Short Account of The Life and Death of the late Mr. N. Aspden, Surgeon, of Blackburn* (Blackburn, 1798); idem, *Memoirs of Mr. James H. Wood, Late Surgeon, &c. &c. To the Dispensary and Work House, at Blackburn, Lancashire; who died December 30, 1814, aged 19 Years: Including His Conversion and Happy Death, &c. &c.*, 2nd ed. (London, 1816), 16-19.

[21.] Wood, *Memoirs of James Wood*, 9, 21-28, 32ff., 51-54, 61-62, 98-100, 116. For a defense of the theater against "persons of morose and narrow minds," see Whittle, *History of Preston*, I: 93-94.

[22.] "S. H.," *Memorial of a Beloved Aunt*, 11-16, 21-22, 36-37, 57, 59. And also see Rev. Frederick F. Woolley, *A Brief Memorial of the Christian Character of the Late Mrs. R. Topping, of Bolton* (Bolton, 1850).

[23.] James Clegg, *Annals of Bolton: History, Chronology, Politics* (Bolton, 1888), 89.

[24.] *A Brief memoir of the Late Mrs. De Manneville, of Acres' Field* (Bolton, 1843), 3-10, 17, 23-24.

[25.] Rev. William Kirkman, *Memorials of Mr. Thomas Crouch Hincksman of Lytham, Lancashire* (London, 1885), 3-6, 28, 41-53, 58-59, 71-72, 109, 115-21, 124-25, 127.

[26.] Rev. John Hannah, *The Story of the Wreck of the 'Maria' Mail Boat: With a Memoir of Mrs. Hincksman, the Only Survivor* (London, [1877?]), 5-6, 14-16, 20-30, 40ff., 88-91. Samuel Leach, *Old Age Reminiscences* (printed for private circulation, 1923), who grew up in Winckley Square near the Hincksmans, described them (p. 24) as Wesleyans "of a pronounced type." He recounts his fascination with hearing her story of being wrecked, but suspected it had been a good deal embroidered during its many recountings.

27. *Friendship's Tribute to the Memory of the Late Mrs. Fishwick, of Springfield, near Garstang* (Lancaster, 1852), 5-7, 32-34, 36.

28. Anon., *Memoir of Mrs. George Barnes, of Farnworth* (Manchester, 1853), 4-9, 47, 72-75.

29. Quoted by B. T. Barton, *History of Farnworth and Kersley* (Bolton, 1887), 276-79.

30. Richard Edgcumbe, ed., *The Diary of Frances Lady Shelley 1787-1817* (London, 1912), 2, 8-9.

31. BALS, Bolton Biographical Notes, B4, p. 204, obit. from *BC*, Apr. 16, 1864.

32. Catherine Jacson, *Desultory Retracings: A Personal and Family Record* (London, 1895), 34-38, 59, 62-63.

33. BRL, Hindle Papers, G3 HIN, John Fowden Hindle to William Hindle, Apr. 12, 1817.

34. Cunliffe to Ainsworth, Mar. 1817, quoted by William Alexander Abram, "Sketches in Local History," vol. 4 (articles in *PG*, 1877-84), Aug. 27, 1881.

35. BALS, Bolton Biographical Notes, B1, sermons on the death of Thomasson (Mar. 8, 1876) by the Rev. Robert Best of Mawdsley Street Chapel (pp. 57-59), and J. K. Applebee, minister of Bolton Free Christian Church (pp. 60-62).

36. R. S. Crossley, *Accrington Captains of Industry* (Accrington, 1930), 189-90.

37. William Alexander Abram, *Blackburn Characters of a Past Generation* (Blackburn, 1894), 260, 265.

38. James Barlow, "On the Great Utility of Contemplating the Works of the Creator, as Displayed in the Wonderful Structure, Analogy, and Economy of Animals and Vegetables" (MS in BRL, 1831), 6-8, 18, 28, 44, 66.

39. Quoted by T. A. I. McQuay, "A Blackburn Surgeon: James Barlow (1767-1839)," *The Practitioner* 195 (July 1965): 108.

40. *Autobiography of Joseph Livesey* (London, [1881?]), 17-18, 55-57.

41. Anthony Hogg, *The Hulton Diaries 1832-1928: A Gradely Lancashire Chronicle* (Chichester: Solo Mio, 1989), 14, 25-26. He entered the Church and eventually became vicar of Emberton near Newport Pagnell.

42. *PP*, May 4, 1839, p. 2.

43. *PP*, Jan. 20, 1838, p. 2.

44. Quoted by Thomas Shaw, BRL, G3 MOR, typescript notes on Lord Morley (1924). For the rounding up of Sabbath-breakers (those out in the streets during divine service), see, e.g., BALS, Bolton Biographical Notes, B1, p. 173, and Barrie M. Ratcliffe and W. H. Chaloner, trans. and eds., *A French Sociologist Looks at Britain: Gustave d'Eichthal and British Society in 1828* (Manchester: Manchester University Press, 1977), 94 (the Bolton boroughreeve and constables "seize those who don't look like gentlemen and take them to church by the scruff of the neck").

45. LRO, Pedder Papers, DD Pd/17/16, Jane Pedder, Clifton, Bristol, to Richard Pedder, Fishergate, Preston, Mar. 5, 1839.

46. Arthur Noel Walker, *The Walker Family 1681-1946* (printed for private circulation, 1947), 15-20, 31.

47. Kirkman, *Hincksman*, 43-44.

48. *PC*, Apr. 16, 1836, p. 3; Apr. 30, p. 4.

49. *PC*, Aug. 2, 1845, p. 2. See also the Rev. Edward Girdlestone's appeal for petitions from every parish in the country in support of the government's proposal to stop

all postal labor on Sundays (letter in *Church and State Gazette*, Apr. 2, 1850; clipping in CMA, Rushton's Visitation Returns, vol. 21, Deane).

[50.] *BC*, Mar. 10, 1849, p. 5.

[51.] Walter Lowe Clay, *The Prison Chaplain: A Memoir of the Rev. John Clay, B.D.* (Cambridge, 1861), 577-79.

[52.] "Annual Report of the Rev. John Clay, Chaplain to the Preston House of Correction. Presented to the Visiting Justices at the October Sessions, 1838," *Journal of the Statistical Society of London* II (1839): 93.

[53.] *PC*, Sept. 13, 1826, quoted by Peter Whittle, *Marina; or, An Historical and Descriptive Account of Southport, Lytham, and Blackpool, Situate on the Western Coast of Lancashire* (Preston 1831), "Lytham," 30.

[54.] Whittle, *Marina*, "Southport," 103.

[55.] Letter to Aunt Barton, Sept. 5, 1810, in Edward Hall, ed., *Miss Weeton: Journal of a Governess 1807-1811* (London: Oxford University Press, 1936), 294.

[56.] *BS*, July 28, 1841, p. 3.

[57.] John Taylor, *Autobiography of A Lancashire Lawyer, Being the Life and Recollections of John Taylor, Attorney-at-Law, And First Coroner of the Borough of Bolton* (Bolton, 1883), 7, 21-25.

[58.] Ibid., 27.

[59.] Ibid., 38-39.

[60.] Ibid., 75-76.

[61.] Ibid., 90-91, 102.

[62.] Ibid., 105-106.

[63.] Ibid., 108, 111.

[64.] Ibid., 117, 121-22, 129.

[65.] Ibid., 134-35.

[66.] Ibid., 194 and passim.

[67.] Ibid., 222.

[68.] Ibid., 239.

[69.] Ibid., 255-56.

[70.] LRO, Cross Papers, DDX 841, Richard Assheton Cross, "Sketches of My Father's Life" (rough draft, later published as *A Family History* (London, 1900)). Park, a judge in the Court of Common Pleas and Exchequer, was the author of *An Earnest Exhortation to a frequent reception of the holy-sacrament of the Lord's-supper* (see Peter Whittle, *History of Preston*, vol. II, *The History of the Borough of Preston* (Preston, 1837), 299).

[71.] *Speech of [J.] H. Ainsworth, Esquire, at the Tea Party, held in the School Room, St. Paul's, Halliwell, on Tuesday January 2nd, 1849. The Rev. W. Milton, M.A., in the Chair* (London and Bolton, 1849), 8 (in BALS, ZHB/3/2).

[72.] "J. H. A., A Lay Member of the Church," *Texts of Scripture, Suggested to the serious consideration of those who deny the Necessity and Efficacy of the Two Holy Sacraments, Baptism and the Supper of the Lord; And who object to forms of Praise, Thanksgiving, and Prayer, in Public Worship* (London and Bolton, 1848); BALS, Ainsworth Papers, ZAH/1/3, Account Book: this lists Ainsworth's donations for churches, schools, parsonages, clergymen, and miscellaneous purposes in Britain and Ireland. In Britain the donations were geographically widespread, mainly reserved for Anglican institutions or religious societies, and between August 1842 and September 1850 amounted to £4441 13s. 10d. For similar purposes in supporting the Establishment in Ireland, he spent more than £3500 from 1845 to the end of 1850. See Taylor, *Autobiography*, 171-72, for a testimony to Ainsworth's charitability: "This gentleman did many godlike acts during his life, and 'had a heart open as day to melting charity.'" Although he frequently attended and casually donated to Dissenting chapels, the limits of his charitability are outlined in the Ainsworth Papers, ZAH/4/22, July 12, 1847: "The Revd Mr Smith (R.C. Priest,) Mr Duntill & Mr Waterhouse called to ask for a Subscription for the R.C. School in Higher Bridge Street but I declined giving them any money on the plea that I considered their Church in error."

[73.] Ainsworth Papers, ZAH/4/3, e.g., Jan. 17, Oct. 25, 1823; /4, Jan. 31, Feb. 1, July 19, 25, Oct. 26, 30, 31, and end of year thoughts, 1824; /5, Mar. 19, May 1, 4 ("Severe Mathematical study is the only way of attaining the improvement you desire"), 30, June 26, Aug. 22 ("Was called at five—Make a point of rising early 6 days in the week; the seventh, please yourself—"), Oct. 30, Dec. 24 ("When I reflect upon the little improvement I make, how little I keep up to the plans laid down, I feel discouraged—perseverance & resolution be my motto"), 1825; /6, Mar. 12, 14, May 16, Dec. 8, 1826; /11, Mar. 15, 1831; /14, Feb. 8, 1839; /16, Dec. 31, 1841; /22, readings during parts of year in back of diary.

[74.] Ainsworth Papers, Journal, ZAH/4/1, 2, passim, a rich catalogue of such events; /3, July 22, 1823; /5, June 25, Aug. 23, 24, 25, 30, 1825, for examples of free-flowing dinners.

[75.] ZAH/4/15, July 1, 1840; /16, Mar. 21, 1841, for his gout. He did not dwell in as much detail in the 1840s on what he had eaten, but the dinners were plentiful in number, any event of significance in his life (birthday, birth of a child, new steam engine, and so on) was celebrated with much champagne, and see the contents of his wine cellar below.

[76.] ZAH/4/11, Dec. 16, 24, 1831.

[77.] Ainsworth Papers, ZAH/1/4, Wine Book.

[78.] BALS, Heywood Papers, ZHE/71/52, Nov. 1830; /3, week of Oct. 9, 1820. See John Seed, "Theologies of Power: Unitarianism and the Social Relations of Religious Discourse, 1800-50," in R. J. Morris, ed., *Class, Power and Social Structure in British Nineteenth-Century Towns* (Leicester: Leicester University Press, 1986), 135, who describes how rational Dissent's breaking with Calvinism also entailed a breaking with Puritan asceticism.

[79.] Heywood Papers, ZHE/18-27, Heywood ("A friend to even handed justice") to editor of *BC* (draft), June 12, 1828.

[80.] ZHE/18-27, cousins to Heywood, Mar. 3, 1824; Heywood to cousins, Mar. 3.

[81.] ZHE/26/3, Letter Book, Heywood to James Heywood, Sept. 11, 1836; and see Heywood to Samuel Gaskell, July 27, 1837, regarding a relative of his ("whose lamentable condition has been occasioned by intemperance") being sent to Gaskell's asylum.

[82.] ZHE/26/3, Heywood to Jacob Brettell, July 6, 17, 1838.

[83.] ZHE/38, Heywood to Mr. Phillips, July 24, 1842; /40, Heywood to J. H. McKeand, July 23, 1844; sister to Heywood, Aug. 8. Heywood's distaste for smoking surfaces repeatedly. See his *A Journey to America in 1834* (privately printed, 1919), 11-12: May 18, 1834, on board the *Britannia*, sailing for America, a long discussion at breakfast about smoking: "I considered it hurtful, and particularly as generally it was accompanied by drinking." And his *A Journey to Italy in 1826* (privately printed, 1919), 64: June 25, 1826, at Coire in northern Italy: "Smoking appears to be a terrible habit here; old and young have one of these nasty though ornamental things hanging from their mouths, many whilst at work"; 74: July 3 at Freiburg: "Quite disgusting to see so much smoking, some with long sticks contrived all sorts of ways."

[84.] ZHE/36, Jan. 2, 1840, George Egerton to Heywood; Jan. 2, Heywood to Egerton (copy).

85. ZHE/28, Aug. 14, 1832, Heywood to James Heywood; /26/3, Feb. 4, 1840, Heywood to Noah Makinson.

86. Louisa Potter, *Lancashire Memories* (London, 1879), 96. This is a semi-fictionalized account of people she had known, with all their names changed.

87. Ibid., 81-82.

88. Edgcumbe, ed., *Diary of Lady Shelley*, 11.

89. A. Hewitson, *Our Churches and Chapels* (Preston, 1869), 19, 26-27, 49-50, 73-75.

90. BALS, Edgworth Preparitive [*sic*] Meeting Book, FRM 11/1, "The Quarterly Meeting's Queries" (in back of minute book), 1-9; Minutes of Women's Preparative Meeting, Edgworth and Bolton, FRM/11/7, "Answers to queries" (separate sheets at back), Apr. 2, 1848, Mar. 29, 1846.

91. PRO, HO 45/249, Hulton to Derby, Aug. 19, 1842, enclosing copy of Ashworth to Hulton, Aug. 19.

92. BALS, Heywood Papers, ZHE/38, Ashworth to Heywood, Aug. 19; and see Heywood copy of letter intended to have been sent to the lord chancellor, Aug. 25, testifying to Ashworth's fitness in all other respects to be a magistrate; /39, Heywood to Ashworth, Jan. 4, 1843, asserting that Lord Holland was fully aware of Ashworth's scruples when he inserted his name in the commission of the peace.

93. PRO, HO 45/249, Derby to Graham, Aug. 20, 1842, Jan. 12, 1843; Graham to Derby, Aug. 22, Dec. 24, 1842 (copies); Arthur G. Rose, "Truckling Magistrates of Lancashire in 1842," *TLCAS* 83 (1985): 60-63.

94. BALS, FRM 11/1, Sept. 13, 1795, epistle from Yearly Meeting.

95. BALS, Bolton Biographical Notes, B1, p. 83, obit. in *MG*, 1880.

96. Rhodes Boyson, *The Ashworth Cotton Enterprise: The Rise and Fall of a Family Firm* (Oxford: Clarendon Press, 1970), 247-54.

97. Recently covered in fascinating detail by Pat Jalland, *Death in the Victorian Family* (Oxford: Oxford University Press, 1996). For a longer-term and comparative perspective, see Philippe Ariès, *The Hour of Our Death*, trans. Helen Weaver (New York: Vintage Books, 1982).

98. Anon., *Memoir of Mrs George Barnes*, 51 (letter of Feb. 20, 1845).

99. LRO, Parker of Browsholme Papers, DDB/72/499, St. Clare to Parker, Dec. 22, 1802.

100. LRO, Palmer Papers, DDX 398/110, Esther Mary Grimshaw, Liverpool, to Mr. and Mrs. James Palmer, Sept. 23, 1825.

101. Taylor, *Autobiography*, 147-49. On childhood deaths, see Jalland, *Death in the Victorian Family*, chap. 6.

102. A phrase used by Mrs. William Feilden on hearing of the birth of her thirteenth grandchild (LRO, Coucher Book of Feniscowles, vol. I, PR 2846/2/1, Mary Haughton Feilden to J. W. Whittaker, Apr. 1, 1834).

103. BRL, Whittaker Papers, 921 WHI, McGrath to Whittaker, Jan. 9, 1837.

104. William Thistlethwaite, *The Prodigal Child Reclaimed; or, the History of Betty Bridge: to which is added The Life and Happy Death of Betty Ann Hawkins* (Bolton, 1816), 18-22.

105. Wood, *Memoirs of James Wood*, 116, 149, 151.

106. Pilkington, *Makers of Wesleyan Methodism in Preston*, 146. For the distance between narrativized ideals of "triumphant deaths" and painful and prosaic reality, see Jalland, *Death in the Victorian Family*, chap. 1.

107. William Jones, *The Fainting of a Standard-Bearer. A Sermon Preached at Mawdsley-Street Chapel, Bolton, on Sunday, January 14th, 1838, Occasioned by the La-*

mented Death of the Rev. William Thistlethwaite, M.A., 2nd ed. (Bolton, 1838), 20-21.

[108.] BL, Gladstone Papers, Add. MS 44356, Hulton to Gladstone, Apr. 25, 1840. See also Catherine Rothwell, "A History of Fleetwood-on-Wyre 1834-1934" (FLA thesis, 1974), 43-46, on the trials of Peter Hesketh Fleetwood, MP for Preston. His wife died aged 26 in 1833, and his five children all died young before 1838. He himself lost the sight of an eye through scarlet fever in 1833. But in 1839, after seeing a blind man, he wrote, "How thankful did I feel to a merciful God who, when he took away one, left one eye to me."

[109.] *Memoir of Mrs George Barnes*, 26-27 (letter to sister, Apr. 26, 1844).

Notes to Chapter 3

[1.] B. T. Barton, *Historical Gleanings of Bolton and District* (Bolton, 1881), 1st ser., I: 43-44.

[2.] See, e.g., David Goodway, *London Chartism 1838-1848* (Cambridge: Cambridge University Press, 1982); John K. Walton, "The North-West," in *The Cambridge Social History of Britain 1750-1950*, ed. F. M. L. Thompson (Cambridge: Cambridge University Press, 1990), I: 379; Stanley H. Palmer, *Police and Protest in England and Ireland 1780-1850* (Cambridge: Cambridge University Press, 1988); Dorothy Thompson, review of *1848*, by John Saville, *HW(J)* 28 (Autumn 1989): 160-66; Robert Sykes, "Physical-Force Chartism: The Cotton District and the Chartist Crisis of 1839," *IRSH* XXX, 2 (1985): 207-36; Clive Emsley, "The Impact of War and Military Participation on Britain and France 1792-1815," in *Artisans, Peasants and Proletarians 1760-1860: Essays Presented to Gwyn A. Williams*, ed. Emsley and James Walvin (London: Croom Helm, 1985), 75-76; idem, "Repression, 'Terror' and the Rule of Law in England During the Decade of the French Revolution," *EHR* 100, 397 (Oct. 1985): 801-25. As Alan D. Gilbert notes ("Religious and Political Stability in Early Industrial England," in *The Industrial Revolution and British Society*, ed. Patrick O'Brien and Roland Quinault (Cambridge: Cambridge University Press, 1993), 81): what is more puzzling is not the maintenance of public order but the ease with which it was maintained.

[3.] The most prominent recent example is John Saville, *1848: The British State and the Chartist Movement* (Cambridge: Cambridge University Press, 1987).

[4.] Pierre Bourdieu, "Les Modes de Domination," *Actes de la Recherche en Sciences Sociales* (1976): 122-32, quoted in Alf Lüdtke, "The Role of State Violence in the Period of Transition to Industrial Capitalism: the example of Prussia from 1815 to 1848," *SH* 4 (May 1979): 177.

[5.] See the Marquess of Anglesey's assertion (*A History of the British Cavalry 1816 to 1919* (London: Leo Cooper, 1973), I: 84) concerning the ability of properly directed mounted troops to break up immense bodies without injury to anyone— "By feints, by backing, by rearing and by dexterous horse management."

[6.] PRO, HO 42/180, T. D. Whitaker to Sidmouth, Sept. 17, 1818, quoted by Robert G. Hall, "Tyranny, Work and Politics: The 1818 Strike Wave in the English Cotton District," *IRSH* xxxiv, 3 (1989): 466; BALS, Handbill Collection, ZZ/130/13/9, July 19, 1819; /10, Oct. 11, 1819; LRO, DDHu 53/82, printed notice to inhabitants of Great and Little Bolton, Aug. 3, 1819.

[7.] HO 52/1, Starkie to Sidmouth, Feb. 5, 1820; to ?, Apr. 11; minutes of Whalley meeting of Feb. 17; Whitaker to Sidmouth, Feb. 23; Col. John Hargreaves to Sidmouth, Apr. 22; resolutions of Burnley meeting of Apr. 21; HO 40/12, Starkie to ?, Apr. 2; Whitaker to Sidmouth, Apr. 10; Shaw to Whitaker, Apr. 9.

[8.] HO 52/1, "Memorial to Lords Commissioners of H. M. Treasury," [1820]; HO 40/13, Fletcher to Sidmouth, May 25; Byng to undersecretary, May 27, and private letter. Ralph Fletcher pointed out to Sidmouth (HO 40/14, Aug. 14) that the General Annual Session of the county had allowed several orders for money for temporary barracks out of the county rate under an Act of 44 Geo. 3, but not without considerable opposition. And see HO 40/16, Byng to Hobhouse, Apr. 29, 1821, not recommending that expense be incurred to keep on the Bolton barracks after Christmas, given the quiet state of the country and the proximity of the military in Manchester; boroughreeve and constables of Great Bolton to Fletcher, Apr. 23, saying that as the people of Little Bolton had resolved at their town's meeting not to pay their share for the barracks after December, Great Bolton could not shoulder the entire cost.

[9.] HO 40/19, Whittaker to Eckersley, Apr. 15, 1826.

[10.] *PC*, Apr. 29, 1826, p. 3: many in the crowd reassured the shopkeepers who were shutting up their shops, "'Never mind yer shops, folk, we shallna meddle whe yo.'" Charles James Darbishire of Bolton, in a letter to his business partner, Robert Heywood, traveling in Europe, June 6, 1826 (BALS, Heywood Papers, ZHE/18-27), also commented on this good order: "I had no fear of the security of the property in the town [Bolton] even if the rioters ventured here since they showed themselves very wise even in their madness & universally declared their respect for every kind of property except the Power Looms."

[11.] *David Whitehead and Sons Limited: A Short History of the Firm* (n.p., n.d.), 10.

[12.] HO 40/19, John Fowden Hindle and Rev. Richard Noble to Peel, Apr. 27, enclosing depositions of John Kay and Eccles Shorrock.

[13.] Ibid., depositions of John Haughton and Rev. Richard Noble.

[14.] HO 40/19, Eckersley to Hobhouse, Apr. 25; Hindle and Noble to Peel, Apr. 27, deposition of William Halton Carr; *David Whitehead*, 11-12.

[15.] HO 40/19, Fletcher, Hulton, and Ridgway to Peel, Apr. 27. See also HO 40/19, Hulton to ?, Apr. 29 (also in LRO, Hulton Papers, DDHu 48/134).

[16.] LRO, DDHu 48/135, H. Hobhouse to Fletcher, Hulton, and Joseph Ridgway, Apr. 29; /139, Peel to Hulton, May 1.

[17.] HO 40/19, Byng to Hobhouse, May 1, 2; Fletcher to Peel, May 3. For the preparations to resist loomwreckers with brown besses, blunderbusses, and paving stones at a Horrocks mill in Preston, see Thomas Whittaker, *Battles in Temperance Armour*, quoted by W. Pilkington, *The Makers of Wesleyan Methodism in Preston* (London and Preston, 1890), 194-96.

[18.] BALS, Heywood Papers, ZHE/18-27, Darbishire to Robert Heywood, June 6, 1826.

[19.] *David Whitehead*, 12-13.

[20.] HO 40/19, Skinner to Byng, May 5, 7; J. F. Hindle and Charles Whitaker to Byng, May 23.

[21.] HO 40/20, deposition of Thomas Dowson of Further Gate, Blackburn, July 8; deposition of Thomas Howson [*sic*], weaver, Blackburn, before Whitaker and Hindle, July 10; Eckersley to Byng, July 4. Byng's communications (Byng to ?, June 17; to Hobhouse, June 19, July 9, 12; to ?, July 28; to Peel, Aug. 22 (enclosing notes of aide-de-camp, Capt. Hodgson), 29) indicate considerable dissatisfaction with timid mayors (like the mayor of Preston) who called in troops unnecessarily, and with the Bolton magistrates. (Fletcher "was always timid and now gets old, and is not very efficient"; Watkins "is also old, and not at all respected. I am told he was a bankrupt, only paid 5s in the Pound, and no one knows by what means he lives.") Nor was he impressed by the exaggerated reports of Fletcher's spies.

22. HO 40/20, Hobhouse to Lt. Gen. Sir Herbert Taylor, July 20, 1826; Fletcher to Hobhouse, July 22, Aug. 2; Byng to Hobhouse, July 9, 12, 22; to ?, July 28, 29; to Peel, Aug. 29.

23. HO 40/21, Byng to home secretary, Oct. 7, 1826, Sept. 4; A. L. Howarth to Neville and Eccles, Sept. 9; Eckersley to Byng, Sept. 10, 12; HO 40/22, Byng to undersecretary, Jan. 14, 1827, Dec. 22; to quartermaster general, Dec. 11.

24. HO 40/20, Eckersley to Byng (extract), Dec. 5; HO 40/21, Eckersley to Hobhouse, Sept. 14, 19; Byng to home secretary, Oct. 7; Rev. J. W. Whittaker to Eckersley, Dec. 6.

25. LRO, DDHu 48/140, earl of Derby to Hulton, May 1, 1826.

26. HO 40/22, Rogerson to Peel, Jan. 1, 182[7].

27. HO 40/22, Eckersley to Byng (extract), Jan. 11, 1827; Lt. Col. G. H. Hewett to Byng (copy), Jan. 13; Capt. E. B. Brooks to Col. Burslem (copy), Dec. 2; Eckersley to Byng (copy), Dec. 3; Thomas Rogerson to Peel, July 19, 1828; Burslem to Maj. Gen. Sir H. Torrens, Aug. 1; John Fleming et al. to Burslem, July 30; Lt. J. Dickson to Major A. Poyntz, July 31; Capt. ? to Poyntz, Aug. 1.

28. HO 40/23, Whittaker to Peel, May 2, 5; Bouverie to undersecretary, May 6. For troop distributions in Manchester and the cotton belt to the north, see HO 40/23, May 8, 1929.

29. HO 40/23, J. F. Hindle and John Taylor to Peel, May 6, 12; Thomas Clayton, John Hargreaves, John Aspinall, Hindle, Philip Abbott, James Whitaker, Taylor, William Gray, and John Hopwood, magistrates of Blackburn Hundred, to Peel, May 9; Bouverie to Peel, May 10; to Phillips, May 11, 12; Shaw and Artindale to Bouverie, May 11.

30. HO 40/26, Bouverie to Phillips, July 2, 1830. For the land purchase of Apr. 13, 1830, LRO, DDX/156/1.

31. HO 40/26 confidential memo. by ?, n.d.; HO 40/31(1), Bouverie to Phillips, Aug. 26, 1833.

32. For labor and trades union disputes, see HO 40/26, Bouverie to undersecretary, Nov. 20, 1830; HO 52/8, Fletcher, Hulton, Ridgway, James Kearsley, and Robert Lomax to Melbourne, and Hulton to Melbourne, Dec. 15; Rhodes Boyson, *The Ashworth Cotton Enterprise: The Rise and Fall of a Family Firm* (Oxford: Clarendon Press, 1970), 146-47. The Eighteenth Royal Irish Regiment's unpopularity with a section of the population, partly because of its antilabor role, was expressed in antimilitary, anti-Irish brawls and meetings in Bolton in July and August 1831. See HO 40/29, Bouverie to Fitzroy Somerset, Apr. 7, 1831; to Phillips, May 17, 22, Aug. 13; Capt. Huddleston to Shaw, Aug. 17, with enclosures; poster advertising antimilitary meeting, Aug. 5; *BC*, Aug. 13.

33. HO 52/8, Nicholas Grimshaw to Melbourne, Dec. 18, 1830; anon., Preston, to Derby, Dec. 21; Gorst and Birchall to Derby, Dec. 25; HO 52/13, Grimshaw to [Melbourne?], Jan. 5, 1831; HO 40/26, Bouverie to Phillips, Dec. 24.

34. HO 52/8, Gorst and Birchall to Derby, Dec. 25, 27; William Rawstorne to Derby, Dec. 26; Laurence Rawstorne to Derby, Dec. 26; Grimshaw to [Melbourne?], Dec. 28; J. Norris to Derby, Dec. 28; resolutions of meeting at Whalley, Dec. 29; proceedings of adjourned meeting at Bull Inn, Preston, Dec. 29.

35. HO 40/29, R. Hardman, Preston Post Office, to Sir Francis Freeling, postmaster general, Nov. 7, 8, 1831; HO 52/13, James Dixon to Melbourne, Nov. 7, 9; Richard Palmer to Melbourne, Nov. 8.

[36.] HO 52/13, Charles Swainson to Melbourne, Nov. 8, 11; requisition of leading inhabitants to mayor, Nov. 9; Derby to Melbourne, Nov. 10; Dixon to Melbourne, Nov. 14; Addison, Horrocks, Marshall, and Rawstorne to Melbourne, Nov. 15.

[37.] HO 52/13, J. F. Hindle and Rev. John Hopwood to Melbourne, Nov. 9; deposition of John Kay, Nov. 8; list of persons appointed as special constables.

[38.] HO 40/30, Shaw to Phillipps, Nov. 18, 1832, Dec. 12, 13, 14; Dixon Robinson to Shaw (copy), Nov. 21, 24; HO 52/13, Richard Noble and John Taylor to Melbourne, Sept. 25, 1832; James Watkins and R. Lomax to Melbourne, Nov. 29, Dec. 13, 15; Watkins, Lomax, and John Fletcher to Melbourne, Dec. 12; John Addison to Melbourne, Dec. 13; Richard Palmer to Phillipps, Dec. 17; Carr, Robinson, Neville, and Eccles to Melbourne, Dec. 6.

[39.] HO 40/31 (1), Bouverie to Phillipps, Aug. 26, 1833.

[40.] HO 52/26, Hindle and John Lister to home secretary, Jan. 21, 1835; HO 52/29, Thomas Miller to Russell, Nov. 2, 1836; Phillipps to Miller, Nov. 4; Peter Haydock to Russell, Nov. 7; Derby to Russell, Nov. 3; Miller to Russell, Nov. 6 (quotation); HO 40/34, Maj. Gen. Sir R. Jackson to Phillipps, Nov. 12, 1836; Derby to Wemyss, Nov. 3; Wemyss to Derby, Nov. 3; HO 52/34, Haydock to Russell, Feb. 15, Aug. 10, 1837; HO 40/35, Wemyss to Phillipps, Apr. 25, 26, 27, 31, July 22, 26, 27, 31, Aug. 13, 1837; James Watkins to Wemyss, Apr. 24; Jackson to Phillipps, July 23, 29, Aug. 4, 13; Wemyss to Thomas Ward, July 26; Preston magistrates to Wemyss, July 20; to Major Smith, July 29.

[41.] Lt. Gen. Sir William Napier, *The Life and Opinions of General Sir Charles James Napier* (London, 1857), II: 1, 46. See J. R. Dinwiddy, "Chartism," in his *Radicalism and Reform in Britain, 1780-1850* (London: Hambledon Press, 1992), 408: the Newport Rising, involving seven thousand men, the largest insurrection in nineteenth-century Britain, was dispersed by thirty soldiers.

[42.] Napier, *Napier*, 69, and see 93 (journal, Dec. 1).

[43.] CUL, Sir James Graham's Papers (microfilm), Wellington to Graham, Aug. 22, 1842; Peel to Graham, Aug. 31; Graham to J. K. Shuttleworth, Aug. 30.

[44.] HO 40/44, Darbishire to Lord ?, July 14, 1839; Robert Lomax to Russell, July 15; Darbishire to Russell, July 21, Aug. 4, 11, 12; J. Winder to Russell, Aug. 4.

[45.] HO 40/44, statement of Winder, Aug. 16; Darbishire to Russell, Aug. 13, 14, 15, 16, 18; Wemyss to Phillipps, Aug. 14, 15; E. Campbell, postmistress, to ?, Aug. 14; Winder to [Russell?], Aug. 14, 17; Major Braddyll to Russell, Aug. 15; John Fletcher to Russell, Aug. 24; BALS, Heywood Papers, ZHE/35, notes on Chartism, 1839; statement about the riot at Little Bolton Town Hall, Sept. 1839; Heywood to Robert Lomax, Sept. 19. On Darbishire's patience, see Thomas H. Winder, *Records and Reminiscences of Some of the Winder Family, for 200 Years* (Bolton, 1902), 33: James Winder "used to relate how the officer commanding the military, with sword drawn and flashing eyes, demanded authority to fire on the mob," a demand refused by the mayor.

[46.] HO 40/44, Winder to [Russell?], Aug. 14, 17; Mangnall to Russell, Aug. 24, enclosing memorial of council to Russell, Aug. 23; Darbishire to Russell, Sept. 3.

[47.] HO 40/44, Wemyss to Phillipps, Aug. 14; Braddyll to Russell, Aug. 15; HO 45/43, Wemyss to J. H. Manners Sutton, Oct. 14, 1841.

[48.] A point well-argued by Robert Sykes, "Physical-Force Chartism: The Cotton District and the Chartist Crisis of 1839," *IRSH* xxx, 2 (1985): 220, 235.

[49.] Napier, *Napier*, 102.

[50.] Ibid., 51 (Napier to Col. W. Napier, June 29, 1839).

[51.] Ibid., 66 (journal, July 30).

[52.] Ibid., 82 (Napier to Sir H. Ross, Aug. 28). See also pp. 47 (journal, June 19), 55, 58 (to undersecretary, July 24) 63, 66, 79, 92, 101-102, 141, 153.

[53.] HO 50/451, map of barracks, 1840.

[54.] Napier, *Napier*, 47 (journal, June 19, 1839). See also HO 50/451, "Report on Barracks" by Napier [1840].

[55.] HO 50/451, "Rough Sketch . . . for a Barrack on the Ordnance Ground at Blackburn," July 1839; Napier to Normanby, May 23, 1840; Major Rivers to Napier (copy), May 14, June 9; Napier to Phillipps, June 12; "Report on Barracks" by Napier; D. Burrows to Napier (copy), Mar. 18; and see Peter Catterall to Napier, June 9, and A. W. Hopkins to Lord Holland (copy), Feb. 13, both advocating barracks at Preston; HO 45/41, Napier to Phillipps, Feb. 13, 1841, Mar. 2; Phillipps to Napier, Mar. 31; HO 45/249F, Ordnance Office to Phillipps, Feb. 17, 1842; BL, Peel Papers, Add. MS 40501, memorial of leading inhabitants of Blackburn to Peel, Jan. 27, 1842; John Hornby to Peel, Jan. 29, 1842; Peel to John Hornby, Feb. 14, 1842. For troop deployments against Chartists and election rioters in 1840-41, see HO 40/54, Sir Charles Shaw to Fox Maule, Jan. 23, 1840; to Phillipps, Feb. 11; HO 45/41, Napier to Phillipps, July 2, 3, 1841; HO 45/43, Wemyss to Phillipps, June 26, 30, July 1; Capt. P. L. P. French to Major Simmonds, July 2; George Jacson to Wemyss, July 3; BALS, Heywood Papers, ZHE/36, Heywood to Normanby, Feb. 11, 1840.

[56.] HO 45/249F, memorial of Joseph Feilden, John Fowden Hindle, John Taylor, John Hopwood, John Lister, William Henry Hornby, and Montague Joseph Feilden, county magistrates of the lower division of Blackburn Hundred, to Wellington, Sept. 30; J. F. Hindle to Graham, Oct. 15. Note also that in 1845 the military (in the guise of Capt. Thomas Bickham, a staff officer stationed in Preston) joined Preston businessmen in their successful lobbying for a direct line from Preston to Liverpool via Ormskirk, so as to hasten the movement of troops from the Liverpool docks to the new barracks. See LRO, Liverpool, Ormskirk, and Preston Railway, DDH 1124/3-4, 1125/1.

[57.] All liberals: Charles James Darbishire, Robert Heywood, J. Arrowsmith, Andrew Knowles, and Robert Walsh.

[58.] HO 45/43, Wemyss to J. H. Manners Sutton, Oct. 14, 1841.

[59.] HO 45/43, Manners Sutton to Wemyss, Nov. 10, 1841; memo signed by Cullen, Nov. 13; Cullen to Wemyss, Nov. 18; Wemyss to Manners Sutton, Nov. 19, enclosing newspaper account of meeting. Dr. John Bowring, MP for Bolton, later pointed out in the Commons (*Hansard*, 3rd ser., 67 (1843): 748-50) the opposition to barracks by denying the allegation, in a debate on Ordnance estimates, that all parties were in favor. His liberal colleague for Bolton, Peter Ainsworth, contended that the opposition was not representative, and that he, the mayor, and the borough magistrates all thought it necessary for the military to remain in Bolton.

[60.] HO 45/268, Gomm to Phillipps, May 2, 1842, June 4, 6; *Hansard*, 3rd ser., 67 (1843): 749; HO 45/269, Wemyss to Phillipps, June 5.

[61.] HO 45/249A, Horrocks to Graham, June 13; HO 45/249F, George Jacson to Graham, Aug. 20; HO 45/268, Lt. Gen. Thomas Arbuthnot to Manners Sutton, Aug. 23, 25; HO 45/269, Horrocks to Wemyss (copy), June 19, 24; Wemyss to Horrocks (copy), June 21; to Phillipps, June 25. But note that, after the troubles of 1842 were over, the mayor and magistrates sent a memorial to the home secretary requesting reimbursement for the amount spent on barracks. Graham declined, pointing out that those who asked for troops and had their property protected by them must pay accordingly, either by subscription or a borough rate (LRO, DDPr 130/26, Phillipps to Palmer, Feb. 3, 1843).

[62.] HO 45/249, Thomas Cullen to Graham, Aug. 12, 1842; deposition of John Boyd, Bolton commissioner of police, Aug. 12; Winder to Graham, Aug. 12, 13. For an overall account of the crisis, see A. G. Rose, "The Plug Riots of 1842 in Lancashire and Cheshire," *TLCAS* 67 (1957): 76-112; and F. C. Mather, *Public Order in the Age of the Chartists* (Manchester: Manchester University Press, 1959).

[63.] HO 45/249, Elizabeth Campbell to Lt. Col. Maberley, Aug. 13, 15; Robert Thompson, schoolmaster, to [Graham?]; Winder to [Graham?], Aug. 15; Cullen to Graham, Aug. 16, 19, 22; Winder to Graham, Aug. 17, 18, 20, 24.

[64.] BALS, Heywood Papers, ZHE/38, Heywood to Daniel Maude, Aug. 16; BALS, Ainsworth Papers, ZAH/4/17; B. T. Barton, *History of Farnworth and Kersley* (Bolton, 1887), 110-17, 122-23.

[65.] HO 45/249, John Lister and William Henry Hornby to Graham, Aug. 13; Lister, Hornby, and John Fowden Hindle to Graham, Aug. 15.

[66.] HO 45/249, Joseph Feilden, Hindle, Lister, James Simpson, Hornby, and Montague Joseph Feilden to Graham, Aug. 19. On the arrangements at the Hargreaves' Broad Oak works, R. S. Crossley, *Accrington Captains of Industry* (Accrington, 1930), 57.

[67.] HO 45/249, Arbuthnot to mayor of Clitheroe, Aug. 20; HO 45/249F, Hindle to Graham, Oct. 15.

[68.] HO 45/249A, Horrocks to Graham, Aug. 13; HO 45/268, Warre to Graham, Aug. 13; Horrocks, T. B. Addison, John Bairstow, and George Jacson to Warre, Aug. 13; Horrocks to Col. Broke, Aug. 25; R. G. Gammage, *History of the Chartist Movement 1837-1854* (1894; reprint, London: Merlin Press, 1976), 221.

[69.] HO 45/249A, poster, "Copy of the Mayor's Speech," Aug. 13; Horrocks to Graham, Aug. 13.

[70.] *PP*, Aug. 20, 1842, p. 2.

[71.] HO 45/249A, Horrocks to Graham, Aug. 15.

[72.] HO 45/249A, Woodford to Phillipps, Aug. 17; T. B. Addison to Graham, Aug. 18.

[73.] HO 45/249A, Addison to Graham, Aug. 18; Jacson to Graham, Aug. 20; notice of mayor and magistrates, Aug. 20.

[74.] HO 45/249A, William Clayton to Graham, Aug. 24; Woodford to Phillipps, Aug. 26 (2 letters), 28; Gorst and Birchall to Graham, Aug. 26.

[75.] CUL, Graham Papers, Graham to Warre, Aug. 12, 13; Graham to Wellington, Aug. 16, on the usefulness of post office reports from the main towns. See also Derek Gregory, "The Friction of Distance? Information Circulation and the Mails in Early Nineteenth-Century England," *JHG* 13, 2 (Apr. 1987): 131.

[76.] CUL, Graham Papers, Graham to Warre, Aug. 15; to queen, Aug. 16, 17, 18, 20; to Wellington, Aug. 16, 20; queen to Graham, Aug. 17; Wellington to Graham, Aug. 19; Graham to Lord Francis Egerton, Aug. 20; to Townley Parker, Aug. 24; Peel to Graham, Aug. 26; Graham to Peel, Sept. 2; to Lord Wharncliffe, Sept. 2. And see HO 45/249B, "Censure on Magistrates for truckling with the rioters." Also Arthur G. Rose, "Truckling Magistrates of Lancashire in 1842," *TLCAS* 83 (1985): cases were prepared against four JPs, including Thomas Cullen, mayor of Bolton (p. 42), but no action was taken. J. W. Croker, in the *Quarterly Review* 71 (Dec. 1842) (quoted by Norman McCord, *The Anti-Corn Law League 1838-1846* (London: George Allen and Unwin, 1958), 121), wrote that out of the fifty-nine JPs in Manchester, Stockport, and Bolton, "there was hardly one magistrate (except the seven Conservatives) who was not a member, and most of them very active members, of the Anti-Corn-Law Association and League."

[77.] John Saville, *The Consolidation of the Capitalist State, 1800-1850* (London: Pluto Press, 1994), 60, notes that by the mid-1840s a regiment took nine hours to travel from London to Manchester by rail—or seventeen days on foot.

[78.] HO 45/2410B, Carswell to Woodford, Jan. 16, 1848; HO 45/2410D, Arbuthnot (at Manchester) to Phillipps, Jan. 18, 1848; Sheppard to Arbuthnot, Jan. 17; H. Barnard (for Arbuthnot) to Temple, Jan. 17.

[79.] HO 45/2410B, J. Winder to Sir George Grey, Mar. 20, Apr. 10, 1848; Woodford to Phillipps, Mar. 10, 12, 14, 23; memo of Lt. Col. Alexander M. Tulloch, War Office, Apr. 6; HO 45/2410D, Arbuthnot to Sir Denis Le Marchant, Apr. 12.

[80.] See Saville, *Consolidation of the Capitalist State*, 76-77.

[81.] HO 45/2410B, Winder to Grey, July 30, 1848; report of Supt. James Harris of the Bolton Borough Police, July 29; notice re arming and drilling from the mayor, Thomas Ridgway Bridson (quoting 60 Geo. 3 and 1 Geo. 4, c. 1, s. 1), n.d.; notice from mayor, July 29; deposition of Robert Lomax, July 28, enclosed in Bridson, Stephen Blair, J. Winder, and James Harris to Grey; printed private letter to millowners and employers of hands from the mayor, July 28; report of Harris, July 28; copy of decisions of meeting of magistrates, July 28; Bridson to Grey, July 29; and see Winder to Grey, June 12 (2 letters), and Robert Greenhalgh, Bolton postmaster, to Maberly, June 12.

[82.] BALS, Council Minutes, AB/1/2, May 10, 1848.

[83.] *PP*, Apr. 15, 1848, p. 5; Apr. 22, p. 4.

[84.] LRO, Council Minutes, CBP/1/1, May 11, 1848.

[85.] *PG*, Apr. 15, 1848, p. 4.

[86.] *PC*, Apr. 15, 1848, p. 4; April 22, p. 4.

[87.] *PC*, Nov. 18, 1848, p. 4. And see *PC*, Mar. 9, 1850, p. 4; Dec. 7, p. 4.

[88.] HO 45/2410D, Maj. Gen. Sir John F. Burgoyne, report "On Barracks," contained in G. Butler, Office of Ordnance, to D. Le Marchant, Oct. 27, 1848; Wellington to Grey, Dec. 18, 1849; report on state of troops in Northern and Midland Districts, Sept. 16, 1849.

[89.] In this sense, as Dinwiddy notes in his "Chartism," 416-20, Chartism was a partial success in provoking a change in the attitudes and policies of the governing classes.

Notes to Chapter 4

[1.] LRO, Cross Papers, DDX 841/3/1, "Observations made upon a Tour thro' Part of North Wales," Sept. 1790. His son, Richard Assheton Cross, "Sketch of my Father's Life" (DDX 841), commented on his father's account of "their strange secluded life which he seems by no means to have approved of." Lillian Faderman, *Surpassing the Love of Men: Romantic Friendship and Love Between Women from the Renaissance to the Present* (New York: William Morrow, 1981), 74-75, 84, 121-25, 152; Elizabeth Mavor, *The Ladies of Llangollen: A Study in Romantic Friendship* (London: Michael Joseph, 1971), 202-3.

[2.] Tom did not repay these years of frugality (mother and sister mainly lived on a diet of bread and potatoes) with gratitude. Nelly later alleged: "[L]ike all his sex, when he was grown up, he considered what had been done for him was his right; that he owed no gratitude to us, for we were but *female* relatives, and had only done our duty." Edward Hall, ed., *Miss Weeton: Journal of a Governess 1807-1811* (London: Oxford University Press, 1936), 23.

[3.] Hall, *Miss Weeton*, 4-6, 13, 19, 200-201 (Weeton to brother, Dec. 9, 1909), 202, 204, 209, 218 (Weeton to Miss Winkley, Dec. 28).

[4.] M. Jeanne Peterson, "The Victorian Governess: Status Incongruence in Family and Society," in *Suffer and Be Still: Women in the Victorian Age*, ed. Martha Vicinus (Bloomington: Indiana University Press, 1972).

[5.] Hall, *Miss Weeton*, 231-37, Weeton to brother, Feb. 25, 1810, describing Pedder's drunken mauling of his daughter's corpse after she burnt to death in the parlor fire.

[6.] Hall, *Miss Weeton*, 253-55 (Weeton to Mrs. Whitehead, Apr. 18), 256-60 (journal, undated, latter part of April 1810), 267-68 (Weeton to brother, July 1), 277-78 (journal, undated, start Aug. 1810), 301 (Weeton to brother, Sept. 15), 315-16 (Weeton to brother, Nov. 11-15).

[7.] Hall, *Miss Weeton*, 239 (to brother, Feb. 25, 1810; to Miss Winkley, Feb. 25), 241-42 (to Mrs. Chorley, Mar. 14), 254-55 (to Mrs. Whitehead, Apr. 18), 257 (journal, undated, latter part of Apr. 1810), 276-77 (journal, undated, start Aug. 1810). See also 282 (to brother, Aug. 15), saying that Pedder took no pains to get his wife introduced, seldom even taking her to church or accompanying her in a visit, and never joining her in a walk; and 311 (to Mrs. Whitehead, Oct. 18), reporting the comment of Mrs. Pedder's father, a local farmer: "'People,' he says, 'do not always do well that marry so much above them, for they only get despised and abused by their fine new relations.'"

[8.] Hall, *Miss Weeton*, 259 (journal, undated, latter part of Apr. 1810), 283 (to brother, Aug. 15), 311-13 ("An Essay," Oct.-Nov.), 322 (to Miss Winkley, Feb. 4, 1811).

[9.] Hall, *Miss Weeton*, xvii (letter to brother, n.d.). Weeton went on to become a governess near Huddersfield before marrying a Wigan cotton spinner, Aaron Stock, in 1814. Her truly miserable marriage, her husband's cruelty, and her struggle for custody of their child are detailed in ibid., pp. 324-26; in Hall (ed.), *Miss Weeton's Journal of a Governess*, vol. 2 (London: Oxford University Press, 1939); and by Amanda Vickery, *The Gentleman's Daughter: Women's Lives in Georgian England* (New Haven: Yale University Press, 1998), 77-81.

[10.] Catherine Jacson, *Desultory Retracings. A Personal and Family Record* (London, 1895), 133-37, 143-44, 160-61. Henry Formby, the son of a clergymen, had been in the calico-printing and manufacturing business with the first Sir Robert Peel and had married a daughter of Jonathan Peel of Accrington House, Sir Robert's brother (pp. 2-3).

[11.] Jacson, *Desultory Retracings*, 210-11.

[12.] For the pervasiveness of domesticity, see, e.g., Walter E. Houghton, *The Victorian Frame of Mind 1830-1870* (New Haven: Yale University Press, 1957), 341-44; Steven Mintz, *A Prison of Expectations: The Family in Victorian Culture* (New York: New York University Press, 1983); Bonnie G. Smith, *Changing Lives: Women in European History Since 1700* (Lexington, Mass.: D. C. Heath, 1989), 177-87; F. M. L. Thompson, *The Rise of Respectable Society: A Social History of Victorian Britain, 1830-1900* (London: Fontana, 1988), 58-59, 157-58, 175, 250-53. For studies of separate-spheres ideology in theory and practice, see, e.g., Leonore Davidoff and Catherine Hall, *Family Fortunes: Men and Women of the English Middle Class, 1780-1850* (London: Hutchinson, 1987); Nancy F. Cott, *The Bonds of Womanhood: "Woman's Sphere" in New England, 1780-1835* (New Haven: Yale University Press, 1977); Catherine Hall, "The Early Formation of Victorian Domestic Ideology," in *Fit Work for Women*, ed. Sandra Burman (London: Croom Helm, 1979), 15-32; idem, "Private Persons Versus Public Someones: Class, Gender and Politics in England, 1780-1850," in *Language, Gender and Childhood*, ed. Carolyn Steedman, Cathy Urwin, and Valerie Walkerdine (London: Routledge and Kegan Paul, 1985); idem, "The Sweet Delights of Home," in

From the Fires of Revolution, ed. Perrot; idem, "The Tale of Samuel and Jemima: Gender and Working-Class Culture in Nineteenth-Century England," in *E. P. Thompson: Critical Perspectives*, ed. Harvey J. Kaye and Keith McClelland (Philadelphia: Temple University Press, 1990), 78-102; Leonore Davidoff, *Worlds Between: Historical Perspectives on Gender and Class* (Cambridge: Polity Press, 1995), 8-9 and passim; Lawrence Stone, *The Family, Sex and Marriage In England 1500-1800* (London: Penguin, 1979), 169, 413-14, 422; Lynn Hunt, "The Unstable Boundaries of the French Revolution," in *From the Fires of Revolution*, ed. Perrot; Joan B. Landes, *Women and the Public Sphere in the Age of the French Revolution* (Ithaca: Cornell University Press, 1988); Geoff Eley, "Nations, Publics, and Political Cultures: Placing Habermas in the Nineteenth Century," in *Habermas and the Public Sphere*, ed. Craig Calhoun (Cambridge, Mass.: MIT Press, 1992), 309-11; Thomas Laqueur, *Making Sex: Body and Gender from the Greeks to Freud* (Cambridge, Mass.: Harvard University Press, 1990), 4-11, 150-52, 194-207; Bonnie Smith, *Ladies of the Leisure Class: The Bourgeoises of Northern France in the Nineteenth Century* (Princeton: Princeton University Press, 1981); Mary Poovey, *Uneven Developments: The Ideological Work of Gender in Mid-Victorian England* (Chicago: University of Chicago Press, 1988), chap. 1; Barbara Caine, *English Feminism 1780-1980* (Oxford: Oxford University Press, 1997), chap. 1. For strong reservations, see Linda Colley, *Britons: Forging the Nation 1707-1837* (New Haven: Yale University Press, 1992), 239-81; Amanda Vickery, "Golden Age to Separate Spheres? A Review of the Categories and Chronology of English Women's History," *HJ* 36, 2 (1993): 383-414; idem, "Shaking the Separate Spheres," *Times Literary Supplement*, Mar. 12, 1993, 6-7; idem, *Gentleman's Daughter*; M. Jeanne Peterson, *Family, Love, and Work in the Lives of Victorian Gentlewomen* (Bloomington: Indiana University Press, 1989).

[13.] See Davidoff, *Worlds Between*, 227-28.

[14.] Thomas Bancroft, *The Chain of Duty; or, An Exhortation to Civil and Religious Obedience* (Bolton, 1797), 3-5, 10-11, 14-20.

[15.] Thomas Starkie, *A Sermon, Occasioned by the Present Times—1 January 1793, before the Friendly Societies of Mechanics* (Blackburn, 1793), 8-9.

[16.] Joseph Fletcher, *Admonitions to Youth: A Sermon, Preached in the Independent Chapel, Blackburn, January 13, 1811* (Blackburn, 1811), 11.

[17.] Joseph Fletcher Jr., ed., *Memoirs of the Life and Correspondence of the late Rev. Joseph Fletcher, D.D.* (London, 1846), 279-80.

[18.] William Jones, *An Essay on Improper and Unhappy Marriages: Or A Guide in Forming Connexions for Life* (London, 1842), 11-12, 22-23.

[19.] Edward Girdlestone, *Home; or, The Friend of His Family The Friend of God* (London, n.d.), 51-52.

[20.] Leonore Davidoff, *The Best Circles: Society, Etiquette and the Season* (London: Croom Helm, 1973), 42ff.

[21.] See the references in n. 12.

[22.] See Dror Wahrman, "*Percy*'s Prologue: From Gender Play to Gender Panic in Eighteenth-Century England," *P&P* 159 (May 1998): 156-60.

[23.] Thomas W. Laqueur, "The Queen Caroline Affair: Politics as Art in the Reign of George IV," *JMH* 54, 3 (Sept. 1982): 417-66; Davidoff and Hall, *Family Fortunes*, 150-55.

[24.] For the plebeian radical side of the affair and its gender implications, see Anna Clark, "Queen Caroline and the Sexual Politics of Popular Culture in London, 1820," *Representations* 31 (Summer 1990): 47-68.

25. Jackson Porter, *The Vanity and Dignity of Man. A Sermon Preached in the Parish Church, Blackburn, July 15th, 1830, Being the Evening of the Interment of his late Majesty, George the Fourth* (Blackburn, 1830), 14-15.

26. *BM*, Oct. 25, 1820.

27. *BM*, Dec. 6, 1820, p. 2.

28. *PC*, Dec. 23, 1820, p. 2.

29. *BM*, Aug. 23, 1820, p. 3.

30. *BM*, Nov. 12, 1817, p. 1; Nov. 26, pp. 2-3.

31. Duncan Bythell, "Women in the Workforce," in *The Industrial Revolution and British Society*, ed. Patrick K. O'Brien and Roland Quinault (Cambridge: Cambridge University Press, 1993), 48, notes that women only formed about 4 percent of the total coal mine workforce in 1841. But in banning women and children from working underground, the 1842 Mines Act for the first time made it unlawful for women to do a particular type of work.

32. At least before mid-century. Sonya O. Rose, *Limited Livelihoods: Gender and Class in Nineteenth-Century England* (Berkeley and Los Angeles: University of California Press, 1992), 45-47, suggests that there was a growing consensus toward the end of the century on the evils of married women working—domestic ideology overriding economic logic. The number of such women working in 1900 was possibly half what it had been in 1850.

33. Franklin Baker, *The Moral Tone of the Factory System Defended: in a Letter to the Lord Bishop of Manchester* (London, 1850), 10-16.

34. *BG*, July 10, 1833, p. 8.

35. F. H. Thicknesse, *Happy Homes and How to Make Them. A Lecture to Working Men, Delivered in Holy Trinity Schools, Bolton* (Bolton, 1861), 13-14. He was son of a rector of Stafford and a prebendary of Lichfield (see Edward Baines, *The History of the County Palatine and Duchy of Lancashire*, 4th ed., revised, enlarged, and edited by James Croston (Manchester and London, 1888), III: 131).

36. E.g., *BS*, Mar. 29, 1843, p. 2; *PC*, May 26, 1849, p. 6.

37. Medal contained in BALS, Ainsworth Papers, ZAH/6/4.

38. The original painting, dated 1822, is missing. The only known reproduction of it is a rather poor-quality photograph in the form of a *carte de visite* at the Harris Museum and Art Gallery. I am grateful to Francis Marshall, the Keeper of Fine Art, for showing it to me. For descriptions see J. H. Spencer in the *Preston Herald*, Dec. 1, 1944, and T. S. Hodkinson, "Thomas Batty Addison 1787-1874" (thesis, Chorley College of Education, 1973), 5-6.

39. See Caine, *English Feminism*, 82-83, 86-87.

40. This was true across a wide range of retailing and small manufacturing concerns. For example, the *Blackburn Mail* was continued by Ellen Waterworth for five years after the death of her husband, Jonathan, in 1799 before it was bought by Thomas Butler (see Alan W. Waterworth, *Waterworth —The Story of a Lancashire Family* (1986), 2-3). Mary, the widow of Thomas Cropp, similarly continued the *Bolton Chronicle* after his death in 1831 (*BC*, Mar. 26, 1831), until A. R. Martin took over in Sept. 1833 (*BC*, Sept. 21, 1833); she placed an advertisement on Sept. 6, 1834, stating that she was beginning a business as a grocer and provision dealer in Old Hall Street and that she had genteel apartments to let. Thomas Thomasson owned a quarry in Edgworth, and from there he expanded into cotton carding and spinning. He died in 1782, leaving debts of more than £600 and six children, and his widow took over the management of the concern until Thomas, her eldest son, turned twenty-one and assumed control (see

R. Lindop, *Turton Tales: A Collection of Historical Family Stories* (Turton Local History Society, 1978), 15).

[41.] E.g., the parents of Richard Palmer (born 1773), future county coroner and Preston town clerk, moved to Preston from Lancaster when he was young and became innkeepers, first at the Plough, then at the White Horse, which Mrs. Palmer continued to run for many years after her husband's death. (LRO, Palmer Papers, DDX 398/19, Notes on Richard Palmer (anon., n.d.).)

[42.] Of the heads of household identified as bourgeois in Table 1.3, seventy-nine were women, variously described (if any occupation was given) as annuitants, gentlewomen, landed proprietors, proprietors of houses, ladies, fundholders, a "baronetess," or proprietors of railway shares and mortgage securities. All but two were widowed or unmarried (for the two listed as married, no other mention is made of a husband). Only four women, all of them marginally bourgeois, had other occupations: a confectioner (Alice Fair, twenty-four, unmarried, with two servants who probably helped with the baking rather than being domestics), a brush manufacturer (Margaret Pickering, a widow, only included in the sample because her mother and aunt, living with her, are listed as ladies and as proprietors of land and houses), a grocer (Ann Walsh, a widow, only in the sample because her son Eli, twenty-nine, was a master cotton manufacturer), and a counterpane manufacturer (Mary Ann Cunliffe, a widow, employing fourteen workers and presumably looking after the business until her two sons, aged eighteen and sixteen, and listed as assistants to her, were old enough to take over). But at the lower edge of the bourgeoisie, at the defining point of the practical application of the ideology of public and private, even though the leading woman in the household did not work, her relatives, especially her daughters, often did: typically as schoolteachers, governesses, dressmakers, or retailers.

[43.] Davidoff and Hall, *Family Fortunes*, chap. 6.

[44.] See Theodore Koditschek, *Class Formation and Urban-Industrial Society: Bradford, 1750-1850* (Cambridge: Cambridge University Press, 1990), 210 n., 214 n.

[45.] PRO, RAIL 458/1, Manchester, Bolton and Bury Canal Minute Book, Sept. 20, 1790.

[46.] PRO, RAIL 59/2, Minutes of the Proceedings of the Directors of the Bolton and Preston Railway Company, Mar. 31, 1842.

[47.] LRO, *Addresses from One of the 3730 Electors in Preston*, Jan. 14, 1832.

[48.] In the words of Joan Scott, "The Imagination of Olympe de Gouges," in *Mary Wollstonecraft and 200 Years of Feminisms*, ed. Eileen Janes Yeo (London: Rivers Oram Press, 1997), 37.

[49.] See Anna Clark, "Manhood, Womanhood, and the Politics of Class in Britain, 1790-1845," in *Gender and Class in Modern Europe*, ed. Laura L. Frader and Sonya O. Rose (Ithaca: Cornell University Press, 1996), 265-68, 273; Lynn Hunt, "Forgetting and Remembering: The French Revolution Then and Now," *AHR* 100, 4 (Oct. 1995): 1130-32.

[50.] *BC*, Feb. 26, 1831, p. 1.

[51.] Sally Alexander, "Women, Class and Sexual Differences in the 1830s and 1840s: Some Reflections on the Writing of a Feminist History," *HW(J)* 17 (Spring 1984): 136-37.

[52.] Clark, "Manhood, Womanhood," 274-79.

[53.] In Anna Clark's phrase, "Manhood, Womanhood," 275.

[54.] This was vigorously attacked in the loyalist press (see *BM*, July 7, 1819, p. 3—a wholly facetious account), including an unflattering print by George Cruikshank, 'The Belle Alliance: or, The Female Reformers of Blackburn!!!" See James Epstein, "Understanding the Cap of Liberty: Symbolic Practice and Social Conflict in Early Nineteenth-Century England," *P&P* (Feb. 1989): 102-6; John Belchem, *'Orator' Hunt: Henry Hunt and English Working-Class Radicalism* (Oxford: Clarendon Press, 1985), 112; E. P. Thompson, *The Making*, 455-56.

[55.] Barbara Taylor, *Eve and the New Jerusalem: Socialism and Feminism in the Nineteenth Century* (Cambridge, Mass.: Harvard University Press, 1993), 80-81. See also Alexander, "Women, Class and Sexual Differences," 142.

[56.] See Joan Scott, "On Language, Gender, and Working-Class History," in her *Gender and the Politics of History* (New York: Columbia University Press, 1988), 63-65.

[57.] LRO, DDPr 138, Ashworth Cuttings, n.d., quoted by Alison Andrew, "The Working Class and Education in Preston 1830-1870: A Study of Social Relations" (Ph.D. diss., Leicester University, 1987), 69.

[58.] Sonya Rose, "Protective Labor Legislation in Nineteenth-Century Britain: Gender, Class, and the Liberal State," in *Gender and Class*, ed. Frader and Rose, 210.

[59.] *PC*, Apr. 25, 1835, p. 3.

[60.] *Preston Protestant Association: Report of Addresses . . . March 9th 1852* (Preston, 1852), 27.

[61.] BALS, FRM/1/72, Marsden Yearly Meeting, 1792.

[62.] BALS, FRM/11/7, Minutes of Women's Preparative Meeting, Edgworth and Bolton, 1823ff.

[63.] See F. K. Prochaska, "Philanthropy," in *The Cambridge Social History*, ed. F. M. L. Thompson, 3: 385, 392.

[64.] PRL, "Preston Auxiliary Bible Society—Addresses and Reports: First Report of Preston Bible Association," 4-7, 11 (Appendix: "Address to the Mistresses of Families"); and see 12, "Address to Female Servants."

[65.] LRO, DDHu 53/82/102, "Report of the Ladies' Charity," 1806.

[66.] BALS, "Report of the Ladies' Charity, for the Relief of Poor Lying-in Women, in or near the towns of Great and Little Bolton," Mar. 30, 1837-Mar. 29, 1838 (Bolton, 1838), 3-5.

[67.] BALS, "Second Report of the Bolton Clothing Charity," Nov. 1817-Nov. 1818 (Bolton, 1818), 4, 6-9.

[68.] "Third Report," Nov. 1818-Nov. 1819, 3-4; "Sixth Report," Nov. 1821-Nov. 1822, 4-5.

[69.] George Thistlethwaite, *Memoirs of the Life of the Rev. W. Thistlethwaite* (London, 1838), 57-58; BALS, "The Fifth Report of the Bolton Ladies' Auxiliary Society, in Aid of the London Society for Promoting Christianity Amongst the Jews," 1817. The patroness was Mrs. Hulton of Hulton Park.

[70.] *PC*, Jan. 31, 1835, p.2.

[71.] LRO, PR 1551, Coucher Book of Minutes of National and Sunday Schools: Trinity Sunday School. Heading the list of patronesses was the Dowager Queen Adelaide.

[72.] Frederick W. Briscoe, *History of St. George's Church and Schools, Bolton* (Bolton, 1893), 47-49.

[73.] LRO, CUBt/2/44, Mawdsley Street Church Sick Society Minute Book, 1837ff., Mar. 5, Sept. 4, 1838.

[74.] For example, a Grand Fancy Ball for the benefit of the Preston Ladies' Charity in December 1828 (*PC*, Nov. 15, 1828, p. 2) had as its patronesses a number of wealthy ladies from the vicinity. Presumably they were merely for decoration and dancing on this occasion, whatever role they might have played in the Ladies' Charity, since leading elite males made up the committee of Hon. Stewards. At a ball at the opening of

Little Bolton Town Hall (*BC*, Feb. 2, 1828, p. 1), Ladies Patronesses shared the public honors with the male patrons and stewards.

⁷⁵· *The Preston Institution Bazaar Gazette*, 4, Apr. 30, 1849, pp. 4-5, 7-8.

⁷⁶· See, e.g., *BM*, Jan. 10, 1810, "Fashions for Ladies. January, 1810"; Mar. 7, p. 2, description from *La Belle Assemblée*, 2, new series; Apr. 4, p. 2, "Fashions for ladies and gentlemen from Ackerman's Repository of Arts, Fashions, Manufactures, &c."

⁷⁷· E.g., Isaac Wilcockson, *Authentic Records of the Guild Merchant of Preston, 1822* (Preston, 1822), 66-74: a complete list of ladies in the mayoress's procession, with a description of the dress of each.

⁷⁸· As just one example among many, at a dinner to celebrate the opening of the Blackburn market house in 1848 (*BS*, Feb. 2, 1848, p. 3), Randle Feilden, "with an appropriate allusion to the universally acknowledged beauty of the females of the county, gave 'the standing toast of the county,'—'The Lancashire Witches,'" which was drunk with enthusiasm.

⁷⁹· See, e.g., Perrot, "At Home," in *From the Fires of Revolution*, ed. idem, 346.

⁸⁰· David Cannadine, "Through the Keyhole," *New York Review of Books*, Nov. 21, 1991, 34-38; W. L. Burn, *The Age of Equipoise: A Study of the Mid-Victorian Generation*, 2nd ed. (New York: Norton, 1965), 248.

⁸¹· Smith, *Changing Lives*, 197, 200-203; idem, *Ladies of the Leisure Class*, 54-57; Peter Williams, "Constituting Class and Gender: A Social History of the Home, 1700-1901," in *Class and Space: The Making of Urban Society*, ed. Nigel Thrift and Peter Williams (London: Routledge and Kegan Paul, 1987), 193, 202; Jonas Frykman and Orvar Löfgren, *Culture Builders: A Historical Anthropology of Middle-Class Life*, trans. Alan Crozier (New Brunswick: Rutgers University Press, 1979), 93-102, 127; Davidoff and Hall, *Family Fortunes*, 114, 221-22, 360; Geoffrey Best, *Mid-Victorian Britain 1851-1875* (London: Weidenfeld and Nicolson, 1971), 279-81; Stephen Kern, *The Culture of Love: Victorians to Moderns* (Cambridge, Mass.: Harvard University Press, 1992), 23-24. Samplings of the kinship connections across the area are detailed in Brian Lewis, "Bourgeois Ideology and Order: Middle-Class Culture and Politics in Lancashire, 1789-1851" (Ph.D. diss., Harvard University, 1994), 41-51.

⁸²· LRO, "The Diaries of Laurence Rawstorne from 1810-1849," Nov. 23, 1817, Jan. 15, 1818.

⁸³· They married in July. William Kirkman, *Memorials of Mr. Thomas Crouch Hincksman of Lytham, Lancashire* (London, 1885), 34-35. On the rituals of courting, see Davidoff, *Best Circles*, 49-50.

⁸⁴· BALS, Ainsworth Papers, ZAH/4/1, Apr. 21, 23, 26, 29, 30, 1824. Maybe he too would have described this as providential, as Miss de Manneville died on May 2, 1826, a fact he noted without comment.

⁸⁵· As related by Rhodes Boyson, *The Ashworth Cotton Enterprise: The Rise and Fall of a Family Firm* (Oxford: Clarendon Press, 1970), 251.

⁸⁶· Jacson, *Desultory Retracings*, 234-35.

⁸⁷· E.g., Whittaker while on honeymoon in Paris to mother, July 10, 1825: "I know nothing upon earth that is left me to wish for,—so completely are all my most sanguine expectations & hopes realized in my charming Mary." Mary Whittaker to mother-in-law, Sept. 16, 1829: "I certainly think that no woman could possibly be more blessed in a husband than I am; for I think him a pattern of excellence in all respects." BRL, 921 WHI, Whittaker Correspondence.

⁸⁸· Ibid., Whittaker to mother, Sept. 12, 1824.

⁸⁹· SJC, Whittaker I, Whittaker to mother, June 3, 1824.

[90.] Quoted by E. M. Hall (ed.), "The Knutsford Letters," 242 (typescript in CMA, MS F 823 89 G69).

[91.] Series of letters in BRL, 921 WHI, Whittaker Correspondence.

[92.] BALS, Heywood Papers, ZHE/44, Heywood to Elizabeth Shawcross, Dec. 30, 1847, Jan. 2, 3, 1848; Shawcross to Heywood, Jan. 2, 1848; and subsequent letters. William Shawcross (Elizabeth's brother) to Heywood, Apr. 9, claimed that he had watched over his sister ever since their mother's early death: "All my exertions & cares have been now amply repaid," and she would be "all that 'a good wife' expresses."

[93.] Jones, *Improper Marriages*, 32-33.

[94.] James C. Scholes, *History of Bolton* (Bolton, 1892), 287-88.

[95.] Susan Maria ffarington, *The History of the ffaringtons of Farington and Worden* (reprinted from *Chorley Guardian*, 1936).

[96.] Lawrence Stone, *Road to Divorce: England 1530-1987* (Oxford: Oxford University Press, 1990), chaps. 6-10. There were only 276 Acts of divorce, 1765-1857. Before a bill for divorce could be introduced, there had to be a prior grant of legal separation *a mensa et thoro* ("from bed and board") from the ecclesiastical courts and a verdict of damages for "criminal conversation" against the wife's "seducer" by a husband in the common law courts. See Joan Perkin, *Women and Marriage in Nineteenth-century England* (London: Routledge, 1989), 22-23.

[97.] LRO, Hoghton Papers, DDHo/530, "Act to Dissolve the Marriage of Henry Hoghton, Esquire, with Louisa Josephine Hoghton, 28 July, 1849."

[98.] W. Beamont, *A History of the House of Lyme* (Warrington, 1876), 200-3, 203-4 n.; Sidney Lee, ed., *Dictionary of National Biography* (New York, 1899), 58: 449-52; V. A. C. Gatrell, *The Hanging Tree: Execution and the English People 1770-1868* (Oxford: Oxford University Press, 1994), 2 and passim.

[99.] Stone, *Road to Divorce*, 158-59, 184.

[100.] LRO, DDX 1008/1/14, indenture of Jan. 15, 1803. Anthony Hewitson, *Northward. Historic, Topographic, Residential, and Scenic Gleanings, &c. Between Preston and Lancaster* (Preston, 1900), 42, recounts that Louisa, daughter of John Grimshaw (five-time mayor of Preston), also separated from her husband, Thomas Butler-Cole of Kirkland Hall, after many years of married life together.

[101.] See Anna Clark, *The Struggle for the Breeches* (Berkeley and Los Angeles: University of California Press, 1995), chap. 5; Deborah Valenze, review of ibid., *AHR* (Dec. 1995): 1513-15.

[102.] Richard Edgcumbe, ed., *The Diary of Frances Lady Shelley 1787-1817* (London, 1912), 2-3, 10.

[103.] *Statement by Mr. Leonard Thomas de Manneville, A French Nobleman, Knight of various Orders, etc. Residing near Honfleur, in Normandy, of Facts, by means of which, all Safe and Free Intercourse Between Himself and Caroline Thomas de Manneville, His Only Child, Now in her Fifteenth year of age, was, for fourteen years, suspended in England* (Paris, 1817); Archibald Sparke, *Bibliographia Boltoniensis* (Manchester, 1913), 56; Stone, *Road to Divorce*, 171, 173.

[104.] LRO, Whitaker Papers, DDWh/4/27, Eliza to Charles Whitaker, Aug. 12, 1813; /29, Aug. 17, 1813; /132, A. E. Robbins to Sarah Horrocks, n.d.

[105.] As most famously described by Blackstone, *Commentaries on the Laws of England* (Oxford, 1765-69), I: 430: if husband and wife are one body before God, they are one person in law, and that person is represented by the husband. Quoted by Mary Lyndon Shanley, *Feminism, Marriage, and the Law in Victorian England, 1850-1895* (Princeton: Princeton University Press, 1989). And see her discussion of the common law doctrine of coverture, pp. 7-9. A positive side for a married woman was that her husband was responsible for debts that she incurred. Preston's MP, Sir Henry Hoghton, apparently ran into considerable financial problems catching up with his wife's high spending in the 1790s (see LRO, Hoghton Papers, DDHo/391, Hoghton to John Fletcher, Mar. 8, 1794; /392, J. Gill to Fletcher, n.d.; /393, Gill to Fletcher, n.d.; /394, Gill to ?, n.d.). Also Ursula Vogel, "Property Rights and the Status of Women in Germany and England," in *Bourgeois Society in Nineteenth-Century Europe*, ed. Jürgen Kocka and Allen Mitchell (Oxford: Berg, 1993), 251: as the unmarried woman enjoyed the same property rights and liabilities as a man, this provided an important precedent for campaigns for equality of rights for married women.

[106.] LRO, Whitaker Papers, DDWh 3/110, will of William St. Clare of Preston, 1812.

[107.] Though note that R. J. Morris's sample of middle-class wills in Leeds reveals that few testators deviated from the custom that the widow and children should each receive a third of the wealth, with the remaining third to be disposed of as the testator wished. Gendered equity customarily applied—i.e. fair shares for all offspring—but sons would normally receive their fortunes free of all restraint at the age of twenty-one, daughters usually only the income from capital invested in trust. All this was very different from patterns of primogeniture and entail among the landed classes. Morris, "Reading the Will: Cash Economy Capitalists and Urban Peasants in the 1830s," in *The Making of the British Middle Class? Studies of Regional and Cultural Diversity Since the Eighteenth Century*, ed. Alan Kidd and David Nicholls (Stroud, Gloucestershire: Sutton, 1998), 120-21, 128.

[108.] BRL, G13 FEI, copy of will of Sir William Feilden, May 13, 1850.

[109.] See Perkin, *Women and Marriage*. She writes (pp. 66, 70-71, 74) that beyond the marriage settlement (which raised jointures for the widow, pin money for the wife, and portions for daughters and younger sons on coming of age) the rich often made gifts of separate property to their married daughters by the doctrine of trusts, upheld by Equity in Chancery. Such separate incomes considerably altered wives' relationships with their husbands. But in the absence of such agreements—i.e. so far as the bulk of the middle class was concerned—the husband could assert his Common Law rights (pp. 7, 16). For the evidence of more middling women possessing separate estates than was once thought, see Margaret R. Hunt, *The Middling Sort: Commerce, Gender, and the Family in England, 1680-1780* (Berkeley and Los Angeles: University of California Press, 1996), 158-61; Davidoff and Hall, *Family Fortunes*, 209-10.

[110.] LRO, DX/605, indenture of Sept. 11, 1832.

[111.] LRO, Whitaker Papers, DDWh/4/141, T. S. Shuttleworth, Preston, to the Rev. Charles Whitaker, Symonstone, Oct. 22, 1846. In the event, none of the beneficiaries wished to live there, being settled elsewhere, so Eliza, Samuel's widow, had a deed drawn up and signed by all of them in 1855 leaving the trustees free to sell the house. She went to live near Grange over Sands. Margaret Burscough, *The History of Lark Hill, Preston* (Preston, 1989), 35-36.

[112.] But see Hunt, *Middling Sort*, 136-37.

[113.] Jacson, *Desultory Retracings*, 267.

[114.] BALS, Ainsworth Papers, ZAH/4/22, Jan. 1, 1847, Feb. 19; /23, Feb. 5, 1848, Mar. 27, May 4, 10.

[115.] BRL, Whittaker Papers, 921 WHI, Mary Haughton Whittaker to her mother-in-law, Aug. 14, 19, 1836.

[116.] Dr. Charles Rothwell relates that he had to be carried piggyback by his groom, sometimes to his gig, sometimes (if after dark) even to a patient. "A History of the Changes in Medical Men and Manners in Bolton; being the Introductory Lecture read before the Medical Society, By its President for 1879" (typescript in BALS, B610 ROT), 27.

[117.] Hall, *Miss Weeton*, 272-74 (Weeton to Miss Winkley, July 8, 1810).

[118.] LRO, DDX 76/1, advertisement for Mr. and Mrs. Stretton's boarding school in Blackburn, Jan. 6, 1800; /4, for Miss Clayton's, Penny St., Blackburn, Aug. 27, 1805, and for Miss Lang's, King St., to open on Mar. 4, 1805.

[119.] Whittle, *History of Preston*, I: 84.

[120.] Franklin Baker, *The Rise and Progress of Nonconformity in Bolton* (London, 1854), 71.

[121.] Louisa Potter, *Lancashire Memories* (London, 1879), 165-74.

[122.] Jacson, *Desultory Retracings*, 136, 143-44.

[123.] Edgcumbe, ed., *Diaries of Lady Shelley*, 14.

[124.] LRO, Cross Papers, DDX 841, Richard Assheton Cross, "Sketch of my Father's Life." Note that, in spite of the testimony of his mother's input, it was his father's life—the public face of the family—that he considered of most significance and as the guiding narrative.

[125.] LRO, Coucher Book of Feniscowles, PR 2846/2/1, vol. I, Mary Haughton Feilden to bishop of Chester, Dec. 23, 1833; bishop of Chester to Mrs. Feilden, Dec. 24, 1833; Whittaker to Mrs. Feilden, Feb. 27, 1834; to William Feilden, Apr. 3 (extract); Mrs. Feilden to Whittaker, Apr. 5; Whittaker to Mrs. Georgiana Willis, May 12; Mrs. Feilden to Whittaker, May 11, 27, June 3, 5.

[126.] LRO, PR 2846/2/1, Mrs. Feilden to Whittaker, Jan. 25, 27, 1835. The newspaper account was indeed enthusiastic, paying tribute to the Feildens' "beautiful mansion" and their "splendid hospitality." The editor stated that his aim was to "furnish so complete a statement of the particulars as to render it worthy of lengthened preservation in the cottages of the poor, as well as in the portfolio of those in more fortunate circumstances." *BS*, Feb. 11, 1835, supplement.

[127.] PR 2846/2/1, Mrs. Feilden to [Whittaker ?], Jan. 12, 1836.

[128.] LRO, DDX/510, Diaries of Dolly Clayton, passim.

[129.] Potter, *Lancashire Memories*, 66-67, 69-70, 73.

[130.] BALS, "Diary of Charles James Darbishire of Rivington, J.P., for 1852" (incomplete copy), May 28, July 27, Sept. 1.

[131.] Potter, *Lancashire Memories*, 25-43. The Darbishires were her cousins, and she describes them at "Old Court," her name for Lomax Fold. See G. M. Ramsden, "A Record of the Kay Family of Bury Lancashire in the Seventeenth and Eighteenth Centuries. With Notes on the Families of Gaskell, Mangnall, Darbishire" (typescript in BALS, 1978), 55-57.

[132.] For differing assessments of the confines and the latitude, see, e.g., Steven Marcus, *The Other Victorians: A Study of Sexuality and Pornography in Mid-Nineteenth-Century England* (New York: Basic Books, 1964); J. A. Banks, *Victorian Values: Secularism and the Size of Families* (London: Routledge and Kegan Paul, 1981), 89; M. Jeanne Peterson, "Dr. Acton's Enemy: Medicine, Sex, and Society in Victorian England," *Victorian Studies* 29, 4 (Summer 1986): 569-90; F. B. Smith, *The People's Health 1830-1910* (London: Croom Helm, 1979), 295-96; Steven Seidman, "The Power of Desire and the Danger of Pleasure: Victorian Sexuality Reconsidered," *JSH* 24, I (Fall 1990): 47-67; Peter Gay, *The Bourgeois Experience: Victoria to Freud*, vol. 2, *The Tender Passion* (Oxford: Oxford University Press, 1986); Carol Z. Stearns and Peter N. Stearns, "Victorian Sexuality: Can Historians Do It Better?" *JSH* (Summer 1985): 625-34; Paul Langford, *A Polite and Commercial People: England 1727-1783* (Oxford: Clarendon Press, 1989), 637-39; John D'Emilio and Estelle B. Freedman, *In-*

timate Matters: A History of Sexuality in America (New York: Harper and Row, 1988), xiii, 67-72, 84; Laqueur, *Making Sex*, passim; idem, "Orgasm, Generation, and the Politics of Reproductive Biology," in *The Making of the Modern Body: Sexuality and Society in the Nineteenth Century*, ed. Catherine Gallagher and Laqueur (Berkeley and Los Angeles: University of California Press, 1987); idem, "Sex and Desire in the Industrial Revolution," in *Industrial Revolution*, ed. O'Brien and Quinault, 104; Stephen Kern, *The Culture of Love: Victorians to Moderns* (Cambridge, Mass.: Harvard University Press, 1992), 331, 337-39, 403-4; Michael Mason, *The Making of Victorian Sexuality* (Oxford: Oxford University Press, 1994), 19-20, 203; Tim Hitchcock, "Redefining Sex in Eighteenth-Century England," *HW* 41 (1996): 73-90; Roy Porter, "The Literature of Sexual Advice Before 1800," in *Sexual Knowledge, Sexual Science: The History of Attitudes to Sexuality*, ed. Porter and Mikulás Teich (Cambridge: Cambridge University Press, 1994), 134-35.

[133.] BRL, G3 BAR, notes on Barlow and Winstanley Families (extracted from Bannister Cuttings vols. of local history in Chorley Local Studies Collection); W. A. Abram, *Blackburn Characters of a Past Generation* (Blackburn, 1894), 260, 265-66. Note also that John Burgoyne, MP for Preston 1768-92, after the death of his wife, Lady Charlotte Stanley, had four children by an actress, Susan Caulfield, to whom he bequeathed the bulk of his property with reversion to their son, John. See R. G. Thorne, *The History of Parliament: The House of Commons 1790-1820* (London: Secker and Warburg, 1986), III: 318-19; Edward Barrington De Fonblanque, *Political and Military Episodes in the Latter Half of the Eighteenth Century: Derived from the Life and Correspondence of the Rt. Hon. John Burgoyne* (London, 1876), 465.

[134.] Gladys Whittaker, *The Every-Claytons of Carr Hall* (Pendle Libraries Local History Note Sheets, 12, n.d.), 1-2; Leslie Chapples, *Of Yeoman Stock . . . The Halsteads of Rowley* (Farnham, Surrey, n.d.), 34-35.

[135.] LRO, Whitaker Papers, DDWh /3/148, will of Samuel Horrocks, proved at Chester Apr. 30, 1846. There was no issue from his marriage to Eliza, daughter of Thomas Miller.

[136.] *MG*, May 10, 1880, quoted by John Bailey, "Thomas Birchall Jr. of Ribbleton Hall" (thesis, Chorley College of Education, 1969), 28-29.

[137.] Michel Foucault, *The History of Sexuality*, vol.1, *An Introduction*, trans. Robert Hurley (New York: Vintage Books, 1990), 25-35 and passim.

[138.] *BFP*, Aug. 21, 1847, p. 1; Jan. 16, 1847, p. 2.

[139.] LRO, DDHu 53/82/266-295, advert of J. Gardner, Bolton bookseller, n.d.

[140.] *BM*, Jan. 10, 1810, p. 2.

[141.] Leon Radzinowicz, *A History of English Criminal Law*, vol. IV, *Grappling for Control* (London: Stevens and Son, 1968), 329: from 1842 to 1849, between 49 and 96 people in Britain were sentenced to death each year, the highest number (13-22) for murder, the second for sodomy (12-18); but in the decade after 1841 only murderers were executed. For earlier executions see Gatrell, *Hanging Tree*, 618: 28 men were hanged for sodomy in England and Wales, 1805-18 (3 percent of all those executed), and 22 (2 percent), 1819-32. A record of those committed, convicted, and executed between 1798 and 1818 at Lancaster Assizes (LRO, DDCm 1/9) shows that all of the 6 men convicted of sodomy were hanged. The 11 people convicted of murder were also hanged. Executions were higher in other categories that did not carry the death penalty by the 1840s, but by no means all those convicted were hanged (e.g. 30/121 for burglary, 48/75 for forging and uttering forged bank notes, 31/86 for highway robbery).

[142.] To paraphrase Kern, *Culture of Love*, 194.

[143.] Introduction, John Boswell, "Revolutions, Universals, and Sexual Categories," 18-19, 22-23, 34, Robert Padgug, "Sexual Matters: Rethinking Sexuality in History," 59-60, and Martha Vicinus, "Distance and Desire: English Boarding School Friendships, 1870-1920," 214, in *Hidden from History: Reclaiming the Gay and Lesbian Past*, ed. Martin Bauml Duberman, Martha Vicinus, and George Chauncey Jr. (New York: NAL Books, 1989); Anthony Giddens, *Sociology* (Cambridge: Polity Press, 1989), 159-62; Jeffrey Weeks, *Sex, Politics and Society: The Regulation of Sexuality Since 1800* (London: Longman, 1981), chap. 6 and passim; E. Anthony Rotundo, "Learning About Manhood: Gender Ideals and the Middle-Class Family in Nineteenth-Century America," Jeffrey Richards, "'Passing the Love of Women': Manly Love and Victorian Society," and introduction to *Manliness and Morality: Middle-Class Masculinity in Britain and America 1800-1940*, ed. J. A. Mangan and James Walvin (Manchester: Manchester University Press, 1987); Randolph Trumbach, "Sex, Gender, and Sexual Identity in Modern Culture: Male Sodomy and Female Prostitution in Enlightenment London," in *Forbidden History: The State, Society, and the Regulation of Sexuality in Modern Europe*, ed. John C. Fout (Chicago: University of Chicago Press, 1992), 94-96; Faderman, *Surpassing the Love of Men*, 152; Richard Davenport-Hines, *Sex, Death and Punishment: Attitudes to Sex and Sexuality in Britain since the Renaissance* (London: Collins, 1990), 116. For an alternative, anti-constructionist reading, see Rictor Norton, *The Myth of the Modern Homosexual: Queer History and the Search for Cultural Unity* (London: Cassell, 1997).

Notes to Chapter 5

[1.] E. Whitehead, *A Sermon Preached in the Parish Church of Bolton, on Sunday the 24th of September, 1786; Being the Next Lord's day After the execution of James Holland, On Bolton Moor, for Croft-Breaking* (Bolton, 1786), 11-12.

[2.] *BM*, Sept. 4, 1793, p. 3, a reference to a man about to be executed for the murder of a Warrington postboy.

[3.] Peter Whittle, *Bolton-le-Moors, and the Townships in the Parish* (Bolton, [1857]), 428.

[4.] *PC*, Nov. 24, 1849, p. 6.

[5.] See, e.g., David Rothman, *The Discovery of the Asylum: Social Order and Disorder in the New Republic* (Boston: Little, Brown, 1971); Michel Foucault, *Discipline and Punish: The Birth of the Prison*, trans. Alan Sheridan (New York: Pantheon, 1977); Michael Ignatieff, *A Just Measure of Pain* (New York: Columbia University Press, 1978); Hubert L. Dreyfus and Paul Rabinow, *Michel Foucault: Beyond Structuralism and Hermeneutics* (Chicago: University of Chicago Press, 1982), 147-60; Michael Walzer, "The Politics of Michel Foucault," in *Foucault: A Critical Reader*, ed. David Couzens Hoy (Oxford: Blackwell, 1986), 62-63; Colin Jones and Roy Porter, introduction, 1-3, 9, and Randall McGowen, "Power and Humanity, Or Foucault Among the Historians," 95, 110, in *Reassessing Foucault: Power, Medicine and the Body*, ed. Jones and Porter (London: Routledge, 1994).

[6.] James Miller, *The Passion of Michel Foucault* (New York: Simon and Schuster, 1993), 222.

[7.] See, e.g., Jürgen Habermas, *Der Philosophische Diskurs der Moderne: Zwölf Vorlesungen* (Frankfurt, 1985), 338, cited by Hoy, *Foucault*, 9; Margaret DeLacy, *Prison Reform in Lancashire, 1700-1850: A Study in Local Administration* (Manchester: Chetham Society, 1986); idem, "Grinding Men Good? Lancashire's Prisons at Mid-Century," in *Policing and Punishment in Nineteenth-Century Britain*, ed. Victor Bailey (London: Croom Helm, 1981); Bailey, introduction to *Policing and Punishment*;

Michael Ignatieff, "State, Civil Society and Total Institutions: A Critique of Recent Social Histories of Punishment," 83-91, and David Philips, "'A Just Measure of Crime, Authority, Hunters and Blue Locusts': The 'Revisionist' Social History of Crime and the Law in Britain, 1780-1850," 60-68, in *Social Control and the State: Historical and Comparative Essays*, ed. Stanley Cohen and Andrew Scull (Oxford: Martin Robertson, 1983); Anthony Giddens, *A Contemporary Critique of Historical Materialism*, vol. I, *Power, Property and the State* (Berkeley and Los Angeles: University of California Press, 1981), 169-73; idem, *Sociology* (Cambridge: Polity Press, 1989), 290; Terry Eagleton, *Ideology: An Introduction* (London: Verso, 1991), 6-8, 165-66; Lynn Hunt, "History, Culture, and Text," in *The New Cultural History*, ed. idem (Berkeley and Los Angeles: University of California Press, 1989), 8; Jeffrey Weeks, "Foucault for Historians," *HW(J)* 14 (Autumn 1982): 115-18. For Foucault's own, belated, appreciation of the positive aspects of nineteenth-century liberalism (representative democracy, the market economy as a bulwark against state power, the rule of law), see Miller, *Passion*, 310-12.

[8.] V. A. C. Gatrell, "Crime, Authority and the Policeman-State," in *The Cambridge Social History of Britain 1750-1950*, ed. F. M. L. Thompson (Cambridge: Cambridge University Press, 1990), III: 243-310.

[9.] Eric C. Midwinter, *Law and Order in Early Victorian Lancashire* (Borthwick Papers, 34, University of York Borthwick Institute of Historical Research, 1968), 9.

[10.] PP 1835, XXV, "Reports of the Commissioners Appointed to Inquire into the Municipal Corporations in England and Wales: Report on the Borough of Preston," 1692.

[11.] Though no change was made without the consent of the Feildens as the lords of the moiety of the manor, and they continued to appoint constables to attend at the court leet of the Honor of Clitheroe. See LRO, Feilden Papers, DDCm 2/167, printed letters of appointment, Oct. 8, 1800, Oct. 7, 1812, Oct. 15, 1822; /195, letter of May 21, 1838.

[12.] BALS, Great Bolton Improvement Trustees' Minutes, TGB/1/1, Aug. 28, 31, 1793, Mar. 4, 1795.

[13.] A town meeting had previously set up a rota for patrols by 120 special constables (LRO, DDHu 53/82/1, printed notice of meeting of Jan. 4, 1790), primarily targeting disorderly conduct (keepers of disorderly lodging houses and "all foot-ball players, or other persons, who shall cause riotous meetings, shall be prosecuted at the expence of the town"). But it is unclear whether this is the birth of the Special Constables' Society or an earlier, short-lived scheme.

[14.] BALS, FP/2/6, Great Bolton Special Constables' Society; FP/2/5, Roll of Special Constables, 1816-32; FP/2/4, Minute Book, 1829-34; FP/2/3, Watch and Ward, Magistrates' Occurrence Book, 1812-20; FP/2/2, Constable's Occurrence Book, 1808-28; FP/2/1, Account Book, 1812-31. And see T. K. Campbell, "Watch and Ward—The Great Bolton Constables' Society" (typescript in BALS, 1976), 1-2.

[15.] PRO, PC/1/759, report of Capt. Jebb, Apr. 3, 1838; PC/1/761 (papers in connection with 1/758), E, deposition of John Lockwood; F, deposition of Robert Morris; and see also D, strictures of Judge Alderson at Lancaster Assizes, Mar. 23, 1833; and G, [S.?] W. [Paulton?] to James Winder, Mar. 24, 1838; PC/1/757, "Counter Statement of Deputation against a Charter of Incorporation"; /758, "Further Statements of Petitioners for Charter."

[16.] LRO, CBP /50, Watch Committee Minutes, Jan. 18, 1836. Banister's salary was increased to a fixed rate of £300 on Jan. 1, 1841 (CBP/1/1).

[17.] LRO, CBP/1/1, Council Minutes, Aug. 2, 1839, Feb. 24, 1842, Aug. 24, 1848; CBP/50, July 29, 1839, Aug. 6; CBP/50/3, Apr. 8, 1847.

[18.] E.g., CBP/50, Nov. 5, 1839.

[19.] It should also be remembered that the police were intended only to supplement, and not to replace, the military. See, e.g., CBP/50, the watch committee's resolution on Sept. 4, 1837, to invite the millowners and JPs to a meeting to consider applying to government for the town to be made a military station.

[20.] CBP/1/1, Jan. 31, Apr. 27, 1840.

[21.] BALS, AB/24/1 (1), Bolton Borough Council, Watch Committee Minutes, Dec. 20, 31, 1838, Jan. 9, 16, 29, 31, 1839.

[22.] See, e.g., AB/24/1 (1), Mar. 2, 5, 11, 12, Apr. 8, 19, May 17, July 12, Aug. 30, Oct. 28, 1839.

[23.] *BFP*, Sept. 28, 1839, p. 3.

[24.] BALS, AJB/5, Bolton Borough Police, Daily Memorandum Book, July-Aug. 1839; /6, Sept.-Oct. 1839.

[25.] HO 52/39, notice of Jan. 28, 1839.

[26.] HO 40/44, Darbishire to Russell, July 29, Aug. 4, 1839, and see Aug. 12. The council agreed on Aug. 5 (BALS, AB/1/1, Council Minutes). See also F. C. Mather, *Public Order in the Age of the Chartists* (Manchester: Manchester University Press, 1959), 121; Leon Radzinowicz, *A History of English Criminal Law and its Administration from 1750*, vol. IV, *Grappling for Control* (London: Stevens and Sons, 1968), 258; Stanley H. Palmer, *Police and Protest in England and Ireland 1780-1850* (Cambridge: Cambridge University Press, 1988), 418-20.

[27.] W. Brimelow, *Political and Parliamentary History of Bolton* (Bolton, 1882), 373-74.

[28.] *BFP*, Aug. 24, 1839, p. 2; *BC*, July 27, 1839, p. 2.

[29.] PRO, HO 52/39, Angelo to Fox Maule, Oct. 5, 1839.

[30.] *The Times*, Oct. 14, 1839, p. 5, quoted by Mather, *Public Order*, 122.

[31.] PRO, HO 52/39, Darbishire to Normanby, Oct. 11, 1839.

[32.] BALS, ABJ/3, Bolton Borough Police, Morning State Book, Nov. 6, 1839; PRO, HO 52/39, Shaw to Normanby, Dec. 5, 1839. For praise of their conduct at the fires, HO 40/44, Wemyss to Phillipps, Dec. 3.

[33.] BALS, ABJ/1, Bolton Borough Police, Examination Book 1839-1861.

[34.] A phrase of Brutus in *Julius Caesar* 4.3.27.

[35.] PRO, HO 40/44, Hurley to Boyd, Nov. 13, 1839; Shaw to Phillipps, Dec. 2; BALS, ABJ/1, Bolton Borough Police, Examination Book 1839-1861.

[36.] ABJ/1, Bolton Borough Police, Examination Book 1839-1861. It was a force made up largely of laborers, spinners, weavers, and craftsmen.

[37.] BALS, AB/1/1, Council Minutes, July 15, Aug. 9, 1842; ABJ/1, Bolton Borough Police, Examination Book 1839-1861; AB/24/1 (1), Watch Committee Minutes, Dec. 14, 21, 1842, Sept. 6, 1843, Apr. 3, June 5, 1844, May 7, June 4, Dec. 3, Dec. 24, 1845, June 2, 1847, July 27, 28, Aug. 2, 1848.

[38.] BALS, AB/24/1 (1), Watch Committee Minutes, Nov. 16, 1842, Apr. 3, July 3, Sept. 4, 1844.

[39.] *PC*, Feb. 2, 1839. And see *PP*, Nov. 9, 1839, p. 2; Nov. 30, 1839, p. 2.

[40.] *BFP*, Apr. 20, p. 2. And see *BC*, Dec. 21, 1839, p. 3.

[41.] See David Taylor, *The New Police in Nineteenth-Century England: Crime, Conflict and Control* (Manchester: Manchester University Press, 1997), 27-30, 39-40.

[42.] *PC*, Feb. 2, 1839, p. 3; Robert Hindle, *An Account of the Expenditure of the County Palatine of Lancaster* (London, 1843), 201-2.

[43.] *PC*, Nov. 9, 1839, p. 2; May 2, 1840, p. 2.

[44.] Robert B. Storch, "The Plague of Blue Locusts. Police Reform and Popular Resistance in Northern England, 1840-57," *IRSH* XX (1975): 69-70.

[45.] BALS, Heywood Papers, ZHE/37, Edmund Grundy, John Haslam, John Fletcher, Andrew Knowles, William Scowcroft, George Piggot, James Knowles, and E. and W. Bolling to magistrates in Bolton neighborhood, Jan. 23, 1841.

[46.] See *BS*, Dec. 16, 1840, p. 2; Dec. 30, p. 2.

[47.] *BS*, Jan. 6, 1841.

[48.] *PC*, Dec. 3, 1840, p. 2.

[49.] Hindle, *Expenditure of Lancashire*, 203-5.

[50.] *BFP*, Mar. 12, 1842, p. 2.

[51.] Hindle, *Expenditure of Lancashire*, 205-6; *BS*, Apr. 6, 1842, p. 2. Home Secretary Graham agreed on May 20 to the formation of the police districts, pursuant to 3 & 4 Vic. c. 88, and to the overall reduction of the constabulary force to 350 men. See PRO, HO 65/4, Phillipps to Messrs. Gorsts and Birchall, clerks of the peace, May 20, 1842. See also Mather, *Public Order*, 133-34; Radzinowicz, *Criminal Law*, IV: 278; David Foster, "Public Opinion and the Police in Lancashire 1838-1842" (MA thesis, Sheffield University, 1965), 68-71; Palmer, *Police and Protest*, 444; Clive Emsley, *The English Police: A Political and Social History* (Hemel Hempstead: Harvester Wheatsheaf, 1991), 44.

[52.] *PC*, July 5, 1845, p. 2. But the police did, the paper claimed, keep an especial eye on all suspected poachers and disturbers of game, thus allowing magisterial landowners to shift the costs of gamekeeping onto the ratepayers. And see *PC*, Oct. 28, 1848, p. 6.

[53.] Mather, *Public Order*, 139. But he also notes that both the Bolton Borough Police (p. 122) and generally the county police (p. 138) were ineffective, because of the paucity of their numbers, unless supported by the military. Palmer, *Police and Protest*, 446, comments that such an example of police being able to curtail riots unaided was rare.

[54.] *PC*, June 10, 1848, p. 4.

[55.] *PG*, Feb. 4, 1854, p. 6, quoted by Marian Roberts, *The Story of Winckley Square, Preston* (Preston, 1988), 34.

[56.] Clive Emsley, "The English Bobby," in *Myths of the English*, ed. Roy Porter (Cambridge: Polity Press, 1993), 118-22; idem, *The English Police*, 59-61; Douglas Hay and Francis Snyder, "Using the Criminal Law, 1750-1850. Policing, Private Prosecution, and the State," in *Policing and Prosecution in Britain 1750-1850*, ed. idem (Oxford: Clarendon Press, 1989), 47: during the second half of the nineteenth century the English police became part of the national landscape: "The policed society came to be perceived as the normal society."

[57.] David Foster, "The Changing Social and Political Composition of the Lancashire County Magistracy, 1821-1851" (Ph.D. diss., Lancaster University, 1971), 131-36. When Joseph Lister, Blackburn manufacturer, was nominated in 1824, the chancellor of the Duchy of Lancaster recognized that "the necessity of a magistrate in that populous district and the difficulty of finding one out of business were so great that (he did not) think he could refuse the appointment." Duchy Papers, Bexley to F. Harper, Nov. 6-7, 1824 (quoted by Foster, 133-34).

[58.] Ibid., 132, 136, 140, 142ff., 206, 208, 229, 245-50, 254ff., 274-75, and appendix. For the questioning of the suitability of clergymen for the job (because of the incompatibility of the roles of counselor and judge), see ibid., 242; PRO, HO 42/61, Bancroft to J. King, Feb. 9, 1801 ("the Clergyman of a Parish does not appear to advantage in the character of an Informer."); LRO, DDHu 48/147, Lord Aberdeen to William Hulton, Mar. 11, 1828, /148, idem, Mar. 24, /150, idem, Apr. 7 (re the appointment of the Rev. William Allen); and for the Rev. J. W. Whittaker's grounds for refusing magistracy, plus the advice from his family, in spite of heavy pressure, see WRO, "The Whittaker Letters," D/D2 EHC/205, Miss Bessy Whittaker of Lytham to Whittaker, Apr. 26, 1822; /207, mother to Whittaker, July 14, 1822; Edward Hall, ed., "The Knutsford Letters," 180, Aunt Sharpe to Whittaker, Feb. 23, 1822 (CMA, MS F 823 89 G69) ; LRO, PR 1549/3, Coucher Book of St. Mary's, "Report of the Vicar of Blackburn to the Bishop of Chester," Aug. 7, 1835; BRL, 921 WHI, Blackburn Industrial Disturbances (1826-29), inhabitants of Blackburn to Whittaker, May 1826.

[59.] HO 52/29, [E.?] Rishton to Russell, Feb. 8, 1836; Joseph Bray to [Russell?], Feb. 9; Richard Palmer to Russell, Apr. 30; T. B. Addison to Palmer, May 2; John Addison to Palmer, May 2; HO 90/1, returns to a circular letter to town clerks from H. Manners Sutton, Oct. 27, 1841; LRO, CBP/1/1, Aug. 5, 1846.

[60.] HO 52/39, petition of Bolton Council to queen, Dec. 19, 1838; second petition, Dec. 19; Winder to Messrs. Parkes and Preston, Westminster, Dec. 20, 1838 (quotation); Winder to Russell, Dec. 20; memorial of council to Russell, Dec. 29; Darbishire to Russell, Jan. 5, 1839; Winder to Russell, July 18; Thomasson to Russell, Aug. 31; BALS, AB/1/1, Dec. 5, 19, 28, 1838 (including letter from Phillipps to town clerk, Dec. 25). See also BALS, Heywood Papers, ZHE/26/3, Robert Heywood to Henry Ashworth, June 10, 1838, commenting on the paucity of suitable candidates among the reformers.

[61.] BALS, AB/1/1, Feb. 13, 1839, Apr. 5, May 22, 29, June 8; BALS, Heywood Papers, ZHE/35, Heywood to Normanby, Dec. 2, 1839; Home Office to Heywood, Dec. 4; [John?] Potter to Heywood, Dec. 3; Heywood to Thomas Potter, mayor of Manchester, Dec. 10; PRO, HO 52/39, minutes of meeting of borough magistrates, Apr. 5, 1839; /44, Arrowsmith to Normanby, Dec. 1840; Winder to Normanby, Dec. 16.

[62.] HO 52/39, memorial to Russell from Darbishire, Heywood, Ainsworth, Ashworth, Barnes, and Andrews, n.d.; memorial to Russell from Bolton Council, Apr. 5, 1839; Winder to Russell, Apr. 17; BALS, Heywood Papers, ZHE/35, Heywood to Joseph Ridgway, Mar. 27.

[63.] BALS, AB/1/1, Apr. 8, Aug. 11, 1841; *Statement Relating to the Burthens and Expences Intended to be Inflicted on the Borough of Bolton, by the Establishment of Borough Quarter Sessions. Published for the Information of the Ratepayers, by the Committee of Ratepayers, opposed to the Bolton Charter* (Bolton, 1841), 3-5, 11; Brimelow, *Political and Parliamentary*, 444; John Taylor, *Autobiography of a Lancashire Lawyer* (Bolton, 1883), 113-16.

[64.] HO 90/1, returns to a circular letter to town clerks by H. Manners Sutton, Oct. 27, 1841; BALS, Heywood Papers, ZHE/45, Heywood to Walmsley, May 4, 1849; /46, Heywood to Walmsley, July 25, Aug. 13, 1850; Walmsley to Heywood, Aug. 12.

[65.] Though it should be noted that responsibility for many prosecutions lay primarily with the aggrieved party, who might be reluctant because of the prohibitive expense. One solution was the prosecution society, a form of voluntary association. For example, the eighteen landowners and inhabitants of Turton who formed the Turton Society for the Prosecution of Felons in May 1789 each paid 2s. 6d. annually into a fund, up to a stock of £20. The society apparently continued in existence until 1856, disbursing sums for apprehending suspects, for briefs, counsel, attending the sessions, and the like. BALS, Turton Society for the Prosecution of Felons, FP/1/1, May 30, 1789; and see, e.g., /5, Feb. 25, 1812, Sept. 1, 1817. For another example, see LRO, Rawstorne Papers, DDR 9/5, "Bond for Prosecuting Felons in Penwortham and Howick," 1801.

And see Hay and Snyder, "Using the Criminal Law," 27, 38: the prosecuting associations were gradually superseded by the new police, especially after 1856. Bolton had an earlier borough prosecutor: John Gaskell, presumably the first, held the office from 1842 to 1858 (Brimelow, *Political and Parliamentary,* 172 (entry under Gaskell, Samuel)).

[66.] PRO, PC/1/759, report of Capt. Jebb, Apr. 3, 1838.

[67.] Taylor, *Autobiography,* 37.

[68.] David Philips, "Crime, Law and Punishment in the Industrial Revolution," in *The Industrial Revolution and British Society,* ed. Patrick K. O'Brien and Roland Quinault (Cambridge: Cambridge University Press, 1985), 166-69. For a description of particular vindictiveness against poachers by county JPs, see the Rev. Walter Lowe Clay, *The Prison Chaplain: A Memoir of the Rev. John Clay, B.D.* (Cambridge, 1861), 563-64 (letter of Clay to Lord Stanley, Feb. 2, 1855).

[69.] BALS, Heywood Papers, ZHE/31, minutes of Magistrates' Court, Sept. 14, 17, 24, Oct. 15, Nov. 12, Dec. 3, 1835.

[70.] J. M. Beattie, *Crime and the Courts in England 1660-1800* (Princeton: Princeton University Press, 1986), 13 and chaps. 9-10; Joanna Innes and John Styles, "The Crime Wave: Recent Writing on Crime and Criminal Justice in Eighteenth-century England," in *Rethinking Social History: English Society 1570-1920 and its Interpretation,* ed. Adrian Wilson (Manchester: Manchester University Press, 1993), 227-40; Randall McGowen, "The Well-Ordered Prison. England, 1780-1865," in *The Oxford History of the Prison: The Practice of Punishment in Western Society,* ed. Norval Morris and David J. Rothman (New York: Oxford University Press, 1995), 80-85.

[71.] McGowen, "Well-Ordered Prison," 85, 89-90; DeLacy, *Prison Reform,* 58ff.

[72.] Sidney and Beatrice Webb, *English Prisons Under Local Government* (London: Longmans, Green, 1922), 51, 83; Hardwick, *Preston,* 439.

[73.] T. H. B. Oldfield, *The Representative History of Great Britain and Ireland* (London, 1816), 93; Clay, *Prison Chaplain,* 105.

[74.] Clay, *Prison Chaplain,* 107; Hindle, *Expenditure of Lancashire,* 78. Also see W. Cooke Taylor's comment in *An Illustrated Itinerary of the County of Lancaster* (London, 1842), 158: "[W]e were somewhat startled in seeing cannon mounted upon the angles of the building, and pointed up and down the streets. We were told that they were placed there some time ago, upon an apprehension of violence in the town; but that apprehension over, they should have been removed from a building where the moral force of the laws alone should be exhibited, not instruments of violence."

[75.] See above, nn. 5-7, and especially DeLacy, *Prison Reform.*

[76.] Quoted by Morris and Rothman, introduction to *Oxford History of the Prison,* viii. And see Felix Driver, "Bodies in Space. Foucault's account of disciplinary power," in *Reassessing Foucault,* ed. Jones and Porter, 119-20.

[77.] James Neild, *Gentleman's Magazine,* June 1806, idem, *State of the Prisons* (1812), and J. J. Gurney, *Notes on a Visit to Some of the Prisons in Scotland and the North of England* (1819), cited by Webb and Webb, *English Prisons,* 83; McGowen, "Well-Ordered Prison," 95-96.

[78.] See, e.g., Samuel Leach, *Old Age Reminiscences* (printed for private circulation, 1923), 25: Clay's annual reports "were looked forward to by all men in the country who were interested in improvement in prison discipline and amendment of the then conditions"; and *PP,* Oct. 22, 1842, p. 2.

[79.] LRO, QGR/2/1, General Report of Preston House of Correction, October 1823; /3, General Report, 1824. The acts also abolished gambling and the sale of liquor in prisons, appointed salaried governors, and defined chaplains' duties. None of this was enforced until prison inspectors were appointed in 1835. See Leon Radzinowicz and Roger Hood, *A History of English Criminal Law and its Administration from 1750*, vol. V, *The Emergence of Penal Policy* (London: Stevens and Sons, 1986), 145.

[80] QGR/2/10, Chaplain's Report, Oct. 1825.

[81] QGR/2/13, Chaplain's Report, 1826; /17, Chaplain's Report, Oct. 1828.

[82] QGR/2/20, Chaplain's Report, Oct. 1829.

[83] Clay, *Prison Chaplain*, 108, 114-15.

[84] MS minutes, Quarter Sessions, Lancashire, Sept. 11, 1834, cited by Webb and Webb, *English Prisons*, 95.

[85] *BG*, Mar. 4, 1835, p. 7.

[86] Clay, *Prison Chaplain*, 116.

[87] LRO, QGR/2/36, Chaplain's Report, Oct. 1837, pp. 3-4; /29, Chaplain's Report, Oct. 1839, p. 3; /31, Chaplain's Report, Oct. 1840, p. 3.

[88] QGR/2/37, Chaplain's Report, Oct. 1838, p. 12.

[89] QGR/2/37, Chaplain's Report, Oct. 1838, pp. 10-11; U. R. Q. Henriques, "The Rise and Decline of the Separate System of Prison Discipline," *P&P* 54 (Feb. 1972): 76-78.

[90] QGR/2/31, Chaplain's Report, Oct. 1840, p. 5. According to Hardwick, *Preston*, 441, flogging continued even later, in rare cases, for criminals under the "Juvenile Act."

[91] QGV/2/4, rules for House of Correction, 1842.

[92] QGV/2/1, Major J. Jebb to Thomas Rawson, May 13, 1843.

[93] Clay, *Prison Chaplain*, 122.

[94] QGR/2/39, Chaplain's Report, Oct. 1844, pp. 6-8; QGR/2/33, Chaplain's Report, Dec. 1846, p. 5. The prison dress was now a uniform gray, rather than the previous range of colors for each different category (p. 16).

[95] QGR/2/39, Chaplain's Report, Oct. 1844, p. 14.

[96] Ibid., p. 9.

[97] QGR/2/40, Chaplain's Report, Oct. 1845, p. 12.

[98] Ibid., p. 8.

[99] QGR/2/33, Dec. 1846, p. 5.

[100] QGR/2/33, Chaplain's Report, Dec. 1846, pp. 3-4, 6, 17-20; QGR/2/42, Chaplain's Report, Oct. 1848, pp. 32-33.

[101] Philip Priestley, *Victorian Prison Lives: English Prison Biography 1830-1914* (London: Methuen, 1985), 38. For his reiterated insistence that Preston was different from Pentonville and Reading, see QGR/2/41, Chaplain's Report, Oct. 1847, pp. 9-10, and letters to Charles Dickens, Mar. 1853, and to Capt. O'Brien, Aug. 1, 1853, in Clay, *Prison Chaplain*, 325-27, 330-31.

[102] QGR/2/43, Chaplain's Report, Dec. 1849, p. 20; QGR/2/34, Chaplain's Report, Dec. 1850, pp. 12-13, 25-26.

[103] QGR/2/33, Chaplain's Report, Dec. 1846, pp. 24-26; QGR/2/43, Chaplain's Report, Dec. 1849, p. 39.

[104] QGR/2/34, Chaplain's Report, Dec. 1850, p. 54.

[105] See Clay, *Prison Chaplain*, 393, 577.

[106] Feb. 2, 1855, in Clay, *Prison Chaplain*, 569.

[107] See David Eastwood, *Government and Community in the English Provinces, 1700-1870* (New York: St. Martin's Press, 1997), 137-39, 162-63.

[108] Clay, *Prison Chaplain*, 108.

[109] Ibid., 232, 576, 583.

[110] Ibid., 620, letter to Miss Carpenter, Aug. 25, 1854.

[111.] *BC*, Dec. 17, 1842, p. 2.

[112.] *PC*, July 4, 1840, p. 4.

[113.] *PC*, Sept. 30, 1848, p. 4.

[114.] Clay, *Prison Chaplain*, 111, 204, 310.

[115.] Ibid., 103.

[116.] Hindle, *Expenditure of Lancashire*, 226-28, 230, 273; QGR/2/38, Chaplain's Report, Oct. 1841, memorial to magistrates, Aug. 1, 1839.

[117.] Clay, *Prison Chaplain*, 587-88, 598; and see his lament (613) to M. D. Hill, Feb. 4, 1851.

[118.] McGowen, "Well-Ordered Prison," 101-5; Henriques, "Prison Discipline," 84-86.

[119.] See Martin J. Wiener, *Reconstructing the Criminal: Culture, Law, and Policy in England, 1830-1914* (Cambridge: Cambridge University Press, 1990), 44-49 and passim; Philip Abrams, *The Origins of British Sociology 1834-1914* (Chicago: University of Chicago Press, 1968), 10-11, 31-37; M. J. Cullen, *The Statistical Movement in Early Victorian Britain: The Foundations of Empirical Social Research* (New York: Barnes and Noble, 1975); Theodore M. Porter, *The Rise of Statistical Thinking 1820-1900* (Princeton: Princeton University Press, 1986); Anthony Giddens, *Sociology* (Cambridge: Polity Press, 1989), 118-33; Gatrell, "Crime, Authority and the Policeman State," passim; Stan Cohen, *Folk Devils and Moral Panics: The Creation of the Mods and Rockers* (Oxford: Blackwell, 1987), 55, 60-61, 199.

[120.] See Wilbur R. Miller, *Cops and Bobbies: Police Authority in New York and London, 1830-1870* (Chicago: University of Chicago Press, 1977), 12ff.; Mike Brogden, "'All Police is Conning Bastards'—Policing and the Problem of Consent," in *Law, State and Society*, ed. Bob Fryer et al. (London: Croom Helm, 1981), 212; John Field, "Police, Power and Community in a Provincial English Town: Portsmouth 1815-1875," in *Policing and Punishment*, ed. Bailey, 46-48; Gatrell, "Crime, Authority and the Policeman State," 257-59.

Notes to Chapter 6

[1.] "Testimonial of Respect to the Rev. James Slade, Vicar of Bolton," Nov. 30, 1836, printed circular in CMA, MS F 942.72 R121, Archdeacon Rushton's Visitation Returns, vol. 11, Parish Church.

[2.] He was a moderate High Churchman, though he cannot be slotted neatly into any category. See Peter Nockles, "Church parties in the pre-Tractarian Church of England 1750-1833: the 'Orthodox'—some problems of definition and identity," in *The Church of England c.1689-c.1833: From Toleration to Tractarianism*, ed. John Walsh, Colin Haydon, and Stephen Taylor (Cambridge: Cambridge University Press, 1993), 335-36, 439-50; idem, *The Oxford Movement in Context: Anglican High Churchmanship, 1760-1857* (Cambridge: Cambridge University Press, 1994), pp. 25-26; Peter Virgin, *The Church in an Age of Negligence: Ecclesiastical Structure and Problems of Church Reform 1700-1840* (Cambridge: James Clarke, 1989), 22.

[3.] BRL, Whittaker Correspondence, 921 WHI, Mary Whittaker to his mother, Aug. 14, 1836: her husband sat up late to write his letters on weekday nights: "His writing hours are very agreeable to him." Edward M. Hall of Surbiton, a manuscripts collector, bought a four-volume collection of (mainly) family letters from a London bookshop in the 1950s, and subsequently dispersed them to libraries having a local interest in Whittaker (see introductory items to the Edward Hall MSS Collection in WRO). Individual churches retained most of the official correspondence before handing them on to the LRO.

4. J. G. Shaw, *Short History of the Church of S. John the Evangelist Blackburn* (Blackburn, 1933).

5. LRO, PR1555/6, Parish Church Rebuilding Papers, 1818-35; LRO, PR1549/2, Coucher Book of St. Mary's; Thomas Rogerson, *A Short Statement of Facts Relative to the Taking Down, and Re-Building, of the Parish Church of Blackburn* (Blackburn, 1827).

6. LRO, PR1549/13, Coucher Book of St. Peter's.

7. LRO, PR3340/2/1, Records of St. Paul's Church Blackburn; *John Bull*, Jan. 10, 1830; *St. Paul's Blackburn Centenary Souvenir, 1830-1930* (Blackburn, 1930).

8. A phrase in *The Clerical Journal*, Mar. 8, 1855, p. 109.

9. CMA, MS F 823 89 G69, Edward Hall, ed., "The Knutsford Letters 1803-1824," iv; MS F 929/2/W126, Whittaker Family Letters 1783-1837, vol. 1.

10. Sidney Lee, ed., *Dictionary of National Biography* (New York, 1900), 61: 145; Whittaker, *An Historical and Critical Inquiry into the Interpretation of the Hebrew Scriptures, with Remarks on Mr. Bellamy's New Translation* (Cambridge, 1819). He became an accomplished scholar, noted for his polemical works on theology and church government and also for his facility with languages, mostly Eastern, but also ancient etymologies, especially Celtic (*The Gentleman's Magazine*, obituary, Oct. 1854, p. 397). In addition, he was a founding Fellow of the Royal Astronomical Society, and evolved an (unpublished) theory of the universe reconciling biblical, astronomical, and geological time (*Monthly Notices, Royal Astronomical Society*, 15 (1855): 119-20).

11. SJC, Whittaker I, JWW to mother, June 1, 7, 14, 1820, Mar. 6, 1821 (quotation); WRO, D/D2 EHC/207, Whittaker Letters, mother to JWW, June 10, 1820.

12. £845 11s. 5d. BRL, Whittaker Correspondence, 921 WHI, James Neville, attorney, to T. Calvert, Jan. 23, 1822. By 1835 it had risen to £918 gross, £893 net (PP, 1835, XXII, "Report of the Ecclesiastical Revenues Commission").

13. SJC, Whittaker I, JWW to mother, Jan. 20, 1822; and see July 14, 1824 for his continuing ambitions.

14. For his own assessment, see LRO, PR1549/3, Coucher Book of St. Mary's, "Report of the Vicar of Blackburn to the Bishop of Chester," Aug. 7, 1835; /4, JWW to secretary of Subdivision of Parishes Commission, July 27, 1849 ("Perhaps nowhere else have such remarkable exertions been made in advancing the moral amelioration of the people under the auspices of the Church as here"). For one example of praise in high quarters for his efforts, see LRO, PR1549/29, Coucher Book of Tockholes, vol.1, Viscount Palmerston to JWW, Apr. 26, 1830, on being solicited for a contribution for Tockholes Church: "It is always gratifying to see the indefatigable Industry with which Dissenters from the Church of England work out the attainment of objects of this kind, imitated successfully by members of the Establishment."

15. For favorable assessments of Hanoverian church-building until the 1790s, before a quarter of a century or more of stagnation, see Mark Smith, "The reception of Richard Podmore: Anglicanism in Saddleworth 1700-1830," 113-15, and John Walsh and Stephen Taylor, "Introduction: the Church and Anglicanism in the 'long' eighteenth century," 10, in *Church of England*, ed. Walsh et al. See also Alan D. Gilbert, *Religion and Society in Industrial England* (London: Longman, 1976), 27-29, and Geoffrey Best, *Mid-Victorian Britain 1851-1875* (London: Weidenfeld and Nicolson, 1971), 186-90, who suggest a somewhat later chronology for the main phase of Church revitalization, which Whittaker clearly anticipated.

16. See James Obelkevich, *Religion and Rural Society: South Lindsey 1825-1875* (Oxford: Clarendon Press, 1976), ix, 321, and passim.

[17.] See LRO, PR1549/31, Coucher Book of Walton-le-Dale, Rev. Henry McGrath to JWW, Nov. 4, 1833: "Now, in these matters [grant applications], I consider you one of 'the giants in the Earth in *these* days'!"; PR2846/2/1, Coucher Book of Feniscowles, bishop of Chester to JWW, June 16, 1834: the ICBS granted half the cost of the building of Immanuel Church and the bishop believed this to be unprecedentedly high, reflecting the fact that "the sense of your great exertions in the Parish of Blackburn was so strong."

[18.] LRO, PR1549/17, Coucher Book of Bamber Bridge, letters of July 1, 20, 22, and Aug. 16, 19, 1824.

[19.] LRO, PR1549/8, Coucher Book of All Saints', letter of Aug. 12, 1837; LRO, PR1549/15, Coucher Book of Trinity Church, JWW to archbishop of Canterbury, Nov. 9, 1835.

[20.] For his attempts to build relatively cheap but spiritually uplifting churches, see CERC, 15,218, JWW to secretary of Church commissioners, Apr. 29, 1837; JWW to commissioners, Apr. 29, 1825, in T. Counsell, *Mellor in Blackburnshire* (Blackburn, 1929), 46-47; LPL, ICBS B4524, Blackburn Witton, memorial to Incorporated Church Building Society, Dec. 10, 1835; LRO, PR1549/8, Coucher Book of All Saints', JWW to secretary of Curates' Aid Society, Mar. 5, 1852.

[21.] LRO, PR3002/3/2, St. Michael's Letter Book, JWW to secretary of ICBS, May 17, 1844.

[22.] Ibid., JWW answer to CPAS questionnaire [1841].

[23.] Ibid., JWW to the Rev. William Pullen of CPAS, Aug. 19, 1839.

[24.] Ibid., JWW to Frederick Sandog of CPAS, Oct. 21, 1840.

[25.] Ibid., JWW to bishop of Chester, July 20, 1837; to the Rev. Henry Raikes of Diocesan Society, July 22, 1837.

[26.] Ibid., JWW to archbishop of Canterbury, Aug. 23, 1837.

[27.] Ibid., JWW to Raikes, Apr. 3, 1839.

[28.] Ibid., JWW to bishop of Chester, May 7, 1844.

[29.] LRO, PR1549/32, Coucher Book of Witton, JWW to Mrs. Joseph Feilden, Nov. 24, 1835; Mrs. Joseph Feilden to JWW, Nov. 24, 1835; JWW to archbishop, Mar. 22, 1836. For the dispute with his parents-in-law over the patronage at Feniscowles, see PR2846/2/1, Coucher Book of Feniscowles, William and Joseph Feilden to JWW, Dec. 11, 1833; JWW to W. and J. Feilden, Dec. 12, 1833; JWW to bishop of Chester, Dec. 14, 1833; Mrs. W. Feilden to bishop of Chester, Dec. 23, 1833; bishop of Chester to Mrs. W. Feilden, Dec. 24, 1833; W. Feilden to JWW, Jan. 23, 1834.

[30.] LRO, PR1549/32, Coucher Book of Witton, JWW to the Rev. William Cooke, July 19, 1839; JWW to Joseph Feilden, Sept. 19, 1839; PR2846/2/1, Coucher Book of Feniscowles, JWW to the Rev. Leeds Comyns Booth, May 26, 1836; JWW to the Rev. J. S. Hodgson, July 4, 1836; PR2846/2/2, JWW to the Rev. George Edmundson, Mar. 22, 1838; the Rev. Jonathan Beilby to JWW, Nov. 24, 1845; W. Feilden to JWW, Nov. 26, 1845; Mrs. W. Feilden to JWW, Nov. 17, 1845.

[31.] LRO, PR1549/23, Coucher Book of Salesbury, Hugh Wallace (de Tabley's agent) to JWW, June 9, 1842; JWW to Wallace, June 14, 1842; JWW to S. J. Allen, Nov. 25, 1842; JWW to bishop of London, Oct. 31, 1843.

[32.] LRO, PR1549/17, Coucher Book of Bamber Bridge, JWW to the Rev. R. H. Feilden of Walton-le-Dale, May 10, 1831, blaming Bishop Blomfield of Chester for not giving the project enough backing in 1825; Townley Parker to Feilden, Apr. 2, blaming the vicar for dropping the project in the hope of collecting a larger grant for a church nearer the town.

[33.] Ibid., Parker to R. H. Feilden, Apr. 2, 1831; McGrath to JWW, Jan. 25, 1836; Edmund Sharpe to JWW, Feb. 6, 1836; Parker to JWW, Aug. 19, 1836; JWW to Parker, Aug. 27, 1836; JWW to McGrath, May 11, 17, 1837; JWW to bishop of Chester, July 7, 1837; bishop of Chester to JWW, July 10, 1837; JWW to McGrath, July 13, 1837. For another example of Whittaker's refusal to concede the patronage, see LRO, PR1549/8, Coucher Book of All Saints', JWW to William Dodsworth, Aug. 12, 16, 23, 28, Sept. 2, Oct. 25, 1837: he turned down a grant to build All Saints' from the trustees of a fund called Hyndman's Trust when he discovered that the money was conditional on the patronage being vested in the trustees.

[34.] LPL, ICBS B4524, Blackburn Witton, memorial of JWW to ICBS, Dec. 10, 1835.

[35.] Quoted by Paul T. Phillips, *The Sectarian Spirit: Sectarianism, Society, and Politics in Victorian Cotton Towns* (Toronto: University of Toronto Press, 1982), 114.

[36.] LRO, PR1549/20, Coucher Book of Lower Darwen, Arnold to JWW, May 7, 1841.

[37.] LRO, PR1549/8, Coucher Book of All Saints', circular of Mar. 15, 1851.

[38.] Ibid., CPAS to JWW, Aug. 5, 1847.

[39.] LRO, PR1549/32, Coucher Book of Witton, Ashe to Rushton, Jan. 6, 1854; LRO, PR1549/15, Coucher Book of Trinity, vol. 2, Robinson to JWW, July 16, 1852.

[40.] LRO, PR1549/8, Coucher Book of All Saints', Burgess to JWW, July 31, 1851, Jan. 5, 1852. Burgess may have been feeling the backlash of lay antipathy to Whittaker on the parish subdivision issue (see below). He was a parish church curate, with duties to perform there, which irked those who wanted him to devote all his energies to All Saints'. (See letters of Jan. 5, 7, 17, 1852).

[41.] Mar. 8, p. 109; Apr. 23, pp. 183-84; June 8, pp. 258-59; Sept. 8, p. 399. Burgess had been a Dissenting Minister in London before joining the Established Church. On his appointment by Whittaker in August 1850 he professed much esteem for the vicar (LRO, PR1549/8, Coucher Book of All Saints'): on August 29 he wrote that he could "but rejoice that my lot should be cast with one who, as Solomon saith, '*intermeddleth with* all *wisdom*'."

[42.] Whittaker estimated his income in 1850 at £900 (LRO, PR1549/8, Coucher Book of All Saints', Mar. 7). Burgess thought that such a figure was based on an antiquated assessment and that the true figure was around £1,500 (*Clerical Journal*, Apr. 23, 1855, p. 184).

[43.] Whittaker did not waver in his belief that the poor would come if the accommodation were provided. See, e.g., LRO, PR1549/20, Coucher Book of Lower Darwen, clipping of *BM* (report on laying of foundation stone, Feb. 22, 1827); PR1549/8, Coucher Book of All Saints', circular of Mar. 15, 1851: "From careful observation on the spot it is clearly ascertained that it is want of accommodation alone which stands in the way of a manifestation of deep interest in the Church of England in this district: and that if a Church were erected it would be speedily filled." For contrary evidence of unoccupied free seats, see, e.g., PR1549/13, Coucher Book of St. Peter's, JWW to the Rev. John Hull, Oct. 16, 1828. The 1851 Religious Census figures (PRO, HO 129/480, 482) are flawed (see, e.g., David M. Thompson, "The 1851 Religious Census: Problems and Possibilities," *Victorian Studies* XI (1967): 87-97; Paul S. Ell and T. R. Slater, "The Religious Census of 1851: a Computer-Mapped Survey of the Church of England," *JHG* 20, 1 (1994): 44-61, and they do not give a clear indication of the extent of lower-class alienation (see K. S. Inglis, *Churches and the Working Classes in Victorian England* (London: Routledge and Kegan Paul, 1963) for a strong statement of alienation and, for more nuanced approaches, Hugh McLeod, *Religion and Society in England, 1850-1914* (New York: St. Martin's Press, 1996), 221-22, and Callum G.

Brown, "The Mechanism of Religious Growth in Urban Societies. British Cities Since the Eighteenth Century," in *European Religion in the Age of Great Cities 1830-1930*, ed. Hugh McLeod (London: Routledge, 1995), 239-42). But if we take the Blackburn figures as a rough estimate of order of magnitude, from the churches, chapels and schoolrooms that gave returns or averages it appears that—not including Sunday School children—around 5,369 people attended in the morning, 4,942 in the afternoon, and 1,049 in the evening. Even though the Nonconformists scored nearly as highly, the figures compared favorably with other cotton towns. But what is beyond doubt is that the attendance was far below the accommodation available.

[44.] LRO, PR1549/13, Coucher Book of St. Peter's, undated copy of a note of Jan. 16, 1849. The following account is taken from *BS*, Jan. 24, 1849, and *MG*, Jan. 20, 1849.

[45.] Walter Chamberlain, *Parochial Centralization; or Remarks on the Present State of the Church of England* (Bolton, [1850]), 22.

[46.] W. R. Ward, *Religion and Society in England 1790-1850* (London: B. T. Batsford, 1972), 227, refers to a "clerical proletariat" who "in hard times . . . would keep quiet no longer."

[47.] This was mentioned by the Rev. Thomas Sharples at the Accrington meeting. For a report on the Stone meeting, see *BS*, Dec. 20, 1848. The Rev. J. Beilby of Immanuel Church, Feniscowles, spoke at the meeting and claimed to represent all the incumbents of the new districts in Blackburn.

[48.] *BS*, Feb. 14, pp. 1-3; Feb. 7, p. 4; Feb. 21, p. 3; Mar. 7, p. 1; Mar. 14, p. 3; Apr. 18 1849, p. 2. But a number of Whittaker's clergymen—mostly outside the town—did continue to stand by him, including the incumbents of Great Harwood, Tockholes, Balderstone, Trinity, Walton-le-Dale, Samlesbury, and Lower Darwen, and the curates of Over Darwen and Salesbury, as did some of Blackburn's leading inhabitants. (LRO, PR1549/13, Coucher Book of St. Peter's, note of Jan. 18, 1849).

[49.] LRO, PR1549/10, Coucher Book of the Division of the Parish into separate and distinct Parishes, Jan. 24, 1849.

[50.] *BS*, Jan. 24, 1849.

[51.] *MG*, Jan. 20, 1849, p. 6.

[52.] *MC*, Jan. 27, 1849.

[53.] Geoffrey B. A. M. Finlayson, *The Seventh Earl of Shaftesbury 1801-1885* (London: Eyre Methuen, 1981), 311-12; Edwin Hodder, *The Life and Work of the Seventh Earl of Shaftesbury* (London, 1886), II: 279.

[54.] Chalmers, *The Christian and Civic Economy of Large Towns* (Glasgow, 1821-26); Boyd Hilton, *The Age of Atonement: The Influence of Evangelicalism on Social and Economic Thought, 1795-1865* (Oxford: Clarendon Press, 1988), chaps. 2-3.

[55.] *Hansard*, 3rd ser., 103: 12-48.

[56.] Quoted by Hodder, *Shaftesbury*, 279.

[57.] PP, 1854, LXIX, Minutes of Evidence taken before the Subdivision of Parishes Commissioners, 101.

[58.] Ibid., 34.

[59.] Ibid., 47-48.

[60.] Ibid., 128-29.

[61.] Ibid., 84-87.

[62.] Ibid., 87-91. And see R. A. Soloway, *Prelates and People* (London: Routledge and Kegan Paul, 1969), 344.

[63.] *BS*, Dec. 20, 1848, p. 2.

[64.] Minutes of Evidence, 53-60.

[65.] Ibid., 124-25.

[66.] PP, July 1849, XXII, "First Report of the Subdivision of Parishes Commissioners"; PP, May 1850, XX, "Second Report"; PP, May 1850, XX, "Third Report . . . Respecting the Proposed Removal of Some of the City Churches." See also PP, Apr. 1851, XLII, "Copy of an Address to Her Majesty . . . on CHURCH EXTENSION," and PP, Dec. 1852, LXXVIII, "Particulars of all Information . . . respecting the immediate Want . . . for Six Hundred NEW CHURCHES. . . ."

[67.] This was needed in particular to transfer the powers of portioning out districts and building churches from the Church Building Commission, which had expired, to the Ecclesiastical Commission. *Hansard*, 3rd ser., 139: 221-37; 140: 681-89; 142: 574-75; 143: 554, 947, 1090-93, 1418.

[68.] "The Patronage Act," (Oct. 15, 1831), 1 & 2 Will. 4, c. 38; "An Act to make better Provision for the Spiritual Care of Populous Parishes," (July 28, 1843), 6 & 7 Vic., c. 37. See Virgin, *Age of Negligence*, 142-43. The first Church Building Act, of 1818 (58 Geo. 3, c. 45), as well as establishing the Church Building Commissioners with the power to spend £1M. of public money on new churches, was the first to enable the division of parishes without a separate act. The subsequent Church Building Acts made this incrementally easier. See G. F. A. Best, *Temporal Pillars: Queen Anne's Bounty, the Ecclesiastical Commissioners, and the Church of England* (Cambridge: Cambridge University Press, 1964), 195, 357-58.

[69.] "New Parishes Act," (July 29, 1856), 19 & 20 Vic., c. 104.

[70.] LRO, PR1549/4, Coucher Book of St. Mary's, JWW to secretary of Subdivision of Parishes Commission, July 27, 1849. In a letter to the bishop of Manchester of May 22, 1849, on the question of double fees he claimed that, "No objection has ever been made to this practice by the laity, who have always most cheerfully acquiesced in it" (LRO, PR1549/15, Coucher Book of Trinity Church, vol. 2).

[71.] CERC, 15,218, May 18, 1849.

[72.] LRO, PR1549/22, Coucher Book of Mellor Brook, letter of Feb. 15.

[73.] *BS*, Nov. 24, 1858, p. 2; Dec. 1, 1858, p. 3; Jan. 5, 1859, p. 3. Whittaker had died in August 1854 and was accorded a large, ceremonial funeral in his parish church conducted by the bishop of Manchester, after a procession of more than six hundred people led by the police, ministers of different denominations, and the mayor and aldermen of the newly incorporated borough (*PP*, Aug. 12 1854, p. 8). But in the same month, nine Blackburn incumbents sent a memorial to the archbishop of Canterbury requesting that, now the vicar was dead, the chapelries be made into district parishes (LRO, PR1549/10, Coucher Book of the Division of the Parish). John Rushton, the new vicar, relinquished his half of the double fees in 1854, and the division in 1859 made this permanent. Fifteen district chapelries became New Parishes, equal in rights and privileges to the ancient chapelries of Walton-le-Dale, Samlesbury, and Great Harwood, and to the New Parish of Bamber Bridge (which had held that status since the vacancy in the incumbency of Walton-le-Dale, since it had been formed out of the Walton-le-Dale chapelry). The incumbent of the mother church was still to be styled the "Vicar of the Parish and Parish Church of Blackburn," and the incumbents of the New Parishes were still perpetual curates.

[74.] *BS*, Jan. 24, 1849; *MG*, Jan. 20, 1849.

[75.] In particular, Whittaker wanted no minister in his parish who supported the Bible Society, the Church Missionary Society, and the Society for the Conversion of the Jews. See LRO, PR1549/31, Coucher Book of Walton-le-Dale, JWW to the Rev. E. M. Hall, Feb. 7, 16, 1826.

[76.] LRO, PR1549/20, Coucher Book of Lower Darwen, July 20, 1836. For other examples, see LRO, PR1549/32, Coucher Book of Witton, Mar. 2, 1838, and Sept. 25,
28, Oct. 16, 1839.

[77.] LRO, PR1549/23, Coucher Book of Salesbury, Apr. 9, 10, 12, 17, 26, and May
10.

[78.] LRO, PR 2318, St. George's Chapel, Preston: Minutes of Meetings of Pew Proprietors, Nov. 15, 1798, Feb. 22, 1804, Apr. 19, 1843, Apr. 8, 1844, Mar. 27, 1845,
Apr. 11, 1849, and passim; A. Hewitson ("Atticus"), *Our Churches and Chapels* (Preston, 1869), 36-37.

[79.] LRO, Preston Trinity Church, PR 2307/1/1, resolutions of meeting, June 21,
1813; PR 2313/1, Trinity Church Minute Book, Sept. 27, 1813; PR 2307/4, resolutions
of meeting, Aug. 9, 1813; /1/1, June 21, 1813; /1/2, July 25; /1/7, draft letter, n.d.; PR
2307/1/7, draft letter, n.d.; /6, *PC*, Apr. 2, 1814; PR 2310/3, Joseph Harrison to mayor
and corporation (draft), n.d.; PR 2307/1/23, minute of May 18, 1815; /1/35-38, Thomas Batty Addison to William Ward (draft), Nov. 4, 1815; /1/39-40, Addison to
[bishop of Chester?], Nov. 10, 1815; /1/47, minute of Dec. 2, 1815; /1/54, minute of
May 7, 1817; PR 2311/7, Swainson to Harrison, n.d.; PR 2313/1, Oct. 22, 1816; July
5, 1817. For the purchasers of pews, see PR 2307/6/22, ground plan of Trinity, n.d.;
PR.2311/6, statement of sale of pews, Dec. 15, 1815. The minister's salary was later
augmented by Queen Anne's Bounty (see PR 2307/1/69, Christopher Hodgson to Rev.
Thomas Raven, Mar. 15, 1825; PR 2310/1, n.d.).

[80.] Hewitson, *Our Churches*, 62.

[81.] W. Makin, *St. Peter's Church, Preston* (Preston, 1975), 15; Rev. Ernest Hudson,
Sketches of the History of the Parish of S. Paul, Preston 1826-1926, 17-18; Hewitson,
Preston, 483-86; idem, *Our Churches and Chapels*, 105-6; Hardwick, *Preston*, 477;
LPL, ICBS 3701, St. James, Preston, Rev. J. Cousins to Bowdler, Dec. 10, 1845, June 3,
July 11, 1846; certificate and plan, 1846.

[82.] Hewitson, *Preston*, 492-93; idem, *Our Churches and Chapels*, 127-29.

[83.] LRO, Hoghton Papers, DDHo/128, indenture of 1813 between Hoghton and Wilson; /492, for a copy of the grant of the Rectory of Preston by James I to Sir Richard
Hoghton; Edward Baines, *The History of the County Palatine and Duchy of Lancaster*,
4th ed., revised, enlarged, and edited by James Croston (Manchester and London,
1888), V: 326; Hewitson, *Preston*, 453. On Hulme's Charity see B. T. Barton, *History
of Farnworth and Kersley* (Bolton, 1887), 196, 212: William Hulme, born at Kersley
Hall, founded the trust in 1691, and stipulated that none but graduates of Brasenose
College, Oxford, be appointed. On the Carus Wilsons see Herbert Carus-Wilson and
Harold I. Talboys, eds., *Genealogical Memoirs of the Carus-Wilson Family* (Hove,
1899).

[84.] LRO, DDHo/134, Parr to Hoghton, Feb. 27, 1846; /135, Hoghton to Parr, Mar.
2, 1846 (copy); /136, Parr to Hoghton, n.d.; /138, Parr to Hoghton, May 9, 1849;
/139, Hoghton to Parr, May 25 (extract); /140, Parr to Hoghton, May 26; /141, memo
of reply, June 3; Parr to Hoghton, June 12; /143, Hoghton to Parr, June 14 (copy);
/144, Hoghton to Messrs. Pilkington and Walker, June 14; /145, Parr to Hoghton, June
15; /146, Joseph Walker to Hoghton, June 16; /147, Hoghton to Pilkington and
Walker, June 22; /148, Walker to Hoghton, July 7; /149, Parr to Walker, July 11.

[85.] LRO, PR 2307/4, Aug. 9, 1813; /1/1, June 21; /1/5, J. Harrison's minutes of con-
versation with Sir H. P. Hoghton, Oct. 5, 1813; /1/20, Rev. James Penny to trustees,
Apr. 18, 1815; /1/22, St. Clare and Addison to Penny, Apr. 21; PR 2313/1, Hoghton to
Harrison, Aug. 22, 1813; Hoghton to ?, Oct. 20; minute of Oct. 21; bishop of Chester

to Hoghton, Oct. 28; George Jacson to bishop, Nov. 6; bishop to Jacson, Nov. 10; minute of Nov. 13, 1813; Jacson to Bishop, n.d.; sentence of consecration, Dec. 8, 1815.

[86.] LPL, ICBS 4449, Christ Church, Preston, Rev. Thomas Clark to Bowdler, Feb. 2, 1852.

[87.] PP, 1835, XXII, "Report of the Ecclesiastical Revenues Commission"; LRO, PR 1495/2, "Minutes of Information with Reference to the Parish and Vicarage of Preston," [1840]; W. E. Cunliffe, *A Historical Sketch of the Church and Parish of Ashton-on-Ribble* (in *St. Michael's New Church Bazaar Souvenir*, Preston, 1908), 15, 17; Douglas B. Cochrane, *A History of the Parish of St. Andrew's, Ashton-on-Ribble* (Preston, n.d.), 6-11. In addition the secretary of war nominated to the Garrison Chapel at Fulwood Barracks, and the county justices to the House of Correction Chapel.

[88.] LRO, PR 2313/1, Penny to Rev. Thomas Selkirk, n.d.; PR 2307, Penny to ?, Jan. 22, 1816.

[89.] CERC, 17,894, Preston St. George, St. James, St. Paul, St. Peter, Holy Trinity, Parr to commissioners, Oct. 13, 1842.

[90.] See Best, *Temporal Pillars*, 351-59.

[91.] CERC, 17,894, Parr to commissioners, Nov. 30, 1842.

[92.] PP, 1835, XXII, "Report of the Ecclesiastical Revenues Commission": £751 gross, £665 net; LRO, PR 1495/2, "Minutes of Information with Reference to the Parish and Vicarage of Preston," [1840]: the income included approximately £154 in rent on buildings in town, £52 in Easter dues in Preston township, over £200 for vicarial tithes and mortuaries throughout the parish and for Easter dues in the out-townships (all being commuted into a fixed sum for each township), more than £200 in surplice fees (the vicar received dues from all churches except on funerals at St. Peter's and St. Paul's), and £8 from the corporation as trustees of an estate that provided an annual sum for a "preaching Minister" in Preston.

[93.] CERC, 17,894, Parr to commissioners, Nov. 30, 1842; note of Mar. 5, 1869. Note also the opposition of the Rev. Robert Atherton Rawstorne, incumbent of Penwortham (CERC, 18,121, Farington St. Paul, Rawstorne to Jelf, Nov. 17, 1842), to marriages in the proposed district of St. Paul, Farington, in his parish. As the income of the parish church was so small, he did not think he was justified to himself or his successors in giving up any of the emoluments.

[94.] James C. Scholes, *Memoir of the Rev. Edward Whitehead, M.A., Vicar of Bolton from 1737 to 1789* (Bolton, 1889), 22.

[95.] Frederick W. Briscoe, *History of St. George's Church and Schools, Bolton* (Bolton, 1893), 10-12, 14; BALS, Ainsworth Papers, ZAH/3/3, Richard Ainsworth to ?, Sept. 10, 1796.

[96.] For recognition of the need, see the observation of the Rev. Robert Bullock of All Saints', LRO, Hulton of Hulton Papers, DD Hu/53/53, return re church accommodation, Mar. 3, 1814.

[97.] *Holy Trinity Church, Bolton: Centenary 1826-1926* (Bolton, 1926), 8; CMA, Rushton, vol. 13, Holy Trinity, Bolton.

[98.] "Testimonial of Respect to the Rev. James Slade, Vicar of Bolton," Nov. 30, 1836, printed circular in Rushton, vol. 11, Parish Church. Built for £2,200, it was consecrated in 1839 (Rushton, vol. 13, Emmanuel, Bolton).

[99.] Rev. C. J. Street, "Two Hundred Years of Free Religion," part I, in *Bank Street Chapel, Bolton: Bi-Centenary Commemoration, 1696-1896* (London, 1896), 54-57; J. A. Atkinson, *Memoir of the Rev. Canon Slade* (Bolton, 1892), 254-55; Rushton, vol. 10, Christ Church, Bolton: the expense of purchase and alterations was around £1,920

(£500 from the Diocesan Society, £250 from the ICBS, £250 from the Ecclesiastical Commissioners, and £1,000 in local subscriptions).

[100.] Rushton, vol. 10, St. Paul's, Astley Bridge; vol. 10, St. John, Little Bolton.

[101.] Rushton, vol. 10, St. Stephen's, Leverbridge. For its pretensions to being the first entirely terra-cotta church in the country, see BALS, file on St. Stephen's, B283 B. LEV., including photocopies of *Illustrated London News*, Feb. 1, 1845; *The Builder*, May 5, 1845, p. 214 (letter from John Fletcher, Apr. 29), n.d., p. 248 (letter from Edmund Sharpe, the architect, May 14), and June 10, 1876, p. 553 (paper by Sharpe).

[102.] Rushton, vol. 13, Christ Church, Harwood; LPL, ICBS 2268, Harwood, application of Richard Heslop, Jan. 10, 1838; Jean Vickers, *A History of Christ's Church, Harwood, 1840-1990* (Horwich, 1990), 14-16; G. E. Rees, *Notes on Portions of the Townships of Harwood and Breightmet* (Bolton, 1892), 17, 21-23.

[103.] For further examples, see CMA, Walmsley Chapel, L99/2/3/1 and /2 (subscription books); /3, A. L. Haworth to Rev. L. Grisdale, n.d.; /4, Grisdale to bishop of Chester, Dec. 1, 1836; L99/2/2/1, account book; LPL, ICBS 2140, Turton, letter from Rev. J. Spencer, Jan. 18, 1840; Rushton, vol. 12, Turton, circular, n.d.

[104.] PP, 1835, XXII, "Report of the Ecclesiastical Revenues Commission," lists the vicar of Bolton (the bishop of Chester's appointee) as patron of Blackrod, Trinity, Bradshaw, Lever, and Walmsley, and the vicar of Deane (a Crown appointee) as patron of Horwich and Westhoughton; T. Tipping nominated to All Saints', Little Bolton, trustees to St. George's, Little Bolton, Lord Kenyon to Peel, "Inhabitants" to Rivington, and G. M. Hoare to Turton. According to the 1851 Religious Census returns (PRO, HO 129/468), nine of the Bolton and Deane churches were under the patronage of the vicars, three in the gift of individual patrons, five in the Crown and the bishop alternately, and three in trustees. At Rivington, the minister was chosen by "Popular Election" (a poll at a meeting of the inhabitants); the previous time a vacancy had occurred, in 1823, and subsequently in 1856, this was presided over by Robert Andrews, Esq., of Rivington Hall, a Unitarian (see Thomas Hampson, *History of Rivington* (Wigan and Horwich, 1893), 108, 110; G. N. Shawcross, *Rivington Church: A Short History* (Blackburn, 1929), 19, 22. On the role of Hulton at Deane Parish Church, see LRO, Hulton of Hulton Papers, DDHu 10/14/1, bishop of London to William Hulton, May 18, 1829; Thomas Brocklebank to bishop of Chester, June 9; bishop of Chester to Hulton, July 4, 9; Brocklebank to Hulton, Aug. 13, 21, Oct. 5, 19, 21, Nov. 6; Lyndhurst to Hulton, Nov. 13; CMA, L85/2/12/1, Deane Church Minutes 1818-85, July 2, Dec. 17, 1818, Apr. 9, 1822, July 18, 1833, Sept. 1, 1833, May 25, 1842; J. H. Dawson, *Deane Church*, 3rd ed. (Bolton, 1969), 7, 17, 20, 41.

[105.] LRO, Additional Allen Papers, DDX/633/2, Allen to bishop of Chester, Feb. 2, 1816; /3, bishop of Chester to Allen, Feb. 10, 1816; LRO, Papers, handbills, etc., collected by Rev. William Allen, DP 279/24A, bishop of Chester to Allen, Jan. 30, 1816; /36, bishop of Chester to Allen, Jan. 17, 1831.

[106.] CERC, 17,837 (2), Farnworth with Kearsley, St. John, answers to queries [1826?]; note of May 4, 1870; Brocklebank to Jenner, Mar. 24, 1827; Rev. George Marriott to Jelf, Jan. 1, [1830]; Girdlestone to commissioners, Nov. 16, 1830; Girdlestone to Marriott, Dec. 22, 1830; Rev. Thomas Alfred Ashworth to commissioners, May 10, 1831.

[107.] Atkinson, *Slade*, 65 (Oct. 7).

[108.] CERC, 15276, Bolton le Moors, Slade to secretary of Church Commissioners, [June?] 20, July 4, Dec. 14, 1836; to bishop of Chester, Dec. 5, 1836; bishop of Chester to Jelf, Oct. 17, 1840, and answers to queries. Slade did not object to Trinity forming a separate district under the terms of the 1818 Church Building Act. For clerical income, see Slade's answers to queries, Feb. 8, 1827: parish church: £450 (£36 from Lord Bradford, rents £100, land £28, surplice fees c. £286); Trinity: pew rents—value not yet known; St. George's: £174 [*sic*] (land £52, pew rents £125, fees £4); All Saints': £120 (parliamentary grants £88, land £28, pew rents, and fees); Bradshaw: £111 (parliamentary grants £36, land £65, pew rents, and fees); Turton: £175 [*sic*] (land £100, Queen Anne's Bounty £8, bequest £19, pew rents and fees £40); Walmsley: £85 (interest of £200 from Queen Anne's Bounty, rest in land); Rivington: £100 [*sic*] (land £80, rent charge £10, fees £4); Little Lever: £145 (land £100, pews £40, fees £5). Maintenance expenditure at the parish church and Trinity was met by a parish rate, St. George's and Little Lever by a charge on the pews, Blackrod by a township rate, the rest (except Rivington—unspecified) by subscription. PP, 1835, XXII, "Report of the Ecclesiastical Revenues Commission," lists the revenue of the parish church as £464.

[109.] CERC, 679, St. John, Little Bolton, Lyons to commissioners, Sept. 1, 1845; Leach to Murray, Sept. 5, 1845.

[110.] Chamberlain, *Parochial Centralization*, 8, 22-23.

[111.] BALS, Loxham Diaries, SLB/27/3/1 and /2.

[112.] Atkinson, *Slade*, 25-26.

[113.] CERC, 17,597, Horwich Holy Trinity: William Hulton to bishop of Chester, Oct. 31, 1826; petition to commissioners, Dec. 11; petition to bishop of Chester, Oct. 26.

[114.] Thomas Hampson, *Horwich: Its History, Legends, and Church* (Wigan, 1883), 71-73.

[115.] CERC, 17,597, Francis Bedford (architect of church) to George Jelf, June 18, July 4, 1831; sketch of pews and rents, 1832.

[116.] Hampson, *Horwich*, 75-81.

[117.] BALS, Ainsworth Diaries, ZHA/4/19, Nov. 30, 1844. The church, only built between 1838 and 1840 (with Ainsworth as the chief subscriber), fell victim to dry rot in 1843. Its restoration was the opportunity for a substantial enlargement. See B. Crompton, *St. Peter's Halliwell 1840-1940: Centenary of Consecration: A Brief History of the Parish* (Bolton, 1940).

[118.] Rushton, vol. 22, St. Paul's, Halliwell.

[119.] BALS, Ainsworth Papers, ZHA/4/22, Mar. 19, 1847; /23, Dec. 7, 14, 15, 16, 18, 30, 1848.

[120.] J. E. Batty, "God, Mammon and the Ainsworth Bleachworks" (typescript in BALS, 1990), 2-4; BALS, ZHA/4/23, June 19, 22, 1848. Ainsworth's brand of Anglicanism is not clear. In appointing Milton and in inviting Dr. Walter Hook of Leeds to preach at the consecration of St. Paul's, a High Church stance is suggested; but at a later date (1855), when he advertised for a new incumbent, he stipulated that the man must be married, an Oxbridge graduate, Evangelical, and in strict accordance with the plain teachings of the catechism on the subject of baptism (Rushton, vol. 22).

[121.] MC, Mar. 20, 1850, letter of Milton (also in Rushton, vol. 22).

[122.] Batty, "God, Mammon," 5ff. (quotations about Egyptian slavery, p. 16); MC, Mar. 20, 1850.

[123.] As Hugh McLeod, *Religion and the Working Class in Nineteenth-Century Britain* (London: Macmillan, 1984), 53, 58, argues, even those members of the lower orders who shared their masters' religion did not necessarily share their values.

[124.] LRO, QDV/9/1-412, Sectarian Returns 1929. And see the figures for church and chapel attendance on Jan. 9, 1834, in Whittle, *Preston*, II: 147-48.

[125.] Hewitson, *Our Churches and Chapels*, 19, 25, 50, 59, 73-75, 86, 95, 116, 123-25, 135.

[126.] Kenneth T. Jarvis, *History and Progress of Fishergate Baptist Church: Centenary Celebrations of Present Chapel and 175th Church Anniversary* (Preston, 1958), 5-6; William Shaw, *History of the Fishergate Baptist Church Preston* (Preston, 1883), 3-5. The Ansties were relatives of John Anstie, a Devizes clothier, who in 1778 went into a calico-printing partnership with Robert Livesey, a local putter-out, Josephus Smith, a London merchant and banker, and William Hall, probably a local manager. See S. D. Chapman and S. Chassagne, *European Textile Printers in the Eighteenth Century: A Study of Peel and Oberkampf* (London: Heinemann, 1981), 28-30.

[127.] William Alexander Abram, *A History of Blackburn, Town and Parish* (Blackburn, 1877), 364-65.

[128.] Hewitson, *Our Churches and Chapels*, 56; Rev. Dennis Duckworth, *The Story of a Church* (Preston, n.d.), 5, 10, 13 (recording that when the Rev. Elias de la Roche Rendell became minister in 1844 he had a salary of £90, which he supplemented with lectures and teaching).

[129.] James Dakeyne, *History of the Bolton New Church Society 1781-1888* (London and Bolton, 1888), 5, 13. As well as providing financial support, Crompton built the chapel organ and was the choirmaster.

[130.] John Seed, "Theologies of Power: Unitarianism and the Social Relations of Religious Discourse, 1800-50," in *Class, Power and Social Structure in British Nineteenth-Century Towns*, ed. R. J. Morris (Leicester: Leicester University Press, 1986), 121; Paul T. Phillips, *Sectarian Spirit*, 47.

[131.] See V. A. C. Gatrell, "Incorporation and the Pursuit of Liberal Hegemony in Manchester 1790-1839," in *Municipal Reform and the Industrial City*, ed. Derek Fraser (Leicester: Leicester University Press, 1982); Alan Kidd, *Manchester*, 2nd ed. (Keele: Keele University Press, 1996), 66.

[132.] *Bank Street Chapel, Bolton, Bi-Centenary Commemoration, 1696-1896* (London and Manchester, 1896), 96, 142-43; G. M. Ramsden, *A Responsible Society: The Life and Times of the Congregation of Bank Street Chapel, Bolton* (Horsham, West Sussex, 1985). Bank Street survived a split in 1821 when, because of a difference of opinion over the choice of a minister, part of the congregation broke away and set up first in a private house, then in the Cloth Hall, and finally in a former Calvinist Baptist Chapel in Moor Lane, under the pastorship of the Rev. George Harris, before being reunited in Bank Street in 1843 (Street, "Two Hundred Years of Free Religion," II: 48-54). Robert Heywood wrote in 1833 to the Rev. William Smith that, although a good deal of unpleasant feeling had been softened by time, he still remained unconvinced of the propriety of the separation: "No one would rejoice more than myself to find that both societies could be well supported but I fear the *rational* part of the population is not such as to justify the most favorable expectation." (BALS, Heywood Papers, ZHE 26/3, Letter Book, Heywood to Smith, Mar. 31, 1833; and see Heywood to the Rev. James Yates, Apr. 13, 1833.)

[133.] BALS, Minutes of the Transactions of the Monthly Meeting of Marsden, FRM/1/5, vol. IV, Nov. 18, 1790, Mar. 17, 1791, and passim. For the names of leading Quakers, see Edgworth Preparitive [*sic*] Meeting Book, FRM/11/1 (1776ff.) and Minutes and Proceedings of the Bolton Preparative Meeting of the Society of Friends, FRM/11/2 (1829ff.).

[134.] Rev. John Ward, *The Rise and Progress of Wesleyan Methodism in Blackburn and the Neighbourhood* (Blackburn, 1871), 18, 21, 25-26, 56-62, 65, 68-69, and passim.

[135.] W. Pilkington, *The Makers of Wesleyan Methodism in Preston* (London and Preston, 1890), 17, 24, 52-53, 106, and passim; W. F. Richardson, *Preston Methodism's*

200 Fascinating Years (Preston, 1975), 208: the Wesleyan chapels in Preston were Back Lane (in the Orchard), 1787-1817, replaced by Lune Street Chapel in 1817, and Wesley Chapel, opened in 1839.

[136.] Rev. G. Rodney Hugman, *Withnell Fold Methodist Church Centenary Celebrations* (n.p., 1852), 6.

[137.] BALS, Bolton Biographical Notes, passim; *Report of the Wesleyan Methodist Auxiliary Missionary Society, for the Bolton District, 1833* (Bolton, 1834). The periodic tendency of Methodism to fragment plagued the cause. See, for example, *A Plain Statement of Facts, Shewing Some Reasons for a Considerable Number of Persons Seceding from the Wesleyan Methodist Society* (Bolton, 1834); John Rylands Library, Methodist Archives, "Declaration of the Wesleyan Methodists in Bolton," Dec. 1, 1834.

[138.] Joseph Fletcher Jr., *The Select Works and Memoirs of the Late Rev. Joseph Fletcher, D.D.*, vol. I, *Memoirs of the Life and Correspondence of the late Rev. Joseph Fletcher, D.D.* (London, 1846), 5, 33, 48, 64-66, 117, 129 (letter to the Rev. R. Wardlaw, Sept. 7, 1808), 133, 140-44; Rev. B. Nightingale, *Lancashire Nonconformity; or, Sketches, Historical and Descriptive, of the Congregational and Old Presbyterian Churches in the County: The Churches of the Blackburn District* (Manchester, 1891), 42, 47, 56, 60-62, 69-72.

[139.] Nightingale, *The Story of the Lancashire Congregational Union 1806-1906* (Manchester, 1906), 11, 24-25, 30-31, 47 (letter of Kay-Shuttleworth of Sept. 1867), 49-50. For details of the plans and fluctuating progress of the union, see LRO, Minute Book of the Lancashire County Congregational Union, Blackburn District, 1830-62, CUBk 1/1. And see Fletcher to the Rev. Ralph Wardlaw, 1811, quoted by Fletcher, *Memoirs of Fletcher*, 175: "The County Unions formed in Lancashire and Cheshire, since I came here, have done more good to the 'perishing souls' of men in the dark and semibarbarous parts of both counties, than the occasional itinerant excursions of regular ministers for the last twenty years."

[140.] Nightingale, *Congregational Union*, 56-60; Fletcher, *Memoirs of Fletcher*, 207-10. And see Kenneth D. Brown, *A Social History of the Nonconformist Ministry in England and Wales 1800-1930* (Oxford: Clarendon Press, 1988), 64-67.

[141.] Fletcher, *Memoirs of Fletcher*, 298-99, 307 (letter to Cunliffe, 1822).

[142.] Dr. Williams' Library, "An Appendix of the Blackburn Academy Correspondence," extract from Cunliffe's will, n.d.; Daniel Moses, John Murdoch, William Lyall, Edward Edwards, R. Elliot, John Wild, James Gwyther, John Morfitt, Richard Jones, and William Williams, students, to chairman of committee, Apr. 3, 1827.

[143.] Rev. Richard Slate, *A Brief History of the Rise and Progress of the Lancashire Congregational Union; and of the Blackburn Independent Academy* (London, 1840); Abram, *Blackburn*, 364. The actual move, after the necessary fund-raising and building in Manchester, came in 1843.

[144.] Hewitson, *Our Churches and Chapels*, 6.

[145.] Sketch by the Rev. J. A. James of Birmingham, quoted by Fletcher, *Memoirs of Fletcher*, 578.

[146.] Dr. Williams' Library, "Blackburn Academy Correspondence," Porter to Raffles, Dec. 16, 1841, note of Raffles, and John Kelly to Raffles.

[147.] LRO, ÇUBk 1/1, Feb. 17, 1848, Feb. 15, 1849; *Centenary of Belthorn Independent Chapel, August 24, 1918* (Darwen, 1918), 11.

[148.] LRO, CUBl 1/1, "Summary of Faith and Order," James Street Chapel, Blackburn, Minute Book, Jan. 23, 1842; and see the investigations of members' conduct, e.g., July 1, 30, 1847, Oct. 2, Dec. 31, 1851. In Preston (Rev. Samuel R. Antliff, *Inde-*

pendency in Preston: Historical Sketches of Cannon Street Independent Church (Preston, 1880), 13), people desiring admission to the church had to write to the pastor stating their views on Christian doctrine and polity, and the reasons why they wished to associate with the professed disciples of Christ; and to face a searching interview by the minister and two deacons as to their doctrinal sentiments, religious experience, moral deportment, and views of church government.

[149.] Preston Independency, for example, expanded into a new chapel in Cannon Street in 1826 under the vigorous pastorship of the Rev. David Thompson Carnson, 1820-47, among the first batch of graduates from the Blackburn Academy. See Nightingale, *History of the Parent Sunday School, now meeting in Bairstow Street, Preston, 1812-1912* (Preston, 1912) 14, 63-66; Antliff, *Independency in Preston*, 25-26. For Independency's strength in Farnworth, Egerton, and Edgworth, see Nightingale, *Lancashire Nonconformity: The Churches of Bolton, Bury, Rochdale, &c.* (Manchester, 1892), 64-65, 70-73, 137. But there are reports of chapels and mission stations foundering or struggling to survive, especially when the union cut off their external funding because of shortage of money. See, e.g., Nightingale, *Lancashire Nonconformity: Blackburn District*, 114-15 (a chapel in Mellor Brook, opened in 1824, had to sell to the vicar of Blackburn in 1832); LRO, CUBk 1/1, Mar. 18, 1842 (re Belthorn); Feb. 17, 1848 (re Great Harwood).

[150.] See, e.g., *Centenary of Belthorn Chapel*, 6-7; LRO, James Street Chapel, Blackburn, deeds, CUBl 1/39, indenture of 16 Dec., 1842; LRO, CUBk 1/1, Sept. 28, 1830, and passim; *Pickup Bank Congregational Chapel, Hoddlesden, Centenary* (1928), 3-4.

[151.] Nightingale, *Lancashire Nonconformity: Blackburn District*, 88-90, 93-94; BFP, Oct. 23, 1847, p. 4.

[152.] J. Roe, *A History of St. Mary's Church, Friargate, Preston* (Preston, 1967), 14-18; T. G. Holt, S.J., "Joseph Dunn of Preston from his Correspondence," in *Catholic Englishmen: Essays Presented to Rt. Rev. Brian Charles Foley, Bishop of Lancaster*, ed. J. A. Hilton (Wigan, n.d.), 29-30; Rev. J. Quinn, "'Daddy' Dunn (1746-1827)," *The Monthly Magazine of St. Wilfrid's and St. Mary's Churches, Preston* 16 (1949), I-V; Joseph Gillow, *A Literary and Biographical History, or Bibliographical Dictionary of the English Catholics: From the Breach with Rome, in 1534, to the Present Time* (London, c. 1885; reprint, New York: B. Franklin, 1968), II: 143-48, and see V: 121-22, for details of the Rev. Richard Morgan (1746-1814), a significant coworker in the Preston vineyard; Leslie Shawcross, *Stonyhurst: Centenary, 1894* (London, 1894), 8-10; Fr. John Gerard, *Stonyhurst Handbook* (n.p., n.d.); A. S. Bennett, *Samuel Clegg and Stonyhurst College* (North West Gas Historical Society, 1986), 2-8, 11, 26. On his efforts for the spread of Catholicism (through fund-raising) and of gas in the United States, especially Cincinnati, see ASJ, Dunn Papers, E. Fenwick, bishop of Cincinnati, to Dunn, Oct. 19, [1824?], Dec. 2, 1824, Apr. 12, 1825, Jan. 17, 1826; John Power, rector of St. Peter's, New York City, to Dunn, Feb. 28, 1827.

[153.] He was an indefatigable letter-writer and fund-raiser. The portrait of him (c. 1820, artist unknown) in the Harris Museum and Art Gallery has him standing by a stack of such letters on his desk, with the schools visible behind him and a prominent place given to a letter of 1816 from Pius VII, congratulating him on his endeavors. See also ASJ, Dunn Papers, Archbishop P. Curtis of Armagh to Dunn, Oct. 2, 1825, who stated that Dunn (then aged seventy-nine) far surpassed his own six to eight letters a day.

[154.] Dunn Papers, bishop of Norwich to Dunn, Mar. 1815; Sir Robert Peel to Dunn, Mar. 14, 1816; Robert Peel [Jr.] to Dunn, Mar. 15, 1816, May 21, 1817, Apr. 10, 1818; Dunn to Peel Jr., n.d. (reply to last letter); Dunn to Castlereagh (draft), n.d. [c.

1818]; Charles Plowden to Dunn, Mar. 26, 1818 (Luke 11:8: "I say unto you, Though he will not rise and give him because he is his friend, yet because of his importunity he will rise and give him as many as he needeth"). On the origins of the loyal address, ASJ, St. Wilfrid's, Preston, 1713-1841, Dunn to Castlereagh, Apr. 10, 1817. See also John Corry, *The History of Lancashire* (London, 1825) II: 219, concerning a circular from Dunn of Mar. 17, 1819, drawing attention to the large number of Protestants who had contributed; Whittle, *Preston*, I: 90-91 (and 71, describing how the town's two MPs were patrons of an oratorio in St. Wilfrid's for the benefit of the Catholic school during race week, July 1820).

[155.] Dunn Papers, John Gore to Dunn, Oct. 16, 1816; Rev. Charles Plowden to Dunn, Feb. 3, 1818; note of Dunn, Aug. 27, 1819; Dunn to John Gage, Aug. 29, 1819; Dunn to Rt. Rev. Dr. Smith, Durham, n.d.; ASJ, St. Wilfrid's, Preston, 1713-1841, copies of correspondence re chapel trust, especially James Blanchard, John and George Gradwell (linen importers and provision merchants), Henry Sherrington (cotton spinner and manufacturer), Richard Arrowsmith (woolen draper and importer, later a banker), Robert Holme, J. H. Wilkinson (grocer), Lawrence Teebay (liquor merchant), and Thomas Gregson to John Dalton, Apr. 27, 1818.

[156.] Dunn Papers, Plowden to Dunn, Feb. 11, Mar. 26, Apr. 20, 1818; Dunn to Plowden, n.d. Dunn lived the life of a gentleman. A codicil to his will, of Mar. 11, 1816, bequeathed the residue of his estate to the priests of Preston if they did not have sufficient income "to live like gentlemen." He noted his own assets in a note of Oct. 30, 1822: £100 in the savings bank, £153 2s. 1d. in the Preston Bank, £200 in the gas company, two houses in Chapel Street which let for £22 and £20 p.a., a warehouse in Mount Street—£21 p.a., and two shares in the Lancaster Canal for c. £26 each.

[157.] Dunn Papers, Tristram to Dunn, June 2, 1820, Jan. 16, 1821. And see T. Glover to Dunn, Oct. 1822; Bishop Thomas Penwick to Dunn, Oct. 20, 1825.

[158.] ASJ, St. Ignatius, Preston, printed accounts, Nov. 3, 1835; note of Brother Thomas Barry, n.d. [c. 1841]; Barry to Fr. Barrow, n.d. [same time]; note of Barry, May 24, 1841; "Prospectus for Raising a Foundation for Sisters of Charity, to be Established in Preston" (patronized by all the local Catholic families); donation list for same, July 1, 1836; minute of meeting of Aug. 17, 1837, re establishment of a girls' school near St. Ignatius's; Anthony Holden, *History of the Church and Parish of St. Ignatius, Preston 1833-1933* (Preston, 1933); Leo Warren, *St Ignatius': A Preston Congregation 1833-1983* (Preston, 1983), 25-29 (also detailing, 26-28, the withdrawal of the Christian Brothers in 1847 after disputes over the control of the schools with the Catholic Poor Schools' Fund, and with Bishop Brown, the vicar apostolic; and the withdrawal of the Sisters of Charity in 1848); idem, "Hard Times in Catholic Preston," in *Catholic Englishmen*, ed. Hilton, 47.

[159.] B. F. Page, *Our Story, Being the History of St. Walburge's Parish, Preston* (Preston, 1929).

[160.] Though W. J. Lowe, *The Irish in Mid-Victorian Lancashire: The Shaping of a Working-Class Community* (New York: P. Lang, 1989), 119, estimates that in Preston in 1855 the Irish accounted for less than a third of the Catholic population.

[161.] John Bossy, *The English Catholic Community 1570-1850* (New York: Oxford University Press, 1976), 303-8, 322-23, 355. This is Bossy's estimate (424-25) of Catholic congregations in Preston, where [ ] = conjecture and { }= probably seriously inflated: 1783: 1,200; 1790: [2,000]; 1800: [3,000]; 1810: [4,000]; 1819: 6,000; 1829: {10,900}; 1834: 8,892; 1851: {19,420}.

[162.] For the national picture, see Alan Haig, *The Victorian Clergy* (London: Croom Helm, 1984), chaps. 5, 7, 8; Virgin, *Church in an Age of Negligence*, chaps. 2, 10;

Walsh and Taylor, "Introduction: the Church and Anglicanism," 6-7; Brian Heeney, *A Different Kind of Gentleman: Parish Clergy as Professional Men in Early and Mid-Victorian England* (Hamden, Conn.: Archon Books, 1976). For Nonconformist ministers, see Michael R. Watts, *The Dissenters*, vol. II, *The Expansion of Evangelical Nonconformity* (Oxford: Clarendon Press, 1995), 240-65.

[163.] We should not forget the drive to provide a parsonage for every incumbent, or that building substantial and costly parsonage houses meant a competition for funds from the well-disposed, and that the incumbent himself would be expected to pay his share. Of the thirty-six livings in the four parishes in 1835 (PP, 1835, XXII, "Report of the Ecclesiastical Revenues Commission"), twenty did not have a glebe house, and of the sixteen that did, two were unfit for residence.

[164.] See, e.g., CERC, 677, Bolton, Holy Trinity, Rev. Alfred Hadfield to Murray, Mar. 26, 1845, and Hadfield's answers to queries, Apr. 17, 1845, describing his subscriptions to religious societies, school sick societies, clothing institutions, the National School, the dispensary, etc., as well as making up the shortfall in contributions for church maintenance, at a time when income from pew rents was falling because other, newer churches were drawing away the wealthier members of his congregation.

[165.] PP, 1835, XXII, "Report of the Ecclesiastical Revenues Commission," indicates only a limited number of pluralists: Slade of Bolton (also prebend in Chester Cathedral and rector of West Kirby), W. Marsden of Blackrod (perpetual curate of St. Michael's, Manchester; he employed a stipendiary curate at Blackrod), M. Y. Starkie of Over Darwen (rector of Rushbury, Salop; he employed a curate at Over Darwen), R. N. Whitaker of Langho (perpetual curate of the family chapel at the Holme), and R. Hewitt of Lever (rector of Westhorpe, Sussex).

[166.] LRO, PR1549/20, Coucher Book of Lower Darwen, note of Mar. 9, 1830; JWW to Christopher Hodson of the Bounty Office, Feb. 19, 1830; JWW to the Rev. J. Steele, Oct. 8, 1836; John Burnet to JWW, June 20, 1836. Asking for a CPAS augmentation on Dec. 28, 1839, in a letter to Frederick Sandog, the vicar said that the living—or "starving"—could not maintain a minister.

[167.] LRO, PR2397/1, Coucher Book of Langho, Dent to JWW, Jan. 1, 1845; JWW to bishop of Chester, Jan. 3; JWW to Thomas Ainsworth, Jan. 9; JWW to tithe commissioners, Apr. 29; Rev. Jonathan Beilby to JWW, July 3; Coates to JWW, June [19?] 1846.

[168.] HO 129/480, Religious Census Returns, 1851, John F. Coates of Langho.

[169.] CERC, 15,218, Parker to secretary of commissioners, Apr. 26, 1849.

[170.] PRO, HO 129/480, Religious Census Returns, 1851. This was a slight improvement on 1835 (PP, 1835, XXII, "Report of the Ecclesiastical Revenues Commission"): Mellor was the poorest (£39), St. Peter's the wealthiest (£168), with an average of £109. Note that only three of Blackburn's fourteen churches in 1835 came above the Church's "poverty line" of £150, whereas two-thirds of livings nationally came above this line. See Walsh and Taylor, "Introduction: the Church and Anglicanism," 6-7.

[171.] PRO, HO 129/482, Religious Census Returns, 1851.

[172.] LRO, PR1549/32, Coucher Book of Witton, Ashe to the Rev. John Rushton, Mar. 14, 1855. And recall (chap. 5) the Rev. John Clay's statement along the same lines in trying to get his prison chaplain's salary raised (LRO, QGR/2/38, memorial to magistrates, Aug. 1, 1839).

[173.] Rushton, vol. 11, Parish Church, Hardcastle to Rushton, Jan. 26, 1847; newspaper clipping, July 1853 (detailing how, in the sell off of the remaining Church lands in the parish by the Church Estate Commissioners, the earl of Bradford (as lay impropriator) and the bishop of Chester (as lay rector) were to be the chief beneficiaries, and not the local Church).

[174.] Rushton, vol. 13, St. George's, Little Bolton, Jones to Rushton, Aug. 31, Dec. 22, 1847; memo, n.d. According to PRO, HO 129/468, Religious Census returns 1851, Bolton and Deane Parish incomes (not including the parish churches: Bolton at c. £460 and Deane at £234) varied between £90 5s. (plus a parsonage valued at £10 p.a.) for the clergyman at Rivington, and £230 for the minister of Christ Church. They averaged roughly £150. In Preston Parish (PRO, HO 129/481-2) incomes ranged from the £75 at St. Thomas's to the nearly £320 at Christ Church, with again an average falling somewhere close to £150. The contrasting figures for 1835 (PP, 1835, XXII, "Report of the Ecclesiastical Revenues Commission") are averages of £119 for Bolton, £189 for Deane, and £114 for Preston. And see n. 108 for the 1827 figures in Bolton.

[175.] Anon., *All Saints' Church, Bolton—Bi-Centenary 1726-1926*, 5, 8; Rushton, vol. 12, All Saints', Little Bolton. The Rev. John Leach in turn held the living in commendam until Tipping began his ministrations in 1852. Birley (1805-83), son of William Birley of Kirkham and grandson of Charles Swainson, the Preston millowner, was part of the hugely successful Birley-Hornby dynasty that had made its money in flax importing and sailcloth manufacturing on the Fylde plain and had stretched its tentacles into all forms of bourgeois wealth across the milltowns. He married Anne, daughter of John Hargreaves of Hart Common, Westhoughton, thereby extending a tentacle to the family of railway promoters and carriers who became part of the leading Bolton ironfounding firm, Hick Hargreaves. See BALS, Bolton Biographical Notes, B1, pp. 186-87, obit. of the Rev. Birley, July 1883; B3, p. 30, "Centenary of Hick, Hargreaves," in *Journal and Guardian*, Nov. 10, 1833; LRO, Birley Pedigree, 1875.

[176.] Anon., *Holy Trinity Church Bolton: Centenary 1826-1926* (Bolton, 1926), 12-13.

[177.] Rushton, vol. 33, St. George's. Whittle, *Preston*, I: 85-86, lists a number of schools and "academies" for "young gentlemen" in Preston run by local curates.

[178.] Robert Walmsley, *A Short History of St. Bartholomew's Church, Westhoughton* (Manchester, 1955), 24.

[179.] Rushton, vol. 13, Harwood, Christ Church.

[180.] LRO, PR 1549/23, Coucher Book of Salesbury, Dickenson to bishop of Chester, Oct. 29, 1846; JWW to bishop, Nov. 2, 1846.

[181.] Rushton, vol. 4, Feniscowles.

[182.] George Thistlethwaite, *Memoirs of the Life of the Rev. W. Thistlethwaite, M.A., By his Son* (London, 1838), 89, 109; Briscoe, *St. George's*, 32, 34; Barton, *Bolton*, 1st ser., I: 152.

[183.] Rushton, vol. 4, St. James, Over Darwen.

[184.] John Taylor, *Autobiography of A Lancashire Lawyer, Being the Life and Recollections of John Taylor, Attorney-at-Law, And First Coroner of the Borough of Bolton* (Bolton, 1883), 268-69.

[185.] Rushton, vol. 8, Tockholes, Robinson [to Rushton?], Apr. 1854.

[186.] LRO, PR 2846/2/2, Coucher Book of Feniscowles, vol. 2, R. N. Whitaker to JWW, Nov. 27, 1845. Catherine Jacson, *Desultory Retracings. A Personal and Family Record* (London, 1895), 104, looking back to time spent in Accrington around 1830, described the Rev. John Hopwood, the "worthy" clergyman, as "one of the then simple order of yeomen clerics from St. Bee's [*sic*]." On St. Bees College, Cumberland—founded by the bishop of Chester in 1816 to provide a two-year, nongraduate education for prospective ordinands who could not afford Oxbridge, and who would go on to staff the poorer and less appealing curacies of the diocese—see Haig, *Victorian Clergy*, chap 3.

[187.] LRO, PR2846/2/2, Coucher Book of Feniscowles, JWW to William Feilden, Mar. 17, 1838; Feilden to JWW, Nov. 30, 1837. The living was improved, principally by a £1,000 endowment from the Feildens (Feilden to JWW, Mar. 31, 1838).

[188.] Rev. John Bedford, *A Correspondence Between the Rev. William Sutcliffe, Curate of Farnworth, near Bolton; and the Rev. John Bedford, Wesleyan Minister; Relative to the Doctrines, Ministry, and System of the Wesleyan Methodists, &c.* (Bolton, 1842), iii-v, 9 (Bedford to Sutcliffe, Mar. 11, 1842), 11-12 (Sutcliffe to Bedford, Mar. 14), 15-17 (Bedford to Sutcliffe, Mar. 21), 26-29 (Sutcliffe to Bedford, Mar. 28), 31 (Burns to Bedford, Mar. 31); and see W. Burns, *A Letter from a Clergyman to his Parishioners Against the Interference of a Wesleyan Preacher in his Parish* (Preston, 1842) and Bedford, *A Wesleyan Minister's Answer to "A Letter from a Clergyman"* (Bolton, 1842).

[189.] Fletcher, *Memoirs of Fletcher*, 204-5.

[190.] See, e.g., *Sermon, Preached by the Rev. Edward Kenyon, on the Opening of Pleasington Priory, August 24, 1819* (Blackburn, 1819), 10; Rev. Roger Baxter, S.J., *Letters which Appeared in the Preston Chronicle, in Defence of the Trinity; Against the letters of the Rev. T. C. Holland* (Preston, 1816), iii-v; Whittle, *Preston*, II: 77, 268-70.

[191.] *A Circular Letter, from the Independent Ministers, Assembled at Bolton le Moors, August 31ˢᵗ, 1796, to the Independent Congregations in the County of Lancaster*, 7-8.

[192.] Thomas Macconell, *Popery Consumptive, But Protestantism Sound. The Substance of a Speech Made in Grimshaw-Street Chapel, Preston* (Preston [1824]), 21-23. And see the exchange between George Harris, *The Causes of Deism and Atheism; A Lecture, Delivered in the Unitarian Meeting-House, Moor-Lane, Bolton, On Sunday Evening, January 19th, 1823* (London, 1823), and Joseph Fox, *Lectures on Modern Socinianism, Delivered in Duke's Alley Chapel, Bolton* (London, 1824).

[193.] LRO, PR 1549/3, Coucher Book of St. Mary's, "Report to the Bishop of Chester," Aug. 7, 1835.

[194.] Rev. Dennis Duckworth, *The Story of a Church* (Preston, n.d.), 7-8, 11.

[195.] Thomas Hampson, *History of Rivington* (Wigan, 1893), 170-72.

[196.] Ibid., 172-73.

[197.] See G. I. T. Machin, *Politics and the Churches in Great Britain 1832 to 1868* (Oxford: Clarendon Press, 1977), 42-46, 56-60; J. P. Ellens, "Lord John Russell and the Church Rate Conflict: The Struggle for a Broad Church, 1834-1868," *JBS* (Apr. 1987): 233-41.

[198.] See, for example, Samuel James Allen, *The Christian's Duty in Times of National Degeneracy* (Blackburn, 1830), 10-11: a sermon in Whalley Parish Church for the SPCK, June 29, 1830. For the views of Dr. Whittaker of Blackburn against governmental tampering, see BRL, 921WHI, Whittaker Correspondence, JWW to Richard Withington, Nov. 18, 1829; to mother, Apr. 29, 1835; Whittaker, *The Present Posture and Future Prospects of the Church of England, Being A Sermon Preached Before the University of Cambridge* (London, 1830), 32; LRO, PR 2846/2/1, Coucher Book of Feniscowles, Dr. Charles Wordsworth of Trinity, Cambridge, to JWW, Aug. 8, 1834. But for widespread local clerical support for Peel's Ecclesiastical Commission in 1835, see *PP*, Feb. 7, 1835, p. 2, a report on a meeting of the clergy of Amounderness Deanery.

[199.] *Memorial of the Rev. Francis Skinner, D.D., first Minister of the United Presbyterian Church, Mount Street, Blackburn, Lancashire* (Manchester, 1867), 3, and sermon of Rev. William McKerrow, Jan. 6, 1867, printed in ibid., 43-44. Skinner's prominence in the local Dissenting elite was confirmed by both his marriages: to Martha, eldest daughter of John Eccles of Lower Darwen and sister of Banister Eccles, leading Independent millowners, in 1837; and to Catherine, eldest daughter of William Martin of Bolton, in 1844 (Nightingale, *Lancashire Nonconformity*, 74).

[200.] See the comment of the Rev. Gilbert Wardlaw of Blackburn Independent Academy to George Hadfield, Dec. 8, 1836 (Dr. Williams' Library, "An Appendix of the Blackburn Academy Correspondence"): "There is at present a controversy here on the Church question between the Vicar and our presbyterian friend, Mr. Skinner, but it has unhappily become very personal." Whittaker already had a low opinion of Skinner. In his 1835 Report to the bishop of Chester (LRO, PR1549/3, Coucher Book of St. Mary's), he stated that the congregation of the "Secession Kirk of Scotland" consisted chiefly of Scots of the lowest class, violent radicals, and outrageous bigots, and that the minister kept his head above water only by being a violent partisan in politics.

[201.] Marsyas was a satyr in Greek mythology who challenged Apollo to a musical contest and was flayed alive when he lost.

[202.] *Church Property, Ecclesiastical Establishments, the Alliance Between Church and State, and the King's Supremacy Considered with Reference to the Purposes of the Church Destructionists, in a Series of Letters to William Eccles, Esq., Attorney at Law* (Blackburn, 1837).

[203.] LRO, PR1549/32, Coucher Book of Witton, clipping of letter from "Alpha," *BG*, Nov. 16, 1836. See also clippings from *BS*, Oct. 26, *BG*, Nov. 9.

[204.] BRL, 921 WHI, Whittaker Correspondence, McGrath to JWW, Jan. 9, 1837. And see Rev. M. A. Gathercole to JWW, Nov. 2, 1836; JWW copy of a letter from W. W. Bolton to Mrs. J. Reid, Nov. 7, 1838.

[205.] Rev. Joseph Hague, *An Answer to the Letter of James Greenway, Esq. on the Union of Church and State* (Over Darwen, 1834), 10, 15, 27-28, 31-33, 35.

[206.] Franklin Baker, *A Lecture on the Evils of Church Establishments, and Particularly the Church of England, Delivered at Bank Street Chapel, Bolton, on Sunday Evening, May 19th, 1832*, 2nd ed. (London, 1832), 4-15. See also the comments of his fellow Unitarian, George Harris, on Church Establishments in *The Causes of Deism and Atheism*, 46-47.

[207.] Atkinson, *Slade*, 107-10 (at an Operative Conservative Association dinner, 1837).

[208.] Rev. Charles P. Wilbraham, *Scenes Beyond the Atlantic; A Lecture, Delivered to the Parish Church Schools, at Bolton-le-Moors* (Bolton, 1846), 25-26.

[209.] John Owen Parr, *The Duty and Advantage of National Union in the National Church: A Sermon Preached Before the Mayor and Corporation of the Borough of Preston, on Occasion of the Guild, September 6, 1842* (Preston, 1842), 8-9, 12-14.

[210.] Thomas Rogerson, *Taking Down, and Re-Building, of the Parish Church of Blackburn*.

[211.] According to the Rev. Joseph Hague, *Answer to Greenway*, 32, the majority of the leypayers objected to paying in 1834, and the decision had been taken to begin a voluntary subscription in lieu.

[212.] LPL, ICBS 7146, Blackburn St. Mary, printed circular of meeting of principal inhabitants, Jan. 24, 1831.

[213.] CMA, Deane Church Minutes 1818-85, L85/2/12/1, Oct. 25, 1832, Dec. 15, 1833, Mar. 30, 1869. For the maneuverings to secure a rate in defiance of the vestry in the new district parish of St. John's, Farnworth, see CERC, 17,837(2), Farnworth with Kersley, St. John, Rev. George Marriott to Jelf, Sept. 7, 1829; petition of vestry meeting to commissioners, Feb. 17, 1830; Rev. T. A. Ashworth to commissioners, May 10, June 7, 1831; list of vestrymen, Jan. 31, 1832; Ashworth, J. S. Troutbeck, Benjamin Rawson, John and T. B. Crompton, George Cottingham, George Lomas, and W. J. Clough to commissioners, Feb. 25, 1832; appointment of select vestry, Mar. 1832; Ashworth to commissioners, June 12, 1832.

214. LPL, ICBS 2030, Preston Parish Church, Wilson to Rodber, June 18, 1836.

215. Peter F. Taylor, "Popular Politics and Labour-Capital Relations in Bolton, 1825-1850" (Ph.D. diss., Lancaster University, 1991), 48. There had been an earlier protest about the rates (for an enlargement of the parish church churchyard), but this had hinged on a demand for a more equitable and up-to-date distribution of the burden between country and urban townships (BALS, *Case and Opinion, why the Country Townships object to the Resolution made and carried at the Parish Meeting, Held on Wednesday the 6th March, 1816* (Bolton, 1816)).

216. BC, May 12, 1849, p. 7; Rushton, vol. 11, Bolton Parish Church, newspaper clipping of May 1849.

217. E.g., *BA*, Apr. 17, 1833, p. 8, report of lectures by Skinner against the rate; Mar. 13, 1833, p. 8, letter from John Sparrow, Blackburn millowner and Catholic; reports of meetings in all three towns against the rate, *PC*, Jan. 21, 1837, p. 3; Apr. 22, p.3; *BS*, Jan. 18, p. 2; Jan. 25, p. 2; *BFP*, Mar. 25, pp. 2-3; and for meetings in Darwen of the friends of the separation of church and state, *PC*, May 25, 1850, p. 7.

218. LPL, ICBS 3334, Emmanuel, Bolton, Levy to Rodber, Nov. 25, 1843; to Rev. J. Bowdler, July 31, 1844. Levy noted in his application (received Jan. 1, 1844) that "There are no church-rates in the parish of Bolton owing to the opposition of the parishioners."

219. Fletcher, *Memoirs of Fletcher*, 158 (letter to parents, Aug. 1810).

220. The interdenominational nature of the Bible Society, though Anglican led, is seen in *Eighth Report of the Bolton Auxiliary Bible Society* (Bolton, 1822; in BALS).

221. George Thistlethwaite, *W. Thistlethwaite*, 57-63.

222. William Jones, *The Fainting of a Standard-Bearer: A Sermon Preached at Mawdsley-Street Chapel, Bolton, on Sunday, January 14th, 1838, Occasioned by the Lamented Death of the Rev. William Thistlethwaite, M.A.*, 2nd ed. (Bolton, 1838), 4, 7-8, 19, 22.

223. B. T. Barton, *History of Farnworth and Kersley* (Bolton, 1887), 180-82.

224. BC, Mar. 10, 1849, p. 5.

225. They brought together the town's leading Churchmen, clerical and lay, for the distribution of tracts and books in the district. See *Report of the Blackburn District Committee of the Society for the Promotion of Christian Knowledge for the Year 1824* (Blackburn, 1825; in BRL); 1834 Report (Blackburn, 1835); *Sermon Preached Before the Committee of the Association in the Deanery of Blackburn, to Aid the Incorporated Society for the Propagation of the Gospel in Foreign Parts, by the Rev. R. N. Whitaker, M.A., Vicar of Whalley, on Ascension day, 1845: And the report of the Committee at the 20th Annual Meeting, on the 3rd day of November, 1845* (Blackburn, 1846). A further Anglican concern was the Blackburn Association in Aid of the London Hibernian Society, begun in 1832 to support scriptural education. See *BA*, Mar. 20, 1833, p. 1 (report of the first annual meeting, chaired by Joseph Feilden, attended by the vicar and most of the Anglican clergy of the neighborhood); *BA*, Mar. 12, 1834, p. 1.

226. Fletcher, *Memoirs of Fletcher*, 194 (letter to Dr. Wardlaw, May 1814), 281 (letter to Jane France, Oct. 19, 1821).

227. BS, Oct. 21, 1835, p. 8; May 24, 1837, p. 3.

[228.] PRL, Preston Auxiliary Bible Society—Addresses and Reports: "Report of the Preston Auxiliary Bible Society" (1815), 5-6, 9-16, 28, 34-36.

[229.] Ibid., "Third Annual Report" (1817), i.

[230.] *PC*, Dec. 14, 1833, pp. 2-3.

[231.] *PC*, Dec. 7, 1833, p. 2, letter of Wilson; Dec. 14, p. 2.

[232.] *PC*, Apr. 16, 1836, p. 3; Apr. 30, p. 4, letter of Slate of Apr. 21.

[233.] E.g., *BG*, Nov. 28, 1832, p. 1; *PC*, May 19, 1838, p. 3.

[234.] Whitaker, *Whalley*, 4th ed., II: 477 n.

[235.] Abram, "Sketches," 7: 45, Shuttleworth to Charles Abbot, Dec. 16, 1816. Shuttleworth, son of the Rev. Humphrey Shuttleworth, vicar of Preston 1782-1809, became warden of New College, Oxford, and in 1830, bishop of Cirencester (Whittle, *Preston*, II: 234, and (appended to the same vol.), *The Commercial Directory of Preston* (Preston, 1841), 13).

[236.] Taylor, *Autobiography*, 19.

[237.] *Sermon, Preached by the Rev. Edward Kenyon, on the Opening of Pleasington Priory, August 24, 1819* (Blackburn, 1819), 13-14. On Kenyon and Butler see Gillow, *Dictionary of English Catholics*, IV: 13-16, 364-66. See Hewitson's comment, *Preston*, 504, writing in the 1880s of Fr. Dunn: "In his days, the boundary of denominationalism was by no means so sharply defined, nor was the spirit of sectarianism so keenly manifested in Preston, as it is now." (Hewitson is referring to a rise in sectarianism in Preston after 1864, documented by Lowe, *The Irish in Mid-Victorian Lancashire*, 165.) Nevertheless, anti-Catholic tracts and sermons continued to be penned and preached in Preston throughout this period: e.g., by the vicar, Shuttleworth (d. 1812), by the Rev. William Towne, parish church curate, in November 1813, and at a gathering of Calvinist ministers at Grimshaw Street Chapel in February 1821; and in February 1818, Fr. Dunn had a published exchange with the Rev. Law of Trinity (Whittle, *Preston*, I: 62, 314-15, 322, II: 234, 258). Gillow, II: 143-47, writes of a published reply (n.d.) Dunn gave to a printed letter of 1802 by the Rev. Henry Wilson, formerly minister of St. George's who had moved on to Wexford, which accused the bishop of Wexford and his clergy of responsibility for the massacres in the area in 1798 and asserted that Catholics aimed to destroy every Protestant in Ireland.

[238.] James J. Sack, *From Jacobite to Conservative: Reaction and Orthodoxy in Britain, c.1760-1832* (Cambridge: Cambridge University Press, 1993), 227, 230-32, 238-42, traces this seachange in the right-wing press over the period from 1801 to the 1820s, away from the relative toleration of Pitt and Burke. He points to the aggressive regime of Pius VII, the Concordat with Napoleon (undermining the sympathy for Catholics persecuted by the French Revolution), the propagandizing of the 1798 Irish rebellion as another in a tradition of popish massacres, and in the 1820s to the proselytizing activities of Bishop Milner and the threat posed by Daniel O'Connell's Catholic Association.

[239.] W. Brimelow, *Political and Parliamentary History of Bolton* (Bolton, 1882), 56.

[240.] BL, Peel Papers, Add. MS 40394, Hulton to Peel, May 31.

[241.] Barton, *Bolton*, 1st ser., I: 144-45.

[242.] Brimelow, *Political and Parliamentary*, 57.

[243.] BL, Peel Papers, Add. MS 40393, Peel to Hulton, Apr. 23.

[244.] Brimelow, *Political and Parliamentary*, 60-62.

[245.] Atkinson, *Slade*, 100-101.

[246.] Brimelow, *Political and Parliamentary*, 64-65, 72-73. Slade sent the petition to the Rev. W. Jones, Independent minister, but Jones refused to sign, not because he disagreed with its sentiments, but because of Slade's attack on the repeal of the Test and Corporation Acts at the previous Church and King dinner.

[247.] Mary Conlon, *St Alban's, Blackburn 1773-1973: A Study in Two Centuries of Blackburn Catholicism* (Chorley: Brewer, 1973).

[248.] LRO, DDPR/50/2a, *A Full and Accurate report of the Speeches Delivered at an Important Meeting of the Friends of Civil and Religious Liberty, Held at Blackburn, on the 22nd of December, 1828.*

[249.] LRO, PR 1549/3, Coucher Book of St. Mary's, requisition to Whittaker, Feb. 4, 1829; petition to Lords from clergy, gentry, etc., of Blackburn.

[250.] Whittaker, *Series of Letters Addressed to the Reverend Nicholas Wiseman, D.D. . . . On the Contents of his Late Publications* (London, 1836) (a response to the first public presentation of Roman Catholic doctrines in England intended for non-Catholic audiences. See Edward Norman, *The English Catholic Church in the Nineteenth Century* (Oxford: Clarendon Press, 1984), 122-23).

[251.] Whittaker, *The Catholic Church. Five Sermons Preached in the Parish Church of Blackburn, on occasion of the Commemoration of the Reformation, Celebrated October 4th, 1835* (Blackburn, 1836), 45.

[252.] *BM*, July 29, 1829, p. 3.

[253.] Whittaker, *Catholic Church*, 93. See also idem, *Correspondence Occasioned by an Invitation from the Clergy of Blackburn, to a Public Discussion, of the Differences in Faith Between the Churches of England and Rome* (Blackburn, 1829); idem, *A Treatise on the Church of Christ, Intended for Young Persons* (Blackburn, 1832), 113, 230.

[254.] Whittaker, *Present Posture*, 43.

[255.] BRL, 921 WHI, Whittaker Correspondence, JWW to archbishop of Canterbury, June 4, 1829.

[256.] In his 1835 "Report to the Bishop of Chester," Whittaker commented that the papists were on the increase because of the influx of Irish laborers. See Gilbert, *Religion and Society*, 45; E. P. Thompson, *The Making*, 478-80.

[257.] Atkinson, *Slade*, 115-17.

[258.] William Burdett, *God's Providence A Nation's Safeguard. A Sermon Preached in the Parish Church of Deane, On Tuesday, November 5th, 1839, (Being the Anniversary of the Gunpowder Treason)* (Bolton, 1839), 12-13.

[259.] The Gunpowder Plot of 1605 and the landing of William of Orange at Torbay in 1688.

[260.] *BS*, Nov. 8, 1843, p. 3.

[261.] See John Wolffe, *The Protestant Crusade in Great Britain 1829-1860* (Oxford: Clarendon Press, 1991), 147, 290, 303; Bossy, *English Catholic Community*, 387; and below, chap. 12.

[262.] Wolffe, *Protestant Crusade*, 150, suggests that the distribution of the nearly fifty branches, 1836-44, points to a heavy dependence on the enthusiasm generated by visiting speakers.

[263.] BALS, *Authentic Report of the Great Protestant Meeting held in St. George's School Room, Little Bolton, November 9th, 1840, for the purpose of forming a Branch Association, to be called the Bolton and Halliwell Association* (Bolton, 1840), 1-9, 24, 30.

[264.] *PC*, Apr. 12, 1845, 3.

[265.] *Preston Protestant Association: Report of Addresses by the Rev. Hugh M'Neile, D.D., and other Gentlemen, Delivered at a Public Meeting, Held in the Theatre, Preston—March 9th 1852—to Petition Parliament for the Repeal of the Maynooth Endowment Act* (Preston; in PRL), 3-5, 30-36.

^{266.} See Machin, *Politics and the Churches*, 209-18; and on moral panics, Stanley Cohen, *Folk Devils and Moral Panics: The Creation of the Mods and Rockers*, 2nd ed. (Oxford: Blackwell, 1987).

^{267.} *BS*, Dec. 11, 1850, p. 2. The editor alleged (Jan. 1, 1851, p. 2) that beside the Papal Aggression everything else during the past year paled in significance.

^{268.} *BS*, Dec. 18, 1850, pp. 2-3. Reprinted in *What Blackburn Churchmen said in 1850. Report of the Proceedings at a Protestant Meeting held in St. John's School, Blackburn, on Saturday, December 14th, 1850* (Blackburn, 1893), 3-46.

^{269.} *BC*, Nov. 23, 1850, p. 6.

^{270.} *PP*, Nov. 9, 1850, p. 4; *PC*, Oct. 26, 1850, p. 4; Nov. 23, p. 4; *PG*, Oct. 26, 1850, quoted by William J. Lowe, "The Irish in Lancashire, 1846-71: A Social History" (Ph.D. diss., Trinity College, Dublin, 1974), 406. Lowe, *The Irish in Mid-Victorian Lancashire*, 150-51, cites other liberal or moderate Lancashire newspapers (e.g., *Liverpool Mercury*, Oct. 25, Nov. 1, 1850; *MG*, Nov. 23, 1850) that followed a similar editorial line.

^{271.} *PC*, Dec. 7, 1850, p. 6.

^{272.} J. O. Parr, *Restrictive Laws Against Rome Necessary. A Sermon Preached in the Parish Church, Preston, before the Mayor and Corporation, on Sunday Morning, March 9th, 1851* (Preston, 1851), 5-6, 8.

^{273.} Rushton, vol. 11, Bolton Parish Church, clipping from the *Times* re Protestant meeting.

^{274.} This is the subject of John Henry Newman's first tract, "Thoughts on the ministerial commission," Sept. 9, 1833, in *Tracts for the Times by Members of the University of Oxford* (London, 1834), 1-2, quoted by Frank M. Turner, *Contesting Cultural Authority: Essays in Victorian Intellectual Life* (Cambridge: Cambridge University Press, 1993), 27.

^{275.} Rushton, vol. 13, Emmanuel, Bolton, clipping of Dec. 1851.

^{276.} Catherine Jacson, *Desultory Retracings*, 221-22, 252-59.

^{277.} Series of letters in *BS*, Mar. and Apr. 1846, especially Mar. 11 and 25. John Baynes of the Park Place Mills accused many of the Blackburn clergy of Tractarianism in the *Lancaster Gazette*. The clergymen implicated indignantly refuted this, and Whittaker took up their cause. See also Nigel Yates, *The Oxford Movement and Anglican Ritualism* (London: Historical Association, 1983), 18.

^{278.} Rev. James Bonwell, ed., *The Preston Magazine and Christian's Miscellany* 1, Jan. 2, 1843, pp. 1-3, 8 (letter from "A Parish Priest"), 12 (editor's agreement); 2, Feb. 1, p. 23 (letters); 3, Mar. 1, pp. 29-30, 40; 4, Apr. 1, pp. 48, 50, 54-55 (anon. letter). Hewitson, *Our Churches*, 56-57, says that Bonwell was later disrobed for immorality. On patronage and Tractarianism in Lytham, see LRO, Clifton Papers, DDCl 1201/32, Charles Swainson to James Fair, May 18, 1847.

^{279.} Edward Girdlestone, *Facts and Thoughts for the Additional Curates' Aid Society, in Connexion with the Diocese of Manchester* (London, 1849), 5-19. The Rev. J. Irvine, vicar of Leigh, replied in *A Review of a Pamphlet by the Rev. E. Girdlestone* (London, 1850).

^{280.} Rushton, vol. 21, Westhoughton-St. Mary, newspaper clippings from *MC* (partly copied from *Morning Chronicle*), Jan.-Apr. 1851, including letter of Thomas Dickinson, Apr. 30; clipping from *BC*, Sept., re first stone ceremony at Wingates; Robert Walmsley, *A Short History of St. Bartholomew's Church, Westhoughton* (Manchester, 1955), 24.

^{281.} Rushton, vol. 21, Deane, private circular of Rev. Girdlestone, Apr. 1851.

[282.] Atkinson, *Slade*, 256-60; Rushton, vol. 11, Bolton Parish Church, clipping from the *Times* re Protestant meeting (quoting Girdlestone as saying, "They had also the Curates Aid Society and the National Society, which were in the hands of the Tractarians, and were infinitely more dangerous than Popery"); *BC*, Nov. 30, 1850, p. 8; Dec. 7, p. 8; Dec. 14, p. 8.

[283.] Thomas Laqueur, *Religion and Respectability: Sunday Schools and Working Class Culture, 1780-1850* (New Haven: Yale University Press, 1976).

[284.] Rev. Edward Whitehead, *A Sermon Preached in the Parish Church of Bolton, on Sunday the 24th of September, 1786; Being the Next Lord's Day After the Execution of James Holland, On Bolton Moor, for Croft-Breaking* (Bolton, 1786), 15.

[285.] William Thistlethwaite, *Twenty-One Sermons Preached in St. George's Church, Bolton in Behalf of St. George's and All Saints' Sunday Schools* (London, 1838), 16-18 ("On the Training Up of Children," Aug. 1809).

[286.] LRO, Hulton Papers, DDHu 53/82/98a, program of Sept. 20, 1807.

[287.] Thistlethwaite, *Twenty-One Sermons*, 27-28 ("On the Religious Instruction of Children," Sept. 1811).

[288.] Whittle, *Bolton*, iii. And see his *Blackburn*, 144. For allied sentiments, Timothy Grimshaw, *The Cogitations and Opinions of Timothy Grimshaw Esq., formerly of Dean, Consisting of Critical Observations upon the Customs, Manners, &c. of the People of Bolton* (Bolton, 1839; incomplete), 11-12, 48, 51-52; Laurence Rawstorne, *Some Remarks on Lancashire Farming* (London, 1843), 115.

[289.] For the committee of the first National School in Blackburn, *BM*, Apr. 29, 1812, p. 1. For Blackburn schools, LRO, PR 1549/11, Accounts of the National and Sunday Schools; PR 1551, Coucher Book of Minutes of National and Sunday Schools, 1829-43; J. G. Shaw, albums of articles in *BT*, Feb. 25, 1933. For Preston schools, Henry Cartmell, *The Preston Churches and Sunday Schools* (Preston, 1892); Meg Whittle, "Philanthropy in Preston: The Changing Face of Charity in a 19th Century Provincial Town" (Ph.D. diss., Lancaster University, 1990), chap. 1; T. J. Bakewell, *History of the Preston Church of England Middle Class School, Known as "The Commercial School"* (Preston, 1892); Hardwick, *Preston*, 495. For Bolton schools, Atkinson, *Slade*, 14; Allen Collection, DP 280/12, "Rules for the Sunday School belonging to the Parish Church of Bolton," drawn up Jan. 1, 1813 (Bolton, 1817); Briscoe, *St. George's Church and Schools*.

[290.] E.g., Brimelow, *Political and Parliamentary*, 262.

[291.] BALS, Bolton Biographical Notes, obit., 1880.

[292.] As the Rev. Edward Girdlestone of Deane, *The Education Question* (London, 1852), 14-16, put it.

[293.] E.g., meeting at Maudsley Street schoolroom, Bolton, May 1843 (Brimelow, *Political and Parliamentary*, 470-71).

[294.] Girdlestone, *Education Question*, 10.

[295.] Brimelow, *Political and Parliamentary*, 382-84. For similar opposition from the Blackburn National and Sunday School committee, LRO, PR 1551, Coucher Book of Minutes of National and Sunday Schools, Feb. 14, 1839. And see Machin, *Politics and the Churches*, 65ff.

[296.] *BFP*, Oct. 3, 1846, p. 3, letter from "Humanitas."

[297.] *BFP*, Nov. 14, 1846, p. 3.

[298.] BALS, ZZ/130/10/6.

[299.] *BFP*, Nov. 21, 1846, p. 2.

300. BALS, Heywood Papers, ZHE/42, Heywood to E. Ashvorth, Oct. 29; drafts to James A. Turner et al., Nov. 25, 26; John Butler, Isle of Wight, to Heywood, Dec. 7; Heywood to Butler, Dec. 9; to Noah Jones, Dec. 21, 1846.

301. Atkinson, *Slade*, 137-40; *BFP*, Dec. 26, 1846, p. 3.

302. Taylor, "Popular Politics," 286-87. The Church Institute did not immediately prosper. The plan had to be shelved because of the trade depression, but was revived in 1851 and opened in 1855.

303. BALS, Heywood Papers, ZHE/42, Heywood to Butler and James Cocker, Apr. 26; printed letter of T. R. Bridson, chairman of Mechanics' Institute, Apr. 10, 1847.

304. CMA, National Public School Association letters, M136/2/3/417, Bridson to LPSA, Nov. 25, 1850. This point was reinforced by the speakers at an LPSA meeting in Preston (*PC*, May 4, 1850, p. 8).

305. CMA, M136/2/3/602, Clay to R. W. Smiles, July 12, 1851; /1081, Fort to J. Espinasse, Aug. 21, 1849; /1833, Johnson to NPSA, June 15, 1852; /2620, Probert to George Elliot, Oct. 4, 1847; /3440, Verity to Elliot, Sept. 1847.

306. Rev. Canon Parr, *A Lecture on Capital and Labour, Delivered at the [Mechanics'] Institution, Preston, on Tuesday, November 27th, 1860* (Preston).

307. See Eileen Yeo, "Christianity in Chartist Struggle 1838-1842," *P&P* 91 (1981): 109-37; Harold Faulkner, *Chartism and the Churches: A Study in Democracy* (New York: Columbia University Press, 1916), 59-68.

308. On the class divisions within Preston's churches, see, e.g., Hewitson, *Our Churches*, 4-5, 9-10: the religious fabrics "are cut up into patrician and plebeian quarters, into fashionable coteries for the perfumed portion of humanity, and into half-starved benches with the brand of poverty upon them for the poor."

309. Owen Chadwick, *The Victorian Church* (London: Adam and Charles Black, 1966), I: 335.

310. *BS*, Aug. 7, 1839.

311. *Dr. Whittaker's Sermon to the Chartists. A Sermon Preached at the Parish Church, Blackburn, on Sunday, August 4th, 1839*. Within six months, ten thousand copies had been sold in eleven editions, including two in Welsh.

312. Rushton, vol. 6, note by Rushton, [1855?]. There is no evidence for this assertion: the Blackburn Chartists were not noticeably reticent in 1842. See David Gadian, "Class formation and class action in north-west industrial towns, 1830-50," in *Class, Power and Social Structure in British Nineteenth-Century Towns*, ed. R. J. Morris (Leicester: Leicester University Press, 1986), 47; and above, chap. 3.

313. "Christianity in Chartist Struggle," 134.

314. James 2:15-16: "If a brother or sister be naked, and destitute of daily food,/And one of you say unto them, Depart in peace, be *ye* warmed and filled; notwithstanding ye give them not those things which are needful to the body; what *doth it* profit?"; Job 34:29: "When he giveth quietness, who then can make trouble? and when he hideth *his* face, who then can behold him? whether *it be done* against a nation, or against a man only."

315. *PC*, Aug. 17, 1839, p. 3.

316. Philippians 4:11-12. James Slade, *Lessons for Sunday Schools Selected from the Scriptures, with Spelling Exercises Prefixed, and A Few Explanatory Notes* (London, 1831), iv, 58, 67, 69, and passim.

317. *BFP*, Dec. 22, 1838, p. 2. See also Franklin Baker, *A Letter to the Rev. John Lyons, M.A., Occasioned by A Sermon Preached in St. George's Church, Little Bolton, on Sunday, June 27, 1841, By that Gentleman, Being the Sunday Previous to the Elec-*

tion of Members for the Borough of Bolton (London and Bolton, 1841)—a response to Lyons's warning against voting for a Unitarian candidate.

318. For examples of his political stance, Atkinson, *Slade*, 92-94, 96-97, 104-6, 112-14, 119.

Notes to Chapter 7

1. PRO, MH 12/5594, Official Circular of Poor Law Commissioners, Dec. 24, 1840: evidence of John Ashworth Jr., land agent.

2. PP 1834, "Report of Poor Laws Commission," XXVII, 343-44.

3. PRO, MH 12/5593, Henry Ashworth to Edwin Chadwick, June 9, 1834; Edmund Ashworth to Chadwick, June 9. In 1835-36, some families and individuals were sent from rural parishes in the south to work in the mills of the Ashworths, R. H. Greg, and others. J. R. Barnes of Farnworth, and Brooks and Smith of Bolton also expressed interest in the scheme during the labor shortage of 1835. See Henry Ashworth to Chadwick, Jan. 2, Feb. 13, Mar. 21, Apr. 4, 15, 25, May 2, 1835; Edmund Ashworth to Chadwick, Jan. 7; J. R. Barnes to ?, Mar. 9; Brooks and Smith to commissioners, Mar. 11; Ashworths to Henry Gibbons (copy), June 2. See also MH 12/5529, Banister Eccles and Co. of Blackburn to Chadwick, Mar. 21, 1835.

4. In the phrase of Felix Driver, *Power and Pauperism: The Workhouse System, 1834-1884* (Cambridge: Cambridge University Press, 1993), 19, building on Karl Polanyi, *The Great Transformation* (Boston: Beacon Press, 1957), 140.

5. Driver, *Power and Pauperism*, 41-42, 56-57, 134-35; Martin J. Daunton, *Progress and Poverty: An Economic and Social History of Britain 1700-1850* (Oxford: Oxford University Press, 1995), 455-59, 492-95; Gertrude Himmelfarb, *The Idea of Poverty: England in the Early Industrial Age* (New York: Knopf, 1984), 163-67; David Eastwood, *Government and Community in the English Provinces, 1700-1870* (New York: St. Martin's Press, 1997), 131-33; George W. Stocking Jr., *Victorian Anthropology* (London: Free Press, 1987), 34-36; Patricia Hollis, "Anti-Slavery and British Working-Class Radicalism in the Years of Reform," in *Anti-Slavery, Religion and Reform*, ed. Christine Bolt and Seymour Drescher (Hamden, Conn.: Archon Books, 1980), 302-7; Boyd Hilton, *The Age of Atonement: The Influence of Evangelicalism on Social and Economic Thought, 1795-1865* (Oxford: Clarendon Press, 1988).

6. Peter Mandler, "The Making of the New Poor Law *Redivivus*," *P&P* 117 (Nov. 1987): 131-57; Anthony Brundage, *The Making of the New Poor Law: The Politics of Inquiry, Enactment and Implementation, 1832-39* (New Brunswick, NJ: Rutgers University Press, 1978), 182-83.

7. Michael E. Rose, introduction to *The Poor and the City: The English Poor Law in its Urban Context, 1834-1914* (Leicester: Leicester University Press, 1985), ed. idem, 3-9; Driver, *Power and Pauperism*, 33, 49, 134-35, 145; Himmelfarb, *Idea of Poverty*, 168, 177; Nicholas C. Edsall, *The Anti-Poor Law Movement 1834-44* (Manchester: Manchester University Press, 1971).

8. Mandler, "The Making," 150, 156-57; Driver, *Power and Pauperism*, 33, 135.

9. *BC*, Nov. 24, 1838, p. 2; Mar. 5, 1842, p. 2; May 28, 1842, p. 2; July 20, 1844, p. 2; PRO, MH 12/5593, John Foster to commissioners, Feb. 16, 1836 (and draft reply, Feb. 18), May 31; and letter of Henry and Edmund Ashworth in *BFP*, May 13.

10. *BFP*, Jan. 28, 1837, p. 2; Feb. 10, 1838, p. 2; Mar. 23, 1839, p. 2.

11. BALS, Heywood Papers, ZHE/30, Darbishire to Robert Heywood, May 27, 1834.

12. *BFP*, Jan. 21, 1837, p. 2.

13. *BFP*, Feb. 4, p. 3; Feb. 11, p. 3; BALS, Bolton Poor Law Union Records, GBO/1/1, Feb. 9; MH 12/5593, Richard Muggeridge to commissioners, Feb. 13. The four Tory

ex officio guardians in question were Ridgway, Fletcher, Robert Lomax of Harwood, and William Ford Hulton of Hulton Park. Note that William Naisby, veteran radical draper and guardian for Great Bolton, also registered his strong opposition to the New Poor Law at this meeting.

14. BALS, GBO/1/1, Mar. 25.

15. MH 12/5593, Mott to commissioners, Oct. 18, Dec. 11; Woodhouse to commissioners, Dec. 20, 1838.

16. *BFP*, Feb. 9, 1839, p. 3; MH 12/5593, Winder to commissioners, Feb. 12; commissioners to Winder, Feb. 21; Woodhouse to Mott, Feb. 26; commissioners to Woodhouse, Mar. 2; memo. of Richard Dunderdale, Richard Nightingale, William Barton, John Ashworth, Thomas Thomasson, Thomas Wallwork, Thomas Evans, William Naisby, and Joshua Crook, Mar. 4; Richard Nightingale to commissioners, Mar. 5; William Naisby to commissioners, Mar. 5; John Smith to commissioners, Mar. 6; memo of Mott, Mar. 9; memo of Power, Mar. 11, 1840; Woodhouse to commissioners, Apr. 4; Winder to commissioners, Apr. 4; BALS, GBO/1/1, Feb. 25, 1839, Mar. 4; Mar. 27, 1840, Apr. 5, 10.

17. MH 12/5593, John Ashworth to Chadwick, July 22.

18. GBO/1/1, Feb. 5, 12, 1841.

19. MH 12/5594, poster of Bolling et al. to ratepayers, n.d.; Mott to commissioners, Mar. 30, Apr. 30, 1841. On the earlier debate on the workhouse, see MH 12/5593, Woodhouse to commissioners, Oct. 5, 1839; commissioners to Woodhouse, Oct. 12; Power to commissioners, Nov. 9; memo of Power, Mar. 11, 1840; John Ashworth to Chadwick, July 22; Power to commissioners, July 24; memorial of Great Bolton overseers to commissioners, July 16; GBO/1/1, Apr. 26, 1839, May 10, Oct. 4, 18, Nov. 1, 8; Feb. 14, 1840, July 10; *BFP*, Apr. 4, p. 2.

20. MH 12/5594, Thomas Dawson to Mott, Apr. 19, 1841; commissioners to Woodhouse, June 3, Dec. 6; Dawson to Henry Ashworth, June 11; Mott to commissioners, July 23, Oct. 12, Nov. 27; John Ashworth to Mott, July 19; Woodhouse to Chadwick, Jan. 22, Feb. 5, Mar. 4, 1842; Mott to commissioners, Jan. 27, Apr. 7; Thomas Hart to commissioners, Feb. 20; memo of commissioners, n.d.; J. S. Scowcroft, Thomas Dawson, Robert Makant, and John Smith, overseers of Bolton, to Mott, Apr. 18; John Bolling to Graham, May 19; Woodhouse to Mott, July 1; John Ashworth to Chadwick, June 30; Mott to commissioners, Aug. 4; Clements to Edmund Head, Oct. 1; GBO/1/2, July 23, 1841, Nov. 5, Dec. 10; Jan. 21, 1842, Mar. 4, Apr. 1, May 6, Sept. 23. This was the composition of the guardians elected during the year from March 1842 (GBO/1/2, Mar. 26, 1842): fifteen farmers, four attorneys, four gentlemen, three shopkeepers, two manufacturers, one cotton spinner, one land surveyor, one coal merchant, one coal proprietor, one bleacher, one slate merchant, and one draper.

21. MH 12/5594, Flitcroft to commissioners, Dec. 20, 1842: he reported Ralph Shaw of Lostock as saying that the best way to remove the vermin would be to boil the pauper, vermin, clothes, and all; Heap to Bolling, Dec. 18; GBO/1/2, Dec. 16; *BFP*, Mar. 9, 1844, p. 3.

22. MH 12/5594, Flitcroft to commissioners, Dec. 20, 1842; MH 12/5595, Clements to commissioners, Jan. 9, 1843.

23. MH 12/5594, commissioners to Woodhouse, Jan. 17, 1843; BALS, Heywood Papers, ZHE/39, Ashworth to Robert Heywood, Jan. 30, 1843.

24. GBO/1/3, Jan. 27, 1843; MH 12/5594, Clements to commissioners, Feb. 27, 1843.

25. GBO/1/3, Feb. 24, 1843, Mar. 31, Apr. 28, July 7, 28, Aug. 4, Sept. 22, Nov. 17, Dec. 8; May 24, 1844, July 5, 12; Jan. 17, 1845, Jan. 24; GBO/1/4, June 9, July 28,

Aug. 11; MH 12/5594, commissioners to Woodhouse, Oct. 5, 1843; commissioners to Richard Brimelow, Dec. 11; Brimelow to commissioners, Dec. 12; Clements to commissioners, Dec. 20; MH 12/5597, commissioners to Woodhouse, July 21, 1845.

[26.] GBO/1/4, Dec. 1.

[27.] MH 12/5597, commissioners to Woodhouse, Oct. 3, 1846; GBO/1/4, Oct. 12.

[28.] MH 12/5594, memorial from guardians and overseers of townships wishing to form a separate union, Jan. 6, 1843; memorial of Little Bolton ratepayers re same, Feb. 7; memorial of Halliwell ratepayers re same, Feb. 2; memorial of vicar, clergy, and magistrates re same; Clements to commissioners, May 4, June 21, 25, 27; James Cooper to Clements, June 19; John Smith to Clements, May 24, June 21; Woodhouse to Clements, June 21; Cooper to commissioners, June 24; commissioners to Woodhouse, June 29; Woodhouse to George Coode, June 30.

[29.] *BFP*, Mar. 9, 1844, p. 3; *MG*, Mar. 9, p. 6.

[30.] MH 12/5597, commissioners to Mott, Oct. 3, 1846; Mott to commissioners, Oct. 24; MH 12/5598, Thomas Hodson to commissioners, Jan. 6, 1848; Flitcroft to commissioners, Jan. 17, Feb. 19; *Bolton Times*, Jan. 15, including letter from 'A Ratepayer'; memorial of Bolton ratepayers to commissioners, received Feb. 15; memorial of vicar et al., Jan. 31; Thomas Balshaw to commissioners, Feb. 4, 12; Balshaw to Poor Law Board, Feb. 28, Mar. 16; John Harwood and William Taylor to Lord Elrington, Feb. 29; D. Knott to PLB, Mar. 6; *MG*, Feb. 19; *Manchester Courier*, Feb. 19; PLB to Woodhouse, Apr. 14; Flitcroft to PLB, Apr. 11, 18, Mar. 29; Joseph Slater Platt to PLB, Apr. 15; Woodhouse to Lumley, Apr. 27, June 19; John Lomax to PLB, June 25; Assistant Commissioner Austin to George Nicholls, July 10; John Gaskell to PLB, July 12; PLB to Flitcroft, Sept. 1; MH 12/5599, Ralph Shaw to PLB, Feb. 6, 1850; memorial of Great Bolton guardians and overseers, received June 27; memo of Austin, July 5; overseers of Great Bolton to PLB, July 3; Austin to Lumley, Oct. 25; petition of Halliwell inhabitants to PLB, received Aug. 12; GBO/1/4, May 5, 1847, May 19, 26, June 30; GBO/1/5, July 28, 1847, Aug. 18, Sept. 22, Oct. 13, 20, Dec. 29; Jan. 12, 1848, Mar. 29, Apr. 26, May 24, Aug. 2, Dec. 13; *BC*, Apr. 15, 1848, p. 4. Rhodes Boyson, "The New Poor Law in North-East Lancashire, 1834-71," *TLCAS* 70 (1960): 55, notes that Lostock only came into the union when one large ratepayer refused to pay the voluntary rate.

[31.] *PC*, Jan. 14, 1837, p. 2; Mar. 10, 1838, p. 2. For an overview, see Winifred Proctor, "Poor Law Administration in Preston Union, 1838-1848," *THSLC* 117 (1965): 146-64.

[32.] *PP*, Apr. 29, 1837, p. 2; Jan. 12, 1839, p. 2; Apr. 24, 1841, p. 2.

[33.] *PG*, Feb. 10, 1844, p. 2.

[34.] Letter to guardians, reprinted in *PC*, Feb. 25, 1837, p. 3, and *PP*, Feb. 25, p. 3.

[35.] *PC*, Mar. 11, p. 2; Apr. 8, p. 2; *PP*, Mar. 25, p. 2.

[36.] LRO, Poor Law Union Records, PUT/1/5, Mar. 31, 1840; PUT/1/6, Apr. 6, 13, 20, 1841, July 13, 20, Aug. 10, 24.

[37.] PUT/1/3, Sept. 4, 18, 25, 1838, Oct. 30, Dec. 18; Jan. 22, 29, 1839; PUT/1/4, Dec. 3, 10, 17, 24, 1839; PUT/1/5, Feb. 18, 1840, May 12, June 2.

[38.] PUT/1/7, Nov. 16, 1841 (letters of Mott to Lomas of May 22 and Nov. 13 read out by chairman, Lomas).

[39.] PUT/1/7, Dec. 7, 1841.

[40.] MH 12/6112, Mott to commissioners, Feb. 21, 1842.

[41.] MH 12/6112, Thackeray to commissioners, Feb. 22, 1842, Mar. 1, 9; Mott to Thackeray, Feb. 25; Lawe to commissioners, Mar. 7; PUT/1/7, Feb. 22, 1842, Mar. 1, 8, 15.

42. MH 12/6112, Lomas and Carr to commissioners, Mar. 9. Also see *List of Persons Who Voted* (Preston, 1841): of the elected Preston guardians, Lomas, James Carr (painter), and Christopher Ward (hatter) had voted a straight conservative (Parker/Swainson) ticket in the 1841 parliamentary election, and Livesey and John Hawkins (spinner) had voted straight liberal (Fleetwood/Strickland). In Preston, union politics were not party politics.

43. MH 12/6112, poster "To the Ratepayers of this Town," Mar. 3; Lomas to Duncombe, printed letter in *PC*, Feb. 28.

44. MH 12/6112, Marshall to commissioners, Mar. 12; and see Addison to commissioners, Mar. 16.

45. MH 12/6112, Marshall to commissioners, Mar. 24.

46. MH 12/6112, Marshall to commissioners, Mar. 24, 25, 29, [Apr. 15?]; commissioners to Marshall, Apr. 1; Thackeray to commissioners, Apr. 7; Robert Addison to Thackeray (copy), Mar. 17; Lomas, Andrew Halliday, Livesey (Preston guardians), Henry Breakell (Woodplumpton), and Seth Eccles (Alston) to commissioners, Apr. 12; William Ainsworth to commissioners, Apr. 12; James Carr to commissioners, Apr. 13; Walmsley to commissioners, Apr. 14; commissioners to Thackeray, Apr. 21; commissioners to W. Gilbert, May 19; Walmsley to commissioners, May 30; Gilbert to commissioners, May 30, 31; Thackeray to commissioners, June 11; printed notice to guardians re new elections, June 18; commissioners to Thackeray, June 16; Marshall to commissioners, June 13; Addison to commissioners, June 15; commissioners to Addison, June 23; PUT/1/7, Mar. 29, Apr. 12, June 14.

47. MH 12/6112, Marshall to commissioners, Apr. 20.

48. MH 12/6112, Marshall to commissioners, June 13; Gilbert to commissioners, May 30.

49. MH 12/6112, Mott to guardians, June 15 [N.B. this letter is out of sequence and is to be found at the end of Feb. in the file]; and see Mott to commissioners, June 2.

50. MH 12/6112, Thackeray to commissioners, July 14, and note on back by Mott of July 19.

51. MH 12/6112, report of committee on obtaining labor, Sept. 22; Mott to commissioners, Oct. 1; PUT/1/8, July 26, Aug. 30, Sept. 27, Oct. 11, 18.

52. MH 12/6112, order of Oct. 10; proceedings of board, Oct. 25, 28; PUT/1/8, 25, 28.

53. PUT/1/8, Nov. 1.

54. MH 12/6112, Marshall to commissioners, Nov. 1.

55. PUT/1/8, Aug. 2, 23; MH 12/6112, Thackeray to commissioners, Aug. 24, 29: he commented, on the attempt to dissolve the union, that it was "an attack upon the great principle of Centralization," that it was voted through because "The Country Guardians without Education or judgement speaking generally are easily led by such Characters as Lomas or Livesey," and that he hoped the commissioners would repulse the attempt "in a decisive & peremptory manner—in order to discourage all similar futile attempts"; memo of Mott, Sept. 12; commissioners to Thackeray, Sept. 13.

56. MH 12/6112, Marshall to commissioners, Nov. 1; PUT/1/8, Dec. 6.

57. PUT/1/9, Feb. 6, 1844.

58. PUT/1/8, Apr. 4, 1843; PUT/1/10, Oct. 10, 1844, Dec. 17; Chadwick to Dixon, Nov. 15, 1844; Jan. 14, 28, 1845, Feb. 4, 11, 25, Mar. 4, 18, 25, May 20, 27, June 17, 24, July 8; PUT/1/11, Feb. 3, 1846.

59. MH 12/6113, Livesey to commissioners, Feb. 24, enclosing memorial; Thackeray to commissioners, Mar. 3; memorial of William Ainsworth (cotton spinner), Michael Satterthwaite (currier), James Carr (painter and guilder), John Noble (maltster), Peter

Dobson (gentleman), Christopher Ward (hatter), and the Rev. John Owen Parr, Preston guardians, to commissioners, May.

60. MH 12/6113, Thackeray to commissioners, Mar. 17; memo of board meeting, June 15.

61. MH 12/6113, Ainsworth to commissioners, Sept. 10, and note on same by "A. A." [Alfred Austin].

62. MH 12/6113, Addison to commissioners, Mar. 17; note by A. A., Apr. 11; commissioners to Thackeray, May 28; PUT/1/12, June 1; PUT/1/13, Mar. 7, 1848. The six Preston guardians and the vicar (ex officio guardian) had again crossed party lines: in the 1847 election (PRL, "Preston Poll List, 1847," from *PG*, Sept. 18, 1847), Ainsworth, Satterthwaite, and Noble voted for the liberals (Strickland/Grenfell), and Carr, Dobson, Ward, and Parr voted conservative (Parker).

63. Indeed, Rawstorne had claimed in his *Some Remarks on Lancashire Farming* (London, 1843), 71, that "The labour test in the workhouse is nugatory and valueless. No industrious habits can be enforced by penal enactments"; and that (pp. 93-94) "Many persons were sanguine enough to expect that the new poor law system would bring with it a salutary relief. This hope seems now to have vanished, and it is believed that the work houses on which such large sums have been expended, have served rather to aggravate the evils complained of, than to remove them." And see p. 105.

64. Joseph Livesey, *Autobiography of Joseph Livesey* (London, [1881?]), 38-39.

65. PUT/1/13, Apr. 18, 25, 1848, May 2; *PC*, Apr. 22, 1848, p. 6; Apr. 29, p. 6; May 6, pp. 4, 6 (quotations). The initial vote (Apr. 18) was a tie; Parr's intervention came before a second vote (May 2).

66. PUT/1/13, Aug. 1, 1848, Sept. 25.

67. PUT/1/14, Apr. 24, 1849; *PC*, Mar. 31, 1849, pp. 3-4; Apr. 28, p. 6.

68. *PC*, Apr. 20, 1850, p. 4.

69. PUT/1/14, Nov. 16, 20, 27, Dec. 4, 11.

70. *BS*, Jan. 18, 1837, p. 2; Jan. 3, 1838, p. 3; *BG*, Jan. 25, 1837, p. 4.

71. MH 12/5529, John Brandwood and John Bury to commissioners, Nov. 13, 1837; Banister Eccles, Thomas Wilcock, and Benjamin Tattersall to commissioners, Nov. 16; memo of Power, Nov. 28; Power to commissioners, June 21, 1838; Ellingthorpe to commissioners, Sept. 29, Nov. 3; PUK/1/1, Sept. 23, 1837, Oct. 21; PUK/10/1, Ellingthorpe to Power, Dec. 15, 1838.

72. MH 12/5529: Mott to commissioners, Aug. 27, 1842; Mott to guardians (copy), Aug. 27.

73. MH 12/5529, Ellingthorpe to Mott, Sept. 6; and see Mott to Ellingthorpe, Sept. 13.

74. MH 12/5530, Ellingthorpe to commissioners, Jan. 6, 20, May 29; Clements to commissioners, May 21.

75. MH 12/5530, Ellingthorpe to commissioners, Dec. 6, 19, 1843; Clements to commissioners, Dec. 12; commissioners to Ellingthorpe, Dec. 21, 28; Richard Eccles to commissioners, Dec. 6; Clements to commissioners, Jan. 26, 1844; Ellingthorpe to commissioners, Feb. 19; memo by H. W. Sass, Feb. 26; memo by Clements, Feb. 27; Clements to commissioners, June 27, 1845, July 17 (quotation); Clements to Ellingthorpe, May 8.

76. MH 12/5530, Ainsworth to commissioners, Nov. 8, 1843.

77. MH 12/5530, "A Rate Payer" to commissioners, Oct. 1, 1846; Richard Haworth to commissioners, Dec. 22; MH 12/5531, Haworth to commissioners, Jan. 21, 1847.

78. MH 12/5531, Oliver Roylance to commissioners, Jan. 30, 1847; *PG*, Jan. 30.

79. MH 12/5531, Ellingthorpe to commissioners, Feb. 10.

[80.] MH 12/5531, reports of Austin, Mar. 20, 1847, July 15; commissioners to Ellingthorpe, Aug. 6; report on insane in workhouse, Aug. 14, enclosing copy of remarks of J. Hancock Hall and Thomas Turner, commissioners in lunacy, Sept. 17, 1845, and of Austin, June 24, 1846; Ellingthorpe to commissioners, Aug. 18, 1847; petition of twenty-four inmates to commissioners, Sept. 5, 1848 (postmark); "J. M." to Austin, Sept. 8; memo of Austin, Jan. 12, 1849; Robert Gorell to PLB, Mar. 27; MH 12/5532, report of Mainwaring, Jan. 7, 1850; Ellingthorpe to commissioners, May 22; memo of Austin, May 27.

[81.] See Boyson, "New Poor Law," 35ff.; Eric C. Midwinter, "State Intervention at the Local Level: The New Poor Law in Lancashire," *HJ* X, 1 (1967): 106-12; idem, *Social Administration in Lancashire 1830-1860: Poor Law, Public Health and Police* (Manchester: Manchester University Press, 1969), 60-61 and passim.

[82.] M. A. Crowther, *Workhouse System*, 225, 236.

[83.] F. M. L. Thompson, *The Rise of Respectable Society: A Social History of Victorian Britain, 1830-1900* (London: Fontana, 1988), 349-55; Michael E. Rose, "The Disappearing Pauper: Victorian Attitudes to Relief of the Poor," in *In Search of Victorian Values: Aspects of Nineteenth-Century Thought and Society*, ed. Eric M. Sigsworth (Manchester: Manchester University Press, 1988), 57-59, 67; David Eastwood, "Debate: The Making of the New Poor Law *Redivivus*," *P&P* 127 (May 1990): 192.

[84.] Edwin Waugh, *Home-Life of the Lancashire Factory Folk During the Cotton Famine* (London, 1867), 15-17; William Alexander Abram, *Blackburn Characters of a Past Generation* (Blackburn, 1894), 286, in describing Dr. Henry Ainsworth Grimes's free treatment for poor patients. For an earlier example, see BALS, Bolton Infirmary Reports 1818-1860, HBO/1/10/1, report for 1840-41, p. 4, which refers to those who, "with a spirit of independence which would scornfully reject the alternative of parish pay, resolve to endure any privation, and even consign to the pawnbroker their furniture and all their goods, rather than submit to what they conceive to be so great a degradation."

[85.] It was also working in the sense that poor relief, which had risen to around 2 percent of national product from the end of the eighteenth century, dropped to a steady 1 percent between 1834 and 1914. See Peter H. Lindert, "Unequal living standards," in *The Economic History of Britain Since 1700*, ed. Roderick Floud and Donald McCloskey, 2nd ed. (Cambridge: Cambridge University Press, 1994), 381-86.

[86.] See, e.g., Noel Parry and José Parry, *The Rise of the Medical Profession: A Study of Collective Social Mobility* (London: Croom Helm, 1976), 117 and passim; Michael Durey, "Medical Elites, the General Practitioner and Patient Power in Britain During the Cholera Epidemic of 1831-2," in *Metropolis and Province: Science in British Culture, 1780-1850*, ed. Ian Inkster and Jack Morrell (Philadelphia: University of Pennsylvania Press, 1983), 258-61, 274; Robert Gray, "Medical Men, Industrial Labour and the State in Britain, 1830-1850," *SH* 16, 1 (Jan. 1991): 19-43; Ivan Waddington, "The Movement Towards the Professionalisation of Medicine," and Irvine Loudon, "Obstetrics and the General Practitioner," *British Medical Journal* 301, 6754 (Oct. 3, 1990): 688-89, 703; F. B. Smith, *The People's Health 1830-1910* (London: Croom Helm, 1979), 48-49, 346-47, 355-60, and passim; Hilary Marland, *Medicine and Society in Wakefield and Huddersfield 1780-1870* (Cambridge: Cambridge University Press, 1987), 72-77; Penelope J. Corfield, *Power and the Professions in Britain 1700-1850* (London: Routledge, 1995), 141-43, 149.

[87.] Black, *A Medico-Topographical, Geological, and Statistical Sketch of Bolton and its Neighbourhood* (Bolton, 1837), 84.

[88.] Ibid., 86.

[89.] As practiced by the Hahnemannists, the followers of Samuel Hahnemann (1755-1843), German physician and founder of homeopathy.

[90.] Rothwell, "A History of the Changes in Medical Men and Manners in Bolton; Being the Introductory Lecture read before the Medical Society, By its President for 1879" (typescript in BALS), 12, 14, 17. See also Virginia Berridge, "Health and Medicine," in *The Cambridge Social History of Britain 1750-1950*, ed. F. M. L. Thompson (Cambridge: Cambridge University Press, 1990), 3: 180-82, 189.

[91.] *PC*, Mar. 3, 1832, p. 3.

[92.] Black, *Bolton*, 59, 84-85.

[93.] James Barlow, *An Address to the Medical and Surgical Pupils, on the Studies and Duties of their Profession* (Blackburn, 1839), 3, 8, 25-37, 44-45, 48-49, 54, 58-59, 100-105. On the competition for lower-class patients and the impact of the New Poor Law, see, e.g., John V. Pickstone, "Establishment and Dissent in Nineteenth-Century Medicine: An Exploration of Some Correspondence and Connections Between Religious and Medical Belief Systems in Early Industrial England," in *The Church and Healing*, ed. W. J. Sheils (Oxford: Blackwell, 1982), 174-75; Katherine A. Webb, "The Development of the Medical Profession in Manchester 1750-1860" (Ph.D. diss., Manchester University, 1988), 44, 141, 266, and passim; Ivan Waddington, *The Medical Profession in the Industrial Revolution* (Dublin: Gill and Macmillan, 1984); Frederick F. Cartwright, *A Social History of Medicine* (London: Longman, 1977).

[94.] MH 12/5530, Ellingthorpe to commissioners, Mar. 7; memo re appointment of MOs, Sept.; commissioners to Ellingthorpe, Sept. 20; Ellingthorpe to commissioners, Sept. 27. And see memo re appointment of MOs in the out-districts, Dec. 1843; commissioners to Ellingthorpe, Jan. 3, 1844.

[95.] MH 12/5531, *BS*, Mar. 17, 1847; Ellingthorpe to commissioners, April 5.

[96.] See, e.g., LRO, PUT/ 1/4, Oct. 8, 1939; PUT/1/6, May 18, 1841; PUT/1/9, Aug. 29, 1843; Jan. 9, 1844; Feb. 6, 20.

[97.] MH 12/5595, Woodhouse to Chadwick, Jan. 21; commissioners to Woodhouse, Jan. 26, Feb. 11; memo re appointment of MOs, Feb. 3; Woodhouse to Chadwick, Mar. 25; J. B. Garstang to Chadwick, June 15; G. L. Anderton to Chadwick, June 18; Chadwick to James P. Tyrer, July 11; memo re appointment of James Heaton, June 15, and re Ranby Thomas Snape, n.d., and James Pendlebury, n.d.; commissioners to Woodhouse, July 10, 1843; BALS, GBO/1/2, Apr. 1, 15, 1842; GBO/1/3, Feb. 17, 1843, letter from meeting of medical practitioners Johnson (chairman), Moore, Ramforth, Durham, Mallett, Heap, Robinson, Bancroft, Ferguson, Scowcroft, Chadwick, Garstang, Hatton, Featherstonhaugh, Wimpenny, Snape, and Thomas Haworth (secretary). Featherstonhaugh and Garstang later said that they had objected to the resolution (Feb. 24), while Dr. Haworth stated that Featherstonhaugh had voted in favor of it (letter of Mar. 3).

[98.] MH 12/5595, Featherstonhaugh to Chadwick, Aug. 12, 1843.

[99.] MH 12/5595, Woodhouse to Chadwick, Sept. 1, 1843; MH 12/5596, Robert Yates Greenhalgh to Lumley, Mar. 18, 1844; MH 12/5597, Featherstonhaugh to commissioners, Mar. 15, 1845.

[100.] MH 12/5599, Marshall to guardians, Apr. 2, 1850.

[101.] MH 12/5598, memorial of guardians to PLB, Mar. 20, 1848; commissioners to Woodhouse, Mar. 31; MH 12/5531, Ellingthorpe to commissioners, July 7, 1847; BALS, GBO/1/5, July 21, 1847; Sept. 1, 15. A nurse, Elizabeth Irlam, also died of fever on Dec. 15, 1848 (GBO/1/5, Dec. 20). On typhus and the risks to medical personnel, see Anne Hardy, "Urban Famine or Urban Crisis? Typhus in the Victorian City," *Medical History*, 32 (1988), reprinted in *Victorian City: A Reader in British Urban*

History 1820-1914, ed. R. J. Morris and Richard Rodger (London: Longman, 1993), 215, 224, and passim.

[102.] MH 12/5598, Marshall to commissioners, March 13, 23, 1848. Marshall was appointed MO for Westhoughton on Aug. 19.

[103.] See, e.g., MH 12/5599, John Carruthers (RCS, Edinburgh, MD, Glasgow) to PLB, Mar. 28, 1850; PLB to Woodhouse, June 1, re appointment of Johnson Martin; memo re appointment of James Parkinson Scowcroft, Sept. See also LRO, PUT/1/8, Feb. 14, Mar. 14, 1843: the commissioners objected to the appointment of Bernard Haldan (MRCS, Edinburgh, and the MO of the Preston District and the dispensary for several years) because he had only a Scottish qualification. They suggested that a temporary replacement be found while Haldan was obtaining a diploma from the RCS of London, and this was in fact done (Apr. 18). But later in the year, they wrote (PUT/1/9, Sept. 5) that after consultations with the home secretary and the attorney general it appeared that persons with a surgical diploma from a Royal College or university in Scotland or Ireland were legally competent to be MOs under the Poor Law Amendment Act, but they could not practice pharmacy in England and Wales.

[104.] PRO, MH 12/5529, Wraith to commissioners, June 24, 1842.

[105.] MH 12/5595, Hawley to commissioners, Sept. 2, 1843; GBO/1/3, Aug. 25, Sept. 29, 1843.

[106.] MH 12/5594, Mott to commissioners, Dec. 25, 1841; evidence before John Taylor, coroner, Dec. 3, 1841; Woodhouse to Lumley, Aug. 26, 1842; MH 12/5595, memo re proceedings in Chancery, Jan. 10, 1844; GBO/1/2, Oct. 22, Dec. 10, 1841.

Notes to Chapter 8

[1.] LRO, DDHu 53/82/96, Address of the Rev. Thomas Jones, Oct. 1, 1797.

[2.] And maybe also his creditworthiness. In 1803, when John Horrocks, MP, the Preston cotton lord, was affected by the cutting off of trade to Hamburg, he apparently donated £1,000 toward the Royal Preston Volunteers to confirm his credit. See Kenneth Garlick and Angus Macintyre, eds., *Diary of Joseph Farington*, IV: 2126 (Sept. 11, 1803), quoted by Austin Gee, "The British Volunteer Movement 1793-1807" (D.Phil. diss., Oxford University, 1989), 207.

[3.] R. J. Morris, "Organization and Aims of the Principal Secular Voluntary Organizations of the Leeds Middle Class, 1830-1851" (D.Phil. diss., Oxford University, 1970); idem, *Class, Sect and Party: The Making of the British Middle Class, Leeds 1820-1850* (Manchester: Manchester University Press, 1990); idem, "Clubs, Societies and Associations," in *The Cambridge Social History of Britain 1750-1950*, ed. F. M. L. Thompson (Cambridge: Cambridge University Press, 1990), 3: 401-43; Stana S. Nenadic, "The Structure, Values and Influence of the Scottish Urban Middle Class; Glasgow 1800 to 1870" (Ph.D. diss., Glasgow University, 1986), 191, 242ff.; Frederic Cople Jaher, *The Urban Establishment: Upper Strata in Boston, New York, Charleston, Chicago, and Los Angeles* (Urbana: University of Illinois Press, 1982), 57-63; Edward Pessen, *Riches, Class and Power Before the Civil War* (Lexington, Mass.: D. C. Heath, 1973), 258-78; David Blackbourn, "The Discreet Charm of the Bourgeoisie: Reappraising German History in the Nineteenth Century," in *The Peculiarities of German History: Bourgeois Society and Politics in Nineteenth-Century Germany*, by Blackbourn and Geoff Eley (Oxford: Oxford University Press, 1984), 196-97.

[4.] See Robert D. Putnam, *Making Democracy Work: Civic Traditions in Modern Italy* (Princeton: Princeton University Press, 1993), 89-90, 173, 175-76.

[5.] Alexis de Tocqueville, *Democracy in America*, part II (1840), chaps. 29-31; Jürgen Habermas, *The Structural Transformation of the Public Sphere: An Inquiry into a*

Category of Bourgeois Society, trans. Thomas Burger (Cambridge, Mass.: MIT Press, 1989).

⁶· See note 3.

⁷· And see Patrick Joyce, review of *Class, Sect and Party*, by R. J. Morris, *JEH* 52, I, (Mar. 1992): 229-30; Michael Winstanley, ibid., *UH(Y)* 18 (1991): 200-2. They question whether the fluctuating membership of these associations and the haphazard success of their efforts could ever offset the more deeply ingrained divisions. Many members of the middle class, particularly those further down the social scale, played little or no role in any type of society.

⁸· The building of the railway network provides a supreme example of this. For a detailed discussion, see Brian Lewis, "Bourgeois Ideology and Order: Middle-Class Culture and Politics in Lancashire, 1789-1851" (Ph.D. diss., Harvard University, 1994), 509-29. Other varieties of professional or business association included the master spinners', manufacturers' and bleachers' societies (see chap. 9); ad hoc dinners or meetings of doctors to promote good feeling or to petition the government (see *BC*, Mar. 8, 1834, p. 3; *BS*, Nov. 20, 1844, p. 3); committees of businessmen for commercial purposes such as the building of the Blackburn Exchange Buildings (*BS*, July 17, 1850, p. 1), or the formation of the Blackburn Fire and Life Insurance Company (*BS*, July 23, 1845, p. 1); and commercial lobbies such as the Blackburn Association for the Effecting the Abolition of the East India Company's Monopoly of Salt, formed in September 1846, and a sister Association for Effecting a Reduction of the Duty on Tea, founded in November. These two were harbingers of a Commercial Association, or Chamber of Commerce, launched at a meeting in September 1847. Rule 1 laid out the terms on which disparate members of the bourgeoisie could come together: "The objects of this association being solely and entirely for the consideration of mercantile subjects, calculated to benefit the general trade of the town and neighbourhood of Blackburn, all discussions of a political character are expressly prohibited." BRL, "Minutes and Reports of the proceedings of the Blackburn Associations for the effecting the abolition of the East India Company's Monopoly of Salt, and reduction of the duty on Tea, and of the Commercial Association from Sep. 24, 1846 to Febr. 9, 1848."

⁹· R. J. Morris and Richard Rodger, "An Introduction to British Urban History, 1820-1914," in *The Victorian City: A Reader in British Urban History 1820-1914*, ed. idem (London: Longman, 1993), 34.

¹⁰· E.g., *BM*, Feb. 27, 1811; LRO, Allen Collection, DP 281/37, "Report of the Committee for the Relief of the Poor resident in the Township of Little Bolton," 1817 (partly distributing funds from the London Association for the Relief of the Manufacturing and Labouring Poor); *BM*, Jan. 19, 1820, p. 2.

¹¹· PRO, HO 40/20, J. W. Whittaker to Francis Fortune, London, May 8, 1826. For reports of the distress, see, e.g., HO 40/19, Fletcher to Hobhouse, Feb. 23, 1826; Messrs. Cunliffe to ?, Apr. 22; J. W. Paget to ?, Apr. 27; J. W. Whittaker to Eckersley, Apr. 15. Also note HO 40/21, the deposition of the county gentlemen assembled as the grand jury for the county palatine at the summer assizes in Lancaster, Aug. 12, on the distress.

¹²· HO 40/19, select vestry and other principal inhabitants of Lower Darwen to Peel, May 1, 1826.

¹³· HO 40/19, Thomas Rogerson to Peel, Apr. 12, 1826, plus enclosure of printed appeal from Whittaker. For one expression of "Sincere and Unfeigned thanks" for relief, see *BM*, Apr. 12, 1826, p. 3. The distress does not seem to have been as great in Preston (*PC*, Apr. 15, 1826, p. 3). Horrocks and Miller were still paying the same wages in April that they had been a year earlier, and only one factory in town was

closed. A public meeting chaired by the mayor was not well attended by the respectable, and those present were divided on whether to start a subscription or to continue to rely on the poor rate (still only 9 1/2d. in the pound). When a Mr. Huffman claimed that those opposing a subscription wanted to pauperize the people so that they could not vote in the coming election, the mayor, Nicholas Grimshaw, dissolved the meeting without a resolution.

[14.] HO 40/19, Whittaker to Eckersley, Apr. 22; Slade to Peel, Apr. 29, May 3; Hulton to ?, May 4. And see HO 40/20, Whittaker to W. H. Hyett, July 7. For other expressions of joy at monarchical donations, HO 40/19, inhabitants of Lower Darwen to Peel, May 3; Rogerson to Peel, May 20. See also LRO, Allen Papers, DP 282/9, London Manufacturers' Relief Committee exhortation to the distressed to be obedient and patient, May 6.

[15.] For example, *PC*, May 13, 1826, p. 3, drew attention to the charity of William Heatley of Brindle Lodge, who for two months had been distributing £20-worth of provisions and money a day in Hoghton Bottoms. A letter of May 16 (*PC*, May 20, p. 4) from John Banning of the Hoghton relief committee also pointed to the considerable aid of Sir H. P. Hoghton and William Feilden. The contrast was with places with no resident gentry to alleviate the distress. According to the London Committee on October 25 (LRO, Allen Collection, DP 281/43, appeals, extracts and remittances of the London Committee, Dec. 1826), in the townships of Salesbury, Clayton-le-Dale, Wilpshire, Dinkley, and Osbaldeston, "it is the misfortune of this district to be without a single resident family of property by whom the wants of the poor may be alleviated, as has been very liberally done in many surrounding places."

[16.] HO 40/19, Rogerson to Peel, May 20; HO 40/21, printed resolutions of meeting, Aug. 12; McAdam to James McAdam (his son), Aug. 13; to J. C. [Herries?], Sept. 6; to E. Mortimer, Sept. 6; A. L. Howarth to Neville and Eccles, Sept. 9; Byng to Peel, Oct. 7; Rogerson to Peel, Dec. 11. For local committee compliance with the London resolution to discontinue gratuitous relief, *BM*, Sept. 20, 1826, p. 3. For the mixed results of public works projects in Darwen (including making a reservoir for the papermakers), Turton, and Bolton (where the weavers were not suited to roadwork and little roadmaking was done), see PRO, MH 12/5594, circular of Poor Law commissioners, Dec. 24, 1840, evidence of John Ashworth Jr. For the public-works building of a new well at Alleys Spring, Blackburn, *BM*, Oct. 11, 1826, p. 3. For an example of relief expenditure, including work on the roads in Great Harwood and the turnpike from Fecit Brow to Accrington, LRO, PR 163, Great Harwood Relief Committee, 1826-27: Thomas Carr to Rev. Robert Dobson (printed), Sept. 6; W. H. Hyett to Dobson, Sept. 2 (and draft reply on reverse); PR 163/5, Relief Book.

[17.] PP 1841 (ii), II, 261, "Copies of Extracts of Correspondence between Home Office and Poor Law Commissioners on subject of Distress in Bolton; with Report of Assistant Commissioner sent by Her Majesty's Government to inquire into alleged Cases of Destitution and Death," 1-9; PP 1842, XXXV, 69, "Copies of Communications to Home Office regarding Mott's Report; &c": especially p. 3, evidence of Nancy Beswick, weaver, and William Coop, combmaker; pp. 6-7, 13, statement of Naisby; pp. 14-15, 19-20, replies of Mott; pp. 16-18, petition to Graham of Edmund Ashworth, John Entwisle, George Knott, Jacob Lomax, James Barry, Thomas Lee, Thomas Thomasson, John Goodbrand, James Haigh, John Mackinnell, John Vickers, Robert Walsh, and Nathaniel Wilson. (A copy of this letter is also in PRO, MH 12/5594, Bowring to Graham, Dec. 14, 1841.) MH 12/5594, Naisby to Woodhouse, Sept. 11, 1841; Mott to commissioners, Sept. 24, Dec. 24; Bowring to Graham, Dec. 14, expressing his dissatisfaction at the biased nature of Mott's investigation; *BFP*, Sept. 25,

1841, p. 2. See also Henry Ashworth to Richard Cobden (BL, Cobden Papers, Add. MS 43653, Sept. 24, 1841) on the commissioners' investigations of Bowring's statements.

[18.] Archibald Prentice, *History of the Anti-Corn-Law League* (1853; reprint, London: Cass, 1968), I: 270-71.

[19.] Quoted in ibid., 281-82. And see W. Cooke Taylor, *Notes of a Tour in the Manufacturing Districts of Lancashire*, 3rd ed. (New York: A. M. Kelley, 1968), 40, 167-79.

[20.] Cooke Taylor, *Tour in the Manufacturing Districts*, 42-43.

[21.] BALS, Poor Protection Society Reports 1841-58, B361 BOL, "Report of the Bolton Society for the Protection of the Poor," Bolton, 1841; *BFP*, July 4, 1840, p. 1.

[22.] Bolton District Provident Society Report, 1840, pp. 30-33.

[23.] 1842 Report, 7-11.

[24.] 1841 Report, 7-8; 1842 Report, 9-10; PRO, MH 12/5594, Mott to commissioners, Dec. 24, 1841.

[25.] As did the revived Blackburn relief committee. *BS*, Dec. 1, 1841, pp. 1, 3; Nov. 17, p. 2.

[26.] Arrowsmith, *Essay on Mechanics' Institutes, with a Particular Relation to the Institute Recently Established in Bolton* (Bolton, 1825), 5, 7, 10, 12-13, 15-20, 23-26.

[27.] "The First Annual Report of the Bolton Mechanics Institute," Bolton (1826), 5, 8, 12. The annual subscription for mechanics was 10s., half price for members' sons under 21 and fatherless orphans (pp. 9-10).

[28.] BALS, Reports of the Bolton Mechanics Institute: Report for 1830-1 (from *BC*, Oct. 8, 1831).

[29.] Barrie M. Ratcliffe and W. H. Chaloner, trans. and ed., *A French Sociologist Looks at Britain: Gustave d'Eichthal and British Society in 1828* (Manchester: Manchester University Press, 1977), 93.

[30.] Reports for 1833-34 (*BC*, Sept. 27, 1834); 1835-36 (*BFP*, Jan. 21, 1837); 1836-37 (*BFP*, Sept. 30, 1837); 1837-38; 1838-39.

[31.] BALS, Heywood Papers, ZHE/37, 16th Annual Report of Bolton Mechanics' Institution, Oct. 1, 1841, indicates that the trustees were still bipartisan, but the hon. committee members were apparently all liberal. The "general" members of the committee were "mechanics": two tailors, a cutler, a wire worker, a printer, three mechanics, a clerk, a spinner, a bookkeeper, a plumber, two schoolmasters, and a moulder.

[32.] Reports, 1840-41; 1846-47 (*BC*, Oct. 30, 1847); 1847-48 (*BC*, Nov. 4, 1848); 1849-50 (*BC*, Oct. 26, 1850) (when it was noted that from the library "A vast proportion of the works taken out has been works of fiction, a taste for which class of reading is indulged in to an extent which is incompatible with true mental culture and healthy intellectual progress"); 1850-51 (*BC*, Nov. 8, 1851).

[33.] Joseph Livesey had organized a meeting for the same purpose on September 11, 1828. Six people showed up. This was one of a number of his attempts to establish reading rooms for the working classes. See the *Autobiography of Joseph Livesey* (London [1881?]), 41-43.

[34.] PC, Nov. 15, 1828, p. 3. According to Peter Whittle, *The History of the Borough of Preston* (Preston, 1837), II: 280-82, John Gilbertson, surgeon, played a key role.

[35.] Alison Andrew, "The Working Class and Education in Preston 1830-1870: A Study of Social Relations" (Ph.D. diss., Leicester University, 1987), 139-41.

[36.] LRO, QDS/1/4/131, Preston Institution for the Diffusion of Knowledge, Oct. 1837.

[37.] PC, Apr. 21, 1849, p. 4; Apr. 28, pp. 4, 7; *The Preston Institution Bazaar Gazette*, 4, Apr. 30, 1849, p. 2; Hewitson, *Preston*, 449-50.

[38.] BRL, B374.2, Minute Book for the Mechanics' Institution, 1844-46: Mar. 27, Apr. 4, 1844.

[39.] *BS,* Jan. 5, 1848, p. 3.

[40.] Whittle, *Blackburn,* 32-33. Darwen had its own Mechanics' Institute, founded in February 1839 largely by the clerical and manufacturing elite. Reflecting the prevalence of Nonconformity in the village, the main elite patronage of the institute was liberal. See Margaret B. S. Doyle, "Social Control in Over Darwen, Lancashire" (MA thesis, Lancaster University, 1972), 47-48; *BS,* Jan. 26, 1848, p. 3.

[41.] LRO, HRPD, Preston Dispensary, "Draft First Report, Oct. 1809-Oct. 1810"; Derby to John Taylor, Nov. 25, 1809. See also "Marmaduke Tulketh" [Peter Whittle], *History of Preston,* vol. I, *A Topographical, Statistical, and Historical Account of the Borough of Preston* (Preston, 1821), 80-81.

[42.] Meg Whittle, "Philanthropy in Preston: The Changing Face of Charity in a 19th Century Provincial Town" (Ph.D. diss., Lancaster University, 1990), 99-100; HRPD, report of Oct. 26, 1835.

[43.] HRPD, Chew to S. Crane, Nov. 14, 1814; to John Taylor, Nov. 19; ? to committee, Nov. 23; memo of general meeting of Dec. 16.

[44.] HRPD, 2nd report, Oct. 1811, and ff.; 7th report, Oct. 1816; 8th report, Oct. 1817; William Taylor, Thomas Troughton, and James Bell, overseers, to committee, June 10, 1823; Thomas Birchall to committee, June 14, 1823; 15th report, Oct. 1824; 20th report, Oct. 24, 1829; AGM, Oct. 25, 1832. And see Whittle, *Preston,* II: 128, 135; John V. Pickstone, *Medicine and Industrial Society: A History of Hospital Development in Manchester and its Region, 1752-1946* (Manchester: Manchester University Press, 1985), 69-71; Meg Whittle, "Philanthropy in Preston," 88-89, 102-4, 108-11.

[45.] HRPD, committee minutes, Jan. 27, Feb. 3, 5, June 9, Oct. 26, 1835, Jan. 5, 1836; note of Alexander Moore, William Alexander, J. H. Norris, Robert Brown, Richard Inman, and James Harrison, Jan. 28, 1835; *The Lancet,* Nov. 21, 1835, pp. 297-99, letter of Brown, Inman, and Harrison (dated Nov. 12).

[46.] BALS, Bolton Dispensary Minute Book 1813-18, HBO/1/1/1, Dec. 2, 11, 1813, Mar. 4, 1814.

[47.] BALS, HBO/1/10/1, Bolton Infirmary Reports 1818-60, 1818-19 Report, 4-5, 21, 23-24.

[48.] This in spite of the comment of a later report (1831-32, p. 7) that "That individual is but a poor philanthropist, whose motive in helping his fellow creatures is the anticipation of their gratitude."

[49.] LRO, Allen Collection, DP 282/22, printed letter from Black to the subscribers to the Bolton Dispensary, Sept. 22, 1823; /23, printed letter from the surgeons to the dispensary, presented at the monthly committee meeting on Oct. 3, 1823.

[50.] Reports for 1825-26, pp. 3-4; 1826-27, pp. 10, 12; 1827-28, pp. 6-7; 1828-29, pp. 3-5, 11; 1829-30, pp. 4-6.

[51.] Reports for 1830-31, pp. 4-5, 7; 1836-37, pp. 3-4, 6; 1837-38, pp. 3-5; 1838-39, pp. 4-5.

[52.] Report for 1841-42, p. 4.

[53.] Report for 1843-44, p. 4.

[54.] Report for 1845-46, p. 3.

[55.] Reports for 1840-41, p. 10; 1844-45, pp. 3-5, 22; 1846-47, pp. 3, 5; 1847-48, p. 4.

[56.] Report for 1848-49, pp. 3-5.

[57.] Reports for 1849-50, pp. 3-5; 1850-51, pp. 4, 6; 1851-52, pp. 4-5.

[58.] *BC,* Mar. 4, 1848, p. 5.

[59.] Though the overseers had employed a surgeon to attend paupers since at least 1794 (Pickstone, *Medicine and Society*, 72), and, according to the obituary of one such surgeon (*Memoirs of Mr. James H. Wood, Late Surgeon, &c. &c. To the Dispensary and Work House, at Blackburn*, 2nd ed. (London, 1816)), who died in 1814, there was some kind of rate-supported dispensary for paupers. The charity General Dispensary was for non-paupers as well.

[60.] This ignored smaller-scale institutions like the Preston House of Recovery.

[61.] BRL, B614, Blackburn General Dispensary Annual Reports 1824-34, 1st Report (prepared for AGM at start of 1825).

[62.] Adam Cottam £200, James Cunliffe £100, Joseph Feilden £500, William Feilden £300, John Fleming £150, John Hornby £300, John Lister £150, Henry Sudell £300, and John Turner £150.

[63.] See LRO, DD Pr/50/6, Report of Blackburn Infirmary, Dec. 12, 1862.

[64.] BRL, B614, 2nd-11th Reports (1826-35).

[65.] W. E. Moss, *Blackburn's First Temperance Society Centenary: Its Origin and History* (Blackburn, 1931; reprinted from *BT*, Apr. 4 and 11, 1931), pp. 6-8; *BA*, Aug. 27, 1832, p. 8. Note that, in spite of Whittaker and Skinner working together, this did not prevent the pair of them having a bitter public dispute over religion in 1836 (see above, chap. 6). On the reasons behind and timing of the anti-spirits crusade, see Brian Harrison, *Drink and the Victorians: The Temperance Question in England 1815-1872* (Pittsburgh: University of Pittsburgh Press, 1971), 91ff.

[66.] D. O'Connor, "The Temperance Movement in Bolton" (typescript in BALS, 1974), 3-4.

[67.] *BFP*, Jan. 4, 1840; O'Connor, "Temperance Movement," 6, 20, 25-26, 30-31, 37-41.

[68.] Moss, *Blackburn's First Temperance Society*, 5, 9-11.

[69.] *PC*, Mar. 24, 1832, p. 3.

[70.] Frank Hodgkinson, "The Social Origins of the Teetotal Movement in Preston 1820-1835" (Cert. Ed. thesis, Chorley College of Education, 1974), 46-47, 52-53, 58-59, 61, 68, 71-73; Harrison, *Drink*, 113-26, 134-38, 169; Thomas Walmsley, *Reminiscences of the Preston Cockpit and the Old Teetotallers* (Preston, 1892), 52-63; idem, *The First Juvenile Temperance Society* (Preston, 1892), 5-8; LRO, DDPR 130/24, Fleetwood to Henry Bradley (secretary to Preston Temperance Society), Jan. 26, 1835; 130/25, Townley Parker to Bradley, Oct. 20, 1838.

[71.] Rev. Walter Lowe Clay, *The Prison Chaplain: A Memoir of the Rev. John Clay, B.D.* (Cambridge, 1861), 494-96 (quotation on p. 496).

[72.] LRO, QGR/2/14, "General Report of Preston House of Correction," 1827; and see /20, Chaplain's Report, Oct. 1829.

[73.] LRO, QGR/2/29, Chaplain's Report, Oct. 1839, p. 9.

[74.] LRO, QGR/2, Chaplain's Reports, /34, Dec. 1850, pp. 51, 54, 56; Dec. 1849, pp. 47-49, 52; /40, Oct. 1845, p. 6.

[75.] Rudd, *An Address . . . May 13 1811; At the Commencement of a Course of Lectures to the Society, on Natural and Experimental Philosophy* (Preston, 1811), 9-10. And see Roy Porter, "Science, Provincial Culture and Public Opinion in Enlightenment England," *British Journal of Eighteenth-Century Studies* 3 (1980): 20-46.

[76.] PRL, Minutes of the Preston Literary and Philosophical Society, Mar. 12, 20, Apr. 30, May 3, 14, Dec. 3, 1810, Jan. 13, 20, Nov. 23, Dec. 7, 1812, Jan. 6, Apr. 12, May 3, Oct. 20, 1813, Apr. 30, Nov. 13, 1816, May 29 [1817?].

[77.] Hewitson, *Preston*, 298-99; Marian Roberts, *The Story of Winckley Square, Preston* (Preston, 1988), 50; Hardwick, *Preston*, 451-52.

[78.] Rainforth, *Address to the Bolton Philosophical and Literary Society*, read Aug. 13, 1813; LRO, Allen Collection, DP 282/14, printed circular of Oct. 18, 1813. The members were to meet once a month for two hours. Literary and philosophical intelligence from members or correspondents was to occupy no more than the first half hour, and any essay no longer than the second. The final hour was to be given over to conversation on the essay.

[79.] *BM*, Aug. 27, 1823, p. 2; George C. Miller, *Blackburn: The Evolution of a Cotton Town* (Blackburn, 1951), 222; *BS*, Oct. 30, 1844, p. 3; Nov. 6.

[80.] Edwin Butterworth, *A Statistical Sketch of the County Palatine of Lancaster* (London, 1841), 9; Moss, *Blackburn's First Temperance Society*, 10-11.

[81.] There were, naturally, exceptions. For example, the Horrockses had an impressive library at Penwortham Lodge (*A Catalogue of the Library at Penwortham Lodge. A.D. 1823* (Preston)), John Skaife of Blackburn, surgeon, collector and bibliophile, had around ten thousand volumes (Abram, *Blackburn Characters*, 103); and Edward Pedder of the Preston banking family had a fine collection at Dove Nest, Ambleside (Hall, ed., *Miss Weeton*, 255, letter to Mrs. Whitehead, Apr. 18, 1810: "The collection is numerous, valuable, and well selected. How rich I should be in books if I had all in Mr P's library that had never been read.")

[82.] Tom Dunne, "A History of Public Libraries in Bolton from the Beginnings to 1974" (Ph.D. diss., Strathclyde University, 1981), 46ff. Thomas Thomasson, in a letter to the Rev. Robert Best, Feb. 4, 1871 (BALS, Bolton Biographical Notes, B1, obit., 1876), described the three circulating libraries in town around 1820: the Church and King; Gowland's in Mealhouse Lane; and Kell's in Deansgate, where he obtained copies of Hume, Smollett, Gibbon, the British essayists and poets, and Byron in mutilated editions.

[83.] *BC*, Sept. 9, 1837, p. 2.

[84.] Dunne, "Libraries in Bolton," 85-91; LRO, Allen Collection, DP 282/10, printed letter from J. Gardner, librarian, to Allen, Aug. 20, 1818.

[85.] BALS, Heywood Papers, ZHE/24/3, draft of Heywood to various newspapers [Mar. 1829].

[86.] Ibid.

[87.] LRO, Allen Collection, DP 282/18, notice of Nov. 2, 1827, for annual meeting; BALS, Exchange Newsroom subscribers' names for 1848.

[88.] *BFP*, Dec. 26, 1835, p. 23, letter of Heywood indicating the lack of public support. On the newsroom and its travails, see Dunne, "Libraries in Bolton," 105-11; and for a small subscription newsroom at the Ship Inn, at least in 1816-23, p. 85.

[89.] James T. Heyes, "Libraries in Blackburn: A History of the Major Library Institutions from 1787 to 1974" (FLA thesis, 1979), 25-27, 33-36, 44-47.

[90.] BRL, "Exchange News Room a/c's &c."

[91.] Whittle, *Preston*, I: 45-46; DDPR 138/30, "Rules for the . . . Preston Subscription Library, agreed to at a General Meeting of the Subscribers held February 21st, 1825," cited in Susan Bullen, "The Cultural Life of Preston 1742-1842" (MA thesis, Leicester University, 1970), 43-44; Butterworth, *Statistical Sketch*, 113; Hardwick, *Preston*, 448-49, 452; LRO, QDS/1/4/126, Preston Law Library.

[92.] Dunne "Libraries in Bolton," 161ff.

[93.] But they did print one of Wilson's poems that referred to "foul winds," "Jupiter's thunder," and peas; but perhaps the scatological double entendre was lost on the editors.

[94.] *Records of the Preston Oyster and Parched Pea Club 1773-1841* (Preston, 1861, reprinted from *PC*); LRO, Pedder Papers, DDPd 25/27, extracts concerning the Oyster

Club from Richard Pedder's Commonplace Book; Rev. F. R. Raines, *Miscellanies: Being a Selection from the Poems and Correspondence of the Rev. Thomas Wilson, B.D.* (Manchester, 1857), 100-102, 148 n. 1.

[95.] B. T. Barton, *Historical Gleanings of Bolton and District* (Bolton, 1881), 1st ser., I: 139-45; LRO, DDHu 53/82/11.

[96.] *BM*, June 4, 1828, p. 3. As Sack, *Jacobite to Conservative*, notes, p. 103, Pitt Clubs did nothing more than this to promote a right-wing agenda. They did not act as a point of organization for the distribution of loyal pamphlets or for serious discussion of political matters. For a dinner of the Preston Pitt Club at The Mitre, May 28, 1822, see Whittle, *Preston*, II: 110-11.

[97.] BALS, Heywood papers, ZHE/18-27, Robert Heywood to editor of *Morning Chronicle*, Mar. 15, 1828; George Harris, *Letter to the Inhabitants of Bolton on Church and King Clubs* (Liverpool, 1825); an address in *BC*, from "A Dissenter," to the Church and King Club (included in Heywood Papers, ZHE/24/3 [Mar. 1829]).

[98.] *BFP*, Sept. 6, 1845, p. 2.

[99.] *BC*, Oct. 13, 1827, p. 4.

[100.] Whittle, *Bolton*, 140.

[101.] Henry Whittaker, *The Union Club, Blackburn 1849-1949: A Short History* (Blackburn, 1950), 4-12.

[102.] John Taylor, *Autobiography of a Lancashire Lawyer, Being the Life and Recollections of John Taylor, Attorney-at-Law, And First Coroner of the Borough of Bolton* (Bolton, 1883), 122-24. Also see BALS, "Diary of Charles James Darbishire of Rivington, J.P., for 1852" (incomplete copy), for references to the Delta Club, e.g., Feb. 11, Mar. 10.

[103.] Taylor, *Autobiography*, 68-69.

[104.] Hewitson, *Preston*, 250; Hardwick, *Preston*, 453; Whittle, *Preston*, I: 39-41, writes in 1821 of the newsroom at the Guild Hall, one nearly opposite the Bull Inn, and minor newsrooms at The Mitre, The George, and The Castle.

[105.] BALS, "Rules of the Bolton Billiard Club," Bolton (1847).

[106.] BRL, "Rules of Blackburn Subscription Bowling Green," Blackburn (1850), 10-11.

[107.] *BS*, June 25, 1845; Dec. 5, 1849, p. 1.

[108.] James Watkins, "The Hollins Leases 1756-1829 and Reminiscences of the Hollins 1830-1842" (typescript in BALS, 1902), 19-20.

[109.] Whittle, *Preston*, I: 43, II: 106; *Catalogue of Books Belonging to the Preston Natural History Society* (Preston, 1827); *PC*, Mar. 26, 1826, p. 2; DDPR 37/91, "Rules of Preston Floral and Horticultural Society," 1844 (the mayor, John Addison, president).

[110.] *BC*, July 12, 1834, p. 1; LRO, Clifton Papers, DDCl 1188/37, William Henry Turner to P. Fair, Sept. 9, 1840 (re Blackburn Agricultural Society); 1188/50, William Jackson to Fair, Sept. 1840 (re Preston Agricultural Society).

[111.] LRO, DDPR 37/80, "Report of proceedings of Preston Phrenological Society," Apr. 1839.

[112.] *BS*, Oct. 30, 1844, p. 3; Nov. 6.

[113.] Such as the Preston Catch and Glee Club (PRL, "Preston Catch and Glee Club—Rules, Minutes, &c."), going strong in the thirties and rather less elitist than many of the other organizations (though the admission fee was 2s. 6d., with an additional 12s. 6d. per annum for refreshments).

[114.] LRO, Allen Collection, DP 282/17, notice of concert, Dec. 4, 1823.

[115.] Abram, *Blackburn Characters*, 111-14; *BS*, Nov. 27, 1850, p. 2.

116. *BC*, June 1, 1850, p. 5; Whittle, *Preston*, I: 42, reports a choral society in Preston from 1819. H. C. Robbins Landon, "Music," in *The Cambridge Cultural History of Britain*, vol. 6, *The Romantic Age in Britain*, ed. Boris Ford (Cambridge: Cambridge University Press, 1992), 247, notes that *The Messiah* and *The Creation* were the most popular with choral societies in the Anglo-Saxon world, only rivaled toward mid-century by *Elijah* (first performed in 1846, in Birmingham Town Hall).

117. LRO, QDS/2/1/45, Lodge of Peace and Unity, Preston; QDS/2/1/13, Society of Benevolence, Blackburn, 1799; QDS 2/1/28 and 2/2/14, Lodge of Anchor and Hope, Bolton, Sept. 7, 1799 and Mar. 22, 1800; QDS 2/1/14 and 2/2/5, Lodge of Antiquity, Bolton, Sept. 6, 1799 and Mar. 22, 1800; QDS 2/1/31, 2/2/25, 2/3/27, 2/4/2, 2/5/10, Lodge of St. John (later of His Grace the Duke of Atholl), Bolton, Sept. 6, 1799, Mar. 19, 1800, Mar. 1801, Feb. 25, 1802, Mar. 14, 1803; Brother James Rostron, *History of the Lodge of Fidelity, No. 269, 1788-1914* (Blackburn, 1914), passim and membership roll; BRL, B366.1/Fid., "Copy of an Address Presented by the Freemasons of Blackburn, to Mrs. Henry Brock-Hollinshead," Mar. 19, 1858.

118. BALS, Bolton Biographical Notes, B1, portrait of Stephen Blair, 122-23.

119. *BM*, Feb. 16, 1820, p. 3; Feb. 23, p. 3.

120. *BFP*, June 30, 1838, p. 3; *PC*, June 30, supplement.

121. *BC*, Apr. 25, 1829, p. 4.

122. *PC*, May 20, 1837, p. 2; May 27, p. 3.

123. Grimshaw, *Cogitations*, 108-12; Brimelow, *Political and Parliamentary*, 364-65.

124. *BS*, Apr. 24, 1844, p. 3.

125. *PP*, Apr. 2, 1842, p. 2. And see eulogy on Mar. 26, p. 3.

126. *BC*, Sept. 9, 1848, p. 8.

127. *BC*, Feb. 25, 1832, p. 4; Mar. 3, p. 4.

128. William Alexander Abram, *Preston Guild Merchant, 1882. Memorials of the Preston Guilds* (Preston, 1882, reprinted from *PG*), 113 (quoting *Harrop's Manchester Mercury*, Aug. 31, 1802), and passim.

129. Ibid., 117.

130. *The Kaleidoscope*, quoted by Abram, *Guild*, 125. For further details of the 1822 Guild, see Isaac Wilcockson, *Authentic Records of the Guild Merchant of Preston, 1822* (Preston, 1822).

131. *A Full and Detailed Account of the Guild Merchant of Preston* (Preston, 1842).

132. Though the correspondent for the *Illustrated London News* (clipping in LRO, Horrocks, Crewdson and Co. Papers, DDHs/75) thought that some of rank and from a distance had been deterred "owing to the recent riots in the borough. It has indeed been rumoured that the Chartists would endeavour to get up a meeting or counter demonstration; but, from the excellent arrangements of the mayor and magistrates, any such attempt would have been immediately frustrated."

133. Abram, *Guild*, 138-42. For the ladies' procession, with the ladies walking two and two, with a gentleman on either side, from the town hall to the parish church along a matted path, see Campbell B. A. G. Hulton, *Gleanings*, Sept. 7, 1842, quoted by Hogg, *Hulton Diaries*, 15. The distance between plebeian and patrician activities was revealed quite clearly in the pricing of admission. In 1822, for example, no one could attend a ball, concert, or oratorio for less than half a guinea. See R. D. Parker, "The Changing Character of Preston Guild Merchant 1762-1862," *Northern History* 20 (1984): 119.

134. BALS, Ainsworth Papers, ZAH/4/1, Sept. 2-13, Nov. 6, 1822, Apr. 21, 23, 1824, Jan. 11, 1825; /2, Jan. 9, 1833.

135. *BM*, Apr. 27, 1814, quoted by Abram, "Sketches," vol. 2 (*PG*, Nov. 1, 1879).

[136.] LRO, Allen Collection, DP 282/15, notice of Bolton Assemblies for the 1816-17 season; *BC*, Oct. 13, 1827, p. 1; Feb. 2, 1828, p. 1.

[137.] *PC*, Jan. 25, 1845, p. 3.

[138.] *BS*, Mar. 13, 1850, p. 2.

[139.] BALS, B708 (P. B.) BOL, *Bolton Dispensary. Catalogue of the Exhibition of Pictures . . . 28th June, 1838.*

[140.] *PC*, Nov. 25, 1837, p. 2. On exhibitions and museums as means of conciliation and instruction of the working classes, see Tony Bennett, "The Exhibitionary Complex," in *Culture/Power/History: A Reader in Contemporary Social Theory*, ed. Nicholas B. Dirks, Geoff Eley, and Sherry B. Ortner (Princeton: Princeton University Press, 1994).

[141.] Whittle, *Preston*, II: 150, 169; *PC*, Dec. 16, 1837, p. 3; Dec. 23, p. 3.

[142.] *PC*, Nov. 9, 1839, pp. 2-3; *Catalogue of the Preston Exhibition of Works of Art, Models, &c. At the Corn-Exchange* (Preston, 1840). For a discussion of art and exhibitions in northern cities, see Caroline Arscott, "'Without Distinction of Party': the Polytechnic Exhibitions in Leeds 1839-45," and John Seed, "'Commerce and the Liberal Arts': the Political Economy of Art in Manchester, 1775-1860," in *The Culture of Capital: Art, Power and the Nineteenth-Century Middle Class*, ed. Janet Wolff and John Seed (Manchester: Manchester University Press, 1988). Also the essays in Alan Kidd and David Nicholls, eds., *Gender, Civic Culture and Consumerism: Middle-Class Identity in Britain, 1800-1940* (Manchester: Manchester University Press, 1999).

[143.] *BC*, Dec. 22, 1849, p. 4; Dec. 29, p. 5; Jan. 5, 1850, p. 1.

[144.] *PC*, Nov. 30, 1850, p. 5.

Notes to Chapter 9

[1.] Gilbert J. French, *The Life and Times of Samuel Crompton*, 2nd ed. (Manchester, 1860), 119; Archibald Sparke, *Bibliographia Boltoniensis* (Manchester, 1913), 65-66.

[2.] A line from the rules in the Ashworth's Turton Mill, quoted by William Dodd, *The Factory System Illustrated in a Series of Letters to the Right Honourable Lord Ashley* (1841; reprint, New York: A. M. Kelley, 1968), 88.

[3.] PP 1834, X, "Report from S. C. on Hand-Loom Weavers' Petitions," 428, evidence of Richard Needham, a Bolton weaver.

[4.] C. Bruyn Andrews, ed., *The Torrington Diaries* (New York: Barnes and Noble, 1970), III: 110-17, entries for June 23, 1792 ff. And see John Holt, *General View of the Agriculture of the County of Lancaster* (London, 1795), 213: "Another evil arising from manufactories is, the propagation of vice, insubordination, and diseases."

[5.] Thomas Dunham Whitaker, *An History of Richmondshire* (London, 1823), I: 15.

[6.] Ibid., II: 432-33. See also idem, *An History of the Original Parish of Whalley*, 4th ed. (London, 1872), II: 140-43, 232, 388, 576-77; idem, *Loidis and Elmete* (Leeds, 1816), 380. For similar sentiments, see the Rev. S. J. Allen in his obituary for Whitaker, *Gentleman's Magazine*, cited in John Gough Nichols, "Biographical Memoirs of Thomas Dunham Whitaker," preface to Whitaker, *Whalley*, 4th ed., xlviii; John Britton and Edward Wedlake Brayley, *Beauties of England and Wales*, vol. IX, *A Topographical and Historical Description of Lancashire* (London, 1810), 251. For critiques of Whitaker, see Edward Baines, *History of the County Palatine and Duchy of Lancaster*, 1st ed. (London, 1836), I: vi, IV: 367; Charles Hardwick, *History of the Borough of Preston and its Environs* (Preston, 1857), 380-81.

[7.] John Corry, *The History of Lancashire* (London, 1825), II: 162-63, 165-66, 265, 333-34 (quotation), 340-43, 351-52.

8. James Black, *A Medico-Topographical, Geological, and Statistical Sketch of Bolton and its Neighbourhood* (Bolton, 1837), 57, 61.

9. *BC*, Feb. 16, 1850, p. 5.

10. Franklin Baker, *The Moral Tone of the Factory System Defended* (London, 1850), 10 (quotation), 11, 13-16, 19-21, 25-26.

11. LRO, QGR/2/14, "General Report of Preston House of Correction," 1827; Chaplain's Report, Dec. 1849, pp. 53-54. See also the comment of R. Raynsford Jackson, cotton manufacturer, during a debate on the incorporation of the borough of Blackburn (*BS*, Dec. 4, 1850, pp. 1-3): "He wished to ask whether in a manufacturing town, we should always require to have the same police force. ('No, no.') Were not the great mass of the population during the day enclosed in the mills, and, at night, fatigued with toil, did they not seek repose, instead of disturbing the peace, and thus giving employment to the police force? (Applause.) But there were times when these people were not employed, and it was unfortunate that there were idle people, there were also evil-disposed people. (Hear, hear.) Then it was that an extensive and powerful police force were required."

12. See Theodore Koditschek, *Class Formation and Urban-Industrial Society: Bradford, 1750-1850* (Cambridge: Cambridge University Press, 1990), 414-15, 422-23; David Roberts, *Paternalism in Early Victorian England* (New Brunswick, NJ: Rutgers University Press, 1979); Patrick Joyce, "Work," in *The Cambridge Social History of Britain 1750-1950*, ed. F. M. L. Thompson (Cambridge: Cambridge University Press, 1990), II: 168-69.

13. Edward Baines Jr., "Cotton Manufacture," in *County of Lancaster*, by Baines, II: 508-9, 516-17, 521.

14. See Patrick Joyce, *Work, Society and Politics: The Culture of the Factory in Later Victorian England* (Brighton: Harvester Press, 1980), chap. 4.

15. *BM*, Dec. 11, 1805, p. 3; Jan. 9, 1799, p. 3; Jan. 10, 1810, p. 3; Nov. 1, 1809, p. 3; Nov. 8, 1809, p. 3.

16. See E. P. Thompson, "The Moral Economy of the English Crowd in the Eighteenth Century," *P&P* 50 (Feb. 1971): 76-136; idem, *The Making of the English Working Class* (London, 1980), passim; Douglas Hay and Nicholas Rogers, *Eighteenth-Century English Society: Shuttles and Swords* (Oxford: Oxford University Press, 1997), chap. 7; Koditschek, *Class Formation*, 67, 74; Martin Daunton, *Progress and Poverty: An Economic and Social History of Britain 1700-1850* (Oxford: Oxford University Press, 1995), 16, 117, 327-30, 484-85, and passim; John Rule, *Albion's People: English Society, 1714-1815* (London: Longman, 1992), 28-29; idem, *The Vital Century: England's Developing Economy 1714-1815* (London: Longman, 1992), 78-79, 313-14. For example, parliamentary reports on the question of a minimum wage for weavers (e.g., PP 1809, III; PP 1811, II), a response to extensive agitation, came down firmly against any interference of the legislature in the liberty of every individual to dispose of his time and labor. See John Dinwiddy, "Luddism and Politics in the Northern Counties," *SH* 4 (Jan. 1979): 37.

17. Edwin Chadwick, *Report on the Sanitary Condition of the Labouring Population of Great Britain, 1842* (Edinburgh: Edinburgh University Press, 1965, with an introduction by M. W. Flinn), 303-4, testimony of Henry Ashworth.

18. Leon Faucher, *Manchester in 1844: Its Present Condition and Future Prospects* (reprint, London: Cass, 1969), 113; PP 1846, VI (i), S. C. of Lords on Burdens on Real Property, 1846: Evidence of Henry Ashworth, 345; and see 321, Ashworth's statement that a fair return in the commercial world for manufacturing capital was considered to be 8 or 9 percent.

[19.] PP 1846, VI (i), S. C. Burdens on Real Property, 321; PP 1834, XX, "Supplementary Report of Factories Inquiry Commission," Part II: D1 Lancashire, 280.

[20.] See Roberts, *Paternalism*, 173-78 (and note his comment, 173, that "True paternalism is never without a dictatorial edge, and Henry Ashworth was a true paternalist"). For another example of a commonplace authoritarianism, see B. T. Barton, *Historical Gleanings of Bolton and District*, 1st ser. (Bolton, 1881), I: 65-67.

[21.] Timothy Grimshaw, *The Cogitations and Opinions of Timothy Grimshaw Esq.* (Bolton, 1839), 76.

[22.] Angus Bethune Reach, *Manchester and the Textile Districts*, ed. Chris Aspin, ([Rossendale]: Helmshore Local History Society, 1972), 65-69; Faucher, *Manchester*, 113; Dodd, *The Factory System*, 89-90, 92.

[23.] William Cooke Taylor, *Notes of a Tour in the Manufacturing Districts of Lancashire*, 3rd ed. (New York: A. M. Kelley, 1968), 30-36. On the internalization of values, see Henry Ashworth's comment in his *Letter to the Right Honourable Lord Ashley, on the Cotton Factory Question, and the Ten Hours' Factory Bill; with An Appendix, containing an Abstract of the Bill. By a Lancashire Cotton Spinner*, 17, reprinted in *British Labour Struggles: Contemporary Pamphlets 1727-1850: The Factory Act of 1833*, ed. Kenneth E. Carpenter (New York: Arno Press, 1972): there was a feeling of good order and wholesome discipline in his colony, and the workers appointed from among themselves a number of Sabbath-wardens or constables to apprehend and admonish idlers and enforce Sabbath regulations. These appointments, he claimed, were not enforced by him.

[24.] Reach, *Manchester and the Textile Districts*, 67; Dodd, *Factory System*, 83: The spinners were paid 10 percent less than the Bolton list of prices (see below, n. 97).

[25.] Cooke Taylor, *Tour in the Manufacturing Districts*, 163-64.

[26.] PP 1833, XX, "First Report of Factories Inquiry," E5, 7; Ashworth, *Letter to Ashley*, 28; PP 1834, XX, "Supplementary Report of Factories Inquiry Commission," Part II, D1, 281; PP 1846, VI (i), S. C. on Burdens on Real Property, 333-34, 340-41.

[27.] PP 1833, XX, "First Report of Factories Inquiry," E5, 7.

[28.] Faucher, *Manchester*, 112-13.

[29.] Whittle, *Bolton*, 372-74; P. John Smalley, "A Study of Model Villages with Particular Reference to Bank Top, Eagley and Egerton" (thesis, Manchester Polytechnic, 1983), 49-56. On the Philips dynasty, see David Brown, "From 'Cotton Lord' to Landed Aristocrat: the Rise of Sir George Philips Bart., 1766-1847," *BIHR* 69, 168 (Feb. 1996): 62-64 and passim; V. A. C. Gatrell, "The Commercial Middle Class in Manchester, c.1820-1857" (Ph.D. diss., Cambridge University, 1971), 160-65.

[30.] *Illustrated London News*, Oct. 25, 1851; Whittle, *Bolton*, 340-42. For details of the schools—the children paid 1 1/2d. a week, the proprietors paid for the teachers, coal, gas, books, and writing materials—see school inspector's report, 1848, contained in CMA, MS F 942.72 R121, Archdeacon Rushton's Visitation Returns, vol. 22, St. Paul's, Halliwell. As Robert Gray, *The Factory Question and Industrial England, 1830-1860* (Cambridge: Cambridge University Press, 1996), 137, n. 21, points out, Dean Mills was celebrated in fictional guise by Benjamin Disraeli, *Coningsby*, book IV, chaps. 1-3; by G. Jewsbury, *Marian Withers* (1851), II: 33-57; and by Frances Trollope, *The Life and Adventures of Michael Armstrong the Factory Boy* (1840; reprint, London: Cass, 1968), 236-38. But note that Roberts, *Paternalism*, 178, sees something of the Ashworths in Disraeli's Mr. Millbank in *Coningsby* and in his Mr. Trafford in *Sybil*.

[31.] This did not preclude some of these Manchester Men from having or developing extensive landed connections themselves. On the Philipses, see Brown, "From 'Cotton

Lord' to Landed Aristocrat," 62-82; on Bazley, ("the epitome of Manchester man"), who became a large landowner in Oxfordshire and Gloucestershire, see Anthony Howe, "The Business Community," in *The Lancashire Cotton Industry: A History Since 1700*, ed. Mary B. Rose (Preston: Lancashire County Books, 1996), 102-5. On Robert Gardner, ("probably the most successful of Manchester's self-made men of the postwar generation"), see Stanley Chapman, "The Commercial Sector," in ibid., 78. In contrast to Bazley and his own son, Gardner was a conservative and apparently opposed the Anti-Corn Law League's agitation (see his obit. in *PG*, June 1866, quoted by Denis O'Connor, "Barrow Bridge, Bolton, Lancashire: A Model Industrial Community of the Nineteenth Century" (typescript in BALS, 1971), 99-100); but note that this did not prevent the firm of Gardner and Bazley from donating £500 to the League's £250,000 fund in 1845 (*BFP*, Dec. 27, 1845, p. 3).

[32.] Roberts, *Paternalism*, 180-83.

[33.] See Martin J. Daunton, "Housing," in *The Cambridge Social History of Britain 1750-1950*, ed. F. M. L. Thompson (Cambridge: Cambridge University Press, 1990), II: 223-24: most housing in towns was owned by small-scale, lower-middle-class investors.

[34.] See Sidney Pollard, *The Genesis of Modern Management: A Study of the Industrial Revolution in Great Britain* (Cambridge, Mass.: Harvard University Press, 1965), 201: from the returns of the 881 large firms to the Factory Commission in 1833, 299 gave no details regarding housing, 414 made no housing provisions, and 168 provided some houses—but generally only a few. More houses seem to have been employer-owned in Blackburn than in the other towns—10-15 percent in the 1850s is Patrick Joyce's estimate ("The Factory Politics of Lancashire in the Later Nineteenth Century," *HJ* XVIII, 3 (1975): 546). And see David Walsh, "Working Class Development, Control and New Conservatism; Blackburn 1820-1850" (MSc. thesis, Salford University, 1986), 161-72. In Preston, Horrocks and Miller were the most noted providers of workforce housing (small, but neat and clean, each with a privy and piped water). See George Thomas Clark, *Report to the General Board of Health, on a Preliminary Inquiry into the Sewerage, Drainage, and Supply of Water, and the Sanitary Condition of the Inhabitants of the Borough of Preston* (London, 1849), 13-14.

[35.] Joyce, *Work, Society and Politics*. For doubts about the reach and stabilizing impact of these spheres of influence, particularly in the mid-century period, see H. I. Dutton and J. E. King, "The Limits of Paternalism: the Cotton Tyrants of North Lancashire, 1836-54," *SH* 7, 1 (Jan. 1982): 59-74; Koditschek, *Class Formation*, 427-33; John K. Walton, "The North-West," in *Cambridge Social History*, ed. Thompson, I: 377-78; idem, *Lancashire: A Social History, 1558-1939* (Manchester: Manchester University Press, 1987), 165.

[36.] Cyrus Redding, ed., *An Illustrated Itinerary of the County of Lancaster* (London, 1842), 289. Redding expresses his debt to Dr. J. R. Beard of Manchester for sketches of the hundreds of Salford and Blackburn, and to Cooke Taylor for descriptions of the manufacturing districts. The attribution of this quotation to the latter is my presumption.

[37.] *BFP*, June 30, 1838, p. 3.

[38.] *BC*, Nov. 2, 1850, p. 5.

[39.] *PC*, July 7, 1849, p. 4; July 28, p. 4; Aug. 11, p. 8; Aug. 25, p. 4.

[40.] *PC*, Aug. 11, 1849, p. 8.

[41.] Whittle, *Bolton*, 59. And see idem, *Blackburn*, 223, 230.

[42.] Whittle, *Bolton*, 175-82.

[43.] BC, June 11, 1859, quoted by Peter F. Taylor, "The New Paternalism and Labour-Capital Relations in the Bolton Cotton Industry, c. 1848-1877" (BA thesis, Manchester Polytechnic, 1986), 52.

[44.] PP 1816, III, "Report of the Minutes of Evidence taken Before the S. C. on the State of the Children employed in the Manufactories of the United Kingdom," 258-76, 294-305 (quotations of William Tomlinson, a retired Preston medical man, and of Joseph Dutton, a Liverpool ironmonger; case against legislation put by William Taylor, manager for Horrocks, Miller and Co., on behalf of twenty-four Preston cotton mills).

[45.] BL, Peel Papers, Add. MS 40275, Roger Holland to Peel, Mar. 25, 1818.

[46.] Peel's Factory Act stipulated that in cotton mills no child could be employed under the age of nine, and that the working day be limited to twelve hours for those aged nine to sixteen; but there was no provision for inspection.

[47.] E.g., PRO, HO 52/3, Report of Joseph Ridgway and the Rev. Thomas Brocklebank, Oct. 9-11, 1822; Report of James Shuttleworth, Thomas Batty Addison, and Richard Moore, Preston October Sessions 1823; Report of Ralph Fletcher to Hobhouse, Oct. 28; Report of Henry Hoghton to Peel, Dec. 13.

[48.] LRO, QSP 2841/29, Report of Charles Whitaker and Rev. James Quartley, Feb. 26, 1824. See also the entries for Richard Haworth's mill, Blackburn, and James Livesey's, Hoghton Bottoms, for more straightforward infringements of the act by reducing the dinner hour.

[49.] BL, Peel Papers, Add. MS 40378, William Bolling to Peel, May 25, 1825.

[50.] [Ashworth], Letter to Ashley, 9; PP 1833, XX, "First Report of Factories Inquiry Commission," E5, Evidence of Henry Ashworth, 6-7; E27, "Resolutions of Committee of Master Cotton Spinners, London, 18 June, 1833." See also Robert E. Zegger, John Cam Hobhouse: A Political Life, 1819-1852 (Columbia: University of Missouri Press, 1973), 170-74.

[51.] [Ashworth], Letter to Ashley, 6-9, 19-20, 28-33. Ashworth's position on the employment of children is echoed by Clark Nardinelli, Child Labor and the Industrial Revolution (Bloomington: Indiana University Press, 1990). See also PP 1833, XX, "First Report of Factories Inquiry Commission," D1, Lancashire District, Examinations taken by Mr. Cowell, 128-31.

[52.] PP 1833, XXI, "Second Report of Factories Inquiry Commission," D3, Lancashire District, 1; D2, Evidence of Thomas Bott (surgeon to Prestolee New Mills), 56; E1, Report, evidence of two Bolton surgeons, Richard Johnson and George Wolstenholme (quotation), 9; James Harrison (Preston surgeon), Edinburgh Medical and Surgical Journal, XLIV (1835): 428, quoted by F. B. Smith, The People's Health 1830-1910 (London: Croom Helm, 1979), 171-72.

[53.] PP 1834, XIX, "Supplementary Report," D1, Lancashire District, 160 (and see the comments of John Bolling, 173-74); W. Brimelow, Political and Parliamentary History of Bolton (Bolton, 1882), 211-14.

[54.] Peter Ormrod of Bolton and William Townley of Feilden, Throp, and Townley of Blackburn, for example, took this position.

[55.] PP 1834, XX, "Supplementary Report Part II," D1, Lancashire, Answers to Queries, 122-45, 162-64, 182, 210-11, 259-60, 266-69, 278-81, 304-9.

[56.] E.g., with various reservations, the Ashworths, Abraham Haigh of Bolton, and William Sharrock of Roach Mill, Samlesbury, thought they could manage without children under twelve, and Thomas Cullen of Bolton without children under eleven.

[57.] See Gray, Factory Question, 97-109.

[58.] PP 1834, XX, D1, 127.

[59.] R. A. Sykes, "Popular Politics and Trades Unionism in South-East Lancashire, 1829-42" (Ph.D. diss., Manchester University, 1982), 142-44, 290, 306-7, 332-33, 340-42, 345; G. W. Daniels, "A 'Turn-Out' of Bolton Machine-Makers in 1831," *Economic Journal* (Jan. 1929): 591-602; Peter F. Taylor, "Popular Politics and Trades Unionism in South-East Lancashire, 1829-42," (Ph.D. diss., Lancaster University, 1991), 213-15, 241-42.

[60.] Rhodes Boyson, *The Ashworth Cotton Enterprise: The Rise and Fall of a Family Firm* (Oxford: Clarendon Press, 1970), 142-49.

[61.] LRO, DDHu 53/72, poster from Hulton to the Hulton colliers, "MY FRIENDS, THE LABOURER IS WORTHY OF HIS HIRE," Mar. 21, 1831; /73, typed copy of colliers' reply from *BC*, Apr. 2, 1831, and poster from Hulton to the colliers who have "Come In," Apr. 4.

[62.] *BC*, Apr. 27, 1833, p. 4; PP 1834, X, "Report from S. C. on Hand-Loom Weavers' Petitions," 343-46, 360, 380-82, 388-91, 417, 419-22, 436, 449; Brimelow, *Political and Parliamentary*, 228-37, 279-83; Sykes, "Popular Politics," 235-36; I. J. Prothero, *Artisans and Politics in Early Nineteenth-Century London: John Gast and his Times* (Folkestone: Dawson, 1979), 176-77; Taylor, "Popular Politics," 166-67. And see *BS*, Feb. 28, 1838, p. 2.

[63.] Duncan Bythell, *The Handloom Weavers: A Study in the English Cotton Industry During the Industrial Revolution* (Cambridge: Cambridge University Press, 1969), 160-67.

[64.] "Hand-Loom Weavers Speech of Dr. Bowring, M.P., in the House of Commons, On Tuesday, July 28, 1835," pp. 3, 7, 14, and "A Letter Addressed to the Members of . . . Parliament, on the Distresses of the Hand Loom Weavers" (Bolton, 1834), reprinted in *British Labour Struggles: The Framework Knitters and Hand Loom Weavers*, ed. Carpenter.

[65.] Howe, "The Business Community," 108.

[66.] Sykes, "Popular Politics," 133-34. And see below, n. 97.

[67.] *PP*, Dec. 31, 1836, p. 2.

[68.] The dispute can be traced in Henry Ashworth, *An Inquiry into the Origin, Progress, and Results of the Strike of the Operative Cotton Spinners of Preston, from October, 1836, to February, 1837* (Manchester, 1838), 1-13, reprinted in *British Labour Struggles: Rebirth of the Trades Union Movement*, ed. Carpenter; and in PC, especially Oct. 29, 1836, p. 2; Nov. 5, p. 2; Nov. 12, p. 2; Nov. 19, p. 3; Nov. 26, p. 2; Dec. 3, p. 3; Dec. 17, p. 2; Dec. 31, p. 2; Jan. 14, 1837, pp. 2-3; Jan. 21, p. 2; Jan. 28, p. 2; Feb. 18, p. 3; *BFP*, Mar. 11, p. 1.

[69.] PRO, HO 40/35, "Letter to Workmen," Jan. 24, 1837; "To the Public at Large," from United Trades of Preston, Feb. 14; Swainson to Russell, Feb. 15.

[70.] The wage increase in Bolton, for example, was taken off again in April 1837, and this was soon followed by moves to partial working. See Sykes, "Popular Politics," 121, 135.

[71.] Anthony Howe, *The Cotton Masters 1830-1860* (Oxford: Clarendon Press, 1984), 181-86; Gray, *Factory Question*, chap. 7.

[72.] William Kenworthy, *Inventions and Hours of Labour. A Letter to Master Cotton Spinners, Manufacturers, and Mill-Owners in General* (Blackburn, 1842). Howe, *Cotton Masters*, 186, lists him as one of only four Lancashire textile masters to take a leading role in the factory movement.

[73.] *BS*, Dec. 14, 1842, p. 2. Kenworthy's original letter drew high praise from the editor, Nov. 23, p. 2.

[74.] See Gray, *Factory Question*, 7, 52, 56, 183; idem, "The Languages of Factory Reform"; J. T. Ward, "The Factory Movement in Lancashire 1830-1855," *TLCAS* 75-76 (1965-66): 195-99, 205.

[75.] *BFP*, Mar. 7, 1846, p. 3; and see Jan. 23, 1847, p. 2, for names to a requisition for a public meeting, surgeons, ministers, and lawyers being prominent.

[76.] E.g., *PC*, Jan. 30, 1847, p. 6, report of a meeting in Blackburn Theatre attended by at least five manufacturers.

[77.] E.g., *BFP*, Mar. 16, 1844, p. 3; Dec. 21, p. 3; May 30, 1846, p. 2; *PC*, May 2, 1846, p. 4; May 16, p. 3.

[78.] *BS*, Apr. 24, 1844, p. 2.

[79.] *BS*, May 1, 1844, p. 2.

[80.] *BS*, Apr. 24, 1844, p. 2.

[81.] Howe, "Business Community," 108.

[82.] LRO, DDX 1116/1/2, Master Spinners Association Cotton and Flax. Note also (*BFP*, Aug. 8, 1846, p. 2) the reason for a meeting of the Blackburn Cotton Spinners' and Cotton Manufacturers' Association in August 1846: to make a unanimous, coordinated decision to give a fortnight's notice of moving to a four-day week.

[83.] *BFP*, Nov. 29, 1845, p. 3; *PC*, Nov. 29, 1845, p. 2.

[84.] *PC*, Mar. 15, 1845, p. 2; Gray, *Factory Question*, 193-94; Michael Huberman, *Escape from the Market: Negotiating Work in Lancashire* (Cambridge: Cambridge University Press, 1996), 122, quoting Gardner (n. 43): "I am satisfied [that] those mills that work short hours will have a choice of hands, and [that] individual interest will accomplish what is necessary without the intervention of the legislature."

[85.] *PC*, Feb. 7, 1846, pp. 2-3; Feb. 21, p. 3, letter of James Walsh to Bright, explaining that the engine *was* speeded, but only because eighty-five looms were added, not increasing in speed the machinery overall.

[86.] LRO, Horrocks, Crewdson and Co. Papers, DDHs/80, Letter Book, Horrocks, Miller and Co. to editor of *PG*, Apr. 2, 1846; Huberman, *Escape from the Market*, 122-23.

[87.] *PC*, May 2, 1846, p. 4.

[88.] *PC*, Mar. 7, 1846, p. 3.

[89.] *BS*, Aug. 1, 1849, p. 2. For reports of other meetings, see *BS*, Oct. 31, p. 2; Mar. 27, 1850, pp. 2-3; Apr. 24, p. 2; *BC*, July 21, 1849, p. 6; Oct. 27, p. 7.

[90.] *BC*, Mar. 9, 1850, p. 6.

[91.] *PC*, Mar. 23, 1850, p. 4.

[92.] *PC*, Mar. 16, 1850, p. 6.

[93.] *BS*, Aug. 1, 1849, p. 2.

[94.] BALS, Bolton Council Minutes, AB/1/2, May 8, 1850. The 1850 Factory Act stopped relays by preventing mills from working before 6 a.m. and after 6 p.m.

[95.] *BS*, June 13, 1849, p. 3; June 27, p. 3. And see July 4, p. 2. For his earlier, unsuccessful, experiment with eleven hours, BRL, B338.4, *Alteration of Working Hours at Mr. Joseph Eccles' Mill to Eleven Hours Per Day. To the Workpeople in My Employ* (open letter of March 20, 1846); *PC*, May 2, 1846, p. 4.

[96.] Anon., *The Strike. A Tale* (London, n.d.), 44.

[97.] Huberman, *Escape from the Market*, 133, 139-40; Michael Winstanley, "The Factory Workforce," in *Lancashire Cotton Industry*, ed. Rose, 136. Lists established in Bolton (for fine spinning) and in Oldham (for coarse spinning) became widely adopted, as did the 1853 Blackburn list for weaving. But Huberman (pp. 133-35) points out that Bolton's list, stipulating prices per lb. of yarn (depending on count), dates back to 1813 (BALS, ZZ/220, "A General List of Prices of Spinning"), and seems to have had a continuous existence in the town and neighborhood thereafter. Bolton's large firms were willing to accept it—and thus infringe on free-market nostrums—in the hope of reducing both work stoppages and undercutting by smaller competitors. Preston masters chose the more confrontational route (pp. 6, 53-57). Note also the evidence of William Taylor, manager for Horrocks, Miller, and Co. of Preston (PP 1816, III, "Report of the Minutes of Evidence taken Before the S. C. on the State of the Children Employed in the Manufactories of the United Kingdom"), suggesting Bolton masters' earlier predisposition to compromise: the Cotton Arbitration Act of 1800, which provided rudimentary machinery for the arbitration of wage disputes, was, he claimed, begun in Bolton and had been abandoned in every town except Bolton (where it was working badly). On the Arbitration Act, see Bythell, *Handloom Weavers*, 148-53; Dinwiddy, "Luddism and Politics," 37.

[98.] PP 1842, XXII, "Reports of Inspectors of Factories": Report of Horner, pp. 4, 27; appx. 5, Horner to Ewings, superintendent, Mar. 31, 1842.

[99.] See the discussion of Bolton's "factory cripples" in Dodd, *The Factory System*, 72-79. For an instance of brutality to children see Harriet Carson, *From the Loom to the Lawyer's Gown . . . Incidents in the Life of Mr. Mark Knowles*, 3rd ed. (London, 1885), 20: "Mr. Knowles well remembers seeing his brother Edward, a boy of eight, returning from the mill at which he worked, his back and shoulders scored with dark lines of whip-marks that lay scarcely half-an-inch apart." For other instances of employers flouting the law—to some extent as a strategy of resistance—see Gray, *Factory Question*, chap. 6, and Prosecution Returns, PP 1839, XLII etc., (cited in ibid., 189): H. and E. Ashworth and Robert Hopwood in particular were repeatedly fined for, among other things, employing children under age and young persons for too many hours.

[100.] PP 1842, XVII, "Reports to Commissioners on Employment of Children: Report by John L. Kennedy Esq. on the Employment of Children and Young Persons in the Collieries of Lancashire, Cheshire, and Part of Derbyshire," 163-64, 186-87, 190, 208-14, 230.

[101.] Ibid., "Report by Anthony Austin, Esq., on the Employment . . . in Mines and Quarries in the North of Lancashire," 787-91, 811-15.

[102.] PRO, MH 12/5529, Mott to commissioners, Jan. 31, 1842.

[103.] *Hansard*, 3rd ser., 64 (July 5, 1842): 999-1002. And see A. J. Heesom, "The Northern Coal-Owners and the Opposition to the Coal Mines Act of 1842," *IRSH* 25, 2 (1980): 236-71.

[104.] PP 1843, XIV, "Reports to Commissioners on Employment of Children": Appx. I, B, "Report by Kennedy on Employment of Children and Young Persons in Print Grounds and Miscellaneous Trades, in Lancashire," b.4-5, 20, 31-32; PP 1843, XV, "Report by A. Austin Esq. on the Employment of Children and Young Persons in Trades and Manufactures in the West and North of Lancashire," M.64, 66-7, m.60, 67, 70.

[105.] Bryan Narey, "The 1853-60 Ten Hours Movement in the Bleaching Industry with Particular Reference to the Master Bleachers of Bolton" (MA thesis, Manchester Polytechnic, 1988). The master bleachers had a long history of association, dating back to a Society of Bleachers which met at inns in Manchester and Bolton and lobbied against Pitt's Fustian Tax in 1784. It is uncertain whether it continued to meet on a regular basis. But it seems that by the 1820s a uniform price list was in operation, and a Bleachers' Association met routinely to petition governments, to keep wages down, and to break unions (recorded in the diaries of John Horrocks Ainsworth). See Sir Alan John Sykes et al., *Concerning the Bleaching Industry* (Manchester, 1925), 26-28;

BALS, Ainsworth diary, ZAH/4/2, May 8, 1830, Dec. 10, 1831, Aug. 29, 1833; /21, Feb. 23-26, 1846.

[106.] *PC*, Aug. 3, 1850, p. 4.

[107.] B. Nightingale, *The Story of the Lancashire Congregational Union 1806-1906* (Manchester, 1906), 91-92.

[108.] See, e.g., F. M. L. Thompson, "Social Control in Victorian Britain," *Econ HR* 2nd ser., XXXIV, 2 (May 1981): 189ff.

Notes to Chapter 10

[1.] Reach, *Manchester and the Textile Districts*, ed. Chris Aspin ([Rossendale]: Helmshore Local History Society, 1972), 1.

[2.] Cyrus Redding, ed., *An Illustrated Itinerary of the County of Lancaster* (London, 1842), 156, 158, 287. (See chap. 9, n. 36.)

[3.] John Aikin, MD, *A Description of the Country from Thirty to Forty Miles Round Manchester* (London, 1795), 283, 286-87.

[4.] Whitaker, *An History of Richmondshire* (London, 1823), II: 416.

[5.] Dickens visited Preston during the great lockout of 1853-54 and recorded his impressions in "On Strike," *Household Words* 203 (Feb. 11, 1854). His famous description of Coketown in *Hard Times* (1854; reprint, London: Penguin, 1969), 65-67, drew strongly on his experience of Preston. See, e.g., Sheila M. Smith, *The Other Nation: The Poor in English Novels of the 1840s and 1850s* (Oxford: Clarendon Press, 1980), 77.

[6.] Sir George Head, *A Home Tour Through the Manufacturing Districts of England, in the Summer of 1835* (London, 1836), 408.

[7.] Hardwick, *History of the Borough of Preston and its Environs* (Preston, 1857), 506, and see 525.

[8.] See David Eastwood, *Government and Community in the English Provinces, 1700-1870* (New York: St. Martin's Press, 1997), 63-68.

[9.] The act appointed for life forty trustees holding property to the value of £1,000 in Great Bolton, and thirty trustees holding property to the value of £500 in Little Bolton. See Michael Winstanley, "Owners and Occupiers: Property, Politics and Middle-Class Formation in Early Industrial Lancashire," in *The Making of the British Middle Class? Studies of Regional and Cultural Diversity Since the Eighteenth Century*, ed. Alan Kidd and David Nicholls (Stroud, Gloucestershire: Sutton, 1998), 99.

[10.] BALS, Great Bolton Improvement Trustees Minutes, TBG/1/1, e.g., Apr. 11, 25, 1793, May 20, June 7, 24, Aug. 9 on sewers; Aug. 23, 28, 31, Sept. 7 on watchmen; May 14, 1794, Nov. 2, 1796, June 14, 1797 on roads; July 27, 1796 on the new shambles; Jan. 5, 1797 on the town hall; TBG/1/2, Apr. 1, June 24, 1801, Apr. 2, 1803, Aug. 5, 1807, Jan. 2, Feb. 3, 1808, Mar. 15, June 7, 1809, Mar. 3, 1810, Sept. 4, Dec. 11, 1816, July 24, 25, Nov. 18, 1818, July 10, Dec. 11, 1819, Feb. 23, Mar. 1, Apr. 29, Nov. 1, 1820, Oct. 2, 1822 on the town hall, marketplace, workhouse, and intended applications to Parliament for amended acts.

[11.] This is treated in some detail by Peter F. Taylor, *Popular Politics in Early Industrial Britain: Bolton 1825-1850* (Keele: Ryburn, 1995), 30-39; idem, "Popular Politics and Labour-Capital Relations in Bolton, 1825-1850" (Ph.D. diss., Lancaster University, 1991), 38-47. And see William Naisby, *A Peep at Corruption; Shewing the Unequal, Unjust, and Partial Assessment of the Rate on the Leypayers of Great Bolton; the Extravagant Expenditure of the Township's Money; and the Necessity of Correcting such Abuses* (Bolton, 1827).

[12.] BALS, TGB/1/2, July 12, 1824, Aug. 15, 16, Nov. 17, 1825.

[13.] TGB/1/2, Dec. 2, 1829, Mar. 10, 17, June 2, 1830.

[14.] BALS, Proceedings of the Trustees of Little Bolton, TLB/1/1, Mar. 5, Apr. 5, 8, 12, 19, 21, 1830. For those elected during its two-decade life, see TLB/3/1, Register of Little Bolton Trustees. Many were reelected over and over every three years; but counting each occupation at each election (so that the same individual might be counted several times over the course of the years), the composition of the trust can be categorized thus: 119 textile employers, 30 gentlemen, 17 other industrial employers, 47 retailers and wholesalers, 11 "craftsmen," 3 farmers, 1 banker, 1 surgeon, 11 miscellaneous.

[15.] TGB/1/3, Oct. 27, Nov. 3, 1830.

[16.] BALS, Heywood Papers, ZHE/34, Robert Heywood to Capt. Jebb, Mar. 24, 1838; TGB/1/3, Mar. 1, 1837; Taylor, "Popular Politics," 52.

[17.] 43 Geo. 3, c. cxxv: "An Act for regulating the markets within the Town of Blackburn . . . and for improving the streets and other places" [Blackburn Police Act, 1803]. See *BM*, Sept. 17, 1800, p. 3, for notice of intent to apply for an act.

[18.] LRO, Feilden Papers, DDCm 2/169, case and opinion of Richard Preston, Apr. 15, 1802; /171, brief for Henry Feilden for himself and archbishop against Police Bill; /178, Carr and Hargreaves to Feilden, Sept. 14, 1824; Feilden to Carr and Hargreaves, n.d.; proceedings of trustees, Nov. 11; Shuttleworth and Hopkins to Carr and Hargreaves, Jan. 19, 1825; /179, resolutions of trustees, Nov. 8, 1824; /180, draft heads of bill, n.d. The Feildens had acquired through purchase during the course of the eighteenth century a moiety of the lordship of the manor of Blackburn, and they leased from the archbishop of Canterbury (who held the other moiety) the Rectory of Blackburn (432 acres, the tithes, and some buildings). By his own estimation, Joseph Feilden owned a sixth in value (not including the cotton manufactories) of the town and township of Blackburn by the 1840s. See William Alexander Abram, *A History of Blackburn, Town and Parish* (Blackburn, 1877), 284-85; LRO, Feilden Papers, Rectory and Manor of Blackburn, DDCm 2/45, Abstract of Messrs. Feilden's Title to the Rectory of Blackburn; indentures between archbishop and Henry and John Feilden, Dec. 25, 1808, Apr. 20-21, 1809; BM, Feilden Papers, 3/51, brief in support of John and Joseph Feilden and William Townley against Blackburn Water Works Bill.

[19.] PP 1835, XXV, "Reports of the Commissioners Appointed to Inquire into the Municipal Corporations in England and Wales: Report on the Borough of Preston," 1692.

[20.] Brian G. Awty, "The Introduction of Gas Lighting to Preston," *THSLC* 125 (1974): 84-100. Both the Blackburn Gas-Light Company and the Bolton Gas Company started in 1818. See William Alexander Abram, *History of the Blackburn Gas-Light Company* (Blackburn, 1879); James Clegg, *The Bolton Gas Company: 1818-1872. An Historical Retrospect* (Bolton, 1872, reprinted from *BC*); BALS, UGB/1/1, Proceedings of the Bolton Gas Company; /2/1, Minutes of General Meetings.

[21.] PP 1835, XXV, Report on Preston, 1691: the Borough Quarter Sessions was held before the mayor, aldermen and recorder, the Civil Court of Record before the mayor and at least two aldermen.

[22.] PP 1835, XXV, Report on Preston, 1686, 1689, 1693; Edward Baines, *History of the County Palatine and Duchy of Lancaster*, 1st ed. (London, 1836), IV: 343-44.

[23.] See Derek Fraser, *Urban Politics in Victorian England: The Structure of Politics in Victorian Cities* (Leicester: Leicester University Press, 1976), 115ff.; idem, *Power and Authority in the Victorian City* (Oxford: Blackwell, 1979), 5-14.

[24.] PC, Aug. 15, 1835, p. 3.

[25.] PP, June 27, 1835, p. 3; Aug. 8, p. 2; Aug. 29, p. 2; Sept. 12, p. 2.

[26.] *PC*, Oct. 10, 1835, p. 3.

[27.] *PC*, Nov. 14, 1835, p. 2; Nov. 21, p. 3; Nov. 28, p. 3; Dec. 5, p. 2.

[28.] *PC*, Jan. 2, 1836, pp. 2-3; Jan. 9, p. 2.

[29.] *PC*, Nov. 5, 1836, pp. 2-3.

[30.] See E. P. Hennock, *Fit and Proper Persons: Ideal and Reality in Nineteenth-Century Urban Government* (Montreal: McGill-Queen's University Press, 1973), 182-86, 308-9; R.G. Wilson, *Gentlemen Merchants: The Merchant Community in Leeds 1700-1830* (Manchester: Manchester University Press, 1971), 176; Fraser, *Urban Politics*, passim.

[31.] Three things helped ensure this: the Municipal Corporations Act's requirement that councillors own real or personal property worth £1,000, or occupy property of £30 rateable value; the fact that council service was unpaid; and the fact that council meetings were held during normal working hours. The act introduced a ratepayer franchise but with a three-year residency requirement. This, plus the tendency to resort to compounding (levying the rate on the owner rather than the renter of small property), or not to rate smaller properties at all, in practice prevented the bulk of the lower orders from voting. See Hennock, *Fit and Proper Persons*, 10-12, 312; Eastwood, *Government and Community*, 83.

[32.] LRO, Borough of Preston, Council Minutes, CBP/1/1; LRO, PRS-DOB (5), *Preston Municipal Elections. Reprinted from the Preston Chronicle* (Preston, 1859).

[33.] *PP*, Nov. 10, 1838, pp. 2-3.

[34.] E.g., *PC*, Nov. 3, 1849, p. 4: "We have forty-eight gentlemen who have met for fourteen years to manage an estate of less value than the private property of some of the individual members, and in what state is it?"

[35.] Hewitson, *Preston Town Council. Or Portraits of Local Legislators* (Preston, 1870), 56.

[36.] In some years the *Chronicle* reported a general decay in partisan hostility, e.g., *PC*, Nov. 30, 1844, p. 2; Aug. 8, 1846, p. 4; but something fairly minor could revive it—like the home secretary's substitution of a liberal for a conservative in an appointment to the borough bench (Nov. 14, 1846, p. 4).

[37.] W. Brimelow, *Political and Parliamentary History of Bolton* (Bolton, 1882), 275-78.

[38.] Fraser, *Power and Authority*, 86.

[39.] *BFP*, Jan. 13, 1838, p. 2.

[40.] Henry Ashworth, *Recollections of Richard Cobden, M.P., and The Anti-Corn-Law League*, 2nd ed. (London, 1876), 16; *BFP*, Jan. 20, 1838, pp. 1-2.

[41.] PRO, PC/1/758, Further Statement of Petitioners for Charter; BALS, Heywood Papers, ZHE/34, Heywood to Capt. Jebb, Mar. 24, 1838.

[42.] BALS, Heywood Papers, ZHE/34, Heywood to Capt. Jebb, Mar. 24, 1838.

[43.] *BFP*, Jan. 27, 1838, p. 2. See also Ashworth's account, *Recollections*, 17, of the deputations from each side traveling to London to plead their cases before the Privy Council. Ashworth, Robert Heywood, and James Winder appeared for the incorporators, a dozen Bolton Tories, plus William Bolling, MP, and the agents of the earl of Bradford and of Thomas Tipping for the anti-incorporators. This heavyweight opposition apparently dismayed Heywood, but Ashworth assured him "*we* had a *democratic* case, whilst *they* had a *baronial* one, and that I did not dread the result."

[44.] PRO, PC/1/755, "Petition of the Lords of the Manor of Great Bolton," Mar. 1838; /756, "Petition of Thomas Tipping of Davenport Hall, Cheshire"; /749, "Petition from Great Bolton against incorporation"; /757, "Counter Statement of Deputation against a Charter of Incorporation." See also /752, petitions against from the proprietors of Bolton Gas Light and Coke Company, and of Great and Little Bolton Water Works Company, on the grounds of lack of necessity and increased taxation. Both of these companies contained a heavy proportion of Great Bolton trustees.

45. PRO, PC/1/753, "Petition of inhabitant householders and occupiers of property in Little Bolton township"; /757, "Counter Statement of Deputation against a Charter of Incorporation"; /751, "Petition from inhabitant householders and occupiers of property in Haulgh District, Bolton Borough."

46. PRO, PC/1/759, "Report of Capt. Jebb in respect of Bolton Charter," Apr. 3, 1838. See also BALS, Heywood Papers, ZHE/34, Heywood to Jebb, Mar. 24, 1838.

47. 171 women had signed the pro-reform petition, but the petitioners had subsequently withdrawn their names in the belief that the Privy Council would not recognize them. Jebb, determined not to allow undue advantage to the antireformers, struck off all the female names on their petition as well.

48. PRO, PC/1/759, Report of Capt. Jebb.

49. See *BC*, Nov. 17, 1838, p. 2; Nov. 24, p. 2.

50. John Garrard, *Leadership and Power in Victorian Industrial Towns 1830-80* (Manchester: Manchester University Press, 1983), 165, 188-89.

51. LRO, DDPr/51/5, *Bolton Municipal Registration. The Disfranchising Whigs. The Revision of the Burgess Lists; Taken from the Bolton Chronicle of October 7 and 14, 1843* (Bolton), i-iii, 3; James Clegg, *Annals of Bolton: History, Chronology, Politics* (Bolton, 1888), section II: 62-63.

52. Clegg, *Annals*, II: 65-67, 86; Baines, *County of Lancaster*, 4th ed., III: 200.

53. Garrard, *Leadership and Power*, passim.

54. For a classic statement, see Lewis Mumford, *The City in History: Its Origins, Its Transformations, and Its Prospects* (London: Secker and Warburg, 1961), 447, 474, 489-94. For the deterioration in housing quality, see Martin Daunton, "Housing," in *Cambridge Social History*, ed. Thompson, 2: 202-3; idem, *Progress and Poverty: An Economic and Social History of Britain 1700-1850* (Oxford: Oxford University Press, 1995), 257-58.

55. For the rise of "fact-gathering," see Mary Poovey, *Making a Social Body: British Cultural Formation 1830-1864* (Chicago: University of Chicago Press, 1995), 10-11; M. J. Cullen, *The Statistical Movement in Early Industrial Britain: The Foundations of Empirical Social Research* (New York: Barnes and Noble, 1975); Theodore M. Porter, *The Rise in Statistical Thinking 1820-1900* (Princeton: Princeton University Press, 1986). For condition-of-England writings, see T. W. Heyck, *The Transformation of Intellectual Life in Victorian England* (New York: St. Martin's Press, 1982), 28, 44; Kathleen Tillotson, *Novels of the Eighteen-Forties* (Oxford: Clarendon Press, 1954); Raymond Williams, *Culture and Society 1780-1950* (New York: Harper and Row, 1958).

56. See, e.g., V. A. C. Gatrell, "The Commercial Middle Class in Manchester, c.1820-1857" (Ph.D. diss., Cambridge University, 1971), 11-13; Anthony Howe, *The Cotton Masters 1830-1860* (Oxford: Clarendon Press, 1984), 306-9; Alan J. Kidd, "Introduction: The Middle Class in Nineteenth-Century Manchester," 10-12, and Michael E. Rose, "Culture, Philanthropy and the Manchester Middle Classes," 109-13, in *City, Class and Culture: Studies of Social Policy and Cultural Production in Victorian Manchester*, ed. Kidd and K. W. Roberts (Manchester: Manchester University Press, 1985); Robert Fishman, *Bourgeois Utopias: The Rise and Fall of Suburbia* (New York: Basic Books, 1987), 4 and passim; John Archer, "Ideology and Aspiration: Individualism, the Middle Class, and the Genesis of the Anglo-American Suburb," *JUH* 14, 2 (Feb. 1988):

214-53; Jonas Frykman and Orvar Löfgren, *Culture Builders: A Historical Anthropology of Middle-Class Life* (New Brunswick, NJ: Rutgers University Press, 1987), 51-55.

[57.] Christopher Hamlin, *Public Health and Social Justice in the Age of Chadwick: Britain, 1800-1854* (Cambridge: Cambridge University Press, 1998), 7-11.

[58.] BRL, Blackburn General Dispensary Annual Reports 1824-1834: 8th (quotation), 9th, and 11th reports; *BA*, Aug. 27, 1832; LRO, HRPD, Preston Dispensary, Nov. 17, 30, 1831, Oct. 25, 1832; *PC*, Nov. 26, 1831, p. 3, June 9, 1832, p. 3; R. J. Morris, *Cholera 1832: The Social Response to an Epidemic* (London: Croom Helm, 1976), 197-200; Michael Durey, *The Return of the Plague: British Society and the Cholera 1831-2* (Dublin: Gill and Macmillan, 1979), 205.

[59.] *BFP*, Nov. 21, 1835, p. 2.

[60.] James Black, *A Medico-Topographical, Geological, and Statistical Sketch of Bolton and its Neighbourhood* (Bolton, 1837), 37-44, 75-81, 98.

[61.] For examples of routine business, see LRO, Borough of Preston Council Minutes, CBP/1/1: July 27, 1837, Dec. 14, 1840, June 10, 1842, Sept. 25, 1847—memorials to the royal family; Jan. 1, Apr. 18, 1839, May 27, Nov. 9, 1841, Aug. 29, 1844—complaints about the mail; Feb. 8, 1836, Aug. 2, 1839, Jan. 1, Aug. 30, 1841, Aug. 5, 1846, Aug. 26, 1847—concerns of the borough police force, the raising of a watch-rate, and the magistracy; Nov. 9, 1839, June 19, 1846, June 16, 1847—concerns of the grammar school; Aug. 23, 1841, Feb. 24, 1842—plans for a covered market.

[62.] Rev. Walter Lowe Clay, *The Prison Chaplain: A Memoir of the Rev. John Clay, B.D.* (Cambridge, 1861), 492-93, 577.

[63.] M.W. Flinn, introduction to *Report on the Sanitary Condition of the Labouring Population of Great Britain, 1842*, by Chadwick (Edinburgh: Edinburgh University Press, 1965), 58-59; but see John V. Pickstone, "Dearth, Dirt and Fever Epidemics: Rewriting the History of British 'Public Health', 1780-1850," in *Epidemics and Ideas: Essays on the Historical Perception of Pestilence*, ed. Terence Ranger and Paul Slack (Cambridge: Cambridge University Press, 1992), 134-35.

[64.] The figures are for Preston in the six years up to June 1843. The average for tradesmen's families was 31.63.

[65.] PP 1844, XVII, "First Report of the Commissioners for Inquiring into the State of Large Towns and Populous Districts" [The Buccleuch Commission]: Rev. J. Clay, "Report on the Sanatory Condition of Preston," 33-55.

[66.] E. C. Oakes, *Water Supplies Through Three Centuries* (Preston, 1953), 10.

[67.] PP 1845, XVIII, "Second Report of the Commissioners for Inquiring into the State of Large Towns and Populous Districts": Appx., pt. II, "Report on the Sanatory Condition of the Large Towns in Lancashire by Dr. Lyon Playfair," 6, 9, 16-17, 21, 72-73.

[68.] Friedrich Engels, *The Condition of the Working Class in England*, trans. and ed. W. O. Henderson and W. H. Chaloner (Palo Alto: Stanford University Press, 1958), 51.

[69.] A meeting in 1841 chaired by Robert Heywood established a committee to find shareholders to build public baths (*BFP*, May 1, 1841, p. 2, May 8, p. 2); but progress seems to have been slow until the Bolton Baths Company, under the chairmanship of John Horrocks Ainsworth, began work in 1845 (*Extracts from Various Authors on the General Advantages of Bathing* (Bolton, 1846)).

[70.] John Entwisle, *A Report of the Sanatory Condition of the Borough of Bolton, in a Letter Addressed to Thomas Ridgway Bridson, Esq., Mayor* (Bolton, 1848), 1-5, 11, 28-50, 57-67, 73-91. Again, he made a contrast between Little and Great Bolton. In the former, the elected trustees could raise £3,000 a year; in the latter, unelected trustees dared not risk the unpopularity of a rate, and the Improvement Act limited expenditure from their scanty funds to lighting and repairing roads.

[71] *PC*, Nov. 16, 1844, p. 2.

[72] *PC*, Nov. 23, p. 2. See also Dec. 14, p. 2; Jan. 11, 1845, p. 2. And see its praise for the second report of the Health of Towns Commissioners, Mar. 1, p. 2. See also the stinging comments in *Dr. Granville's Spas of England*, quoted at length in *PG*, Nov. 30, 1844 (quoted by Nigel Morgan, *Vanished Dwellings: Early Industrial Housing in a Lancashire Cotton Town* (Preston, 1988), 20): "Of all the rising manufacturing towns in the north, Preston is probably the only one which has contrived to add to its population, its wealth, its factories, to a very considerable extent, without at the same time having made any corresponding advances in civilization, cleanliness, and the ameliorations in the material part of the city. . . . It would take half a century of steady good will and a considerable expenditure of money, to make Preston what Manchester, Halifax, Bradford, Wakefield, or even Huddersfield, are, and have been for a long time."

[73] See *PC*, Nov. 4, 1848, p. 5, praising Clay for his latest Prison Chaplain's Report: "The public are under great obligations to our valued townsman for this addition to its stock of information on the *classe dangereuse*; and we trust the circulation of this Report will, like the publication of its predecessors, be productive of national good." The point is that any kind of information—criminal statistics, details of drainage, accounts of alcoholism—helped form a composite picture of the dangerous class. See also Iorwerth Prothero, *Radical Artisans in England and France, 1830-1870* (Cambridge: Cambridge University Press, 1997), 196-97.

[74] LRO, CBP/53/1, Minutes of Commissioners for Improvement of Borough of Preston, Sept. 4, 1843, and passim. The meeting to consider a new Improvement Act on Nov. 4, 1844, also saw a large attendance.

[75] James Barron, *A History of the Ribble Navigation From Preston to the Sea* (Preston, 1938), 51-58, 476; H. N. B. Morgan, "Origins of Preston's Dock Problem: The Corporation and the Ribble Navigation Company," *University of Lancaster Regional Bulletin* 6:19 (Summer 1977): 3; Jack M. Dakres, *The Last Tide: A History of the Port of Preston* (Preston, 1986), 12-20. For Hesketh Fleetwood's grandiose plans and his squandering of much of the family fortune on their very imperfect realization, see Catherine Rothwell, "A History of Fleetwood-on-Wyre 1834-1934" (F.L.A. thesis, 1974), 28-49; Joseph H. Sutton, "Early Fleetwood, 1835-1847" (M.Litt thesis, Lancaster University, 1968); PRO, Preston and Wyre Docks Company Minute Book, RAIL 577/1; LRO Reading Room, Box 28, "Prospectus for Fleetwood," Mar. 25, 1837; Christopher Monkhouse, "A New Lanark by the Sea," *Country Life*, July 17, 1975, pp. 126-28, July 31, 1975, pp. 290-93.

[76] See memorial of merchants to the proprietors, presented by Peter Haydock, July 31, 1835, cited by Barron, *Ribble Navigation*, 57-58.

[77] Cited by Morgan, "Origins," 3. Baines, *County of Lancaster*, IV: 362, wrote in 1836 that the merchants of Preston could accomplish much if the river project were controlled by them and not the landowners en route: "The example of the Clyde is before them; and it is not improbable that Preston, Freckleton, and Lytham, might be made to rival Glasgow, Port Glasgow, and Grenock [*sic*], as they are similarly situated with respect to each other."

[78] LRO, CBP/40/1, Ribble Navigation Committee Minutes, July 27, 1836 (report of Captain Belcher); "Ribble Navigation: Report of Robert Stevenson and Son to Mayor and Council of Borough of Preston, 16 March 1837," pp. 1-8.

[79] LRO, CBP/1/1, Aug. 30, 1837; CBP 63/1, Minutes of Directors of Ribble Navigation Company, Sept. 29, 1837. Morgan remarks ("Origins," 5) that there were no political and religious divisions among the subscribers to the navigation. Thus the Ribble, like other business organizations, was a means of bringing the middle classes together for collective action.

[80] Cited by Morgan, "Origins," 4-5.

[81] CBP 63/1, Minutes of Directors of Ribble Navigation Company, Apr. 12, 1838, Jan. 1, Feb. 24 , Apr. 1, 1842.

[82] Barron, *Ribble Navigation*, 64-69, 71-76, 97, 488; Morgan, "Origins," 4-5 (citing Catterall); Dakres, *Last Tide*, 39-40; LRO, CBP/1/1, Jan. 1, 1851.

[83] LRO, CBP/1/1, Nov. 9, 1850, report of Philip Park, borough treasurer (and treasurer to the Ribble Navigation Company—a further conflict of interest), suggesting that mercantile interests had already greatly benefited from the improvement of the navigation, and that it was in the council's interest (both as a landowner and to stimulate the reviving spirits of the shareholders) to help the company finance further dredging.

[84] *PC*, Aug. 31, 1850, p. 4.

[85] *PG*, Oct. 30, 1867, cited by Morgan, "The Port of Preston: a Victorian Community and the Perils of a Marginal Natural Asset," in *Ports and Resorts in the Regions*, ed. E. M. Sigsworth (papers at a conference of regional history tutors, Hull College of Higher Education, July 1980), 42.

[86] *Pace* Morgan, "Origins," 6.

[87] LRO, Borough of Preston Council Minutes, CBP/1/1, Aug. 28, 1838, Aug. 29, 1844 (quotation), Nov. 9, 1846, Apr. 29, 1847.

[88] Ibid., Aug. 29, 1850.

[89] Edwin Waugh, *Home-Life of the Lancashire Factory Folk During the Cotton Famine* (London, 1867), 24.

[90] LRO, DDH 1114/1-3, House of Commons Select Committee on Railway Bills, May 21, 31, 1847; DDH 1114/5-7, 9, House of Lords Select Committee, June 30, July 1, 2, 5, 1847; DDH 1116/7, petition of mayor, aldermen, and burgesses against bill; CBP/1/1, Apr. 29, Aug. 26, 1847; Robert W. Rush, *The East Lancashire Railway* (Trowbridge: Oakwood Press, 1983), 5-7.

[91] DDH 1114/3. These are the words of Robert Segar, who was posing the questions.

[92] DDH 1114/7.

[93] DDH 1116/1-2, petitions of property owners and occupiers against ELR Bill.

[94] CBP/53/1, Minutes of Commissioners, Nov. 4, 1844; CBP 53/23, Minute Book of Special Improvement Committee, Apr. 5, 19, 30, 1847; CBP/1/1, Apr. 26, 1847, Mar. 13, 1848 (quotations).

[95] *PC*, Apr. 15, 1848, p. 4.

[96] *PC*, May 8, 1847, p. 4. See also Feb. 6, 1847, p. 4; Apr. 3, p. 4; Mar. 18, 1848, p. 4; June 9, 1849, p. 4, a further attack on the commissioners: "Their sole qualifications are property; and, as in almost all cases where authority is based exclusively on that interest, they limit their views to the narrowest consideration of its paramount importance. The comfort, convenience, wants, and welfare of those who are less affluent, weigh lightly in the scale compared with their selfish requirements, or selfish objections to expense."

[97] John Prest, *Liberty and Locality: Parliament, Permissive Legislation, and Ratepayers' Democracies in the Nineteenth Century* (Oxford: Clarendon Press, 1990), 29, 35-36.

[98.] *PC*, May 8, p. 6, reporting a lecture in the Theatre by R. D. Grainger, FRS, attended by the mayor and some of the most influential inhabitants, at which it was unanimously resolved to form a branch of the new Health of Towns Association of London.

[99.] Notably John Foster, *Class Struggle and the Industrial Revolution: Early Industrial Capitalism in Three English Towns* (London: Weidenfeld and Nicolson, 1974); Theodore Koditschek, *Class Formation and Urban-Industrial Society: Bradford, 1750-1850* (Cambridge: Cambridge University Press, 1990), 527-30; idem, "Class Formation and the Bradford Bourgeoisie" (Ph.D. diss., Princeton University, 1981), 837-39 and passim.

[100.] CBP/1/1, May 11, 1848; *PC*, May 20, 1848, p. 4.

[101.] CBP/1/1, Oct. 23, 1848; *PC*, Oct. 28, pp. 4, 6.

[102.] LRO, PUT 1/14, Oct. 17, 1848.

[103.] CBP/1/1, Nov. 9, 1848. The procedure is detailed by Prest, *Liberty and Locality*, 29-35.

[104.] George Thomas Clark, *Report to the General Board of Health, on a Preliminary Inquiry into the Sewerage, Drainage, and Supply of Water, and the Sanitary Condition of the Inhabitants of the Borough of Preston* (London, 1849), 3, 5-6, 16-17, 26, 31, 33, and passim.

[105.] LRO, PUT 1/14, Apr. 17, July 31, Aug. 7, 14, Sept. 18, 1849; William J. Lowe, "The Irish in Lancashire, 1846-71: A Social History" (Ph.D. diss., Trinity College, Dublin, 1974), 204.

[106.] LRO, CBP/1/1, Aug. 29, Sept. 13, Oct. 7, 1850; CBP 55/16, Public Health Act Committee, Nov. 22, 1849, Apr. 22, 1850; PRO, MH13/148, Richard Palmer (town clerk) to Austin, Jan. 9, 1849; Palmer to General Board of Health, Apr. 5, Dec. 7; GBH to Palmer, May 3; Palmer to Alexander Bain (GBH assistant secretary), Apr. 22, 1850; GBH to Palmer, Apr. 25; *PC*, June 2, 1849, p. 7.

[107.] *PP*, Aug. 24, 1850, p. 4; *PC*, Aug. 31, 1850, p. 4.

[108.] PRO, MH 13/148, Catterall and Catterall to GBH, July 16, 27 (enclosing memorial), 30, 1850; GBH memo, July 26; GBH to Catterall and Catterall, July 24, 29, Aug. 2.

[109.] CBP/1/1, Nov. 9, 1848, Nov. 9, Dec. 10, 1849, Feb. 7, 1850; PRO, MH 13/148, Palmer to GBH, Nov. 10, 13, 1848; GBH to Palmer, Nov. 14; Palmer to GBH, June 18, 1850; James German to GBH, July 10; GBH to German, July 12. On the public baths and washhouses, and the importance of James German in pushing for them, see Nigel Morgan, *An Introduction to the Social History of Housing in Victorian Preston* (Preston: Curriculum Development Centre, 1982), 36-37, 60. On the state of the graveyards, see Clark, *Report on Preston*, 28-29.

[110.] BALS, Great Bolton Improvement Trustees Minutes, TGB/1/3, Feb. 24, June 16, 1842, Nov. 1, Dec. 6, 13, 1843; Garrard, *Leadership and Power*, 188-91.

[111.] *BFP*, Nov. 19, 1842, p. 2; BALS, Bolton Council Minutes, AB/1/1, Sept. 17, 1845.

[112.] *BFP*, Sept. 20, 1845, pp. 2-3.

[113.] TGB/1/3, Oct. 8, 15, 1845.

[114.] *BFP*, Aug. 15, p. 2.

[115.] *BFP*, Sept. 21, 1846, p. 3; Sept. 28, p. 3; Oct. 17, p. 2; BALS, Proceedings of Trustees of Little Bolton, TLB/1/2, Aug. 7, Oct. 2, 1846, Mar. 5, 1847.

[116.] Garrard, *Leadership and Power*, 191-92.

[117.] The council's battle with the Water Works Company had arisen in 1843 in opposition to a private bill to increase the company's capital and to its pricing policy, and

this evolved into the struggle to take over the powers of the trusts. Agreement was finally reached in March 1846: the council was to lease the waterworks, with an option
to buy it outright. The Improvement Act ratified this. See BALS, Bolton Council Minutes, AB/1/1, Apr. 19, May 10, Aug. 9, Sept. 27, Nov. 9, Dec. 6, 1843, Feb. 11, Mar.
13, 31, July 10, Oct. 14, Nov. 18, 1846; ABPP/3/1, Bolton Improvement Bill, 1847; /3,
Report of H.M. Commissioners re Bolton Improvement, 27 Feb., 1847; /4, Minutes of
Evidence before Commissioners, 5 Feb., 1847 (evidence of James Kyrke Watkins); /7,
agreement for lease of waterworks to corporation, 30 Mar., 1846; James C. Scholes,
History of Bolton (Bolton, 1892), 493-94; Garrard, *Leadership and Power*, 189-91.
And see BALS, Heywood Papers, ZHE/42, for letters on a rival scheme of the Lanca-
shire Water Works Company, and for the final compromise.

[118.] BALS, Public Health Committee Minute Book, AB/16/1, Nov. 9, 1847, Feb. 3,
1848.

[119.] BC, Mar. 11, 1848, pp. 5, 8; AB/16/1, Apr. 10, 1848.

[120.] BC, July 1, 1848, p. 5 (quotations); July 8, pp. 4-5; July 22, p. 5; Sept. 2, p. 7;
Oct. 21, pp. 4-5.

[121.] BALS, B361 BOL, Report of Bolton Society for the Protection of the Poor (1848),
p. 9.

[122.] AB/16/1, Nov. 13, 22, 1848, May 7, 1849, June 14, 27, July 4, 25, Aug. 1, 29;
BC, Sept. 8, 1849, p. 5.

[123.] BC, Feb. 23, 1850, p. 6.

[124.] AB/16/1, Oct. 29, 1849.

[125.] He addressed the letter to the Great Bolton Trustees (AB/1/2, Aug. 17, 1849) and
sent a copy to the Little Bolton Trustees (TLB/1/3, Aug. 3, 1849).

[126.] TGB/1/3, Aug. 8, 1849.

[127.] PRO, MH13/26, Bolton Correspondence re Local Government Act: J. Knowles to
Henry Austin (secretary to GBH), Sept. 13, Oct. 15, 1849; GBH to Knowles, Oct. 9;
BALS, AB/1/2, Oct. 17, 1849; BC, Oct. 20, p. 6; Oct. 27, p. 5.

[128.] AB/1/2, Jan. 18, 1850; BC, Jan. 26, p. 5; BALS, Bolton Biographical Notes, B1,
obit. of Thomasson, 1876, p. 47.

[129.] BC, Feb. 23, 1850, pp. 5-6; TLB/1/3, Feb. 1, 21, 1850.

[130.] BC, Aug. 10, p. 5. The act cost £2,568. Little Bolton and Haulgh petitioners were
partially appeased by a clause guaranteeing that improvements applying to one township would be paid only from that township's own rates. Among other dilutions, some
manufacturers were appeased by the weakening of proposed smoke regulation, ratepayers by a rate limitation of 2s. 6d. in the pound (rather than the 3s. 6d. the council
wanted), cellar-owners by a five-year moratorium on the closing up of cellar dwellings.
See Garrard, *Leadership and Power*, 193-94.

[131.] E. C. Midwinter, *Social Administration in Lancashire 1830-1860: Poor Law,
Public Health and Police* (Manchester: Manchester University Press, 1969), 83; Garrard, *Leadership and Power*, 193.

[132.] AB/1/2, Nov. 9, letter from C. E. Trevelyan, Treasury.

[133.] Jacson, *Desultory Retracings*, 58.

[134.] E.g., BS, Sept. 25, 1844, p. 3, letter of "W.T.W."; Oct. 16, 1844, p. 3, letter of
"Amicus"; Aug. 6, 1845, supplement, re the rectorial glebe lands of the archbishop of
Canterbury, which hampered the expansion of the town to the south-west; Aug. 9,
1843, p. 3, letter of "Anti-Smoke."

[135.] BS, Aug. 5, 1846, p. 3. Lloyd stated that in other respects Blackburn was favorably placed: there were no cesspools as in other manufacturing towns, on the whole the
town was not densely built, it was well ventilated, and green fields impinged on the

center. See also letter of "Civis," May 5, 1841, p. 3, and letter of "Commercial Traveller," Sept. 23, 1846, p. 3.

[136.] *BS*, Mar. 29, 1843, p. 2.

[137.] *BG*, July 31, 1833, pp. 1, 4; Aug. 14, p. 4; Aug. 21, p. 4; Aug. 28, p. 4; *BA*, Sept. 11, 1833, p. 8; Sept. 18, p. 8; *BG*, Dec. 16, 1835, p. 4; Jan. 20, 1836, pp. 4-5.

[138.] LRO, Feilden Papers, DDCm 2/185-88, 190, 192, 194, 200-203 (on the circus case); /204, resolutions of trustees, Sept. 10, 1840; /205, notice of application for an act, Oct. 19; /206, minutes of interview with Feilden, Oct. 23, 1840; /207, R. W. Hopkins to Feilden, May 17, 1841.

[139.] 5 Vic., c. cxii: "An Act for Improving the Streets and Public Places, and erecting a Town Hall, and Improving the Markets in the Township of Blackburn."

[140.] *BS*, Apr. 12, 1843, p. 3; BM, Feilden Papers, 2/303a, Oct. 20, 1843 (stating the agreed price of £2,081 5s.); /304, Jan. 22, 1844. The *BS* reported on Jan. 17, 1844, p. 2, that the differences between the commissioners and Joseph Feilden had been entirely removed.

[141.] *BS*, Aug. 7, 1844, p. 2; Aug. 28, p. 3; BM, Feilden Papers, 3/51, "Brief in Support of the Petition of John Feilden and Joseph Feilden Esqs. and Mr. William Townley against the Bill," 1845; 14/5, report of Watson.

[142.] Expressed thus in *BS*, Mar. 29, 1843, p. 2.

[143.] *BS*, Aug. 10, 1842, Apr. 12, 1843, p. 2.

[144.] BM, Feilden Papers, 8/15, Local Acts—Preliminary Inquiries 9 & 10 Vic. c. 106: Blackburn Improvement and Market, Report of Commissioners; 11 Vic., c. cclv: "An Act for Improving the Streets and Public Places, and erecting a Town Hall, and improving the Markets in the Township of Blackburn."

[145.] *BS*, Feb. 2, 1848, p. 3.

[146.] *PC*, Feb. 27, 1847, p. 8, letter of "Examiner."

[147.] *BS*, Mar. 28, 1849, p. 3, letter of "W.W.T."

[148.] *BS*, Feb. 2, 1848, p. 3.

[149.] See, e.g., editorials and letters in *PC*, Feb. 6, 1847, p. 4; Feb. 27, p. 8; Mar. 6, p. 8; Mar. 20, p. 5; Apr. 3, p. 4; and below.

[150.] See, e.g., *BS*, Nov. 27, 1850, pp. 1-2; and below.

[151.] W. H. Hornby, R. Raynsford Jackson, and John Livesey (cotton manufacturers), Dugdale (surgeon), Hoole (schoolmaster), Charles Tiplady (stationer and printer), R. H. Hutchinson (mill manager), Daniel Thwaites (master brewer), James Boyle (confectioner), J. Parkinson and C. Parkinson (wholesale grocers), George Dewhurst (reedmaker), and Thomas Ainsworth (attorney).

[152.] *BS*, Apr. 11, 1849, p. 2; Apr. 18, p. 3; Dec. 5, p. 2; Oct. 2, 1850, p. 3, letter of "Alpha"; Oct. 9, p. 3, letter of "A Ratepayer"; Oct. 23, p. 3, letter of "M. S. A."; Nov. 27, pp. 1-2; Dec. 4, 1850, pp. 1-3; *PC*, Oct. 19, p. 5; PRO, PC/1/744, "Petition of the Inhabitants of the Parliamentary Borough of Blackburn."

[153.] *BS*, Sept. 26, 1849, p. 3, reported that only thirty had died in Blackburn.

[154.] Abram, *History of Blackburn*, 375; J. Withers, *Report on the Sanitary Condition of the Borough* (1853). See also the assessment of Peter Whittle, *Blackburn As It Is: A Topographical, Statistical, and Historical Account of the Borough of Blackburn* (Preston, 1852), 35, 98, 103, 114-15, 123, 144, 148-49, 293, 303.

[155.] To borrow the terminology of Jeffrey Williamson, "Coping with city growth," in *The Economic History of Britain Since 1700*, ed. Roderick Floud and Donald McCloskey, 2nd ed. (Cambridge: Cambridge University Press, 1994), I: 352-56.

[156.] See Poovey, *Making a Social Body*, 116-30.

[157.] *PC*, Nov. 3, p. 4.

[158.] Hamlin, *Public Health*, 12-15, 213-15, 243-44.

[159.] For a spectrum of perspectives, see Anthony Sutcliffe, "The Growth of Public Intervention in the British Urban Environment During the Nineteenth Century: A Structural Approach," in *The Structure of Nineteenth Century Cities*, ed. James H. Johnson and Colin Pooley (London: Croom Helm, 1982), 110-14; Anthony S. Wohl, *Endangered Lives: Public Health in Victorian Britain* (London: J. M. Dent, 1983), 3-6, 140, and passim; Asa Briggs, "Victorian Values," in *In Search of Victorian Values: Aspects of Nineteenth-Century Thought and Society*, ed. Eric M. Sigsworth (Manchester: Manchester University Press, 1988), 16; Hamlin, *Public Health*, 4, 13, 218; Daunton, *Progress and Poverty*, 254-58; F. B. Smith, *The People's Health 1830-1910* (London: Croom Helm, 1979), 229; Mark Girouard, *The English Town: A History of Urban Life* (New Haven: Yale University Press, 1990), 198; Jeffrey G. Williamson, *Inequality, Poverty, and History: The Kuznets Memorial Lectures* (Oxford: Blackwell, 1991), 126-29; idem, *Coping with City Growth During the Industrial Revolution* (Cambridge: Cambridge University Press, 1990), 280 and passim.

[160.] Flinn, introduction to *Report on the Sanitary Condition*, 69-70.

[161.] See R. J. Morris, "Middle-Class Culture, 1700-1914," in *A History of Modern Leeds*, ed. Derek Fraser (Manchester: Manchester University Press, 1980), 200.

[162.] See Hamlin, *Public Health*, 281-82, 289.

[163.] John Thompson Jr., *A History of the Public Park, Blackburn* (from *PG*, Oct. 24, 1857), 4, contrasted all this with the previous Blackburn, once "a bye-word for its ungainly exterior, for the narrowness of its streets, the irregularity of its dwellings, and the utter absence of anything like a decent structure." The development of the archiepiscopal lands (the 317-acre Audley rectorial estate to the south of Darwen Street, and the 78-acre Brookhouse estate) came after 1853 when the Ecclesiastical Commissioners assumed control. See Abram, *History of Blackburn*, 284-85.

[164.] For the poor state of Darwen, as detailed in a report by J. Paton, engineer, see *PC*, Sept. 15, 1849, p.7.

[165.] Midwinter, *Social Administration*, 83, 85, 88-89, 98, 104, 109; Oakes, *Water Supplies*, 15-19.

[166.] BALS, Bolton Biographical Notes, B1, portrait of Rushton, 1877, pp. 129-30; obit., 1883, p. 195.

Notes to Chapter 11

[1.] Peter Whittle, *Bolton-le-Moors, and the Townships in the Parish* (Bolton, [1857]), 419.

[2.] Henry Ashworth, *A Tour in the United States, Cuba, and Canada* (London and Manchester, 1861), 145-46, 188.

[3.] BALS, Bolton Biographical Notes, B1, p. 83, *Manchester Examiner* obit. of Henry Ashworth, 1880.

[4.] See, e.g., François Crouzet, *The First Industrialists: The Problem of Origins* (Cambridge: Cambridge University Press, 1985); Katrina Honeyman, *Origins of Enterprise: Business Leadership in the Industrial Revolution* (Manchester: Manchester University Press, 1983); Anthony Howe, *The Cotton Masters 1830-1860* (Oxford: Clarendon Press, 1984); Harold Perkin, *The Origins of Modern English Society 1780-1880* (London: Routledge and Kegan Paul, 1969), 225.

[5.] James Bullough, Henry Ward, both manufacturers, and John Dugdale, Blackburn ironfounder and manufacturer, respectively. See R. S. Crossley, *Accrington Captains of Industry* (Accrington, 1930), 86; William Alexander Abram, *Blackburn Characters of a Past Generation* (Blackburn, 1894), 197; J. G. Shaw, "John Dugdale and Sons, Iron-Founders," *BT*, July 19, 1930.

[6.] As Ernest Gellner, *Nations and Nationalism* (Oxford: Blackwell, 1983), 22, 24, points out, for the illusion of social mobility to take root there must be at least some convergence with reality. For a discussion of the origins of the local bourgeoisie, see Brian Lewis, "Bourgeois Ideology and Order: Middle-Class Culture and Politics in Lancashire, 1789-1851" (Ph.D. diss., Harvard University, 1994), 36-40.

[7.] John Thompson Jr., *A History of the Public Park, Blackburn* (reprinted from *PG*, Oct. 24, 1857), 16.

[8.] Quoted by Crossley, *Accrington Captains*, 30-39.

[9.] See, e.g., the gradations of smaller gentry, squire, and yeoman in Ribblesdale, c. 1815, in Sir James Kay-Shuttleworth, *Ribblesdale or Lancashire Sixty Years Ago* (London, 1874), I: 6-9.

[10.] Abram, *Blackburn Characters*, 58-59. For the meaning of gentleman as "retired on rentier income," the commonest usage by the 1830s, see R. J. Morris, "Reading the Will: Cash Economy Capitalists and Urban Peasants in the 1830s," in *The Making of the British Middle Class? Studies of Regional and Cultural Diversity Since the Eighteenth Century*, ed. Alan Kidd and David Nicholls (Stroud, Gloucestershire: Sutton, 1998), 118-19.

[11.] See Penelope J. Corfield, "The Rivals: Landed and Other Gentlemen," in *Land and Society in Britain, 1700-1914*, ed. Negley Harte and Roland Quinault (Manchester: Manchester University Press, 1996), 12, 16, 21, 23.

[12.] Richard Edgcumbe, ed., *The Diary of Frances Lady Shelley 1787-1817* (London, 1912), 3.

[13.] See Paul Langford, *Public Life and the Propertied Englishman 1689-1798* (Oxford: Clarendon Press, 1991), 9.

[14.] According to Samuel Crompton's survey of mule spinning mills in the cotton industry, 1811 (cited by S. D. Chapman and S. Chassagne, *European Textile Printers in the Eighteenth Century: A Study of Peel and Oberkampf* (London: Heinemann, 1981), 42), the eight Horrocks mills in Preston topped the list with 107,136 spindles, far outpacing the second largest, McConnel and Kennedy of Manchester (85,000). Sidney Pollard, *The Genesis of Modern Management: A Study of the Industrial Revolution in Great Britain* (Cambridge, Mass.: Harvard University Press, 1965), 92-93, notes from blue books of 1816 and 1818 that the Horrockses employed seven thousand handloom weavers in the countryside around Preston.

[15.] Margaret Burscough, *The History of Lark Hill, Preston* (Preston, 1989), pedigree, 15, 19, 23, 27-28; Rev. George Streynsham Master, *Some Notices of the Family of Master, of East Langdon and Yotes in Kent, New Hall and Croston in Lancashire, and Barrow Green in Surrey* (London, 1874), 25-35. See also Amanda J. Vickery, "Women of the Local Elite in Lancashire, 1750-c.1825" (Ph.D. diss., London University, 1991), 28-30, 332, and passim.

[16.] BALS, Bolton Biographical Notes, B1, p. 10, "The Peter Rothwells of Bolton."

[17.] BALS, Bolton Biographical Notes, B3, p. 56, article on Hardcastle in *Bolton Journal and Guardian*, Apr. 12, 1935. Tim Bobbin was the famous Lancashire dialect poet.

[18.] See John Langton, "The Industrial Revolution and the Regional Geography of England," *TIBG* 9 (1984): 159-61; K. C. Phillipps, *Language and Class in Victorian England* (Oxford: Blackwell, 1984); Peter Burke, introduction to *The Social History of Language*, ed. Burke and Roy Porter (Cambridge: Cambridge University Press, 1987), 1-17.

[19.] Abram, *Blackburn Characters*, 3.

[20.] See Stana S. Nenadic, "The Structure, Values and Influence of the Scottish Urban Middle Class; Glasgow 1800 to 1870" (Ph.D. diss., Glasgow University, 1986), 106-7, 168.

[21.] BALS, Ainsworth Papers, ZAH/10/1/1, 4, 5, photos of portraits. And see Leonore Davidoff and Catherine Hall, *Family Fortunes: Men and Women of the English Middle Class, 1780-1850* (London: Hutchinson, 1987), 410-14; Eric J. Hobsbawm, *The Age of Capital 1848-1875* (London: Sphere Books, 1988), 275; Walter E. Houghton, *The Victorian Frame of Mind 1830-1870* (New Haven: Yale University Press, 1957), 201-2; Bonnie G. Smith, *Changing Lives: Women in European History Since 1700* (Lexington, Mass.: D. C. Heath, 1989), 195-97.

[22.] Abram, *Blackburn Characters*, 66-67.

[23.] Middle-class insecurity and its repercussions receive excellent treatment in Margaret R. Hunt, *The Middling Sort: Commerce, Gender, and the Family in England, 1680-1780* (Berkeley and Los Angeles: University of California Press, 1996), chap. 1 and passim.

[24.] George Elwick, *The Bankrupt Directory, December 1820-April 1843* (London, 1843). Prominent casualties, apart from Sudell, included the Turners, Blackburn cotton spinners, 1843; William Garnett Taylor, Little Bolton cotton spinner, 1840; the Sleddons, Preston machine makers and cotton spinners, 1826; Henry Hilton, Over Darwen bleacher, 1842; Edward Hilton and Nathaniel Walsh, Over Darwen papermakers, 1842; John Haughton, Blackburn cotton spinner, 1837; Roger Haslam, Little Bolton cotton spinner, 1841; William Dickinson and Thomas Throp, Blackburn ironfounders, 1837; the Carrs, Over Darwen cotton spinners, 1826 and 1827; Henry Briggs, Blackburn cotton spinner, 1841; Thomas Ainsworth and Peter Cort, Turton and Bradshaw bleachers, 1828; and John Abbott, Blackburn cotton manufacturer, 1842. See also John Graham, "The Chemistry of Calico Printing from 1790 to 1835 and History of Printworks in the Manchester District from 1760-1846" (MS, 1846, in MCL, Reference Library), which, in giving a detailed firm-by-firm account, incidentally points to a great deal of fluctuation in fortunes and a high degree of failure.

[25.] William Alexander Abram, *A History of Blackburn, Town and Parish* (Blackburn, 1877), 405; *BT*, May 6, 1922 (see BRL, L 25 Woo, file of cuttings on Woodfold Park).

[26.] *Autobiographical Memoirs of Thomas Fletcher of Liverpool* (Liverpool, 1893; written 1843), 45-46.

[27.] BL, Peel Papers, Add. MS 40,508, Hulton to Peel, May 14, 1842; Peel to Hulton, May 18.

[28.] BALS, Bolton Biographical Notes, B1, p. 26, obit. of William Ford Hulton, 1879.

[29.] See, e.g., Richard Rodger, *Housing in Urban Britain 1780-1914* (Basingstoke: Macmillan, 1989), chap. 5; M. A. Simpson and T. H. Lloyd, eds., *Middle Class Housing in Britain* (Newton Abbot: David and Charles, 1977).

[30.] Chris Aspin, "Cotton's Legacy," in *The Lancashire Cotton Industry: A History Since 1700*, ed. Mary B. Rose (Preston: Lancashire County Books, 1996), 354.

[31.] John Corry, *The History of Lancashire* (London, 1825), II: 338-39.

[32.] BALS, Bolton Biographical Notes, B1, pp. 1-6, obit. of Peter Ormrod, 1875.

[33.] Burscough, *Lark Hill*, 19, 30.

[34.] John Holt, *General View of the Agriculture of the County of Lancaster* (London, 1795), 15-16.

[35.] R. W. Dickson, *General View of the Agriculture of Lancashire* (London, 1815), 95.

[36.] Which can be found in the LRO.

[37.] Whittle, *Bolton*, 354-55.

[38.] Abram, *Blackburn*, passim; George C. Miller, *Blackburn Worthies of Yesterday* (Blackburn, 1959), passim. For the Hornbys, later residents, see *BT*, Jan. 7, 1899. The 1851 bourgeois data sample (see Table 3) includes the following heads of household resident on King St.: four surgeons, two solicitors, three cotton spinners, an engineer, an auctioneer and accountant, a superintendent of the county police, a boarding-schoolmaster, a cotton manufacturer, a ropemaker, a cotton merchant, a gentleman, a gentlewoman, a landed proprietor, a master house painter, and a proprietor of houses. Three of them were JPs.

[39.] In 1824 the residents included the Rev. James Dodgson of St. John's; the Rev. Richard Garnett, a curate at the parish church; James Lund, John Alston, Eccles Shorrock, Banister Eccles, and Moses Sharples, cotton manufacturers; Richard Moulden, gentleman; Christopher Parkinson, tallow chandler; and Richard Martland, physician. See BRL, A33, J. G. Shaw, Albums of articles: *BT*, Feb. 11, 1933; Edward Baines, *History, Directory and Gazetteer of Lancashire*, vol. I (Liverpool, 1824).

[40.] BM, Feilden Papers, 7/10, deed of covenants and grant of ground rents, Dr. Martland and others with John and Joseph Feilden, Dec. 12, 1839. In 1851 the occupants from the sample were: a master painter, a professor of music, three cotton manufacturers, three retired cotton manufacturers, a retired ironfounder, a gentlewoman, an attorney, two wholesale grocers, a woolen draper, a retired silk mercer, a coppersmith, a druggist, two surgeons, a landed proprietor, and a pawnbroker.

[41.] Peter Whittle, *Blackburn As It Is: A Topographical, Statistical, and Historical Account of the Borough of Blackburn* (Preston, 1852), 270-71.

[42.] Shaw, Albums of articles, passim; Whittle, *Blackburn*, 235; for the Dugdales, Brian Hall, *Lowerhouse and the Dugdales: The Story of a Lancashire Mill Community* (Burnley and District Historical Society, 1976), 7.

[43.] For example (J. G. Shaw, *History and Traditions of Darwen and its People* (Blackburn, 1889), 30, 141, 149, 160), Joseph Eccles, cotton spinner, lived at Lower Darwen House, and his son Richard after him; another son, Thomas, lived in The Elms. Eccles Shorrock, cotton spinner, lived at Low Hill House, Over Darwen (built and first occupied by Samuel Crompton, the inventor of the spinning mule, who was then unsuccessfully trying his hand at bleaching), then at Hollinshead Hall, Tockholes. Richard Kershaw Smalley built Astley Bank. Henry Hilton, papermaker, lived at Whitehall before he failed in 1843.

[44.] Abram, *Blackburn*, 493-94.

[45.] B. T. Barton, *Historical Gleanings of Bolton and District*, 1st ser. (Bolton, 1881), I: 239; William E. Brown, *Buildings of Bolton* (Bolton and District Civic Trust, 1983), 26. In the early 1830s (MCL, Local History Library, MS 942.72 S154 v.XIV, Giles Shaw MSS: Edwin Butterworth, MS History of Bolton-le-Moors, 1833ff., pp. 86ff.), peripheral big houses included Chamber Hall (Peter Ormrod, cotton spinner) and Sunning Hill (Peter Rothwell, ironfounder), both in Great Bolton; West Cottage (the seat of the late John Pilkington, merchant and manufacturer) and Mort Field (James Cross), in Little Bolton; The Hollins (John Fletcher, land and coalowner) in Haulgh; Hill Top (Thomas Wright) and The Thorns (William Garnett Taylor, cotton spinner) in Sharples; Egerton Hall (Edmund Ashworth) and Rose Hill (J. Ogden) in Turton; Orrell House (the Orrell family) in Edgworth; Bradshaw Hall (Thomas Hardcastle; "if the long chimnies of the adjoining works were not visible this place would be a most desirable retreat on account of the woods & meadows adjoining"), Birch House and Vale House (both long occupied by the Horrockses of Preston) in Bradshaw; Lomax Fold (Robert Lomax) in Harwood; Crompton Fold (John Bolling, cotton spinner) in Breightmet; Darcy Lever New Hall (William Bolling, MP, cotton spinner; a "splendid" brick mansion built by the Bradshaws in the previous century, with "beautiful pleasure grounds") in Darcy Lever. A sampling of other notable houses of the first decades of the century includes those of Roger Holland, Manchester dimity manufacturer and owner of the Four Factories in Bolton, who moved to Birch House, Farnworth, in 1806 (W. P. Crankshaw and Alfred Blackburn, *A Century and a Half of Cotton Spinning 1797-1947: The History of Knowles, Ltd. of Bolton* (Bolton, n.d.), 11); Thomas Barnes, millowner, who resided at Summerfield, Great Lever, and afterwards built Limefield, Moses Gate (B. T. Barton, *History of Farnworth and Kersley* (Bolton, 1887), 247); John Smith of Great Lever, extensive bleacher, who lived at Great Lever Hall; Major Watkins of Great Lever Bleachworks, who built Mayfield House on the Manchester Road (Barton, *Bolton*, 2nd ser. (Bolton, 1882), 241); and John Ashworth Sr., who built The Oaks (twelve bedrooms) in 1820, and Henry lived there after his marriage in 1823 (Rhodes Boyson, *The Ashworth Cotton Enterprise: The Rise and Fall of a Family Firm* (Oxford: Clarendon Press, 1970), 247). Near to the Fletchers' The Hollins in Haulgh were three other large properties of closely intermarried families: Wheatfield (the Grays), Vale Bank (the Watkins), and Haulgh Cottage (built by James Watkins when John Fletcher took Vale Bank on marrying in 1836) (James Watkins, "The Hollins Leases 1756-1829 and Reminiscences of the Hollins 1830-1842" (typescript in BALS, 1902), 10-14.)

[46.] Butterworth, "Bolton," 72.

[47.] St. George's St. had the following heads of household who met the criteria established in Table 3: two cotton spinners, two gentlewomen, a millwright, a draper, a pawnbroker, a timber dealer and builder, a watchmaker, two attorneys, an engineer, a fundholder, a clergyman, a surgeon, an annuitant, and a muslin manufacturer. Newport Terrace had a master tanner, a cotton spinner, two annuitants, and a cotton manufacturer and bleacher.

[48.] From the 1851 sample: six spinners and manufacturers, an annuitant, a coalmaster, a timber dealer and builder, two solicitors, a proprietor of houses, and a master druggist and grocer.

[49.] BALS, Bolton Biographical Notes, B1, pp. 101-2, obit. of Dr. Chadwick, May 1876. The speech is undated, but was apparently one of his last on the council, 1859-61.

[50.] Alan Crosby, *Penwortham in the Past* (Preston, 1988), 97; LRO, DDX 1/11, inquisition re enclosing part of a highway and setting out another, Feb. 10, 1800; Burscough, *Lark Hill*, 10-13; Whittle, *History of Preston*, I: 170 (and for other examples, scattered across town, 154).

[51.] PC, Feb. 27, 1836, p. 3.

[52.] Marian Roberts, *The Story of Winckley Square, Preston* (Preston, 1988), 7-8. Cross had recently returned from legal studies in London and presumably took the London squares as his model.

[53.] LRO, Pedder Papers, DDPd 11/59, conditions for building, c. 1805; /60, draft articles for regulation, Apr. 15, 1807.

[54.] Whittle, *Preston*, I: 146, II: 183-84.

[55.] Charles Hardwick, *History of the Borough of Preston and its Environs* (Preston, 1857), 434.

[56.] Anthony Hewitson, *History of Preston* (Preston, 1883), 390.

[57.] PC, Feb. 27, 1836, p. 3. For the estates being sold off for housing, see Hardwick, *Preston*, 431-32, 498.

[58.] Though Brian R. Bristow, "Residential Differentiation in Mid-Nineteenth Century Preston" (Ph.D. diss., Lancaster University, 1982), 78-79, notes that this only met limited success because the terminus of the Longridge Railway and the building of cotton mills close by soon surrounded the posher housing with humbler dwellings.

[59.] Hardwick, *Preston*, 508-10; Crosby, *Penwortham*, 119-21; Whittle, *Preston*, I: 158. Joseph Bray bought Tulketh Hall (used as a school) and estate from the Hesketh family around 1848 (Henry Fishwick, *The History of the Parish of Preston* (Rochdale, 1900), 266). Another prominent resident of Ashton was the banker John Lawe, who built The Larches in 1838 (for this and further discussion of the houses of the wealthy, see Nigel Morgan, *An Introduction to the Social History of Housing in Victorian Preston* (Preston: Curriculum Development Centre, 1982), 7-8). On Ashton Park, see *PP*, June 8, 1861, in LRO, Pedder Papers, DDPd 842/3, items re Old Bank, Preston.

[60.] Bristow, "Residential Differentiation," 79-81, 95-97, 177-79, 205-11, 274-79, 416, and passim.

[61.] E.g., Colin G. Pooley, "Residential Differentiation in Victorian Cities: A Reassessment," *TIBG* 9 (1984): 131-44; idem, "Choice and Constraint in the Nineteenth-Century City: A Basis for Residential Differentiation," in *The Structure of Nineteenth Century Cities*, ed. James H. Johnson and Colin G. Pooley (London: Croom Helm, 1982), 200-204; Richard Dennis, "Stability and Change in Urban Communities: A Geographical Perspective," in ibid., 256; David Cannadine, "Victorian cities: how different?" *SH* 4 (Jan. 1977): 458-67; David Ward, "Environs and neighbours in the 'Two Nations': residential differentiation in mid-nineteenth-century Leeds," *JHG* 6, 2 (1980): 133-62; F. M. L. Thompson, "Town and City," in *Cambridge Social History*, ed. idem, I: 60-62.

[62.] See R. J. Morris, *Class, Sect and Party: The Making of the British Middle Class, Leeds 1820-1850* (Manchester: Manchester University Press, 1990), 54-56, 163; Cannadine, "Victorian cities," 460-61.

[63.] PP 1844, XVII, appendix to "First Report of Commissioners of Inquiry into State of Large Towns: Report on Sanatory Condition of Preston" by J. Clay, 54-55; LRO, QGR/2/39, Chaplain's Report, Oct. 1844, pp. 13-14.

[64.] Engels, *Condition of the Working Class,* 54-56.

[65.] See Edward Pessen, *Riches, Class and Power Before the Civil War* (Lexington, Mass.: D. C. Heath, 1973), 174-201.

[66.] Cf. Davidoff and Hall, *Family Fortunes*. And see F. M. L. Thompson, "The Rise of Suburbia," in *The Victorian City: A Reader in British Urban History 1820-1914*, ed. R. J. Morris and Richard Rodger (London: Longman, 1993), 165-70; H. J. Dyos, *Victorian Suburb: A Study of the Growth of Camberwell* (Leicester: Leicester University Press, 1961), chap. 1.

[67.] LRO, DDPr 124/1, *Catalogue of Very Valuable Household Furniture . . . October 1828; /2*, "Ground Plan and Elevation of the Hall at Woodfold Park," 1831.

[68.] Whittle, *Bolton*, 370-71.

[69.] According to the 1851 census.

[70.] Samuel Leach, *Old Age Reminiscences* (printed for private circulation, 1923), 14-16, 18-20, 23-26, 29-31.

[71.] Sir Charles Brown, *Sixty-Four Years a Doctor* (Preston, 1922), 2-3. The governess earned £20 a year, the cook £12, the housemaid £11, the parlourmaid £10, the nurse £8, and the coachman 14s. a week with a £2 bonus on Christmas Day.

[72.] Leach, *Old Age Reminiscences*, 18-20.

[73.] WRO, D/D2 EHC/207, Whittaker Letters, mother to JWW, Feb. 22, 1822.

[74.] BRL, Whittaker Papers, 921 WHI, Mary Haughton Whittaker to mother-in-law, Aug. 1, 1825; JWW to mother, Mar. 22, 1834.

[75.] Ibid., JWW to mother, Mar. 22, 1834, Aug. 8, 1835, Aug. 19, 1836.

[76.] Louisa Potter, *Lancashire Memories* (London, 1879), 57-71, 83, 88-89, 125-39. At one stage (p. 71) she consulted with a few intimate friends on whether to call Cicely, the maid, "Farrar," as ladies' maids were usually called by their surnames. Note that at the Feilden household, for example, the ladies' maid was "Baldwin." See, for one instance, LRO, PR 2846/2/1, Coucher Book of Feniscowles, vol. I, Caroline Feilden to JWW, June 16, 1834.

[77.] Whittle, *Blackburn*, 333.

[78.] R. S. Crossley, *Accrington Captains of Industry* (Accrington, 1930), 42, 83.

[79.] Sir Charles Brown, *Origin and Progress of Horrockses, Crewdson and Co. A Lesson in Perseverance for Everyone. Interesting, Instructive, and Amusing* (Preston, n. d.), 21-22. A number of these collections are discussed in Edward Twycross, *The Mansions of England and Wales. Illustrated in a Series of Views of the Principal Seats; with Historical and Topographical Descriptions* (London, 1847), vols. I-III, passim. On Newsham's collection (which he bequeathed to the town, and which became an important part of the collection in the Harris Art Gallery), see also William Powell Frith, *My Autobiography and Reminiscences* (New York, 1888), 149-50.

[80.] See LRO, PR 2846/2/1, Coucher Book of Feniscowles, vol. I, William Feilden to JWW, June 19, 1834, discussing his purchases at Christie's.

[81.] *The Art Union*, Jan. 1, 1843, p. 10, quoted by Cornelius P. Darcy, *The Encouragement of the Fine Arts in Lancashire 1760-1860* (Manchester: Chetham Society, 1976), 143.

[82.] *Catalogue of the Exhibition of the Works of Local Artists (Living and Deceased)* (Manchester, 1857), 7, quoted by Darcy, *Fine Arts*, 150-51.

[83.] Darcy, *Fine Arts*, 143-45.

[84.] *PC*, July 1, 1865, quoted by David Hunt, *A History of Preston* (Preston, 1992), 179-80.

[85.] Frith, *Autobiography*, 111.

[86.] Darcy, *Fine Arts*, 148, 157-58. And see Disraeli's depiction of Millbank in *Coningsby* (reprint, New York, 1962), 188, quoted by Darcy, 148.

[87.] LRO, Cross Papers, DDX 841/3/23, list of pictures at Red Scar, n.d.

[88.] LRO, Cross Papers, DDX 841, Richard Assheton Cross, "Sketch of My Father's Life."

[89.] This paragraph is heavily indebted to the fascinating anthropological investigation of the late nineteenth-century Swedish bourgeoisie by Jonas Frykman and Orvar Löfgren, *Culture Builders: A Historical Anthropology of Middle-Class Life*, trans. Alan Crozier (New Brunswick, NJ: Rutgers University Press, 1987).

[90.] Catherine Jacson, *Desultory Retracings. A Personal and Family Record* (London, 1895), 92-93.

[91.] For discussions of urban time-consciousness and time-discipline, from meetings, assemblies, markets, and the mail to factories, see David S. Landes, *Revolution in Time: Clocks and the Making of the Modern World* (Cambridge, Mass.: Harvard University Press, 1983); Michael Adas, *Machines as the Measure of Men: Science, Technology, and Ideologies of Western Dominance* (Ithaca: Cornell University Press, 1989), 251, 259-63; Richard Whipp, "'A Time To Every Purpose': An Essay on Time and Work," in *The Historical Meanings of Work*, ed. Patrick Joyce (Cambridge: Cambridge University Press, 1987), 217-19; Mark Harrison, *Crowds and History: Mass Phenomena in English Towns, 1790-1835* (Cambridge: Cambridge University Press, 1988), 106-8; Anthony Giddens, *Social Theory and Modern Sociology* (Cambridge: Polity Press, 1987), 95-96. For the importance of the railway timetable in fixing mental boundaries of time units, see Leonore Davidoff, *The Best Circles: Society Etiquette and the Season* (London: Croom Helm, 1973), 34, and note Catherine Jacson's comment (*Desultory Retracings*, 191), looking back to the 1830s: "There was a wider margin of time. There were no railway stations to be reached, no imperative Bradshaw to compel to inexorable minutes, no telegrams or telephones."

[92.] A phrase of Lucy Deane in George Eliot's *The Mill on the Floss* (1860; reprint, London, 1967), 370.

[93.] LRO, Whitaker Papers, DDWh 4/78, Alice Ainsworth to Eliza Whitaker, May 1, 1816.

[94.] BALS, Heywood Papers, ZHE 26/3, Heywood to Noah Makinson, Feb. 4, 1840.

[95.] Frykman and Löfgren, *Culture Builders*, 31-33.

[96.] D. J. Oddy, "Food, Drink and Nutrition," in *Cambridge Social History*, ed. Thompson, 2: 258-59.

[97.] E.g., *BM*, July 19, 1797, p. 3; Aug. 20, 1806, p. 3; July 8, 1807, p. 3; Aug. 5, 1807, p. 4. When Catherine Hutton, daughter of an upwardly mobile Birmingham businessman, visited Blackpool back in 1788, she found three guest houses occupied by gentry, Manchester manufacturers, and Liverpool merchants, and a fourth filled by "rich, rough, honest manufacturers of the town of Bolton, whose coarseness of manners is proverbial even among their own countrymen." Quoted by C. H. Beale, *Reminiscences of a Gentlewoman of the Last Century* (Birmingham, 1891), 56-57, quoted by Paul Langford, *A Polite and Commercial People: England 1727-1783* (Oxford: Clarendon Press, 1989), 72.

[98.] Peter Whittle, *Marina; or, An Historical and Descriptive Account of Southport, Lytham, and Blackpool, Situate on the Western Coast of Lancashire* (Preston, 1831): "Southport," 23-24; "Lytham," 5, 29; "Blackpool," 18; Alan Stott, *A History of Norbreck and Little Bispham* (Fylde, 1982), 15-17.

[99.] BRL, Shaw, Albums of articles: *BT*, Nov. 23, 1929.

[100.] BALS, B920B EDE, miscellaneous items re James Eden: *Bolton Journal*, May 2, 1874, obit. of James Eden.

[101.] Jacson, *Desultory Retracings*, 168-71.

[102.] LRO, Cross Papers, DDX 841, Richard Assheton Cross, "Sketch of My Father's Life."

[103.] LRO, Whitaker Papers, DDWh 4/102, St. Clare to Eliza Whitaker, June 11, 1820; /111, ibid., [1821?].

[104.] LRO, PR 2846/2/1, Coucher Book of Feniscowles, vol. I, JWW to William Feilden, June 10, 1834.

[105.] Watkins, "Hollins Leases," 16. Thomas Leach and his family, described above, frequently resorted in school-holiday time to Lytham and Blackpool (Leach, *Old Age Reminiscences*, 21-22).

[106.] Denis Lyddon and Peter Marshall, *Paper in Bolton: A Papermaker's Tale* (Altrincham, 1975), 38; Barton, *Farnworth and Kersley*, 271.

[107.] John B. Trappes-Lomax and Christopher N. Trappes-Lomax, eds., *Otter Hunting Diary 1829 to 1871 of the Late James Lomax, Esq. of Clayton Hall* (Blackburn, 1910), entry for May 1832, and passim.

[108.] Jacson, *Desultory Retracings*, 189-90.

[109.] Edward Hall, ed., *Miss Weeton: Journal of a Governess 1807-1811* (London: Oxford University Press, 1936), 273-74.

[110.] LRO, Whitaker Papers, DDWh 4/120, Alice Ainsworth to Eliza Whitaker, Oct. 11 [1821?].

[111.] David Punter, "Romantics to Early Victorians," in *Cambridge Cultural History*, ed. Ford, 6: 20-21, 27; Keith Thomas, *Man and the Natural World: Changing Atti-*

tudes in England 1500-1800 (London: Penguin, 1984), 243-69; Maurice Cranston, *The Romantic Movement* (Oxford: Blackwell, 1994), chap. 3; John Brewer, *The Pleasures of the Imagination: English Culture in the Eighteenth Century* (London: Harper Collins, 1997), chap. 16. Note also Peter Gay's Freudian suggestion (*The Bourgeois Experience: Victoria to Freud*, vol. II, *The Tender Passion* (Oxford: Oxford University Press, 1986), 259-62, 270-73, 286) that bourgeois enjoyment of nature, music, and religion could act as sexual substitutes—as intense, emotional climaxes of feeling.

[112.] J. A. Atkinson, *Memoir of the Rev. Canon Slade* (Bolton, 1892), 223-34.

[113.] LRO, Cross Papers, DDX 841/3/1, "Observations made upon a Tour thro' Part of North Wales," Sept. 1790.

[114.] For a valuable study of the English abroad, see John Pemble, *The Mediterranean Passion: Victorians and Edwardians in the South* (Oxford: Clarendon Press, 1987).

[115.] LRO, Whitaker Papers, DDWh 4/75, Horrocks to Eliza Whitaker, Aug. 16, 1814.

[116.] Jacson, *Desultory Retracings*, 46-47, 64-84. They had already been in France in 1824-25, and journeyed between Brittany and Paris in post chaises and diligences.

[117.] C. Martin, Manchester, to Jaques [*sic*] Martin, Genève, Apr. 20, 1826, in Heywood, *A Journey to Italy in 1826* (privately printed, 1919), 90.

[118.] LRO, "The Diaries of Laurence Rawstorne from 1810-1849" (typescript).

[119.] SJC, Whittaker I, JWW to mother, Aug. 2, 15, Sept. 16, 21, 1819.

[120.] BRL, Whittaker Papers, 921 WHI, JWW to mother, July 10, 1825.

[121.] Not quite *the* best traveled: the prize probably goes to Montague Joseph Feilden, millowner and son of William Feilden, who apparently spent several years on the Continent, took a tour through the Canadas and the United States, had a lengthy stay in the East (Constantinople, Asia Minor, and Palestine), and lived for two and a half years in India. His brother, John Leyland Feilden, traveled to the United States and Cuba, to Jamaica to look after some of his mother's property, and to Port Natal in South Africa (Whittle, *Blackburn*, 347). Another noted traveler was John Skaife, Blackburn surgeon, naturalist, collector, bibliophile, and opium addict, who journeyed in France, Germany, Switzerland, Italy, and the Netherlands (Abram, *Blackburn Characters*, 96-109).

[122.] BALS, Heywood Papers, ZHE/30, J. Black to Dr. J. H. Griscom, New York, Apr. 24, 1834.

[123.] On one occasion, traveling from Delhi, New York, on August 18, "I took my seat on the top, but was told by the driver that he had another going with him, but I did not yield, and he put a negro to drive both me and the horses, but it did not do. I was glad to have an opportunity of showing the Americans that I made no distinction."

[124.] Dr. Williams' Library, Diaries of Robert and Mrs. Heywood and other papers: 28.157, Italy, 1826; 28.164 (a), Journey to Ireland, 1823; 28.163, Journey to Paris, Italy & Switzerland, 1848; Egypt, 1845; Robert Heywood, *A Journey to the Levant in 1845* (privately printed [by his daughter], 1919); *A Journey to America in 1834* (privately printed, 1919); *A Journey to Italy in 1826* (privately printed, 1919); BALS, Heywood Papers, ZHE/18-27, Heywood to father, Sept. 1823 (2 letters) (on going to Ireland; he indicates that this was not his first trip to Dublin).

[125.] Celia Ann Temple, *Records of the Family of John Ainsworth Horrocks, Pioneer and Founder of the Ruined Village of Penwortham and its Church, on the River Hut, Stanley County, South Australia* (Bedford, 1890), 107-8.

[126.] BALS, Ainsworth Papers, ZAH/1, JHA to sister, Sarah, Aug. 26, 1820 (from Dieppe to Rouen the country is fine; but "We saw but few, very few Chateaux and

those far inferior to the beautiful seats which we saw almost every mile in England"),
Oct. 7; to brother, Peter, Jan. 17, 1821 (describing the road from Rome to Naples with
reference to e.g. *The Aeneid*); /4/1, "Tour of Scotland in 1819"; "Continental Tour in
1820-21"; "Tour in Wales," 1823; and diary entries, June 2-July 1, 1824 (June 14: saw
David's "Venus Disarming Mars": "not pleased with it—Mars holding out his sword;
countenance not interested: Venus like a peasant.—Two graces shewing their teeth—
Building in the clouds—Design a bad one—"); Aug. 23-Sept. 2, 1826; Aug. 20-Sept.
30, 1827; July 10-Aug. 2, 1833.

[127.] Charles Wilbraham, *Two Lectures on Palestine, Delivered in the Parish Church
Sunday School, Bolton-le-Moors, on the 2nd and 9th October 1844* (Bolton, 1844), 7,
17-18, 65.

[128.] Wilbraham, *Scenes Beyond the Atlantic; A Lecture, Delivered to the Parish
Church Schools, at Bolton-le-Moors* (Bolton, 1846), 13, 39-40.

[129.] See Geoff Eley and Ronald Grigor Suny, "Introduction: From the Moment of Social History to the Work of Cultural Representation," in *Becoming National: A
Reader*, ed. idem (New York: Oxford University Press, 1996), 9: "What looks from
outside and from a distance as a bounded group appears much more divided and contested at closer range. Culture is more often not what people share, but what they
choose to fight over."

Notes to Chapter 12

[1.] Clifton to James Fair, n.d., quoted by John Kennedy, *The Clifton Chronicle* (Preston, 1990), 75.

[2.] *PC*, June 17, 1848, p. 2.

[3.] *PC*, Jan. 5, 1850, p. 4.

[4.] Mr. Alderman Baynes, *The Cotton Trade. Two Lectures . . . delivered before the
members of the Blackburn Literary, Scientific and Mechanics' Institution* (on Apr. 2
and June 11, 1857; Blackburn, 1857), II, "Its Mission: Politically, Socially, Morally,
and Religiously," 56-57, 60, 66-68, 74-77.

[5.] Obit., *BT*, Oct. 11, 1873, p. 6.

[6.] As noted by, e.g., D. A. Farnie, *The English Cotton Industry and the World Mar-
ket 1815-1896* (Oxford: Clarendon Press, 1979), 40; Anthony Howe, *The Cotton Mas-
ters 1830-1860* (Oxford: Clarendon Press, 1984), 229-49; Wendy Hinde, *Richard
Cobden: A Victorian Outsider* (New Haven: Yale University Press, 1987), 70-71, 282;
Norman McCord, *The Anti-Corn Law League 1838-1846* (London: George Allen and
Unwin, 1958), 208-12; W. H. Greenleaf, *The British Political Tradition*, vol. 2, *The
Ideological Heritage* (London: Methuen, 1983), 38-42; Geoffrey Best, *Mid-Victorian
Britain 1851-1875* (London: Weidenfeld and Nicolson, 1971), 239; Gary S. Messinger,
Manchester in the Victorian Age: The Half-Known City (Manchester: Manchester Uni-
versity Press, 1985), 73-78.

[7.] See also, e.g., the statement of the cotton lord, Thomas Bazley, *A Lecture upon
Cotton as an Element of Industry* (London, 1852), 25, at the Society of Arts in London, Prince Albert in the chair, in connection with the Great Exhibition: "[T]he hand-
maid of Industry is Peace!"

[8.] Baynes, *The Cotton Trade*, 88-89. For similar reactions, see Paul Adelman, *Victorian Radicalism: The Middle-Class Experience, 1830-1914* (London: Longman, 1984),
chap. 2.

[9.] The distinction between milltown radicals and liberals along a spectrum of reforming opinion is not clearcut, though the more radical tended to be especially exercised by aristocratic privileges and values. For useful attempts at clarification, see T. A.

Jenkins, *The Liberal Ascendancy, 1830-1886* (New York: St. Martin's Press, 1994), 10-14.

[10.] BALS, Bolton Biographical Notes, B1, pp. 147-49.

[11.] For a particularly candid expression of this, see *PC*, Sept. 28, 1839, p. 2: "A neighbouring nation, at the mouth of a few guns, forced the free and recently recognised states of South America, to enter into commercial and reciprocal treaties. These states undoubtedly have no desire to trade with France, or be in alliance with her; but France says they *must*, and as she backs her demands with hints and omens which cannot be mistaken, why the states are compelled to yield—to yield reluctantly to terms which, though they are too ignorant to know it, are mutually beneficial to both countries. Let us do this with China, and the tea trade and every other branch of commerce will be placed on a much safer foundation."

[12.] BL, Cobden Papers, vol. VII, Add. MS 43653, Ashworth to Cobden, Sept. 22, Oct. 3, 1849, Oct. 12, 1852.

[13.] BL, Peel papers, Add. MS 40589, Whittaker to Peel, 15 Apr., 1846; LRO, Coucher Book of Trinity, PR 1549/14.

[14.] For a good summary of the "feudalization"/"bourgeoisification" debate, see Simon Gunn, "The 'Failure' of the Victorian Middle Class: A Critique," in *The Culture of Capital: Art, Power and the Nineteenth-century Middle Class*, ed. Janet Wolff and John Seed (Manchester: Manchester University Press, 1988).

[15.] R. G. Thorne, *The History of Parliament: The House of Commons 1790-1820* (London: Secker and Warburg, 1986), II: 237.

[16.] Around 3,500 loyalists at the time and subsequently signed the original address and protested against the amendment. DDHu 53/55, address and amended address to Prince Regent, Feb. 25, 1817; notice from "A Freeholder," Preston, Feb. 26; notice of magistrates, clergy, and freeholders who were not at the meeting, approving the original address. These were published together by William Addison (Preston, May 1, 1817), to demonstrate that Lancashire still retained a high character of loyalty.

[17.] PRO, HO 40/3, extract, "Mr. J. W." to Fletcher, Jan. 4, 1817. The Mr. Turner was presumably a member of the Mill Hill cotton-manufacturing and calico-printing family (there are no other Turners listed in Rogerson's *Lancashire Directory* of 1818). One member of this family, William Turner, a Whig Churchman, purchaser of Shrigley Hall in Cheshire, and soon to be high sheriff of Cheshire, became one of Blackburn's first MPs in 1832. It is rather startling that individuals like Turner and Cunliffe should have been the objects of such spying.

[18.] HO 40/12, Fletcher to Sidmouth, Apr. 19, 1820; Alpha to J. Langshaw, Apr. 17 (Heywood quotation); HO 40/14, Fletcher to Sidmouth, Aug. 14, 1820; Alpha to Langshaw, Aug. 13.

[19.] LRO, DDHu 53/82/82, notice of meeting, Sept. 25, 1816; /83, notice of requisition and reply, Sept. 9; /85, notice of John Pilkington, John Cockshott, and the Rev. William Thistlethwaite, Sept. 27.

[20.] BALS, Heywood Papers, ZHE/15, draft notice "To the Public," Oct. 11, 1819; copy of notice to magistrates of the Division of Warrington, Oct. 11; reply of J. A. Borron, Oct. 20, enclosing Derby to Borron, Oct. 19; resolutions of meeting, n.d.

[21.] William Alexander Abram, *Blackburn Characters of a Past Generation* (Blackburn, 1894), 17.

[22.] DDHu 53/61, requisitions to Hulton, 1820; John Gorst, Preston, to Hulton, Mar. 11; Hulton to "Gentlemen," Mar. 10; Henry Philip Hoghton of Walton Hall to Hulton, Mar. 12.

[23.] *PC*, Nov. 18, 1820, p. 3; Nov. 25, p. 2; Dec. 9, p. 2; Dec. 23, p. 2.

[24.] *BM*, Nov. 22, 1820, p. 3. And see letters excoriating the queen, Oct. 25, p. 2; Dec. 6, pp. 2-3; Dec. 13, p. 2; and comments on loyal addresses, Dec. 20, p. 4; Dec. 27, p. 3. But see James J. Sack, *From Jacobite to Conservative: Reaction and Orthodoxy in Britain, c.1760-1832* (Cambridge: Cambridge University Press, 1993), 141ff.: although most of the national loyalist press supported the king, Lord Kenyon of Peel, a prominent Orangeman, and his journal the *True Briton*, championed the queen. For the affair and domesticity, see above, chap. 4.

[25.] William Dobson, *History of the Parliamentary Representation of Preston*, 2nd ed. (Preston, 1868), 66; LRO, *Preston Election Squibs*, 1818, pp. i-v.

[26.] His active backers included John Lawe (banker), W. Ormerod Pilkington (gentleman, attorney), Thomas Howard (attorney), Charles Buck (attorney), Peter Haydock (attorney), James Holland (attorney), William Woodcock (timber merchant), and Thomas Emmett (timber merchant).

[27.] Stephen W. Urbanski, "Parliamentary Politics, 1796-1832, in an Industrializing Borough: Preston, Lancashire" (Ph.D. diss., Emory University, 1976), 20-30, 84-85, 92-95; Dobson, *Parliamentary Representation*, 66-70; *Preston Election Squibs*, 1820: pp. 3-7, proceedings at hustings; p. 20, notice from Williams's committee room, Mar. 6; p. 32, Robert Middleton of Hunt's committee to independent electors, Mar. 13; pp. 34-36, proceedings on the riot; p. 47, notice from Williams's committee room, Mar. 23; LRO, DDK 1683/20-31, letters of J. Walton to James Heyes, Mar. 9-22; /32, William Rawstorne to Heyes, Mar. 22.

[28.] *An Alphabetical List . . .* (Preston, 1820). The assessment is imperfect partly because of the inconsistency in designation of occupations, partly because of the difficulties in telling whether a retailer, timber merchant, coal merchant, or draper, to name but a few, were wealthy men with substantial premises or kept tiny shops. For this and later poll books I have erred on the side of selectivity. Here I have counted only the following occupations: manufacturer, surgeon, gentleman, attorney, minister, spinning master, banker, clerk (which generally meant an Anglican clergyman), barrister, and physician.

[29.] See Frank O'Gorman, *Voters, Patrons, and Parties: The Unreformed Electoral System of Hanoverian England 1734-1832* (Oxford: Clarendon Press, 1989), 137, 187.

[30.] LRO, DDK 1683/28, Walton to Heyes, Mar. 18.

[31.] LRO, DDK 1683/26, Walton [to Heyes?] (letter incomplete), Mar. 15.

[32.] *PC*, Apr. 22, 1826, p. 2; *Preston Election Squibs*, 1826: p. 3, Stanley to electors, Apr. 22; pp. 6, 8, Thomas Smith to electors, May 4, 8; p. 25, Samuel Horrocks Jr. to electors, May 29; p. 34, Robert Barrie to electors, June 8; pp. 39-47, the hustings; p. 103, "Dissenters!," June 17; p. 113, "Address of Dissenting Ministers to Preston Dissenters," June 19; pp. 115-16, "A Trinitarian Dissenter to Trinitarian Dissenters," June 20; p. 118, "An Elector to Electors of Preston," June 23; p. 121, "To Roman Catholic Electors," June 26; pp. 121-23, close of poll; Urbanski, "Parliamentary Politics," 102-6, 111; Dobson, *Parliamentary Representation*, 72-74. For details of Wood, see his obituary in *MG*, Oct. 22, 1856, quoted by William Alexander Abram, "Sketches in Local History," vol. 7.

[33.] *Cobbett's Poor Man's Friend* 1, letter 1: "To the Working Classes of Preston," Aug. 1, 1826.

[34.] LRO, QDE/3, "1826—List of Voters." I have counted these occupations: attorneys, esquires, gentlemen, manufacturers, clerks, surgeons, cotton merchants, ironfounders, land surveyors and agents, ministers, cotton spinners (who in this case were masters; operatives were listed simply as "spinners"), spinning masters, bankers, "Drs.," physicians, and the governor of the House of Correction.

[35.] See Mark Harrison, *Crowds and History: Mass Phenomena in English Towns, 1790-1835* (Cambridge: Cambridge University Press, 1988), 183-91; Frank O'Gorman, "Campaign Rituals and Ceremonies: The Social Meaning of Elections in England 1780-1860," *P&P* 135 (May 1992): 79-115.

[36.] LRO, DDH/48, "Preston Election 1826: Case"; /50, opinion of W. G. Adam, Lincoln's Inn.

[37.] LRO, DDPR 130/13, Stanley to R. Palmer, Mar. 2, 1828.

[38.] LRO, DDH/62, William Cross to William Clayton, n.d.; and see related correspondence and memos, /49, /51-53, /56, /58, /60, /76, /81-82, /90. See also James Aldridge, "The Parliamentary Franchise at Preston and the Reform Act of 1832" (BA thesis, Manchester University, 1948), 38, 55-57; Dobson, *Parliamentary Representation*, 74.

[39.] See, e.g., *Preston Election Squibs*, 1826, p. 109, one of a series of squibs on "The Tyrants' Looking Glass," suggesting the numbers of tinmen, cane-makers, drapers, hackhorse men, attorneys, manufacturers, etc. who could expect to benefit from future patronage if they voted correctly. The author concluded, "After all our boast of freedom, the country and its important interests, are bought and sold for bread and cheese."

[40.] Urbanski, "Parliamentary Politics," 127, 131, 135; Dobson, *Parliamentary Representation*, 75-76; Winifred Proctor, "Orator Hunt, M.P. for Preston, 1830-32," *THSLC* 114 (1962): 131-44; John Belchem, *'Orator' Hunt: Henry Hunt and English Working-Class Radicalism* (Oxford: Clarendon Press, 1985), 207-11, 216-17; Anthony Hewitson, *History of Preston* (Preston, 1883), 134.

[41.] According to Abram, *Blackburn Characters*, 240-41, Stanley's agents took no effective precautions against the impersonation of nonresident electors. James Boyle, a Blackburn radical confectioner (and later an alderman), claimed that he went to Preston with another Blackburn radical to impersonate unknown out-voters, and between them they voted fourteen times for Hunt. See also Joseph Livesey, *Autobiography of Joseph Livesey* (London [1881?]), 51: the result was "by no means the result of fair play."

[42.] *An Alphabetical List . . .* (Preston, 1831).

[43.] See James Vernon, *Politics and the People: A Study in English Political Culture, c.1815-67* (Cambridge: Cambridge University Press, 1993).

[44.] See *PP*, Apr. 28, 1832, p. 2; Roland Quinault, "The Industrial Revolution and Parliamentary Reform," in *The Industrial Revolution and British Society*, ed. Patrick O'Brien and Quinault (Cambridge: Cambridge University Press, 1993), 183-84, 196-201.

[45.] *BC*, Feb. 26, 1831, pp. 1, 3.

[46.] *BC*, Feb. 12, 1831, p. 4.

[47.] *PC*, Apr. 2, 1831, p. 3. On Mitchell and Johnston see Belchem, *'Orator' Hunt*, 207ff.

[48.] *BC*, Feb. 12, 1831, p. 4.

[49.] LRO, DDHu 53/82/20, "Letter from A Tradesman and Independent Elector," quoting speech of July 6.

[50.] *PP*, Mar. 12, 1831, p. 2.

[51.] *PC*, Oct. 1, p. 3; Oct. 8, p. 3.

[52.] *PC*, Oct. 15, p. 2.

[53.] *BC*, May 12, 1832, p. 4; May 19, p. 2.

[54.] *BC*, May 19, p. 3.

[55.] *PC*, May 12, p. 3.

[56.] *BC*, May 19, p. 3.

[57.] *BC*, May 19, p. 4.

[58.] *PC*, May 26, p. 3. And see W. L. Burn, *The Age of Equipoise: A Study of the Mid-Victorian Generation*, 2nd ed. (New York: Norton, 1965), 74, for a similar comment about Joseph Parkes, Birmingham radical attorney.

[59.] LRO, DDHu 53/82/35, "Address to Electors"; /39, "Speech at Election Dinner," Dec. 1, 1832; William Brimelow, *Political and Parliamentary History of Bolton* (Bolton, 1882), 128-29, 131.

[60.] BALS, Heywood Papers, ZHE/28, Darbishire to Heywood, June 20, 1832.

[61.] BALS, Heywood Papers, ZHE/28, draft to editor of *BC*, n.d. See also LRO, DDHu 53/82/50, to the inhabitants of Bolton.

[62.] Frank Whitson Fetter, "Robert Torrens: Colonel of Marines and Political Economist," *Economica* (May 1962): 152-65; Cobbett's *Political Register* XXXIII (Jan. 3, 1818): 5 (quotation, cited by Fetter, 159); LRO, DDHu 53/82/29, letter to the electors of Bolton, from William Cobbett, July 4, 1832.

[63.] Brimelow, *Political and Parliamentary*, 125-46, 150-56; LRO, DDHu 53/82/36, address to electors by Yates, Nov. 27, 1832; BALS, Heywood Papers, ZHE/28, Darbishire to Heywood, June 20, 1832. For anti-Unitarian broadsides, see LRO, DDHu 53/82/19, /21, /22, /24.

[64.] Brimelow, *Political and Parliamentary*, 147-49; *BC*, Dec. 8, 1832, p. 3.

[65.] *Autobiographical Recollections of Sir John Bowring. With a Brief Memoir by Lewin B. Bowring* (London, 1877), 14, 61, 65, 337-39, 349-50, and passim; Bowring, *Matins and Vespers with Hymns and Poems. With a Memoir of his Life by Lady Bowring* (London, 1895), 11, 16-17, 18-19, 26-29; LRO, DD Pr/50/4, poster-letters from Bowring to the electors of Blackburn, Aug. 3-Oct. 22, 1832.

[66.] *BG*, June 27, 1832, p. 4; July 18, pp. 3-4; Aug. 1, p. 4; Aug. 8, p. 4; Dec. 12, p. 5; Dec. 19, pp. 4-5.

[67.] BRL, PO5, broadsheet of a newspaper advertisement, Mar. 14, 1831.

[68.] *BG*, Sept. 12, 1832, p. 1; *BC*, Dec. 15, p. 3. Just before the election (*BG*, Nov. 28, 1832, pp. 1, 4) he joined prominent reformers on the founding committee of the Blackburn East India Association, which was dedicated to ending the East India Company's monopoly on trade with China and to removing restrictions on the settlement of British subjects in the interior of India. But for an attack on Feilden's legal, army, Church, and slave-owning connections, see LRO, *Addresses from One of the 3730 Electors of Preston*, letter from "Egalite," Feb. 4, 1832.

[69.] Cited in *BG*, July 18, 1832, p. 5. Note also Bolling's family ties to the Church: he married a sister of James Slade, vicar of Bolton, and Slade and his brother William (a partner in the Bolling cotton mills) married sisters of Bolling. See the Rev. J. A. Atkinson, *Memoir of the Rev. Canon Slade* (Bolton, 1892), 5, 7; BALS, Bolton Biographical Notes, B1, p. 40, obit. of Mrs. William Bolling, May 1881.

[70.] *BA*, Aug. 27, p. 8.

[71.] William Durham, *History of the Parliamentary Elections for the Borough of Blackburn from 1832 to 1865* (Preston, 1866), 9-10.

[72.] PRO, HO 52/13, anon. to mayor of Preston, Nov. 14, 1831.

[73.] *Addresses from One of the 3730*, June 23, 1832; Jan. 5, 1833.

[74.] *PC*, Dec. 15, pp. 2-3; Urbanski, *Parliamentary Politics*, 138-44; Dobson, *Parliamentary Representation*, 78-80; Proctor, "Orator Hunt," 151-53; Aldridge, "Parliamentary Franchise," 70-73, 118. One of the sitting candidates, John Wood, had retired to become chairman of the Board of Stamps and Taxes. On Forbes, see Belchem, *'Orator' Hunt*, 265.

[75.] But seventy-two of them apparently did not vote, possibly including some disgruntled Cromptonites like Robert Segar. *A List of Persons Entitled to Vote, Distinguishing those who Voted* (Preston, 1833). I have counted these occupations: esquire, gentleman, attorney or solicitor, barrister, physician, surgeon, doctor, minister, vicar, clerk, priest, manufacturer, linen manufacturer, banker, cotton spinner, flax spinner, merchant, ironfounder, and governor of the House of Correction.

[76.] See John A. Phillips and Charles Wetherell, "The Great Reform Act of 1832 and the Political Modernization of England," *AHR* 100, 2 (Apr. 1995): 411-36.

[77.] John A. Phillips, *The Great Reform Bill in the Boroughs: English Electoral Behaviour, 1818-1841* (Oxford: Clarendon Press, 1992), 298-301. This was the national pattern: as we have seen, in wide-suffrage boroughs like Preston, elections had long been "participatory, partisan and popular" (O'Gorman, *Voters, Patrons and Parties*, 392-93).

[78.] *BA*, Feb. 18, 1833, p. 8.

[79.] Ibid.

[80.] LRO, DDHu 53/82/57, poster "To the Protestants of Great Britain," Dec. 1, 1834.

[81.] LRO, DDHu 53/81, report of election riot in Bolton [1841].

[82.] Brimelow, *Political and Parliamentary*, 116-21. See also BL, Peel Papers, Add. MS 40402, Hulton to Peel, Dec. 24, 1831; DDHu 53/56, handwritten extract from Alison's *History of Europe*, II: 403, detailing Peterloo, with Hulton's own account juxtaposed: "The Town was saved from such pillage and conflagration, as, afterwards destroy'd a great part of the city of Bristol." And DDHu 53/80, memorial to Hulton from the boroughreeve, constables, and leading Tories of Great Bolton, Mar. 30, 1835, appealing to him that, with the change in the administration, "your invaluable Services as a Magistrate which have always done honor to yourself and conferred a benefit on the Public may be restored to the Community."

[83.] BL, Peel Papers, Add. MS 40404, Hulton to Peel, Dec. 4, 1834; Peel to Hulton, Dec. 11.

[84.] David Walsh, "Operative Conservatism in Lancashire, 1833-1846. Some Comments on a Changing Political Culture," occasional paper in Politics and Contemporary History, 11 (Salford University, 1987), 22, 27; idem, "Working Class Development, Control and New Conservatism; Blackburn 1820-1850" (MSc. thesis, Salford University, 1986), 254; BALS, Bolton Biographical Notes, B1, obit. of William Ford Hulton, 1879.

[85.] *PC*, June 6, 1835, p. 3. Note also the Preston Conservative Registration Club, begun under the presidency of John Paley Jr., cotton spinner, in September 1837, to ensure Tory names were on the electoral register (LRO, DDPR 37/72, resolution of meeting of Sept. 28, 1837).

[86.] *BS*, Feb. 4, p. 4; Feb. 11, p. 4; Peter A. Whittle, *Blackburn As It Is: A Topographical, Statistical, and Historical Account of the Borough of Blackburn* (Preston, 1852), 161.

[87.] *BC*, Nov. 7, 1835, p. 2. The paper had changed hands in September 1834 and its editorial line switched from radical to conservative. See Sept. 13, 1834, pp. 1-2; Dec. 20, 1834, p. 2; Jan. 3, 1835, p. 2.

[88.] *PC*, Feb. 6, 1836, p. 2; Walsh, "Working Class Political Integration," chaps. 9-10.

[89.] See James Vernon, ed., *Re-reading the Constitution: New Narratives in the Political History of England's Long Nineteenth Century* (Cambridge: Cambridge University Press, 1996), 2 and passim.

[90.] LRO, DDPr/51/3a, *Report of the Proceedings at the Meeting of the Bolton Operative Conservative Association, held in the Little Bolton Town Hall, June 1st, 1836* (Bolton, 1836), 3-11, 16-18, 27-28.

[91.] *Report of the Proceedings at the First Anniversary Dinner of the Horwich Operative Conservative Association* (Bolton, 1836), 3-16.

[92.] See, e.g., Boyd Hilton, "Peel: A Reappraisal," *HJ* 22, 3 (1979): 585-614.

[93.] *BS*, Nov. 27, 1839, quoted by Walsh, "Operative Conservatism," 54.

[94.] *PP*, Nov. 30, 1839, p. 4.

[95.] Sykes, "Popular Politics and Trades Unionism in South-East Lancashire, 1829-42" (Ph.D. thesis, Manchester University, 1982), 432-34, 456-61, 465, 467. He suggests (446) that because of the unusual identification of the anti-Poor Law agitation in Bolton with conservatism, popular protest was muted in 1837-38. But note that, although there was some conservative attempt to run with opposition to the New Poor Law as a way of attracting lower-class support—at the Horwich OCA meeting cited above, for example, Charles Rothwell, an operative, condemned the cruelty of the Whigs' measure, and Ridgway himself was a staunch opponent—it was difficult to make it convincing given Tory support for it at a national level. Locally, Hulton on behalf of his son and Foster of the *Chronicle* had both solicited appointments in the early days of the new system's operation. See BL, Peel Papers, Add. MS 40409, Hulton to Peel, Jan. 7, 1835; for Foster, see chap. 7. Also see Peter F. Taylor, "Popular Politics and Labour-Capital Relations in Bolton, 1825-1850" (Ph.D. diss., Lancaster University, 1991), 94, who notes that, as the town's leading employers were conservative and committed to industrial society, the scope for the development of Tory-radicalism was limited. For Robert Heywood's assessment, see ZHE/26/3, Heywood to editor of *BFP*, June 6, 1836.

[96.] Walsh, "Operative Conservatism," 38, 53, 56, and passim; idem, "Working Class Development," 254-58, 273. He discusses the formation of short-lived Conservative Trades Associations to appeal to the middling orders, but these apparently merged with the OCAs around 1837 or soon after. The upshot in Blackburn was an OCA where the middling sort formed a majority of the officeholders by the mid-1840s. In 1837, only one of the committee—Charles Tiplady, bookbinder—had the vote; in 1847, this had increased to fourteen out of twenty.

[97.] *BFP*, Aug. 18, 1838, p. 3.

[98.] *BG*, Aug. 12, 1835, p. 4.

[99.] See, e.g., Robert Segar's denial of impending betrayal, *PC*, May 26, 1832, p. 3. For clear statements of middle-class reformers reneging on their radicalism as soon as Reform was safe, see Belchem, '*Orator' Hunt*, 259-60, 265-66; Iorwerth Prothero, *Radical Artisans in England and France, 1830-1870* (Cambridge: Cambridge University Press, 1997), 186, 191 (quoting a Bolton radical in *BC*, Mar. 19, 1831, p. 3: "[I]f the middle classes obtained what they were now seeking for, they would in two years from this time join the aristocracy, and again call them a rabble and swinish multitude").

[100.] *BFP*, Nov. 21, 1835, p. 2. This manifesto was signed "A. W. P."—presumably A. W. Paulton, soon to be a prominent anti-Corn Law speaker.

[101.] *BFP*, Sept. 22, 1838, p. 3.

[102.] *PC*, Nov. 10, 1838, pp. 2-3.

[103.] *BFP*, Feb. 10, 1838, p. 2; Feb. 17, p. 3; Feb. 24, p. 2 (quotations).

[104.] *BFP*, Sept. 14, p. 2. The reference was to the Tory-radical Richard Oastler, and the Chartist leaders Feargus O'Connor and James Bronterre O'Brien. On the mixed hostility to both "aristocrats" and "capitalists," see J. R. Dinwiddy, "Chartism," in his

Radicalism and Reform in Britain, 1780-1850 (London: Hambledon Press, 1992), 412-14.

[105.] *BFP*, Sept. 22, 1838, p. 3.

[106.] *BFP*, Aug. 24, p. 2. See also *BFP*, Aug. 31, p. 2; *BC*, Aug. 10, p. 2; Aug. 17, p. 2; Aug. 24, p. 2; Robert Sykes, "Physical-Force Chartism: The Cotton District and the Chartist Crisis of 1839," *IRSH* xxx, 2 (1985): 220, 235.

[107.] *BFP*, July 17, 1841, p. 2.

[108.] *BFP*, Feb. 26, 1842, p. 2.

[109.] *BFP*, Aug. 27, 1842, p. 2.

[110.] *BFP*, Aug. 20, p. 2. See also Mar. 5, p. 2; July 23, p. 2; Aug. 13, p. 2. For the charges of incitement, see above, chap. 3.

[111.] LRO, DDPr/51/4, Bowring to the electors of Bolton, June 10, 1841.

[112.] For indications of this, see BALS, Heywood Papers, ZHE/35, Heywood to Thornley, Dec. 11, 1839; *BFP*, Nov. 15, 1845, p. 3; Nov. 22, p. 4; Nov. 7, 1846, p. 3; Taylor, "Popular Politics," p. 124; W. A. Abram, *Members of the Hornby Family who have Represented Blackburn in Parliament* (Manchester, 1892), 8.

[113.] See Henry Ashworth, *Recollections of Richard Cobden, M.P., and the Anti-Corn-Law League*, 2nd ed. (London, 1876), 13.

[114.] H. I. Hunt, "David Whitehead of Rawtenstall: A Transcription from the Manuscript of the First David Whitehead" (1956), 76, 81.

[115.] Quoted by Archibald Prentice, *History of the Anti-Corn-Law League*, 2nd ed. (London, 1968), I: 69. And see Bowring's speech in Manchester, Sept. 10, 1839, quoted by Burn, *Age of Equipoise*, 64.

[116.] BL, Cobden Papers, Add. MS 43,653, Ashworth to Cobden, Apr. 14, 1842.

[117.] Prentice, *Anti-Corn-Law League*, I: 64, 107, 120, 137, 185, 399; II: 147, 415-16; Ashworth, *Recollections of Cobden*, 13, 57-62, 200; BALS, Heywood Papers, ZHE/38, R. Cunliffe, secretary of Bolton ACLA, to Heywood, Jan. 24, 1842.

[118.] *BFP*, Dec. 27, 1845, p. 3.

[119.] George Jacob Holyoake, *Bygones Worth Remembering* (New York, 1905), I: 162-69.

[120.] *BFP*, Dec. 27, 1845, p. 3; Prentice, *Anti-Corn-Law League*, I: 145, 415-16; II: 15, 23, 415-16; *BS*, Dec. 14, 1842, pp. 2-3.

[121.] *PC*, Feb. 9, 1839, p. 2; Jan. 4, 1845, p. 3; Dec. 6, p. 2; Dec. 13, p. 2; Prentice, *Anti-Corn-Law League*, I: 145; II: 12, 15.

[122.] And see *Report of the Conference of Ministers of all Denominations on the Corn Laws, held in Manchester August 17-20, 1841* (Manchester, 1841), for the names of local ministers present.

[123.] *BFP*, Feb. 16, 1839, pp. 2-3.

[124.] Information gleaned from J. E. King, *Richard Marsden and the Preston Chartists 1837-1848*, occasional paper 10 (Centre for North-West Regional Studies, University of Lancaster, 1980), 6, 33-34, 41; *Preston Election Squibs*, 1841, pp. 17-18, "The Council of the Preston Chartists," June 17.

[125.] *MG*, Jan. 20, 1844, p. 7.

[126.] *BFP*, Mar. 16, 1844, p. 3; Mar. 23, p. 3.

[127.] For a classic account, see J. R. Vincent, *The Formation of the Liberal Party 1857-1868* (London: Constable, 1966). For emphasis on the continuities of radicalism over the mid-century period, see Eugenio F. Biagini and Alastair J. Reid, eds., *Currents of Radicalism: Popular Radicalism, Organized Labour and Party Politics in Britain, 1850-1914* (Cambridge: Cambridge University Press, 1991); Margot Finn, *After Chartism: Class and Nation in English Radical Politics, 1848-1874* (Cambridge: Cambridge

University Press, 1993); David Nicholls, "The English Middle Class and the Ideological Significance of Radicalism, 1760-1886," *JBS* 24 (Oct. 1985): 415-33; Miles Taylor, *The Decline of British Radicalism, 1847-1860* (Oxford: Clarendon Press, 1995).

[128.] Ashworth, *Recollections*, 218.

[129.] BALS, Heywood Papers, ZHE/43, Heywood to Bowring, Jan. 22, 1847; *BFP*, July 24, 1847, p. 2; Nov. 27, p. 2; Dec. 24. The paper ceased on Jan. 23, was revived on July 24 in time for the election, and printed its last edition on Dec. 24. The *Bolton Times*, a more extended liberal paper, replaced it the following week but only lasted until July 15, 1848. The editor of the *Bolton Times* wrote (reported in *BC*, July 15, 1848, p. 4), "Without a local newspaper, the Reformers of Bolton are powerless as a party—with a local newspaper, well supported and carried on with becoming spirit and energy, they might accomplish much good for the borough."

[130.] The Freehold Land Societies bought up estates and parceled them out to thrifty working-class investors, who could then qualify for the 40s.-freehold county franchise. See J. Ewing Ritchie, *Freehold Land Societies: Their History, Present Position, and Claims* (London, 1853). For the Freehold Land Society in Preston, presided over by John Goodair, millowner, which bought a forty-five-acre farm in Fulwood and laid it out for building in 1850-51, see Anthony Hewitson, *Northward. Historic, Topographic, Residential, and Scenic Gleanings, &c. Between Preston and Lancaster* (Preston, 1900), 5-6.

[131.] Nicholas C. Edsall, "A Failed National Movement: the Parliamentary and Financial Reform Association, 1848-54," *BIHR* XLIX, 119 (May 1976): 108-14; Hugh Mulleneux Walmsley, *The Life of Sir Joshua Walmsley* (London, 1879), 1ff., 160-66, 198-214.

[132.] Add. MS 43383, Bright to Cobden, Sept. 26, 1851, quoted by Edsall, "Failed National Movement," 122.

[133.] Note the tension in playing to both sides of the gallery in the 1849 Bolton election. At one meeting, with few of the wealthier classes in attendance, he was asked, "Where, sir, are your Broadcloths to-night?" He replied, pointing to the "Fustian Jackets" before him, "'There are my Broadcloths.'" (Walmsley, *Walmsley*, 213-14.) But at the nomination, Thomas Thomasson reassured the electorate that Walmsley's standing in society "was a guarantee that he would countenance no 'wild or undigested scheme of change.' Sir Joshua had got too much wool on his back to partake in any dangerous experiments." (BALS, Bolton Biographical Notes, B1, p. 67, obit., 1867.)

[134.] Edsall, "Failed National Movement," 114-31; Walmsley, *Walmsley*, 215ff.; Michael R. Watts, *The Dissenters*, vol. II, *The Expansion of Evangelical Nonconformity* (Oxford: Clarendon Press, 1995), 565-66.

[135.] Walmsley, *Walmsley*, 227-29.

[136.] Ibid., 225-26. See also BALS, Heywood Papers, ZHE/47, Heywood to Z. Hubbersty, Sept. 8, 1851.

[137.] See Edsall, "Failed National Movement," 130; P. J. Cain and A. G. Hopkins, *British Imperialism*, vol. 1, *Innovation and Expansion 1688-1914* (London: Longman, 1993), 79, 99-100, 141-42, 202; Philip Harling, *The Waning of 'Old Corruption': The Politics of Economical Reform in Britain, 1779-1846* (Oxford: Clarendon Press, 1996); Michael Winstanley, "Oldham Radicalism and the Origins of Popular Liberalism, 1830-52," *HJ* 36, 3 (1993): 642-43; Gareth Stedman Jones, "Rethinking Chartism," in his *Languages of Class: Studies in English Working Class History 1832-1982* (Cambridge: Cambridge University Press, 1983), 174-77; Miles Taylor, "Rethinking the Chartists: Searching for Synthesis in the Historiography of Chartism," *HJ* 39, 2 (1996): 488-92.

[138.] See John Breuilly, *Labour and Liberalism in Nineteenth-Century Europe: Essays in Comparative History*, 2nd ed. (Manchester: Manchester University Press, 1994), 208 and passim.

[139.] See Dinwiddy, "Chartism," 416-20.

[140.] See Patrick O'Brien, "Political Preconditions for the Industrial Revolution," in *Industrial Revolution*, ed. O'Brien and Quinault, 125-51; John Brewer, *The Sinews of Power: War, Money and the English State, 1688-1783* (London: Unwin Hyman, 1989); Lawrence Stone, introduction to *An Imperial State at War*, ed. idem (London: Routledge, 1994); John Prest, *Liberty and Locality: Parliament, Permissive Legislation, and Ratepayers' Democracies in the Nineteenth Century* (Oxford: Clarendon Press, 1990).

[141.] *BS*, Feb. 27, 1850, pp. 1-2. For a recent overview, see Jeffrey A. Auerbach, *The Great Exhibition of 1851: A Nation on Display* (New Haven: Yale University Press, 1999).

[142.] For the national picture, see Harling, *Waning of 'Old Corruption,'* 257. For the statue to Peel in Preston (see above, chap. 8), *PC*, July 6, p. 4; July 20, pp. 4, 6; Nov. 30, p. 5. In neither of the other towns could the initial momentum be sustained. For Blackburn, where there seems to have been all-party approval of the principle but not of a specific project, see *BS*, July 10, 1850, p. 4; July 17, p. 1; Aug. 7, p. 1 (listing the extensive committee) and p. 2; Aug. 14, p. 2; Sept. 18, p. 2; Mar. 21, 1855, p. 3; Dec. 16, 1882, p. 8. The project for a park in Bolton failed to raise sufficient funds to pay the asking price of local landowners (some of whom—most notably the earl of Bradford—were averse to aiding the creation of a park named after Peel; see *BC*, Oct. 23, 1852, p. 8). The scheme's rise and fall can be traced in *BC*, July 20, 1850, p. 4; July 27, p. 2; Aug. 10, p. 5; Sept. 14, p. 5; Apr. 17, 1852, p. 8; May 1, p. 5; Oct. 23, p. 8; May 26, 1866, p. 7 (opening of the rate-financed Queen's Park); BALS, Heywood Papers, ZHE/46, Heywood to Walmsley, Aug. 13; Thomas Lever Rushton to Heywood, n.d.; Heywood to W. R. Scott, n.d.; John Hick to Heywood, Nov. 23; Heywood to John Butler, Dec. 4; Rushton to Heywood, Dec. 19, 1850; /47, Heywood to J. A. Turner, Jan. 22, 1851; Richard Marsden to Heywood, Jan. 28; S. D. Darbishire to Heywood, n.d. (and draft reply, Feb. 1); Walmsley to Heywood, Feb. 4, Feb. 8, Feb. 25, Mar. 14, July 21, June 4 (and draft reply, June 5); Stephen Blair to Rushton, Feb. 7; Heywood to Blair, Feb. 12; Blair to Heywood, Feb. 21; Scott to Heywood, n.d.; J. P. Fletcher to Heywood, May 10; Rushton to Heywood, Aug. 8; Heywood to Henry Ashworth, Aug. 26; /48, Elijah Rigby to Heywood, Apr. 13, 1852 (and draft reply, Apr. 15); Rushton to Heywood, Oct. 4; Fletcher to Heywood, Oct. 18 (and draft reply, Oct. 20); /51, Heywood draft to editor of *BC*, Mar. 29, 1855. And see Peter Bailey, *Leisure and Class in Victorian England: Rational Recreation and the Contest for Control, 1830-1885* (Toronto: University of Toronto Press, 1978), 52-53.

[143.] Baynes, *The Cotton Trade*, I, "The Origin, Rise, Progress and Present Extent of the Cotton Trade," 30-31.

[144.] *BC*, July 20, 1850, p. 4.

[145.] Baynes, *The Cotton Trade*, I: 30-31.

[146.] *BC*, Apr. 6, 1850, p. 4.

[147.] Gilbert J. French, *The Life and Times of Samuel Crompton*, 2nd ed. (Manchester, 1860), 232-34.

Notes to Conclusion

[1.] BL, Cobden Papers, vol. VII, Add. MS 43653, Ashworth to Cobden, May 25, 1850, Oct. 22, 1851.

[2.] See K. Theodore Hoppen, *The Mid-Victorian Generation 1846-1886* (Oxford: Oxford University Press, 1998), 1.

Notes to Appendix 4

[1.] BALS, Heywood Papers, ZHE/26/3, Heywood to James Silk Buckingham, May 2, 1836.

[2.] ZHE/26/3, Heywood to Henry Ashworth, June 10, 1838.

[3.] ZHE/26/3, Heywood to James Coppoch, n.d.

[4.] ZHE/36, Thomas Thornley to Heywood, July 29, 1840.

[5.] LRO, DDHu 53/82, "£10 Reward" (incomplete); /73, "Borough Election, Nomination of Candidates," July 25, 1837; *BFP*, July 29, 1837, p. 2. For the bitterness between Torrens and Ainsworth, see ZHE/31, Bolton election petition (extract), Mar. 10, 1835; Ainsworth to Heywood, Mar. 21, May 9, June 29.

[6.] William Naisby, *A Reply to Col. Torrens's Speech, &c.* (Bolton, Feb. 4, 1834). For other attacks on Torrens see LRO, DDHu 53/82/47, "To the Electors of Bolton"; /49, "Address to the Electors of Bolton"; /66, "Dialogue between two Tories!! Mr. Simpleton and Mr. Wisdom."

[7.] BALS, Heywood Papers, ZHE/26/3, Heywood to William Bowker, Dec. 22, 1834.

[8.] ZHE/35, Heywood to Thornley, Dec. 11, 1839; /36, Ainsworth to Heywood, May 29, 1840; Heywood to Ainsworth, May 29; C. J. Darbishire to Heywood, June 1; Heywood to Ainsworth, June 30; Ainsworth to Heywood, July 6; Heywood to Ainsworth, July 9, 13; Ainsworth to Heywood, July 11; Heywood to Ainsworth, July 14; Joseph Brotherton to Heywood, July 14; Thomas Thornley to Heywood, n.d. and July 29; *BFP*, Apr. 7, 1838, p. 2; Mar. 14, 1840, p. 3; May 30, pp. 2-3; July 18, p. 3; Nov. 7, pp. 2-3; June 19, 1841, p. 2; July 3, p. 2; W. Brimelow, *Political and Parliamentary History of Bolton* (Bolton, 1882), 263, 287-89, 397-402, 413.

[9.] A continuation of Frank O'Gorman's finding, *Voters, Patrons and Parties: The Unreformed Electoral System of Hanoverian England 1734-1832* (Oxford: Clarendon Press, 1989), 368-76, that in eighteenth-century elections where two candidates of one party faced two of another, very few split their votes; that plumping in four-cornered contests was rare; and that in three-cornered contests, split voting was significantly higher.

[10.] *BFP*, Jan. 7, 1843, p. 3; Jan. 28, p. 3 (a meeting of electors voted on the motion of Thomas Thomasson and C. J. Darbishire to replace Ainsworth with a better man); Heywood Papers, ZHE/39, "Mr. Ainsworth's Reply to the Requisitionists, Calling upon him to resign his seat for the Borough of Bolton," Feb. 10, 1843.

[11.] Quoted by Brimelow, *Political and Parliamentary*, 462-63.

[12.] Heywood Papers, ZHE/39, Joseph Brotherton to Heywood, Dec. 26, 1846; /43, Heywood to Bowring, Apr. 30, 1847, May 3; Bowring to Heywood, May 4; Heywood to Bowring, May 25; Bowring to Heywood, May 27; James Wardle to Heywood, July 6.

[13.] BALS, Ainsworth Papers, ZAH/3/16, letter to electors from Ainsworth, July 3, 1847 (quotation); Ainsworth Diary, ZAH/4/22, July 4, 1847, July 20.

[14.] See *BFP*, July 31, 1847, pp. 1-3.

[15.] BALS, Heywood Papers, ZHE/45, Richard Cobden to Edmund Ashworth, Feb. 9, 1849; Walmsley to Heywood, Feb. 11, 14, 20; Edmund Ashworth to Heywood, Feb. 16; Thomas Thomasson to Heywood, Feb. 17; Heywood to Walmsley, Feb. 21; John Smith to Heywood, Mar. 19; *BC*, Dec. 23, 1848, p. 8; Jan. 27, 1849, p. 3; Feb. 3, p. 5.

[16.] *BS*, Aug. 4, 1835, quoted by David Walsh, "Working Class Political Integration and the Conservative Party: A Study of Class Relations and Party Political Development in the North-West, 1800-1870" (Ph.D. diss., Salford University, 1991), 450.

[17.] BALS, Crompton Papers, ZCR/54/1, "A List of the 163 . . . Plumpers for Dr. Bowring." The Eccleses and the Pilkingtons (James, James Jr., and William), leading Independents, were prominent plumpers. Banister Eccles was rated at over £418, and Joseph Eccles at over £319.

[18.] *BG*, Feb. 11, p. 4; Feb. 18, pp. 4-5.

[19.] *BG*, Jan. 14, 1835, p. 1, "Letter to Electors," Jan. 10.

[20.] *BG*, Jan. 28, p. 4.

[21.] *BS*, Aug. 2, 1837, and see July 26, 1837, p. 3.

[22.] Michael J. Turner, *Reform and Respectability: The Making of a Middle-Class Liberalism in Early Nineteenth-Century Manchester* (Manchester: Chetham Society, 1995), 27-28.

[23.] CMA, J. B. Smith's Papers: Blackburn, Dundee, and Walsall Elections (Elections, vol. III), MS 923.2 S.336, draft of election address (and printed address, July 20, 1837).

[24.] Ibid., Smith to William Longsdon, Sept. 20, 1837.

[25.] Ibid., July 31.

[26.] Ibid., Aug. 7.

[27.] BL, Peel Papers, Add. MS 40425, Feilden to Peel, Oct. 17, 1838.

[28.] BL, Peel Papers, Add. MS 40486, Feilden to Peel, Aug. 2, 1841.

[29.] *BS*, June 2, 1841, p. 2; June 9, p. 1; June 16, p. 2; June 30, pp. 2-3; W. A. Abram, ed., "Extracts from the Diary of Mr Charles Tiplady, 1840-1873" (typescript in BRL), entry of July 12, 1841.

[30.] *List of Persons Who Voted* (Blackburn, 1841). This poll book does not list occupations.

[31.] William Durham, *History of the Parliamentary Elections for the Borough of Blackburn from 1832 to 1865* (Preston, 1866). On Hargreaves, see R. S. Crossley, *Accrington Captains of Industry* (Accrington, 1930), 54-55.

[32.] William Dobson, *History of the Parliamentary Representation of Preston*, 2nd ed. (Preston, 1868), 82.

[33.] *PC*, Jan. 3, 1835, p. 2; Jan. 10, p. 2; Jan. 24, p. 2.

[34.] Dobson, *Parliamentary Representation*, 83-85; LRO, *Preston Election Squibs*, 1837: p. 5, extract from letter of Cobden, July 4; pp. 47-58, "The Nomination"; pp. 53-54, extract from the *PP* (quotation); *PC*, July 29, p. 1.

[35.] Col. Roger Fleetwood Hesketh, *Sir Peter Hesketh-Fleetwood, Bt. A Monograph* (Fleetwood, 1951), 8. For Strickland, see H. W. Clemesha, *A History of Preston in Amounderness* (Manchester, 1912), 266.

[36.] *Preston Election Squibs*, 1841, pp. 37-38, "To the Independent Electors," June 18.

[37.] Dobson, *Parliamentary Representation*, 85; *Preston Election Squibs*, 1841: p. 1, Fleetwood to electors, June 12; pp. 2-3, Strickland to "Liberal and Independent Electors," June 14; Parker to electors, June 14; p. 4, Swainson to "Independent Electors," June 14; p. 21, speech of Parker at Operative Conservative dinner (from *PC*, Sept. 19, 1840); p. 39, the joint addresses of Fleetwood and Strickland and of Parker and Swainson, June 18; p. 61, "Preston Election Races"; LRO, DD PR 130/25, Parker to Bray (expressing unease), May 6, 1841.

[38.] *Preston Election Squibs*: pp. 74-77, "The Nomination" (from *PC*, July 3, p. 3); p. 77, Parker to "Honest and Independent Electors," June 30; p. 78, Fleetwood and

Strickland to electors, June 30 (praising them for firm adherence to free trade); Swainson to "Worthy and Independent Electors," July 1.

[39.] Given the mobility of a town experiencing rapid growth, tracing voting patterns across elections is a frustrating business. But of the 73 individuals in 1835 who voted for Fleetwood/Stanley, and who voted again in 1841 under the same name, address, and, usually, occupation (the only exceptions being where a cotton spinner, say, is described as a gentleman, but is beyond reasonable doubt the same person), 60 voted for Parker/Swainson, 10 for Fleetwood/Strickland, 2 for Fleetwood/Parker, and 1 for Fleetwood/Swainson.

[40.] Dobson, *Parliamentary Representation*, 86-87. The poll list ("Preston Poll List," 1847, extracted from *PG*, Sept. 18, 1847) only lists occupations intermittently. But a comparison of names and addresses of bourgeois voters also listed in the 1841 poll book provides the following sample: 63 who plumped for Parker, 20 who split for Strickland and Grenfell, 8 for Parker and Grenfell, 1 for Parker and Strickland, and 1 who plumped for Grenfell. Of this sample, 53 voted conservative in 1841 and 1847, 16 voted liberal, and 15 voted otherwise.

INDEX